COMPLETE
IRISH
MYTHOLOGY

COMPLETE IRISH MYTHOLOGY

Lady Gregory

Preface by W. B. Yeats

THE SLANEY PRESS

Originally published by John Murray Publishers, London,
in separate volumes: *Gods and Fighting Men* (1904) and
Cuchulain of Muirthemne (1902)

This collection volume published in 1994 by
The Slaney Press

by arrangement with

Reed Consumer Books Ltd
Michelin House
81 Fulham Road
London SW3 6RB
and Auckland, Melbourne, Singapore and Toronto

ISBN 1 85152 680 3

Design and arrangement copyright © Reed Consumer Books Ltd 1994

Printed and bound in Great Britain by
William Clowes Limited, Beccles and London

Contents

GODS AND FIGHTING MEN

THE STORY OF THE TUATHA DE DANAAN AND OF THE FIANNA OF IRELAND, ARRANGED AND PUT INTO ENGLISH BY LADY GREGORY. WITH A PREFACE BY W.B. YEATS

Dedication to the members of

the Irish literary society of New York

My Friends, those I know and those I do not know, I am glad in the year of the birth of your Society to have this book to offer you.

It has given great courage to many workers here—working to build up broken walls—to know you have such friendly thoughts of them in your minds. A few of you have already come to see us, and we begin to hope that one day the steamers across the Atlantic will not go out full, but come back full, until some of you find your real home is here, and say as some of us say, like Finn to the woman of enchantments—

Ní fágfamaoir an dtír féin dá bfagmaoir an doman mór man dúitce agur Tír-na-n-Óg leir.

"We would not give up our own country—Ireland—if we were to get the whole world as an estate, and the Country of the Young along with it."

AUGUSTA GREGORY.

PREFACE

I

A few months ago I was on the bare Hill of Allen, "wide Almhuin of Leinster," where Finn and the Fianna lived, according to the stories, although there are no earthen mounds there like those that mark the sites of old buildings on so many hills. A hot sun beat down upon flowering gorse and flowerless heather; and on every side except the east, where there were green trees and distant hills, one saw a level horizon and brown boglands with a few green places and here and there the glitter of water. One could imagine that had it been twilight and not early afternoon, and had there been vapours drifting and frothing where there were now but shadows of clouds, it would have set stirring in one, as few places even in Ireland can, a thought that is peculiar to Celtic romance, as I think, a thought of a mystery coming not as with Gothic nations out of the pressure of darkness, but out of great spaces and windy light. The hill of Teamhair, or Tara, as it is now called, with its green mounds and its partly wooded sides, and its more gradual slope set among fat grazing lands with great trees in the hedgerows, had brought before one imaginations, not of heroes who were in their youth for hundreds of years, or of women who came to them in the likeness of hunted fawns, but of kings that lived brief and politic lives, and of the five white roads that carried their armies to the lesser kingdoms of Ireland, or brought to the great fair that had given Teamhair its sovereignty, all that sought justice or pleasure or had goods to barter.

II

It is certain that we must not confuse these kings, as did the mediæval chroniclers, with those half-divine kings of Almhuin. The chroniclers, perhaps because they loved tradition too well to cast out utterly much that they dreaded as Christians, and perhaps because popular imagination had begun the mixture, have mixed one with another ingeniously, making Finn the head of a kind of Militia under Cormac MacArt, who is supposed to have reigned at Teamhair in the second century, and making Grania, who travels to enchanted houses under the cloak of Angus, god of Love, and keeps her troubling beauty longer than did Helen hers,

1

Cormac's daughter, and giving the stories of the Fianna, although the impossible has thrust its proud finger into them all, a curious air of precise history. It is only when one separates the stories from that mediæval pedantry, as in this book, that one recognises one of the oldest worlds that man has imagined, an older world certainly than one finds in the stories of Cuchulain, who lived, according to the chroniclers, about the time of the birth of Christ. They are far better known, and one may be certain of the antiquity of incidents that are known in one form or another to every Gaelic-speaking countryman in Ireland or in the Highlands of Scotland. Sometimes a labourer digging near to a cromlech, or Bed of Diarmuid and Grania as it is called, will tell one a tradition that seems older and more barbaric than any description of their adventures or of themselves in written text or story that has taken form in the mouths of professed story-tellers. Finn and the Fianna found welcome among the court poets later than did Cuchulain; and one finds memories of Danish invasions and standing armies mixed with the imaginations of hunters and solitary fighters among great woods. One never hears of Cuchulain delighting in the hunt or in woodland things; and one imagines that the story-teller would have thought it unworthy in so great a man, who lived a well-ordered, elaborate life, and had his chariot and his chariot-driver and his barley-fed horses to delight in. If he is in the woods before dawn one is not told that he cannot know the leaves of the hazel from the leaves of the oak; and when Emer laments him no wild creature comes into her thoughts but the cuckoo that cries over cultivated fields. His story must have come out of a time when the wild wood was giving way to pasture and tillage, and men had no longer a reason to consider every cry of the birds or change of the night. Finn, who was always in the woods, whose battles were but hours amid years of hunting, delighted in the "cackling of ducks from the Lake of the Three Narrows; the scolding talk of the blackbird of Doire an Cairn; the bellowing of the ox from the Valley of the Berries; the whistle of the eagle from the Valley of Victories or from the rough branches of the Ridge of the Stream; the grouse of the heather of Cruachan; the call of the otter of Druim re Coir." When sorrow comes upon the queens of the stories, they have sympathy for the wild birds and beasts that are like themselves: "Credhe wife of Cael came with the others and went looking through the bodies for her comely comrade, and crying as she went. And as she was searching she saw a crane of the meadows and her two nestlings, and the cunning beast the fox watching the nestlings; and when the crane covered one of the birds to save it, he would make a rush at the other bird, the way she had to stretch herself out over the birds; and she would sooner have got her own death by the fox than the nestlings to be killed by him. And Credhe was looking at that, and she said: 'It is no wonder I to have such love for my comely sweetheart, and the bird in that distress about her nestlings.' "

III

One often hears of a horse that shivers with terror, or of a dog that howls at something a man's eyes cannot see, and men who live primitive lives where instinct does the work of reason are fully conscious of many things that we cannot perceive at all. As life becomes more orderly, more deliberate, the supernatural world sinks farther away. Although the gods come to Cuchulain, and although he is the son of one of the greatest of them, their country and his are far apart, and they come to him as god to mortal; but Finn is their equal. He is continually in their houses; he meets with Bodb Dearg, and Angus, and Manannan, now as friend with friend, now as with an enemy he overcomes in battle; and when he has need of their help his messenger can say: "There is not a king's son or a prince, or a leader of the Fianna of Ireland, without having a wife or a mother or a foster-mother or a sweetheart of the Tuatha de Danaan." When the Fianna are broken up at last, after hundreds of years of hunting, it is doubtful that he dies at all, and certain that he comes again in some other shape, and Oisin, his son, is made king over a divine country. The birds and beasts that cross his path in the woods have been fighting men or great enchanters or fair women, and in a moment can take some beautiful or terrible shape. One thinks of him and of his people as great-bodied men with large movements, that seem, as it were, flowing out of some deep below the narrow stream of personal impulse, men that have broad brows and quiet eyes full of confidence in a good luck that proves every day afresh that they are a portion of the strength of things. They are hardly so much individual men as portions of universal nature, like the clouds that shape themselves and re-shape themselves momentarily, or like a bird between two boughs, or like the gods that have given the apples and the nuts; and yet this but brings them the nearer to us, for we can remake them in our image when we will, and the woods are the more beautiful for the thought. Do we not always fancy hunters to be something like this, and is not that why we think them poetical when we meet them of a sudden, as in these lines in "Pauline":

> "An old hunter
> Talking with gods; or a nigh-crested chief
> Sailing with troops of friends to Tenedos

IV

One must not expect in these stories the epic lineaments, the many incidents, woven into one great event of, let us say, the story of the War for the Brown Bull of Cuailgne, or that of the last gathering at Muirthemne. Even Diarmuid and Grania, which is a long story, has nothing of the clear outlines of Deirdre, and is indeed but a succession of detached episodes. The men who imagined the Fianna had the imagination of children, and as soon as they had invented one wonder, heaped another on top of it. Children—or, at any rate, it is so I remember my own childhood—do not understand large design, and they delight in little shut-in places where they can play at houses more than in great expanses where a country-side takes, as it were, the impression of a thought. The wild creatures and the green things are more to them than to us, for they creep towards our light by little holes and crevices. When they imagine a country for themselves, it is always a country where one can wander without aim, and where one can never know from one place what another will be like, or know from the one day's adventure what may meet one with to-morrow's sun. I have wished to become a child again that I might find this book, that not only tells one of such a country, but is fuller than any other book that tells of heroic life, of the childhood that is in all folk-lore, dearer to me than all the books of the western world.

V

Children play at being great and wonderful people, at the ambitions they will put away for one reason or another before they grow into ordinary men and women. Mankind as a whole had a like dream once; everybody and nobody built up the dream bit by bit, and the ancient story-tellers are there to make us remember what mankind would have been like, had not fear and the failing will and the laws of nature tripped up its heels. The Fianna and their like are themselves so full of power, and they are set in a world so fluctuating and dream-like, that nothing can hold them from being all that the heart desires.

I have read in a fabulous book that Adam had but to imagine a bird, and it was born into life, and that he created all things out of himself by nothing more important than an unflagging fancy; and heroes who can make a ship out of a shaving have but little less of the divine prerogatives. They have no speculative thoughts to wander through eternity and waste heroic blood; but how could that be otherwise, for it is at all times the proud angels who sit thinking upon the hill-side and not the people of Eden. One morning we meet them hunting a stag that is "as joyful as the leaves of a tree in summer-time"; and whatever they do, whether they listen to the harp or follow an enchanter over-sea, they do for the sake of joy, their joy in one another, or their joy in pride and movement; and even their battles are fought more because of their delight in a good fighter than because of any gain that is in victory. They live always as if they were playing a game; and so far as they have any deliberate purpose at all, it is that they may become great gentlemen and be worthy of the songs of poets. It has been said, and I think the Japanese were the first to say it, that the four essential virtues are to be generous among the weak, and truthful among one's friends, and brave among one's enemies, and courteous at all times; and if we understand by courtesy not merely the gentleness the story-tellers have celebrated, but a delight in courtly things, in beautiful clothing and in beautiful verse, one understands that it was no formal succession of trials that bound the Fianna to one another. Only the Table Round, that is indeed, as it seems, a rivulet from the same river, is bound in a like fellowship, and there the four heroic virtues are troubled by the abstract virtues of the cloister. Every now and then some noble knight builds himself a cell upon the hill-side, or leaves kind women and joyful knights to seek the vision of the Grail in lonely adventures. But when Oisin or some kingly forerunner—Bran, son of Febal, or the like—rides or sails in an enchanted ship to some divine country, he but looks for a more delighted companionship, or to be in love with faces that will never fade. No thought of any life greater than that of love, and the companionship of those that have drawn their swords upon the darkness of the world, ever troubles their delight in one another as it troubles Iseult amid her love, or Arthur amid his battles. It is one of the ailments of our speculation that thought, when it is not the planning of something, or the doing of something or some memory of a plain circumstance separates us from one another because it makes us always more unlike, and because no thought passes through another's ear unchanged. Companionship can only be perfect when it is founded on things, for things are always the same under the hand, and at last one comes to hear with envy the voices of boys lighting a lantern to ensnare moths, or of the maids chattering in the kitchen about the fox that carried off a turkey before breakfast. This book is full of fellowship untroubled like theirs, and made noble by a courtesy that has gone perhaps out of the world. I do not know in literature better friends and lovers. When one of the Fianna finds Osgar dying the proud death of a young man, and asks is it well with him, he is answered, "I am as you would have me be." The very heroism of the Fianna is indeed but their pride and joy in one another, their good fellowship. Goll, old and savage, and letting himself die of hunger in a cave because he is angry and sorry, can speak lovely words to the wife whose help he refuses. " 'It is best as it is,' he said, 'and I never took the advice of a woman east or west, and I never will take it. And oh, sweet-voiced queen,' he said, 'what ails you to be fretting after me? and remember now your silver and your gold, and your silks . . . and do not be crying tears after me, queen with the white hands,' he said, 'but remember your constant lover Aodh, son of the best woman of the world, that came from Spain asking for you, and that I fought on Corcar-an-Dearg; and go to him now,' he said, 'for it is bad when a woman is without a good man.' "

VI

A

They have no asceticism, but they are more visionary than any ascetic, and their invisible life is but the life about them made more perfect and more lasting, and the invisible people are their own images in the water. Their gods may have been much besides this, for we know them from fragments of mythology picked out with trouble from a fantastic history running backward to Adam and Eve, and many things that may have seemed wicked to the monks who imagined that history, may have been altered or left out; but this they must have been essentially, for the old stories are confirmed by apparitions among the country-people to-day. The Men of Dea fought against the mis-shapen Fomor, as Finn fights against the Cat-Heads and the Dog-Heads; and when they are overcome at last by men, they make themselves houses in the hearts of hills that are like the houses of men. When they call men to their houses and to their country Under-Wave they promise them all that they have upon earth, only in greater abundance. The god Midhir sings to Queen Etain in one of the most beautiful of the stories: "The young never grow old; the fields and the flowers are as pleasant to be looking at as the blackbird's eggs; warm streams of mead and wine flow through that country; there is no care or no sorrow on any person; we see others, but we ourselves are not seen." These gods are indeed more wise and beautiful than men; but men, when they are great men, are stronger than they are, for men are, as it were, the foaming tide-line of their sea. One remembers the Druid who answered, when some one asked him who made the world, "The Druids made it." All was indeed but one life flowing everywhere, and taking one quality here, another there. It sometimes seems to one as if there is a kind of day and night of religion, and that a period when the influences are those that shape the world is followed by a period when the greater power is in influences that would lure the soul out of the world, out of the body. When Oisin is speaking with S. Patrick of the friends and the life he has outlived, he can but cry out constantly against a religion that has no meaning for him. He laments, and the country-people have remembered his words for centuries: "I will cry my fill, but not for God, but because Finn and the Fianna are not living."

VII

Old writers had an admirable symbolism that attributed certain energies to the influence of the sun, and certain others to the lunar influence. To lunar influence belong all thoughts and emotions that were created by the community, by the common people, by nobody knows who, and to the sun all that came from the high disciplined or individual kingly mind. I myself imagine a marriage of the sun and moon in the arts I take most pleasure in; and now bride and bridegroom but exchange, as it were, full cups of gold and silver, and now they are one in a mystical embrace. From the moon come the folk-songs imagined by reapers and spinners out of the common impulse of their labour, and made not by putting words together, but by mixing verses and phrases, and the folk-tales made by the capricious mixing of incidents known to everybody in new ways, as one deals out cards, never getting the same hand twice over. When one hears some fine story, one never knows whether it has not been hazard that put the last touch of adventure. Such poetry, as it seems to me, desires an infinity of wonder or emotion, for where there is no individual mind there is no measurer-out, no marker-in of limits. The poor fisher has no possession of the world and no responsibility for it; and if he dreams of a love-gift better than the brown shawl that seems too common for poetry, why should he not dream of a glove made from the skin of a bird, or shoes made from the skin of a fish, or a coat made from the glittering garment of the salmon? Was it not Aeschylus who said he but served up fragments from the banquet of Homer?—but Homer himself found the great banquet on an earthen floor and under a broken roof. We do not know who at the foundation of the world made the banquet for the first time, or who put the pack of cards into rough hands; but we do know that, unless those that have made many inventions are about to change the nature of poetry, we may have to go where Homer went if we are to sing a new song. Is it because all that is under the moon thirsts to escape out of bounds, to lose itself in some unbounded tidal stream, that the songs of the folk are mournful, and that the story of the Fianna, whenever the queens lament for their lovers, reminds us of songs that are still sung in country-places? Their grief, even when it is to be brief like Grania's, goes up into the waste places of the sky. But in supreme art or in supreme life there is the influence of the sun too, and the sun brings with it, as old writers tell us, not merely discipline but joy; for its discipline is not of the kind the multitudes impose upon us by their weight and pressure, but the expression of the individual soul turning itself into a pure fire and imposing its own pattern, its own music, upon the heaviness and the dumbness that is in others and in itself. When we have drunk the cold cup of the moon's intoxication, we thirst for something beyond ourselves, and the mind flows outward to a natural immensity; but if we have drunk from the hot cup of the sun, our own fullness awakens, we desire little, for wherever one goes one's heart goes too; and if any ask what music is the sweetest, we can but answer, as Finn answered, "what happens." And yet the songs and stories that have come from either influence are a part, neither less than the other, of the pleasure that is the bride-bed of poetry.

VIII

Gaelic-speaking Ireland, because its art has been made, not by the artist choosing his material from wherever he has a mind to, but by adding a little to something which it has taken generations to invent, has always had a popular literature. One cannot say how much that literature has done for the vigour of the race, for one cannot count the hands its praise of kings and high-hearted queens made hot upon the sword-hilt, or the amorous eyes it made lustful for strength and beauty. One remembers indeed that when the farming people and the labourers of the towns made their last attempt to cast out England by force of arms they named themselves after the companions of Finn. Even when Gaelic has gone, and the poetry with it, something of the habit of mind remains in ways of speech and thought and "come-all-ye"s and poetical saying; nor is it only among the poor that the old thought has been for strength or weakness. Surely these old stories, whether of Finn or Cuchulain, helped to sing the old Irish and the old Norman-Irish aristocracy to their end. They heard their hereditary poets and story-tellers, and they took to horse and died fighting against Elizabeth or against Cromwell; and when an English-speaking aristocracy had their place, it listened to no poetry indeed, but it felt about it in the popular mind an exacting and ancient tribunal, and began a play that had for spectators men and women that loved the high wasteful virtues. I do not think that their own mixed blood or the habit of their time need take all, or nearly all, credit or discredit for the impulse that made our modern gentlemen fight duels over pocket-handkerchiefs, and set out to play ball against the gates of Jerusalem for a wager, and scatter money before the public eye; and at last, after an epoch of such eloquence the world has hardly seen its like, lose their public spirit and their high heart and grow querulous and selfish as men do who have played life out not heartily but with noise and tumult. Had they understood the people and the game a little better, they might have created an aristocracy in an age that has lost the meaning of the word. When one reads of the Fianna, or of Cuchulain, or of some great hero, one remembers that the fine life is always a part played finely before fine spectators. There also one notices the hot cup and the cold cup of intoxication; and when the fine spectators have ended, surely the fine players grow weary, and aristocratic life is ended. When O'Connell covered with a dark glove the hand that had killed a man in the duelling field, he played his part; and when Alexander stayed his army marching to the conquest of the world that he might contemplate the beauty of a plane-tree, he played his part. When Osgar complained as he lay dying, of the keening of the women and the old fighting men, he too played his part; "No man ever knew any heart in me," he said, "but a heart of twisted horn, and it covered with iron; but the howling of the dogs beside me," he said, "and the keening of the old fighting men and the crying of the women one after another, those are the things that are vexing me." If we would create a great community—and what other game is so worth the labour?—we must recreate the old foundations of life, not as they existed in that splendid misunderstanding of the eighteenth century, but as they must always exist when the finest minds and Ned the beggar and Seaghan the fool think about the same thing, although they may not think the same thought about it.

IX

When I asked the little boy who had shown me the pathway up the Hill of Allen if he knew stories of Finn and Oisin, he said he did not, but that he had often heard his grandfather telling them to his mother in Irish. He did not know Irish, but he was learning it at school, and all the little boys he knew were learning it. In a little while he will know enough stories of Finn and Oisin to tell them to his children some day. It is the owners of the land whose children might never have known what would give them so much happiness. But now they can read this book to their children, and it will make Slieve-naman, Allen, and Benbulben, the great mountain that showed itself before me every day through all my childhood and was yet unpeopled, and half the country-sides of south and west, as populous with memories as are Dundealgan and Emain Macha and Muirthemne; and after a while somebody may even take them to some famous place and say, "This land where your fathers lived proudly and finely should be dear and dear and again dear"; and perhaps when many names have grown musical to their ears, a more imaginative love will have taught them a better service.

X

I need say nothing about the translation and arrangement of this book except that it is worthy to be put beside "Cuchulain of Muirthemne." Such books should not be commended by written words but by spoken words, were that possible, for the written words commending a book, wherein something is done supremely well, remain, to sound in the ears of a later generation, like the foolish sound of church bells from the tower of a church when every pew is full.

W. B. YEATS

CONTENTS

PART I. THE GODS

PART II THE FIANNA

13

PART I

The Gods

The Coming of the Tuatha de Danaan

CHAPTER I

The Fight with the Firbolgs

It was in a mist the Tuatha de Danaan, the people of the gods of Dana, or as some called them, the Men of Dea, came through the air and the high air to Ireland.

It was from the north they came; and in the place they came from they had four cities, where they fought their battle for learning: great Falias, and shining Gorias, and Finias, and rich Murias that lay to the south. And in those cities they had four wise men to teach their young men skill and knowledge and perfect wisdom: Senias in Murias; and Arias, the fair-haired poet, in Finias; and Urias of the noble nature in Gorias; and Morias in Falias itself. And they brought from those four cities their four treasures: a Stone of Virtue from Falias, that was called the Lia Fail, the Stone of Destiny; and from Gorias they brought a Sword; and from Finias a Spear of Victory; and from Murias the fourth treasure, the Cauldron that no company ever went away from unsatisfied.

It was Nuada was king of the Tuatha de Danaan at that time, but Manannan, son of Lir, was greater again. And of the others that were chief among them were Ogma, brother to the king, that taught them writing, and Diancecht, that understood healing, and Neit, a god of battle, and Credenus the Craftsman, and Goibniu the Smith. And the greatest among their women were Badb, a battle goddess; and Macha, whose mast-feeding was the heads of men killed in battle; and the Morrigu, the Crow of Battle; and Eire and Fodla and Banba, daughters of the Dagda, that all three gave their names to Ireland afterwards; and Eadon, the nurse of poets; and Brigit, that was a woman of poetry, and poets worshipped her, for her sway was very great and very noble. And she was a woman of healing along with that, and a woman of smith's work, and it was she first made the whistle for calling one to another through the night. And the one side of her face was ugly, but the other side was very comely. And the meaning of her name was Breo-saighit, a fiery arrow. And among the other women there were many shadow-forms and great queens; but Dana, that was called the Mother of the Gods, was beyond them all.

And the three things they put above all others were the plough and the sun and the hazel-tree, so that it was said in the time to come that Ireland was divided between those three, Coll the hazel, and Cecht the plough, and Grian the sun.

And they had a well below the sea where the nine hazels of wisdom were growing; that is, the hazels of inspiration and of the knowledge of poetry. And their leaves and their blossoms would break out in the same hour, and would fall on the well in a shower that raised a purple wave. And then the five salmon that were waiting there would eat the nuts, and their colour would come out in the red spots of their skin, and any person that would eat one of those salmon would know all wisdom and all poetry. And there were seven streams of wisdom that sprang from that well and turned back to it again; and the people of many arts have all drank from that well.

It was on the first day of Beltaine, that is called now May Day, the Tuatha de Danaan came, and it was to the north-west of Connacht they landed. But the Firbolgs, the Men of the Bag, that were in Ireland before them, and that had come from the South, saw nothing but a mist, and it lying on the hills.

Eochaid, son of Erc, was king of the Firbolgs at that time, and messengers came to him at Teamhair, and told him there was a new race of people come into Ireland, but whether from the earth or the skies or on the wind was not known, and that they had settled themselves at Magh Rein.

They thought there would be wonder on Eochaid when he heard that news; but there was no wonder on him, for a dream had come to him in the night, and when he asked his Druids the meaning of the dream, it is what they said, that it would not be long till there would be a strong enemy coming against him.

Then King Eochaid took counsel with his chief advisers, and it is what they agreed, to send a good champion of their own to see the strangers and to speak with them. So they chose out Sreng, that was a great fighting man, and he rose up and took his strong red-brown shield, and his two thick-handled spears, and his sword, and his head-covering, and his thick iron club, and he set out from Teamhair, and went on towards the place the strangers were, at Magh Rein.

But before he reached it, the watchers of the Tuatha de Danaan got sight of him, and they sent out one of their own champions, Bres, with his shield and his sword and his two spears, to meet him and to talk with him.

So the two champions went one towards the other slowly, and keeping a good watch on one another, and wondering at one another's arms, till they came near enough for talking; and then they stopped, and each put his shield before his body and struck it hard into the ground, and they looked at one another over the rim. Bres was the first to speak, and when Sreng heard it was Irish he was talking, his own tongue, he was less uneasy, and they drew nearer, and asked questions as to one another's family and race.

And after a while they put their shields away, and it was what Sreng said, that he had raised his in dread of the thin, sharp spears Bres had in his hand. And Bres said he himself was in dread of the thick-handled spears he saw with Sreng, and he asked were all the arms of the Firbolgs of the same sort. And Sreng took off the tyings of his spears to show them better, and Bres wondered at them, being so strong and so heavy, and so sharp at the sides though they had no points. And Sreng told him the name of those spears was Craisech, and that they would break through shields and crush flesh and bones, so that their thrust was death or wounds that never healed. And then he looked at the sharp, thin, hard-pointed spears that were with Bres. And in the end they made an exchange of spears, the way the fighters on each side would see the weapons the others were used to. And it is the message Bres sent to the Firbolgs, that if they would give up one half of Ireland, his people would be content to take it in peace; but if they would not give up that much, there should be a battle. And he and Sreng said to one another that whatever might happen in the future, they themselves would be friends.

Sreng went back then to Teamhair and gave the message and showed the spear; and it is what he advised his people, to share the country and not to go into battle with a people that had weapons so much better than their own. But Eochaid and his chief men consulted together, and they said in the end: "We will not give up the half of the country to these strangers; for if we do," they said, "they will soon take the whole."

Now as to the Men of Dea, when Bres went back to them, and showed them the heavy spear, and told them of the strong, fierce man he had got it from, and how sturdy he was and well armed, they thought it likely there would soon be a battle. And they went back from where they were to a better place, farther west in Connacht, and there they settled themselves, and made walls and ditches on the plain of Magh Nia, where they had the great mountain, Belgata, in their rear. And while they were moving there and putting up their walls, three queens of them, Badb and Macha and the Morrigu, went to Teamhair where the Firbolgs were making their plans. And by the power of their enchantments they brought mists and clouds of darkness over the whole place, and they sent showers of fire and of blood over the people, the way they could not see or speak with one another through the length of three days. But at the end of that time, the three Druids of the Firbolgs, Cesarn and Gnathach and Ingnathach, broke the enchantment.

The Firbolgs gathered their men together then, and they came with their eleven battalions and took their stand at the eastern end of the plain of Magh Nia.

And Nuada, king of the Men of Dea, sent his poets to make the same offer he made before, to be content with the half of the country if it was given up to him. King Eochaid bade the poets to ask an answer of his chief men that were gathered there; and when they heard the offer they would not consent. So the messengers asked them when would they begin the battle. "We must have a delay," they said; "for we want time to put our spears and our armour in order, and to brighten our helmets and to sharpen our swords, and to have spears made like the ones you have. And as to yourselves," they said, "you will be wanting to have spears like

19

our Craisechs made for you." So they agreed then to make a delay of a quarter of a year for preparation.

It was on a Midsummer day they began the battle. Three times nine hurlers of the Tuatha de Danaan went out against three times nine hurlers of the Firbolgs, and they were beaten, and every one of them was killed. And the king, Eochaid, sent a messenger to ask would they have the battle every day or every second day. And it is what Nuada answered that they would have it every day, but there should be just the same number of men fighting on each side. Eochaid agreed to that, but he was not well pleased, for there were more men of the Firbolgs than of the Men of Dea.

So the battle went on for four days, and there were great feats done on each side, and a great many champions came to their death. But for those that were alive at evening, the physicians on each side used to make a bath of healing, with every sort of healing plant or herb in it, the way they would be strong and sound for the next day's fight.

And on the fourth day the Men of Dea got the upper hand, and the Firbolgs were driven back. And a great thirst came on Eochaid, their king, in the battle, and he went off the field looking for a drink, and three fifties of his men protecting him; but three fifties of the Tuatha de Danaan followed after them till they came to the strand that is called Traigh Eothaile, and they had a fierce fight there, and at the last King Eochaid fell, and they buried him there, and they raised a great heap of stones over his grave.

And when there were but three hundred men left of the eleven battalions of the Firbolgs, and Sreng at the head of them, Nuada offered them peace, and their choice among the five provinces of Ireland. And Sreng said they would take Connacht; and he and his people lived there and their children after them. It is of them Ferdiad came afterwards that made such a good fight against Cuchulain, and Erc, son of Cairbre, that gave him his death. And that battle, that was the first fought in Ireland by the Men of Dea, was called by some the first battle of Magh Tuireadh.

And the Tuatha de Danaan took possession of Teamhair, that was sometimes called Druim Cain, the Beautiful Ridge, and Liathdruim, the Grey Ridge, and Druim na Descan, the Ridge of the Outlook, all those names were given to Teamhair. And from that time it was above all other places, for its king was the High King over all Ireland. The king's rath lay to the north, and the Hill of the Hostages to the north-east of the High Seat, and the Green of Teamhair to the west of the Hill of the Hostages. And to the north-east, in the Hill of the Sidhe, was a well called Nemnach, and out of it there flowed a stream called Nith, and on that stream the first mill was built in Ireland.

And to the north of the Hill of the Hostages was the stone, the Lia Fail, and it used to roar under the feet of every king that would take possession of Ireland. And the Wall of the Three Whispers was near the House of the Women that had seven doors to the east, and seven doors to the west; and it is in that house the feasts of Teamhair used to be held. And there was the Great House of a Thousand Soldiers, and near it, to the south, the little Hill of the Woman Soldiers.

CHAPTER II

The Reign of Bres

But if Nuada won the battle, he lost his own arm in it, that was struck off by Sreng; and by that loss there came troubles and vexation on his people.

For it was a law with the Tuatha de Danaan that no man that was not perfect in shape should be king. And after Nuada had lost the battle he was put out of the kingship on that account.

And the king they chose in his place was Bres, that was the most beautiful of all their young men, so that if a person wanted to praise any beautiful thing, whether it was a plain, or a dun, or ale, or a flame, or a woman, or a man, or a horse, it is what he would say, "It is as beautiful as Bres." And he was the son of a woman of the Tuatha de Danaan, but who his father was no one knew but herself.

But in spite of Bres being so beautiful, his reign brought no great good luck to his people; for the Fomor, whose dwelling-place was beyond the sea, or as some say below the sea westward, began putting tribute on them, the way they would get them under their own rule.

It was a long time before that the Fomor came first to Ireland; dreadful they were to look at, and maimed, having but one foot or one hand, and they under the leadership of a giant and his mother. There never came to Ireland an army more horrible or more dreadful than that army of the Fomor. And they were friendly with the Firbolgs and content to leave Ireland to them, but there was jealousy between them and the Men of Dea.

And it was a hard tax they put on them, a third part of their corn they asked, and a third part of their milk, and a third part of their children, so that there was not smoke rising from a roof in Ireland but was under tribute to them. And Bres made no stand against them, but let them get their way.

And as to Bres himself, he put a tax on every house in Ireland of the milk of hornless dun cows, or of the milk of cows of some other single colour, enough for a hundred men. And one time, to deceive him, Nechtan singed all the cows of Ireland in a fire of fern, and then he smeared them with the ashes of flax seed, the way they were all dark brown. He did that by the advice of the Druid Findgoll, son of Findemas. And another time they made three hundred cows of wood with dark brown pails in place of udders, and the pails were filled with black bog stuff. Then Bres came to look at the cows, and to see them milked before him, and Cian,

21

father of Lugh, was there. And when they were milked it was the bog stuff that was squeezed out; and Bres took a drink of it thinking it to be milk, and he was not the better of it for a long time.

And there was another thing against Bres; he was no way open-handed, and the chief men of the Tuatha de Danaan grumbled against him, for their knives were never greased in his house, and however often they might visit him there was no smell of ale on their breath. And there was no sort of pleasure or merriment in his house, and no call for their poets, or singers, or harpers, or pipers, or horn-blowers, or jugglers, or fools. And as to the trials of strength they were used to see between their champions, the only use their strength was put to now was to be doing work for the king. Ogma himself, the shining poet, was under orders to bring firing to the palace every day for the whole army from the Islands of Mod; and he so weak for want of food that the sea would sweep away two-thirds of his bundle every day. And as to the Dagda, he was put to build raths, for he was a good builder, and he made a trench round Rath Brese. And he used often to be tired at the work, and one time he nearly gave in altogether for want of food, and this is the way that happened. He used to meet in the house an idle blind man, Cridenbel his name was, that had a sharp tongue, and that coveted the Dagda's share of food, for he thought his own to be small beside it. So he said to him: "For the sake of your good name let the three best bits of your share be given to me." And the Dagda gave in to that every night; but he was the worse of it, for what the blind man called a bit would be the size of a good pig, and with his three bits he would take a full third of the whole.

But one day, as the Dagda was in the trench, he saw his son, Angus Og, coming to him. "That is a good meeting," said Angus; "but what is on you, for you have no good appearance to-day?" "There is a reason for that," said the Dagda, "for every evening, Cridenbel, the blind man, makes a demand for the three best bits of my share of food, and takes them from me." "I will give you an advice," said Angus. He put his hand in his bag then, and took out three pieces of gold and gave them to him.

"Put these pieces of gold into the three bits you will give this evening to Cridenbel," he said, "and they will be the best bits in the dish, and the gold will turn within him the way he will die."

So in the evening the Dagda did that; and no sooner had Cridenbel swallowed down the gold than he died. Some of the people said then to the king: "The Dagda has killed Cridenbel, giving him some deadly herb." The king believed that, and there was anger on him against the Dagda, and he gave orders he should be put to death. But the Dagda said: "You are not giving the right judgment of a prince." And he told all that had happened, and how Cridenbel used to say, "Give me the three best bits before you, for my own share is not good to-night," "And on this night," he said, "the three pieces of gold were the best things before me, and I gave them to him, and he died."

The king gave orders then to have the body cut open. And they found the gold inside it, and they knew it was the truth the Dagda had told.

And Angus came to him again the next day, and he said: "Your work will soon be done, and when you are given your wages, take nothing they may offer you till the cattle of Ireland are brought before you, and choose out a heifer then, black and black-maned, that I will tell you the signs of."

So when the Dagda had brought his work to an end, and they asked him what reward he wanted, he did as Angus had bidden him. And that seemed folly to Bres; he thought the Dagda would have asked more than a heifer of him.

There came a day at last when a poet came to look for hospitality at the king's house, Corpre, son of Etain, poet of the Tuatha de Danaan. And it is how he was treated, he was put in a little dark narrow house where there was no fire, or furniture, or bed; and for a feast three small cakes, and they dry, were brought to him on a little dish. When he rose up on the morrow he was no way thankful, and as he was going across the green, it is what he said: "Without food ready on a dish; without milk enough for a calf to grow on; without shelter; without light in the darkness of night; without enough to pay a story-teller; may that be the prosperity of Bres."

And from that day there was no good luck with Bres, but it is going down he was for ever after. And that was the first satire ever made in Ireland.

Now as to Nuada: after his arm being struck off, he was in his sickness for a while, and then Diancecht, the healer, made an arm of silver for him, with movement in every finger of it, and put it on him. And from that he was called Nuada Argat-lamh, of the Silver Hand, for ever after.

Now Miach, son of Diancecht, was a better hand at healing than his father, and had done many things. He met a young man, having but one eye, at Team-hair one time, and the young man said: "If you are a good physician you will put an eye in the place of the eye I lost." "I could put the eye of that cat in your lap in its place," said Miach. "I would like that well," said the young man. So Miach put the cat's eye in his head; but he would as soon have been without it after, for when he wanted to sleep and take his rest, it is then the eye would start at the squeaking of the mice, or the flight of the birds, or the movement of the rushes; and when he was wanting to watch an army or a gathering, it is then it was sure to be in a deep sleep.

And Miach was not satisfied with what his father had done to the king, and he took Nuada's own hand that had been struck off, and brought it to him and set it in its place, and he said: "Joint to joint, and sinew to sinew." Three days and three nights he was with the king; the first day he put the hand against his side, and the second day against his breast, till it was covered with skin, and the third day he put bulrushes that were blackened in the fire on it, and at the end of that time the king was healed.

But Diancecht was vexed when he saw his son doing a better cure than himself, and he threw his sword at his head, that it cut the flesh, but the lad healed the wound by means of his skill. Then Diancecht threw it a second time, that it reached the bone, but the lad was able to cure the wound. Then he struck him the third time and the fourth, till he cut out the brain, for he knew no physician could cure him after that blow; and Miach died, and he buried him.

And herbs grew up from his grave, to the number of his joints and sinews, three hundred and sixty-five. And Airmed, his sister, came and spread out her cloak and laid out the herbs in it, according to their virtue. But Diancecht saw her doing that, and he came and mixed up the herbs, so that no one knows all their right powers to this day.

Then when the Tuatha de Danaan saw Nuada as well as he was before, they gathered together to Team-hair, where Bres was, and they bade him give up the kingship, for he had held it long enough. So he had to give it up, though he was not very willing, and Nuada was put back in the kingship again.

There was great vexation on Bres then, and he searched his mind to know how could he be avenged on those that had put him out, and how he could gather an army against them; and he went to his mother, Eri, daughter of Delbaith, and bade her tell him what his race was.

"I know that well," she said; and she told him then that his father was a king of the Fomor, Elathan, son of Dalbaech, and that he came to her one time over a level sea in some great vessel that seemed to be of silver, but she could not see its shape, and he himself having the appearance of a young man with yellow hair, and his clothes sewed with gold, and five rings of gold about his neck. And she that had refused the love of all the young men of her own people, gave him her love, and she cried when he left her. And he gave her a ring from his hand, and bade her give it only to the man whose finger it would fit, and he went away then the same way as he had come.

And she brought out the ring then to Bres, and he put it round his middle finger, and it fitted him well. And they went then together to the hill where she was the time she saw the silver vessel coming, and down to the strand, and she and Bres and his people set out for the country of the Fomor.

And when they came to that country they found a great plain with many gatherings of people on it, and they went to the gathering that looked the best, and the people asked where did they come from, and they said they were come from Ireland. "Have you hounds with you?" they asked them then, for it was the custom at that time, when strangers came to a gathering, to give them some friendly challenge. "We have hounds," said Bres. So the hounds were matched against one another, and the hounds of the Tuatha de Danaan were better than the hounds of the Fomor. "Have you horses for a race?" they asked then. "We have," said Bres. And the horses of the Tuatha de Danaan beat the horses of the Fomor.

Then they asked was any one among them a good hand with the sword, and they said Bres was the best. But when he put his hand to his sword, Elathan, his father, that was among them, knew the ring, and he asked who was this young man. Then his mother answered him and told the whole story, and that Bres was his own son.

There was sorrow on his father then, and he said: "What was it drove you out of the country you were king over?" And Bres said: "Nothing drove me out but my own injustice and my own hardness; I took away their treasures from the people, and their jewels, and their food itself. And there were never taxes put on them before I was their king."

"That is bad," said his father; "it is of their prosperity you had a right to think more than of your own king-ship. And their good-will would be better than their curses," he said; "and what is it you are come to look for here?" "I am come to look for fighting men," said Bres, "that I may take Ireland by force." "You have no right to get it by injustice when you could not keep it by justice," said his father. "What advice have you for me then?" said Bres.

And Elathan bade him go to the chief king of the Fomor, Balor of the Evil Eye, to see what advice and what help would he give him.

BOOK II

Lugh of the Long Hand

CHAPTER I

The coming of Lugh

Now as to Nuada of the Silver Hand, he was holding a great feast at Teamhair one time, after he was back in the kingship. And there were two door-keepers at Teamhair, Gamal, son of Figal, and Camel, son of Riagall. And a young man came to the door where one of them was, and bade him bring him in to the king. "Who are you yourself?" said the door-keeper. "I am Lugh, son of Cian of the Tuatha de Danaan, and of Ethlinn, daughter of Balor, King of the Fomor," he said; "and I am foster-son of Taillte, daughter of the King of the Great Plain, and of Echaid the Rough, son of Duach." "What are you skilled in?" said the door-keeper; "for no one without an art comes into Teamhair." "Question me," said Lugh; "I am a carpenter." "We do not want you; we have a carpenter ourselves, Luchtar, son of Luachaid." "Then I am a smith." "We have a smith ourselves, Colum Cuaillemech of the Three New Ways." "Then I am a champion." "That is no use to us; we have a champion before, Ogma, brother to the king." "Question me again," he said; "I am a harper." "That is no use to us; we have a harper ourselves, Abhean, son of Bicelmos, that the Men of the Three Gods brought from the hills." "I am a poet," he said then, "and a teller of tales." "That is no use to us; we have a teller of tales ourselves, Erc, son of Ethaman." "And I am a magician." "That is no use to us; we have plenty of magicians and people of power." "I am a physician," he said. "That is no use; we have Diancecht for our physician." "Let me be a cup-bearer," he said. "We do not want you; we have nine cup-bearers ourselves." "I am a good worker in brass." "We have a worker in brass ourselves, that is Credne Cerd."

Then Lugh said: "Go and ask the king if he has any one man that can do all these things, and if he has, I will not ask to come into Teamhair." The door-keeper went into the king's house then and told him all that. "There is a young man at the door," he said, "and his name should be the Ildánach, the Master of all Arts, for all the things the people of your house can do, he himself is able to do every one of them." "Try him with the chess-boards," said Nuada. So the chessboards were brought out, and every game that was played, Lugh won it. And when Nuada was told that, he said: "Let him in, for the like of him never came into Teamhair before."

Then the door-keeper let him pass, and he came into the king's house and sat down in the seat of knowledge. And there was a great flag-stone there that could hardly be moved by four times twenty yoke of oxen, and Ogma took it up and hurled it out through the house, so that it lay on the outside of Teamhair, as a challenge to Lugh. But Lugh hurled it back again that it lay in the middle of the king's house. He played the harp for them then, and he had them laughing and crying, till he put them asleep at the end with a sleepy tune. And when Nuada saw all the things Lugh could do, he began to think that by his help the country might get free of the taxes and the tyranny put on it by the Fomor. And it is what he did, he came down from his throne, and he put Lugh on it in his place, for the length of thirteen days, the way they might all listen to the advice he would give.

This now is the story of the birth of Lugh. The time the Fomor used to be coming to Ireland, Balor of the Strong Blows, or, as some called him, of the Evil Eye, was living on the Island of the Tower of Glass. There was danger for ships that went near that island, for the Fomor would come out and take them. And some say the sons of Nemed in the old time, before the Firbolgs were in Ireland, passed near it in their ships, and what they saw was a tower of glass in the middle of the sea, and on the tower something that had the appearance of men, and they went against it with Druid spells to attack it. And the Fomor worked against them with Druid spells of their own; and the sons of Nemed attacked the tower, and it vanished, and they thought it was destroyed. But a great wave rose over them then, and all their ships went down and all that were in them.

And the tower was there as it was before, and Balor living in it. And it is the reason he was called "of the Evil Eye," there was a power of death in one of his eyes, so that no person could look at it and live. It is the way it got that power, he was passing one time by a house where his father's Druids were making spells of death, and the window being open he looked in, and the smoke of the poisonous spells was rising up, and it went into his eye. And from that time he had to keep it closed unless he wanted to be the death of some enemy, and then the men that were with him would lift the eyelid with a ring of ivory.

Now a Druid foretold one time that it was by his own grandson he would get his death. And he had at that time but one child, a daughter whose name was Ethlinn; and when he heard what the Druid said, he shut her up in the tower on the island. And he put twelve women with her to take charge of her and to guard her, and he bade them never to let her see a man or hear the name of a man.

So Ethlinn was brought up in the tower, and she grew to be very beautiful; and sometimes she would see men passing in the currachs, and sometimes she would see a man in her dreams. But when she would speak of that to the women, they would give her no answer.

So there was no fear on Balor, and he went on with war and robbery as he was used, seizing every ship that passed by, and sometimes going over to Ireland to do destruction there.

Now it chanced at that time there were three brothers of the Tuatha de Danaan living together in a place that was called Druim na Teine, the Ridge of the Fire, Goibniu and Samthainn and Cian. Cian was a lord of land, and Goibniu was the smith that had such a great name. Now Cian had a wonderful cow, the Glas Gaibhnenn, and her milk never failed. And every one that heard of her coveted her, and many had tried to steal her away, so that she had to be watched night and day.

And one time Cian was wanting some swords made, and he went to Goibniu's forge, and he brought the Glas Gaibhnenn with him, holding her by a halter. When he came to the forge his two brothers were there together, for Samthainn had brought some steel to have weapons made for himself; and Cian bade Samthainn to hold the halter while he went into the forge to speak with Goibniu.

Now Balor had set his mind for a long time on the Glas Gaibhnenn, but he had never been able to get near her up to this time. And he was watching not far off, and when he saw Samthainn holding the cow, he put on the appearance of a little boy, having red hair, and came up to him and told him he heard his two brothers that were in the forge saying to one another that they would use all his steel for their own swords, and make his of iron. "By my word," said Samthainn, "they will not deceive me so easily. Let you hold the cow, little lad," he said, "and I will go in to them." With that he rushed into the forge, and great anger on him. And no sooner did Balor get the halter in his hand than he set out, dragging the Glas along with him, to the strand, and across the sea to his own island.

When Cian saw his brother coming in he rushed out, and there he saw Balor and the Glas out in the sea. And he had nothing to do then but to reproach his brother, and to wander about as if his wits had left him, not knowing what way to get his cow back from Balor. At last he went to a Druid to ask an advice from him; and it is what the Druid told him, that so long as Balor lived, the cow would never be brought back, for no one would go within reach of his Evil Eye.

Cian went then to a woman – Druid, Birog of the Mountain, for her help. And she dressed him in a woman's clothes, and brought him across the sea in a blast of wind, to the tower where Ethlinn was. Then she called to the women in the tower, and asked them for shelter for a high queen she was after saving from some hardship, and the women in the tower did not like to refuse a woman of the Tuatha de Danaan, and they let her and her comrade in. Then Birog by her enchantments put them all into a deep sleep, and Cian went to speak with Ethlinn. And when she saw him she said that was the face she had seen in her dreams. So she gave him her love; but after a while he was brought away again on a blast of wind.

And when her time came, Ethlinn gave birth to a son. And when Balor knew that, he bade his people put the child in a cloth and fasten it with a pin, and throw him into a current of the sea. And as they were carrying the child across an arm of the sea, the pin dropped out, and the child slipped from the cloth into the water, and they thought he was drowned. But he was brought away by Birog of the Mountain, and she brought him to his father Cian; and he gave him to be fostered by Taillte, daughter of the King of the Great Plain. It is thus Lugh was born and reared.

And some say Balor came and struck the head off Cian on a white stone, that has the blood marks on it to this day; but it is likely it was some other man he struck the head off, for it was by the sons of Tuireann that Cian came to his death.

And after Lugh had come to Teamhair, and made his mind up to join with his father's people against the Fomor, he put his mind to the work; and he went to a quiet place in Grellach Dollaid, with Nuada and the Dagda, and with Ogma; and Goibniu and Diancecht were called to them there. A full year they stopped there, making their plans together in secret, the way the Fomor would not know they were going to rise against them till such time as all would be ready, and till they would know what their strength was. And it is from that council the place got the name afterwards of "The Whisper of the Men of Dea."

And they broke up the council, and agreed to meet again that day three years, and every one of them went his own way, and Lugh went back to his own friends, the sons of Manannan.

And it was a good while after that, Nuada was holding a great assembly of the people on the Hill of Uisnech, on the west side of Teamhair. And they were not long there before they saw an armed troop coming towards them from the east, over the plain; and there was a young man in front of the troop, in command over the rest, and the brightness of his face was like the setting sun, so that they were not able to look at him because of its brightness.

And when he came nearer they knew it was Lugh Lamh-Fada, of the Long Hand, that had come back to them, and along with him were the Riders of the Sidhe from the Land of Promise, and his own foster-brothers, the sons of Manannan, Sgoith Gleigeil, the White Flower, and Goitne Gorm-Shuileach, the Blue-eyed Spear, and Sine Sindearg, of the Red Ring, and Donall Donn-Ruadh, of the Red-brown Hair. And it is the way Lugh was, he had Manannan's horse, the Aonbharr, of the One Mane, under him, that was as swift as the naked cold wind of spring, and the sea was the same as dry land to her, and the rider was never killed off her back. And he had Manannan's breast-plate on him, that kept whoever was wearing it from wounds, and a helmet on his head with two beautiful precious stones set in the front of it and one at the back, and when he took it off, his forehead was like the sun on a dry summer day. And he had Manannan's sword, the Freagarthach, the Answerer, at his side, and no one that was wounded by it would ever get away alive; and when that sword was bared in a battle, no man that saw it coming against him had any more strength than a woman in child-birth.

And the troop came to where the King of Ireland was with the Tuatha de Danaan, and they welcomed one another.

And they were not long there till they saw a surly, slovenly troop coming towards them, nine times nine of the messengers of the Fomor, that were coming to ask rent and taxes from the men of Ireland; and the names of the four that were the hardest and the most cruel were Eine and Eathfaigh and Coron and Compar; and there was such great dread of these four on the Tuatha de Danaan, that not one of them would so much as punish his own son or his foster-son without leave from them.

They came up then to where the King of Ireland was with the Riders of the Sidhe, and the king and all the Tuatha de Danaan stood up before them. And Lugh of the Long Hand said: "Why do you rise up before that surly, slovenly troop, when you did not rise up before us?"

"It is needful for us to do it," said the king; "for if there was but a child of us sitting before them, they would not think that too small a cause for killing him." "By my word," said Lugh, "there is a great desire coming on me to kill themselves." "That is a thing would bring harm on us," said the king, "for we would meet our own death and destruction through it." "It is too long a time you have been under this oppression," said Lugh. And with that he started up and made an attack on the Fomor, killing and wounding them, till he had made an end of eight nines of them, but he let the last nine go under the protection of Nuada the king. "And I would kill you along with the others," he said, "but I would sooner see you go with messages to your own country than my own people, for fear they might get any ill-treatment."

So the nine went back then till they came to Lochlann, where the men of the Fomor were, and they told them the story from beginning to end, and how a young well-featured lad had come into Ireland and had killed all the tax-gatherers but themselves, "and it is the reason he let us off," they said, "that we might tell you the story ourselves."

"Do you know who is the young man?" said Balor of the Evil Eye then.

"I know well," said Ceithlenn, his wife; "he is the son of your daughter and mine. And it was foretold," she said, "that from the time he would come into Ireland, we would never have power there again for ever."

Then the chief men of the Fomor went into a council, Eab, son of Neid, and Seanchab, grandson of Neid, and Sital Salmhor, and Liath, son of Lobais, and the nine poets of the Fomor that had learning and the gift of foreknowledge, and Lobais the Druid, and Balor himself, and his twelve white-mouthed sons, and Ceithlenn of the Crooked Teeth, his queen.

And it was just at that time Bres and his father Elathan were come to ask help of the Fomor, and Bres said: "I myself will go to Ireland, and seven great battalions of the Riders of the Fomor along with me, and I will give battle to this Ildánach, this master of all arts, and I will strike his head off and bring it here to you, to the green of Berbhe." "It would be a fitting thing for you to do," said they all. "Let my ships be made ready for me," said Bres, "and let food and provisions be put in them."

So they made no delay, but went and got the ships ready, and they put plenty of food and drink in them, and the two swift Luaths were sent out to gather the army to Bres. And when they were all gathered, they made ready their armour and their weapons, and they set out for Ireland.

And Balor the king followed them to the harbour, and he said: "Give battle to that Ildánach, and strike off his head; and tie that island that is called Ireland to the back of your ships, and let the destroying water take its place, and put it on the north side of Lochlann, and not one of the Men of Dea will follow it there to the end of life and time."

Then they pushed out their ships and put up their painted sails, and went out from the harbour on the untilled country, on the ridges of the wide-lying sea, and they never turned from their course till they came to the harbour of Eas Dara. And from that they sent out an army through West Connacht and destroyed it alto-gether, through and through. And the King of Connacht at that time was Bodb Dearg, son of the Dagda.

CHAPTER II

The Sons of Tuireann

And Lugh of the Long Hand was at that time at Teamhair with the King of Ireland, and it was showed to him that the Fomor were after landing at Eas Dara. And when he knew that, he made ready Manannan's horse, the Aonbharr, at the time of the battle of the day and night; and he went where Nuada the king was, and told him how the Fomor had landed at Eas Dara and had spoiled Bodb Dearg's country; "and it is what I want," he said, "to get help from you to give battle to them." But Nuada was not minded to avenge the destruction that was done on Bodb Dearg and not on himself, and Lugh was not well pleased with his answer, and he went riding out of Teamhair westward. And presently he saw three armed men coming towards him, his own father Cian, with his brothers Cu and Ceithen, that were the three sons of Cainte, and they saluted him. "What is the cause of your early rising?" they said. "It is good cause I have for it," said Lugh, "for the Fomor are come into Ireland and have robbed Bodb Dearg; and what help will you give me against them?" he said.

"Each one of us will keep off a hundred from you in the battle," said they. "That

31

is a good help," said Lugh; "but there is a help I would sooner have from you than that: to gather the Riders of the Sidhe to me from every place where they are."

So Cu and Ceithen went towards the south, and Cian set out northward, and he did not stop till he reached the Plain of Muirthemne. And as he was going across the plain he saw three armed men before him, that were the three sons of Tuireann, son of Ogma. And it is the way it was between the three sons of Tuireann and the three sons of Cainte, they were in hatred and enmity towards one another, so that whenever they met there was sure to be fighting among them.

Then Cian said: "If my two brothers had been here it is a brave fight we would make; but since they are not, it is best for me to fall back." Then he saw a great herd of pigs near him, and he struck himself with a Druid rod that put on him the shape of a pig of the herd, and he began rooting up the ground like the rest.

Then Brian, one of the sons of Tuireann, said to his brothers: "Did you see that armed man that was walking the plain a while ago?" "We did see him," said they. "Do you know what was it took him away?" said Brian. "We do not know that," said they. "It is a pity you not to be keeping a better watch over the plains of the open country in time of war," said Brian; "and I know well what happened him, for he struck himself with his Druid rod into the shape of a pig of these pigs, and he is rooting up the ground now like any one of them; and whoever he is, he is no friend to us." "That is bad for us," said the other two, "for the pigs belong to some one of the Tuatha de Danaan, and even if we kill them all, the Druid pig might chance to escape us in the end."

"It is badly you got your learning in the city of learning," said Brian, "when you cannot tell an enchanted beast from a natural beast." And while he was saying that, he struck his two brothers with his Druid rod, and he turned them into two thin, fast hounds, and they began to yelp sharply on the track of the enchanted pig.

And it was not long before the pig fell out from among the others, and not one of the others made away but only itself, and it made for a wood, and at the edge of the wood Brian gave a cast of his spear that went through its body. And the pig cried out, and it said: "It is a bad thing you have done to have made a cast at me when you knew me." "It seems to me you have the talk of a man," said Brian. "I was a man indeed," said he; "I am Cian, son of Cainte, and give me your protection now." "I swear by the gods of the air," said Brian, "that if the life came back seven times to you, I would take it from you every time." "If that is so," said Cian, "give me one request: let me go into my own shape again." "We will do that," said Brian, "for it is easier to me to kill a man than a pig."

So Cian took his own shape then, and he said: "Give me mercy now." "We will not give it," said Brian. "Well, I have got the better of you for all that," said Cian; "for if it was in the shape of a pig you had killed me there would only be the blood money for a pig on me; but as it is in my own shape you will kill me, there never was and never will be any person killed for whose sake a heavier fine will be paid than for myself. And the arms I am killed with," he said, "it is they will tell the deed to my son."

"It is not with weapons you will be killed, but with the stones lying on the ground," said Brian. And with that they pelted him with stones, fiercely and roughly, till all that was left of him was a poor, miserable, broken heap; and they buried him the depth of a man's body in the earth, and the earth would not receive that murder from them, but cast it up again. Brian said it should go into the earth again, and they put it in the second time, and the second time the earth would not take it. And six times the sons of Tuireann buried the body, and six times it was cast up again; but the seventh time it was put underground the earth kept it. And then they went on to join Lugh of the Long Hand for the battle.

Now as to Lugh; upon parting with his father he went forward from Teamhair westward, to the hills that were called afterwards Gairech and Ilgairech, and to the ford of the Shannon that is now called Athluain, and to Bearna nah-Eadar-gana, the Gap of Separation, and over Magh Luirg, the Plain of Following, and to Corr Slieve na Seaghsa, the Round Mountain of the Poet's Spring, and to the head of Sean-Slieve, and through the place of the bright-faced Corann, and from that to Magh Mor an Aonaigh, the Great Plain of the Fair, where the Fomor were, and the spoils of Connacht with them.

It is then Bres, son of Elathan, rose up and said: "It is a wonder to me the sun to be rising in the west to-day, and it rising in the east every other day." "It would be better for us it to be the sun," said the Druids. "What else is it?" said he. "It is the shining of the face of Lugh, son of Ethlinn," said they.

Lugh came up to them then and saluted them. "Why do you come like a friend to us?" said they. "There is good cause for that," he said, "for there is but one half of me of the Tuatha de Danaan, and the other half of yourselves. And give me back now the milch cows of the men of Ireland," he said. "May early good luck not come to you till you get either a dry or a milch cow here," said a man of them, and anger on him.

But Lugh stopped near them for three days and three nights, and at the end of that time the Riders of the Sidhe came to him. And Bodb Dearg, son of the Dagda, came with twenty-nine hundred men, and he said: "What is the cause of your delay in giving battle?" "Waiting for you I was," said Lugh.

Then the kings and chief men of the men of Ireland took their armour on them, and they raised the points of their spears over their heads, and they made close fences of their shields. And they attacked their enemies on Magh Mor an Aonaigh, and their enemies answered them, and they threw their whining spears at one another, and when their spears were broken they drew their swords from their blue-bordered sheaths and began to strike at one another, and thickets of brown flames rose above them from the bitterness of their many-edged weapons.

And Lugh saw the battle pen where Bres, son of Elathan, was, and he made a fierce attack on him and on the men that were guarding him, till he had made an end of two hundred of them.

When Bres saw that, he gave himself up to Lugh's protection. "Give me my life this time," he said, "and I will bring the whole race of the Fomor to fight it out with you in a great battle; and I bind myself to that, by the sun and the moon, the sea and the land," he said.

On that Lugh gave him his life, and then the Druids that were with him asked his protection for themselves. "By my word," said Lugh, "if the whole race of the Fomor went under my protection they would not be destroyed by me." So then Bres and the Druids set out for their own country.

Now as to Lugh and the sons of Tuireann. After the battle of Magh Mor an Aonaigh, he met two of his kinsmen and asked them did they see his father in the fight. "We did not," said they. "I am sure he is not living," said Lugh; "and I give my word," he said, "there will no food or drink go into my mouth till I get knowledge by what death my father died."

Then he set out, and the Riders of the Sidhe after him, till they came to the place where he and his father parted from one another, and from that to the place where his father went into the shape of a pig when he saw the sons of Tuireann.

And when Lugh came to that place the earth spoke to him, and it said: "It is in great danger your father was here, Lugh, when he saw the sons of Tuireann before him, and it is into the shape of a pig he had to go, but it is in his own shape they killed him."

Then Lugh told that to his people, and he found the spot where his father was buried, and he bade them dig there, the way he would know by what death the sons of Tuireann had made an end of him.

Then they raised the body out of the grave and looked at it, and it was all one bed of wounds. And Lugh said: "It was the death of an enemy the sons of Tuireann gave my dear father." And he gave him three kisses, and it is what he said: "It is bad the way I am myself after this death, for I can hear nothing with my ears, and I can see nothing with my eyes, and there is not a living pulse in my heart, with grief after my father. And you gods I worship," he said, "it is a pity I not to have come here the time this thing was done. And it is a great thing that has been done here," he said, "the people of the gods of Dana to have done treachery on one another, and it is long they will be under loss by it and be weakened by it. And Ireland will never be free from trouble from this out, east and west," he said.

Then they put Cian under the earth again, and after that there was keening made over his grave, and a stone was raised on it, and his name was written in Ogham. And Lugh said: "This hill will take its name from Cian, although he himself is stripped and broken. And it was the sons of Tuireann did this thing," he said, "and there will grief and anguish fall on them from it, and on their children after them. And it is no lying story I am telling you," he said; "and it is a pity the way I am, and my heart is broken in my breast since Cian, the brave man, is not living."

Then he bade his people to go before him to Team-hair, "But do not tell the story till I tell it myself," he said.

And when Lugh came to Teamhair he sat in the high seat of the king, and he looked about him and he saw the three sons of Tuireann. And those were the three that were beyond all others at Teamhair at that time for quickness and skill, for a good hand in battle, for beauty and an honourable name.

Then Lugh bade his people to shake the chain of silence, and they did so, and they all listened. And Lugh said: "What are your minds fixed on at this time, Men of Dea?" "On yourself indeed," said they. "I have a question to ask of you," he said. "What is the vengeance each one of you would take on the man that would kill your father?"

There was great wonder on them when they heard that, and one of the chief men among them said: "Tell us was it your own father that was killed?" "It was indeed," said Lugh; "and I see now in this house," he said, "the men that killed him, and they know themselves what way they killed him better than I know it." Then the king said: "It is not a death of one day only I would give the man that had killed my father, if he was in my power, but to cut off one of his limbs from day to day till I would make an end of him." All the chief men said the same, and the sons of Tuireann like the rest.

"There are making that answer," said Lugh, "the three men that killed my father; and let them pay the fine for him now, since you are all together in the one place. And if they will not," he said, "I will not break the protection of the king's house, but they must make no attempt to quit this house till they have settled with me."

"If it was I myself had killed your father," said the king, "I would be well content you to take a fine from me for him."

"It is at us Lugh is saying all this," said the sons of Tuireann among themselves. "Let us acknowledge the killing of his father to him," said Iuchar and Iucharba. "I am in dread," said Brian, "that it is wanting an acknowledgment from us he is, in the presence of all the rest, and that he will not let us off with a fine afterwards." "It is best to acknowledge it," said the others; "and let you speak it out since you are the eldest."

Then Brian, son of Tuireann, said: "It is at us you are speaking, Lugh, for you are thinking we went against the sons of Cainte before now; and we did not kill your father," he said, "but we will pay the fine for him the same as if we did kill him." "I will take a fine from you that you do not think of," said Lugh, "and I will say here what it is, and if it is too much for you, I will let you off a share of it." "Let us hear it from you," said they. "Here it is," said Lugh; "three apples, and the skin of a pig, and a spear, and two horses, and a chariot, and seven pigs, and a dog's whelp, and a cooking-spit, and three shouts on a hill. That is the fine I am asking," he said; "and if it is too much for you, a part of it will be taken off you presently, and if you do not think it too much, then pay it."

"It is not too much," said Brian, "or a hundred times of it would not be too much. And we think it likely," he said, "because of its smallness that you have some treachery towards us behind it." "I do not think it too little of a fine," said Lugh; "and I give you the guarantee of the Tuatha de Danaan I will ask no other thing, and I will be faithful to you, and let you give the same pledge to me." "It is a pity you to ask that," said Brian, "for our own pledge is as good as any pledge in the world." "Your own pledge is not enough," said Lugh, "for it is often the like of you promised to pay a fine in this way, and would try to back out of it after."

So then the sons of Tuireann bound themselves by the King of Ireland, and by Bodb Dearg, son of the Dagda, and by the chief men of the Tuatha de Danaan, that they would pay that fine to Lugh.

"It would be well for me now," said Lugh, "to give you better knowledge of the fine." "It would be well indeed," said they.

"This is the way of it then," said Lugh. "The three apples I asked of you are the three apples from the Garden in the East of the World, and no other apples will do but these, for they are the most beautiful and have most virtue in them of the apples of the whole world. And it is what they are like, they are of the colour of burned gold, and they are the size of the head of a child a month old, and there is the taste of honey on them, and they do not leave the pain of wounds or the vexation of sickness on any one that eats them, and they do not lessen by being eaten for ever. And the skin I asked of you," he said, "is the pig skin of Tuis, King of Greece, and it heals all the wounds and all the sickness of the world, and whatever danger a man may be in, if it can but overtake the life in him, it will cure him; and it is the way it was with that pig, every stream of water it would go through would be turned into wine to the end of nine days after, and every wound it touched was healed; and it is what the Druids of Greece said, that it is not in itself this virtue was, but in the skin, and they skinned it, and the skin is there ever since. And think, too, it will not be easy for you to get it, with or without leave."

"And do you know what is the spear I am asking of you?" he said. "We do not," said they. "It is a very deadly spear belonging to the King of Persia, the Luin it is called, and every choice thing is done by it, and its head is kept steeped in a vessel of water, the way it will not burn down the place where it is, and it will be hard to get it. And do you know what two horses and what chariot I am asking of you? They are the chariot and the two wonderful horses of Dobar, King of Siogair, and the sea is the same as land to them, and there are no faster horses than themselves, and there is no chariot equal to that one in shape and in strength.

"And do you know what are the seven pigs I asked of you? They are the pigs of Easal, King of the Golden Pillars; and though they are killed every night, they are found alive again the next day, and there will be no disease or no sickness on any person that will eat a share of them.

"And the whelp I asked of you is Fail-Inis, the whelp belonging to the King of Ioruaidh, the Cold Country. And all the wild beasts of the world would fall down at the sight of her, and she is more beautiful than the sun in his fiery wheels, and it will be hard to get her.

"And the cooking-spit I asked of you is a spit of the spits of the women of Inis Cenn-fhinne, the Island of Caer of the Fair Hair. And the three shouts you are to give on a hill must be given on the Hill of Miochaoin in the north of Lochlann. And Miochaoin and his sons are under bonds not to allow any shouts to be given on that hill; and it was with them my father got his learning, and if I would forgive you his death, they would not forgive you. And if you get through all your other voyages before you reach to them, it is my opinion they themselves will avenge him on you. And that is the fine I have asked of you," said Lugh.

There was silence and darkness on the sons of Tuireann when they heard that. And they went to where their father was, and told him the fine that had been put on them. "It is bad news that is," said Tuireann; "and it is to your death and your destruction you will be going, looking for those things. But for all that, if Lugh himself had a mind to help you, you could work out the fine, and all the men of the world could not do it but by the power of Manannan or of Lugh. Go then and ask the loan of Manannan's horse, the Aonbharr, from Lugh, and if he has any wish to get the fine, he will give it to you; but if he does not wish it he will say the horse is not his, and that he would not give the loan of a loan. Ask him then for the loan of Manannan's curragh, the Scuabtuinne, the Sweeper of the Waves. And he will give that, for he is under bonds not to refuse a second request, and the curragh is better for you than the horse," he said.

So the sons of Tuireann went to where Lugh was, and they saluted him, and they said they could not bring him the fine without his own help, and for that reason it would be well for them to get a loan of the Aonbharr. "I have that horse only on loan myself," said Lugh, "and I will not give a loan of a loan."

"If that is so, give us the loan of Manannan's curragh," said Brian. "I will give that," said Lugh. "What place is it?" said they. "At Brugh na Boinn," said Lugh.

Then they went back again to where Tuireann was, and his daughter Ethne, their sister, with him, and they told him they had got the curragh. "It is not much the better you will be for it," said Tuireann, "although Lugh would like well to get every part of this fine he could make use of before the battle with the Fomor. But he would like yourselves to come to your death looking for it."

Then they went away, and they left Tuireann sorrowful and lamenting, and Ethne went with them to where the curragh was. And Brian got into it, and he said: "There is place but for one other person along with me here." And he began to find fault with its narrowness. "You ought not to be faulting the curragh," said Ethne; "and O my dear brother," she said, "it was a bad thing you did, to kill the father of Lugh of the Long Hand; and whatever harm may come to you from it, it is but just." "Do not say that, Ethne," they said, "for we are in good heart, and we will do brave deeds. And we would sooner be killed a hundred times over," they said, "than to meet with the death of cowards." "My grief," said Ethne, "there is nothing more sorrowful than this, to see you driven out from your own country."

Then the three pushed out their curragh from the beautiful clear-bayed shore of Ireland. "What course shall we take first?" said they. "We will go look for the apples," said Brian, "as they were the first thing we were bade bring. And so we ask of you, curragh of Manannan that is under us, to sail to the Garden in the East of the World."

And the curragh did not neglect that order, but it sailed forward over the green-sided waves and deep places till it came to its harbour in the east of the world.

And then Brian asked his brothers: "What way have you a mind to get into the garden? for I think," he said, "the king's champions and the fighting men of the country are always guarding it, and the king himself is chief over them." "What should we do," said his brothers, "but to make straight at them and attack them, and bring away the apples or fall ourselves, since we cannot escape from these dangers that are before us without meeting our death in some place." "It would be better," said Brian, "the story of our bravery and our craftiness to be told and to live after us, than folly and cowardice to be told of us. And what is best for us to do now," he said, "is to go in the shape of swift hawks into the garden, and the watchers have but their light spears to throw at us, and let you take good care to keep out of their reach; and after they have thrown them all, make a quick flight to the apples and let each of you bring away an apple of them in your claws, and I will bring away the third."

They said that was a good advice, and Brian struck himself and the others with his Druid rod, and changed them into beautiful hawks. And they flew towards the garden, and the watchers took notice of them and shouted on every side of them, and threw showers of spears and darts, but the hawks kept out of their reach as Brian had bade them, till all the spears were spent, and then they swept down bravely on the apples, and brought them away with them, without so much as a wound.

And the news went through the city and the whole district, and the king had three wise, crafty daughters, and they put themselves into the shape of three ospreys, and they followed the hawks to the sea, and sent flashes of lightning before them and after them, that scorched them greatly.

"It is a pity the way we are now," said the sons of Tuireann, "for we will be burned through and through with this lightning if we do not get some relief." "If I can give you relief I will do it," said Brian. With that he struck himself and his brothers with the Druid rod, and they were turned into three swans, and they went down quickly into the sea, and the ospreys went away from them then, and the sons of Tuireann went into their boat.

After that they consulted together, and it is what they agreed, to go to Greece and to bring away the skin of the pig, with or without leave. So they went forward till they came near to the court of the King of Greece.

"What appearance should we put on us going in here?" said Brian. "What appearance should we go in with but our own?" said the others. "That is not what I think best," said Brian; "but to go in with the appearance of poets from Ireland, the way the high people of Greece will hold us in respect and in honour." "It would be hard for us to do that," they said, "and we without a poem, and it is little we know how to make one."

However, they put the poet's tie on their hair, and they knocked at the door of the court, and the door-keeper asked who was in it. "We are poets of Ireland," said Brian, "and we are come with a poem to the king."

The door-keeper went in and told the king that there were poets from Ireland at the door. "Let them in," said the king, "for it is in search of a good man they came so far from their own country." And the king gave orders that everything should be well set out in the court, the way they would say they had seen no place so grand in all their travels.

The sons of Tuireann were let in then, having the appearance of poets, and they fell to drinking and pleasure without delay; and they thought they had never seen, and there was not in the world, a court so good as that or so large a household, or a place where they had met with better treatment.

Then the king's poets got up to give out their poems and songs. And then Brian, son of Tuireann, bade his brothers to say a poem for the king. "We have no poem," said they; "and do not ask any poem of us, but the one we know before, and that is to take what we want by the strength of our hand if we are the strongest, or to fall by those that are against us if they are the strongest." "That is not a good way to make a poem," said Brian. And with that he rose up himself and asked a hearing. And they all listened to him, and it is what he said:

"O Tuis, we do not hide your fame; we praise you as the oak among kings; the skin of a pig, bounty without hardness, this is the reward I ask for it.

"The war of a neighbour against an ear; the fair ear of his neighbour will be against him; he who gives us what he owns, his court will not be the scarcer for it.

"A raging army and a sudden sea are a danger to whoever goes against them. The skin of a pig, bounty without hardness, this is the reward I ask, O Tuis."

"That is a good poem," said the king; "but I do not know a word of its meaning." "I will tell you its meaning," said Brian. " 'O Tuis, we do not hide your fame; we praise you as the oak above the kings.' That is, as the oak is beyond the kingly trees of the wood, so are you beyond the kings of the world for open-handedness and for grandeur.

" 'The skin of a pig, bounty without hardness.' That is, the skin of a pig you own is what I would wish to get from you as a reward for my poem.

" 'The war of a neighbour against an ear, the fair ear of his neighbour will be against him.' That is, you and I will be by the ears about the skin, unless I get it with your consent.

"And that is the meaning of the poem," said Brian.

"I would praise your poem," said the king, "if there was not so much about my pig-skin in it; and you have no good sense, man of poetry," he said, "to be asking that thing of me, and I would not give it to all the poets and the learned men and the great men of the world, since they could not take it away without my consent. But I will give you three times the full of the skin of gold as the price of your poem," he said.

"May good be with you, king," said Brian, "and I know well it was no easy thing I was asking, but I knew I would get a good ransom for it. And I am that covetous," he said, "I will not be satisfied without seeing the gold measured myself into the skin."

The king sent his servants with them then to the treasure-house to measure the gold. "Measure out the full of it to my brothers first," said Brian, "and then give good measure to myself, since it was I made the poem."

But when the skin was brought out, Brian made a quick sudden snatch at it with his left hand, and drew his sword and made a stroke at the man nearest him, and made two halves of him. And then he kept a hold of the skin and put it about himself, and the three of them rushed out of the court, cutting down every armed man before them, so that not one escaped death or wounding. And then Brian went to where the king himself was, and the king made no delay in attacking him, and they made a hard fight of it, and at the end the King of Greece fell by the hand of Brian, son of Tuireann.

The three brothers rested for a while after that, and then they said they would go and look for some other part of the fine. "We will go to Pisear, King of Persia, said Brian, "and ask him for the spear."

So they went into their boat, and they left the blue streams of the coast of Greece, and they said: "We are well off when we have the apples and the skin." And they stopped nowhere till they came to the borders of Persia.

"Let us go to the court with the appearance of poets," said Brian, "the same as we went to the King of Greece." "We are content to do that," said the others, "as all turned out so well the last time we took to poetry; not that it is easy for us to take to a calling that does not belong to us."

So they put the poet's tie on their hair, and they were as well treated as they were at the other court; and when the time came for poems Brian rose up, and it is what he said:

"It is little any spear looks to Pisear; the battles of enemies are broken, it is not too much for Pisear to wound every one of them.

"A yew, the most beautiful of the wood, it is called a king, it is not bulky. May the spear drive on the whole crowd to their wounds of death."

"That is a good poem," said the king, "but I do not understand why my own spear is brought into it, O Man of Poetry from Ireland."

"It is because it is that spear of your own I would wish to get as the reward of my poem," said Brian. "It is little sense you have to be asking that of me," said the king; "and the people of my court never showed greater respect for poetry than now, when they did not put you to death on the spot."

When Brian heard that talk from the king, he thought of the apple that was in his hand, and he made a straight cast and hit him in the forehead, so that his brains were put out at the back of his head, and he bared the sword and made an attack on the people about him. And the other two did not fail to do the same, and they gave him their help bravely till they had made an end of all they met of the people of the court. And then they found the spear, and its head in a cauldron of water, the way it would not set fire to the place.

And after a while they said it was time for them to go and look for the rest of the great fine that was on them, and they asked one another what way should they go. "We will go to the King of the Island of Siogair," said Brian, "for it is with him are the two horses and the chariot the Ildánach asked of us."

They went forward then and brought the spear with them, and it is proud the three champions were after all they had done. And they went on till they were come to the court of the King of Siogair.

"It is what we will do this time," said Brian, "we will go in with the appearance of paid soldiers from Ireland, and we will make friends with the king, the way we will get to know in what place the horses and the chariot are kept." And when they had settled on that they went forward to the lawn before the king's house.

The king and the chief men that were with him rose up and came through the fair that was going on there, and they saluted the king, and he asked who were they. "We are trained fighting men from Ireland," they said, "and we are earning wages from the kings of the world." "Is it your wish to stop with me for a while?" said the king. "That is what we are wanting," said they. So then they made an agreement and took service with him.

They stopped in the court a fortnight and a month, and they never saw the horses through that time. Then Brian said: "This is a bad way we are in, to have no more news of the horses now than the first day we came to the place." "What is best for us to do now?" said his brothers. "Let us do this," said Brian, "let us take our arms and gather our things together, and go to the king and tell him we will leave the country and this part of the world unless he will show us those horses."

So they went to the king that very day, and he asked them what did they mean by getting themselves ready for a journey. "You will hear that, high king," said Brian; "it is because trained fighting men from Ireland, like ourselves, have always trust put in them by the kings they guard, and we are used to be told the secrets and the whispers of any person we are with, and that is not the way you have treated us since we came to you. For you have two horses and a chariot that are

41

the best in the world, as we have been told, and we have not been given a sight of them yet." "It would be a pity you to go on that account," said the king, "when I would have showed them to you the first day, if I had known you had a wish to see them. And if you have a mind to see them now," he said, "you may see them; for I think there never came soldiers from Ireland to this place that were thought more of by myself and by my people than yourselves."

He sent for the horses then, and they were yoked to the chariot, and their going was as fast as the cold spring wind, and the sea was the same as the land to them.

And Brian was watching the horses closely, and on a sudden he took hold of the chariot and took the chariot driver out and dashed him against the nearest rock, and made a leap into his place himself, and made a cast of the Persian spear at the king, that went through his heart. And then he and his brothers scattered the people before them, and brought away the chariot.

"We will go now to Easal, the King of the Golden Pillars," said Brian, "to look for the seven pigs the Ildánach bade us bring him."

They sailed on then without delay or drawback to that high country. And it is the way the people of that country were, watching their harbours for fear of the sons of Tuireann, for the story of them had been told in all parts, how they had been sent out of Ireland by force, and how they were bringing away with them all the gifted treasures of the whole world.

Easal came to the edge of the harbour to meet them, and he asked was it true what he heard, that the king of every country they had gone to had fallen by them. Brian said it was true, whatever he might wish to do to them for it. "What was it made you do that?" said Easal. Brian told him then it was the oppression and the hard sentence of another had put them to it; and he told him all that had happened, and how they had put down all that offered to stand against them until that time.

"What did you come to this country now for?" said the king. "For the pigs belonging to yourself," said Brian; "for to bring them away with us is a part of the fine." "What way do you think to get them?" said the king. "If we get them with good-will," said Brian, "we are ready to take them thankfully; and if we do not, we are ready to do battle with yourself and your people on the head of them, that you may fall by us, and we may bring away the pigs in spite of you." "If that is to be the end of it," said the king, "it would be a pity to bring my people into a battle." "It would be a pity indeed," said Brian.

Then the king whispered and took advice with his people about the matter, and it is what they agreed, to give up the pigs of their own free will to the sons of Tuireann, since they could not see that any one had been able to stand against them up to that time.

Then the sons of Tuireann gave their thanks to Easal, and there was wonder on them to have got the pigs like that, when they had to fight for every other part of the fine. And more than that, they had left a share of their blood in every other place till then.

Easal brought them to his own house that night, and they were served with food, and drink, and good beds, and all they could wish for. And they rose up on the morrow and came into the king's presence, and the pigs were given to them. "It is well you have done by us, giving us these pigs," said Brian, "for we did not get any share of the fine without fighting but these alone." And he made a poem for the king then, praising him, and putting a great name on him for what he had done.

"What journey are you going to make now, sons of Tuireann?" said Easal. "We are going," they said, "to the country of Ioruaidh, on account of a whelp that is there." "Give me one request," said Easal, "and that is to bring me with you to the King of Ioruaidh, for a daughter of mine is his wife, and I would wish to persuade him to give you the whelp without a battle." "That will please us well," they said.

So the king's ship was made ready, and we have no knowledge of what happened till they came to the delightful, wonderful coast of Ioruaidh. The people and the armies were watching the harbours and landing-places before them, and they knew them at once and shouted at them.

Then Easal went on shore peaceably, and he went to where his son-in-law, the king, was, and told him the story of the sons of Tuireann from beginning to end. "What has brought them to this country?" said the King of Ioruaidh. "To ask for the hound you have," said Easal. "It was a bad thought you had coming with them to ask it," said the king, "for the gods have not given that much luck to any three champions in the world, that they would get my hound by force or by good-will." "It would be better for you to let them have the hound," said Easal, "since they have put down so many of the kings of the world."

But all he could say was only idleness to the king. So he went then to where the sons of Tuireann were, and gave them the whole account. And when they heard the king's answer, they made no delay, but put quick hands on their arms, and offered to give battle to the army of Ioruaidh. And when they met, there was a brave battle fought on both sides. And as for the sons of Tuireann, they began to kill and to strike at the men of Ioruaidh till they parted from one another in the fight, so that Iuchar and Iucharba chanced to be on one side, and Brian by himself on the other side. It was a gap of danger and a breaking of ranks was before Brian in every path he took, till he came to the King of Ioruaidh in the battle pen where he was. And then the two brave champions began a fierce fight together, and they did not spare one another in it. And at the last Brian overcame the king, and bound him, and brought him through the middle of the army, till he came to the place where Easal was, and it is what he said: "There is your son-in-law for you, and I swear by my hand of valour, I would think it easier to kill him three times than to bring him to you once like this."

So then the whelp was given to the sons of Tuireann, and the king was unbound, and peace was made between them. And when they had brought all this to an end, they bade farewell to Easal and to all the rest.

Now as to Lugh of the Long Hand, it was showed to him that the sons of Tuireann had got all the things that were wanting to him against the battle with the Fomor; and on that he sent a Druid spell after them to put forgetfulness on them of the rest of the fine that they had not got. And he put a great desire and longing on them to go back to Ireland; so they forgot that a part of the fine was wanting to them, and they turned back again toward home.

And it is the place where Lugh was at the time, at a gathering of the people for a fair on the green outside Teamhair, and the King of Ireland along with him. And it was made known to Lugh that the sons of Tuireann were landed at Brugh na Boinn. And he went into the city of Teamhair, and shut the gate after him, and he put on Manannan's smooth armour, and the cloak of the daughters of Flidais, and he took his own arms in his hand.

And the sons of Tuireann came where the king was, and they were made welcome by him and by the Tuatha de Danaan. And the king asked them did they get the fine. "We did get it," said they; "and where is Lugh till we give it to him?" "He was here a while ago," said the king. And the whole fair was searched for him, but he was not found.

"I know the place where he is," said Brian; "for it has been made known to him that we are come to Ireland, and these deadly arms with us, and he is gone into Teamhair to avoid us."

Messengers were sent to him then, and it is the answer he gave them that he would not come, but that the fine should be given to the king.

So the sons of Tuireann did that, and when the king had taken the fine they all went to the palace in Teamhair; and Lugh came out on the lawn and the fine was given to him, and it is what he said: "There is a good payment here for any one that ever was killed or that ever will be killed. But there is something wanting to it yet that it is not lawful to leave out. And where is the cooking-spit?" he said; "and where are the three shouts on the hill that you did not give yet?"

And when the sons of Tuireann heard that there came clouds of weakness on them. And they left the place and went to their father's house that night, and they told him all they had done, and the way Lugh had treated them.

There was grief and darkness on Tuireann then, and they spent the night together. And on the morrow they went to their ship, and Ethne, their sister, with them, and she was crying and lamenting, and it is what she said:

"It is a pity, Brian of my life, it is not to Teamhair your going is, after all the troubles you have had before this, even if I could not follow you.

"O Salmon of the dumb Boinn, O Salmon of the Lifé River, since I cannot keep you here I am loath to part from you.

"O Rider of the Wave of Tuaidh, the man that stands best in the fight, if you come back again, I think it will not be pleasing to your enemy.

"Is there pity with you for the sons of Tuireann leaning now on their green shields? Their going is a cause for pity, my mind is filled up with it.

"You to be to-night at Beinn Edair till the heavy coming of the morning, you who have taken forfeits from brave men, it is you have increased our grief.

"It is a pity your journey is from Teamhair, and from the pleasant plains, and from great Uisnech of Midhe; there is nothing so pitiful as this."

After that complaint they went out on the rough waves of the green sea; and they were a quarter of a year on the sea without getting any news of the island.

Then Brian put on his water dress and he made a leap, and he was a long time walking in the sea looking for the Island of the Fair-Haired Women, and he found it in the end. And he went looking for the court, and when he came to it, all he found was a troop of women doing needlework and embroidering borders. And among all the other things they had with them, there was the cooking-spit.

And when Brian saw it, he took it up in his hand and he was going to bring it with him to the door. And all the women began laughing when they saw him doing that, and it is what they said: "It is a brave deed you put your hand to; for even if your brothers were along with you, the least of the three times fifty women of us would not let the spit go with you or with them. But for all that," they said, "take a spit of the spits with you, since you had the daring to try and take it in spite of us."

Brian bade them farewell then, and went to look for the boat. And his brothers thought it was too long he was away from them, and just as they were going to leave the place they were, they saw him coming towards them, and that raised their courage greatly.

And he went into the boat, and they went on to look for the Hill of Miochaoin. And when they came there, Miochaoin, that was the guardian of the hill, came towards them; and when Brian saw him he attacked him, and the fight of those two champions was like the fight of two lions, till Miochaoin fell at the last.

And after Miochaoin had fallen, his three sons came out to fight with the three sons of Tuireann. And if any one ever came from the east of the world to look at any fight, it is to see the fight of these champions he had a right to come, for the greatness of their blows and the courage of their minds. The names of the sons of Miochaoin were Corc and Conn and Aedh, and they drove their three spears through the bodies of the sons of Tuireann, and that did not discourage them at all and they put their own three spears through the bodies of the sons of Miochaoin, so that they fell into the clouds and the faintness of death.

And then Brian said: "What way are you now, my dear brothers?" "We are near our death," said they. "Let us rise up," he said, "and give three shouts upon the hill, for I see the signs of death coming on us." "We are not able to do that," said they. Then Brian rose up and raised each of them with one hand, and he shedding blood heavily all the time, until they gave the three shouts.

After that Brian brought them with him to the boat, and they were travelling the sea for a long time, but at last Brian said: "I see Beinn Edair and our father's dun, and Teamhair of the Kings." "We would have our fill of health if we could see that," said the others; "and for the love of your good name, brother," they said, "raise up our heads on your breast till we see Ireland again, and life or death will be the same to us after that. And O Brian," they said, "Flame of Valour without treachery, we would sooner death to bring ourselves away, than to see you with wounds upon your body, and with no physician to heal you."

Then they came to Beinn Edair, and from that they went on to their father's house, and Brian said to Tuireann: "Go, dear father, to Teamhair, and give this spit to Lugh, and bring the skin that has healing in it for our relief. Ask it from him for the sake of friendship," he said, " for we are of the one blood, and let him not give hardness for hardness. And O dear father," he said, "do not be long on your journey, or you will not find us alive before you."

Then Tuireann went to Teamhair, and he found Lugh of the Long Hand before him, and he gave him the spit, and he asked the skin of him to heal his children, and Lugh said he would not give it. And Tuireann came back to them and told them he had not got the skin. And Brian said: "Bring me with you to Lugh, to see would I get it from him."

So they went to Lugh, and Brian asked the skin of him. And Lugh said he would not give it, and that if they would give him the breadth of the earth in gold for it, he would not take it from them, unless he was sure their death would come on them in satisfaction for the deed they had done.

When Brian heard that, he went to the place his two brothers were, and he lay down between them, and his life went out from him, and out from the other two at the same time.

And their father cried and lamented over his three beautiful sons, that had the making of a king of Ireland in each of them, and his strength left him and he died; and they were buried in the one grave.

CHAPTER III

The Great Battle of Magh Tuireadh

And it was not long after Lugh had got the fine from the sons of Tuireann that the Fomor came and landed at Scetne.

The whole host of the Fomor were come this time, and their king, Balor, of the Strong Blows and of the Evil Eye, along with them; and Bres, and Indech, son of De Domnann, a king of the Fomor, and Elathan, son of Lobos, and Goll and Ingol, and Octriallach, son of Indech, and Elathan, son of Delbaeth.

Then Lugh sent the Dagda to spy out the Fomor, and to delay them till such time as the men of Ireland would come to the battle.

So the Dagda went to their camp, and he asked them for a delay, and they said he might have that. And then to make sport of him, the Fomor made broth for him, for he had a great love for broth. So they filled the king's cauldron with four times twenty gallons of new milk, and the same of meal and fat, and they put in goats and sheep and pigs along with that, and boiled all together, and then they poured it all out into a great hole in the ground. And they called him to it then, and told him he should eat his fill, the way the Fomor would not be reproached for want of hospitality the way Bres was. "We will make an end of you if you leave any part of it after you," said Indech, son of De Domnann.

So the Dagda took the ladle, and it big enough for a man and a woman to lie in the bowl of it, and he took out bits with it, the half of a salted pig, and a quarter of lard a bit would be. "If the broth tastes as well as the bits taste, this is good food," he said. And he went on putting the full of the ladle into his mouth till the hole was empty; and when all was gone he put down his hand and scraped up all that was left among the earth and the gravel.

Sleep came on him then after eating the broth, and the Fomor were laughing at him, for his belly was the size of the cauldron of a great house. But he rose up after a while, and, heavy as he was, he made his way home; and indeed his dress was no way sightly, a cape to the hollow of the elbows, and a brown coat, long in the breast and short behind, and on his feet brogues of horse hide, with the hair outside, and in his hand a wheeled fork it would take eight men to carry, so that the track he left after him was deep enough for the boundary ditch of a province. And on his way he saw the Battle-Crow, the Morrigu, washing herself in the river Unius of Connacht, and one of her two feet at Ullad Echne, to the south of the water, and the other at Loscuinn, to the north of the water, and her hair hanging in nine loosened locks. And she said to the Dagda, that she would bring the heart's blood of Indech, son of De Domnann, that had threatened him, to the men of Ireland.

And while he was away Lugh had called together the Druids, and smiths, and physicians, and law-makers, and chariot-drivers of Ireland, to make plans for the battle.

And he asked the great magician Mathgen what could he do to help them. "It is what I can do," said Mathgen, "through my power I can throw down all the mountains of Ireland on the Fomor, until their tops will be rolling on the ground. And the twelve chief mountains of Ireland will bring you their help," he said, "and will fight for you: Slieve Leag and Denda Ulad, and Bennai Boirche and Bri Ruri, and Slieve Bladma and Slieve Snechtae, and Slieve Mis and Blai-Slieve, and Nemthann and Slieve Macca Belgodon, and Segois and Cruachan Aigle."

Then he asked the cup-bearers what help they could give. "We will put a strong thirst on the Fomor," they said, "and then we will bring the twelve chief lochs of Ireland before them, and however great their thirst may be, they will find no water in them: Derc-Loch, Loch Luimnech, Loch Orbsen, Loch Righ, Loch Mescdhae, Loch Cuan, Loch Laeig, Loch Echach, Loch Febail, Loch Decket, Loch Riach, Mor-Loch. And we will go," they said, "to the twelve chief rivers of Ireland: the Buas, the Boinn, the Banna, the Nem, the Laoi, the Sionnan, the Muaid, the Sligech, the Samair, the Fionn, the Ruirtech, the Siuir; and they will all be hidden away from the Fomor the way they will not find a drop in them. But as for the men of Ireland," they said, "there will be drink for them if they were to be in the battle to the end of seven years."

And Figol, son of Mamos, the Druid, was asked then what he would do, and he said: "It is what I will do, I will cause three showers of fire to pour on the faces of the army of the Fomor, and I will take from them two-thirds of their bravery and their strength, and I will put sickness on their bodies, and on the bodies of their horses. But as to the men of Ireland," he said, "every breath they breathe will be an increase of strength and of bravery to them; and if they are seven years in the battle they will never be any way tired."

Then Lugh asked his two witches, Bechulle and Dianan: "What power can you bring to the battle?" "It is easy to say that," they said. "We will put enchantment on the trees and the stones and the sods of the earth, till they become an armed host against the Fomor, and put terror on them and put them to the rout."

Then Lugh asked Carpre, the poet, son of Etain, what could he do. "It is not hard to say that," said Carpre. "I will make a satire on them at sunrise, and the wind from the north, and I on a hill-top and my back to a thorn-tree, and a stone and a thorn in my hand. And with that satire," he said, "I will put shame on them and enchantment, the way they will not be able to stand against fighting men."

Then he asked Goibniu the Smith what would he be able to do. "I will do this," he said. "If the men of Ireland stop in the battle to the end of seven years, for every sword that is broken and for every spear that is lost from its shaft, I will put a new one in its place. And no spear-point that will be made by my hand," he said, "will ever miss its mark; and no man it touches will ever taste life again. And that is more than Dolb, the smith of the Fomor, can do," he said.

"And you, Credne," Lugh said then to his worker in brass, "what help can you give to our men in the battle?" "It is not hard to tell that," said Credne, "rivets for their spears and hilts for their swords and bosses and rims for their shields, I will supply them all."

"And you, Luchta," he said then to his carpenter, "what will you do?" "I will give them all they want of shields and of spear shafts," said Luchta.

Then he asked Diancecht, the physician, what would he do, and it is what he said: "Every man that will be wounded there, unless his head is struck off, or his brain or his marrow cut through, I will make him whole and sound again for the battle of the morrow."

Then the Dagda said: "Those great things you are boasting you will do, I will do them all with only myself." "It is you are the good god!" said they, and they all gave a great shout of laughter.

Then Lugh spoke to the whole army and put strength in them, so that each one had the spirit in him of a king or a great lord.

Then when the delay was at an end, the Fomor and the men of Ireland came on towards one another till they came to the plain of Magh Tuireadh. That now was not the same Magh Tuireadh where the first battle was fought, but it was to the north, near Ess Dara.

And then the two armies threatened one another. "The men of Ireland are daring enough to offer battle to us," said Bres to Indech, son of De Domnann. "I give my word," said Indech, "it is in small pieces their bones will be, if they do not give in to us and pay their tribute."

Now the Men of Dea had determined not to let Lugh go into the battle, because of the loss his death would be to them; and they left nine of their men keeping a watch on him.

And on the first day none of the kings or princes went into the battle, but only the common fighting men, and they fierce and proud enough.

And the battle went on like that from day to day with no great advantage to one or the other side. But there was wonder on the Fomor on account of one thing. Such of their own weapons as were broken or blunted in the fight lay there as they were, and such of their own men as were killed showed no sign of life on the morrow; but it was not so with the Tuatha de Danaan, for if their men were killed or their weapons were broken to-day, they were as good as before on the morrow.

And this is the way that happened. The well of Slaine lay to the west of Magh Tuireadh to the east of Loch Arboch. And Diancecht and his son Octruil and his daughter Airmed used to be singing spells over the well and to be putting herbs in it; and the men that were wounded to death in the battle would be brought to the well and put into it as dead men, and they would come out of it whole and sound, through the power of the spells. And not only were they healed, but there was such fire put into them that they would be quicker in the fight than they were before.

And as to the arms, it is the way they were made new every day. Goibniu the Smith used to be in the forge making swords and spears, and he would make a spear-head by three turns, and then Luchta the Carpenter would make the shaft by three cuts, and the third cut was a finish, and would set it in the ring of the spear. And when the spear-heads were stuck in the side of the forge, he would throw the shaft and the rings the way they would go into the spear-head and want no more setting. And then Credne the Brazier would make the rivets by three turns and would cast the rings of the spears to them, and with that they were ready and were set together.

And all this went against the Fomor, and they sent one of their young men to spy about the camp and to see could he find out how these things were done. It was Ruadan, son of Bres and of Brigit daughter of the Dagda they sent, for he was a son and grandson of the Tuatha de Danaan. So he went and saw all that was done, and came back to the Fomor.

And when they heard his story it is what they thought, that Goibniu the Smith was the man that hindered them most. And they sent Ruadan back again, and bade him make an end of him.

So he went back again to the forge, and he asked Goibniu would he give him a spear-head. And then he asked rivets of Credne, and a shaft of the carpenter, and all was given to him as he asked. And there was a woman there, Cron, mother to Fianlug, grinding the spears.

And after the spear being given to Ruadan, he turned and threw it at Goibniu, that it wounded him. But Goibniu pulled it out and made a cast of it at Ruadan, that it went through him and he died; and Bres, his father, and the army of the Fomor, saw him die. And then Brigit came and keened her son with shrieking and with crying.

And as to Goibniu, he went into the well and was healed. But after that Octriallach, son of Indech, called to the Fomor and bade each man of them bring a stone of the stones of Drinnes and throw them into the well of Slane. And they did that till the well was dried up, and a cairn raised over it, that is called Octriallach's Cairn.

And it was while Goibniu was making spear-heads for the battle of Magh Tuireadh, a charge was brought against his wife. And it was seen that it was heavy news to him, and that jealousy came on him. And it is what he did, there was a spear-shaft in his hand when he heard the story, Nes its name was; and he sang spells over the spear-shaft, and any one that was struck with that spear afterwards, it would burn him up like fire.

And at last the day of the great battle came, and the Fomor came out of their camp and stood in strong ranks. And there was not a leader or a fighting man of them was without good armour to his skin, and a helmet on his head, a broad spear in his right hand, a heavy sword in his belt, a strong shield on his shoulder. And to attack the army of the Fomor that day was to strike the head against a rock, or to go up fighting against a fire.

And the Men of Dea rose up and left Lugh and his nine comrades keeping him, and they went on to the battle; and Midhir was with them, and Bodb Dearg and Diancecht. And Badb and Macha and the Morrigu called out that they would go along with them.

And it was a hard battle was fought, and for a while it was going against the Tuatha de Danaan; and Nuada of the Silver Hand, their King, and Macha, daughter of Emmass, fell by Balor, King of the Fomor. And Cassmail fell by Octriallach, and the Dagda got a dreadful wound from a casting spear that was thrown by Ceithlenn, wife of Balor.

But when the battle was going on, Lugh broke away from those that were keeping him, and rushed out to the front of the Men of Dea. And then there was a fierce battle fought, and Lugh was heartening the men of Ireland to fight well, the way they would not be in bonds any longer. For it was better for them, he said, to die protecting their own country than to live under bonds and under tribute any longer. And he sang a song of courage to them, and the hosts gave a great shout as they went into battle, and then they met together, and each of them began to attack the other.

And there was great slaughter, and laying low in graves, and many comely men fell there in the stall of death. Pride and shame were there side by side, and hardness and red anger, and there was red blood on the white skin of young fighting men. And the dashing of spear against shield, and sword against sword, and the shouting of the fighters, and the whistling of casting spears and the rattling of scabbards was like harsh thunder through the battle. And many slipped in the blood that was under their feet, and they fell, striking their heads one against another; and the river carried away bodies of friends and enemies together.

Then Lugh and Balor met in the battle, and Lugh called out reproaches to him; and there was anger on Balor, and he said to the men that were with him: "Lift up my eyelid till I see this chatterer that is talking to me." Then they raised Balor's eyelid, but Lugh made a cast of his red spear at him, that brought the eye out through the back of his head, so that it was towards his own army it fell, and three times nine of the Fomor died when they looked at it. And if Lugh had not put out that eye when he did, the whole of Ireland would have been burned in one flash. And after this, Lugh struck his head off.

And as for Indech, son of De Domnann, he fell and was crushed in the battle, and blood burst from his mouth, and he called out for Leat Glas, his poet, as he lay there, but he was not able to help him. And then the Morrigu came into the

51

battle, and she was heartening the Tuatha de Danaan to fight the battle well; and, as she had promised the Dagda, she took the full of her two hands of Indech's blood, and gave it to the armies that were waiting at the ford of Unius; and it was called the Ford of Destruction from that day.

And after that it was not a battle any more, but a rout, and the Fomor were beaten back to the sea. And Lugh and his comrades were following them, and they came up with Bres, son of Elathan, and no guard with him, and he said: "It is better for you to spare my life than to kill me. And if you spare me now," he said, "the cows of Ireland will never go dry." "I will ask an advice about that from our wise men," said Lugh. So he told Maeltine Mor-Brethach, of the Great Judgments, what Bres was after saying. But Maeltine said: "Do not spare him for that, for he has no power over their offspring, though he has power so long as they are living."

Then Bres said: "If you spare me, the men of Ireland will reap a harvest of corn every quarter." But Maeltine said: "The spring is for ploughing and sowing, and the beginning of summer for the strength of corn, and the beginning of autumn for its ripeness, and the winter for using it."

"That does not save you," said Lugh then to Bres. But then to make an excuse for sparing him, Lugh said: "Tell us what is the best way for the men of Ireland to plough and to sow and to reap."

"Let their ploughing be on a Tuesday, and their casting seed into the field on a Tuesday, and their reaping on a Tuesday," said Bres. So Lugh said that would do, and he let him go free after that.

It was in this battle Ogma found Orna, the sword of Tethra, a king of the Fomor, and he took it from its sheath and cleaned it. And when the sword was taken out of the sheath, it told all the deeds that had been done by it, for there used to be that power in swords.

And Lugh and the Dagda and Ogma followed after the Fomor, for they had brought away the Dagda's harp with them, that was called Uaitne. And they came to a feasting-house, and in it they found Bres and his father Elathan, and there was the harp hanging on the wall. And it was in that harp the Dagda had bound the music, so that it would not sound till he would call to it. And sometimes it was called Dur-da-Bla, the Oak of Two Blossoms, and sometimes Coir-cethar-chuin, the Four-Angled Music.

And when he saw it hanging on the wall it is what he said: "Come summer, come winter, from the mouth of harps and bags and pipes." Then the harp sprang from the wall, and came to the Dagda, and it killed nine men on its way.

And then he played for them the three things harpers understand, the sleepy tune, and the laughing tune, and the crying tune. And when he played the crying tune, their tearful women cried, and then he played the laughing tune, till their women and children laughed; and then he played the sleepy tune, and all the hosts fell asleep. And through that sleep the three went away through the Fomor that would have been glad to harm them. And when all was over, the Dagda brought out the heifer he had got as wages from Bres at the time he was making his dun. And she called to her calf, and at the sound of her call all the cattle of Ireland the Fomor had brought away as tribute, were back in their fields again.

And Cé, the Druid of Nuada of the Silver Hand, was wounded in the battle, and he went southward till he came to Carn Corrslebe. And there he sat down to rest, tired with his wounds and with the fear that was on him, and the journey. And he saw a smooth plain before him, and it full of flowers, and a great desire came on him to reach to that plain, and he went on till he came to it, and there he died. And when his grave was made there, a lake burst out over it and over the whole plain, and it was given the name of Loch Cé. And there were but four men of the Fomor left in Ireland after the battle, and they used to be going through the country, spoiling corn and milk and fruit, and whatever came from the sea, till they were driven out one Samhain night by the Morrigu and by Angus Og, that the Fomor might never be over Ireland again.

And after the battle was won, and the bodies were cleared away, the Morrigu gave out the news of the great victory to the hosts and to the royal heights of Ireland and to its chief rivers and its invers, and it is what she said: "Peace up to the skies, the skies down to earth, the earth under the skies; strength to every one."

And as to the number of men that fell in the battle, it will not be known till we number the stars of the sky, or flakes of snow, or the dew on the grass, or grass under the feet of cattle, or the horses of the Son of Lir in a stormy sea.

And Lugh was made king over the Men of Dea then, and it was at Nas he had his court.

And while he was king, his foster-mother Taillte, daughter of Magh Mor, the Great Plain, died. And before her death she bade her husband Duach the Dark, he that built the Fort of the Hostages in Teamhair, to clear away the wood of Cuan, the way there could be a gathering of the people around her grave. So he called to the men of Ireland to cut down the wood with their wide-bladed knives and bill-hooks and hatchets, and within a month the whole wood was cut down.

And Lugh buried her in the plain of Midhe, and raised a mound over her, that is to be seen to this day. And he ordered fires to be kindled, and keening to be made, and games and sports to be held in the summer of every year out of respect to her. And the place they were held got its name from her, that is Taillten.

And as to Lugh's own mother, that was tall beautiful Ethlinn, she came to Teamhair after the battle of Magh Tuireadh, and he gave her in marriage to Tadg, son of Nuada. And the children that were born to them were Muirne, mother of Finn, the Head of the Fianna of Ireland, and Tuiren, that was mother of Bran.

CHAPTER IV

The Hidden House of Lugh

And after Lugh had held the kingship for a long time, the Dagda was made king in his place.

And Lugh went away out of Ireland, and some said he died at Uisnech, the place where the five provinces meet, and the first place there was ever a fire kindled in Ireland. It was by Mide, son of Brath, it was kindled, for the sons of Nemed, and it was burning through six years, and it was from that fire every chief fire was kindled in Ireland.

But Lugh was seen again in Ireland at the time Conchubar and the Men of the Red Branch went following white birds southward to the Boinn at the time of Cuchulain's birth. And it was he came and kept watch over Cuchulain in his three days' sleep at the time of the War for the Bull of Cuailgne.

And after that again he was seen by Conn of the Hundred Battles, and this is the way that happened.

Conn was in Teamhair one time, and he went up in the early morning to the Rath of the Kings at the rising of the sun, and his three Druids with him, Maol and Bloc and Bhuice; and his three poets, Ethain and Corb and Cesarn. And the reason he had for going up there with them every day, was to look about on every side, the way if any men of the Sidhe would come into Ireland they would not come unknown to him. And on this day he chanced to stand upon a stone that was in the rath, and the stone screamed under his feet, that it was heard all over Teamhair and as far as Bregia.

Then Conn asked his chief Druid how the stone came there, and what it screamed for. And the Druid said he would not answer that till the end of fifty-three days. And at the end of that time, Conn asked him again, and it was what the Druid said: "The Lia Fail is the name of the stone; it is out of Falias it was brought, and it is in Teamhair it was set up, and in Teamhair it will stay for ever. And as long as there is a king in Teamhair it is here will be the gathering place for games, and if there is no king to come to the last day of the gathering, there will be hardness in that year. And when the stone screamed under your feet," he said, "the number of the screams it gave was a foretelling of the number of kings of your race that would come after you. But it is not I myself will name them for you," he said.

And while they were in the same place, there came a great mist about them and a darkness, so that they could not know what way they were going, and they heard the noise of a rider coming towards them. "It would be a great grief to us," said Conn, "to be brought away into a strange country." Then the rider threw three spears at them, and every one came faster than the other. "It is the wounding of a king indeed," said the Druids, "any one to cast at Conn of Teamhair."

The rider stopped casting his spears on that, and he came to them and bade Conn welcome, and asked him to come to his house. They went on then till they came to a beautiful plain, and there they saw a king's rath, and a golden tree at its door, and inside the rath a grand house with a roof of white bronze. So they went into the house, and the rider that had come to meet them was there before them, in his royal seat, and there had never been seen a man like him in Teamhair for comeliness or for beauty, or the wonder of his face.

And there was a young woman in the house, having a band of gold on her head, and a silver vessel with hoops of gold beside her, and it full of red ale, and a golden bowl on its edge, and a golden cup at its mouth. She said then to the master of the house: "Who am I to serve drink to?" "Serve it to Conn of the Hundred Battles," he said, "for he will gain a hundred battles before he dies." And after that he bade her to pour out the ale for Art of the Three Shouts, the son of Conn; and after that he went through the names of all the kings of Ireland that would come after Conn, and he told what would be the length of their lifetime. And the young woman left the vessel with Conn, and the cup and the bowl, and she gave him along with that the rib of an ox and of a hog; twenty-four feet was the length of the ox-rib.

And the master of the house told them the young woman was the Kingship of Ireland for ever. "And as for myself," he said, "I am Lugh of the Long Hand, son of Ethlinn."

BOOK III

The Coming of the Gael

CHAPTER I

The Landing

It is not known, now, for what length of time the Tuatha de Danaan had the sway over Ireland, and it is likely it was a long time they had it, but they were put from it at last.

It was at Inver Slane, to the north of Leinster, the sons of Gaedhal of the Shining Armour, the Very Gentle, that were called afterwards the Sons of the Gael, made their first attempt to land in Ireland to avenge Ith, one of their race that had come there one time and had met with his death.

It is under the leadership of the sons of Miled they were, and it was from the south they came, and their Druids had told them there was no country for them to settle in till they would come to that island in the west. "And if you do not get possession of it yourselves," they said, "your children will get possession of it."

But when the Tuatha de Danaan saw the ships coming, they flocked to the shore, and by their enchantments they cast such a cloud over the whole island that the sons of Miled were confused, and all they could see was some large thing that had the appearance of a pig.

And when they were hindered from landing there by enchantments, they went sailing along the coast till at last they were able to make a landing at Inver Sceine in the west of Munster.

From that they marched in good order as far as Slieve Mis. And there they were met by a queen of the Tuatha de Danaan, and a train of beautiful women attending on her, and her Druids and wise men following her. Amergin, one of the sons of Miled, spoke to her then, and asked her name, and she said it was Banba, wife of Mac Cuill, Son of the Hazel.

They went on then till they came to Slieve Eibhline, and there another queen of the Tuatha de Danaan met them, and her women and her Druids after her, and they asked her name, and she said it was Fodhla, wife of Mac Cecht, Son of the Plough.

They went on then till they came to the hill of Uisnech, and there they saw another woman coming towards them. And there was wonder on them while they were looking at her, for in the one moment she would be a wide-eyed most beautiful queen, and in another she would be a sharp-beaked, grey-white crow. She came on to where Eremon, one of the sons of Miled, was, and sat down before him, and he asked her who was she, and she said: "I am Eriu, wife of Mac Greine, Son of the Sun."

And the names of those three queens were often given to Ireland in the after time.

The Sons of the Gael went on after that to Teamhair, where the three sons of Cermait Honey-Mouth, son of the Dagda, that had the kingship between them at that time held their court. And these three were quarrelling with one another about the division of the treasures their father had left, and the quarrel was so hot it seemed likely it would come to a battle in the end.

And the Sons of the Gael wondered to see them quarrelling about such things, and they having so fruitful an island, where the air was so wholesome, and the sun not too strong, or the cold too bitter, and where there was such a plenty of honey and acorns, and of milk, and of fish, and of corn, and room enough for them all.

Great grandeur they were living in, and their Druids about them, at the palace of Teamhair. And Amergin went to them, and it is what he said, that they must give up the kingship there and then, or they must leave it to the chance of a battle. And he said he asked this in revenge for the death of Ith, of the race of the Gael, that had come to their court before that time, and that had been killed by treachery.

When the sons of Cermait Honey-Mouth heard Amergin saying such fierce words, there was wonder on them, and it is what they said, that they were not willing to fight at that time, for their army was not ready. "But let you make an offer to us," they said, "for we see well you have good judgment and knowledge. But if you make an offer that is not fair," they said, "we will destroy you with our enchantments."

At that Amergin bade the men that were with him to go back to Inver Sceine, and to hurry again into their ships with the rest of the Sons of the Gael, and to go out the length of nine waves from the shore. And then he made his offer to the Tuatha de Danaan, that if they could hinder his men from landing on their island, he and all his ships would go back again to their own country, and would never make any attempt to come again; but that if the Sons of the Gael could land on the coast in spite of them, then the Tuatha de Danaan should give up the kingship and be under their sway.

The Tuatha de Danaan were well pleased with that offer, for they thought that by the powers of their enchantments over the winds and the sea, and by their arts, they would be well able to keep them from ever setting foot in the country again.

So the Sons of the Gael did as Amergin bade them and they went back into their ship and drew up their anchors, and moved out to the length of nine waves from the shore. And as soon as the Men of Dea saw they had left the land, they took to their enchantments and spells, and they raised a great wind that scattered the ships of the Gael, and drove them from one another. But Amergin knew it was not a natural storm was in it, and Arranan, son of Miled, knew that as well, and he went up in the mast of his ship to look about him. But a great blast of wind came against him, and he fell back into the ship and died on the moment. And there was great confusion on the Gael, for the ships were tossed to and fro, and had like to be lost. And the ship that Donn, son of Miled, was in command of was parted from the others by the dint of the storm, and was broken in pieces, and he himself and all with him were drowned, four-and-twenty men and women in all. And Ir, son of Miled, came to his death in the same way, and his body was cast on the shore, and it was buried in a small island that is now called Sceilg Michill. A brave man Ir was, leading the Sons of the Gael to the front of every battle, and their help and their shelter in battle, and his enemies were in dread of his name.

And Heremon, another of the sons of Miled, with his share of the ships, was driven to the left of the island, and it is hardly he got safe to land. And the place where he landed was called Inver Colpa, because Colpa of the Sword, another of the sons of Miled, was drowned there, and he trying to get to land. Five of the sons of Miled in all were destroyed by the storm and the winds the Men of Dea had raised by their enchantments, and there were but three of them left, Heber, and Heremon, and Amergin.

And one of them, Donn, before he was swept into the sea, called out: "It is treachery our knowledgeable men are doing on us, not to put down this wind." "There is no treachery," said Amergin, his brother. And he rose up then before them, and whatever enchantment he did on the winds and the sea, he said these words along with it:

"That they that are tossing in the great wide food giving sea may reach now to the land.

"That they may find a place upon its plains, its mountains, and its valleys; in its forests that are full of nuts and of all fruits; on its rivers and its streams, on its lakes and its great waters.

"That we may have our gatherings and our races in this land; that there may be a king of our own in Teamhair; that it may be the possession of our many kings.

"That the sons of Miled may be seen in this land, that their ships and their boats may find a place there.

"This land that is now under darkness, it is for it we are asking; let our chief men, let their learned wives, ask that we may come to the noble woman, great Eriu."

After he had said this, the wind went down and the sea was quiet again on the moment.

And those that were left of the sons of Miled and of the Sons of the Gael landed then at Inver Sceine.

And Amergin was the first to put his foot on land, and when he stood on the shore of Ireland, it is what he said:

"I am the wind on the sea;
I am the wave of the sea;
I am the bull of seven battles;
I am the eagle on the rock;
I am a flash from the sun;
I am the most beautiful of plants;
I am a strong wild boar;
I am a salmon in the water;
I am a lake in the plain;
I am the word of knowledge;
I am the head of the spear in battle;
I am the god that puts fire in the head;
Who spreads light in the gathering on the hills?
Who can tell the ages of the moon?
Who can tell the place where the sun rests?"

CHAPTER II

The Battle of Tailltin

And three days after the landing of the Gael, they were attacked by Eriu, wife of Mac Greine, Son of the Sun, and she having a good share of men with her. And they fought a hard battle, and many were killed on both sides. And this was the first battle fought between the Sons of the Gael and the Men of Dea for the kingship of Ireland.

It was in that battle Fais, wife of Un, was killed in a valley at the foot of the mountain, and it was called after her, the Valley of Fais. And Scota, wife of Miled, got her death in the battle, and she was buried in a valley on the north side of the mountain near the sea. But the Sons of the Gael lost no more than three hundred men, and they beat back the Men of Dea and killed a thousand of them. And Eriu was beaten back to Tailltin, and as many of her men as she could hold together; and when she came there she told the people how she had been worsted in the battle, and the best of her men had got their death. But the Gael stopped on the battle-field, and buried their dead, and they gave a great burial to two of their Druids, Aer and Eithis, that were killed in the fight.

And after they had rested for a while, they went on to Inver Colpa in Leinster, and Heremon and his men joined them there. And then they sent messengers to the three kings of Ireland, the three sons of Cermait Honey-Mouth, and bade them to come out and fight a battle that would settle the ownership of the country once for all.

So they came out, and the best of the fighters of the Tuatha de Danaan with them, to Tailltin. And there they attacked one another, and the Sons of the Gael remembered the death of Ith, and there was great anger on them, and they fell on the Men of Dea to avenge him, and there was a fierce battle fought. And for a while neither side got the better of the other, but at the last the Gael broke through the army of the Men of Dea and put them to the rout, with great slaughter, and drove them out of the place. And their three kings were killed in the rout, and the three queens of Ireland, Eriu and Fodhla and Banba. And when the Tuatha de Danaan saw their leaders were dead they fell back in great disorder, and the Sons of the Gael followed after them. But in following them they lost two of their best leaders, Cuailgne, son of Breagan, at Slieve Cuailgne, and Fuad, his brother, at Slieve Fuad. But they were no way daunted by that, but followed the Men of Dea so hotly that they were never able to bring their army together again, but had to own themselves beaten, and to give up the country to the Gael.

And the leaders, the sons of Miled, divided the provinces of Ireland between them. Heber took the two provinces of Munster, and he gave a share of it to Amergin; and Heremon got Leinster and Connacht for his share, and Ulster was divided between Eimhir, son of Ir, son of Miled, and some others of their chief men. And it was of the sons of Eimhir, that were called the Children of Rudraighe, and that lived in Emain Macha for nine hundred years, some of the best men of Ireland came; Fergus, son of Rogh, was of them, and Conall Cearnach, of the Red Branch of Ulster.

And from the sons of Ith, the first of the Gael to get his death in Ireland, there came in the after time Fathadh Canaan, that got the sway over the whole world from the rising to the setting sun, and that took hostages of the streams and the birds and the languages.

And it is what the poets of Ireland used to be saying, that every brave man, good at fighting, and every man that could do great deeds and not be making much talk about them, was of the Sons of the Gael; and that every skilled man that had music and that did enchantments secretly, was of the Tuatha de Danaan. But they put a bad name on the Firbolgs and the men of Domnand and the Gaileoin, for lies and for big talk and injustice. But for all that there were good fighters among them, and Ferdiad, that made so good a stand against Cuchulain, in the war for the Bull of Cuailgne was one of them. And the Gaileoin fought well in the same war; but the men of Ireland had no great liking for them, and their Druids drove them out of the country afterwards.

BOOK IV

The Ever-Living Living Ones

CHAPTER I

Bodb Dearg

But as to the Tuatha de Danaan after they were beaten, they would not go under the sway of the sons of Miled, but they went away by themselves. And because Manannan, son of Lir, understood all enchantments, they left it to him to find places for them where they would be safe from their enemies. So he chose out the most beautiful of the hills and valleys of Ireland for them to settle in; and he put hidden walls about them, that no man could see through, but they themselves could see through them and pass through them.

And he made the Feast of Age for them, and what they drank as it was the ale of Goibniu the Smith, that kept whoever tasted it from age and from sickness and from death. And for food at the feast he gave them his own swine, that though they were killed and eaten one day, would be alive and fit for eating again the next day, and that would go on in that way for ever.

And after a while they said: "It would be better for us one king to be over us, than to be scattered the way we are through the whole of Ireland."

Now the men among them that had the best chance of getting the kingship at that time were Bodb Dearg, son of the Dagda; and Ilbrech of Ess Ruadh; and Lir of Sidhe Fionnachaidh, the Hill of the White Field, on Slieve Fuad; and Midhir the Proud of Bri Leith, and Angus Og, son of the Dagda; but he did not covet the kingship at all, but would sooner be left as he was. Then all the chief men but those five went into council together, and it is what they agreed, to give the kingship to Bodb Dearg, for the sake of his father, for his own sake, and because he was the eldest among the children of the Dagda.

It was in Sidhe Femen Bodb Dearg had his house, and he put great enchantments about it. Cliach, the Harper of the King of the Three Rosses in Connacht, went one time to ask one of his daughters in marriage, and he stayed outside the place through the whole length of a year, playing his harp, and able to get no nearer to Bodb or to his daughter. And he went on playing till a lake burst up under his feet, the lake that is on the top of a mountain, Loch Bel Sead.

It was Bodb's swineherd went to Da Derga's Inn, and his squealing pig along with him, the night Conaire, the High King of Ireland, met with his death; and it was said that whatever feast that swineherd would go to, there would blood be shed before it was over.

And Bodb had three sons, Angus, and Artrach, and Aedh. And they used often to be living among men in the time of the Fianna afterwards. Artrach had a house with seven doors, and a free welcome for all that came, and the king's son of Ireland, and of Alban, used to be coming to Angus to learn the throwing of spears and darts; and troops of poets from Alban and from Ireland used to be with Aedh, that was the comeliest of Bodb's sons, so that his place used to be called "The Rath of Aedh of the Poets." And indeed it was a beautiful rath at that time, with golden-yellow apples in it and crimson-pointed nuts of the wood. But after the passing away of the Fianna, the three brothers went back to the Tuatha de Danaan.

And Bodb Dearg was not always in his own place, but sometimes he was with Angus at Brugh na Boinn.

Three sons of Lugaidh Menn, King of Ireland, Eochaid, and Fiacha, and Ruide, went there one time, for their father refused them any land till they would win it for themselves. And when he said that, they rose with the ready rising of one man, and went and sat down on the green of Brugh na Boinn, and fasted there on the Tuatha de Danaan, to see if they could win some good thing from them.

And they were not long there till they saw a young man, quiet and with pleasant looks, coming towards them, and he wished them good health, and they answered him the same way. "Where are you come from?" they asked him then. "From the rath beyond, with the many lights," he said. "And I am Bodb Dearg, son of the Dagda," he said, "and come in with me now to the rath."

So they went in, and supper was made ready for them, but they did not use it. Bodb Dearg asked them then why was it they were using nothing. "It is because our father has refused land to us," said they; "and there are in Ireland but the two races, the Sons of the Gael and the Men of Dea, and when the one failed us we are come to the other."

Then the Men of Dea consulted together. And the chief among them was Midhir of the Yellow Hair, and it is what he said: "Let us give a wife to every one of these three men, for it is from a wife that good or bad fortune comes."

So they agreed to that, and Midhir's three daughters, Doirenn, and Aife, and Aillbhe, were given to them. Then Midhir asked Bodb to say what marriage portion should be given to them. "I will tell you that," said Bodb. "We are three times fifty sons of kings in this hill; let every king's son give three times fifty ounces of red gold. And I myself," he said, "will give them along with that, three times fifty suits of clothing of all colours." "I will give them a gift," said a young man of the Tuatha de Danaan, from Rachlainn in the sea. "A horn I will give them, and a vat. And there is nothing wanting but to fill the vat with pure water, and it will turn into mead, fit to drink, and strong enough to make drunken. And into the horn," he said, "you have but to put salt water from the sea, and it will turn into wine on the moment." "A gift to them from me," said Lir of Sidhe Fionnachaidh, "three times fifty swords, and three times fifty well-riveted long spears." "A gift from me," said Angus Og, son of the Dagda, "a rath and a good town with high walls, and with bright sunny houses, and with wide houses, in whatever place it will please them between Rath Chobtaige and Teamhair." "A gift to them from me," said Aline, daughter of Modharn, "a woman-cook that I have, and there is *geasa* on her not to refuse food to any; and according as she serves it out, her store fills up of itself again." "Another gift to them from me," said Bodb Dearg, "a good musician that I have, Fertuinne, son of Trogain; and although there were women in the sharpest pains of childbirth, and brave men wounded early in the day, in a place where there were saws going through wood, they would sleep at the sweetness of the music he makes. And whatever house he may be in, the people of the whole country round will hear him."

So they stopped in Brugh na Boinne three days and three nights, and when they left it, Angus bade them bring away from the oak-wood three apple-trees, one in full bloom, and one shedding its blossom, and the third covered with ripe fruit.

They went then to their own dun that was given them, and it is a good place they had there, and a troop of young men, and great troops of horses and of greyhounds; and they had three sorts of music that comely kings liked to be listening to, the music of harps and of lutes, and the chanting of Trogain's son; and there were three great sounds, the tramping on the green, and the uproar of racing, and the lowing of cattle; and three other sounds, the grunting of good pigs with the fat thick on them, and the voices of the crowd on the green lawn, and the noise of men drinking inside the house. And as to Eochaid, it was said of him that he never took a step backwards in flight, and his house was never without music or drinking of ale. And it was said of Fiacha that there was no man of his time braver than himself, and that he never said a word too much. And as to Ruide, he never refused any one, and never asked anything at all of any man.

And when their lifetime was over, they went back to the Tuatha de Danaan, for they belonged to them through their wives, and there they have stopped ever since.

And Bodb Dearg had a daughter, Scathniamh, the Flower of Brightness, that gave her love to Caoilte in the time of the Fianna; and they were forced to part from one another, and they never met again till the time Caoilte was old and withered, and one of the last that was left of the Fianna. And she came to him out of the cave of Cruachan, and asked him for the bride-price he had promised her, and that she was never able to come and ask for till then. And Caoilte went to a cairn that was near and that was full up of gold, that was wages earned by Conan Maol and hidden there, and he gave the gold to Bodb Dearg's daughter. And the people that were there wondered to see the girl so young and comely, and Caoilte so grey and bent and withered. "There is no wonder in that," said Caoilte, "for I am of the sons of Miled that wither and fade away, but she is of the Tuatha de Danaan that never change and that never die."

CHAPTER II

The Dagda

And it was at Brugh na Boinne the Dagda, the Red Man of all Knowledge, had his house. And the most noticeable things in it were the Hall of the Morrigu, and the Bed of the Dagda, and the Birthplace of Cermait Honey-Mouth, and the Prison of the Grey of Macha that was Cuchulain's horse afterwards. And there was a little hill by the house that was called the Comb and the Casket of the Dagda's wife; and another that was called the Hill of Dabilla, that was the little hound belonging to Boann. And the Valley of the Mata was there, the Sea-Turtle that could suck down a man in armour.

And it is likely the Dagda put up his cooking oven there, that Druimne, son of Luchair, made for him at Teamhair. And it is the way it was, the axle and the wheel were of wood, and the body was iron, and there were twice nine wheels in its axle, that it might turn the faster; and it was as quick as the quickness of a stream in turning, and there were three times nine spits from it, and three times nine pots. And it used to lie down with the cinders and to rise to the height of the roof with the flame.

The Dagda himself made a great vat one time for Ainge, his daughter, but she was not well satisfied with it, for it would not stop from dripping while the sea was in flood, though it would not lose a drop during the ebb-tide. And she gathered a bundle of twigs to make a new vat for herself, but Gaible, son of Nuada of the Silver Hand, stole it from her and hurled it away. And in the place where it fell a beautiful wood grew up, that was called Gaible's Wood.

And the Dagda had his household at Brugh na Boinne, and his steward was Dichu, and Len Linfiaclach was the smith of the Brugh. It was he lived in the lake, making the bright vessels of Fand, daughter of Flidhais; and every evening when he left off work he would make a cast of the anvil eastward to Indeoin na Dese, the Anvil of the Dese, as far as the Grave End. Three showers it used to cast, a shower of fire, and a shower of water, and a shower of precious stones of pure purple.

But Tuirbe, father of Goibniu the Smith, used to throw better again, for he would make a cast of his axe from Tulach na Bela, the Hill of the Axe, in the face of the flood tide, and he would put his order on the sea, and it would not come over the axe.

And Corann was the best of the harpers of the household; he was harper to the Dagda's son, Diancecht. And one time he called with his harp to Cailcheir, one of the swine of Debrann. And it ran northward with all the strength of its legs, and the champions of Connacht were following after it with all their strength of running, and their hounds with them, till they got as far as Ceis Corain, and they gave it up there, all except Niall that went on the track of the swine till he found it in the oak-wood of Tarba, and then it made away over the plain of Ai, and through a lake. And Niall and his hound were drowned in following it through the lake. And the Dagda gave Corann a great tract of land for doing his harping so well.

But however great a house the Dagda had, Angus got it away from him in the end, through the help of Manannan, son of Lir. For Manannan bade him to ask his father for it for the length of a day and a night, and that he by his art would take away his power of refusing. So Angus asked for the Brugh, and his father gave it to him for a day and a night. But when he asked it back again, it is what Angus said, that it had been given to him for ever, for the whole of life and time is made up of a day and a night, one following after the other.

So when the Dagda heard that he went away and his people and his household with him, for Manannan had put an enchantment on them all.

But Dichu the Steward was away at the time, and his wife and his son, for they were gone out to get provisions for a feast for Manannan and his friends. And when he came back and knew his master was gone, he took service with Angus.

And Angus stopped in Brugh na Boinne, and some say he is there to this day, with the hidden walls about him, drinking Goibniu's ale and eating the pigs that never fail.

As to the Dagda, he took no revenge, though he had the name of being revengeful and quick in his temper. And some say it was at Teamhair he made his dwelling-place after that, but wherever it was, a great misfortune came on him.

It chanced one time Corrgenn, a great man of Connacht, came to visit him, and his wife along with him. And while they were there, Corrgenn got it in his mind that there was something that was not right going on between his wife and Aedh, one of the sons of the Dagda. And great jealousy and anger came on him, and he struck at the young man and killed him before his father's face.

Every one thought the Dagda would take Corrgenn's life then and there in revenge for his son's life. But he would not do that, for he said if his son was guilty, there was no blame to be put on Corrgenn for doing what he did. So he spared his life for that time, but if he did, Corrgenn did not gain much by it. For the punishment he put on him was to take the dead body of the young man on his back, and never to lay it down till he would find a stone that would be its very fit in length and in breadth, and that would make a gravestone for him; and when he had found that, he could bury him in the nearest hill.

So Corrgenn had no choice but to go, and he set out with his load; but he had a long way to travel before he could find a stone that would fit, and it is where he found one at last, on the shore of Loch Feabhail. So then he left the body up on the nearest hill, and he went down and raised the stone and brought it up and dug a grave and buried the Dagda's son. And it is many an Ochone! he gave when he was putting the stone over him, and when he had that done he was spent, and he dropped dead there and then.

And the Dagda brought his two builders, Garbhan and Imheall, to the place, and he bade them build a rath there round the grave. It was Garbhan cut the stones and shaped them, and Imheall set them all round the house till the work was finished, and then he closed the top of the house with a slab. And the place was called the Hill of Aileac, that is, the Hill of Sighs and of a Stone, for it was tears of blood the Dagda shed on account of the death of his son.

CHAPTER III

Angus Og

And as to Angus Og, son of the Dagda, sometimes he would come from Brugh na Boinn and let himself be seen upon the earth.

It was a long time after the coming of the Gael that he was seen by Cormac, King of Teamhair, and this is the account he gave of him.

He was by himself one day in his Hall of Judgment, for he used to be often reading the laws and thinking how he could best carry them out. And on a sudden he saw a stranger, a very comely young man, at the end of the hall; and he knew on the moment it was Angus Og, for he had often heard his people talking of him, but he himself used to be saying he did not believe there was any such person at all. And when his people came back to the hall, he told them how he had seen Angus himself, and had talked with him, and Angus had told him his name, and had foretold what would happen him in the future. "And he was a beautiful young man," he said, "with high looks, and his appearance was more beautiful than all beauty, and there were ornaments of gold on his dress; in his hand he held a silver harp with strings of red gold, and the sound of its strings was sweeter than all music under the sky; and over the harp were two birds that seemed to be playing on it. He sat beside me pleasantly and played his sweet music to me, and in the end he foretold things that put drunkenness on my wits."

The birds, now, that used to be with Angus were four of his kisses that turned into birds and that used to be coming about the young men of Ireland, and crying after them. "Come, come," two of them would say, and "I go, I go," the other two would say, and it was hard to get free of them. But as to Angus, even when he was in his young youth, he used to be called the Frightener, or the Disturber; for the plough teams of the world, and every sort of cattle that is used by men, would make away in terror before him.

And one time he appeared in the shape of a land-holder to two men, Ribh and Eocho, that were looking for a place to settle in. The first place they chose was near Bregia on a plain that was belonging to Angus; and it was then he came to them, leading his horse in his hand, and told them they should not stop there. And they said they could not carry away their goods without horses. Then he gave them his horse, and bade them to put all they had a mind to on that horse and he would carry it, and so he did. But the next place they chose was Magh Find, the Fine Plain, that was the playing ground of Angus and of Midhir. And that time Midhir came to them in the same way and gave them a horse to put their goods on, and he went on with them as far as Magh Dairbthenn.

And there were many women loved Angus, and there was one Enghi, daughter of Elcmair, loved him though she had not seen him. And she went one time looking for him to the gathering for games between Cletech and Sidhe in Broga; and the bright troops of the Sidhe used to come to that gathering every Samhain evening, bringing a moderate share of food with them, that is, a nut. And the sons of Derc came from the north, out of Sidhe Findabrach, and they went round about the young men and women without their knowledge and they brought away Elcmair's daughter. There were great lamentations made then, and the name the place got was Cnoguba, the Nut Lamentation, from the crying there was at that gathering.

And Derbrenn, Eochaid Fedlech's daughter, was another that was loved by Angus, and she had six fosterlings, three boys and three girls. But the mother of the boys, Dalb Garb, the Rough, put a spell on them she made from a gathering of the nuts of Caill Ochuid, that turned them into swine.

And Angus gave them into the care of Buichet, the Hospitaller of Leinster, and they stopped a year with him. But at the end of that time there came a longing on Buichet's wife to eat a bit of the flesh of one of them. So she gathered a hundred armed men and a hundred hounds to take them. But the pigs made away, and went to Brugh na Boinn, to Angus, and he bade them welcome, and they asked him to give them his help. But he said he could not do that till they had shaken the Tree of Tarbga, and eaten the salmon of Inver Umaill.

So they went to Glascarn, and stopped a year in hiding with Derbrenn. And then they shook the Tree of Tarbga, and they went on towards Inver Umaill. But Maeve gathered the men of Connacht to hunt them, and they all fell but one, and their heads were put in a mound, and it got the name of Duma Selga, the Mound of the Hunting.

And it was in the time of Maeve of Cruachan that Angus set his love on Caer Ormaith, of the Province of Connacht, and brought her away to Brugh na Boinn.

CHAPTER IV

The Morrigu

As to the Morrigu, the Great Queen, the Crow of Battle, where she lived after the coming of the Gael is not known, but before that time it was in Teamhair she lived. And she had a great cooking-spit there, that held three sorts of food on it at the one time: a piece of raw meat, and a piece of dressed meat, and a piece of butter. And the raw was dressed, and the dressed was not burned, and the butter did not melt, and the three together on the spit.

Nine men that were outlaws went to her one time and asked for a spit to be made for themselves. And they brought it away with them, and it had nine ribs in it, and every one of the outlaws would carry a rib in his hand wherever he would go, till they would all meet together at the close of day. And if they wanted the spit to be high, it could be raised to a man's height, and at another time it would not be more than the height of a fist over the fire, without breaking and without lessening.

And Mechi, the son the Morrigu had, was killed by Mac Cecht on Magh Mechi, that till that time had been called Magh Fertaige. Three hearts he had, and it is the way they were, they had the shapes of three serpents through them. And if Mechi had not met with his death, those serpents in him would have grown, and what they left alive in Ireland would have wasted away. And Mac Cecht burned the three hearts on Magh Luathad, the Plain of Ashes, and he threw the ashes into the stream; and the rushing water of the stream stopped and boiled up, and every creature in it died.

And the Morrigu used often to be meddling in Ireland in Cuchulain's time, stirring up wars and quarrels. It was she came and roused up Cuchulain one time when he was but a lad, and was near giving in to some enchantment that was used against him. "There is not the making of a hero in you," she said to him, "and you lying there under the feet of shadows." And with that Cuchulain rose up and struck off the head of a shadow that was standing over him, with his hurling stick. And the time Conchubar was sending out Finched to rouse up the men of Ulster at the time of the war for the Bull of Cuailgne, he bade him to go to that terrible fury, the Morrigu, to get help for Cuchulain. And she had a dispute with Cuchulain one time he met her, and she bringing away a cow from the Hill of Cruachan; and another time she helped Talchinem, a Druid of the household of Conaire Mor, to bring away a bull his wife had set her mind on. And indeed she was much given to meddling with cattle, and one time she brought away a cow from Odras, that was of the household of the cow-chief of Cormac Hua Cuined, and that was going after her husband with cattle. And the Morrigu brought the cow away with her to the Cave of Cruachan, and the Hill of the Sidhe. And Odras followed her there till sleep fell on her in the oak-wood of Falga; and the Morrigu awoke her and sang spells over her, and made of her a pool of water that went to the river that flows to the west of Slieve Buane.

And in the battle of Magh Rath, she fluttered over Congal Claen in the shape of a bird, till he did not know friend from foe. And after that again at the battle of Cluantarbh, she was flying over the head of Murchadh, son of Brian; for she had many shapes, and it was in the shape of a crow she would sometimes fight her battles.

And if it was not the Morrigu, it was Badb that showed herself in the battle of Dunbolg, where the men of Ireland were fighting under Aedh, son of Niall; and Brigit was seen in the same battle on the side of the men of Leinster.

CHAPTER V

Aine

And as to Aine, that some said was a daughter of Manannan, but some said was the Morrigu herself, there was a stone belonging to her that was called Cathair Aine. And if any one would sit on that stone he would be in danger of losing his wits, and any one that would sit on it three times would lose them for ever. And people whose wits were astray would make their way to it, and mad dogs would come from all parts of the country, and would flock around it, and then they would go into the sea to Aine's place there. But those that did cures by herbs said she had power over the whole body; and she used to give gifts of poetry and of music, and she often gave her love to men, and they called her the Leanan Sidhe, the Sweetheart of the Sidhe.

And it was no safe thing to offend Aine, for she was very revengeful. Oilioll Oluim, a king of Ireland, killed her brother one time, and it is what she did, she made a great yew-tree by enchantment beside the river Maigh in Luimnech, and she put a little man in it, playing sweet music on a harp. And Oilioll's son was passing the river with his step-brother, and they saw the tree and heard the sweet music from it. And first they quarrelled as to which of them would have the little harper, and then they quarrelled about the tree, and they asked a judgment from Oilioll, and he gave it for his own son. And it was the bad feeling about that judgment that led to the battle of Magh Mucruimhe, and Oilioll and his seven sons were killed there, and so Aine got her revenge.

CHAPTER VI

Aoibhell

And Aoibhell, another woman of the Sidhe, made her dwelling-place in Craig Liath, and at the time of the battle of Cluantarbh she set her love on a young man of Munster, Dubhlaing ua Artigan, that had been sent away in disgrace by the King of Ireland. But before the battle he came back to join with Murchadh, the king's son, and to fight for the Gael. And Aoibhell came to stop him; and when he would not stop with her she put a Druid covering about him, the way no one could see him.

And he went where Murchadh was fighting, and he made a great attack on the enemies of Ireland, and struck them down on every side. And Murchadh looked around him, and he said: "It seems to me I hear the sound of the blows of Dubhlaing ua Artigan, but I do not see himself." Then Dubhlaing threw off the Druid covering that was about him, and he said: "I will not keep this covering upon me when you cannot see me through it. And come now across the plain to where Aoibhell is," he said, "for she can give us news of the battle."

So they went where she was, and she bade them both to quit the battle, for they would lose their lives in it. But Murchadh said to her, "I will tell you a little true story," he said; "that fear for my own body will never make me change my face. And if we fall," he said, "the strangers will fall with us; and it is many a man will fall by my own hand, and the Gael will be sharing their strong places." "Stop with me, Dubhlaing," she said then, "and you will have two hundred years of happy life with myself." "I will not give up Murchadh," he said, "or my own good name, for silver or gold." And there was anger on Aoibhell when he said that, and she said: "Murchadh will fall, and you yourself will fall, and your proud blood will be on the plain tomorrow." And they went back into the battle, and got their death there.

And it was Aoibhell gave a golden harp to the son of Meardha the time he was getting his learning at the school of the Sidhe in Connacht and that he heard his father had got his death by the King of Lochlann. And whoever heard the playing of that harp would not live long after it. And Meardha's son went where the three sons of the King of Lochlann were, and played on his harp for them, and they died.

It was that harp Cuchulain heard the time his enemies were gathering against him at Muirthemne, and he knew by it that his life was near its end.

CHAPTER VII

Midhir and Etain

And Midhir took a hill for himself, and his wife Fuamach was with him there, and his daughter, Bri. And Leith, son of Celtchar of Cualu, was the most beautiful among the young men of the Sidhe of Ireland at that time, and he loved Bri, Midhir's daughter. And Bri went out with her young girls to meet him one time at the Grave of the Daughters beside Teamhair. And Leith came and his young men along with him till he was on the Hill of the After Repentance. And they could not come nearer to one another because of the slingers on Midhir's hill that were answering one another till their spears were as many as a swarm of bees on a day of beauty. And Cochlan, Leith's servant, got a sharp wound from them and he died.

Then the girl turned back to Midhir's hill, and her heart broke in her and she died. And Leith said: "Although I am not let come to this girl, I will leave my name with her." And the hill was called Bri Leith from that time.

After a while Midhir took Etain Echraide to be his wife. And there was great jealousy on Fuamach, the wife he had before, when she saw the love that Midhir gave to Etain, and she called to the Druid, Bresal Etarlaim to help her, and he put spells on Etain the way Fuamach was able to drive her away.

And when she was driven out of Bri Leith, Angus Og, son of the Dagda, took her into his keeping; and when Midhir asked her back, he would not give her up, but he brought her about with him to every place he went. And wherever they rested, he made a sunny house for her, and put sweet-smelling flowers in it, and he made invisible walls about it, that no one could see through and that could not be seen.

But when news came to Fuamach that Etain was so well cared by Angus, anger and jealousy came on her again, and she searched her mind for a way to destroy Etain altogether.

And it is what she did, she persuaded Midhir and Angus to go out and meet one another and to make peace, for there had been a quarrel between them ever since the time Etain was sent away. And when Angus was away from Brugh na Boinn, Fuamach went and found Etain there, in her sunny house. And she turned her with Druid spells into a fly, and then she sent a blast of wind into the house, that swept her away through the window.

But as to Midhir and Angus, they waited a while for Fuamach to come and join them. And when she did not come they were uneasy in their minds, and Angus hurried back to Brugh na Boinn. And when he found the sunny house empty, he went in search of Fuamach, and it was along with Etarlaim, the Druid, he found her, and he struck her head off there and then.

And for seven years Etain was blown to and fro through Ireland in great misery. And at last she came to the house of Etar, of Inver Cechmaine, where there was a feast going on, and she fell from a beam of the roof into the golden cup that was beside Etar's wife. And Etar's wife drank her down with the wine, and at the end of nine months she was born again as Etar's daughter.

And she had the same name as before, Etain; and she was reared as a king's daughter, and there were fifty young girls, daughters of princes, brought up with her to keep her company.

And it happened one day Etain and all the rest of the young girls were out bathing in the bay at Inver Cechmaine, and they saw from the water a man, with very high looks, coming towards them over the plain, and he riding a bay horse with mane and tail curled. A long green cloak he had on him, and a shirt woven with threads of red gold, and a brooch of gold that reached across to his shoulders on each side. And he had on his back a shield of silver with a rim of gold and a boss of gold, and in his hand a sharp-pointed spear covered with rings of gold from heel to socket. Fair yellow hair he had, coming over his forehead, and it bound with a golden band to keep it from loosening.

And when he came near them he got down from his horse, and sat down on the bank, and it is what he said:

"It is here Etain is to-day, at the Mound of Fair Women. It is among little children is her life on the strand of Inver Cechmaine.

"It is she healed the eye of the king from the well of Loch da Lig; it is she was swallowed in a heavy drink by the wife of Etar.

"Many great battles will happen for your sake to Echaid of Midhe; destruction will fall upon the Sidhe, and war on thousands of men."

And when he had said that, he vanished, and no one knew where he went. And they did not know the man that had come to them was Midhir of Bri Leith.

And when Etain was grown to be a beautiful young woman, she was seen by Eochaid Feidlech, High King of Ireland, and this is the way that happened.

He was going one time over the fair green of Bri Leith, and he saw at the side of a well a woman, with a bright comb of gold and silver, and she washing in a silver basin having four golden birds on it, and little bright purple stones set in the rim of the basin. A beautiful purple cloak she had, and silver fringes to it, and a gold brooch; and she had on her a dress of green silk with a long hood, embroidered in red gold, and wonderful clasps of gold and silver on her breasts and on her shoulder. The sunlight was falling on her, so that the gold and the green silk were shining out. Two plaits of hair she had, four locks in each plait, and a bead at the point of every lock, and the colour of her hair was like yellow flags in summer, or like red gold after it is rubbed.

There she was, letting down her hair to wash it, and her arms out through the sleeve-holes of her shift. Her soft hands were as white as the snow of a single night, and her eyes as blue as any blue flower, and her lips as red as the berries of the rowan-tree, and her body as white as the foam of a wave. The bright light of the moon was in her face, the highness of pride in her eyebrows, a dimple of delight in each of her cheeks, the light of wooing in her eyes, and when she walked she had a step that was steady and even like the walk of a queen.

And Eochaid sent his people to bring her to him, and he asked her name, and she told him her name was Etain, daughter of Etar, King of the Riders of the Sidhe. And Eochaid gave her his love, and he paid the bride-price, and brought her home to Teamhair as his wife, and there was a great welcome before her there.

And after a while there was a great feast made at Teamhair, and all the chief men of Ireland came to it, and it lasted from the fortnight before Samhain to the fortnight after it. And King Eochaid's brother Ailell, that was afterwards called Ailell Anglonach, of the Only Fault, came to the feast. And when he saw his brother's wife Etain, he fell in love with her on the moment, and all through the length of the feast he was not content unless he could be looking at her. And a woman, the daughter of Luchta Lamdearg, of the Red Hand, took notice of it, and she said: "What far thing are you looking at, Ailell? It is what I think, that to be looking the way you are doing is a sign of love." Then Ailell checked himself, and did not look towards Etain any more.

But when the feast was at an end, and the gathering broken up, great desire and envy came on Ailell, so that he fell sick, and they brought him to a house in Teffia. And he stopped there through the length of a year, and he was wasting away, but he told no one the cause of his sickness. And at the end of the year, Eochaid came to visit his brother, and he passed his hand over his breast, and Ailell let a groan. "What way are you?" said Eochaid then. "Are you getting any easier, for you must not let this illness come to a bad end." "By my word," said Ailell, "it is not easier I am, but worse and worse every day and every night." "What is it ails you?" said Eochaid. "And what is it that is coming against you." "By my word, I cannot tell you that," said Ailell. "I will bring one here that will know the cause of your sickness," said the king.

With that he sent Fachtna, his own physician, to Ailell; and when he came he passed his hand over Ailell's heart, and at that he groaned again. "This sickness will not be your death," said Fachtna then; "and I know well what it comes from. It is either from the pains of jealousy, or from love you have given, and that you have not found a way out of." But there was shame on Ailell, and he would not confess to the physician that what he said was right. So Fachtna went away then and left him.

As to King Eochaid, he went away to visit all the provinces of Ireland that were under his kingship, and he left Etain after him, and it is what he said: "Good Etain," he said, "take tender care of Ailell so long as he is living; and if he should die from us, make a sodded grave for him, and raise a pillar stone over it, and write his name on it in Ogham." And with that he went away on his journey.

One day, now, Etain went into the house where Ailell was lying in his sickness, and they talked together, and then she made a little song for him, and it is what she said:

"What is it ails you, young man, for it is a long time you are wasted with this sickness, and it is not the hardness of the weather has stopped your light footstep."

And Ailell answered her in the same way, and he said: "I have good cause for my hurt; the music of my own harp does not please me; there is no sort of food is pleasant to me, and so I am wasted away." Then Etain said: "Tell me what is it ails you, for I am a woman that is wise. Tell me is there anything that would cure you, the way I may help you to it?" And Ailell answered her: "O kind, beautiful woman, it is not good to tell a secret to a woman, but sometimes it may be known through the eyes." And Etain said: "Though it is bad to tell a secret, yet it ought to be told now, or how can help be given to you?" And Ailell answered: "My blessing on you, fair-haired Etain. It is not fit I am to be spoken with; my wits have been no good help to me; my body is a rebel to me. All Ireland knows, O king's wife, there is sickness in my head and in my body." And Etain said: "If there is a woman of the fair-faced women of Ireland tormenting you this way, she must come to you here if it pleases you; and it is I myself will woo her for you," she said.

Then Ailell said to her: "Woman, it would be easy for you yourself to put my sickness from me. And my desire," he said, "is a desire that is as long as a year; but it is love given to an echo, the spending of grief on a wave, a lonely fight with a shadow, that is what my love and my desire have been to me."

And it is then Etain knew what was the sickness that was on him, and it was a heavy trouble to her.

But she came to him every day to tend him, and to make ready his food, and to pour water over his hands, and all she could do she did for him, for it was a grief to her, he to wither away and to be lost for her sake. And at last one day she said to him: "Rise up, Ailell, son of a king, man of high deeds, and I will do your healing."

Then he put his arms about her, and she kissed him, and she said: "Come at the morning of to-morrow at the break of day to the house outside the dun, and I will give you all your desire."

That night Ailell lay without sleep until the morning was at hand. And at the very time he should have risen to go to her, it was at that time his sleep settled down upon him, and he slept on till the full light of day.

But Etain went to the house outside the dun, and she was not long there when she saw a man coming towards her having the appearance of Ailell, sick and tired and worn. But when he came near and she looked closely at him, she saw it was not Ailell that was in it. Then he went away, and after she had waited a while, she herself went back into the dun.

And it was then Ailell awoke, and when he knew the morning had passed by, he would sooner have had death than life, and he fretted greatly. And Etain came in then, and he told her what had happened him. And she said: "Come to-morrow to the same place."

But the same thing happened the next day. And when it happened on the third day, and the same man came to meet Etain, she said to him: "It is not you at all I come to meet here, and why is it that you come to meet me? And as to him I came to meet," she said, "indeed it is not for gain or through lightness I bade him come to me, but to heal him of the sickness he is lying under for my sake." Then the man said: "It would be more fitting for you to come to meet me than any other one. For in the time long ago," he said, "I was your first husband, and your first man." "What is it you are saying," she said, "and who are you yourself?" "It is easy to tell that," he said; "I am Midhir of Bri Leith." "And what parted us if I was your wife?" said Etain. "It was through Fuamach's sharp jealousy and through the spells of Bresal Etarlaim, the Druid, we were parted. And will you come away with me now?" he said. But Etain said: "It is not for a man whose kindred is unknown I will give up the High King of Ireland." And Midhir said: "Surely it was I myself put that great desire for you on Ailell, and it was I hindered him from going to meet you, the way you might keep your good name."

And when she went back to Ailell's house, she found his sickness was gone from him, and his desire. And she told him all that had happened, and he said: "It has turned out well for us both: I am well of my sickness and your good name is not lessened." "We give thanks to our gods for that," said Etain, "for we are well pleased to have it so."

And just at that time Eochaid came back from his journey, and they told him the whole story, and he was thankful to his wife for the kindness she had showed to Ailell.

It was a good while after that, there was a great fair held at Teamhair, and Etain was out on the green looking at the games and the races. And she saw a rider coming towards her, but no one could see him but herself; and when he came near she saw he had the same appearance as the man that came and spoke with her and her young girls the time they were out in the sea at Inver Cechmaine. And when he came up to her he began to sing words to her that no one could hear but herself. And it is what he said:

"O beautiful woman, will you come with me to the wonderful country that is mine? It is pleasant to be looking at the people there, beautiful people without any blemish; their hair is of the colour of the flag-flower, their fair body is as white as snow, the colour of the fox-glove is on every cheek. The young never grow old there; the fields and the flowers are as pleasant to be looking at as the blackbird's eggs; warm, sweet streams of mead and of wine flow through that country; there is no care and no sorrow on any person; we see others, but we ourselves are not seen.

"Though the plains of Ireland are beautiful, it is little you would think of them after our great plain; though the ale of Ireland is heady, the ale of the great country is still more heady. O beautiful woman, if you come to my proud people it is the flesh of pigs newly killed I will give you for food; it is ale and new milk I will give you for drink; it is feasting you will have with me there; it is a crown of gold you will have upon your hair, O beautiful woman!

"And will you come there with me, Etain?" he said. But Etain said she would not leave Eochaid the High King. "Will you come if Eochaid gives you leave?" Midhir said then. "I will do that," said Etain.

One day, after that time, Eochaid the High King was looking out from his palace at Teamhair, and he saw a strange man coming across the plain. Yellow hair he had, and eyes blue and shining like the flame of a candle, and a purple dress on him, and in his hand a five-pronged spear and a shield having gold knobs on it.

He came up to the king, and the king bade him welcome. "Who are you yourself?" he said; "and what are you come for, for you are a stranger to me?" "If I am a stranger to you, you are no stranger to me, for I have known you this long time," said the strange man. "What is your name?" said the king. "It is nothing very great," said he; "I am called Midhir of Bri Leith." "What is it brings you here?" said Eochaid. "I am come to play a game of chess with you," said the stranger. "Are you a good player?" said the king. "A trial will tell you that," said Midhir. "The chessboard is in the queen's house, and she is in her sleep at this time," said Eochaid. "That is no matter," said Midhir, "for I have with me a chessboard as good as your own." And with that he brought out his chessboard, and it made of silver, and precious stones shining in every corner of it. And then he brought out the chessmen, and they made of gold, from a bag that was of shining gold threads.

"Let us play now," said Midhir. "I will not play without a stake," said the king. "What stake shall we play for?" said Midhir. "We can settle that after the game is over," said the king.

They played together then, and Midhir was beaten, and it is what the king asked of him, fifty brown horses to be given to him. And then they played the second time, and Midhir was beaten again, and this time the king gave him four hard things to do: to make a road over Moin Lamraide, and to clear Midhe of stones, and to cover the district of Tethra with rushes, and the district of Darbrech with trees.

So Midhir brought his people from Bri Leith to do those things, and it is hard work they had doing them. And Eochaid used to be out watching them, and he took notice that when the men of the Sidhe yoked their oxen, it was by the neck and the shoulder they used to yoke them, and not by the forehead and the head.

And it was after Eochaid taught his people to yoke them that way, he was given the name of Eochaid Airem, that is, of the Plough.

And when all was done, Midhir came to Eochaid again, looking thin and wasted enough with the dint of the hard work he had been doing, and he asked Eochaid to play the third game with him. Eochaid agreed, and it was settled as before, the stake to be settled by the winner. It was Midhir won the game that time, and when the king asked him what he wanted, "It is Etain, your wife, I want," said he. "I will not give her to you," said the king. "All I will ask then," said Midhir, "is to put my arms about her and to kiss her once." "You may do that," said the king, "if you will wait to the end of a month." So Midhir agreed to that, and went away for that time.

At the end of the month he came back again, and stood in the great hall at Teamhair, and no one had ever seen him look so comely as he did that night. And Eochaid had all his best fighting men gathered in the hall, and he shut all the doors of the palace when he saw Midhir come in, for fear he would try to bring away Etain by force.

"I am come to be paid what is due to me," said Midhir. "I have not been thinking of it up to this time," said Eochaid, and there was anger on him. "You promised me Etain, your wife," said Midhir. The redness of shame came on Etain when she heard that, but Midhir said: "Let there be no shame on you, Etain, for it is through the length of a year I have been asking your love, and I have offered you every sort of treasure and riches, and you refused to come to me till such a time as your husband would give you leave." "It is true I said that," said Etain. "I will go if Eochaid gives me up to you." "I will not give you up," said Eochaid; "I will let him do no more than put his arms about you in this place, as was promised him." "I will do that," said Midhir.

With that he took his sword in his left hand, and he took Etain in his right arm and kissed her. All the armed men in the house made a rush at him then, but he rose up through the roof bringing Etain with him, and when they rushed out of the house to follow him, all they could see was two swans high up in the air, linked together by a chain of gold.

There was great anger on Eochaid then, and he went and searched all through Ireland, but there were no tidings of them to be had, for they were in the houses of the Sidhe.

It was to the Brugh of Angus on the Boinn they went first, and after they had stopped there a while they went to a hill of the Sidhe in Connacht. And there was a serving-maid with Etain at that time, Cruachan Croderg her name was, and she said to Midhir: "Is this your own place we are in?" "It is not," said Midhir; "my own place is nearer to the rising of the sun." She was not well pleased to stop there when she heard that, and Midhir said to quiet her: "It is your own name will be put on this place from this out." And the hill was called the Hill of Cruachan from that time.

Then they went to Bri Leith; and Etain's daughter Esa came to them there, and she brought a hundred of every sort of cattle with her, and Midhir fostered her for seven years. And all through that time Eochaid the High King was making a search for them.

But at last Codal of the Withered Breast took four rods of yew and wrote Oghams on them, and through them and through his enchantments he found out that Etain was with Midhir in Bri Leith.

So Eochaid went there, and made an attack on the place, and he was for nine years besieging it, and Midhir was driving him away. And then his people began digging through the hill; and when they were getting near to where Etain was, Midhir sent three times twenty beautiful women, having all of them the appearance of Etain, and he bade the king choose her out from among them. And the first he chose was his own daughter Esa. But then Etain called to him, and he knew her, and he brought her home to Teamhair.

And Eochaid gave his daughter Esa her choice of a place for herself. And she chose it, and made a rath there, that got the name of Rath Esa. And from it she could see three notable places, the Hill of the Sidhe in Broga, and the Hill of the Hostages in Teamhair, and Dun Crimthain on Beinn Edair.

But there was great anger on Midhir and his people because of their hill being attacked and dug into. And it was in revenge for that insult they brought Conaire, High King of Ireland, that was grandson of Eochaid and of Etain, to his death afterwards at Da Derga's Inn.

CHAPTER VIII

Manannan

Now as to Manannan the Proud, son of Lir, after he had made places for the rest of the Tuatha de Danaan to live in, he went away out of Ireland himself. And some said he was dead, and that he got his death by Uillenn Faebarderg, of the Red Edge, in battle. And it is what they said, that the battle was fought at Magh Cuilenn, and that Manannan was buried standing on his feet, and no sooner was he buried than a great lake burst up under his feet in the place that was a red bog till that time. And the lake got the name of Loch Orbson, from one of the names of Manannan. And it was said that red Badb was glad and many women were sorry at that battle.

But he had many places of living, and he was often heard of in Ireland after. It was he sent a messenger to Etain, mother of Conaire the High King, the time she was hidden in the cowherd's house. And it was he brought up Deirdre's children in Emhain of the Apple Trees, and it was said of that place, "a house of peace is the hill of the Sidhe of Emhain." And it was he taught Diarmuid of the Fianna the use of weapons, and it was he taught Cuchulain the use of the Gae Bulg, and some say it was he was Deirdre's father, and that he brought Conchubar, king of Ulster, to the place she was hidden, and he running with the appearance of a hare before the hounds of the men of Ulster to bring them there.

And it is what they say, that the time Conchubar had brought the sons of Usnach to Emain Macha, and could not come at them to kill them because of their bravery, it was to Manannan he went for help. And Manannan said he would give him no help, for he had told him at the time he brought Deirdre away that she would be the cause of the breaking up of his kingdom, and he took her away in spite of him. But Conchubar asked him to put blindness for a while on the sons of Usnach, or the whole army would be destroyed with their blows. So after a while he consented to that. And when the sons of Usnach came out again against the army of Ulster, the blindness came on them, and it was at one another they struck, not seeing who was near them, and it was by one another's hands they fell. But more say Manannan had no hand in it, and that it was Cathbad, the Druid, put a sea about them and brought them to their death by his enchantments.

And some say Culain, the Smith, that gave his name to Cuchulain afterwards, was Manannan himself, for he had many shapes.

Anyway, before Culain came to Ulster, he was living in the Island of Falga, that was one of Manannan's places. And one time before Conchubar came into the kingdom, he went to ask advice of a Druid, and the Druid bade him to go to the Island of Falga and to ask Culain, the smith he would find there, to make arms for him. So Conchubar did so, and the smith promised to make a sword and spear and shield for him.

And while he was working at them Conchubar went out one morning early to walk on the strand, and there he saw a sea-woman asleep on the shore. And he put bonds on her in her sleep, the way she would not make her escape. But when she awoke and saw what had happened, she asked him to set her free. "And I am Tiabhal," she said, "one of the queens of the sea. And bid Culain," she said, "that is making your shield for you, to put my likeness on it and my name about it. And whenever you will go into a battle with that shield the strength of your enemies will lessen, and your own strength and the strength of your people will increase."

So Conchubar let her go, and bade the smith do as she had told him.

And when he went back to Ireland he got the victory wherever he brought that shield.

And he sent for Culain then, and offered him a place on the plains of Muirthemne. And whether he was or was not Manannan, it is likely he gave Cuchulain good teaching the time he stopped with him there after killing his great dog.

Manannan had good hounds one time, but they went hunting after a pig that was destroying the whole country, and making a desert of it. And they followed it till they came to a lake, and there it turned on them, and no hound of them escaped alive, but they were all drowned or maimed. And the pig made for an island then, that got the name of Muc-inis, the Pigs Island afterwards; and the lake got the name of Loch Conn, the Lake of the Hounds.

And it was through Manannan the wave of Tuaig, one of the three great waves of Ireland, got its name, and this is the way that happened.

There was a young girl of the name of Tuag, a fosterling of Conaire the High King, was reared in Teamhair, and a great company of the daughters of the kings of Ireland were put about her to protect her, the way she would be kept for a king's asking. But Manannan sent Fer Ferdiad, of the Tuatha de Danaan, that was a pupil of his own and a Druid, in the shape of a woman of his own household, and he went where Tuag was, and sang a sleep-spell over her, and brought her away to Inver Glas. And there he laid her down while he went looking for a boat, that he might bring her away in her sleep to the Land of the Ever-Living Women. But a wave of the flood-tide came over the girl, and she was drowned, and Manannan killed Fer Ferdiad in his anger.

And one time Manannan's cows came up out of the sea at Baile Cronin, three of them, a red, and a white, and a black, and the people that were there saw them standing on the strand for a while, as if thinking, and then they all walked up together, side by side, from the strand. And at that time there were no roads in Ireland, and there was great wonder on the people when they saw a good wide road ready before the three cows to walk on. And when they got about a mile from the sea they parted; the white cow went to the north-west, towards Luimnech, and the red cow went to the south-west, and on round the coast of Ireland, and the black cow went to the north-east, towards Lis Mor, in the district of Portlairge, and a road opened before each of them, that is to be seen to this day.

And some say it was Manannan went to Finn and the Fianna in the form of the Gilla Decair, the Bad Servant, and brought them away to Land-under-Wave. Anyway, he used often to go hunting with them on Cnoc Aine, and sometimes he came to their help.

CHAPTER IX

Manannan at Play

And it was he went playing tricks through Ireland a long time after that again, the time he got the name of O'Donnell's Kern. And it is the way it happened, Aodh Dubh O'Donnell was holding a feast one time in Bel-atha Senaig, and his people were boasting of the goodness of his house and of his musicians.

And while they were talking, they saw a clown coming towards them, old striped clothes he had, and puddle water splashing in his shoes, and his sword sticking out naked behind him, and his ears through the old cloak that was over his head, and in his hand he had three spears of hollywood scorched and blackened.

He wished O'Donnell good health, and O'Donnell did the same to him, and asked where did he come from. "It is where I am," he said, "I slept last night at Dun Monaidhe, of the King of Alban; I am a day in Ile, a day in Cionn-tire, a day in Rachlainn, a day in the Watchman's Seat in Slieve Fuad; a pleasant, rambling, wandering man I am, and it is with yourself I am now, O'Donnell," he said. "Let the gate-keeper be brought to me," said O'Donnell. And when the gate-keeper came, he asked was it he let in this man, and the gate-keeper said he did not, and that he never saw him before. "Let him off, O'Donnell," said the stranger, "for it was as easy for me to come in, as it will be to me to go out again." There was wonder on them all then, any man to have come into the house without passing the gate.

The musicians began playing their music then, and all the best musicians of the country were there at the time, and they played very sweet tunes on their harps. But the strange man called out: "By my word, O'Donnell, there was never a noise of hammers beating on iron in any bad place was so bad to listen to as this noise your people are making."

With that he took a harp, and he made music that would put women in their pains and wounded men after a battle into a sweet sleep, and it is what O'Donnell said: "Since I first heard talk of the music of the Sidhe that is played in the hills and under the earth below us, I never heard better music than your own. And it is a very sweet player you are," he said. "One day I am sweet, another day I am sour," said the clown.

Then O'Donnell bade his people to bring him up to sit near himself. "I have no mind to do that," he said; "I would sooner be as I am, an ugly clown, making sport for high-up people." Then O'Donnell sent him down clothes, a hat and a striped shirt and a coat, but he would not have them. "I have no mind," he said, "to let high-up people be making a boast of giving them to me."

They were afraid then he might go from them, and they put twenty armed horsemen and twenty men on foot to hold him back from leaving the house, and as many more outside at the gate, for they knew him not to be a man of this world. "What are these men for?" said he. "They are to keep you here," said O'Donnell. "By my word, it is not with you I will be eating my supper to-morrow," he said, "but at Cnoc Aine, where Seaghan, Son of the Earl is, in Desmumain." "If I find you giving one stir out of yourself, between this and morning, I will knock you into a round lump there on the ground," said O'Donnell.

But at that the stranger took up the harp again, and he made the same sweet music as before. And when they were all listening to him, he called out to the men outside: "Here I am coming, and watch me well now or you will lose me." When

81

the men that were watching the gate heard that, they lifted up their axes to strike at him, but in their haste it was at one another they struck, till they were all lying stretched in blood. Then the clown said to the gate-keeper: "Let you ask twenty cows and a hundred of free land of O'Donnell as a fee for bringing his people back to life. And take this herb," he said, "and rub it in the mouth of each man of them, and he will rise up whole and well again." So the gate-keeper did that, and he got the cows and the land from O'Donnell, and he brought all the people to life again.

Now at that time Seaghan, Son of the Earl, was holding a gathering on the green in front of his dun, and he saw the same man coming towards him, and dressed in the same way, and the water splashing in his shoes. But when he asked who was he, he gave himself the name of a very learned man, Duartane O'Duartane, and he said it was by Ess Ruadh he was come, and by Ceiscorainn and from that to Corrslieve, and to Magh Lorg of the Dagda, and into the district of Hy'Conaill Gabhra, "till I came to yourself," he said, "by Cruachan of Magh Ai." So they brought him into the house, and gave him wine for drinking and water for washing his feet, and he slept till the rising of the sun on the morrow. And at that time Seaghan, Son of the Earl, came to visit him, and he said: "It is a long sleep you had, and there is no wonder in that, and your journey so long yesterday. But I often heard of your learning in books and of your skill on the harp, and I would like to hear you this morning," he said. "I am good in those arts indeed," said the stranger. So they brought him a book, but he could not read a word of it, and then they brought him a harp, and he could not play any tune. "It is likely your reading and your music are gone from you," said Seaghan; and he made a little rann on him, saying it was a strange thing Duartane O'Duartane that had such a great name not to be able to read a line of a book, or even to remember one. But when the stranger heard how he was being mocked at, he took up the book, and read from the top to the bottom of the page very well and in a sweet sounding voice. And after that he took the harp and played and sang the same way he did at O'Donnell's house the day before. "It is a very sweet man of learning you are," said Seaghan. "One day I am sweet, another day I am sour," said the stranger.

They walked out together then on Cnoc Aine, but while they were talking there, the stranger was gone all of a minute, and Seaghan, Son of the Earl, could not see where he went.

And after that he went on, and he reached Sligach just at the time O'Conchubar was setting out with the men of Connacht to avenge the Connacht hag's basket on the hag of Munster. And this time he gave himself the name of the Gilla Decair, the Bad Servant. And he joined with the men of Connacht, and they went over the Sionnan westward into Munster, and there they hunted and drove every creature that could be made travel, cattle and horses and flocks, into one place, till they got the hornless bull of the Munster hag and her two speckled cows, and

O'Conchubar brought them away to give to the Connacht hag in satisfaction for her basket.

But the men of Munster made an attack on them as they were going back; and the Gilla Decair asked O'Conchubar would he sooner have the cows driven, or have the Munster men checked, and he said he would sooner have the Munster men checked. So the Gilla Decair turned on them, and with his bow and twenty-four arrows he kept them back till O'Conchubar and his people were safe out of their reach in Connacht.

But he took some offence then, on account of O'Conchubar taking the first drink himself when they came to his house, and not giving it to him, that had done so much, and he took his leave and went from them on the moment.

After that he went to where Tadg O'Cealaigh was, and having his old striped clothes and his old shoes as before. And when they asked him what art he had, he said: "I am good at tricks. And if you will give me five marks I will show you a trick," he said. "I will give that," said Tadg.

With that the stranger put three rushes on the palm of his hand. "I will blow away the middle rush now," he said, "and the other two will stop as they are." So they told him to do that, and he put the tops of two of his fingers on the two outside rushes, and blew the middle one away. "There is a trick now for you, Tadg O'Cealaigh," he said then. "By my word, that is not a bad trick," said O'Cealaigh. But one of his men said: "That there may be no good luck with him that did it. And give me the half of that money now, Tadg," he said, "and I will do the same trick for you myself. "I will give you the half of what I got if you will do it," said the stranger. So the other put the rushes on his hand, but if he did, when he tried to do the trick, his two finger-tips went through the palm of his hand. "Ob-Ob-Ob!" said the stranger, "that is not the way I did the trick. But as you have lost the money," he said, "I will heal you again."

"I could do another trick for you," he said; "I could wag the ear on one side of my head and the ear on the other side would stay still." "Do it then," said O'Cealaigh. So the man of tricks took hold of one of his ears and wagged it up and down. "That is a good trick indeed," said O'Cealaigh. "I will show you another one now," he said.

With that he took from his bag a thread of silk, and gave a cast of it up into the air, that it was made fast to a cloud. And then he took a hare out of the same bag, and it ran up the thread; and then took out a little dog and laid it on after the hare, and it followed yelping on its track; and after that again he brought out a little serving-boy and bade him to follow dog and hare up the thread. Then out of another bag he had with him he brought out a beautiful, well-dressed young woman, and bade her to follow after the hound and the boy, and to take care and not let the hare be torn by the dog. She went up then quickly after them, and it was a delight to Tadg O'Cealaigh to be looking at them and to be listening to the sound of the hunt going on in the air.

All was quiet then for a long time, and then the man of tricks said: "I am afraid there is some bad work going on up there." "What is that?" said O'Cealaigh. "I am thinking," said he, "the hound might be eating the hare, and the serving-boy courting the girl." "It is likely enough they are," said O'Cealaigh. With that the stranger drew in the thread, and it is what he found, the boy making love to the girl and the hound chewing the bones of the hare. There was great anger on the man of tricks when he saw that, and he took his sword and struck the head off the boy. "I do not like a thing of that sort to be done in my presence," said Tadg O'Cealaigh. "If it did not please you, I can set all right again," said the stranger. And with that he took up the head and made a cast of it at the body, and it joined to it, and the young man stood up, but if he did his face was turned backwards. "It would be better for him to be dead than to be living like that," said O'Cealaigh. When the man of tricks heard that, he took hold of the boy and twisted his head straight, and he was as well as before.

And with that the man of tricks vanished, and no one saw where was he gone.

That is the way Manannan used to be going round Ireland, doing tricks and wonders. And no one could keep him in any place, and if he was put on a gallows itself, he would be found safe in the house after, and some other man on the gallows in his place. But he did no harm, and those that would be put to death by him, he would bring them to life again with a herb out of his bag.

And all the food he would use would be a vessel of sour milk and a few crab-apples. And there never was any music sweeter than the music he used to be playing.

CHAPTER X

His Call to Bran

And there were some that went to Manannan's country beyond the sea, and that gave an account of it afterwards.

One time Bran, son of Febal, was out by himself near his dun, and he heard music behind him. And it kept always after him, and at last he fell asleep with the sweetness of the sound. And when he awoke from his sleep he saw beside him a branch of silver, and it having white blossoms, and the whiteness of the silver was the same as the whiteness of the blossoms.

And he brought the branch in his hand into the royal house, and when all his people were with him they saw a woman with strange clothing standing in the house.

And she began to make a song for Bran, and all the people were looking at her and listening to her, and it is what she said:

"I bring a branch of the apple-tree from Emhain, from the far island around which are the shining horses of the Son of Lir. A delight of the eyes is the plain where the hosts hold their games; curragh racing against chariot in the White Silver Plain to the south.

"There are feet of white bronze under it, shining through life and time; a comely level land through the length of the world's age, and many blossoms falling on it.

"There is an old tree there with blossoms, and birds calling from among them; every colour is shining there, delight is common, and music, in the Gentle-Voiced Plain, in the Silver Cloud Plain to the south.

"Keening is not used, or treachery, in the tilled familiar land; there is nothing hard or rough, but sweet music striking on the ear.

"To be without grief, without sorrow, without death, without any sickness, without weakness; that is the sign of Emhain; it is not common wonder that is.

"There is nothing to liken its mists to, the sea washes the wave against the land; brightness falls from its hair.

"There are riches, there are treasures of every colour in the Gentle Land, the Bountiful Land. Sweet music to be listening to; the best of wine to drink.

"Golden chariots in the Plain of the Sea, rising up to the sun with the tide; silver chariots and bronze chariots on the Plain of Sports.

"Gold-yellow horses on the strand, and crimson horses, and others with wool on their backs, blue like the colour of the sky.

"It is a day of lasting weather, silver is dropping on the land; a pure white cliff on the edge of the sea, getting its warmth from the sun.

"The host race over the Plain of Sports; it is beautiful and not weak their game is; death or the ebbing of the tide will not come to them in the Many-Coloured Land.

"There will come at sunrise a fair man, lighting up the level lands; he rides upon the plain that is beaten by the waves, he stirs the sea till it is like blood.

"An army will come over the clear sea, rowing to the stone that is in sight, that a hundred sounds of music come from.

"It sings a song to the army; it is not sad through the length of time; it increases music with hundreds singing together; they do not look for death or the ebb-tide.

"There are three times fifty far islands in the ocean to the west of us, and every one of them twice or three times more than Ireland.

"It is not to all of you I am speaking, though I have made all these wonders known. Let Bran listen from the crowd of the world to all the wisdom that has been told him.

"Do not fall upon a bed of sloth; do not be overcome by drunkenness; set out on your voyage over the clear sea, and you may chance to come to the Land of Women."

With that the woman went from them, and they did not know where she went.

And she brought away her branch with her, for it leaped into her hand from Bran's hand, and he had not the strength to hold it.

Then on the morrow Bran set out upon the sea, and three companies of nine along with him; and one of his foster-brothers and comrades was set over each company of nine.

And when they had been rowing for two days and two nights, they saw a man coming towards them in a chariot, over the sea. And the man made himself known to them, and he said that he was Manannan, son of Lir.

And then Manannan spoke to him in a song, and it is what he said:

"It is what Bran thinks, he is going in his curragh over the wonderful, beautiful clear sea; but to me, from far off in my chariot, it is a flowery plain he is riding on.

"What is a clear sea to the good boat Bran is in, is a happy plain with many flowers to me in my two-wheeled chariot.

"It is what Bran sees, many waves beating across the clear sea; it is what I myself see, red flowers without any fault.

"The sea-horses are bright in summer-time, as far as Bran's eyes can reach; there is a wood of beautiful acorns under the head of your little boat.

"A wood with blossom and with fruit, that has the smell of wine; a wood without fault, without withering, with leaves of the colour of gold.

"Let Bran row on steadily, it is not far to the Land of Women; before the setting of the sun you will reach Emhain, of many-coloured hospitality."

With that Bran went from him; and after a while he saw an island, and he rowed around it, and there was a crowd on it, wondering at them, and laughing; and they were all looking at Bran and at his people, but they would not stop to talk with them, but went on giving out gusts of laughter. Bran put one of his men on the island then, but he joined with the others, and began to stare the same way as the men of the island. And Bran went on rowing round about the island; and whenever they went past his own man, his comrades would speak to him, but he would not answer them, but would only stare and wonder at them. So they went away and left him on that island that is called the Island of Joy.

It was not long after that they reached to the Land of Women. And they saw the chief one of the women at the landing-place, and it is what she said: "Come hither to land, Bran, son of Febal, it is welcome your coming is." But Bran did not dare to go on shore. Then the woman threw a ball of thread straight to him, and he caught it in his hand, and it held fast to his palm, and the woman kept the thread in her own hand, and she pulled the curragh to the landing-place.

On that they went into a grand house, where there was a bed for every couple, three times nine beds. And the food that was put on every dish never came to an end, and they had every sort of food and of drink they wished for.

And it seemed to them they were only a year there when the desire of home took hold on one of them, Nechtan, son of Collbrain, and his kinsmen were begging and praying Bran to go back with him to Ireland. The woman said there would be repentance on them if they went; but in spite of that they set out in the end. And the woman said to them not to touch the land when they would come to Ireland, and she bade them to visit and to bring with them the man they left in the Island of Joy.

So they went on towards Ireland till they came to a place called Srub Bruin. And there were people on the strand that asked them who they were that were coming over the sea. And Bran said: "I am Bran, son of Febal." But the people said: "We know of no such man, though the voyage of Bran is in our very old stories."

Then Nechtan, son of Collbrain, made a leap out of the curragh, and no sooner did he touch the shore of Ireland than he was a heap of ashes, the same as if he had been in the earth through hundreds of years.

And then Bran told the whole story of his wanderings to the people, from the beginning. And after that he bade them farewell, and his wanderings from that time are not known.

CHAPTER XI

His Three Calls to Cormac

And another that went to Manannan's country was Cormac, grandson of Conn, King of Teamhair, and this is the way it happened. He was by himself in Teamhair one time, and he saw an armed man coming towards him, quiet, with high looks, and having grey hair; a shirt ribbed with gold thread next his skin, broad shoes of white bronze between his feet and the ground, a shining branch, having nine apples of red gold, on his shoulder. And it is delightful the sound of that branch was, and no one on earth would keep in mind any want, or trouble, or tiredness, when that branch was shaken for him; and whatever trouble there might be on him, he would forget it at the sound.

Then Cormac and the armed man saluted one another, and Cormac asked where did he come from. "I come," he said, "from a country where there is nothing but truth, and where there is neither age nor withering away, nor heaviness, nor sadness, nor jealousy nor envy, nor pride." "That is not so with us," said Cormac, "and I would be well pleased to have your friendship," he said. "I am well pleased to give it," said the stranger. "Give me your branch along with it," said Cormac. "I will give it," said the stranger, "if you will give me the three gifts I ask in return." "I will give them to you indeed," said Cormac.

Then the strange man left the branch and went away, and Cormac did not know where was he gone to.

He went back then into the royal house, and there was wonder on all the people when they saw the branch. And he shook it at them, and it put them all asleep from that day to the same time on the morrow.

At the end of a year the strange man came back again, and he asked for the first of his three requests. "You will get it," said Cormac. "I will take your daughter, Aille, to-day," said the stranger.

So he brought away the girl with him, and the women of Ireland gave three loud cries after the king's daughter. But Cormac shook the branch at them, until it put away sorrow from them, and put them all into their sleep.

That day month the stranger came again, and he brought Cormac's son, Carpre Lifecar, away with him. There was crying and lamenting without end in Teamhair after the boy, and on that night no one ate or slept, and they were all under grief and very downhearted. But when Cormac shook the branch their sorrow went from them.

Then the stranger came the third time, and Cormac asked him what did he want. "It is your wife, Ethne, I am asking this time," he said. And he went away then, bringing Ethne, the queen, along with him.

But Cormac would not bear that, and he went after them, and all his people were following him. But in the middle of the Plain of the Wall, a thick mist came on them, and when it was gone, Cormac found himself alone on a great plain. And he saw a great dun in the middle of the plain, with a wall of bronze around it, and in the dun a house of white silver, and it half thatched with the white wings of birds. And there was a great troop of the Riders of the Sidhe all about the house, and their arms full of white birds' wings for thatching. But as soon as they would put on the thatch, a blast of wind would come and carry it away again.

Then he saw a man kindling a fire, and he used to throw a thick oak-tree upon it. And when he would come back with a second tree, the first one would be burned out. "I will be looking at you no longer," Cormac said then, "for there is no one here to tell me your story, and I think I could find good sense in your meanings if I understood them," he said.

Then he went on to where there was another dun, very large and royal, and another wall of bronze around it, and four houses within it. And he went in and saw a great king's house, having beams of bronze and walls of silver, and its thatch of the wings of white birds. And then he saw on the green a shining well, and five streams flowing from it, and the armies drinking water in turn, and the nine lasting purple hazels of Buan growing over it. And they were dropping their nuts into the water, and the five salmon would catch them and send their husks floating down the streams. And the sound of the flowing of those streams is sweeter than any music that men sing.

Then he went into the palace, and he found there waiting for him a man and a woman, very tall, and having clothes of many colours. The man was beautiful as to shape, and his face wonderful to look at; and as to the young woman that was with him, she was the loveliest of all the women of the world, and she having yellow hair and a golden helmet. And there was a bath there, and heated stones going in and out of the water of themselves, and Cormac bathed himself in it.

"Rise up, man of the house," the woman said after that, "for this is a comely traveller is come to us; and if you have one kind of food or meat better than another, let it be brought in." The man rose up then and he said: "I have but seven pigs, but I could feed the whole world with them, for the pig that is killed and eaten to-day, you will find it alive again tomorrow."

Another man came into the house then, having an axe in his right hand, and a log in his left hand, and a pig behind him.

"It is time to make ready," said the man of the house, "for we have a high guest with us to-day."

Then the man struck the pig and killed it, and he cut the logs and made a fire and put the pig on it in a cauldron. "It is time for you to turn it," said the master of the house after a while. "There would be no use doing that," said the man, "for never and never will the pig be boiled until a truth is told for every quarter of it." "Then let you tell yours first," said the master of the house. "One day," said the man, "I found another man's cows in my land, and I brought them with me into a cattle pound. The owner of the cows followed me, and he said he would give me a reward to let the cows go free. So I gave them back to him, and he gave me an axe, and when a pig is to be killed, it is with the axe it is killed, and the log is cut with it, and there is enough wood to boil the pig, and enough for the palace besides. And that is not all, for the log is found whole again in the morning. And from that time till now, that is the way they are."

"It is true indeed that story is," said the man of the house.

They turned the pig in the cauldron then, and but one quarter of it was found to be cooked. "Let us tell another true story," they said. "I will tell one," said the master of the house. "Ploughing time had come, and when we had a mind to plough that field outside, it is the way we found it, ploughed, and harrowed, and sowed with wheat. When we had a mind to reap it, the wheat was found in the haggard, all in one thatched rick. We have been using it from that day to this, and it is no bigger and no less."

Then they turned the pig, and another quarter was found to be ready. "It is my turn now," said the woman. "I have seven cows," she said, "and seven sheep. And the milk of the seven cows would satisfy the whole of the men of the world, if they were in the plain drinking it, and it is enough for all the people of the Land of Promise, and it is from the wool of the seven sheep all the clothes they wear are made." And at that story the third quarter of the pig was boiled.

"If these stories are true," said Cormac to the man of the house, "you are Manannan, and this is Manannan's wife; for no one on the whole ridge of the world owns these treasures but himself. It was to the Land of Promise he went to look for that woman, and he got those seven cows with her."

They said to Cormac that it was his turn now. So Cormac told them how his wife, and his son, and his daughter, had been brought away from him, and how he himself had followed them till he came to that place.

And with that the whole pig was boiled, and they cut it up, and Cormac's share was put before him. "I never used a meal yet," said he, "having two persons only in my company." The man of the house began singing to him then, and put him asleep. And when he awoke, he saw fifty armed men, and his son, and his wife, and his daughter, along with them. There was great gladness and courage on him then, and ale and food were given out to them all. And there was a gold cup put in the hand of the master of the house, and Cormac was wondering at it, for the number of the shapes on it, and for the strangeness of the work. "There is a stranger thing yet about it," the man said; "let three lying words be spoken under it, and it will break into three, and then let three true words be spoken under it, and it will be as good as before." So he said three lying words under it, and it broke in three pieces. "It is best to speak truth now under it," he said, "and to mend it. And I give my word, Cormac," he said, "that until to-day neither your wife or your daughter has seen the face of a man since they were brought away from you out of Teamhair, and that your son has never seen the face of a woman." And with that the cup was whole again on the moment. "Bring away your wife and your children with you now," he said, "and this cup along with them, the way you will have it for judging between truth and untruth. And I will leave the branch with you for music and delight, but on the day of your death they will be taken from you again. "And I myself," he said, "am Manannan, son of Lir, King of the Land of Promise, and I brought you here by enchantments that you might be with me to-night in friendship.

"And the Riders you saw thatching the house," he said, "are the men of art and poets, and all that look for a fortune in Ireland, putting together cattle and riches. For when they go out, all that they leave in their houses goes to nothing, and so they go on for ever.

"And the man you saw kindling the fire," he said, "is a young lord that is more liberal than he can afford, and every one else is served while he is getting the feast ready, and every one else profiting by it.

"And the well you saw is the Well of Knowledge, and the streams are the five streams through which all knowledge goes. And no one will have knowledge who does not drink a draught out of the well itself or out of the streams. And the people of many arts are those who drink from them all."

And on the morning of the morrow, when Cormac rose up, he found himself on the green of Teamhair, and his wife, and his son, and his daughter, along with him, and he having his branch and his cup. And it was given the name of Cormac's Cup, and it used to judge between truth and falsehood among the Gael. But it was not left in Ireland after the night of Cormac's death, as Manannan had foretold him.

CHAPTER XII

Cliodna's Wave

And it was in the time of the Fianna of Ireland that Ciabhan of the Curling Hair, the king of Ulster's son, went to Manannan's country.

Ciabhan now was the most beautiful of the young men of the world at that time, and he was as far beyond all other kings' sons as the moon is beyond the stars. And Finn liked him well, but the rest of the Fianna got to be tired of him because there was not a woman of their women, wed or unwed, but gave him her love. And Finn had to send him away at the last, for he was in dread of the men of the Fianna because of the greatness of their jealousy.

So Ciabhan went on till he came to the Strand of the Cairn, that is called now the Strand of the Strong Man, between Dun Sobairce and the sea. And there he saw a curragh, and it having a narrow stern of copper. And Ciabhan got into the curragh, and his people said: "Is it to leave Ireland you have a mind, Ciabhan?" "It is indeed," he said, "for in Ireland I get neither shelter or protection." He bade farewell to his people then, and he left them very sorrowful after him, for to part with him was like the parting of life from the body.

And Ciabhan went on in the curragh, and great white shouting waves rose up about him, every one of them the size of a mountain; and the beautiful speckled salmon that are used to stop in the sand and the shingle rose up to the sides of the curragh, till great dread came on Ciabhan, and he said: "By my word, if it was on land I was I could make a better fight for myself."

And he was in this danger till he saw a rider coming towards him on a dark grey horse having a golden bridle, and he would be under the sea for the length of nine waves, and he would rise with the tenth wave, and no wet on him at all. And he said: "What reward would you give to whoever would bring you out of this great danger?" "Is there anything in my hand worth offering you?" said Ciabhan. "There is," said the rider, "that you would give your service to whoever would give you his help." Ciabhan agreed to that, and he put his hand into the rider's hand.

With that the rider drew him on to the horse, and the curragh came on beside them till they reached to the shore of Tir Tairngaire, the Land of Promise. They got off the horse there, and came to Loch Luchra, the Lake of the Dwarfs, and to Manannan's city, and feast was after being made ready there, and comely serving-boys were going round with smooth horns, and playing on sweet-sounding harps till the whole house was filled with the music.

Then there came in clowns, long-snouted, long-heeled, lean and bald and red, that used to be doing tricks in Manannan's house. And one of these tricks was, a man of them to take nine straight willow rods, and to throw them up to the rafters of the house, and to catch them again as they came down, and he standing on one leg, and having but one hand free. And they thought no one could do that trick but themselves, and they were used to ask strangers to do it, the way they could see them fail.

So this night when one of them had done the trick, he came up to Ciabhan, that was beyond all the Men of Dea or the Sons of the Gael that were in the house, in shape and in walk and in name, and he put the nine rods in his hand. And Ciabhan stood up and he did the feat before them all, the same as if he had never learned to do any other thing.

Now Gebann, that was a chief Druid in Manannan's country, had a daughter, Cliodna of the Fair Hair, that had never given her love to any man. But when she saw Ciabhan she gave him her love, and she agreed to go away with him on the morrow.

And they went down to the landing-place and got into a curragh, and they went on till they came to Teite's Strand in the southern part of Ireland. It was from Teite Brec the Freckled the strand got its name, that went there one time for a wave game, and three times fifty young girls with her, and they were all drowned in that place.

And as to Ciabhan, he came on shore, and went looking for deer, as was right, under the thick branches of the wood; and he left the young girl in the boat on the strand.

But the people of Manannan's house came after them, having forty ships. And Iuchnu, that was in the curragh with Cliodna, did treachery, and he played music to her till she lay down in the boat and fell asleep. And then a great wave came up on the strand and swept her away.

And the wave got its name from Cliodna of the Fair Hair, that will be long remembered.

CHAPTER XIII

His Call to Connla

And it is likely it was Manannan sent his messenger for Connla of the Red Hair the time he went away out of Ireland, for it is to his country Connla was brought; and this is the way he got the call.

It chanced one day he was with his father Conn, King of Teamhair, on the Hill of Uisnach, and he saw a woman having wonderful clothing coming towards him. "Where is it you come from?" he asked her. "I come," she said, "from Tir-nam-

Beo, the Land of the Ever-Living Ones, where no death comes. We use feasts that are lasting," she said, "and we do every kind thing without quarrelling, and we are called the people of the Sidhe." "Who are you speaking to, boy?" said Conn to him then, for no one saw the strange woman but only Connla. "He is speaking to a high woman that death or old age will never come to," she said. "I am asking him to come to Magh Mell, the Pleasant Plain where the triumphant king is living, and there he will be a king for ever without sorrow or fret. Come with me, Connla of the Red Hair," she said, "of the fair freckled neck and of the ruddy cheek; come with me, and your body will not wither from its youth and its comeliness for ever."

They could all hear the woman's words then, though they could not see her, and it is what Conn said to Coran his Druid: "Help me, Coran, you that sing spells of the great arts. There is an attack made on me that is beyond my wisdom and beyond my power, I never knew so strong an attack since the first day I was a king. There is an unseen figure fighting with me; she is using her strength against me to bring away my beautiful son; the call of a woman is bringing him away from the hands of the king."

Then Coran, the Druid, began singing spells against the woman of the Sidhe, the way no one would hear her voice, and Connla could not see her any more. But when she was being driven away by the spells of the Druid, she threw an apple to Connla.

And through the length of a month from that time, Connla used no other food nor drink but that apple, for he thought no other food or drink worth the using. And for all he ate of it, the apple grew no smaller, but was whole all the while. And there was great trouble on Connla on account of the woman he had seen.

And at the end of a month Connla was at his father's side in Magh Archomnim, and he saw the same woman coming towards him, and it is what she said: "It is a high place indeed Connla has among dying people, and death before him. But the Ever-Living Living Ones," she said, "are asking you to take the sway over the people of Tethra, for they are looking at you every day in the gatherings of your country among your dear friends."

When Conn, the king, heard her voice, he said to his people: "Call Coran, the Druid to me, for I hear the sound of the woman's voice again." But on that she said: "O Conn, fighter of a hundred, it is little love and little respect the wonderful tribes of Traig Mor, the Great Strand, have for Druids; and where its law comes, it scatters the spells on their lips."

Then Conn looked to his son Connla to see what he would say, and Connla said: "My own people are dearer to me than any other thing, yet sorrow has taken hold of me because of this woman." Then the woman spoke to him again, and it is what she said: "Come now into my shining ship, if you will come to the Plain of Victory. There is another country it would not be worse for you to look for; though the bright sun is going down, we shall reach to that country before night.

That is the country that delights the mind of every one that turns to me. There is no living race in it but women and girls only."

And when the woman had ended her song, Connla made a leap from his people into the shining boat, and they saw him sailing away from them far off and as if in a mist, as far as their eyes could see. It is away across the sea they went, and they have never come back again, and only the gods know where was it they went.

CHAPTER XIV

Tadg in Manannan's Islands

And another that went to the Land of the Ever-Living Ones, but that came back again, was Tadg, son of Cian, son of Olioll; and this is the way that happened.

It was one time Tadg was going his next heir's round, into the west of Munster, and his two brothers, Airnelach and Eoghan, along with him. And Cathmann, son of Tabarn, that was king of the beautiful country of Fresen that lay to the south-east of the Great Plain, was searching the sea for what he could find just at that time, and nine of his ships with him. And they landed at Beire do Bhunadas, to the west of Munster, and the country had no stir in it, and so they slipped ashore, and no one took notice of them till all were surrounded, both men and cattle. And Tadg's wife Liban, daughter of Conchubar Abratrudh of the Red Brows, and his two brothers, and a great many of the people of Munster, were taken by the foreigners and brought away to the coasts of Fresen. And Cathmann took Liban to be his own wife, and he put hardship on Tadg's two brothers: Eoghan he put to work a common ferry across a channel of the coast, and Airnelach to cut firing and to keep up fires for all the people; and all the food they got was barley seed and muddy water.

And as to Tadg himself, it was only by his courage and the use of his sword he made his escape, but there was great grief and discouragement on him, his wife and his brothers to have been brought away. But he had forty of his fighting men left that had each killed a man of the foreigners, and they had brought one in alive. And this man told them news of the country he came from. And when Tadg heard that, he made a plan in his own head, and he gave orders for a curragh to be built that would be fit for a long voyage. Very strong it was, and forty ox-hides on it of hard red leather, that was after being soaked in bark. And it was well fitted with masts, and oars, and pitch, and everything that was wanting. And they put every sort of meat, and drink, and of clothes in it, that would last them through the length of a year.

When all was ready, and the curragh out in the tide, Tadg said to his people:

"Let us set out now on the high sea, looking for our own people that are away from us this long time."

They set out then over the stormy, heavy flood, till at last they saw no land before them or behind them, but only the hillsides of the great sea. And farther on again they heard the singing of a great flock of unknown birds; and pleasant white-bellied salmon were leaping about the curragh on every side, and seals, very big and dark, were coming after them, breaking through the shining wash of the oars; and great whales after them again, so that the young men liked to be looking at them, for they were not used to see the like before.

They went on rowing through twenty days and twenty nights, and at the end of that time they got sight of a high land, having a smooth coast. And when they reached it they all landed, and they pulled up the curragh and lit their fires, and food was given out to them, and they were not long making an end of it. They made beds for themselves then on the beautiful green grass, and enjoyed their sleep till the rising of the sun on the morrow.

Tadg rose up then and put on his arms, and went out, and thirty of his men along with him, to search the whole island.

They went all through it, but they found no living thing on it, man or beast, but only flocks of sheep. And the size of the sheep was past all telling, as big as horses they were, and the whole island was filled with their wool. And there was one great flock beyond all the others, all of very big rams, and one of them was biggest of all, nine horns he had, and he charged on Tadg's chief men, attacking them and butting at them.

There was vexation on them then, and they attacked him again, and there was a struggle between them. And at the first the ram broke through five of their shields. But Tadg took his spear that there was no escape from, and made a lucky cast at the ram and killed him. And they brought the ram to the curragh and made it ready for the young men to eat, and they stopped three nights on the island, and every night it was a sheep they had for their food. And they gathered a good share of the wool and put it in the curragh because of the wonder and the beauty of it. And they found the bones of very big men on the island, but whether they died of sickness or were killed by the rams they did not know.

They left that island then and went forward till they found two strange islands where there were great flocks of wonderful birds, like blackbirds, and some of them the size of eagles or of cranes, and they red with green heads on them, and the eggs they had were blue and pure crimson. And some of the men began eating the eggs, and on the moment feathers began to grow out on them. But they went bathing after that, and the feathers dropped off them again as quick as they came.

It was the foreigner they had with them gave them the course up to this time, for he had been on the same track before. But now they went on through the length of six weeks and never saw land, and he said then, "We are astray on the great ocean that has no boundaries." Then the wind with its sharp voice began to rise, and there was a noise like the tramping of feet in the sea, and it rose up into great mountains hard to climb, and there was great fear on Tadg's people, for they had never seen the like. But he began to stir them up and to rouse them, and he bade them to meet the sea like men. "Do bravery," he said, "young men of Munster, and fight for your lives against the waves that are rising up and coming at the sides of the curragh." Tadg took one side of the curragh then and his men took the other side, and he was able to pull it round against the whole twenty-nine of them, and to bale it out and keep it dry along with that. And after a while they got a fair wind and put up their sail, the way less water came into the curragh, and then the sea went down and lay flat and calm, and there were strange birds of many shapes singing around them in every part. They saw land before them then, with a good coast, and with that courage and gladness came on them.

And when they came nearer to the land they found a beautiful inver, a river's mouth, with green hills about it, and the bottom of it sandy and as bright as silver, and red-speckled salmon in it, and pleasant woods with purple tree-tops edging the stream. "It is a beautiful country this is," said Tadg, "and it would be happy for him that would be always in it; and let you pull up the ship now," he said, "and dry it out."

A score of them went forward then into the country, and a score stopped to mind the curragh. And for all the cold and discouragement and bad weather they had gone through, they felt no wish at all for food or for fire, but the sweet smell of the crimson branches in the place they were come to satisfied them. They went on through the wood, and after a while they came to an apple garden having red apples in it, and leafy oak-trees, and hazels yellow with nuts. "It is a wonder to me," said Tadg, "to find summer here, and it winter time in our own country."

It was a delightful place they were in, but they went on into another wood, very sweet smelling, and round purple berries in it, every one of them bigger than a man's head, and beautiful shining birds eating the berries, strange birds they were, having white bodies and purple heads and golden beaks. And while they were eating the berries they were singing sweet music, that would have put sick men and wounded men into their sleep.

Tadg and his men went farther on again till they came to a great smooth flowery plain with a dew of honey over it, and three steep hills on the plain, having a very strong dun on every one of them. And when they got to the nearest hill they found a white-bodied woman, the best of the women of the whole world, and it is what she said: "Your coming is welcome, Tadg, son of Cian, and there will be food and provision for you as you want it."

"I am glad of that welcome," said Tadg; "and tell me now, woman of sweet words," he said, "what is that royal dun on the hill, having walls of white marble around it?" "That is the dun of the royal line of the kings of Ireland, from Heremon, son of Miled, to Conn of the Hundred Battles, that was the last to go into it." "What is the name of this country?" Tadg said then. "It is Inislocha, the Lake Island," she said, "and there are two kings over it, Rudrach and Dergcroche, sons of Bodb." And then she told Tadg the whole story of Ireland, to the time of the coming of the Sons of the Gael. "That is well," said Tadg then, "and you have good knowledge and learning. And tell me now," he said, "who is living in that middle dun that has the colour of gold?" "It is not myself will tell you that," she said, "but go on to it yourself and you will get knowledge of it." And with that she went from them into the dun of white marble.

Tadg and his men went on then till they came to the middle dun, and there they found a queen of beautiful shape, and she wearing a golden dress. "Health to you, Tadg," she said. "I thank you for that," said Tadg. "It is a long time your coming on this journey was foretold," she said. "What is your name?" he asked then. "I am Cesair," she said, "the first that ever reached Ireland. But since I and the men that were with me came out of that dark, unquiet land, we are living for ever in this country."

"Tell me, woman," said Tadg, "who is it lives in that dun having a wall of gold about it?" "It is not hard to tell that," she said, "every king, and every chief man, and every noble person that was in a high place of all those that had power in Ireland, it is in that dun beyond they are; Parthalon and Nemed, Firbolgs and Tuatha de Danaan." "It is good knowledge and learning you have," said Tadg. "Indeed I have good knowledge of the history of the world," she said, and this island," she said, "is the fourth paradise of the world; and as to the others, they are Inis Daleb to the south, and Inis Ercandra to the north, and Adam's Paradise in the east of the world." "Who is there living in that dun with the silver walls?" said Tadg then. "I will not tell you that, although I have knowledge of it," said the woman; "but go to the beautiful hill where it is, and you will get knowledge of it."

They went on then to the third hill, and on the top of the hill was a very beautiful resting-place, and two sweethearts there, a boy and a girl, comely and gentle. Smooth hair they had, shining like gold, and beautiful green clothes of the one sort, and any one would think them to have had the same father and mother. Gold chains they had around their necks, and bands of gold above those again. And Tadg spoke to them: "O bright, comely children," he said, "it is a pleasant place you have here." And they answered him back, and they were praising his courage and his strength and his wisdom, and they gave him their blessing.

And it is how the young man was, he had a sweet-smelling apple, having the colour of gold, in his hand, and he would eat a third part of it, and with all he would eat, it would never be less. And that was, the food that nourished the two of them, and neither age or sorrow could touch them when once they had tasted it.

"Who are you yourself?" Tadg asked him then. "I am son to Conn of the Hundred Battles," he said. "Is it Connla you are?" said Tadg. "I am indeed," said the young man, "and it is this girl of many shapes that brought me here." And the girl said: "I have given him my love and my affection, and it is because of that I brought him to this place, the way we might be looking at one another for ever, and beyond that we have never gone."

"That is a beautiful thing and a strange thing," said Tadg, "and a thing to wonder at. And who is there in that grand dun with the silver walls?" he said. "There is no one at all in it," said the girl. "What is the reason of that?" said Tadg. "It is for the kings that are to rule Ireland yet," she said; "and there will be a place in it for yourself, Tadg. And come now," she said, "till you see it."

The lovers went on to the dun, and it is hardly the green grass was bent under their white feet. And Tadg and his people went along with them.

They came then to the great wonderful house that was ready for the company of the kings; it is a pleasant house that was, and any one would like to be in it. Walls of white bronze it had, set with crystal and with carbuncles, that were shining through the night as well as through the day.

Tadg looked out from the house then, and he saw to one side of him a great sheltering apple-tree, and blossoms and ripe fruit on it. "What is that apple tree beyond?" said Tadg. "It is the fruit of that tree is food for the host in this house," said the woman. "And it was an apple of that apple-tree brought Connla here to me; a good tree it is, with its white-blossomed branches, and its golden apples that would satisfy the whole house."

And then Connla and the young girl left them, and they saw coming towards them a troop of beautiful women. And there was one among them was most beautiful of all, and when she was come to them she said: "A welcome to you, Tadg." "I thank you for that welcome," said Tadg; "and tell me," he said "who are you yourself?" "I am Cliodna of the Fair Hair," she said, "daughter of Gebann, son of Treon, of the Tuatha de Danaan, a sweetheart of Ciabhan of the Curling Hair; and it is from me Cliodna's wave on the coast of Munster got its name; and I am a long time now in this island, and it is the apples of that tree you saw that we use for food." And Tadg was well pleased to be listening to her talk, but after a while he said: "It is best for us to go on now to look for our people." "We will be well pleased if you stop longer with us," said the woman.

And while she was saying those words they saw three beautiful birds coming to them, one of them blue and his head crimson, and one was crimson and his head green, and the third was speckled and his head the colour of gold, and they lit on the great apple-tree, and every bird of them ate an apple, and they sang sweet music then, that would put sick men into their sleep.

"Those birds will go with you," Cliodna said then; "they will give you guidance on your way, and they will make music for you, and there will be neither sorrow or sadness on you, by land or by sea, till you come to Ireland. And bring away this beautiful green cup with you," she said, "for there is power in it, and if you do but pour water into it, it will be turned to wine on the moment. And do not let it out of your hand," she said, "but keep it with you; for at whatever time it will escape from you, your death will not be far away. And it is where you will meet your death, in the green valley at the side of the Boinn; and it is a wandering wild deer will give you a wound, and after that, it is strangers will put an end to you. And I myself will bury your body, and there will be a hill over it, and the name it will get is Croidhe Essu."

They went out of the shining house then, and Cliodna of the Fair Hair went with them to the place they had left their ship, and she bade their comrades a kindly welcome; and she asked them how long had they been in that country. "It seems to us," they said, "we are not in it but one day only." "You are in it through the whole length of a year," said she, "and through all that time you used neither food nor drink. But however long you would stop here," she said, "cold or hunger would never come on you." "It would be a good thing to live this way always," said Tadg's people when they heard that. But he himself said: "It is best for us to go on and to look for our people. And we must leave this country, although it is displeasing to us to leave it."

Then Cliodna and Tadg bade farewell to one another, and she gave her blessing to him and to his people. And they set out then over the ridges of the sea; and they were downhearted after leaving that country until the birds began to sing for them, and then their courage rose up, and they were glad and light-hearted.

And when they looked back they could not see the island they had come from, because of a Druid mist that came on it and hid it from them.

Then by the leading of the birds they came to the country of Fresen, and they were in a deep sleep through the whole voyage. And then they attacked the foreigners and got the better of them, and Tadg killed Cathmann, the king, after a hard fight; and Liban his wife made no delay, and came to meet her husband and her sweetheart, and it is glad she was to see him.

And after they had rested a while they faced the sea again, and Tadg and his wife Liban, and his two brothers, and a great many other treasures along with them, and they came home to Ireland safely at the last.

CHAPTER XV

Laegaire in the Happy Plain

And another that went to visit Magh Mell, the Happy Plain, was Laegaire, son of the King of Connacht, Crimthan Cass.

He was out one day with the king, his father, near Loch na-n Ean, the Lake of Birds, and the men of Connacht with them, and they saw a man coming to them through the mist. Long golden-yellow hair he had, and it streaming after him, and at his belt a gold hilted sword, and in his hand two five-barbed darts, a gold-rimmed shield on his back, a five-folded crimson cloak about his shoulders.

"Give a welcome to the man that is coming towards you," said Laegaire, that had the best name of all the men of Connacht, to his people. And to the stranger he said: "A welcome to the champion we do not know."

"I am thankful to you all," said he.

"What is it you are come for, and where are you going?" said Laegaire then.

"I am come to look for the help of fighting men," said the stranger. "And my name," he said, "is Fiachna, son of Betach, of the men of the Sidhe; and it is what ails me, my wife was taken from my pillow and brought away by Eochaid, son of Sal. And we fought together, and I killed him, and now she is gone to a brother's son of his, Goll, son of Dalbh, king of a people of Magh Mell. Seven battles I gave him, but they all went against me; and on this very day there is another to be fought, and I am come to ask help. And to every one that deserves it, I will give a good reward of gold and of silver for that help."

And it is what he said:

"The most beautiful of plains is the Plain of the Two Mists; it is not far from this; it is a host of the men of the Sidhe full of courage are stirring up pools of blood upon it.

"We have drawn red blood from the bodies of high nobles; many women are keening them with cries and with tears.

"The men of the host in good order go out ahead of their beautiful king; they march among blue spears, white troops of fighters with curled hair.

"They scatter the troops of their enemies, they destroy every country they make an attack on; they are beautiful in battle, a host with high looks, rushing, avenging.

"It is no wonder they to have such strength: every one of them is the son of a king and a queen; manes of hair they have of the colour of gold.

"Their bodies smooth and comely; their eyes blue and far-seeing; their teeth bright like crystal, within their thin red lips.

"White shields they have in their hands, with patterns on them of white silver; blue shining swords, red horns set with gold.

"They are good at killing men in battle; good at song-making, good at chess-playing.

"The most beautiful of plains is the Plain of the Two Mists; the men of the Sidhe are stirring up pools of blood on it; it is not far from this place."

"It would be a shameful thing not to give our help to this man," said Laegaire.

Fiachna, son of Betach, went down into the lake then, for it was out of it he had come, and Laegaire went down into it after him, and fifty fighting men along with him.

They saw a strong place before them then, and a company of armed men, and Goll, son of Dalbh, at the head of them.

"That is well," said Laegaire, "I and my fifty men will go out against this troop." "I will answer you," said Goll, son of Dalbh.

The two fifties attacked one another then, and Goll fell, but Laegaire and his fifty escaped with their lives and made a great slaughter of their enemies, that not one of them made his escape.

"Where is the woman now?" said Laegaire. "She is within the dun of Magh Mell, and a troop of armed men keeping guard about it," said Fiachna. "Let you stop here, and I and my fifty will go there," said Laegaire.

So he and his men went on to the dun, and Laegaire called out to the men that were about it: "Your king has got his death, your chief men have fallen, let the woman come out, and I will give you your own lives." The men agreed to that, and they brought the woman out. And when she came out she made this complaint:

"It is a sorrowful day that swords are reddened for the sake of the dear dead body of Goll, son of Dalbh. It was he that loved me, it was himself I loved, it is little Laegaire Liban cares for that.

"Weapons were hacked and were split by Goll; it is to Fiachna, son of Betach, I must go; it is Goll, son of Dalbh, I loved."

And that complaint got the name of "The Lament of the Daughter of Eochaid the Dumb."

Laegaire went back with her then till he put her hand in Fiachna's hand. And that night Fiachna's daughter, Deorgreine, a Tear of the Sun, was given to Laegaire as his wife, and fifty other women were given to his fifty fighting men, and they stopped with them there to the end of a year.

And at the end of that time, Laegaire said: "Let us go and ask news of our own country." "If you have a mind to go," said Fiachna, "bring horses with you; but whatever happens," he said, "do not get off from them."

So they set out then; and when they got back to Ireland, they found a great gathering of the whole of the men of Connacht that were keening them.

And when the men of Connacht saw them coming they rose up to meet them, and to bid them welcome. But Laegaire called out: "Do not come to us, for it is to bid you farewell we are here." "Do not go from us again," said Crimthan, his father, "and I will give you the sway over the three Connachts, their silver and their gold, their horses and their bridles, and their beautiful women, if you will not go from us."

And it is what Laegaire said: "In the place we are gone to, the armies move from kingdom to kingdom, they listen to the sweet-sounding music of the Sidhe, they drink from shining cups, we talk with those we love, it is beer that falls instead of rain.

"We have brought from the dun of the Pleasant Plain thirty cauldrons, thirty drinking horns; we have brought the complaint that was sung by the Sea, by the daughter of Eochaid the Dumb.

"There is a wife for every man of the fifty; my own wife to me is the Tear of the Sun; I am made master of a blue sword; I would not give for all your whole kingdom one night of the nights of the Sidhe."

With that Laegaire turned from them, and went back to the kingdom. And he was made king there along with Fiachna, son of Betach, and his daughter, and he did not come out of it yet.

BOOK V

The Fate of the Children of Lir

Now at the time when the Tuatha de Danaan chose a king for themselves after the battle of Tailltin, and Lir heard the kingship was given to Bodb Dearg, it did not please him, and he left the gathering without leave and with no word to any one; for he thought it was he himself had a right to be made king. But if he went away himself, Bodb was given the kingship none the less, for not one of the five begrudged it to him but only Lir. And it is what they determined, to follow after Lir, and to burn down his house, and to attack himself with spear and sword, on account of his not giving obedience to the king they had chosen. "We will not do that," said Bodb Dearg, "for that man would defend any place he is in; and besides that," he said, "I am none the less king over the Tuatha de Danaan, although he does not submit to me."

All went on like that for a good while, but at last a great misfortune came on Lir, for his wife died from him after a sickness of three nights. And that came very hard on Lir, and there was heaviness on his mind after her. And there was great talk of the death of that woman in her own time.

And the news of it was told all through Ireland, and it came to the house of Bodb, and the best of the Men of Dea were with him at that time. And Bodb said: "If Lir had a mind for it," he said, "my help and my friendship would be good for him now, since his wife is not living to him. For I have here with me the three young girls of the best shape, and the best appearance, and the best name in all Ireland, Aobh, Aoife, and Ailbhe, the three daughters of Oilell of Aran, my own three nurselings." The Men of Dea said then it was a good thought he had, and that what he said was true.

Messages and messengers were sent then from Bodb Dearg to the place Lir was, to say that if he had a mind to join with the Son of the Dagda and to acknowledge his lordship, he would give him a foster-child of his foster-children. And Lir thought well of the offer, and he set out on the morrow with fifty chariots from Sidhe Fionnachaidh; and he went by every short way till he came to Bodb's dwelling-place at Loch Dearg, and there was a welcome before him there, and all the people were merry and pleasant before him, and he and his people got good attendance that night.

And the three daughters of Oilell of Aran were sitting on the one seat with Bodb Dearg's wife, the queen of the Tuatha de Danaan, that was their foster-mother. And Bodb said: "You may have your choice of the three young girls, Lir." "I cannot say," said Lir, "which one of them is my choice, but whichever of them is the eldest, she is the noblest, and it is best for me to take her." "If that is so," said Bodb, "it is Aobh is the eldest, and she will be given to you, if it is your wish." "It is my wish," he said. And he took Aobh for his wife that night, and he stopped there for a fortnight, and then he brought her away to his own house, till he would make a great wedding-feast.

And in the course of time Aobh brought forth two children, a daughter and a son, Fionnuala and Aodh their names were. And after a while she was brought to bed again, and this time she gave birth to two sons, and they called them Fiachra and Conn. And she herself died at their birth. And that weighed very heavy on Lir, and only for the way his mind was set on his four children he would have gone near to die of grief.

The news came to Bodb Dearg's place, and all the people gave out three loud, high cries, keening their nursling. And after they had keened her it is what Bodb Dearg said: "It is a fret to us our daughter to have died, for her own sake and for the sake of the good man we gave her to, for we are thankful for his friendship and his faithfulness. However," he said, "our friendship with one another will not be broken, for I will give him for a wife her sister Aoife."

When Lir heard that, he came for the girl and married her, and brought her home to his house. And there was honour and affection with Aoife for her sister's children; and indeed no person at all could see those four children without giving them the heart's love.

And Bodb Dearg used often to be going to Lir's house for the sake of those children; and he used to bring them to his own place for a good length of time, and then he would let them go back to their own place again. And the Men of Dea were at that time using the Feast of Age in every hill of the Sidhe in turn; and when they came to Lir's hill those four children were their joy and delight, for the beauty of their appearance; and it is where they used to sleep, in beds in sight of their father Lir. And he used to rise up at the break of every morning, and to lie down among his children.

But it is what came of all this, that a fire of jealousy was kindled in Aoife, and she got to have a dislike and a hatred of her sister's children.

Then she let on to have a sickness, that lasted through nearly the length of a year. And the end of that time she did a deed of jealousy and cruel treachery against the children of Lir.

And one day she got her chariot yoked, and she took the four children in it, and they went forward towards the house of Bodb Dearg; but Fionnuala had no mind to go with her, for she knew by her she had some plan for their death or their destruction, and she had seen in a dream that there was treachery against them in Aoife's mind. But all the same she was not able to escape from what was before her.

And when they were on their way Aoife said to her people: "Let you kill now," she said, "the four children of Lir, for whose sake their father has given up my love, and I will give you your own choice of a reward out of all the good things of the world." "We will not do that indeed," said they; "and it is a bad deed you have thought of, and harm will come to you out of it."

And when they would not do as she bade them, she took out a sword herself to put an end to the children with; but she being a woman and with no good courage, and with no great strength in her mind, she was not able to do it.

They went on then west to Loch Dairbhreach, the Lake of the Oaks, and the horses were stopped there. And Aoife bade the children of Lir to go out and bathe in the lake, and they did as she bade them. And as soon as Aoife saw them out in the lake she struck them with a Druid rod, and put on them the shape of four swans, white and beautiful. And it is what she said: "Out with you, children of the king, your luck is taken away from you for ever; it is sorrowful the story will be to your friends; it is with flocks of birds your cries will be heard for ever."

And Fionnuala said: "Witch, we know now what your name is, you have struck us down with no hope of relief; but although you put us from wave to wave, there are times when we will touch the land. We shall get help when we are seen; help, and all that is best for us; even though we have to sleep upon the lake, it is our minds will be going abroad early."

And then the four children of Lir turned towards Aoife, and it is what Fionnuala said: "It is a bad deed you have done, Aoife, and it is a bad fulfilling of friendship, you to destroy us without cause; and vengeance for it will come upon you, and you will fall in satisfaction for it, for your power for our destruction is not greater than the power of our friends to avenge it on you; and put some bounds now," she said, "to the time this enchantment is to stop on us." "I will do that," said Aoife, "and it is worse for you, you to have asked it of me. And the bounds I set to your time are this, till the Woman from the South and the Man from the North will come together. And since you ask to hear it of me," she said, "no friends and no power that you have will be able to bring you out of these shapes you are in through the length of your lives, until you have been three hundred years on Loch Dairbhreach, and three hundred years on Sruth na Maoile between Ireland and Alban, and three hundred years at Irrus Domnann and Inis Gluaire; and these are to be your journeys from this out," she said.

But then repentance came on Aoife, and she said: "Since there is no other help for me to give you now, you may keep your own speech; and you will be singing sweet music of the Sidhe, that would put the men of the earth to sleep, and there will be no music in the world equal to it; and your own sense and your own nobility will stay with you, the way it will not weigh so heavy on you to be in the shape of birds. And go away out of my sight now, children of Lir," she said, "with your white faces, with your stammering Irish. It is a great curse on tender lads, they to be driven out on the rough wind. Nine hundred years to be on the water, it is a long time for any one to be in pain; it is I put this on you through treachery, it is best for you to do as I tell you now.

"Lir, that got victory with so many a good cast, his heart is a kernel of death in him now; the groaning of the great hero is a sickness to me, though it is I that have well earned his anger."

And then the horses were caught for Aoife, and the chariot yoked for her, and she went on to the palace of Bodb Dearg, and there was a welcome before her from the chief people of the place. And the son of the Dagda asked her why she did not bring the children of Lir with her. "I will tell you that," she said. "It is because Lir has no liking for you, and he will not trust you with his children, for fear you might keep them from him altogether."

"I wonder at that," said Bodb Dearg, "for those children are dearer to me than my own children." And he thought in his own mind it was deceit the woman was doing on him, and it is what he did, he sent messengers to the north to Sidhe Fionnachaidh. And Lir asked them what did they come for. "On the head of your children," said they. "Are they not gone to you along with Aoife?" he said. "They are not," said they; "and Aoife said it was yourself would not let them come."

It is downhearted and sorrowful Lir was at that news, for he understood well it was Aoife had destroyed or made an end of his children. And early in the morning of the morrow his horses were caught, and he set out on the road to the south-west. And when he was as far as the shore of Loch Dairbreach, the four children saw the horses coming towards them, and it is what Fionnuala said: "A welcome to the troop of horses I see coming near to the lake; the people they are bringing are strong, there is sadness on them; it is us they are following, it is for us they are looking; let us move over to the shore, Aodh, Fiachra, and comely Conn. Those that are coming can be no others in the world but only Lir and his household."

Then Lir came to the edge of the lake, and he took notice of the swans having the voice of living people, and he asked them why was it they had that voice.

"I will tell you that, Lir," said Fionnuala. "We are your own four children, that are after being destroyed by your wife, and by the sister of our own mother, through the dint of her jealousy." "Is there any way to put you into your own shapes again?" said Lir. "There is no way," said Fionnuala, "for all the men of the world could not help us till we have gone through our time, and that will not be," she said, "till the end of nine hundred years."

When Lir and his people heard that, they gave out three great heavy shouts of grief and sorrow and crying.

"Is there a mind with you," said Lir, "to come to us on the land, since you have your own sense and your memory yet?" "We have not the power," said Fionnuala, "to live with any person at all from this time; but we have our own language, the Irish, and we have the power to sing sweet music, and it is enough to satisfy the whole race of men to be listening to that music. And let you stop here to-night," she said, "and we will be making music for you."

So Lir and his people stopped there listening to the music of the swans, and they slept there quietly that night. And Lir rose up early on the morning of the morrow and he made this complaint:—

"It is time to go out from this place. I do not sleep though I am in my lying down. To be parted from my dear children, it is that is tormenting my heart.

"It is a bad net I put over you, bringing Aoife, daughter of Oilell of Aran, to the house. I would never have followed that advice if I had known what it would bring upon me.

"O Fionnuala, and comely Conn, O Aodh, O Fiachra of the beautiful arms; it is not ready I am to go away from you, from the border of the harbour where you are."

Then Lir went on to the palace of Bodb Dearg, and there was a welcome before him there; and he got a reproach from Bodb Dearg for not bringing his children along with him. "My grief!" said Lir. "It is not I that would not bring my children along with me; it was Aoife there beyond, your own foster-child and the sister of their mother, that put them in the shape of four white swans on Loch Dairbhreach, in the sight of the whole of the men of Ireland; but they have their sense with them yet, and their reason, and their voice, and their Irish."

Bodb Dearg gave a great start when he heard that, and he knew what Lir said was true, and he gave a very sharp reproach to Aoife, and he said: "This treachery will be worse for yourself in the end, Aoife, than to the children of Lir. And what shape would you yourself think worst of being in?" he said.

"I would think worst of being a witch of the air," she said. "It is into that shape I will put you now," said Bodb. And with that he struck her with a Druid wand, and she was turned into a witch of the air there and then, and she went away on the wind in that shape, and she is in it yet, and will be in it to the end of life and time.

As to Bodb Dearg and the Tuatha de Danaan they came to the shore of Loch Dairbhreach, and they made their camp there to be listening to the music of the swans.

And the Sons of the Gael used to be coming no less than the Men of Dea to hear them from every part of Ireland, for there never was any music or any delight heard in Ireland to compare with that music of the swans. And they used to be telling stories, and to be talking with the men of Ireland every day, and with their teachers and their fellow-pupils and their friends. And every night they used to sing very sweet music of the Sidhe; and every one that heard that music would sleep sound and quiet whatever trouble or long sickness might be on him; for every one that heard the music of the birds, it is happy and contented he would be after it.

These two gatherings now of the Tuatha de Danaan and of the Sons of the Gael stopped there around Loch Dairbhreach through the length of three hundred years. And it is then Fionnuala said to her brothers: "Do you know," she said, "we have spent all we have to spend of our time here, but this one night only."

And there was great sorrow on the sons of Lir when they heard that, for they thought it the same as to be living people again, to be talking with their friends and their companions on Loch Dairbhreach, in comparison with going on the cold, fretful sea of the Maoil in the north.

And they came early on the morrow to speak with their father and with their foster-father, and they bade them farewell, and Fionnuala made this complaint:—

"Farewell to you, Bodb Dearg, the man with whom all knowledge is in pledge. And farewell to our father along with you, Lir of the Hill of the White Field.

"The time is come, as I think, for us to part from you, O pleasant company; my grief it is not on a visit we are going to you.

"From this day out, O friends of our heart, our comrades, it is on the tormented course of the Maoil we will be, without the voice of any person near us.

"Three hundred years there, and three hundred years in the bay of the men of Domnann, it is a pity for the four comely children of Lir, the salt waves of the sea to be their covering by night.

"O three brothers, with the ruddy faces gone from you, let them all leave the lake now, the great troop that loved us, it is sorrowful our parting is."

After that complaint they took to flight, lightly, airily, till they came to Sruth na Maoile between Ireland and Alban. And that was a grief to the men of Ireland, and they gave out an order no swan was to be killed from that out, whatever chance there might be of killing one, all through Ireland.

It was a bad dwelling-place for the children of Lir they to be on Sruth na Maoile. When they saw the wide coast about them, they were filled with cold and with sorrow, and they thought nothing of all they had gone through before, in comparison to what they were going through on that sea.

Now one night while they were there a great storm came on them, and it is what Fionnuala said: "My dear brothers," she said, "it is a pity for us not to be making ready for this night, for it is certain the storm will separate us from one another. And let us," she said, "settle on some place where we can meet afterwards, if we are driven from one another in the night."

"Let us settle," said the others, "to meet one another at Carraig na Ron, the Rock of the Seals, for we all have knowledge of it."

And when midnight came, the wind came on them with it, and the noise of the waves increased, and the lightning was flashing, and a rough storm came sweeping down, the way the children of Lir were scattered over the great sea, and the wideness of it set them astray, so that no one of them could know what way the others went. But after that storm a great quiet came on the sea, and Fionnuala was alone on Sruth na Maoile; and when she took notice that her brothers were wanting she was lamenting after them greatly, and she made this complaint:—

"It is a pity for me to be alive in the state I am; it is frozen to my sides my wings are; it is little that the wind has not broken my heart in my body, with the loss of Aodh.

"To be three hundred years on Loch Dairbhreach without going into my own shape, it is worse to me the time I am on Sruth na Maoile.

"The three I loved, Och! the three I loved, that slept under the shelter of my feathers; till the dead come back to the living I will see them no more for ever.

"It is a pity I to stay after Fiachra, and after Aodh, and after comely Conn, and with no account of them; my grief I to be here to face every hardship this night."

She stopped all night there upon the Rock of the Seals until the rising of the sun, looking out over the sea on every side till at last she saw Conn coming to her, his feathers wet through and his head hanging, and her heart gave him a great welcome; and then Fiachra came wet and perished and worn out, and he could not say a word they could understand with the dint of the cold and the hardship he had gone through. And Fionnuala put him under her wings, and she said: "We would be well off now if Aodh would but come to us."

It was not long after that, they saw Aodh coming, his head dry and his feathers beautiful, and Fionnuala gave him a great welcome, and she put him in under the feathers of her breast, and Fiachra under her right wing and Conn under her left wing, the way she could put her feathers over them all. "And Och! my brothers," she said, "this was a bad night to us, and it is many of its like are before us from this out."

They stayed there a long time after that, suffering cold and misery on the Maoil, till at last a night came on them they had never known the like of before, for frost and snow and wind and cold. And they were crying and lamenting the hardship of their life, and the cold of the night and the greatness of the snow and the hardness of the wind. And after they had suffered cold to the end of a year, a worse night again came on them, in the middle of winter. And they were on Carraig na Ron, and the water froze about them, and as they rested on the rock, their feet and their wings and their feathers froze to the rock, the way they were not able to move from it. And they made such a hard struggle to get away, that they left the skin of their feet and their feathers and the tops of their wings on the rock after them.

"My grief, children of Lir," said Fionnuala, "it is bad our state is now, for we cannot bear the salt water to touch us, and there are bonds on us not to leave it; and if the salt water goes into our sores," she said, "we will get our death." And she made this complaint:—

"It is keening we are to-night; without feathers to cover our bodies; it is cold the rough, uneven rocks are under our bare feet.

"It is bad our stepmother was to us the time she played enchantments on us, sending us out like swans upon the sea.

"Our washing place is on the ridge of the bay, in the foam of flying manes of the sea; our share of the ale feast is the salt water of the blue tide.

"One daughter and three sons; it is in the clefts of the rocks we are; it is on the hard rocks we are, it is a pity the way we are."

However, they came on to the course of the Maoil again, and the salt water was sharp and rough and bitter to them, but if it was itself, they were not able to avoid it or to get shelter from it. And they were there by the shore under that hardship till such time as their feathers grew again, and their wings, and till their sores were entirely healed. And then they used to go every day to the shore of Ireland or of Alban, but they had to come back to Sruth na Maoile every night.

Now they came one day to the mouth of the Banna, to the north of Ireland, and they saw a troop of riders, beautiful, of the one colour, with well-trained pure white horses under them, and they travelling the road straight from the south-west.

"Do you know who those riders are, sons of Lir?" said Fionnuala.

"We do not," they said; "but it is likely they might be some troop of the Sons of the Gael, or of the Tuatha de Danaan."

They moved over closer to the shore then, that they might know who they were, and when the riders saw them they came to meet them until they were able to hold talk together.

And the chief men among them were two sons of Bodb Dearg, Aodh Aithfhios-ach, of the quick wits, and Fergus Fithchiollach, of the chess, and a third part of the Riders of the Sidhe along with them, and it was for the swans they had been looking for a long while before that, and when they came together they wished one another a kind and loving welcome.

And the children of Lir asked for news of all the Men of Dea, and above all of Lir, and Bodb Dearg and their people.

"They are well, and they are in the one place together," said they, "in your father's house at Sidhe Fionnachaidh, using the Feast of Age pleasantly and happily, and with no uneasiness on them, only for being without yourselves, and without knowledge of what happened you from the day you left Loch Dairbhreach."

"That has not been the way with us," said Fionnuala, "for we have gone through great hardship and uneasiness and misery on the tides of the sea until this day."

And she made this complaint:—

"There is delight to-night with the household of Lir! Plenty of ale with them and of wine, although it is in a cold dwelling-place this night are the four children of the king.

"It is without a spot our bedclothes are, our bodies covered over with curved feathers; but it is often we were dressed in purple, and we drinking pleasant mead.

"It is what our food is and our drink, the white sand and the bitter water of the sea; it is often we drank mead of hazel-nuts from round four-lipped drinking cups.

"It is what our beds are, bare rocks out of the power of the waves; it is often there used to be spread out for us beds of the breast-feathers of birds.

"Though it is our work now to be swimming through the frost and through the noise of the waves, it is often a company of the sons of kings were riding after us to the Hill of Bodb.

"It is what wasted my strength, to be going and coming over the current of the

Maoil the way I never was used to, and never to be in the sunshine on the soft grass.

"Fiachra's bed and Conn's bed is to come under the cover of my wings on the sea. Aodh has his place under the feathers of my breast, the four of us side by side.

"The teaching of Manannan without deceit, the talk of Bodb Dearg on the pleasant ridge; the voice of Angus, his sweet kisses; it is by their side I used to be without grief."

After that the riders went on to Lir's house, and they told the chief men of the Tuatha de Danaan all the birds had gone through, and the state they were in. "We have no power over them," the chief men said, "but we are glad they are living yet, for they will get help in the end of time."

As to the children of Lir, they went back towards their old place in the Maoil, and they stopped there till the time they had to spend in it was spent. And then Fionnuala said: "The time is come for us to leave this place. And it is to Irrus Domnann we must go now," she said, "after our three hundred years here. And indeed there will be no rest for us there, or any standing ground, or any shelter from the storms. But since it is time for us to go, let us set out on the cold wind, the way we will not go astray."

So they set out in that way, and left Sruth na Maoile behind them, and went to the point of Irrus Domnann, and there they stopped, and it is a life of misery and a cold life they led there. And one time the sea froze about them that they could not move at all, and the brothers were lamenting, and Fionnuala was comforting them, for she knew there would help come to them in the end.

And they stayed at Irrus Domnann till the time they had to spend there was spent. And the Fionnuala said: "The time is come for us to go back to Sidhe Fionnachaidh, where our father is with his household and with all our own people."

"It pleases us well to hear that," they said.

So they set out flying through the air lightly till they came to Sidhe Fionnachaidh; and it is how they found the place, empty before them, and nothing in it but green hillocks and thickets of nettles, without a house, without a fire, without a hearthstone. And the four pressed close to one another then, and they gave out three sorrowful cries, and Fionnuala made this complaint:—

"It is a wonder to me this place is, and it without a house, without a dwelling-place. To see it the way it is now, Ochone! it is bitterness to my heart.

"Without dogs, without hounds for hunting, without women, without great kings; we never knew it to be like this when our father was in it.

"Without horns, without cups, without drinking in the lighted house; without young men, without riders; the way it is to-night is a foretelling of sorrow.

"The people of the place to be as they are now, Ochone! it is grief to my heart! It is plain to my mind to-night the lord of the house is not living.

111

"Och, house where we used to see music and playing and the gathering of people! I think it a great change to see it lonely the way it is to-night.

"The greatness of the hardships we have gone through going from one wave to another of the sea, we never heard of the like of them coming on any other person.

"It is seldom this place had its part with grass and bushes; the man is not living that would know us, it would be a wonder to him to see us here."

However, the children of Lir stopped that night in their father's place and their grandfather's, where they had been reared, and they were singing very sweet music of the Sidhe. And they rose up early on the morning of the morrow and went to Inis Gluaire, and all the birds of the country gathered near them on Loch na-n Ean, the Lake of the Birds. And they used to go out to feed every day to the far parts of the country, to Inis Geadh and to Accuill, the place Donn, son of Miled, and his people that were drowned were buried, and to all the western islands of Connacht, and they used to go back to Inis Gluaire every night.

It was about that time it happened them to meet with a young man of good race, and his name was Aibric; and he often took notice of the birds, and their singing was sweet to him and he loved them greatly, and they loved him. And it is this young man that told the whole story of all that had happened them, and put it in order.

And the story he told of what happened them in the end is this.

It was after the faith of Christ and blessed Patrick came into Ireland, that Saint Mochaomhog came to Inis Gluaire. And the first night he came to the island, the children of Lir heard the voice of his bell, ringing near them. And the brothers started up with fright when they heard it. "We do not know," they said, "what is that weak, unpleasing voice we hear."

"That is the voice of the bell of Mochaomhog," said Fionnuala; "and it is through that bell," she said, "you will be set free from pain and from misery."

They listened to that music of the bell till the matins were done, and then they began to sing the low, sweet music of the Sidhe.

And Mochaomhog was listening to them, and he prayed to God to show him who was singing that music, and it was showed to him that the children of Lir were singing it. And on the morning of the morrow he went forward to the Lake of the Birds, and he saw the swans before him on the lake, and he went down to them at the brink of the shore.

"Are you the children of Lir?" he said.

"We are indeed," said they.

"I give thanks to God for that," said he, "for it is for your sakes I am come to this island beyond any other island, and let you come to land now," he said, "and give your trust to me, that you may do good deeds and part from your sins."

They came to the land after that, and they put trust in Mochaomhog, and he brought them to his own dwelling-place, and they used to be hearing Mass with him. And he got a good smith and bade him make chains of bright silver for them, and he put a chain between Aodh and Fionnuala, and a chain between Conn and Fiachra. And the four of them were raising his heart and gladdening his mind, and no danger and no distress that was on the swans before put any trouble on them now.

Now the king of Connacht at that time was Lairgnen, son of Colman, son of Cobthach, and Deoch, daughter of Finghin, was his wife. And that was the coming together of the Man from the North and the Woman from the South, that Aoife had spoken of.

And the woman heard talk of the birds, and a great desire came on her to get them, and she bade Lairgnen to bring them to her, and he said he would ask them of Mochaomhog.

And she gave her word she would not stop another night with him unless he would bring them to her. And she set out from the house there and then. And Lairgnen sent messengers after her to bring her back, and they did not overtake her till she was at Cill Dun. She went back home with them then, and Lairgnen sent messengers to ask the birds of Mochaomhog, and he·did not get them.

There was great anger on Lairgnen then, and he went himself to the place Mochaomhog was, and he asked was it true he had refused him the birds. "It is true indeed," said he. At that Lairgnen rose up, and he took hold of the swans, and pulled them off the altar, two birds in each hand, to bring them away to Deoch. But no sooner had he laid his hand on them than their bird skins fell off, and what was in their place was three lean, withered old men and a thin withered old woman, without blood or flesh.

And Lairgnen gave a great start at that, and he went out from the place. It is then Fionnuala said to Mochaomhog: "Come and baptize us now, for it is short till our death comes; and it is certain you do not think worse of parting with us than we do of parting with you. And make our grave afterwards," she said, "and lay Conn at my right side and Fiachra on my left side, and Aodh before my face, between my two arms. And pray to the God of Heaven," she said, "that you may be able to baptize us."

The children of Lir were baptized then, and they died and were buried as Fionnuala had desired; Fiachra and Conn one at each side of her, and Aodh before her face. And a stone was put over them, and their names were written in Ogham, and they were keened there, and heaven was gained for their souls.

And that is the fate of the children of Lir so far.

PART II

The Fianna

BOOK I

Finn, Son of Cumhal

CHAPTER I

The Coming of Finn

At the time Finn was born his father Cumhal, of the sons of Baiscne, Head of the Fianna of Ireland, had been killed in battle by the sons of Morna that were fighting with him for the leadership. And his mother, that was beautiful long-haired Muirne, daughter of Tadg, son of Nuada of the Tuatha de Danaan and of Ethlinn, mother of Lugh of the Long Hand, did not dare to keep him with her; and two women, Bodhmall, the woman Druid, and Liath Luachra, came and brought him away to care him.

It was to the woods of Slieve Bladhma they brought him, and they nursed him secretly, because of his father's enemies, the sons of Morna, and they kept him there a long time.

And Muirne, his mother, took another husband that was king of Carraighe; but at the end of six years she came to see Finn, going through every lonely place till she came to the wood, and there she found the little hunting cabin, and the boy asleep in it, and she lifted him up in her arms and kissed him, and she sang a little sleepy song to him; and then she said farewell to the women, and she went away again.

And the two women went on caring him till he came to sensible years; and one day when he went out he saw a wild duck on the lake with her clutch, and he made a cast at her that cut the wings off her that she could not fly, and he brought her back to the cabin, and that was his first hunt.

And they gave him good training in running and leaping and swimming. One of them would run round a tree, and she having a thorn switch, and Finn after her with another switch, and each one trying to hit at the other; and they would leave him in a field, and hares along with him, and would bid him not to let the hares quit the field, but to keep before them whichever way they would go; and to teach him swimming they would throw him into the water and let him make his way out.

But after a while he went away with a troop of poets, to hide from the sons of

Morna, and they hid him in the mountain of Crotta Cliach; but there was a robber in Leinster at that time, Fiacuil, son of Codhna, and he came where the poets were in Fidh Gaible and killed them all. But he spared the child and brought him to his own house, that was in a cold marsh. But the two women, Bodhmall and Liath, came looking for him after a while, and Fiacuil gave him up to them, and they brought him back to the same place he was before.

He grew up there, straight and strong and fair-haired and beautiful. And one day he was out in Slieve Bladhma, and the two women along with him, and they saw before them a herd of the wild deer of the mountain. "It is a pity," said the old women, "we not to be able to get a deer of those deer." "I will get one for you," said Finn; and with that he followed after them, and caught two stags of them and brought them home to the hunting cabin. And after that he used to be hunting for them every day. But at last they said to him: "It is best for you to leave us now, for the sons of Morna are watching again to kill you."

So he went away then by himself, and never stopped till he came to Magh Life, and there he saw young lads swimming in a lake, and they called to him to swim against them. So he went into the lake, and he beat them at swimming. "Fair he is and well shaped," they said when they saw him swimming, and it was from that time he got the name of Finn, that is, Fair. But they got to be jealous of his strength, and he went away and left them.

He went on then till he came to Loch Lein, and he took service there with the King of Finntraigh; and there was no hunter like him, and the king said: "If Cumhal had left a son, you would be that son."

He went from that king after, and he went into Carraighe, and there he took service with the king, that had taken his mother Muirne for his wife. And one day they were playing chess together, and he won seven games one after another. "Who are you at all?" said the king then. "I am a son of a countryman of the Luigne of Teamhair," said Finn. "That is not so," said the king, "but you are the son that Muirne my wife bore to Cumhal. And do not stop here any longer," he said, "that you may not be killed under my protection."

From that he went into Connacht looking for his father's brother, Crimall, son of Trenmor; and as he was going on his way he heard the crying of a lone woman. He went to her, and looked at her, and tears of blood were on her face. "Your face is red with blood, woman," he said. "I have reason for it," said she, "for my only son is after being killed by a great fighting man that came on us." And Finn followed after the big champion and fought with him and killed him. And the man he killed was the same man that had given Cumhal his first wound in the battle where he got his death, and had brought away his treasure-bag with him.

Now as to that treasure-bag, it is of a crane skin it was made, that was one time the skin of Aoife, the beautiful sweetheart of Ilbrec, son of Manannan, that was put into the shape of a crane through jealousy. And it was in Manannan's house it used to be, and there were treasures kept in it, Manannan's shirt and his knife, and the belt and the smith's hook of Goibniu, and the shears of the King of Alban, and the helmet of the King of Lochlann, and a belt of the skin of a great fish, and the bones of Asal's pig that had been brought to Ireland by the sons of Tuireann. All those treasures would be in the bag at full tide, but at the ebbing of the tide it would be empty. And it went from Manannan to Lugh, son of Ethlinn, and after that to Cumhal, that was husband to Muirne, Ethlinn's daughter.

And Finn took the bag and brought it with him till he found Crimall, that was now an old man, living in a lonely place, and some of the old men of the Fianna were with him, and used to go hunting for him. And Finn gave him the bag, and told him his whole story.

And then he said farewell to Crimall, and went on to learn poetry from Finegas, a poet that was living at the Boinn, for the poets thought it was always on the brink of water poetry was revealed to them. And he did not give him his own name, but he took the name of Deimne. Seven years, now, Finegas had stopped at the Boinn, watching the salmon, for it was in the prophecy that he would eat the salmon of knowledge that would come there, and that he would have all knowledge after. And when at the last the salmon of knowledge came, he brought it to where Finn was, and bade him to roast it, but he bade him not to eat any of it. And when Finn brought him the salmon after a while he said: "Did you eat any of it at all, boy?" "I did not," said Finn; "but I burned my thumb putting down a blister that rose on the skin, and after doing that, I put my thumb in my mouth." "What is your name, boy?" said Finegas. "Deimne," said he. "It is not, but it is Finn your name is, and it is to you and not to myself the salmon was given in the prophecy." With that he gave Finn the whole of the salmon, and from that time Finn had the knowledge that came from the nuts of the nine hazels of wisdom that grow beside the well that is below the sea.

And besides the wisdom he got then, there was a second wisdom came to him another time, and this is the way it happened. There was a well of the moon belonging to Beag, son of Buan, of the Tuatha de Danaan, and whoever would drink out of it would get wisdom, and after a second drink he would get the gift of foretelling. And the three daughters of Beag, son of Buan, had charge of the well, and they would not part with a vessel of it for anything less than red gold. And one day Finn chanced to be hunting in the rushes near the well, and the three women ran out to hinder him from coming to it, and one of them that had a vessel of the water in her hand, threw it at him to stop him, and a share of the water went into his mouth. And from that out he had all the knowledge that the water of that well could give.

And he learned the three ways of poetry; and this is the poem he made to show he had got his learning well: –

"It is the month of May is the pleasant time; its face is beautiful; the blackbird sings his full song, the living wood is his holding, the cuckoos are singing and ever singing; there is a welcome before the brightness of the summer.

"Summer is lessening the rivers, the swift horses are looking for the pool; the heath spreads out its long hair, the weak white bog-down grows. A wildness comes on the heart of the deer; the sad restless sea is asleep.

"Bees with their little strength carry a load reaped from the flowers; the cattle go up muddy to the mountains; the ant has a good full feast.

"The harp of the woods is playing music; there is colour on the hills, and a haze on the full lakes, and entire peace upon every sail.

"The corncrake is speaking, a loud-voiced poet; the high lonely waterfall is singing a welcome to the warm pool, the talking of the rushes has begun.

"The light swallows are darting; the loudness of music is around the hill; the fat soft mast is budding; there is grass on the trembling bogs.

"The bog is as dark as the feathers of the raven; the cuckoo makes a loud welcome; the speckled salmon is leaping; as strong is the leaping of the swift fighting man.

"The man is gaining; the girl is in her comely growing power; every wood is without fault from the top to the ground, and every wide good plain.

"It is pleasant is the colour of the time; rough winter is gone; every plentiful wood is white; summer is a joyful peace.

"A flock of birds pitches in the meadow; there are sounds in the green fields, there is in them a clear rushing stream.

"There is a hot desire on you for the racing of horses; twisted holly makes a leash for the hound; a bright spear has been shot into the earth, and the flag-flower is golden under it.

"A weak lasting little bird is singing at the top of his voice; the lark is singing clear tidings; May without fault, of beautiful colours.

"I have another story for you; the ox is lowing, the winter is creeping in, the summer is gone. High and cold the wind, low the sun, cries are about us; the sea is quarrelling.

"The ferns are reddened and their shape is hidden; the cry of the wild goose is heard; the cold has caught the wings of the birds; it is the time of ice-frost, hard, unhappy."

And after that, Finn being but a young lad yet, made himself ready and went up at Samhain time to the gathering of the High King at Teamhair. And it was the law at that gathering, no one to raise a quarrel or bring out any grudge against another through the whole of the time it lasted. And the king and his chief men, and Goll, son of Morna, that was now Head of the Fianna, and Caoilte, son of Ronan, and Conan, son of Morna, of the sharp words, were sitting at a feast in the great house of the Middle Court; and the young lad came in and took his place among them, and none of them knew who he was.

The High King looked at him then, and the horn of meetings was brought to him, and he put it into the boy's hand, and asked him who was he.

"I am Finn, son of Cumhal," he said, "son of the man that used to be head over the Fianna, and king of Ireland; and I am come now to get your friendship, and to give you my service."

"You are son of a friend, boy," said the king, "and son of a man I trusted."

Then Finn rose up and made his agreement of service and of faithfulness to the king; and the king took him by the hand and put him sitting beside his own son, and they gave themselves to drinking and to pleasure for a while.

Every year, now, at Samhain time, for nine years, there had come a man of the Tuatha de Danaan out of Sidhe Finnachaidh in the north, and had burned up Teamhair. Aillen, son of Midhna, his name was, and it is the way he used to come, playing music of the Sidhe, and all the people that heard it would fall asleep. And when they were all in their sleep, he would let a flame of fire out of his mouth, and would blow the flame till all Teamhair was burned.

The king rose up at the feast after a while, and his smooth horn in his hand, and it is what he said: "If I could find among you, men of Ireland, any man that would keep Teamhair till the break of day to-morrow without being burned by Aillen, son of Midhna, I would give him whatever inheritance is right for him to have, whether it be much or little."

But the men of Ireland made no answer, for they knew well that at the sound of the sweet pitiful music made by that comely man of the Sidhe, even women in their pains and men that were wounded would fall asleep.

It is then Finn rose up and spoke to the King of Ireland. "Who will be your sureties that you will fulfil this?" he said. "The kings of the provinces of Ireland," said the king, "and Cithruadh with his Druids." So they gave their pledges, and Finn took in hand to keep Teamhair safe till the breaking of day on the morrow.

Now there was a fighting man among the followers of the King of Ireland, Fiacha, son of Conga, that Cumhal, Finn's father, used to have a great liking for, and he said to Finn: "Well, boy," he said, "what reward would you give me if I would bring you a deadly spear, that no false cast was ever made with?" "What reward are you asking of me?" said Finn. "Whatever your right hand wins at any time, the third of it to be mine," said Fiacha, "and a third of your trust and your friendship to be mine." "I will give you that," said Finn. Then Fiacha brought him the spear, unknown to the sons of Morna or to any other person, and he said: "When you will hear the music of the Sidhe, let you strip the covering off the head of the spear and put it to your forehead, and the power of the spear will not let sleep come upon you."

Then Finn rose up before all the men of Ireland, and he made a round of the whole of Teamhair. And it was not long till he heard the sorrowful music, and he stripped the covering from the head of the spear, and he held the power of it to his forehead. And Aillen went on playing his little harp, till he had put every one in their sleep as he was used; and then he let a flame of fire out from his mouth to burn Teamhair. And Finn held up his fringed crimson cloak against the flame, and it fell down through the air and went into the ground, bringing the four-folded cloak with it deep into the earth.

And when Aillen saw his spells were destroyed, he went back to Sidhe Finnachaidh on the top of Slieve Fuad; but Finn followed after him there, and as Aillen was going in at the door he made a cast of the spear that went through his heart. And he struck his head off then, and brought it back to Teamhair, and fixed it on a crooked pole and left it there till the rising of the sun over the heights and invers of the country.

And Aillen's mother came to where his body was lying, and there was great grief on her, and she made this complaint:—

"Ochone! Aillen is fallen, chief of the Sidhe of Beinn Boirche; the slow clouds of death are come on him. Och! he was pleasant, Och! he was kind, Aillen, son of Midhna of Slieve Fuad.

"Nine times he burned Teamhair. It is a great name he was always looking for, Ochone, Ochone, Aillen!"

And at the breaking of day, the king and all the men of Ireland came out upon the lawn at Teamhair where Finn was. "King," said Finn, "there is the head of the man that burned Teamhair, and the pipe and the harp that made his music. And it is what I think," he said, "that Teamhair and all that is in it is saved."

Then they all came together into the place of counsel, and it is what they agreed, the headship of the Fianna of Ireland to be given to Finn. And the king said to Goll, son of Morna: "Well, Goll," he said, "is it your choice to quit Ireland or to put your hand in Finn's hand?" "By my word, I will give Finn my hand," said Goll.

And when the charms that used to bring good luck had done their work, the chief men of the Fianna rose up and struck their hands in Finn's hand, and Goll, son of Morna, was the first to give him his hand the way there would be less shame on the rest for doing it.

And Finn kept the headship of the Fianna until the end; and the place he lived in was Almhuin of Leinster, where the white dun was made by Nuada of the Tuatha de Danaan, that was as white as if all the lime in Ireland was put on it, and that got its name from the great herd of cattle that died fighting one time around the well, and that left their horns there, speckled horns and white.

And as to Finn himself, he was a king and a seer and a poet; a Druid and a knowledgeable man; and everything he said was sweet-sounding to his people. And a better fighting man than Finn never struck his hand into a king's hand, and whatever any one ever said of him, he was three times better. And of his justice it used to be said, that if his enemy and his own son had come before him to be judged, it is a fair judgment he would have given between them. And as to his generosity it used to be said, he never denied any man as long as he had a mouth to eat with, and legs to bring away what he gave him; and he left no woman without her bride-price, and no man without his pay; and he never promised at night what he would not fulfil on the morrow, and he never promised in the day what he would not fulfil at night, and he never forsook his right-hand friend. And if he was quiet in peace he was angry in battle, and Oisin his son and Osgar his son's son followed him in that. There was a young man of Ulster came and claimed kinship with them one time, saying they were of the one blood. "If that is so," said Oisin, "it is from the men of Ulster we took the madness and the angry heart we have in battle." "That is so indeed," said Finn.

CHAPTER II

Finn's Household

And the number of the Fianna of Ireland at that time was seven score and ten chief men, every one of them having three times nine fighting men under him. And every man of them was bound to three things, to take no cattle by oppression, not to refuse any man, as to cattle or riches; no one of them to fall back before nine fighting men. And there was no man taken into the Fianna until his tribe and his kindred would give securities for him, that even if they themselves were all killed he would not look for satisfaction for their death. But if he himself would harm others, that harm was not to be avenged on his people. And there was no man taken into the Fianna till he knew the twelve books of poetry. And before any man was taken, he would be put into a deep hole in the ground up to his middle, and he having his shield and a hazel rod in his hand. And nine men would go the length of ten furrows from him and would cast their spears at him at the one time. And if he got a wound from one of them, he was not thought fit to join with the Fianna. And after that again, his hair would be fastened up, and he put to run through the woods of Ireland, and the Fianna following after him to try could they wound him, and only the length of a branch between themselves and himself when they started. And if they came up with him and wounded him, he was not let join them; or if his spears had trembled in his hand, or if a branch of a tree had undone the plaiting of his hair, or if he had cracked a dry stick under his foot, and he running. And they would not take him among them till he had made a leap over a stick the height of himself, and till he had stooped under one the height of his knee, and till he had taken a thorn out from his foot with his nail, and he running his fastest. But if he had done all these things, he was of Finn's people.

It was good wages Finn and the Fianna got at that time; in every district a townland, in every house the fostering of a pup or a whelp from Samhain to Beltaine, and a great many things along with that. But good as the pay was, the hardships and the dangers they went through for it were greater. For they had to hinder the strangers and robbers from beyond the seas, and every bad thing, from coming into Ireland. And they had hard work enough in doing that.

And besides the fighting men, Finn had with him his five Druids, the best that ever came into the west, Cainnelsciath, of the Shining Shield, one of them was, that used to bring down knowledge from the clouds in the sky before Finn, and that could foretell battles. And he had his five wonderful physicians, four of them belonging to Ireland, and one that came over the sea from the east. And he had his five high poets and his twelve musicians, that had among them Daighre, son of Morna, and Suanach, son of Senshenn, that was Finn's teller of old stories, the sweetest that ever took a harp in his hand in Ireland or in Alban. And he had his three cup-bearers and his six door-keepers and his horn-players and the stewards of his house and his huntsman, Comhrag of the five hundred hounds, and his serving-men that were under Garbhcronan, of the Rough Buzzing; and a great troop of others along with them.

And there were fifty of the best sewing-women in Ireland brought together in a rath on Magh Feman, under the charge of a daughter of the King of Britain, and they used to be making clothing for the Fianna through the whole of the year. And three of them, that were a king's daughters, used to be making music for the rest on a little silver harp; and there was a very great candlestick of stone in the middle of the rath, for they were not willing to kindle a fire more than three times in the year for fear the smoke and the ashes might harm the needlework.

And of all his musicians the one Finn thought most of was Cnu Deireoil, the Little Nut, that came to him from the Sidhe.

It was at Slieve-nam-ban, for hunting, Finn was the time he came to him. Sitting down he was on the turf-built grave that is there; and when he looked around him he saw a small little man about four feet in height standing on the grass. Light yellow hair he had, hanging down to his waist, and he playing music on his harp. And the music he was making had no fault in it at all, and it is much that the whole of the Fianna did not fall asleep with the sweetness of its sound. He came up then, and put his hand in Finn's hand. "Where do you come from, little one, yourself and your sweet music?" said Finn. "I am come," he said, "out of the place of the Sidhe in Slieve-nam-ban, where ale is drunk and made; and it is to be in your company for a while I am come here." "You will get good rewards from me, and riches and red gold," said Finn, "and my full friendship, for I like you well." "That is the best luck ever came to you, Finn," said all the rest of the Fianna, for they were well pleased to have him in their company. And they gave him the name of the Little Nut; and he was good in speaking, and he had so good a memory he never forgot anything he heard east or west; and there was no one but must listen to his music, and all the Fianna liked him well. And there were some said he was a son of Lugh Lamh-Fada, of the Long Hand.

And the five musicians of the Fianna were brought to him, to learn the music of the Sidhe he had brought from that other place; for there was never any music heard on earth but his was better. These were the three best things Finn ever got, Bran and Sceolan that were without fault, and the Little Nut from the House of the Sidhe in Slieve-nam-ban.

CHAPTER III

Birth of Bran

This, now, is the story of the birth of Bran.

Finn's mother, Muirne, came one time to Almhuin, and she brought with her Tuiren, her sister. And Iollan Eachtach, a chief man of the Fianna of Ulster, was at Almhuin at the time, and he gave his love to Tuiren, and asked her in marriage, and brought her to his own house. But before they went, Finn made him gave his word he would bring her back safe and sound if ever he asked for her, and he bade him find sureties for himself among the chief men of the Fianna. And Iollan did that, and the sureties he got were Caoilte and Goll and Lugaidh Lamha, and it was Lugaidh gave her into the hand of Iollan Eachtach.

But before Iollan made that marriage, he had a sweetheart of the Sidhe, Uchtde-alb of the Fair Breast; and there came great jealousy on her when she knew he had taken a wife. And she took the appearance of Finn's woman-messenger, and she came to the house where Tuiren was, and she said: "Finn sends health and long life to you, queen, and he bids you to make a great feast; and come with me now," she said, "till I speak a few words with you, for there is hurry on me."

So Tuiren went out with her, and when they were away from the house the woman of the Sidhe took out her dark Druid rod from under her cloak and gave her a blow of it that changed her into a hound, the most beautiful that was ever seen. And then she went on, bringing the hound with her, to the house of Fergus Fionnliath, king of the harbour of Gallimh. And it is the way Fergus was, he was the most unfriendly man to dogs in the whole world, and he would not let one stop in the same house with him. But it is what Uchtdealb said to him: "Finn wishes you life and health, Fergus, and he says to you to take good care of his hound till he comes himself; and mind her well," she said, "for she is with young, and do not let her go hunting when her time is near, or Finn will be no way thankful to you." "I wonder at that message," said Fergus, "for Finn knows well there is not in the world a man has less liking for dogs than myself. But for all that," he said, "I will not refuse Finn the first time he sent a hound to me."

And when he brought the hound out to try her, she was the best he ever knew, and she never saw the wild creature she would not run down; and Fergus took a great liking for hounds from that out.

And when her time came near, they did not let her go hunting any more, and she gave birth to two whelps.

And as to Finn, when he heard his mother's sister was not living with Iollan Eachtach, he called to him for the fulfilment of the pledge that was given to the Fianna. And Iollan asked time to go looking for Tuiren, and he gave his word that if he did not find her, he would give himself up in satisfaction for her. So they agreed to that, and Iollan went to the hill where Uchtdealb was, his sweetheart of the Sidhe, and told her the way things were with him, and the promise he had made to give himself up to the Fianna. "If that is so," said she, "and if you will give me your pledge to keep me as your sweetheart to the end of your life, I will free you from that danger." So Iollan gave her his promise, and she went to the house of Fergus Fionnliath, and she brought Tuiren away and put her own shape on her again, and gave her up to Finn. And Finn gave her to Lugaidh Lamha that asked her in marriage.

And as to the two whelps, they stopped always with Finn, and the names he gave them were Bran and Sceolan.

CHAPTER IV

Oisin's Mother

It happened one time Finn and his men were coming back from the hunting, a beautiful fawn started up before them, and they followed after it, men and dogs, till at last they were all tired and fell back, all but Finn himself and Bran and Sceolan. And suddenly as they were going through a valley, the fawn stopped and lay down on the smooth grass, and Bran and Sceolan came up with it, and they did not harm it at all, but went playing about it, licking its neck and its face.

There was wonder on Finn when he saw that, and he went on home to Almhuin, and the fawn followed after him playing with the hounds, and it came with them into the house at Almhuin. And when Finn was alone late that evening, a beautiful young woman having a rich dress came before him, and she told him it was she herself was the fawn he was after hunting that day. "And it is for refusing the love of Fear Doirche, the Dark Druid of the Men of Dea," she said, "I was put in this shape. And through the length of three years," she said, "I have lived the life of a wild deer in a far part of Ireland, and I am hunted like a wild deer. And a serving-man of the Dark Druid took pity on me," she said, "and he said that if I was once within the dun of the Fianna of Ireland, the Druid would have no more power over me. So I made away, and I never stopped through the whole length of a day till I came into the district of Almhuin. And I never stopped then till there was no one after me but only Bran and Sceolan, that have human wits; and I was safe with them, for they knew my nature to be like their own."

Then Finn gave her his love, and took her as his wife, and she stopped in Almhuin. And so great was his love for her, he gave up his hunting and all the things he used to take pleasure in, and gave his mind to no other thing but herself.

But at last the men of Lochlann came against Ireland, and their ships were in the bay below Beinn Edair, and they landed there.

And Finn and the battalions of the Fianna went out against them, and drove them back. And at the end of seven days Finn came back home, and he went quickly over the plain of Almhuin, thinking to see Sadbh his wife looking out from the dun, but there was no sign of her. And when he came to the dun, all his people came out to meet him, but they had a very downcast look. "Where is the flower of Almhuin, beautiful gentle Sadbh?" he asked them. And it is what they said: "While you were away fighting, your likeness, and the likeness of Bran and of Sceolan appeared before the dun, and we thought we heard the sweet call of the Dord Fiann. And Sadbh, that was so good and so beautiful, came out of the house," they said, "and she went out of the gates, and she would not listen to us, and we could not stop her." "Let me go meet my love," she said, "my husband, the father of the child that is not born." And with that she went running out towards the shadow of yourself that was before her, and that had its arms stretched out to her. But no sooner did she touch it than she gave a great cry, and the shadow lifted up a hazel rod, and on the moment it was a fawn was standing on the grass. Three times she turned and made for the gate of the dun, but the two hounds the shadow had with him went after her and took her by the throat and dragged her back to him. "And by your hand of valour, Finn," they said, "we ourselves made no delay till we went out on the plain after her. But it is our grief, they had all vanished, and there was not to be seen woman, or fawn or Druid, but we could hear the quick tread of feet on the hard plain, and the howling of dogs. And if you would ask every one of us in what quarter he heard those sounds, he would tell you a different one."

When Finn heard that, he said no word at all, but he struck his breast over and over again with his shut hands. And he went then to his own inside room, and his people saw him no more for that day, or till the sun rose over Magh Lifé on the morrow.

And through the length of seven years from that time, whenever he was not out fighting against the enemies of Ireland, he went searching and ever searching in every far corner for beautiful Sadbh. And there was great trouble on him all the time, unless he might throw it off for a while in hunting or in battle. And through all that time he never brought out to any hunting but the five hounds he had most trust in, Bran and Sceolan and Lomaire and Brod and Lomluath, the way there would be no danger for Sadbh if ever he came on her track.

But after the end of seven years, Finn and some of his chief men were hunting on the sides of Beinn Gulbain, and they heard a great outcry among the hounds, that were gone into some narrow place. And when they followed them there, they saw the five hounds of Finn in a ring, and they keeping back the other hounds, and in the middle of the ring was a young boy, with high looks, and he naked and having long hair. And he was no way daunted by the noise of the hounds, and did not look at them at all, but at the men that were coming up. And as soon as the fight was stopped Bran and Sceolan went up to the little lad, and whined and licked him, that any one would think they had forgotten their master. Finn and the others came up to him then, and put their hands on his head, and made much of him. And they brought him to their own hunting cabin, and he ate and drank with them, and before long he lost his wildness and was the same as themselves. And as to Bran and Sceolan, they were never tired playing about him.

And it is what Finn thought, there was some look of Sadbh in his face, and that it might be he was her son, and he kept him always beside him. And little by little when the boy had learned their talk, he told them all he could remember. He used to be with a deer he loved very much, he said, and that cared and sheltered him, and it was in a wide place they used to be, having hills and valleys and streams and woods in it, but that was shut in with high cliffs on every side, that there was no way of escape from it. And he used to be eating fruits and roots in the summer, and in the winter there was food left for him in the shelter of a cave. And a dark-looking man used to be coming to the place, and sometimes he would speak to the deer softly and gently, and sometimes with a loud angry voice. But whatever way he spoke, she would always draw away from him with the appearance of great dread on her, and the man would go away in great anger. And the last time he saw the deer, his mother, the dark man was speaking to her for a long time, from softness to anger. And at the end he struck her with a hazel rod, and with that she was forced to follow him, and she looking back all the while at the child, and crying after him that any one would pity her. And he tried hard to follow after her, and made every attempt, and cried out with grief and rage, but he had no power to move, and when he could hear his mother no more he fell on the grass and his wits went from him. And when he awoke it is on the side of the hill he was, where the hounds found him. And he searched a long time for the place where he was brought up, but he could not find it.

And the name the Fianna gave him was Oisin, and it is he was their maker of poems, and their good fighter afterwards.

CHAPTER V

The Best Men of the Fianna

And while Oisin was in his young youth, Finn had other good men along with him, and the best of them were Goll, son of Morna, and Caoilte, son of Ronan, and Lugaidh's Son.

As to Goll, that was of Connacht, he was very tall and light-haired, and some say he was the strongest of all the Fianna. Finn made a poem in praise of him one time when some stranger was asking what sort he was, saying how hardy he was and brave in battle, and as strong as a hound or as the waves, and with all that so kind and so gentle, and open-handed and sweet-voiced, and faithful to his friends.

And the chessboard he had was called the Solustairtech, the Shining Thing, and some of the chessmen were made of gold, and some of them of silver, and each one of them was as big as the fist of the biggest man of the Fianna; and after the death of Goll it was buried in Slieve Baune.

And as to Caoilte, that was a grey thin man, he was the best runner of them all. And he did a good many great deeds; a big man of the Fomor he killed one time, and he killed a five-headed giant in a wheeling door, and another time he made an end of an enchanted boar that no one else could get near, and he killed a grey stag that had got away from the Fianna through twenty-seven years. And another time he brought Finn out of Teamhair, where he was kept by force by the High King, because of some rebellion the Fianna had stirred up. And when Caoilte heard Finn had been brought away to Teamhair, he went out to avenge him. And the first he killed was Cuireach, a king of Leinster that had a great name, and he brought his head up to the hill that is above Buadhmaic. And after that he made a great rout through Ireland, bringing sorrow into every house for the sake of Finn, killing a man in every place, and killing the calves with the cows.

And every door the red wind from the east blew on, he would throw it open, and go in and destroy all before him, setting fire to the fields, and giving the wife of one man to another.

And when he came to Teamhair, he came to the palace, and took the clothes off the door-keeper, and he left his own sword that was worn thin in the king's sheath, and took the king's sword that had great power in it. And he went into the palace then in the disguise of a servant, to see how he could best free Finn.

And when evening came Caoilte held the candle at the king's feast in the great hall, and after a while the king said: "You will wonder at what I tell you, Finn, that the two eyes of Caoilte are in my candlestick." "Do not say that," said Finn, "and do not put reproach on my people although I myself am your prisoner;

for as to Caoilte," he said, "that is not the way with him, for it is a high mind he has, and he only does high deeds, and he would not stand serving with a candle for all the gold of the whole world."

After that Caoilte was serving the King of Ireland with drink, and when he was standing beside him he gave out a high sorrowful lament. "There is the smell of Caoilte's skin on that lament," said the king. And when Caoilte saw he knew him he spoke out and he said: "Tell me what way I can get freedom for my master." "There is no way to get freedom for him but by doing one thing," said the king, "and that is a thing you can never do. If you can bring me together a couple of all the wild creatures of Ireland," he said, "I will give up your master to you then."

When Caoilte heard him say that he made no delay, but he set out from Teamhair, and went through the whole of Ireland to do that work for the sake of Finn. It is with the flocks of birds he began, though they were scattered in every part, and from them he went on to the beasts. And he gathered together two of every sort, two ravens from Fiodh da Bheann; two wild ducks from Loch na Seillein; two foxes from Slieve Cuilinn; two wild oxen from Burren; two swans from blue Dobhran; two owls from the wood of Faradhruim; two polecats from the branchy wood on the side of Druim da Raoin, the Ridge of the Victories; two gulls from the strand of Loch Leith; four woodpeckers from white Brosna; two plovers from Carraigh Dhain; two thrushes from Leith Lomard; two wrens from Dun Aoibh; two herons from Corrain Cleibh; two eagles from Carraig of the stones; two hawks from Fiodh Chonnach; two sows from Loch Meilghe; two water-hens from Loch Erne; two moor-hens from Monadh Maith; two sparrow-hawks from Dubhloch; two stonechats from Magh Cuillean; two tomtits from Magh Tuallainn; two swallows from Sean Abhla; two cormorants from Ath Cliath; two wolves from Broit Cliathach; two blackbirds from the Strand of the Two Women; two roebucks from Luachair Ire; two pigeons from Ceas Chuir; two nightingales from Leiter Ruadh; two starlings from green-sided Teamhair; two rabbits from Sith Dubh Donn; two wild pigs from Cluaidh Chuir; two cuckoos from Drom Daibh; two lapwings from Leanain na Furraich; two woodcocks from Craobh Ruadh; two hawks from the Bright Mountain; two grey mice from Luim-neach; two otters from the Boinn; two larks from the Great Bog; two bats from the Cave of the Nuts; two badgers from the province of Ulster; two landrail from the banks of the Sionnan; two wagtails from Port Lairrge; two curlews from the harbour of Gallimh; two hares from Muirthemne; two deer from Sith Buidhe; two peacocks from Magh Mell; two cormorants from Ath Cliath; two eels from Duth Dur; two goldfinches from Slieve na-n Eun; two birds of slaughter from Magh Bhuilg; two bright swallows from Granard; two redbreasts from the Great Wood; two rock-cod from Cala Chairge; two sea-pigs from the great sea; two wrens from Mios an Chuil; two salmon from Eas Mhic Muirne; two clean deer from Gleann na Smoil; two cows from Magh Mor; two cats from the Cave of

Cruachan; two sheep from bright Sidhe Diobhlain; two pigs of the pigs of the son of Lir; a ram and a crimson sheep from Innis.

And along with all these he brought ten hounds of the hounds of the Fianna, and a horse and a mare of the beautiful horses of Manannan.

And when Caoilte had gathered all these, he brought them to the one place. But when he tried to keep them together, they scattered here and there from him; the raven went away southward, and that vexed him greatly, but he overtook it again in Gleann da Bheann, beside Loch Lurcan. And then his wild duck went away from him, and it was not easy to get it again, but he followed it through every stream to grey Accuill till he took it by the neck and brought it back, and it no way willing.

And indeed through the length of his life Caoilte remembered well all he went through that time with the birds, big and little, travelling over hills and ditches and striving to bring them with him, that he might set Finn his master free.

And when he came to Teamhair he had more to go through yet, for the king would not let him bring them in before morning, but gave him a house having nine doors in it to put them up in for the night. And no sooner were they put in than they raised a loud screech all together, for a little ray of light was coming to them through fifty openings, and they were trying to make their escape. And if they were not easy in the house, Caoilte was not easy outside it, watching every door till the rising of the sun on the morrow.

And when he brought out his troop, the name the people gave them was "Caoilte's Rabble," and there was no wonder at all in that.

But all the profit the King of Ireland got from them was to see them together for that one time. For no sooner did Finn get his freedom than the whole of them scattered here and there, and no two of them went by the same road out of Teamhair.

And that was one of the best things Caoilte, son of Ronan, ever did. And another time he ran from the wave of Cliodna in the south to the wave of Rudraige in the north. And Colla his son was a very good runner too, and one time he ran a race backwards against the three battalions of the Fianna for a chessboard. And he won the race, but if he did, he went backward over Beinn Edair into the sea.

And very good hearing Caoilte had. One time he heard the King of the Luigne of Connacht at his hunting, and Blathmec that was with him said, "What is that hunt, Caoilte?" "A hunt of three packs of hounds," he said, "and three sorts of wild creatures before them. The first hunt," he said, "is after stags and large deer and the second hunt is after swift small hares, and the third is a furious hunt after heavy boars." "And what is the fourth hunt, Caoilte?" said Blathmec. "It is the hunting of heavy-sided, low-bellied badgers." And then they heard coming after the hunt the shouts of the lads and of the readiest of the men and the serving-men that were best at carrying burdens. And Blathmec went out to see the hunting, and just as Caoilte had told him, that was the way it was.

And he understood the use of herbs, and one time he met with two women that were very downhearted because their husbands had gone from them to take other wives. And Caoilte gave them Druid herbs, and they put them in the water of a bath and washed in it, and the love of their husbands came back to them, and they sent away the new wives they had taken.

And as to Lugaidh's Son, that was of Finn's blood, and another of the best men of the Fianna, he was put into Finn's arms as a child, and he was reared up by Duban's daughter, that had reared eight hundred fighting men of the Fianna, till his twelfth year, and then she gave him all he wanted of arms and of armour, and he went to Chorraig Conluain and the mountains of Slieve Bladhma, where Finn and the Fianna were at that time.

And Finn gave him a very gentle welcome, and he struck his hand in Finn's hand, and made his agreement of service with him. And he stopped through the length of a year with the Fianna; but he was someway sluggish through all that time, so that under his leading not more than nine of the Fianna got to kill so much as a boar or a deer. And along with that, he used to beat both his servants and his hounds.

And at last the three battalions of the Fianna went to where Finn was, at the Point of the Fianna on the edge of Loch Lein, and they made their complaint against Lugaidh's Son, and it is what they said: "Make your choice now, will you have us with you, or will you have Lugaidh's Son by himself."

Then Lugaidh's Son came to Finn, and Finn asked him, "What is it has put the whole of the Fianna against you?" "By my word," said the lad, "I do not know the reason, unless it might be they do not like me to be doing my feats and casting my spears among them."

Then Finn gave him an advice, and it is what he said: "If you have a mind to be a good champion, be quiet in a great man's house; be surly in the narrow pass. Do not beat your hound without a cause; do not bring a charge against your wife without having knowledge of her guilt; do not hurt a fool in fighting, for he is without his wits. Do not find fault with high-up persons; do not stand up to take part in a quarrel; have no dealings with a bad man or a foolish man. Let two-thirds of your gentleness be showed to women and to little children that are creeping on the floor, and to men of learning that make the poems, and do not be rough with the common people. Do not give your reverence to all; do not be ready to have one bed with your companions. Do not threaten or speak big words, for it is a shameful thing to speak stiffly unless you can carry it out afterwards. Do not forsake your lord so long as you live; do not give up any man that puts himself under your protection for all the treasures of the world. Do not speak against others to their lord, that is not work for a good man. Do not be a bearer of lying stories, or a tale-bearer that is always chattering. Do not be talking too much; do not find fault hastily; however brave you may be, do not raise factions against you. Do not be going to drinking-houses, or finding fault with old men; do not meddle with low people; this is right conduct I am telling you. Do not refuse to share your meat; do not have a niggard for your friend; do not force yourself on a great man or give him occasion to speak against you. Hold fast to your arms till the hard fight is well ended. Do not give up your opportunity, but with that follow after gentleness."

That was good advice Finn gave, and he was well able to do that; for it was said of him that he had all the wisdom of a little child that is busy about the house, and the mother herself not understanding what he is doing; and that is the time she has most pride in him.

And as to Lugaidh's Son, that advice stayed always with him, and he changed his ways, and after a while he got a great name among the poets of Ireland and of Alban, and whenever they would praise Finn in their poems, they would praise him as well.

And Aoife, daughter of the King of Lochlann, that was married to Mal, son of Aiel, King of Alban, heard the great praise the poets were giving to Lugaidh's Son, and she set her love on him for the sake of those stories.

And one time Mal her husband and his young men went hunting to Slieve-mor-Monaidh in the north of Alban. And when he was gone Aoife made a plan in her sunny house where she was, to go over to Ireland, herself and her nine foster-sisters. And they set out and went over the manes of the sea till they came to Beinn Edair, and there they landed.

And it chanced on that day there was a hunting going on, from Slieve Bladhma to Beinn Edair. And Finn was in his hunting seat, and his fosterling, brown-haired Duibhruinn, beside him. And the little lad was looking about him on every side, and he saw a ship coming to the strand, and a queen with modest looks in the ship, and nine women along with her. They landed then, and they came up to where Finn was, bringing every sort of present with them, and Aoife sat down beside him. And Finn asked news of her, and she told him the whole story, and how she had given her love to Lugaidh's Son, and was come over the sea looking for him; and Finn made her welcome.

And when the hunting was over, the chief men of the Fianna came back to where Finn was, and every one asked who was the queen that was with him. And Finn told them her name, and what it was brought her to Ireland. "We welcome her that made that journey," said they all; "for there is not in Ireland or in Alban a better man than the man she is come looking for, unless Finn himself."

And as to Lugaidh's Son, it was on the far side of Slieve Bladhma he was hunting that day, and he was the last to come in. And he went into Finn's tent, and when he saw the woman beside him he questioned Finn the same as the others had done, and Finn told him the whole story. "And it is to you she is come," he said;

"and here she is to you out of my hand, and all the war and the battles she brings with her; but it will not fall heavier on you," he said, "than on the rest of the Fianna."

And she was with Lugaidh's Son a month and a year without being asked for. But one day the three battalions of the Fianna were on the Hill of the Poet in Leinster, and they saw three armed battalions equal to themselves coming, against them, and they asked who was bringing them. "It is Mal, son of Aiel, is bringing them," said Finn, "to avenge his wife on the Fianna. And it is a good time they are come," he said, "when we are gathered together at the one spot."

Then the two armies went towards one another, and Mal, son of Aiel, took hold of his arms, and three times he broke through the Fianna, and every time a hundred fell by him. And in the middle of the battle he and Lugaidh's Son met, and they fought against one another with spear and sword. And whether the fight was short or long, it was Mal fell by Lugaidh's Son at the last.

And Aoife stood on a hill near by, as long as the battle lasted. And from that out she belonged to Lugaidh's Son, and was a mother of children to him.

BOOK II

Finn's Helpers

CHAPTER I

The Lad of the Skins

Besides all the men Finn had in his household, there were some that would come and join him from one place or another.

One time a young man wearing a dress of skins came to Finn's house at Almhuin, and his wife along with him, and he asked to take service with Finn.

And in the morning, as they were going to their hunting, the Lad of the Skins said to Finn: "Let me have no one with me but myself, and let me go into one part of the country by myself, and you yourself with all your men go to another part." "Is it on the dry ridges you will go," said Finn, "or is it in the deep bogs and marshes, where there is danger of drowning?" "I will go in the deep boggy places," said he.

So they all went out from Almhuin, Finn and the Fianna to one part, and the Lad of the Skins to another part, and they hunted through the day. And when they came back at evening, the Lad of the Skins had killed more than Finn and all his men together.

When Finn saw that, he was glad to have so good a servant. But Conan said to him: "The Lad of the Skins will destroy ourselves and the whole of the Fianna of Ireland unless you will find some way to rid yourself of him." "I never had a good man with me yet, Conan," said Finn, "but you wanted me to put him away; and how could I put away a man like that?" he said. "The way to put him away," said Conan, "is to send him to the King of the Floods to take from him the great cauldron that is never without meat, but that has always enough in it to feed the whole world. And let him bring that cauldron back here with him to Almhuin," he said.

So Finn called to the Lad of the Skins, and he said: "Go from me now to the King of the Floods and get the great cauldron that is never empty from him, and bring it here to me." "So long as I am in your service I must do your work," said the Lad of the Skins. With that he set out, leaping over the hills and valleys till he came to the shore of the sea. And then he took up two sticks and put one of them across the other, and a great ship rose out of the two sticks. The Lad of the Skins went into the ship then, and put up the sails and set out over the sea, and he heard nothing but the whistling of eels in the sea and the calling of gulls in the air till he came to the house of the King of the Floods. And at that time there were hundreds of ships waiting near the shore; and he left his ship outside them all, and then he stepped from ship to ship till he stood on land.

There was a great feast going on at that time in the king's house, and the Lad of the Skins went up to the door, but he could get no farther because of the crowd. So he stood outside the door for a while, and no one looked at him, and he called out at last: "This is a hospitable house indeed, and these are mannerly ways, not to ask a stranger if there is hunger on him or thirst." "That is true," said the king; "and give the cauldron of plenty now to this stranger," he said, "till he eats his fill."

So his people did that, and no sooner did the Lad of the Skins get a hold of the cauldron than he made away to the ship and put it safe into it. But when he had done that he said: "There is no use in taking the pot by my swiftness, if I do not take it by my strength." And with that he turned and went to land again. And the whole of the men of the army of the King of the Floods were ready to fight; but if they were, so was the Lad of the Skins, and he went through them and over them all till the whole place was quiet.

He went back to his ship then and raised the sails and set out again for Ireland, and the ship went rushing back to the place where he made it. And when he came there, he gave a touch of his hand to the ship, and there was nothing left of it but the two sticks he made it from, and they lying on the strand before him, and the cauldron of plenty with them. And he took up the cauldron on his back, and brought it to Finn, son of Cumhal, at Almhuin. And Finn gave him his thanks for the work he had done.

One day, now, Finn was washing himself at the well, and a voice spoke out of the water, and it said: "You must give back the cauldron, Finn, to the King of the Floods, or you must give him battle in place of it."

Finn told that to the Lad of the Skins, but the answer he got from him was that his time was up, and that he could not serve on time that was past. "But if you want me to go with you," he said, "let you watch my wife, that is Manannan's daughter, through the night; and in the middle of the night, when she will be combing her hair, any request you make of her, she cannot refuse it. And the request you will make is that she will let me go with you to the King of the Floods, to bring the cauldron to his house and to bring it back again."

So Finn watched Manannan's daughter through the night, and when he saw her combing her hair, he made his request of her. "I have no power to refuse you," she said; "but you must promise me one thing, to bring my husband back to me, alive or dead. And if he is alive," she said, "put up a grey-green flag on the ship coming back; but if he is dead, put up a red flag."

So Finn promised to do that, and he himself and the Lad of the Skins set out together for the dun of the King of the Floods, bringing the cauldron with them.

No sooner did the king see them than he gave word to all his armies to make ready. But the Lad of the Skins made for them and overthrew them, and he went into the king's dun, and Finn with him, and they overcame him and brought away again the cauldron that was never empty.

But as they were going back to Ireland, they saw a great ship coming towards them. And when the Lad of the Skins looked at the ship, he said: "I think it is an old enemy of my own is in that ship, that is trying to bring me to my death, because of my wife that refused him her love." And when the ship came alongside, the man that was in it called out: "I know you well, and it is not by your dress I know you, son of the King of the Hills." And with that he made a leap on to the ship, and the two fought a great battle together, and they took every shape; they began young like two little boys, and fought till they were two old men; they fought from being two young pups until they were two old dogs; from being two young horses till they were two old horses. And then they began to fight in the shape of birds, and it is in that shape they killed one another at the last. And Finn threw the one bird into the water, but the other, that was the Lad of the Skins, he brought with him in the ship. And when he came in sight of Ireland, he raised a red flag as he had promised the woman.

And when he came to the strand, she was there before him, and when she saw Finn, she said: "It is dead you have brought him back to me." And Finn gave her the bird, and she asked was that what she was to get in the place of her husband. And she was crying over the bird, and she brought it into a little boat with her, and she bade Finn to push out the boat to sea.

And he pushed it out, and it was driven by wind and waves till at last she saw two birds flying, having a dead one between them. And the two living birds let down the dead one on an island; and it was not long till it rose up living, and the three went away together.

And when Manannan's daughter saw that, she said:

"There might be some cure for my man on the island, the way there was for that dead bird."

And the sea brought the boat to the island, and she went searching around, but all she could find was a tree having green leaves. "It might be in these leaves the cure is," she said; and she took some of the leaves and brought them to where the Lad of the Skins was, and put them about him. And on that moment he stood up as well and as sound as ever he was.

They went back then to Ireland, and they came to Almhuin at midnight, and the Lad of the Skins knocked at the door, and he said: "Put me out my wages." "There is no man, living or dead, has wages on me but the Lad of the Skins," said Finn; "and I would sooner see him here to-night," he said, "than the wages of three men." "If that is so, rise up and you will see him," said he.

So Finn rose up and saw him, and gave him a great welcome, and paid him his wages.

And after that he went away and his wife with him to wherever his own country was; but there were some said he was gone to the country of his wife's father, Manannan, Son of the Sea.

CHAPTER II

Black, Brown, and Grey

Finn was hunting one time near Teamhair of the Kings, and he saw three strange men coming towards him, and he asked what were their names. "Dubh and Dun and Glasan, Black, Brown, and Grey, are our names," they said, "and we are come to find Finn, son of Cumhal, Head of the Fianna, and to take service with him."

So Finn took them into his service, and when evening came he said: "Let each one of you watch through a third part of the night." And there was a trunk of a tree there, and he bade them make three equal parts of it, and he gave a part to each of the three men, and he said: "When each one of you begins his watch, let him set fire to his own log, and as long as the wood burns let him watch."

Then they drew lots, and the lot fell to Dubh to go on the first watch. So he set fire to his log, and he went out around the place, and Bran with him. He went farther and farther till at last he saw a bright light, and when he came to the place where it was, he saw a large house. He went inside, and there was a great company of very strange-looking men in it, and they drinking out of a single cup. One of the men, that seemed to be the highest, gave the cup to the man nearest him; and after he had drunk his fill he passed it on to the next, and so on to the last. And while it was going round, he said: "This is the great cup that was taken from Finn, son of Cumhal, a hundred years ago, and however many men may be together, every man of them can drink his fill from it, of whatever sort of drink he has a mind for."

Dubh was sitting near the door, on the edge of the crowd, and when the cup came to him he took a drink from it, and then he slipped away in the dark, bringing it with him. And when he came to the place where Finn was, his log was burned out.

Then it was the turn of Dun to go out, for the second lot had fallen on him, and he put a light to his log, and went out, and Bran with him.

He walked on through the night till he saw a fire that was shining from a large house, and when he went in he saw a crowd of men, and they fighting. And a very old man that was in a high place above the rest called out: "Stop fighting now, for I have a better gift for you than the one you lost to-night." And with that he drew a knife out of his belt and held it up, and said: "This is the wonderful knife, the small knife of division, that was stolen from Finn, son of Cumhal, a hundred years ago; and you have but to cut on a bone with that knife and you will get your fill of the best meat in the world." Then he gave the knife to the man nearest him, and a bare bone with it, and the man began to cut, and there came off the bone slices of the best meat in the world.

The knife and the bone were sent round then from man to man till they came to Dun, and as soon as he had the knife in his hand he slipped out unknown and hurried back, and he had just got to the well where Finn was, when his part of the log burned out.

Then Glasan lighted his log and went out on his watch till he came to the house, the same way the others did. And he looked in and he saw the floor full of dead bodies, and he thought to himself: "There must be some great wonder here. And if I lie down on the floor and put some of the bodies over me," he said, "I will be able to see all that happens."

So he lay down and pulled some of the bodies over him, and he was not long there till he saw an old hag coming into the house, having one leg and one arm and one upper tooth, that was long enough to serve her in place of a crutch. And when she came inside the door she took up the first dead body she met with, and threw it aside, for it was lean. And as she went on, she took two bites out of every fat body she met with, and threw away every lean one.

She had her fill of flesh and blood before she came to Glasan, and she dropped down on the floor and fell asleep, and Glasan thought that every breath she drew would bring down the roof on his head. He rose up then and looked at her, and wondered at the bulk of her body. And at last he drew his sword and hit her a slash that killed her; but if he did, three young men leaped out of her body. And Glasan made a stroke that killed the first of them, and Bran killed the second, but the third made his escape.

Glasan made his way back then, and just when he got to where Finn was, his log of wood was burned out, and the day was beginning to break.

And when Finn rose up in the morning he asked news of the three watchers, and they gave him the cup and the knife and told him all they had seen, and he gave great praise to Dubh and to Dun; but to Glasan he said: "It might have been as well for you to have left that old hag alone, for I am in dread the third young man may bring trouble on us all."

It happened at the end of twenty-one years, Finn and the Fianna were at their hunting in the hills, and they saw a Red-Haired Man coming towards them, and he spoke to no one, but came and stood before Finn. "What is it you are looking for?" said Finn. "I am looking for a master for the next twenty-one years," he said. "What wages are you asking?" said Finn. "No wages at all, but only if I die before the twenty-one years are up, to bury me on Inis Caol, the Narrow Island." "I will do that for you," said Finn.

So the Red-Haired Man served Finn well through the length of twenty years. But in the twenty-first year he began to waste and to wither away, and he died.

And when he was dead, the Fianna were no way inclined to go to Inis Caol to bury him. But Finn said he would break his word for no man, and that he himself would bring his body there. And he took an old white horse that had been turned loose on the hills, and that had got younger and not older since it was put out, and he put the body of the Red-Haired Man on its back, and let it take its own way, and he himself followed it, and twelve men of the Fianna.

And when they came to Inis Caol they saw no trace of the horse or of the body. And there was an open house on the island, and they went in. And there were seats for every man of them inside, and they sat down to rest for a while.

But when they tried to rise up it failed them to do it, for there was enchantment on them. And they saw the Red-Haired Man standing before them in that moment.

"The time is come now," he said, "for me to get satisfaction from you for the death of my mother and my two brothers that were killed by Glasan in the house of the dead bodies." He began to make an attack on them then, and he would have made an end of them all, but Finn took hold of the Dord Fiann, and blew a great blast on it.

And before the Red-Haired Man was able to kill more than three of them, Diarmuid, grandson of Duibhne, that had heard the sound of the Dord Fiann, came into the house and made an end of him, and put an end to the enchantment. And Finn, with the nine that were left of the Fianna, came back again to Almhuin.

CHAPTER III

The Hound

One day the three battalions of the Fianna came to Magh Femen, and there they saw three young men waiting for them, having a hound with them; and there was not a colour in the world but was on that hound, and it was bigger than any other hound.

"Where do you come from, young men?" said Finn. "Out of the greater Iruath in the east," said they; "and our names are Dubh, the Dark, and Agh, the Battle, and Ilar, the Eagle." "What is it you came for?" "To enter into service, and your friendship," said they. "What good will it do us, you to be with us?" said Finn. "We are three," said they, "and you can make a different use of each one of us." "What uses are those?" said Finn. "I will do the watching for all the Fianna of Ireland and of Alban," said one of them. "I will take the weight of every fight and every battle that will come to them, the way they can keep themselves in quiet," said the second. "I will meet every troublesome thing that might come to my master," said the third; "and let all the wants of the world be told to me and I will satisfy them. And I have a pipe with me," he said; "and all the men of the world would sleep at the sound of it, and they in their sickness. And as to the hound," he said, "as long as there are deer in Ireland he will get provision for the Fianna every second night. And I myself," he said, "will get it on the other nights." "What will you ask of us to be with us like that?" said Finn. "We will ask three things," they said: "no one to come near to the place where we have our lodging after the fall of night; nothing to be given out to us, but we to provide for ourselves; and the worst places to be given to us in the hunting." "Tell me by your oath now," said Finn, "why is it you will let no one see you after nightfall?" "We have a reason," said they; "but do not ask it of us, whether we are short or long on the one path with you. But we will tell you this much," they said, "every third night, one of us three is dead and the other two are watching him, and we have no mind for any one to be looking at us."

So Finn promised that; but if he did there were some of the Fianna were not well pleased because of the ways of those three men, living as they did by themselves, and having a wall of fire about them, and they would have made an end of them but for Finn protecting them.

About that time there came seven men of poetry belonging to the people of Cithruadh, asking the fee for a poem, three times fifty ounces of gold and the same of silver to bring back to Cithruadh at Teamhair. "Whatever way we get it, we must find some way to get that," said a man of the Fianna. Then the three young men from Iruath said: "Well, men of learning," they said, "would you sooner get the fee for your poem to-night or to-morrow?" "To-morrow will be time enough," said they.

And the three young men went to the place where the hound had his bed a little way off from the rath, and the hound threw out of his mouth before them the three times fifty ounces of gold and three times fifty of silver, and they gave them to the men of poetry, and they went away.

Another time Finn said: "What can the three battalions of the Fianna do to-night, having no water?" And one of the men of Iruath said: "How many drinking-horns are with you?" "Three hundred and twelve," said Caoilte. "Give me the horns into my hand," said the young man, "and whatever you will find in them after that, you may drink it." He filled the horns then with beer and they drank it, and he did that a second and a third time; and with the third time of filling they were talkative and their wits confused. "This is a wonderful mending of the feast," said Finn. And they gave the place where all that happened the name of the Little Rath of Wonders.

And one time after that again there came to Finn three bald red clowns, holding three red hounds in their hands, and three deadly spears. And there was poison on their clothes and on their hands and their feet, and on everything they touched.

And Finn asked them who were they. And they said they were three sons of Uar, son of Indast of the Tuatha de Danaan; and it was by a man of the Fianna, Caoilte son of Ronan, their father was killed in the battle of the Tuatha de Danaan on Slieve nan Ean, the Mountain of Birds, in the east. "And let Caoilte son of Ronan give us the blood-fine for him now," they said. "What are your names?" said Finn. "Aincel and Digbail and Espaid; Ill-wishing and Harm and Want are our names. And what answer do you give us now, Finn?" they said. "No one before me ever gave a blood-fine for a man killed in battle, and I will not give it," said Finn. "We will do revenge and robbery on you so," said they. "What revenge is that?" said Finn. "It is what I will do," said Aincel, "if I meet with two or three or four of the Fianna, I will take their feet and their hands from them." "It is what I will do," said Digbail, "I will not leave a day without loss of a hound or a serving-boy or a fighting man to the Fianna of Ireland." "And I myself will be always leaving them in want of people, or of a hand, or of an eye," said Espaid. "Without we get some help against them," said Caoilte, "there will not be one of us living at the end of a year." "Well," said Finn, "we will make a dun and stop here for a while, for I will not be going through Ireland and these men following after me, till I find who are the strongest, themselves or ourselves."

So the Fianna made little raths for themselves all about Slieve Mis, and they stopped there through a month and a quarter and a year. And through all that time the three red bald-headed men were doing every sort of hurt and harm upon them.

But the three sons of the King of Iruath came to speak with Finn, and it is what they said: "It is our wish, Finn, to send the hound that is with us to go around you three times in every day, and however many may be trying to hurt or to rob you, they will not have power to do it after that. But let there be neither fire nor arms nor any other dog in the house he goes into," they said. "I will let none of these things go into the one house with him," said Finn, "and he will go safe back to you." So every day the hound would be sent to Finn, having his chain of ridges of red gold around his neck, and he would go three times around Finn, and three times he would put his tongue upon him. And to the people that were nearest to the hound when he came into the house it would seem like as if a vat of mead was being strained, and to others there would come the sweet smell of an apple garden.

And every harm and sickness the three sons of Uar would bring on the Fianna, the three sons of the King of Iruath would take it off them with their herbs and their help and their healing.

And after a while the High King of Ireland came to Slieve Mis with a great troop of his men, to join with Finn and the Fianna. And they told the High King the whole story, and how the sons of Uar were destroying them, and the three sons of the King of Iruath were helping them against them. "Why would not the men that can do all that find some good spell that would drive the sons of Uar out of Ireland?" said the High King.

With that Caoilte went looking for the three young men from Iruath and brought them to the High King. "These are comely men," said the High King, "good in their shape and having a good name. And could you find any charm, my sons," he said, "that will drive out these three enemies that are destroying the Fianna of Ireland?" "We would do that if we could find those men near us," said they; "and it is where they are now," they said, "at Daire's Cairn at the end of the raths." "Where are Garb-Cronan, the Rough Buzzing One, and Saltran of the Long Heel?" said Finn. "Here we are, King of the Fianna," said they. "Go out to those men beyond, and tell them I will give according to the judgment of the King of Ireland in satisfaction for their father." The messengers went out then and brought them in, and they sat down on the bank of the rath.

Then the High King said: "Rise up, Dubh, son of the King of Iruath, and command these sons of Uar with a spell to quit Ireland." And Dubh rose up, and he said: "Go out through the strength of this spell and this charm, you three enemies of the Fianna, one-eyed, lame-thighed, left-handed, of the bad race. And go out on the deep bitter sea," he said, "and let each one of you strike a blow of his sword on the head of his brothers. For it is long enough you are doing harm and destruction on the King of the Fianna, Finn, son of Cumhal."

With that the hound sent a blast of wind under them that brought them out into the fierce green sea, and each of them struck a blow on the head of the others. And that was the last that was seen of the three destroying sons of Uar, Aincel and Digbail and Espaid.

But after the time of the Fianna, there came three times in the one year, into West Munster, three flocks of birds from the western sea having beaks of bone and fiery breath, and the wind from their wings was as cold as a wind of spring. And the first time they came was at reaping time, and every one of them brought away an ear of corn from the field. And the next time they came they did not leave apple on tree, or nut on bush, or berry on the rowan; and the third time they spared no live thing they could lift from the ground, young bird or fawn or silly little child. And the first day they came was the same day of the year the three sons of Uar were put out in the sea.

And when Caoilte, that was one of the last of the Fianna, and that was living yet, heard of them, he remembered the sons of Uar, and he made a spell that drove them out into the sea again, and they perished there by one another.

It was about the length of a year the three sons of the King of Iruath stopped with Finn. And at the end of that time Donn and Dubhan, two sons of the King of Ulster, came out of the north to Munster. And one night they kept watch for the Fianna, and three times they made a round of the camp. And it is the way the young men from Iruath used to be, in a place by themselves apart from the

Fianna, and their hound in the middle between them; and at the fall of night there used a wall of fire to be around them, the way no one could look at them.

And the third time the sons of the King of Ulster made the round of the camp, they saw the fiery wall, and Donn said: "It is a wonder the way those three young men are through the length of a year now, and their hound along with them, and no one getting leave to look at them."

With that he himself and his brother took their arms in their hands, and went inside the wall of fire, and they began looking at the three men and at the hound. And the great hound they used to see every day at the hunting was at this time no bigger than a lap-dog that would be with a queen or a high person. And one of the young men was watching over the dog, and his sword in his hand, and another of them was holding a vessel of white silver to the mouth of the dog; and any drink any one of the three would ask for, the dog would put it out of his mouth into the vessel.

Then one of the young men said to the hound: "Well, noble one and brave one and just one, take notice of the treachery that is done to you by Finn." When the dog heard that he turned to the King of Ulster's sons, and there rose a dark Druid wind that blew away the shields from their shoulders and the swords from their sides into the wall of fire. And then the three men came out and made an end of them; and when that was done the dog came and breathed on them, and they turned to ashes on the moment, and there was never blood or flesh or bone of them found after.

And the three battalions of the Fianna divided themselves into companies of nine, and went searching through every part of Ireland for the King of Ulster's two sons.

And as to Finn, he went to Teamhair Luachra, and no one with him but the serving-lads and the followers of the army. And the companies of nine that were looking for the King of Ulster's sons came back to him there in the one night; but they brought no word of them, if they were dead or living.

But as to the three sons of the King of Iruath and the hound that was with them, they were seen no more by Finn and the Fianna.

CHAPTER IV
Red Ridge

There was another young man came and served Finn for a while; out of Connacht he came, and he was very daring, and the Red Ridge was the name they gave him. And he all but went from Finn one time, because of his wages that were too long in coming to him. And the three battalions of the Fianna came trying to quiet him, but he would not stay for them. And at the last Finn himself came, for it is a power he had, if he would make but three verses he would quiet any one. And it is what he said: "Daring Red Ridge," he said, "good in battle, if you go from me to-day with your great name it is a good parting for us. But once at Rath Cro," he said, "I gave you three times fifty ounces in the one day; and at Carn Ruidhe I gave you the full of my cup of silver and of yellow gold. And do you remember," he said, "the time we were at Rath Ai, when we found the two women, and when we ate the nuts, myself and yourself were there together."

And after that the young man said no more about going from him.

And another helper came to Finn one time he was fighting at a ford, and all his weapons were used or worn with the dint of the fight. And there came to him a daughter of Mongan of the Sidhe, bringing him a flat stone having a chain of gold to it. And he took the stone and did great deeds with it. And after the fight the stone fell into the ford, that got the name of Ath Liag Finn.

And that stone will never be found till the Woman of the Waves will find it, and will bring it to land on a Sunday morning; and on that day seven years the world will come to an end.

BOOK III

The Battle of the White Strand

CHAPTER I

The Enemies of Ireland

Of all the great battles the Fianna fought to keep the foreigners out of Ireland, the greatest was the one that was fought at Finntraigh the White Strand, in Munster; and this is the whole story of it, and of the way the Fianna came to have so great a name.

One time the enemies of Ireland gathered together under Daire Donn, High King of the Great World, thinking to take Ireland and to put it under tribute.

The King of Greece was of them, and the King of France, and the King of the Eastern World, and Lughman of the Broad Arms, King of the Saxons, and Fiacha of the Long Hair, King of the Gairean, and Tor the son of Breogan, King of the Great Plain, and Sligech, son of the King of the Men of Cepda, and Comur of the Crooked Sword, King of the Men of the Dog-Heads, and Caitchenn, King of the Men of the Cat-Heads, and Caisel of the Feathers, King of Lochlann, and Madan of the Bent Neck, son of the King of the Marshes, and three kings from the rising of the sun in the east, and Ogarmach, daughter of the King of Greece, the best woman-warrior that ever came into the world, and a great many other kings and great lords.

The King of the World asked then: "Who is there can give me knowledge of the harbours of Ireland?" "I will do that for you, and I will bring you to a good harbour," said Glas, son of Dremen, that had been put out of Ireland by Finn for doing some treachery.

Then the armies set out in their ships, and they were not gone far when the wind rose and the waves, and they could hear nothing but the wild playing of the sea-women, and the screams of frightened birds, and the breaking of ropes and of sails. But after a while, when the wind found no weakness in the heroes, it rose from them and went up into its own high place. And then the sea grew quiet and the waves grew tame and the harbours friendly, and they stopped for a while at an island that was called the Green Rock. But the King of the World said then: "It is not a harbour like this you promised me, Glas, son of Dremen, but a shore of white sand where my armies could have their fairs and their gatherings the time they would not be fighting." "I know a harbour of that sort in the west of Ireland," said Glas, "the Harbour of the White Strand in Corca Duibhne." So they went into their ships again, and went on over the sea towards Ireland.

CHAPTER II

Cael and Credhe

Now as to Finn, when it was shown to him that the enemies of Ireland were coming, he called together the seven battalions of the Fianna. And the place where they gathered was on the hill that was called Fionntulach, the White Hill, in Munster. They often stopped on that hill for a while, and spear-shafts with spells on them were brought to them there, and they had every sort of thing for food, beautiful blackberries, haws of the hawthorn, nuts of the hazels of Cenntire, tender twigs of the bramble bush, sprigs of wholesome gentian, watercress at the beginning of summer. And there would be brought to their cooking-pots birds out of the oak-woods, and squirrels from Berramain, and speckled eggs from the cliffs, and salmon out of Luimnech, and eels of the Sionnan, and woodcocks of Fidhrinne, and otters from the hidden places of the Doile, and fish from the coasts of Buie and Beare, and dulse from the bays of Cleire.

And as they were going to set out southwards, they saw one of their young men, Cael, grandson of Nemhnain, coming towards them. "Where are you come from, Cael?" Finn asked him. "From Brugh na Boinne," said he. "What were you asking there?" said Finn. "I was asking to speak with Muirenn, daughter of Derg, that was my own nurse," said he. "For what cause?" said Finn. "It was about a high marriage and a woman of the Sidhe that was showed to me in a dream; Credhe it was I saw, daughter of the King of Ciarraighe Luachra." "Do you know this, Cael," said Finn, "that she is the greatest deceiver of all the women of Ireland; and there is hardly a precious thing in Ireland but she has coaxed it away to her own great dun." "Do you know what she asks of every man that comes asking for her?" said Cael. "I know it," said Finn; "she will let no one come unless he is able to make a poem setting out the report of her bowls and her horns and her cups, her grand vessels and all her palaces." "I have all that ready," said Cael; "it was given to me by my nurse, Muirenn, daughter of Derg."

They gave up the battle then for that time, and they went on over every hilly place and every stony place till they came to Loch Cuire in the west; and they came to the door of the hill of the Sidhe and knocked at it with the shafts of their long gold-socketed spears. And there came young girls having yellow hair to the windows of the sunny houses; and Credhe herself, having three times fifty women with her, came out to speak with them. "It is to ask you in marriage we are come," said Finn. "Who is it is asking for me?" said she. "It is Cael, the hundred-killer, grandson of Nemhnain, son of the King of Leinster in the east." "I have heard talk of him, but I have never seen him," said Credhe. "And has he any poem for me?" she said. "I have that," said Cael, and he rose up then and sang his poem;

"A journey I have to make, and it is no easy journey, to the house of Credhe against the breast of the mountain, at the Paps of Dana; it is there I must be going through hardships for the length of seven days. It is pleasant her house is, with men and boys and women, with Druids and musicians, with cup-bearer and door-keeper, with horse-boy that does not leave his work, with distributer to share food; and Credhe of the Fair Hair having command over them all.

"It would be delightful to me in her dun, with coverings and with down, if she has but a mind to listen to me.

"A bowl she has with juice of berries in it to make her eyebrows black; crystal vats of fermenting grain; beautiful cups and vessels. Her house is of the colour of lime; there are rushes for beds, and many silken coverings and blue cloaks; red gold is there, and bright drinking-horns. Her sunny house is beside Loch Cuire, made of silver and yellow gold; its ridge is thatched without any fault, with the crimson wings of birds. The doorposts are green, the lintel is of silver taken in battle. Credhe's chair on the left is the delight of delights, covered with gold of Elga; at the foot of the pleasant bed it is, the bed that was made of precious stones by Tuile in the east. Another bed there is on the right, of gold and silver, it is made without any fault, curtains it has of the colour of the foxglove, hanging on rods of copper.

"The people of her house, it is they have delight, their cloaks are not faded white, they are not worn smooth; their hair is fair and curling. Wounded men in their blood would sleep hearing the birds of the Sidhe singing in the eaves of the sunny house.

"If I have any thanks to give to Credhe, for whom the cuckoo calls, she will get better praise than this; if this love-service I have done is pleasing to her, let her not delay, let her say, 'Your coming is welcome to me.'

"A hundred feet there are in her house, from one corner to another; twenty feet fully measured is the width of her great door; her roof has its thatch of the wings of blue and yellow birds, the border of her well is of crystals and carbuncles.

"There is a vat there of royal bronze; the juice of pleasant malt is running from it; over the vat is an apple-tree with its heavy fruit; when Credhe's horn is filled from the vat, four apples fall into it together.

"She that owns all these things both at low water and at flood, Credhe from the Hill of the Three Peaks, she is beyond all the women of Ireland by the length of a spear-cast.

"Here is this song for her, it is no sudden bride-gift it is, no hurried asking; I bring it to Credhe of the beautiful shape, that my coming may be very bright to her."

Then Credhe took him for her husband, and the wedding-feast was made, and the whole of the Fianna stopped there through seven days, at drinking and pleasure, and having every good thing.

CHAPTER III

Conn Crither

Finn now, when he had turned from his road to go to Credhe's house, had sent out watchmen to every landing-place to give warning when the ships of the strangers would be in sight. And the man that was keeping watch at the White Strand was Conn Crither, son of Bran, from Teamhair Luachra.

And after he had been a long time watching, he was one night west from the Round Hill of the Fianna that is called Cruachan Adrann, and there he fell asleep. And while he was in his sleep the ships came; and what roused him was the noise of the breaking of shields and the clashing of swords and of spears, and the cries of women and children and of dogs and horses that were under flames, and that the strangers were making an attack on.

Conn Crither started up when he heard that, and he said: "It is great trouble has come on the people through my sleep; and I will not stay living after this," he said, "for Finn and the Fianna of Ireland to see me, but I will rush into the middle of the strangers," he said, "and they will fall by me till I fall by them."

He put on his suit of battle then and ran down towards the strand. And on the way he saw three women dressed in battle clothes before him, and fast as he ran he could not overtake them. He took his spear then to make a cast of it at the woman was nearest him, but she stopped on the moment, and she said: "Hold your hand and do not harm us, for we are not come to harm you but to help you." "Who are you yourselves?" said Conn Crither. "We are three sisters," she said, "and we are come from Tir nan Og, the Country of the Young, and we have all three given you our love, and no one of us loves you less than the other, and it is to give you our help we are come." "What way will you help me?" said Conn. "We will give you good help," she said, "for we will make Druid armies about you from stalks of grass and from the tops of the watercress, and they will cry out to the strangers and will strike their arms from their hands, and take from them their strength and their eyesight. And we will put a Druid mist about you now," she said, "that will hide you from the armies of the strangers, and they will not see you when you make an attack on them. And we have a well of healing at the foot of Slieve Iolair, the Eagle's Mountain, she said, "and its waters will cure every wound made in battle. And after bathing in that well you will be as whole and as sound as the day you were born. And bring whatever man you like best with you," she said, "and we will heal him along with you."

Conn Crither gave them his thanks for that, and he hurried on to the strand. And it was at that time the armies of the King of the Great Plain were taking spoils from Traigh Moduirn in the north to Finntraighe in the south. And Conn Crither came on them, and the Druid army with him, and he took their spoils from them, and the Druid army took their sight and their strength from them, and they were routed, and they made away to where the King of the Great Plain was, and Conn Crither followed, killing and destroying. "Stop with me, king-hero," said the King of the Great Plain, "that I may fight with you on account of my people, since there is not one of them that turns to stand against you."

So the two set their banners in the earth and attacked one another, and fought a good part of the day until Conn Crither struck off the king's head. And he lifted up the head, and he was boasting of what he had done. "By my word," he said, "I will not let myself be parted from this body till some of the Fianna, few or many, will come to me."

CHAPTER IV

Glas, Son of Dremen

The King of the World heard that, and he said: "It is a big word that man is saying," he said; "and rise up now, Glas, son of Dremen, and see which of the Fianna of Ireland it is that is saying it."

Glas left the ship then, and he went to where Conn Crither was, and he asked who was he. "I am Conn Crither, son of Bran, from Teamhair Luachra," said he. "If that is so," said Glas, "you are of the one blood with myself, for I am Glas, son of Dremen from Teamhair Luachra." "It is not right for you to come fighting against me from those foreigners, so," said Conn. "It is a pity indeed," said Glas; "and but for Finn and the Fianna driving me from them, I would not fight against you or against one of themselves for all the treasures of the whole world." "Do not say that," said Conn, "for I swear by my hand of valour," he said, "if you had killed Finn's own son and the sons of his people along with him, you need not be in dread of him if only you came under his word and his protection." "I think indeed the day is come for me to fight beside you," said Glas, "and I will go back and tell that to the King of the World."

He went back then to where the king was, and the king asked him which of the men of the Fianna was in it. "It is a kinsman of my own is in it, High King," said Glas; "and it is weak my heart is, he to be alone, and I have a great desire to go and help him." "If you go," said the King of the World, "it is what I ask you, to come and to tell me every day how many of the Fianna of Ireland have fallen by me; and if a few of my own men should fall," he said, "come and tell me who it was they fell by." "It is what I ask you," said Glas, "not to let your armies land till the Fianna come to us, but to let one man only come to fight with each of us until that time," he said.

So two of the strangers were sent against them that day, and they got their death by Glas and by Conn Crither. Then they asked to have two men sent against each of them, and that was done; and three times nine fell by them before night. And Conn Crither was covered with wounds after the day, and he said to Glas: "Three women came to me from the Country of the Young, and they promised to put me in a well of healing for my wounds. And let you watch the harbour to-night," he said, "and I will go look for them." So he went to them, and they bathed him in the well of healing, and he was whole of his wounds.

And as to Glas, son of Dremen, he went down to the harbour, and he said: "O King of the World," he said, "there is a friend of mine in the ships, Madan of the Bent Neck, son of the King of the Marshes; and it is what he said in the great world in the east, that he himself would be enough to take Ireland for you, and that he would bring it under tribute to you by one way or another. And I ask you to let him come alone against me to-night, till we see which of us will fight best for Ireland."

So Madan came to the land, and the two attacked one another, and made a very hard fight; but as it was not in the prophecy that Glas would find his death there, it was the son of the King of the Marshes that got his death by him.

And not long after that Conn Crither came back to Glas, and he gave Glas great praise for all he had done.

CHAPTER V

The Help of the Men of Dea

Then Taistellach that was one of Finn's messengers came to the White Strand asking news; and Conn bade him go back to where Finn was and tell him the way things were. But Taistellach would not go until he had wetted his sword in the blood of one of the enemies of Ireland, the same as the others had done. And he sent a challenge to the ships, and Coimhleathan, a champion that was very big and tall, came and fought with him on the strand, and took him in his arms to bring him back living to the ship of the High King; but Taistellach struck his head off in the sea and brought it back to land.

"Victory and blessing be with you!" said Conn Crither. "And go now to-night," he said, "to the house of Bran, son of Febal my father at Teamhair Luachra, and bid him to gather all the Tuatha de Danaan to help us; and go on to-morrow to the Fianna of Ireland." So Taistellach went on to Bran's house, and he told him the whole story and gave him the message.

Then Bran, son of Febal, went out to gather the Tuatha de Danaan, and he went to Dun Sesnain in Ui Conall Gabra, where they were holding a feast at that time. And there he found three of the best young men of the Tuatha de Danaan, Ilbrec the Many Coloured, son of Manannan, and Nemanach the Pearly, son of Angus Og, and Sigmall, grandson of Midhir, and they made him welcome and bade him to stop with them. "There is a greater thing than this for you to do, Men of Dea," said Bran; and he told them the whole story, and the way Conn Crither his son was. "Stop with me to-night," said Sesnan, "and my son Dolb will go to Bodb Dearg, son of the Dagda, and gather in the Tuatha de Danaan to us."

So he stopped there, and Dolb, son of Sesnan, went to Sidhe Bean Finn above Magh Femen, and Bodb Dearg was there at that time, and Dolb gave him his message. "Young man," said Bodb Dearg, "we are no way bound to help the men of Ireland out of that strait." "Do not say that," said Dolb, "for there is not a king's son or a prince or a leader of the Fianna of Ireland without having a wife or a mother or a foster-mother or a sweetheart of the Tuatha de Danaan; and it is good help they have given you every time you were in want of it." "I give my word," said Bodb Dearg, "it is right to give a good answer to so good a messenger." With that he sent word to the Tuatha de Danaan in every place where they were, and they gathered to him. And from that they went on to Dun Sesnain, and they stopped there through the night. And they rose up in the morning and put on their shirts of the dearest silk and their embroidered coats of rejoicing, and they took their green shields and their swords and their spears. And their leaders at that time besides Bodb Dearg were Midhir of Bri Leith, and Lir of Sidhe Finna-chaidh, and Abarthach, son of Ildathach, and Ilbrec, son of Manannan, and Fionnbhar of Magh Suil, and Argat Lamh, the Silver Hand, from the Sionnan, and the Man of Sweet Speech from the Boinn.

And the whole army of them came into Ciarraighe Luachra, and to red-haired Slieve Mis, and from that to the harbour of the White Strand. "O Men of Dea," said Abarthach then, "let a high mind and high courage rise within you now in the face of the battle. For the doings of every one among you," he said, "will be told till the end of the world; and let you fulfil now the big words you have spoken in the drinking-houses." "Rise up, Glas, son of Dremen," said Bodb Dearg then, "and tell out to the King of the World that I am come to do battle." Glas went then to the King of the World. "Are those the Fianna of Ireland I see?" said the king. "They are not," said Glas, "but another part of the men of Ireland that do not dare to be on the face of the earth, but that live in hidden houses under the earth, and it is to give warning of battle from them I am come." "Who will answer the Tuatha de Danaan for me?" said the King of the World. "We will go against them," said two of the kings that were with him, Comur Cromchenn, King of the Men of the Dog-Heads, and Caitchenn, King of the Men of the Cat-Heads. And they had five red-armed battalions with them, and they went to the shore like great red waves. "Who is there to match with the King of the Dog-Heads for me?" said Bodb Dearg. "I will go against him," said Lir of Sidhe Finnachaidh, "though I heard there is not in the world a man with stronger hands than himself." "Who will be a match for the King of the Cat-Heads?" said Bodb Dearg. "I will be a match for him," said Abarthach, son of Ildathach.

So Lir and the King of the Dog-Heads attacked one another, and they made a hard fight; but after a while Lir was getting the worst of it. "It is a pity the way Lir is," said Bodb Dearg; "and let some of you rise up and help him," he said. Then Ilbrec, son of Manannan, went to his help; but if he did, he got a wound himself and could do nothing. Then Sigmal, grandson of Midhir, went to his help, and after him the five sons of Finnaistucan, and others of the Men of Dea, but they were all driven off by the King of the Dog-Heads. But at that time Abarthach had made an end of the King of the Cat-Heads, and he rose on his spear, and made a leap, and came down between Lir and his enemy. "Leave off now and look on at the fight," he said to Lir, "and leave it to me and the foreigner." With that he took his sword in his left hand and made a thrust with his spear in through the king's armour. And as the king was raising up his shield, he struck at him with the sword that was in his left hand, and cut off both his legs at the knees, and the king let fall his shield then, and Abarthach struck off his head. And the two kings being dead, their people broke away and ran, but the Men of Dea followed them and made an end of them all; but if they did, they lost a good many of their own men.

CHAPTER VI

The March of the Fianna

And Finn and the Fianna were at the house of Credhe yet, and they saw Taistellach coming towards them. It was the custom, now, with Finn when he sent any one looking for news, that it was to himself it was to be told first, the way that if he got bad news he would let on not to mind it; and if it was good news he got, he would have the satisfaction of telling it himself. So Taistellach told him how the foreigners were come to the harbour of the White Strand.

Then Finn turned to his chief men, and he said: "Fianna of Ireland, there never came harm or danger to Ireland to be put aside this great danger that is come against us now. And you get great tribute and great service from the chief men of Ireland," he said, "and if you take that from them it is right for you to defend them now."

And the Fianna all said they would not go back one step from the defence of Ireland. And as to Credhe, she gave every one of them a battle dress, and they were taking leave of her, and Finn said: "Let the woman come along with us till we know is it good or bad the end of this journey will be." So she came with them, bringing a great herd of cattle; and through the whole length of the battle, that lasted a year and a day, she had new milk for them, and it was to her house the wounded were brought for healing.

Then the Fianna set out, and they went to the borders of Ciarraighe Luachra and across by the shores of the Bannlid with their left hand to Slieve Mis, and they made shelters for themselves that night, and kindled fires.

But Caoilte and Oisin and Lugaidh's Son said to one another they would go on to the harbour, the way they would have time to redden their hands in the blood of the foreigners before the rest of the Fianna would come.

And at that time the King of the World bade some of his chief men to go on shore and to bring him back some spoils. So they went to land and they gave out a great shout, and the people of the ships gave out a great shout at the same time. "I swear by the oath my people swear by," said Caoilte, "I have gone round the whole world, but I never heard so many voices together in the one place." And with that he himself and Oisin and Lugaidh's Son made an attack on the strangers, and struck great blows at them. And when Conn Crither and Glas, son of Dremen, heard the noise of those blows, they knew they were struck by some of the Fianna of Ireland, and they came and joined with them, and did great destruction on the strangers, till there was not one left of all that had come to land.

CHAPTER VII

The First Fighters

And in the morning they saw Finn and all his people coming to the rath that is above the harbour. "My father Finn," said Oisin then, "let us fight now with the whole of the foreigners altogether." "That is not my advice," said Finn, "for the number of their armies is too great for us, and we could not stand against them. "But we will send out every day," he said, "some son of a king or of a leader against some king of the kings of the world that is equal in blood to ourselves. And let none of you redden your arms," he said, "but against a king or a chief man at first, for when a king is fallen, his people will be more inclined to give way. And who will give out a challenge of battle from me now?" he said. "I will do that," said the son of Cuban, leader of the Fianna of Munster. "Do not go, my son," said Finn, "for it is not showed to me that you will have good luck in the battle, and I never sent out any man to fight without I knew he would come back safe to me."

"Do not say that," said Cuban's son, "for I would not for the treasure of the whole world go back from a fight on account of a bad foretelling. And as it is my own country they have done their robbery in first," he said, "I will defend it for you." "It is sorrowful I am for that," said Finn, "for whichever of the kings of the world will meet you to-day, yourself and himself will fall together."

Then Glas, son of Dremen, gave out a challenge of fight from Cuban's son, and the King of Greece answered it. And the two fought hand to hand, and the King of Greece made a great cast of his thick spear at Cuban's son, that went through his body and broke his back in two. But he did not take that blow as a gift, but he paid for it with a strong cast of his own golden spear that went through the ringed armour of the King of Greece. And those two fell together, sole to sole, and lip to lip. "There is grief on me, Cuban's son to have fallen," said Finn, "for no one ever went from his house unsatisfied; and a man that I would not keep, or the High King of Ireland would not keep for a week, he would keep him in his house through the length of a year. And let Follamain, his son, be called to me now," he said, "and I will give him his father's name and place."

They stopped there then till the next morning. "Who will go and fight to-day?" said Finn then. "I will do that," said Goll Garb, son of the King of Alban and of the daughter of Goll, son of Morna.

So he put on his battle dress, and there came against him the three kings from the rising of the sun in the east, and their three battalions with them. And Goll Garb rushed among their men, and wounded and maimed and destroyed them, and blinded their eyes for ever, so that their wits went from them, and they called to him to stop his deadly sword for a while. So he did that; and it is what they agreed to take their three kings and to give them over to Goll Garb that he might stop doing destruction with his sword.

"Who will go out and fight to-day?" said Finn, on the morning of the morrow. "I will go," said Oisin, "and the chief men of the sons of Baiscne with me; for we get the best share of all the pleasant things of Ireland, and we should be first to defend her." "I will answer that challenge," said the King of France, "for it is against Finn I am come to Ireland, on account of my wife that he brought away from me; and these men will fall by me now," he said, "and Finn himself at the last; for when the branches of a tree are cut off, it is not hard to cut down the tree itself."

So the King of France and Oisin met one another at the eastern end of the strand, and they struck their banners of soft silk into the green hill, and bared their swords and made a quick attack on one another. And at one time the king struck such a great blow that he knocked a groan out of Oisin. But for all that he was worsted in the end, and great fear came on him, like the fear of a hundred horses at the sound of thunder, and he ran from Oisin, and he rose like a swallow, that his feet never touched the earth at all; and he never stopped till he came to Gleann na-n Gealt, the Valley of Wild Men. And ever since that time, people that have lost their wits make for that valley; and every mad person in Ireland, if he had his way, would go there within twenty-four hours.

And there rose great cries of lamentation from the armies of the World when they saw him going from them, and the Fianna of Ireland raised great shouts of joy.

And when the night was coming on, it is what Finn said: "It is sad and gloomy the King of the World is to-night; and it is likely he will make an attack on us. And which of you will keep watch over the harbour through the night?" he said. "I will," said Oisin, "with the same number that was fighting along with me today; for it is not too much for you to fight for the Fianna of Ireland through a day and a night," he said.

So they went down to the harbour, and it was just at that time the King of the World was saying, "It seems to me, men of the World, that our luck of battle was not good to-day. And let a share of you rise up now," he said, "and make an attack on the Fianna of Ireland." Then there rose up the nine sons of Garb, King of the Sea of Icht, that were smiths, and sixteen hundred of their people along with them, and they all went on shore but Dolar Durba that was the eldest of them. And the sons of Baiscne were ready for them, and they fought a great battle till the early light of the morrow. And not one of them was left alive on either side that could hold a weapon but only Oisin and one of the sons of Garb. And they made rushes at one another, and threw their swords out of their hands, and closed their arms about one another, and wrestled together, so that it was worth coming from the east to the west of the world to see the fight of those two. Then the foreigner gave a sudden great fall to Oisin, to bring him into the sea, for he was a great swimmer, and he thought to get the better of him there. And Oisin thought it would not be worthy of him to refuse any man his place of fighting. So they went into the water together, and they were trying to drown one another till they came to the sand and the gravel of the clear sea. And it was a torment to the heart of the Fianna, Oisin to be in that strait. "Rise up, Fergus of the Sweet Lips," said Finn then, "and go praise my son and encourage him." So Fergus went down to the edge of the sea, and he said: "It is a good fight you are making, Oisin, and there are many to see it, for the armies of the whole world are looking at you, and the Fianna of Ireland. And show now," he said, "your ways and your greatness, for you never went into any place but some woman of high beauty or some king's daughter set her love on you." Then Oisin's courage increased, and anger came on him and he linked his hands behind the back of the foreigner and put him down on the sand under the sea with his face upwards, and did not let him rise till the life was gone from him. And he brought the body to shore then, and struck off his head and brought it to the Fianna.

But there was great grief and anger on Dolar Durba, the eldest of the sons of Garb, that had stopped in the ship, and he made a great oath that he would have satisfaction for his brothers. And he went to the High King, and he said: "I will go alone to the strand, and I will kill a hundred men every day till I have made an end of the whole of the armies of Ireland; and if any one of your own men comes to interfere with me," he said, "I will kill him along with them."

The next morning Finn asked who would lead the battle that day. "I will," said Dubhan, son of Donn. "Do not," said Finn, "but let some other one go."

But Dubhan went to the strand, and a hundred men along with him; and there was no one there before him but Dolar Durba, and he said he was there to fight with the whole of them. And Dubhan's men gave a great shout of laughter when they heard that; but Dolar Durba rushed on them, and he made an end of the whole hundred, without a man of them being able to put a scratch on him. And then he took a hurling stick and a ball, and he threw up the ball and kept it in the air with the hurl from the west to the east of the strand without letting it touch the ground at all. And then he put the ball on his right foot and kicked it high into the air, and when it was coming down he gave it a kick of his left foot and kept it in the air like that, and he rushing like a blast of March wind from one end of the strand to the other. And when he had done that he walked up and down on the strand making great boasts, and challenging the men of Ireland to do the like of those feats. And every day he killed a hundred of the men that were sent against him.

CHAPTER VIII

The King of Ulster's Son

Now it chanced at that time that news of the great battle that was going on reached to the court of the King of Ulster. And the king's son, that was only twelve years of age, and that was the comeliest of all the young men of Ireland, said to his father: "Let me go to help Finn, son of Cumhal, and his men." "You are not old enough, or strong enough, boy; your bones are too soft," said the king. And when the boy went on asking, his father shut him up in some close place, and put twelve young men, his foster-brothers, in charge of him.

There was great anger on the young lad then, and he said to his foster-brothers: "It is through courage and daring my father won a great name for himself in his young youth, and why does he keep me from winning a name for myself? And let you help me now," he said, "and I will be a friend to you for ever." And he went on talking to them and persuading them till he got round them all, and they agreed to go with him to join Finn and the Fianna. And when the king was asleep, they went into the house where the arms were kept, and every lad of them brought away with him a shield and a sword and a helmet and two spears and two greyhound whelps. And they went across Ess Ruadh in the north, and through Connacht of many tribes, and through Caille an Chosanma, the Woods of Defence, that were called the choice of every king and the true honour of every poet, and into Ciarraighe, and so on to the White Strand.

And when they came there Dolar Durba was on the strand, boasting before the men of Ireland. And Oisin was rising up to go against him, for he said he would sooner die fighting with him than see the destruction he was doing every day on his people. And all the wise men and the fighting men and the poets and the musicians of the Fianna gave a great cry of sorrow when they heard Oisin saying that.

And the King of Ulster's son went to Finn and stood before him and saluted him, and Finn asked who was he, and where did he come from. "I am the son of the King of Ulster," he said; "and I am come here, myself and my twelve foster-brothers, to give you what help we can." "I give you a welcome," said Finn.

Just then they heard the voice of Dolar Durba, very loud and boastful. "Who is that I hear?" said the king's son. "It is a man of the foreigners asking for a hundred of my men to go and meet him," said Finn.

Now, when the twelve foster-brothers heard that, they said no word but went down to the strand, unknown to the king's son and to Finn.

"You are not a grown man," said Conan; "and neither yourself or your comrades are fit to face any fighting man at all." "I never saw the Fianna of Ireland till this day," said the young lad; "but I know well that you are Conan Maol, that never says a good word of any man. And you will see now," he said, "if I am in dread of that man on the strand, or of any man in the world, for I will go out against him by myself."

But Finn kept him back and was talking with him; but then Conan began again, and he said: "It is many men Dolar Durba has made an end of, and there was not a man of all those that could not have killed a hundred of the like of you every day."

When the king's son heard that, there was great anger on him, and he leaped up, and just then Dolar Durba gave a great shout on the strand. "What is he giving that shout for?" said the king's son. "He is shouting for more men to come against him," said Conan, "for he is just after killing your twelve comrades." "That is a sorrowful story," said the king's son.

And with that he took hold of his arms, and no one could hold him or hinder him, and he rushed down to the strand where Dolar Durba was. And all the armies of the strangers gave a great shout of laughter, for they thought all Finn's men had been made an end of, when he sent a young lad like that against their best champion. And when the boy heard that, his courage grew the greater, and he fell on Dolar Durba and gave him many wounds before he knew he was attacked at all. And they fought a very hard fight together, till their shields and their swords were broken in pieces. And that did not stop the battle, but they grappled together and fought and wrestled that way, till the tide went over them and drowned them both. And when the sea went over them the armies on each side gave out a great sorrowful cry.

And after the ebb-tide on the morrow, the two bodies were found cold and quiet, each one held fast by the other. But Dolar Durba was beneath the king's son, so they knew it was the young lad was the best and had got the victory. And they buried him, and put a flag-stone over his grave, and keened him there.

CHAPTER IX

The High King's Son

Then Finn said he would send a challenge himself to Daire Donn, the King of the Great World. But Caoilte asked leave to do that day's fighting himself. And Finn said he would agree to that if he could find enough of men to go with him. And he himself gave him a hundred men, and Oisin did the same, and so on with the rest. And he gave out his challenge, and it was the son of the King of the Great Plain that answered it. And while they were in the heat of the fight, a fleet of ships came into the harbour, and Finn thought they were come to help the foreigners. But Oisin looked at them, and he said: "It is seldom your knowledge fails you, Finn, but those are friends of our own: Fiachra, son of the King of the Fianna of the Bretons, and Duaban Donn, son of the King of Tuathmumain with his own people."

And when those that were in the ships, came on shore, they saw Caoilte's banner going down before the son of the King of the Great Plain. And they all went hurrying on to his help, and between them they made an end of the king's son and of all his people.

"Who will keep watch to-night?" said Finn then. "We will," said the nine Garbhs of the Fianna, of Slieve Mis, and Slieve Cua, and Slieve Clair, and Slieve Crot, and Slieve Muice, and Slieve Fuad, and Slieve Atha Moir, and Dun Sobairce and Dundealgan.

And they were not long watching till they saw the King of the Men of Dregan coming towards them, and they fought a fierce battle; and at the end of the night there were left standing but three of the Garbhs, and the King of the Men of Dregan. And they fought till their wits were gone from them; and those four fell together, sole against sole, and lip against lip.

And the fight went on from day to day, and from week to week, and there were great losses on both sides. And when Fergus of the Sweet Lips saw that so many of the Fianna were fallen, he asked no leave but went to Teamhair of the Kings, where the High King of Ireland was, and he told him the way it was with Finn and his people. "That is good," said the High King, "Finn to be in that strait; for there is no labouring man dares touch a pig or a deer or a salmon if he finds it dead before him on account of the Fianna; and there is no man but is in dread to go from one place to another without leave from Finn, or to take a wife till he knows if she has a sweetheart among the Fianna of Ireland. And it is often Finn has given bad judgments against us," he said, "and it would be better for us the foreigners to gain the day than himself."

Then Fergus went out to the lawn where the High King's son was playing at ball. "It is no good help you are giving to Ireland," said Fergus then, "to be playing a game without lasting profit, and strangers taking away your country from you." And he was urging him and blaming him, and great shame came on the young man, and he threw away the stick and went through the people of Teamhair and brought together all the young men, a thousand and twenty of them that were in it. And they asked no leave and no advice from the High King, but they set out and went on till they came to Finntraigh. And Fergus went to where Finn was, and told him the son of the High King of Ireland was come with him; and all the Fianna rose up before the young man and bade him welcome. And Finn said: "Young man," he said, "we would sooner see you coming at a time when there would be musicians and singers and poets and high-up women to make pleasure for you than at the time we are in the straits of battle the way we are now." "It is not for playing I am come," said the young man, "but to give you my service in battle." "I never brought a lad new to the work into the breast of battle," said Finn, "for it is often a lad coming like that finds his death, and I would not wish him to fall through me." "I give my word," said the young man, "I will do battle with them on my own account if I may not do it on yours." Then Fergus of the Fair Lips went out to give a challenge of battle from the son of the High King of Ireland to the King of the World.

"Who will answer the King of Ireland's son for me?" said the King of the World. "I will go against him," said Sligech, King of the Men of Cepda; and he went on shore, and his three red battalions with him. And the High King's son went against them, and his comrades were near him, and they were saying to him: "Take a good heart now into the fight, for the Fianna will be no better pleased if it goes well with you than if it goes well with the foreigner." And when the High King's son heard that, he made a rush through the army of the foreigners, and began killing and overthrowing them, till their chief men were all made an end of. Then Sligech their king came to meet him, very angry and destroying, and they struck at one another and made a great fight, but at the last the King of Ireland's son got the upper hand, and he killed the King of the Men of Cepda and struck off his head.

CHAPTER X

The King of Lochlann and his Sons

And the fighting went on from day to day, and at last Finn said to Fergus of the Sweet Lips: "Go out, Fergus, and see how many of the Fianna are left for the fight to-day." And Fergus counted them, and he said: "There is one battalion only of the Fianna left in good order; but there are some of the men of it," he said, "are able to fight against three, and some that are able to fight against nine or thirty or a hundred." "If that is so," said Finn, "rise up and go to where the King of the World is, and bid him to come out to the great battle."

So Fergus went to the King of the World, and it is the way he was, on his bed listening to the music of harps and pipes. "King of the World," said Fergus, "it is long you are in that sleep; and that is no shame for you," he said, "for it will be your last sleep. And the whole of the Fianna are gone out to their place of battle," he said, "and let you go out and answer them." "In my opinion," said the King of the World, "there is not a man of them is able to fight against me; and how many are there left of the Fianna of Ireland?" "One battalion only that is in good order," said Fergus. "And how many of the armies of the World are there left?" he said. "Thirty battalions came with me to Ireland; and there are twenty of them fallen by the Fianna, and what is left of them is ten red battalions in good order. And there are eight good fighters of them," he said, "that would put down the men of the whole world if they were against me; that is, myself, and Conmail my son, and Ogarmach, the daughter of the King of Greece, that is the best hand in battle of the whole world after myself, and Finnachta of the Teeth, the chief of my household, and the King of Lochlann, Caisel Clumach of the Feathers, and his three sons, Tocha, and Forne of the Broad Shoulders, and Mongach of the Sea."

"I swear by the oath of my people," said the King of Lochlann then, "if any man of the armies goes out against the Fianna before myself and my three sons, we will not go at all, for we would not get the satisfaction we are used to, unless our swords get their fill of blood." "I will go out against them alone," said Forne, the youngest son of the King of Lochlann. With that he put on his battle suit, and he went among the Fianna of Ireland, and a red-edged sword in each of his hands. And he destroyed those of their young men that were sent against him, and he made the strand narrow with their bodies.

And Finn saw that, and it was torment to his heart, and danger of death and loss of wits to him, and he was encouraging the men of Ireland against Forne. And Fergus of the True Lips stood up, and it is what he said: "Fianna of Ireland," he said, "it is a pity the way you are under hardship and you defending Ireland. And one man is taking her from you to-day," he said, "and you are like no other thing but a flock of little birds looking for shelter in a bush from a hawk that is after them. And it is going into the shelter of Finn and Oisin and Caoilte you are," he said; "and not one of you is better than another, and none of you sets his face against the foreigner." "By my oath," said Oisin, "all that is true, and no one of us tries to do better than another keeping him off." "There is not one of you is better than another," said Fergus. Then Oisin gave out a great shout against the King of Lochlann's son. "Stop here with me, king's son," he said, "until I fight with you for the Fianna." "I give my word it is short the delay will be," said Forne.

Then he himself and Oisin made an attack on one another, and it seemed for a while that the battle was going against Oisin. "By my word, Man of Poetry," said Finn then to Fergus of the True Lips, "it is a pity the way you sent my son against the foreigner. And rise up and praise him and hearten him now," he said. So Fergus went down to where the fight was, and he said: "There is great shame on the Fianna, Oisin, seeing you so low in this fight; and there is many a foot messenger and many a horsemen from the daughters of the kings and princes of Ireland looking at you now," he said. And great courage rose in Oisin then, and he drove his spear through the body of Forne, the King of Lochlann's son. And he himself came back to the Fianna of Ireland.

Then the armies of the World gave out a great cry, keening Forne; and there was anger and not fear on his brothers, for they thought it no right thing he to have fallen by a man of the Fianna. And Tocha, the second son of the King of Lochlann, went on shore to avenge his brother. And he went straight into the middle of the Fianna, and gave his sword good feeding on their bodies, till they broke away before him and made no stand till Lugaidh's Son turned round against him. And those two fought a great fight, till their swords were bent and their spears crumbled away, and they lost their golden shields. And at the last Lugaidh's Son made a stroke of his sword that cut through the foreigner's sword, and then he made another stroke that cut his heart in two halves. And he came back high and proud to the Fianna.

Then the third son of the King of Lochlann, Mongach of the Sea, rose up, and all the armies rose up along with him. "Stop here, Men of the World," he said, "for it is not you but myself that has to go and ask satisfaction for the bodies of my brothers." So he went on shore; and it is the way he was, with a strong iron flail in his hand having seven balls of pure iron on it, and fifty iron chains, and fifty apples on every chain, and fifty deadly thorns on every apple. And he made a rush through the Fianna to break them up entirely and to tear them into strings, and they gave way before him. And great shame came on Fidach, son of the King of the Bretons, and he said: "Come here and praise me, Fergus of the True Lips, till I go out and fight with the foreigner." "It is easy to praise you, son," said Fergus, and he was praising him for a long time.

Then the two looked at one another and used fierce, proud words. And then

Mongach of the Sea raised his iron flail and made a great below at the King of the Bretons' son. But he made a quick leap to one side and gave him a blow of his sword that cut off his two hands at the joint; and he did not stop at that, but made a blow at his middle that cut him into two halves. But as he fell, an apple of the flail with its deadly thorns went into Fidach's comely mouth and through his brain, and it was foot to foot those two fell, and lip to lip.

And the next that came to fight on the strand was the King of Lochlann himself, Caisel of the Feathers. And he came to the battle having his shield on his arm; and it is the way the shield was, that was made for him by the smith of the Fomor, there were red flames coming from it; and if it was put under the sea itself, not one of its flames would stop blazing. And when he had that shield on his arm no man could come near him.

And there was never such destruction done on the men of Ireland as on that day, for the flames of fire that he sent from his shield went through the bodies of men till they blazed up like a splinter of oak that was after hanging through the length of a year in the smoke of a chimney; and any one that would touch the man that was burning would catch fire himself. And every other harm that ever came into Ireland before was small beside this.

Then Finn said: "Lift up your hands, Fianna of Ireland, and give three shouts of blessing to whoever will hinder this foreigner." And the Fianna gave those three shouts; and the King of Lochlann gave a great laugh when he heard them. And Druimderg, grandson of the Head of the Fianna of Ulster, was near him, and he had with him a deadly spear, the Croderg, the Red-Socketed, that came down from one to another of the sons of Rudraighe. And he looked at the King of Lochlann, and he could see no part of him without armour but his mouth that was opened wide, and he laughing at the Fianna. Then Druimderg made a cast with the Croderg that hit him in the open mouth, and he fell, and his shield fell along with its master, and its flame went out. And Druimderg struck the head from his body, and made great boasts of the things he had done.

CHAPTER XI

Labran's Journey

It is then Fergus of the True Lips set out again and went through the length of Ireland till he came to the house of Tadg, son of Nuada, that was grandfather to Finn.

And there was great grief on Muirne, Finn's mother, and on Labran of the Long Hand her brother, and on all her people, when they knew the great danger he was in. And Tadg asked his wife who did she think would escape with their lives from the great fighting at the White Strand. "It is a pity the way they are there," said she; "for if all the living men of the world were on one side, Daire Donn, the King of the World, would put them all down; for there are no weapons in the world that will ever be reddened on him. And on the night he was born, the smith of the Fomor made a shield and a sword, and it is in the prophecy that he will fall by no other arms but those. And it is to the King of the Country of the Fair Men he gave them to keep, and it is with him they are now." "If that is so," said Tadg, "you might be able to get help for Finn, son of Cumhal, the only son of your daughter. And bid Labran Lamfada to go and ask those weapons of him," he said. "Do not be asking me," said she, "to go against Daire Donn that was brought up in my father's house." But after they had talked for a while, they went out on the lawn, and they sent Labran looking for the weapons in the shape of a great eagle.

And he went on from sea to sea, till at noon on the morrow he came to the dun of the King of the Country of the Fair Men; and he went in his own shape to the dun and saluted the king, and the king bade him welcome, and asked him to stop with him for a while. "There is a thing I want more than that," said Labran, "for the wife of a champion of the Fianna has given me her love, and I cannot get her without fighting for her; and it is the loan of that sword and that shield you have in your keeping I am come asking now," he said.

There were seven rooms, now, in the king's house that opened into one another, and on the first door was one lock, and on the second two locks, and so on to the door of the last room that had seven locks; and it was in that the sword and the shield that were made by the smith of the Fomor were kept. And they were brought out and were given to Labran, and stalks of luck were put with them, and they were bound together with shield straps.

Then Labran of the Long Hand went back across the seas again, and he reached his father's dun between the crowing of the cock and the full light of day; and the weakness of death came on him. "It is a good message you are after doing, my son," said Tadg, "and no one ever went that far in so short a time as yourself." "It is little profit that is to me," said Labran, "for I am not able to bring them to Finn in time for the fight to-morrow."

But just at that time one of Tadg's people saw Aedh, son of Aebinn, that was as quick as the wind over a plain till the middle of every day, and after that, there was no man quicker than he was. "You are come at a good time," said Tadg. And with that he gave him the sword and the shield to bring to Finn for the battle.

So Aedh, son of Aebinn, went with the swiftness of a hare or of a fawn or a swallow, till at the rising of the day on the morrow he came to the White Strand. And just at that time Fergus of the True Lips was rousing up the Fianna for the great fight, and it is what he said: "Fianna of Ireland," he said, "if there was the length of seven days in one day, you would have work to fill it now; for there never was and there never will be done in Ireland a day's work like the work of to-day."

Then the Fianna of Ireland rose up, and they saw Aedh, son of Aebinn, coming towards them with his quick running, and Finn asked news from him. "It is from the dun of Tadg, son of Nuada, I am come," he said, "and it is to yourself I am sent, to ask how it is you did not redden your weapons yet upon the King of the World." "I swear by the oath of my people," said Finn, "if I do not redden my weapons on him, I will crush his body within his armour." "I have here for you, King of the Fianna," said Aedh then, "the deadly weapons that will bring him to his death; and it was Labran of the Long Hand got them for you through his Druid arts." He put them in Finn's hand then, and Finn took the coverings off them, and there rose from them flashes of fire and deadly bubbles; and not one of the Fianna could stay looking at them, but it put great courage into them to know they were with Finn. "Rise up now," said Finn to Fergus of the True Lips, "and go where the King of the World is, and bid him to come out to the place of the great fight."

CHAPTER XII

The Great Fight

Then the King of the World came to the strand, and all his armies with him; and all that were left of the Fianna went out against them, and they were like thick woods meeting one another, and they made great strokes, and there were swords crashing against bones, and bodies that were hacked, and eyes that were blinded, and many a mother was left without her son, and many a comely wife without her comrade.

Then the creatures of the high air answered to the battle, foretelling the destruction that would be done that day; and the sea chattered of the losses, and the waves gave heavy shouts keening them, and the water-beasts roared to one another, and the rough hills creaked with the danger of the battle, and the woods trembled mourning the heroes, and the grey stones cried out at their deeds, and the wind sobbed telling them, and the earth shook, foretelling the slaughter; and the cries of the grey armies put a blue cloak over the sun, and the clouds were dark; and the hounds and the whelps and the crows, and the witches of the valley, and the powers of the air, and the wolves of the forests, howled from every quarter and on every side of the armies, urging them against one another.

It was then Conan, son of Morna, brought to mind that himself and his kindred had done great harm to the sons of Baiscne, and he had a wish to do some good thing for them on account of that, and he raised up his sword and did great deeds.

And Finn was over the battle, encouraging the Fianna; and the King of the

World was on the other side encouraging the foreigners. "Rise up now, Fergus," said Finn, "and praise Conan for me that his courage may be the greater, for it is good work he is doing on my enemies." So Fergus went where Conan was, and at that time he was heated with the dust of the fight, and he was gone outside to let the wind go about him.

"It is well you remember the old quarrel between the sons of Morna and the sons of Baiscne, Conan," said Fergus; "and you would be ready to go to your own death if it would bring harm on the sons of Baiscne," he said. "For the love of your good name, Man of Poetry," said Conan, "do not be speaking against me without cause, and I will do good work on the foreigners when I get to the battle again." "By my word," said Fergus, "that would be a good thing for you to do." He sang a verse of praise for him then, and Conan went back into the battle, and his deeds were not worse this time than they were before. And Fergus went back to where Finn was.

"Who is best in the battle now?" said Finn. "Duban, son of Cas, a champion of your own people," said Fergus, "for he never gives but the one stroke to any man, and no man escapes with his life from that stroke, and three times nine and eighty men have fallen by him up to this time." And Duban Donn, great-grandson of the King of Tuathmumhain, was there listening to him, and it is what he said: "By my oath, Fergus," he said, "all you are saying is true, for there is not a son of a king or of a lord is better in the battle than Duban, son of Cas; and I will go to my own death if I do not go beyond him." With that he went rushing through the battle like flames over a high hill that is thick with furze. Nine times he made a round of the battle, and he killed nine times nine in every round.

"Who is best in the battle now?" said Finn, after a while. "It is Duban Donn that is after going from us," said Fergus. "For there has been no one ahead of him since he was in his seventh year, and there is no one ahead of him now." "Rise up and praise him that his courage may be the greater," said Finn. "It is right to praise him," said Fergus, "and the foreigners running before him on every side as they would run from a heavy drenching of the sea." So Fergus praised him for a while, and he went back then to Finn.

"Who is best in the battle now?" said Finn. "It is Osgar is best in it now," said Fergus, "and he is fighting alone against two hundred Franks and two hundred of the men of Gairian, and the King of the Men of Gairian himself. And all these are beating at his shield," he said, "and not one of them has given him a wound but he gave him a wound back for it." "What way is Caoilte, son of Ronan?" said Finn. "He is in no great strait after the red slaughter he has made," said Fergus. "Go to him then," said Finn, "and bid him to keep off a share of the foreigners from Osgar." So Fergus went to him. "Caoilte," he said, "it is great danger your friend Osgar is in under the blows of the foreigners, and let you rise up and give him some help," he said.

Caoilte went then to the place where Osgar was, and he gave a straight blow of his sword at the man who was nearest him, that made two halves of him. Osgar raised his head then and looked at him. "It is likely, Caoilte," he said, "you did not dare redden your sword on anyone till you struck down a man that was before my sword. And it is a shame for you," he said, "all the men of the great world and the Fianna of Ireland to be in the one battle, and you not able to make out a fight for yourself without coming to take a share of my share of the battle. And I give my oath," he said, "I would be glad to see you put down in your bed of blood on account of that thing." Caoilte's mind changed when he heard that, and he turned again to the army of the foreigners with the redness of anger on his white face; and eighty fighting men fell in that rout.

"What way is the battle now?" said Finn. "It is a pity," said Fergus, "there never came and there never will come any one that can tell the way it is now. For by my word," he said, "the tree-tops of the thickest forest in the whole of the western world are not closer together than the armies are now. For the bosses of their shields are in one another's hands. And there is fire coming from the edges of their swords," he said, "and blood is raining down like a shower on a day of harvest; and there were never so many leaves torn by the wind from a great forest as there are locks of long golden hair, and of black curled hair, cut off by sharp weapons, blowing into the clouds at this time. And there is no person could tell one man from another, now," he said, "unless it might be by their voices." With that he went into the very middle of the fight to praise and to hearten the men of the Fianna.

"Who is first in the battle now, Fergus?" said Finn, when he came back to him. "By my oath, it is no friend of your own is first in it," said Fergus, "for it is Daire Donn, the King of the World; and it is for you he is searching through the battle," he said, "and three times fifty of his own people were with him. But two of the men of your Fianna fell on them," he said, "Cairell the Battle Striker, and Aelchinn of Cruachan, and made an end of them. But they were not able to wound the King of the World," he said, "but the two of them fell together by him."

Then the King of the World came towards Finn, and there was no one near him but Arcallach of the Black Axe, the first that ever brought a wide axe into Ireland. "I give my word," said Arcallach, "I would never let Finn go before me into any battle." He rose up then and made a terrible great blow of his axe at the king, that went through his royal crown to the hair of his head, but that did not take a drop of blood out of him, for the edge of the axe turned and there went balls of fire over the plain from that blow. And the King of the World struck back at Arcallach, and made two halves of him.

Then Finn and the King of the World turned on one another. And when the king saw the sword and the shield in Finn's hand, he knew those were the weapons that were to bring him to his death, and great dread came on him, and his comeliness left him, and his fingers were shaking, and his feet were unsteady, and the sight of his eyes was weakened.

And then the two fought a great fight, striking at one another like two days of judgment for the possession of the world.

But the king, that had never met with a wound before, began to be greatly weakened in the fight. And Finn gave great strokes that broke his shield and his sword, and that cut off his left foot, and at the last he struck off his head. But if he did, he himself fell into a faint of weakness with the dint of the wounds he had got.

Then Finnachta of the Teeth, the first man of the household of the King of the World, took hold of the royal crown of the king, and brought it where Conmail his son was, and put it on his head.

"That this may bring you success in many battles, my son," he said. And he gave him his father's weapons along with it; and the young man went through the battle looking for Finn, and three fifties of the men of the Fianna fell by him. Then Goll Garbh the Rough, son of the King of Alban, saw him and attacked him, and they fought a hard fight. But the King of Albain's son gave him a blow under the shelter of the shield, in his left side, that made an end of him.

Finnachta of the Teeth saw that, and he made another rush at the royal crown, and brought it to where Ogarmach was, the daughter of the King of Greece. "Put on that crown, Ogarmach," he said, "as it is in the prophecy the world will be owned by a woman; and it will never be owned by any woman higher than yourself," he said.

She went then to look for Finn in the battle, and Fergus of the True Lips saw her, and he went where Finn was. "O King of the Fianna," he said then, "bring to mind the good fight you made against the King of the World and all your victories before that; for it is a great danger is coming to you now," he said, "and that is Ogarmach, daughter of the King of Greece."

With that the woman-fighter came towards him. "O Finn," she said, "it is little satisfaction you are to me for all the kings and lords that have fallen by you and by your people; but for all that," she said, "there is nothing better for me to get than your own self and whatever is left of your people." "You will not get that," said Finn, "for I will lay your head in its bed of blood the same as I did to every other one." Then those two attacked one another like as if there had risen to smother one another the flooded wave of Cliodna, and the seeking wave of Tuaigh, and the big brave wave of Rudraighe. And though the woman-warrior fought for a long time, a blow from Finn reached to her at last and cut through the royal crown, and with a second blow he struck her head off. And then he fell himself in his bed of blood, and was the same as dead, but that he rose again.

And the armies of the World and the Fianna of Ireland were fallen side by side there, and there were none left fit to stand but Cael, son of Crimthan of the Harbours, and the chief man of the household of the King of the World, Finnachta of the Teeth. And Finnachta went among the dead bodies and lifted up the body of the King of the World and brought it with him to his ship, and he said: "Fianna of Ireland," he said, "although it is bad this battle was for the armies of the World, it was worse for yourselves; and I am going back to tell that in the East of the World," he said. Finn heard him saying that, and he lying on the ground in his blood, and the best men of the sons of Baiscne about him, and he said: "It is a pity I not to have found death before I heard the foreigner saying those words. And nothing I myself have done, or the Fianna of Ireland, is worth anything since there is left a man of the foreigners alive to go back into the great world again to tell that story. And is there any one left living near me?" he said. "I am," said Fergus of the True Lips. "What way is the battle now?" said Finn. "It is a pity the way it is," said Fergus, "for, by my word," he said, "since the armies met together to-day, no man of the foreigners or of the men of Ireland took a step backward from one another till they all fell foot to foot, and sole to sole. And there is not so much as a blade of grass or a grain of sand to be seen," he said, "with the bodies of fighting men that are stretched on them; and there is no man of the two armies that is not stretched in that bed of blood, but only the chief man of the household of the King of the World, and your own foster-son, Cael, son of Crimthan of the Harbours." "Rise up and go to him," said Finn. So Fergus went where Cael was, and asked what way was he. "It is a pity the way I am," said Cael, "for I swear by my word that if my helmet and my armour were taken from me, there is no part of my body but would fall from the other; and by my oath," he said, "it is worse to me to see that man beyond going away alive than I myself to be the way I am. And I leave my blessing to you, Fergus," he said; "and take me on your back to the sea till I swim after the foreigner, and it is glad I would be the foreigner to fall by me before the life goes out from my body." Fergus lifted him up then and brought him to the sea, and put him swimming after the foreigner. And Finnachta waited for him to reach the ship, for he thought he was one of his own people. And Cael raised himself up when he came beside the ship, and Finnachta stretched out his hand to him. And Cael took hold of it at the wrist, and clasped his fingers round it, and gave a very strong pull at him, that brought him over the side. Then their hands shut across one another's bodies, and they went down to the sand and the gravel of the clear sea.

CHAPTER XIII

Credhe's Lament

Then there came the women and the musicians and the singers and the physicians of the Fianna of Ireland to search out the kings and the princes of the Fianna, and to bury them; and every one that might be healed was brought to a place of healing.

And Credhe, wife of Cael, came with the others, and went looking through the bodies for her comely comrade, and crying as she went. And as she was searching, she saw a crane of the meadows and her two nestlings, and the cunning beast the fox watching the nestlings; and when the crane covered one of the birds to save it, he would make a rush at the other bird, the way she had to stretch herself out over the birds; and she would sooner have got her own death by the fox than her nestlings to be killed by him. And Credhe was looking at that, and she said: "It is no wonder I to have such love for my comely sweetheart, and the bird in that distress about her nestlings."

Then she heard a stag in Druim Ruighlenn above the harbour, that was making great lamentations for his hind from place to place, for they had been nine years together, and had lived in the wood at the foot of the harbour, Fidh Leis, and Finn had killed the hind, and the stag was nineteen days without tasting grass or water, lamenting after the hind. "It is no shame for me," said Credhe, "I to die for grief after Cael, since the stag is shortening his life sorrowing after the hind."

Then she met with Fergus of the True Lips. "Have you news of Cael for me, Fergus?" she said. "I have news," said Fergus, "for he and the last man that was left of the foreigners, Finnachta Fiaclach, are after drowning one another in the sea."

And at that time the waves had put Cael back on the strand, and the women and the men of the Fianna that were looking for him raised him up, and brought him to the south of the White Strand.

And Credhe came to where he was, and she keened him and cried over him, and she made this complaint:—

"The harbour roars, O the harbour roars, over the rushing race of the Headland of the Two Storms, the drowning of the hero of the Lake of the Two Dogs, that is what the waves are keening on the strand.

"Sweet-voiced is the crane, O sweet-voiced is the crane in the marshes of the Ridge of the Two Strong Men; it is she cannot save her nestlings, the wild dog of two colours is taking her little ones.

170

"Pitiful the cry, pitiful the cry the thrush is making in the Pleasant Ridge, sorrowful is the cry of the blackbird in Leiter Laeig.

"Sorrowful the call, O sorrowful the call of the deer in the Ridge of Two Lights; the doe is lying dead in Druim Silenn, the mighty stag cries after her.

"Sorrowful to me, O sorrowful to me the death of the hero that lay beside me; the son of the woman of the Wood of the Two Thickets, to be with a bunch of grass under his head.

"Sore to me, O sore to me Cael to be a dead man beside me, the waves to have gone over his white body; it is his pleasantness that has put my wits astray.

"A woeful shout, O a woeful shout the waves are making on the strand; they that took hold of comely Cael, a pity it is he went to meet them.

"A woeful crash, O a woeful crash the waves are making on the strand to the north, breaking against the smooth rock, crying after Cael now he is gone.

"A sorrowful fight, O a sorrowful fight, the sea is making with the strand to the north; my beauty is lessened; the end of my life is measured.

"A song of grief, O a song of grief is made by the waves of Tulcha Leis; all I had is gone since this story came to me. Since the son of Crimthann is drowned I will love no one after him for ever; many a king fell by his hand; his shield never cried out in the battle."

After she had made that complaint, Credhe laid herself down beside Cael and died for grief after him. And they were put in the one grave, and it was Caoilte raised the stone over them.

And after that great battle of the White Strand, that lasted a year and a day, there was many a sword and shield left broken, and many a dead body lying on the ground, and many a fighting man left with a foolish smile on his face.

And the great name that was on the armies of the World went from them to the Fianna of Ireland; and they took the ships and the gold and the silver and all the spoils of the armies of the World. And from that time the Fianna had charge of the whole of Ireland, to keep it from the Fomor and from any that might come against it.

And they never lost power from that time until the time of their last battle, the sorrowful battle of Gabhra.

Huntings and Enchantments

CHAPTER I

The King of Britain's Son

Arthur, son of the King of Britain, came one time to take service with Finn, and three times nine men along with him. And they went hunting one day on Beinn Edair, and Finn took his place on the Cairn of the Fianna between the hill and the sea, and Arthur took his stand between the hunt and the sea, the way the deer would not escape by swimming.

And while Arthur was there he took notice of three of Finn's hounds, Bran, and Sceolan and Adhnuall, and he made a plan in his mind to go away across the sea, himself and his three nines, bringing those three hounds along with him. So he did that, and he himself and his men brought away the hounds and crossed the sea, and the place where they landed was Inver Mara Gamiach on the coast of Britain. And after they landed, they went to the mountain of Lodan, son of Lir, to hunt on it.

And as to the Fianna, after their hunting was done they gathered together on the hill; and as the custom was, all Finn's hounds were counted. Three hundred full-grown hounds he had, and two hundred whelps; and it is what the poets used to say, that to be counting them was like counting the branches on a tree.

Now on this day when they were counted, Bran and Sceolan and Adhnuall were missing; and that was told to Finn. He bade his people to search again through the three battalions of the Fianna, but search as they would, the hounds were not to be found.

Then Finn sent for a long-shaped basin of pale gold, and water in it, and he put his face in the water, and his hand over his face, and it was showed him what had happened, and he said: "The King of Britain's son has brought away the hound. And let nine men be chosen out to follow after them," he said. So nine men were chosen out, Diarmuid, grandson of Duibhne; Goll, son of Morna; Oisin, son of Finn; Faolan, the friend of the hounds, son of a woman that had come over the sea to give her love to Finn; Ferdoman, son of Bodb Dearg; two sons of Finn, Raighne Wide Eye and Cainche the Crimson-Red; Glas, son of Enchered Bera, with Caoilte and Lugaidh's Son. And their nine put their helmets on their heads, and took their long spears in their hands, and they felt sure they were a match for any four hundred men from the east to the west of the world.

They set out then, till they came to the mountain of Lodan, son of Lir; and they were not long there till they heard talk of men that were hunting in that place.

Arthur of Britain and his people were sitting on a hunting mound just at that time, and the nine men of the Fianna made an attack on them and killed all of them but Arthur, that Goll, son of Morna, put his two arms about and saved from death. Then they turned to go back to Ireland, bringing Arthur with them, and the three hounds. And as they were going, Goll chanced to look around him and he saw a dark-grey horse, having a bridle with fittings of worked gold. And then he looked to the left and saw a bay mare that was not easy to get hold of, and it having a bridle of silver rings and a golden bit. And Goll took hold of the two, and he gave them into Oisin's hand, and he gave them on to Diarmuid.

They went back to Finn then, bringing his three hounds with them, and the King of Britain's son as a prisoner; and Arthur made bonds with Finn, and was his follower till he died.

And as to the horse and the mare, they gave them to Finn; and the mare bred eight times, at every birth eight foals, and it is of that seed came all the horses of the fair Fianna of the Gael, for they had used no horses up to that time.

And that was not the only time Finn was robbed of some of his hounds. For there was a daughter of Roman was woman-Druid to the Tuatha de Danaan, and she set her love on Finn. But Finn said, so long as there was another woman to be found in the world, he would not marry a witch. And one time, three times fifty of Finn's hounds passed by the hill where she was; and she breathed on the hounds and shut them up in the hill, and they never came out again. It was to spite Finn she did that, and the place got the name of Duma na Conn, the Mound of the Hounds.

And as to Adhnuall, one of the hounds Finn thought most of, and that was brought back from the King of Britain's son, this is the way he came to his death afterwards.

There was a great fight one time between the Fianna and Macoon, son of Macnia, at some place in the province of Leinster, and a great many of the Fianna were killed. And the hound Adhnuall went wandering northward from the battle and went astray; and three times he went round the whole of Ireland, and then he came back to the place of the battle, and to a hill where three young men of the Fianna that had fallen there were buried after their death, and three daughters of a King of Alban that had died for love of them. And when Adhnuall came to that hill, he gave three loud howls and he stretched himself out and died.

CHAPTER II

The Cave of Ceiscoran

Finn called for a great hunt one time on the plains of Magh Chonaill and in the forest parts of Cairbre of the Nuts. And he himself went up to the top of Ceiscoran, and his two dogs Bran and Sceolan with him.

And the Fianna were shouting through the whole country where they were hunting, the way the deer were roused in their wild places and the badgers in their holes, and foxes in their wanderings, and birds on the wing.

And Conaran, son of Imidd, of the Tuatha de Danaan, had the sway in Ceiscoran at that time, and when he heard the shouting and the cry of the hounds all around, he bade his three daughters that had a great share of enchantments, to do vengeance on Finn for his hunting.

The three women went then to the opening of a cave that was in the hills, and there they sat down together, and they put three strong enchanted hanks of yarn on crooked holly-sticks, and began to reel them off outside the cave.

They were not long there till Finn and Conan came towards them, and saw the three ugly old hags at their work, their coarse hair tossed, their eyes red and bleary, their teeth sharp and crooked, their arms very long, their nails like the tips of cows' horns, and the three spindles in their hands.

Finn and Conan passed through the hanks of yarn to get a better look at the hags. And no sooner had they done that, than a deadly trembling came on them and a weakness, and the bold hags took hold of them and put them in tight bonds.

Two other men of the Fianna came up then, and the sons of Menhann along with them, and they went through the spindles to where Finn and Conan were, and their strength went from them in the same way, and the hags tied them fast and carried them into the cave.

They were not long there till Caoilte and Lugaidh's Son came to the place, and along with them the best men of the sons of Baiscne. The sons of Morna came as well, and no sooner did they see the hanks than their strength and their bravery went out of them the same as it went from the others.

And in the end the whole number of them, gentle and simple, were put in bonds by the hags, and brought into the cave. And there began at the mouth of the cave a great outcry of hounds calling for their masters that had left them there. And there was lying on the hillside a great heap of deer, and wild pigs, and hares, and badgers, dead and torn, that were brought as far as that by the hunters that were tied up now in the cave.

Then the three women came in, having swords in their hands, to the place where they were lying, to make an end of them. But first they looked out to see was there ever another man of the Fianna to bring in and to make an end of with the rest.

And they saw coming towards them a very tall man that was Goll, son of Morna, the Flame of Battle. And when the three hags saw him they went to meet him, and they fought a hard battle with him. And great anger came on Goll, and he made great strokes at the witches, and at the last he raised up his sword, and with one blow he cut the two that were nearest him through and through.

And then the oldest of the three women wound her arms about Goll, and he beheading the two others, and he turned to face her and they wrestled together, till at last Goll gave her a great twist and threw her on the ground. He tied her fast then with the straps of a shield, and took his sword to make an end of her. But the hag said: "O champion that was never worsted, strong man that never went back in battle, I put my body and my life under the protection of your bravery. And it is better for you," she said, "to get Finn and the Fianna safe and whole than to have my blood; and I swear by the gods my people swear by," she said, "I will give them back to you again."

With that Goll set her free, and they went together into the hill where the Fianna were lying. And Goll said: "Loose off the fastenings first from Fergus of the True Lips and from the other learned men of the Fianna; and after that from Finn, and Oisin, and the twenty-nine sons of Morna, and from all the rest."

She took off the fastenings then, and the Fianna made no delay, but rose up and went out and sat down on the side of the hill. And Fergus of the Sweet Lips looked at Goll, son of Morna, and made great praises of him, and of all that he had done.

CHAPTER III

Donn, Son of Midhir

One time the Fianna were at their hunting at the island of Toraig to the north of Ireland, and they roused a fawn that was very wild and beautiful, and it made for the coast, and Finn and six of his men followed after it through the whole country, till they came to Slieve-nam-Ban. And there the fawn put down its head and vanished into the earth, and none of them knew where was it gone to.

A heavy snow began to fall then that bent down the tops of the trees like a willow-gad, and the courage and the strength went from the Fianna with the dint of the bad weather, and Finn said to Caoilte: "Is there any place we can find shelter to-night?" Caoilte made himself supple then, and went over the elbow of the hill southward.

And when he looked around him he saw a house full of light, with cups and horns and bowls of different sorts in it. He stood a good while before the door of the house, that he knew to be a house of the Sidhe, thinking would it be best go in and get news of it, or to go back to Finn and the few men that were with him. And he made up his mind to go into the house, and there he sat down on a shining chair in the middle of the floor; and he looked around him, and he saw, on the one side, eight-and-twenty armed men, each of them having a well-shaped woman beside him. And on the other side he saw six nice young girls, yellow-haired, having shaggy gowns from their shoulders. And in the middle there was another young girl sitting in a chair, and a harp in her hand, and she playing on it and singing. And every time she stopped, a man of them would give her a horn to drink from, and she would give it back to him again, and they were all making mirth around her.

She spoke to Caoilte then. "Caoilte, my life," she said, "give us leave to attend on you now." "Do not," said Caoilte, "for there is a better man than myself outside, Finn, son of Cumhal, and he has a mind to eat in this house to-night." "Rise up, Caoilte, and go for Finn," said a man of the house then; "for he never refused any man in his own house, and he will get no refusal from us."

Caoilte went back then to Finn, and when Finn saw him he said: "It is long you are away from us, Caoilte, for from the time I took arms in my hands I never had a night that put so much hardship on me as this one."

The six of them went then into the lighted house and their shields and their arms with them. And they sat down on the edge of a seat, and a girl having yellow hair came and brought them to a shining seat in the middle of the house, and the newest of every food, and the oldest of every drink was put before them. And when the sharpness of their hunger and their thirst was lessened, Finn said: "Which of you can I question?" "Question whoever you have a mind to," said the tallest of the men that was near him. "Who are you yourself then?" said Finn, "for I did not think there were so many champions in Ireland, and I not knowing them."

"Those eight-and-twenty armed men you see beyond," said the tall man, "had the one father and mother with myself; and we are the sons of Midhir of the Yellow Hair, and our mother is Fionnchaem, the fair, beautiful daughter of the King of the Sidhe of Monaid in the east. And at one time the Tuatha de Danaan had a gathering, and gave the kingship to Bodb Dearg, son of the Dagda, at his bright hospitable place, and he began to ask hostages of myself and of my brothers; but we said that till all the rest of the Men of Dea had given them, we would not give them. Bodb Dearg said then to our father: 'Unless you will put away your sons, we will wall up your dwelling-place on you.' So the eight-and-twenty brothers of us came out to look for a place for ourselves; and we searched all Ireland till we found this secret hidden place, and we are here ever since. And my own name," he said, "is Donn, son of Midhir. And we had every one of us ten hundred armed men belonging to himself, but they are all worn away now, and only the eight-and-twenty of us left." "What is it is wearing you away?" said Finn. "The Men of Dea," said Donn, "that come three times in every year to give battle to us on the green outside." "What is the long new grave we saw on the green outside?" said Finn. "It is the grave of Diangalach, a man of enchantments of the Men of Dea; and that is the greatest loss came on them yet," said Donn; "and it was I myself killed him," he said. "What loss came next to that?" said Finn. "All the Tuatha de Danaan had of jewels and riches and treasures, horns and vessels and cups of pale gold, we took from them at the one time." "What was the third greatest loss they had?" said Finn. "It was Fethnaid, daughter of Feclach, the womanharper of the Tuatha de Danaan, their music and the delight of their minds," said Donn.

"And to-morrow," he said, "they will be coming to make an attack on us, and there is no one but myself and my brothers left; and we knew we would be in danger, and that we could make no stand against them. And we sent that bare-headed girl beyond to Toraig in the North in the shape of a foolish fawn, and you followed her here. It is that girl washing herself, and having a green cloak about her, went looking for you.

"And the empty side of the house," he said, "belonged to our people that the Men of Dea have killed."

They spent that night in drinking and in pleasure. And when they rose up in the morning of the morrow, Donn, son of Midhir, said to Finn, "Come out with me now on the lawn till you see the place where we fight the battles every year." They went out then and they looked at the graves and the flag-stones, and Donn said: "It is as far as this the Men of Dea come to meet us." "Which of them come here?" said Finn.

"Bodb Dearg with his seven sons," said Donn; "and Angus Og, son of the Dagda, with his seven sons; and Finnbharr of Cnoc Medha with his seventeen sons; Lir of Sidhe Fionnachaidh with his twenty-seven sons and their sons; Tadg, son of Nuada, out of the beautiful hill of Almhuin; Donn of the Island and Donn of the Vat; the two called Glas from the district of Osraige; Dobhran Dubthaire from the hill of Liamhain of the Smooth Shirt; Aedh of the Island of Rachrainn in the north; Ferai and Aillinn and Lir and Fainnle, sons of Eogobal, from Cnoc Aine in Munster; Cian and Coban and Conn, three sons of the King of Sidhe Monaid in Alban; Aedh Minbhreac of Ess Ruadh with his seven sons; the children of the Morrigu, the Great Queen, her six-and-twenty women warriors, the two Luaths from Magh Lifé; Derg and Drecan out of the hill of Beinn Edair in the east; Bodb Dearg himself with his great household, ten hundred ten score and ten. Those are the chief leaders of the Tuatha de Danaan that come to destroy our hill every year."

Finn went back into the hill then, and told all that to his people.

"My people," he said, "it is in great need and under great oppression the sons of

Midhir are, and it is into great danger we are come ourselves. And unless we make a good fight now," he said, "it is likely we will never see the Fianna again."

"Good Finn," every one of them said then, "did you ever see any drawing-back in any of us that you give us that warning?" "I give my word," said Finn, "if I would go through the whole world having only this many of the Fianna of Ireland along with me, I would not know fear nor fright. And good Donn," he said, "is it by day or by night the Men of Dea come against you?" "It is at the fall of night they come," said Donn, "the way they can do us the most harm."

So they waited till night came on, and then Finn said: "Let one of you go out now on the green to keep watch for us, the way the Men of Dea will not come on us without word or warning."

And the man they set to watch was not gone far when he saw five strong battalions of the Men of Dea coming towards him. He went back then to the hill and he said: "It is what I think, that the troops that are come against us this time and are standing now around the grave of the Man of Enchantments are a match for any other fighting men."

Finn called to his people then, and he said: "These are good fighters are come against you, having strong red spears. And let you all do well now in the battle. And it is what you have to do," he said, "to keep the little troop of brothers, the sons of Midhir, safe in the fight; for it would be a treachery to friendship any harm to come on them, and we after joining them; and myself and Caoilte are the oldest among you, and leave the rest of the battle to us."

Then from the covering time of evening to the edge of the morning they fought the battle. And the loss of the Tuatha de Danaan was no less a number than ten hundred ten score and ten men. Then Bodb Dearg and Midhir and Fionnbhar said to one another: "What are we to do with all these? And let Lir of Sidhe Fionnachaidh give us an advice," they said, "since he is the oldest of us." And Lir said: "It is what I advise, let every one carry away his friends and his fosterlings, his sons and his brothers, to his own place. And as for us that stop here," he said, "let a wall of fire be made about us on the one side, and a wall of water on the other side." Then the Men of Dea put up a great heap of stones, and brought away their dead; and of all the great slaughter that Finn and his men and the sons of Midhir had made, there was not left enough for a crow to perch upon.

And as to Finn and his men, they went back into the hill, hurt and wounded and worn-out.

And they stopped in the hill with the sons of Midhir through the whole length of a year, and three times in the year the Men of Dea made an attack on the hill, and a battle was fought.

And Conn, son of Midhir, was killed in one of the battles; and as to the Fianna, there were so many wounds on them that the clothing was held off from their bodies with bent hazel sticks, and they lying in their beds, and two of them were like to die. And Finn and Caoilte and Lugaidh's Son went out on the green, and

Caoilte said: "It was a bad journey we made coming to this hill, to leave two of our comrades after us." "It is a pity for whoever will face the Fianna of Ireland," said Lugaidh's Son, "and he after leaving his comrades after him." "Whoever will go back and leave them, it will not be myself," said Finn. Then Donn, son of Midhir, came to them. "Good Donn," said Finn, "have you knowledge of any physician that can cure our men?" "I only know one physician could do that," said Donn; "a physician the Tuatha de Danaan have with them. And unless a wounded man has the marrow of his back cut through, he will get relief from that physician, the way he will be sound at the end of nine days." "How can we bring that man here," said Finn, "for those he is with are no good friends to us?" "He goes out every morning at break of day," said Donn, "to gather healing herbs while the dew is on them." "Find some one, Donn," said Caoilte, "that will show me that physician, and, living or dead, I will bring him with me."

Then Aedh and Flann, two of the sons of Midhir, rose up. "Come with us, Caoilte," they said, and they went on before him to a green lawn with the dew on it; and when they came to it they saw a strong young man armed and having a cloak of the wool of the seven sheep of the Land of Promise, and it full of herbs of healing he was after gathering for the Men of Dea that were wounded in the battle. "Who is that man?" said Caoilte. "That is the man we came looking for," said Aedh. "And mind him well now," he said, "that he will not make his escape from us back to his own people."

They ran at him together then, and Caoilte took him by the shoulders and they brought him away with them to the ford of the Slaine in the great plain of Leinster, where the most of the Fianna were at that time; and a Druid mist rose up about them that they could not be seen.

And they went up on a little hill over the ford, and they saw before them four young men having crimson fringed cloaks and swords with gold hilts, and four good hunting hounds along with them. And the young man could not see them because of the mist, but Caoilte saw they were his own two sons, Colla and Faolan, and two other young men of the Fianna, and he could hear them talking together, and saying it was a year now that Finn, son of Cumhal, was gone from them. "And what will the Fianna of Ireland do from this out," said one of them, "without their lord and their leader?" "There is nothing for them to do," said another, "but to go to Teamhair and to break up there, or to find another leader for themselves." And there was heavy sorrow on them for the loss of their lord; and it was grief to Caoilte to be looking at them.

And he and the two sons of Midhir went back then by the Lake of the Two Birds to Slieve-nam Ban, and they went into the hill.

And Finn and Donn gave a great welcome to Luibra, the physician, and they showed him their two comrades that were lying in their wounds. "Those men are brothers to me," said Donn, "and tell me how can they be cured?" Luibra looked then at their wounds, and he said: "They can be cured if I get a good reward."

"You will get that indeed," said Caoilte; "and tell me now," he said, "how long will it take to cure them?" "It will take nine days," said Luibra. "It is a good reward you will get," said Caoilte, "and this is what it is, your own life to be left to you. But if these young men are not healed," he said, "it is my own hand will strike off your head."

And within nine days the physician had done a cure on them, and they were as well and as sound as before.

And it was after that time the High King sent a messenger to bring the Fianna to the Feast of Teamhair. And they all gathered to it, men and women, boys and heroes and musicians. And Goll, son of Morna, was sitting at the feast beside the king. "It is a great loss you have had, Fianna of Ireland," said the king, "losing your lord and your leader, Finn, son of Cumhal." "It is a great loss indeed," said Goll.

"There has no greater loss fallen on Ireland since the loss of Lugh, son of Ethne," said the king. "What orders will you give to the Fianna now, king?" said Goll. "To yourself, Goll," said the king, "I will give the right of hunting over all Ireland till we know if the loss of Finn is lasting." "I will not take Finn's place," said Goll, "till he has been wanting to us through the length of three years, and till no person in Ireland has any hope of seeing him again."

Then Ailbe of the Freckled Face said to the king: "What should these seventeen queens belonging to Finn's household do?" "Let a safe, secret sunny house be given to every one of them," said the king; "and let her stop there and her women with her, and let provision be given to her for a month and a quarter and a year till we have knowledge if Finn is alive or dead."

Then the king stood up, and a smooth drinking-horn in his hand, and he said: "It would be a good thing, men of Ireland, if any one among you could get us news of Finn in hills or in secret places, or in rivers or invers, or in any house of the Sidhe in Ireland or in Alban."

With that Berngal, the cow-owner from the borders of Slieve Fuad, that was divider to the King of Ireland, said: "The day Finn came out from the north, following after a deer of the Sidhe, and his five comrades with him, he put a sharp spear having a shining head in my hand, and a hound's collar along with it, and he bade me to keep them till he would meet me again in the same place." Berngal showed the spear and the collar then to the king and to Goll, and they looked at them and the king said: "It is a great loss to the men of Ireland the man is that owned this collar and this spear. And were his hounds along with him?" he said. "They were," said Berngal; "Bran and Sceolan were with Finn, and Breac and Lainbhui with Caoilte, and Conuall and Comrith with Lugaidh's Son."

The High King called then for Fergus of the True Lips, and he said: "Do you know how long is Finn away from us?" "I know that well," said Fergus; "it is a month and a quarter and a year since we lost him. And indeed it is a great loss he is to the Fianna of Ireland," he said, "himself and the men that were with him." "It is a great loss indeed," said the king, "and I have no hope at all of finding those six that were the best men of Ireland or of Alban."

And then he called to Cithruadh, the Druid, and he said: "It is much riches and many treasures Finn gave you, and tell us now is he living or is he dead?" "He is living," said Cithruadh then. "But as to where he is, I will give no news of that," he said, "for he himself would not like me to give news of it." There was great joy among them when they heard that, for everything Cithruadh had ever foretold had come true. "Tell us when will he come back?" said the king. "Before the Feast of Teamhair is over," said the Druid, "you will see the Leader of the Fianna drinking at it."

And as to Finn and his men, they stopped in the House of the Two Birds till they had taken hostages for Donn, son of Midhir, from the Tuatha de Danaan. And on the last day of the Feast of Teamhair they came back to their people again.

And from that time out the Fianna of Ireland had not more dealings with the people living in houses than they had with the People of the Gods of Dana.

CHAPTER IV

The Hospitality of Cuanna's House

It happened one day Finn and Oisin and Caoilte and Diarmuid and Lugaidh's Son went up on the top of Cairn Feargall, and their five hounds with them, Bran and Sceolan, Sear Dubh, Luath Luachar and Adhnuall. And they were not long there till they saw a giant coming towards them, very tall and rough and having an iron fork on his back and a squealing pig between the prongs of the fork. And there was a beautiful eager young girl behind the giant, shoving him on before her. "Let some one go speak with those people," said Finn. So Diarmuid went towards them, but they turned away before he came to them. Then Finn and the rest rose up and went after them, but before they came to the giant and the girl, a dark Druid mist rose up that hid the road. And when the mist cleared away, Finn and the rest looked about them, and they saw a good light-roofed house at the edge of a ford near at hand. They went on to the house, and there was a green lawn before it, and in the lawn two wells, and on the edge of one well there was a rough iron vessel, and on the edge of the other a copper vessel. They went into the house then, and they found there a very old white-haired man, standing to the right hand of the door, and the beautiful young girl they saw before, sitting near him, and the great rough giant beside the fire, and he boiling a pig. And on the other side of the fire there was an old countryman, having dark-grey hair and twelve eyes in his head, and his twelve eyes were twelve sons of battle. And there was a ram in the house having a white belly and a very black head, and dark-blue horns and green feet. And there was a hag in the end of the house and a worn grey gown on her, and there was no one in the house but those.

And the man at the door gave them a welcome, and then the five of them sat down on the floor of the house, and their hounds along with them.

"Let great respect be shown to Finn, son of Cumhal, and to his people," said the man at the door. "It is the way I am," said the giant, "to be asking always and getting nothing." But for all that he rose up and showed respect to Finn.

Presently there came a great thirst on Finn, and no one took notice of it but Caoilte, and he began complaining greatly. "Why are you complaining, Caoilte?" said the man at the door; "you have but to go out and get a drink for Finn at whichever of the wells you will choose." Caoilte went out then, and he brought the full of the copper vessel to Finn, and Finn took a drink from it, and there was the taste of honey on it while he was drinking, and the taste of gall on it after, so that fierce windy pains and signs of death came on him, and his appearance changed, that he would hardly be known. And Caoilte made greater complaints than he did before on account of the way he was, till the man at the door bade him to go out and to bring him a drink from the other well. So Caoilte did that, and brought in the full of the iron vessel. And Finn never went through such great hardship in any battle as he did drinking that draught, from the bitterness of it; but no sooner did he drink it than his own colour and appearance came back to him and he was as well as before, and his people were very glad when they saw that.

Then the man of the house asked was the pig ready that was in the cauldron. "It is ready," said the giant; "and leave the dividing of it to me," he said. "What way will you divide it?" said the man of the house. "I will give one hind quarter to Finn and his dogs," said the giant, "and the other hind quarter to Finn's four comrades; and the fore quarter to myself, and the chine and the rump to the old man there by the fire and the hag in the corner; and the entrails to yourself and to the young girl that is beside you." "I give my word," said the man of the house, "you have shared it well." "I give my word," said the ram, "it is a bad division to me, for you have forgotten my share in it." With that he took hold of the quarter that was before the Fianna, and brought it into a corner and began to eat it. On that the four of them attacked him with their swords, but with all the hard strokes they gave they could not harm him at all, for the swords slipped from his back the same as they would from a rock. "On my word it is a pity for any one that has the like of you for comrades," said the man with the twelve eyes, "and you letting a sheep bring away your food from you." With that he went up to the ram and took him by the feet and threw him out from the door that he fell on his back, and they saw him no more.

It was not long after that, the hag rose up and threw her pale grey gown over Finn's four comrades, and they turned to four old men, weak and withered, their heads hanging. When Finn saw that there came great dread on him, and the man at the door saw it, and he bade him to come over to him, and to put his head in his breast and to sleep. Finn did that, and the hag took her covering off the four men, the way that when Finn awoke they were in their own shape again, and it is well pleased he was to see that.

"Is there wonder on you, Finn?" said the man at the door, "at the ways of this house?" "I never wondered more at anything I ever saw," said Finn. "I will tell you the meaning of them, so," said the man. "As to the giant you saw first," he said, "having the squealing pig in the prongs of his fork, Sluggishness is his name; and the girl here beside me that was shoving him along is Liveliness, for liveliness pushes on sluggishness, and liveliness goes farther in the winking of an eye than the foot can travel in a year. The old man there beyond with the twelve bright eyes betokens the World, and he is stronger than any other, and he showed that when he made nothing of the ram. The ram you saw betokens the Desires of Men. The hag is Old Age, and her gown withered up your four comrades. And the two wells you drank the two draughts out of," he said, "betoken Lying and Truth; for it is sweet to people to be telling a lie, but it is bitter in the end. And as to myself," he said, "Cuanna from Innistuil is my name, and it is not here I am used to be, but I took a very great love for you, Finn, because of your wisdom and your great name, and so I put these things in your way that I might see you. And the hospitality of Cuanna's house to Finn will be the name of this story to the end of the world. And let you and your men come together now," he said, "and sleep till morning."

So they did that, and when they awoke in the morning, it is where they were, on the top of Cairn Feargall, and their dogs and their arms beside them.

CHAPTER V

Cat-heads and Dog-heads

Nine of the Fianna set out one time, looking for a pup they wanted, and they searched through many places before they found it. All through Magh Leine they searched, and through the Valley of the Swords, and through the storm of Druim Cleibh, and it is pleasant the Plain of the Life looked after it; but not a pup could they find. Then they went searching through Durlass of the generous men, and great Teamhair and Dun Dobhran and Ceanntsaile, men and dogs searching the whole of Ireland, but not a pup could they find.

And while they were going from place to place, and their people with them, they saw the three armies of the sons of the King of Ruadhleath coming towards them. Cat-headed one army was, and the one alongside of it was Dog-headed, and the men of the third army were White-backed.

And when the Fianna saw them coming, Finn held up his shining spear, and light-hearted Caoilte gave out a great shout that was heard in Almhuin, and in Magh Leine, and in Teamhair, and in Dun Reithlein. And that shout was answered by Goll, son of Morna, and by Faolan, Finn's son that was with him, and by the Stutterers from Burren, and by the two sons of Maith Breac, and by Iolunn of the Sharp Edge, and by Cael of the Sharp Sword, that never gave his ear to tale-bearers.

It is pleasant the sound was then of the spears and the armies and of the silken banners that were raised up in the gusty wind of the morning. And as to the banners, Finn's banner, the Dealb-Greine, the Sun-Shape, had the likeness of the sun on it; and Goll's banner was the Fulang Duaraidh, that was the first and last to move in a battle; and Faolan's banner was the Coinneal Catha, the Candle of Battle; and Oisin's banner was the Donn Nimhe, the Dark Deadly One; and Caoilte's was the Lamh Dearg, the Red Hand; and Osgar's was the Sguab Gabhaidh that had a Broom of rowan branches on it, and the only thing asked when the fight was at the hottest was where that Broom was; and merry Diarmuid's banner was the Liath Loinneach, the Shining Grey; and the Craobh Fuileach, the Bloody Branch, was the banner of Lugaidh's Son. And as to Conan, it is a briar he had on his banner, because he was always for quarrels and for trouble. And it used to be said of him he never saw a man frown without striking him, or a door left open without going in through it.

And when the Fianna had raised their banners they attacked the three armies; and first of all they killed the whole of the Cat-Heads, and then they took the Dog-Heads in hand and made an end of them, and of the White-Backs along with them.

And after that they went to a little hill to the south, having a double dun on it, and it is there they found a hound they were able to get a pup from.

And by that time they had searched through the whole of Ireland, and they did not find in the whole of it a hundred men that could match their nine.

And as well as their banners, some of the Fianna had swords that had names to them, Mac an Luin, Son of the Waves, that belonged to Finn; and Ceard-nan Gallan, the Smith of the Branches, that was Oisin's; and Caoilte's Cruadh-Chosgarach, the Hard Destroying One; and Diarmuid's Liomhadoir, the Burnisher; and Osgar's Cosgarach Mhor, the Great Triumphant One.

And it is the way they got those swords: there came one time to where Finn and Caoilte and some others of the Fianna were, a young man, very big and ugly, having but one foot and one eye; a cloak of black skins he had over his shoulders, and in his hand a blunt ploughshare that was turning to red. And he told them he was Lon, son of Liobhan, one of the three smiths of the King of Lochlann. And whether he thought to go away from the Fianna, or to bring them to his smithy, he started running, and they followed after him all through Ireland, to Slieve-na-Righ, and to Luimnech, and to Ath Luain, and by the right side of Cruachan of Connacht, and to Ess Ruadh and to Beinn Edair, and so to the sea.

And wherever it was they found the smithy, they went into it, and there they found four smiths working, and every one of them having seven hands. And Finn and Caoilte and the rest stopped there watching them till the swords were made, and they brought them away with them then, and it is good use they made of them afterwards.

And besides his sword, Mac an Luin, Finn had a shield was called Sgiath Gailbhinn, the Storm Shield; and when it called out it could be heard all through Ireland.

And whether or not it was the Storm Shield, Finn had a wonderful shield that he did great deeds with, and the story of it is this:

At the time of the battle of the Great Battle of Magh Tuireadh, Lugh, after he had struck the head off Balor of the Evil Eye, hung it in the fork of a hazel-tree. And the tree split, and the leaves fell from it with the dint of the poison that dropped from the head. And through the length of fifty years that tree was a dwelling-place of crows and of ravens. And at the end of that time Manannan, son of Lir, was passing by, and he took notice of the tree that it was split and withered, and he bade his men to dig it up. And when they began to dig, a mist of poison rose up from the roots, and nine of the men got their death from it, and another nine after them, and the third nine were blinded. And Luchtaine the Carpenter made a shield of the wood of that hazel for Manannan. And after a while Manannan gave it, and a set of chessmen along with it, to Tadg, son of Nuada; and from him it came to his grandson, Finn, son of Muirne and of Cumhal.

CHAPTER VI

Lomna's Head

Finn took a wife one time of the Luigne of Midhe. And at the same time there was in his household one Lomna, a fool.

Finn now went into Tethra, hunting with the Fianna, but Lomna stopped at the house. And after a while he saw Coirpre, a man of the Luigne, go in secretly to where Finn's wife was.

And when the woman knew he had seen that, she begged and prayed of Lomna to hide it from Finn. And Lomna agreed to that, but it preyed on him to have a hand in doing treachery on Finn. And after a while he took a four-square rod and wrote an Ogham on it, and these were the words he wrote:—

"An alder stake in a paling of silver; deadly night-shade in a bunch of cresses; a husband of a lewd woman; a fool among the well-taught Fianna; heather on bare Ualann of Luigne."

Finn saw the message, and there was anger on him against the woman; and she knew well it was from Lomna he had heard the story, and she sent a message to Coirpre bidding him to come and kill the fool.

So Coirpre came and struck his head off, and brought it away with him.

And when Finn came back in the evening he saw the body, and it without a head. "Let us know whose body is this," said the Fianna. And then Finn did the divination of rhymes, and it is what he said: "It is the body of Lomna; it is not by a wild boar he was killed; it is not by a fall he was killed; it is not in his bed he died; it is by his enemies he died; it is not a secret to the Luigne the way he died. And let out the hounds now on their track," he said.

So they let out the hounds, and put them on the track of Coirpre, and Finn followed them, and they came to a house, and Coirpre in it, and three times nine of his men, and he cooking fish on a spit; and Lomna's head was on a spike beside the fire.

And the first of the fish that was cooked Coirpre divided between his men, but he put no bit into the mouth of the head. And then he made a second division in the same way. Now that was against the law of the Fianna, and the head spoke, and it said: "A speckled white-bellied salmon that grows from a small fish under the sea; you have shared a share that is not right; the Fianna will avenge it upon you, Coirpre." "Put the head outside," said Coirpre, "for that is an evil word for us." Then the head said from outside: "It is in many pieces you will be; it is great fires will be lighted by Finn in Luigne."

And as it said that, Finn came in, and he made an end of Coirpre, and of his men.

CHAPTER VII

Ilbrec of Ess Ruadh

One time Caoilte was hunting on Beinn Gulbain, and he went on to Ess Ruadh. And when he came near the hill of the Sidhe that is there, he saw a young man waiting for him, having a crimson fringed cloak about him, and on his breast a silver brooch, and a white shield, ornamented with linked beasts of red gold, and his hair rolled in a ball at the back, and covered with a golden cup. And he had heavy green weapons, and he was holding two hounds in a silver chain.

And when Caoilte came up to him he gave him three loving kisses, and sat down beside him on the grass. "Who are you, young champion?" said Caoilte. "I am Derg, son of Eoghan of the people of Usnach," he said, "and foster-brother of your own." Caoilte knew him then, and he said: "And what is your life with your mother's people, the Tuatha de Danaan in Sidhe Aedha?" "There is nothing wanting to us there of food or of clothing," said the young man. "But for all that," he said, "I would sooner live the life of the worst treated of the serving-boys of the Fianna than the life I am living in the hill of the Sidhe." "Lonely as you are at your hunting to-day," said Caoilte, "it is often I saw you coming to the Valley of the Three Waters in the south, where the Siuir and the Beoir and the Berba come together, with a great company about you; fifteen hundred young men, fifteen hundred serving-boys, and fifteen hundred women." "That was so," said Derg; "and although myself and my gentle hound are living in the hill of the Sidhe, my mind is always on the Fianna. And I remember well the time," he said, "when you yourself won the race against Finn's lasting black horse. And come now into the hill," he said, "for the darkness of the night is coming on."

So he brought Caoilte into the hill with him, and they were set down in their right places.

It was at that time, now, there was great war between Lir of Sidhe Fionnachaidh and Ilbrec of Ess Ruadh. There used a bird with an iron beak and a tail of fire to come every evening to a golden window of Ilbrec's house, and there he would shake himself till he would not leave sword on pillow, or shield on peg, or spear in rack, but they would come down on the heads of the people of the house; and whatever they would throw at the bird, it is on the heads of some of themselves it would fall. And the night Caoilte came in, the hall was made ready for a feast, and the bird came in again, and did the same destruction as before, and nothing they threw at him would touch him at all. "Is it long the bird has been doing this?" said Caoilte. "Through the length of a year now," said Derg, "since we went to war with Sidhe Fionnachaidh."

Then Caoilte put his hand within the rim of his shield, and he took out of it a copper rod he had, and he made a cast of it at the bird, that brought it down on the floor of the hall. "Did any one ever make a better cast than that?" said Ilbrec. "By my word," said Caoilte, "there is no one of us in the Fianna has any right to boast against another." Then Ilbrec took down a sharp spear, having thirty rivets of gold in it, from its place, and he said: "That is the Spear of Fiacha, son of Congha, and it is with that Finn made an end of Aillen, son of Midhna, that used to burn Teamhair. And keep it beside you now, Caoilte," he said, "till we see will Lir come to avenge his bird on us."

Then they took up their horns and their cups, and they were at drinking and pleasure, and Ilbrec said: "Well, Caoilte," he said, "if Lir comes to avenge his bird on us, who will you put in command of the battle?" I will give the command to Derg there beyond," said he. "Will you take it in hand, Derg?" said the people of the hill. "I will take it," said Derg, "with its loss and its gain."

So that is how they spent the night, and it was not long in the morning till they heard blowing of horns, and rattling of chariots, and clashing of shields, and the uproar of a great army that came all about the hill. They sent some of their people out then to see were there many in it, and they saw three brave armies of the one size. "It would be a great vexation to me," said Aedh Nimbrec, the Speckled, then, "we to get our death and Lir's people to take the hill." "Did you never hear, Aedh," said Caoilte, "that the wild boar escapes sometimes from both hounds and from wolves, and the stag in the same way goes away from the hounds with a sudden start; and what man is it you are most in dread of in the battle?" he said. "The man that is the best fighter of all the Men of Dea," said they all, "and that is Lir of Sidhe Fionnachaidh." "The thing I have done in every battle I will not give up to-day," said Caoilte, "to meet the best man that is in it hand to hand." "The two that are next to him in fighting," they said then, "are Donn and Dubh." "I will put down those two," said Derg.

Then the host of the Sidhe went out to the battle, and the armies attacked one another with wide green spears and with little casting spears, and with great stones; and the fight went on from the rising of the day till midday. And then Caoilte and Lir met with one another, and they made a very fierce fight, and at the last Lir of Sidhe Fionnachaidh fell by the hand of Caoilte.

Then the two good champions Dubh and Donn, sons of Eirrge, determined to go on with the battle, and it is how they fought, Dubh in the front of the whole army, and Donn behind all, guarding the rear. But Derg saw that, and he put his finger into the thong of his spear and made a cast at the one that was nearest him, and it broke his back and went on into the body of the other, so that the one cast made an end of the two. And that ended the battle, and all that was left of the great army of Lir went wearing away to the north. And there was great rejoicing in the hill at Ess Ruadh, and Ilbrec took the spoils of the beaten army for his people, and to Caoilte he gave the enchanted spear of Fiacha, together with nine rich cloaks and nine long swords with hilts and guards of gold, and nine hounds for hunting. And they said farewell to one another, and Caoilte left his blessing to the people of the hill, and he brought their thanks with him. And as hard as the battle had been, it was harder again for Derg to part from his comrade, and the day he was parted from Finn and from all the Fianna was no sadder to him than this day.

It was a long time after that Caoilte went again to the hill of Ilbrec at Ess Ruadh, and this is the way it happened.

It was in a battle at Beinn Edair in the east that Mane, son of the King of Lochlann, made a cast at him in the middle of the battle with a deadly spear. And he heard the whistling of the spear, and it rushing to him; and he lifted his shield to protect his head and his body, but that did not save him, for it struck into his thigh, and left its poison in it, so that he had to go in search of healing. And it is where he went, to the hill of the Sidhe at Ess Ruadh, to ask help of Bebind, daughter of Elcmar of Brugh na Boinne, that had the drink of healing of the

Tuatha de Danaan, and all that was left of the ale of Goibniu that she used to be giving out to them.

And Caoilte called to Cascorach the Musician, son of Caincenn, and bade him bring his harp and come along with him. And they stopped for a night in the hill of the Sidhe of Druim Nemed in Luigne of Connacht, and from that they went forward by Ess Dara, the Fall of the Oaks, and Druim Dearg na Feinne, the Red Ridge of the Fianna, and Ath Daim Glas, the Ford of the Grey Stag and to Beinn Gulbain, and northward into the plain of Ceitne, where the Men of Dea used to pay their tribute to the Fomor; and up to the Footstep of Ess Ruadh, and the High Place of the Boys, where the boys of the Tuatha de Danaan used to be playing their hurling. And Aedh of Ess Ruadh and Ilbrec of Ess Ruadh were at the door of the hill, and they gave Caoilte a true welcome. "I am glad of that welcome," said Caoilte And then Bebind, daughter of Elcmar of Brugh na Boinne, came out, and three times fifty comely women about her, and she sat down on the green grass and gave three loving kisses to the three, to Caoilte and to Cascorach and to Fermaise, that had come with them out of the hill of the Sidhe in Luigne of Connacht. And all the people of the hill welcomed them, and they said: "It is little your friendship would be worth if you would not come to help us and we in need of help." "It was not for bravery I was bade come," said Cascorach; "but when the right time comes I will make music for you if you have a mind to hear it." "It is not for deeds of bravery we are come," said Fermaise, "but we will give you our help if you are in need of it." Then Caoilte told them the cause of his journey. "We will heal you well," said they. And then they all went into the hill and stayed there three days and three nights at drinking and pleasure.

And indeed it was good help Caoilte and Cascorach gave them after that. For there was a woman-warrior used to come every year with the ships of the men of Lochlann to make an attack on the Tuatha de Danaan. And she had been reared by a woman that knew all enchantments, and there was no precious thing in all the hills of the Sidhe but she had knowledge of it, and would bring it away. And just at this time there came a messenger to the door of the hill with news that the harbour was full of ships, and that a great army had landed, and the woman-warrior along with it.

And it was Cascorach the Musician went out against her, having a shield he got the loan of from Donn, son of Midhir; and she used high words when she saw so young a man coming to fight with her, and he alone. But he made an end of her for all her high talk, and left her lying on the strand with the sea foam washing up to her.

And as to Caoilte, he went out in a chariot belonging to Midhir of the Yellow Hair, son of the Dagda, and a spear was given him that was called Ben-badb, the War-Woman, and he made a cast of the spear that struck the King of Lochlann, that he fell in the middle of his army, and the life went from him. And Fermaise went looking for the king's brother, Eolus, that was the comeliest of all the men of the world; and he knew him by the band of gold around his head, and his green armour, and his red shield, and he killed him with a cast of a five-pronged spear. And when the men of Lochlann saw their three leaders were gone, they went into their ships and back to their own country. And there was great joy through the whole country, both among the men of Ireland and the Tuatha de Danaan, the men of Lochlann to have been driven away by the deeds of Caoilte and Fermaise and Cascorach.

And that was not all they did, for it was at that time there came three flocks of beautiful red birds from Slieve Fuad in the north, and began eating the green grass before the hill of the Sidhe. "What birds are those?" said Caoilte. "Three flocks they are that come and destroy the green every year, eating it down to the bare flag-stones, till they leave us no place for our races," said Ilbrec. Then Caoilte and his comrades took up three stones and threw them at the flocks and drove them away. "Power and blessings to you," said the people of the Sidhe then, "that is a good work you have done. And there is another thing you can do for us," they said, "for there are three ravens come to us every year out of the north, and the time the young lads of the hill are playing their hurling, each one of the ravens carries off a boy of them. And it is to-morrow the hurling will be," they said.

So when the full light of day was come on the morrow, the whole of the Tuatha de Danaan went out to look at the hurling; and to every six men of them was given a chess-board, and a board for some other game to every five, and to every ten men a little harp, and a harp to every hundred men, and pipes that were sharp and powerful to every nine.

Then they saw the three ravens from the north coming over the sea, and they pitched on the great tree of power that was on the green, and they gave three gloomy screeches, that if such a thing could be, would have brought the dead out of the earth or the hair off the head of the listeners; and as it was, they took the courage out of the whole gathering.

Then Cascorach, son of Caincenn, took a man of the chessmen and made a cast at one of the ravens that struck his beak and his throat, and made an end of him; and Fermaise killed the second of them, and Caoilte the third of them in the same way.

"Let my cure be done now," said Caoilte, "for I have paid my fee for it, and it is time." "You have paid it indeed," said Ilbrec. "And where is Behind, daughter of Elcmar?" he said. "I am here," said she.

"Bring Caoilte, son of Ronan, with you into some hidden place," he said, "and do his cure, and let him be well served, for he has driven every danger from the Men of Dea and from the Sons of the Gael. And let Cascorach make music for him, and let Fermaise, son of Eogabil, be watching him and guarding him and attending him."

So Elcmar's daughter went to the House of Arms, and her two sons with her, and a bed of healing was made ready for Caoilte, and a bowl of pale gold was brought to her, and it full of water. And she took a crystal vessel and put herbs into it, and she bruised them and put them in the water, and gave the bowl to Caoilte, and he drank a great drink out of it, that made him cast up the poison of the spear that was in him. Five drinks of it he took, and after that she gave him new milk to drink; but with the dint of the reaching he was left without strength through the length of three days and three nights.

"Caoilte, my life," she said then, "in my opinion you have got relief." "I have got it indeed," he said, "but that the weakness of my head is troubling me." "The washing of Flann, daughter of Flidais, will be done for you now," she said, "and the head that washing is done for will never be troubled with pain, or baldness, or weakness of sight." So that cure was done to him for a while; and the people of the hill divided themselves into three parts; the one part of their best men and great nobles, and another of their young men, and another of their women and poets, to be visiting him and making mirth with him as long as he would be on his bed of healing. And everything that was best from their hunting, it was to him they would bring it.

And one day, when Elcmar's daughter and her two sons and Cascorach and Fermaise were with Caoilte, there was heard a sound of music coming towards them from the waters of Ess Ruadh, and any one would leave the music of the whole world for that music. And they put their harps on the corners of the pillars and went out, and there was wonder on Caoilte that they left him. And he took notice that his strength and the strength of his hands was not come to him yet, and he said: "It is many a rough battle and many a hard fight I went into, and now there is not enough strength in me so much as to go out along with the rest," and he cried tears down.

And the others came back to him then, and he asked news of them. "What was that sound of music we heard?" he said. "It was Uaine out of the hill of the Sidhe, at the Wave of Cliodna in the south," said they; "and with her the birds of the Land of Promise; and she is musician to the whole of that country. And every year she goes to visit one of the hills of the Sidhe, and it is our turn this time." Then the woman from the Land of Promise came into the house, and the birds came in along with her, and they pitched on the pillars and the beams, and thirty of them came in where Caoilte was, and began singing together. And Cascorach took his harp, and whatever he would play, the birds would sing to it. "It is much music I have heard," said Caoilte, "but music so good as that I never heard before."

And after that Caoilte asked to have the healing of his thigh done, and the daughter of Elcmar gave herself to that, and all that was bad was sucked from the wound by her serving people till it was healed. And Caoilte stopped on where he was for three nights after that.

And then the people of the hill rose up and went into the stream to swim. And Caoilte said: "What ails me now not to go swim, since my health has come back to me?" And with that he went into the water. And afterwards they went back into the hill, and there was a great feast made that night.

And Caoilte bade them farewell after that, and Cascorach, but Fermaise stopped with them for a while. And the people of the hill gave good gifts to Caoilte; a fringed crimson cloak of wool from the seven sheep of the Land of Promise; and a fish-hook that was called Aicil mac Mogha, and that could not be set in any river or inver but it would take fish; and along with that they gave him a drink of remembrance, and after that drink there would be no place he ever saw, or no battle or fight he ever was in, but it would stay in his memory. "That is a good help from kinsmen and from friends," said Caoilte.

Then Caoilte and Cascorach went out from the hill, and the people of it made a great lamentation after them.

CHAPTER VIII

The Cave of Cruachan

Caoilte was one time at Cruachan of Connacht, and Cascorach was with him, and there he saw sitting on a heap of stones a man with very rough grey hair, having a dark brown cloak fastened with a pin of bronze, and a long stick of white hazel in his hand; and there was a herd of cattle before him in a fenced field.

Caoilte asked news of him. "I am steward to the King of Ireland," said the old man, "and it is from him I hold this land. And we have great troubles on us in this district," he said. "What troubles are those?" said Caoilte. "I have many herds of cattle," he said, "and every year at Samhain time, a woman comes out of the hill of the Sidhe of Cruachan and brings away nine of the best out of every herd. And as to my name, I am Bairnech, son of Carbh of Collamair of Bregia."

"Who was the best man that ever came out of Collamair?" said Caoilte. "I know, and the men of Ireland and of Alban know," said he, "it was Caoilte, son of Ronan. And do you know where is that man now?" he said. "I myself am that man and your own kinsman," said Caoilte.

When Bairnech heard that, he gave him a great welcome, and Caoilte gave him three kisses. "It seems to me that to-night is Samhain night," said Caoilte. "If that is so, it is to-night the woman will come to rob us," said Bernech. "Let me go to-night to the door of the hill of the Sidhe," said Cascorach. "You may do that, and bring your arms with you," said Caoilte.

So Cascorach went then, and it was not long till he saw the girl going past him out of the hill of Cruachan, having a beautiful cloak of one colour about her; a gown of yellow silk tied up with a knot between her thighs, two spears in her hands, and she not in dread of anything before her or after her.

Then Cascorach blew a blast against her, and put his finger into the thong of his spear, and made a cast at the girl that went through her, and that is the way she was made an end of by Cascorach of the Music.

And then Bernech said to Caoilte: "Caoilte," he said, "do you know the other oppression that is on me in this place?" "What oppression is that?" said Caoilte. "Three she-wolves that come out of the Cave of Cruachan every year and destroy our sheep and our wethers, and we can do nothing against them, and they go back into the cave again. And it will be a good friend that will rid us of them," he said. "Well, Cascorach," said Caoilte, "do you know what are the three wolves that are robbing this man?" "I know well," said Cascorach, "they are the three daughters of Airetach, of the last of the people of oppression of the Cave of Cruachan, and it is easier for them to do their robbery as wolves than as women." "And will they come near to any one?" said Caoilte. "They will only come near to one sort," said Cascorach; "if they see the world's men having harps for music, they will come near to them. And how would it be for me," he said, "to go to-morrow to the cairn beyond, and to bring my harp with me?"

So in the morning he rose up and went to the cairn and stopped on it, playing his harp till the coming of the mists of the evening. And while he was there he saw the three wolves coming towards him, and they lay down before him, listening to the music. But Cascorach found no way to make an attack on them, and they went back into the cave at the end of the day.

Cascorach went back then to Caoilte and told him what had happened. "Go up to-morrow to the same place," said Caoilte, "and say to them it would be better for them to be in the shape of women for listening to music than in the shape of wolves."

So on the morrow Cascorach went out to the same cairn, and set his people about it, and the wolves came there and stretched themselves to listen to the music. And Cascorach was saying to them: "If you were ever women," he said, "it would be better for you to be listening to the music as women than as wolves." And they heard that, and they threw off the dark trailing coverings that were about them, for they liked well the sweet music of the Sidhe.

And when Caoilte saw them there side by side, and elbow by elbow, he made a cast of his spear, and it went through the three women, that they were like a skein of thread drawn together on the spear. And that is the way he made an end of the strange, unknown three. And that place got the name of the Valley of the Shapes of the Wolves.

CHAPTER IX

The Wedding at Ceann Slieve

Finn and the Fianna made a great hunting one time on the hill of Torc that is over Loch Lein and Feara Mor. And they went on with their hunting till they came to pleasant green Slieve Echtge, and from that it spread over other green-topped hills, and through thick tangled woods, and rough red-headed hills, and over the wide plains of the country. And every chief man among them chose the place that was to his liking, and the gap of danger he was used to before. And the shouts they gave in the turns of the hunt were heard in the woods all around, so that they started the deer in the wood, and sent the foxes wandering, and the little red beasts climbing rocks, and badgers from their holes, and birds flying, and fawns running their best. Then they let out their angry small-headed hounds and set them hunting. And it is red the hands of the Fianna were that day, and it is proud they were of their hounds that were torn and wounded before evening.

It happened that day no one stopped with Finn but only Diorraing, son of Domhar. "Well, Diorraing," said Finn, "let you watch for me while I go asleep, for it is early I rose to-day, and it is an early rising a man makes when he cannot see the shadow of his five fingers between himself and the light of day, or know the leaves of the hazel from the leaves of the oak." With that he fell into a quiet sleep that lasted till the yellow light of the evening. And the rest of the Fianna, not knowing where he was gone, gave over the hunt.

And the time was long to Diorraing while Finn was asleep, and he roused him and told him the Fianna must have given up the hunt, for he could not hear a cry or a whistle from them. "The end of day is come," said Finn then, "and we will not follow them to-night. And go now to the wood," he said, "and bring timber and dead branches for a shelter, and I will go looking for food for the night." So Diorraing went to the wood, but he was not gone far till he saw a fine well-lighted house of the Sidhe before him on the edge of the wood near at hand, and he went back to Finn with the news. "Let us go to it," said Finn, "for we ought not to be working in this place, and people living so near at hand." They went then to the door of the house and knocked at it, and the door-keeper came to it. "Whose house is this?" said Diorraing. "It belongs to Conan of Ceann Slieve," said the door-keeper. "Tell him," said Diorraing, "there are two of the Fianna of the Gael at the door."

The door-keeper went in then and told Conan there were two men of the Fianna at the door. "The one of them," he said, "is young and strong, and quiet and fair-haired, and more beautiful than the rest of the men of the world, and he

194

has in his hand a small-headed, white-breasted hound, having a collar of rubbed gold and a chain of old silver. And the other of them," he said, "is brown and ruddy and white-toothed, and he is leading a yellow-spotted hound by a chain of bright bronze." "It is well you have made your report of them," said Conan, "and I know them by it; for the man you spoke of first is Finn, son of Cumhal, Head of the Fianna of Ireland, and Bran in his hand; and the other is Diorraing, and Sceolan in his hand. And go now quickly and let them in," he said.

Finn and Diorraing were brought in then, and they got good attendance, and their arms were taken from them, and a grand feast was made ready that pleased them well. And the wife of Conan was at the one side of Finn, and his daughter, Finndealbh, of the Fair Shape, was at his other side. And they had a great deal of talk together, and at last, seeing her so beautiful, the colour of gold on her curled hair, and her eyes as blue as flowers, and a soft four-cornered cloak fastened at her breast with a silver pin, he asked her of Conan for his wife. "Leave asking that, Finn," said Conan, "for your own courage is not greater than the courage of the man she is promised to." "Who is that?" said Finn. "He is Fatha, son of the King of Ess Ruadh," said Conan. "Your wounds and your danger on yourself," said Diorraing; "and it would be right," he said, "that stammering tongue that gave out those words to be tied and to be shortened for ever, and a drink of death to be given to you; for if the whole of the Men of Dea," he said, "could be put into the one body, Finn would be better than them all." "Leave off, Diorraing," said Finn, "for it is not fighting I am here, but asking a wife, and I will get her whether the Men of Dea think good or bad of it." "I will not be making a quarrel with you," said Conan, "but I put you under bonds as a true hero to answer me everything I am going to ask you." "I will do that," said Finn.

With that Conan put questions to Finn as to his birth and his rearing, and the deeds he had done since he came to the Fianna, and Finn gave full answers to them all. And at last he said: "Let us go on with this no longer, but if you have musicians with you, let them be brought to us now; for it is not my custom," he said, "to be for a single night without music." "Tell me this first," said Conan, "who was it made the Dord Fiann, the Mutterer of the Fianna, and when was it made?" "I will tell you the truth of that," said Finn; "it was made in Ireland by the three sons of Cearmait Honey-Mouth; and nine men used to be sounding it, and since it came to me I have fifty men sounding it." "And tell me this," said Conan, "what is the music pleased you best of all you ever heard?" "I will tell you that," said Finn; "the time the seven battalions of the Fianna are gathered in the one place and raise their spear-shafts over their heads, and the sharp whining of the clear, cold wind goes through them, that is very sweet to me. And when the drinking-hall is set out in Almhuin, and the cup-bearers give out the bright cups to the chief men of the Fianna, that is very sweet to me; and it is sweet to me to be listening to the voice of the sea-gull and the heron, and the noise of the waves of Traig Liath, the song of the three sons of Meardha, the whistle of

Lugaidh's Son, and the voice of the cuckoo in the beginning of summer, and the grunting of the pigs on the Plain of Eithne, and the shouting of laughter in Doire." And it is what he said: "The Dord in the green-topped woods, the lasting wash of the waves against the shore, the noise of the waves at Traig Liath meeting with the river of the White Trout; the three men that came to the Fianna, a man of them gentle and a man of them rough, another man of them ploughing the clouds, they were sweeter than any other thing.

"The grey mane of the sea, the time a man cannot follow its track; the swell that brings the fish to the land, it is sleep-music, its sound is sweet.

"Feargall, son of Fionn, a man that was ready-handed, it is long his leap was, it is well marked his track is; he never gave a story that did not do away with secrets; it is his voice was music of sleep to me."

And when Finn had answered all the questions so well, Conan said he would give him his daughter, and that he would have a wedding-feast ready at the end of a month.

They spent the rest of the night then in sleep; but Finn saw a dreadful vision through his sleep that made him start three times from his bed. "What makes you start from your bed, Finn?" said Diorraing. "It was the Tuatha de Danaan I saw," said he, "taking up a quarrel against me, and making a great slaughter of the Fianna."

Now as to the Fianna, they rested at Fotharladh of Moghna that night, and they were downhearted, having no tidings of Finn. And early on the morrow two of them, Bran Beag and Bran Mor, rose up and went to Mac-an-Reith, son of the Ram, that had the gift of true knowledge, and they asked him where did Finn spend the night. And Mac-an-Reith was someway unwilling to tell them, but at the last he said it was at the house of Conan of Ceann Slieve.

The two Brans went on then to Conan's house, and Finn made them welcome; but they blamed him when they heard he was taking a wife, and none of his people with him. "Bid all the Fianna to come to the feast at the end of a month," said Conan then. So Finn and Diorraing and the two Brans went back to where the Fianna were and told them all that had happened, and they went on to Almhuin.

And when they were in the drinking-hall at Almhuin that night, they saw the son of the King of Ireland coming to where they were. "It is a pity the king's son to have come," said Finn; "for he will not be satisfied without ordering everything in the hall in his own way." "We will not take his orders," said Oisin, "but we will leave the half of the hall to him, and keep the other half ourselves."

So they did that; but it happened that in the half of the house that was given up to the King of Ireland's son, there were sitting two of the Men of Dea, Failbhe Mor and Failbhe Beag; and it is what they said, that it is because they were in that side of the hall it was given up. "It is a pity," said Failbhe Beag, "this shame and this great insult to have been put on us to-night; and it is likely Finn has a mind to do more than that again to us," he said, "for he is going to bring away the woman that is promised to the third best man of the Tuatha de Danaan, and against the will of her father and mother." And these two went away early in the morning to Fionnbhar of Magh Feabhail, and told him of the insults Finn and the Fianna of Ireland had a mind to put on the Tuatha de Danaan.

And when Fionnbhar that was king over the Tuatha de Danaan heard that, he sent out messengers through the length of Ireland to gather them all to him. And there came six good battalions to him on the edge of Loch Derg Dheirc at the end of a month; and it was the same day Conan had the wedding-feast made ready for Finn and his people.

And Finn was at Teamhair Luachra at that time, and when he heard the feast was ready, he set out to go to it. And it chanced that the most of the men he had with him at that time were of the sons of Morna. And when they were on their way, Finn said to Goll, "O Goll," he said, "I never felt any fear till now going to a feast. And there are but few of my people with me," he said; "and I know there is no good thing before me, but the Men of Dea are going to raise a quarrel against me and to kill my people." "I will defend you against anything they may do," said Goll.

They went on then to Conan's house, and there was a welcome before them, and they were brought into the drinking-hall, and Finn was put in the place beside the door, and Goll on his right and Finndeilb, of the Fair Shape, on his left, and all the rest in the places they were used to.

And as to Fionnbhar of Magh Feabhail and the Tuatha de Danaan, they put a Druid mist about themselves and went on, hidden and armed, in sixteen battalions, to the lawn before Conan's house. "It is little profit we have being here," they said then, "and Goll being with Finn against us." "Goll will not protect him this time," said Ethne, the woman-Druid, "for I will entice Finn out of the house, however well he is watched."

She went on to the house then, and took her stand before Finn outside. "Who is that before me?" she said then. "It is I myself," said Finn. "I put you under the bonds a true hero never broke," she said, "to come out to me here." When Finn heard that, he made no delay and went out to her; and for all there were so many in the house, not one of them took notice of him going, only Caoilte, and he followed him out. And at the same time the Tuatha de Danaan let out a flock of blackbirds having fiery beaks, that pitched on the breasts of all the people in the house, and burned them and destroyed them, till the young lads and the women and children of the place ran out on all sides, and the woman of the house, Conan's wife, was drowned in the river outside the dun.

But as to Ethne, the woman-Druid, she asked Finn would he run against her. "For it is to run a race against you I called you out," she said. "What length of a race?" said Finn. "From Doire da Torc, the Wood of the Two Boars, to Ath Mor, the Great Ford," she said. So they set out, but Finn got first over the ford. And Caoilte was following after them, and Finn was urging him, and he said: "It is ashamed of your running you should be, Caoilte, a woman to be going past you." On that Caoilte made a leap forward, and when he was in front of the witch he turned about and gave a blow of his sword that made two equal halves of her.

"Power and good luck to you, Caoilte!" said Finn; "for though it is many a good blow you have struck, you never struck a better one than this."

They went back then to the lawn before Conan's dun, and there they found the whole company of the Tuatha de Danaan, that had put the Druid mist off them. "It seems to me, Caoilte," said Finn, "that we are come into the middle of our enemies."

With that they turned their backs to one another, and they were attacked on all sides till groans of weakness from the unequal fight were forced from Finn. And when Goll, that was in the house, heard that, he said: "It is a pity the Tuatha de Danaan to have enticed Finn and Caoilte away from us; and let us go to their help and make no delay," he said.

Then he rushed out, and all that were there of the Fianna with him, and Conan of Ceann Slieve and his sons. And great anger came on Goll, that he looked like a tall mountain under his grey shield in the battle. And he broke through the Tuatha de Danaan till he reached to Fionnbhar their leader, and they attacked one another, cutting and wounding, till at the last Fionnbhar of Magh Feabhail fell by the strokes of Goll. And a great many others fell in that battle, and there never was a harder battle fought in Ireland, for there was no man on one side or the other had a mind to go back one step before whoever he was fighting against. For they were the two hardest fighting troops to be found in the four parts of the world, the strong, hardy Fianna of the Gael, and the beautiful Men of Dea; and they went near to being all destroyed in that battle.

But after a while they saw the rest of the Fianna that were not in the battle coming from all parts of Ireland. And when the Tuatha de Danaan saw them coming, they put the Druid mist about themselves again and made away. And clouds of weakness came on Finn himself, and on them that were with him, with the dint of the fight. And there were many men of the Fianna lost in that battle; and as to the rest, it is a long time they stopped in Almhuin of Leinster, till their wounds were entirely healed.

CHAPTER X

The Shadowy One

And indeed Finn had no great luck in going to look for a wife that time; and he had no better luck another time he asked a wife from among the Sidhe. And this is the way that happened.

It was on the mountain of Bearnas Mor he was hunting, and a great wild pig turned on the hounds of the Fianna and killed the most of them, but Bran made an attack on it then and got the best of it. And the pig began to scream, and with that a very tall man came out of the hill and he asked Finn to let the pig go free. And when he agreed to that, the man brought them into the hill of the Sidhe at Glandeirgdeis; and when they came to the door of the house he struck the pig with his Druid rod, and on the moment it changed into a beautiful young woman, and the name he called her by was Scathach, the Shadowy One.

And he made a great feast for the Fianna, and Finn asked the young girl in marriage, and the tall man, her father, said he would give her to him on that very night.

But when night came on, Scathach asked the loan of a harp, and it was brought to her. One string it had of iron, and one of bronze, and one of silver. And when the iron string would be played, it would set all the hosts of the world crying and ever crying; and when the bright bronze string would be played, it would set them all laughing from the one day to the same hour on the morrow; and when the silver string would be played, all the men of the whole world would fall into a long sleep.

And it is the sleepy silver string the Shadowy One played upon, till Finn and Bran and all his people were in their heavy sleep.

And when they awoke at the rising of the sun on the morrow, it is outside on the mountain of Bearnas they were, where they first saw the wild pig.

CHAPTER XI

Finn's Madness

One time Finn and the Fianna were come to a ford of the Slaine, and they sat down for a while. And as they were sitting there they saw on the round rock up over the ford a young woman, having a dress of silk and a green cloak about her, and a golden brooch in the cloak, and the golden crown that is the sign of a queen on her head. "Fianna of Ireland," she said, "let one of you come now and speak with me."

Then Sciathbreac, of the Speckled Shield, went towards her. "Who is it you are wanting?" he said. "Finn, son of Cumhal," said she. Finn went over then to talk with her. "Who are you?" he said, "and what is it you are wanting?" "I am Daireann, daughter of Bodb Dearg, son of the Dagda," she said; "and I am come to be your wife if you will give me the bride-gift I ask." "What bride-gift is that?" said Finn. "It is your promise," said she, "I to be your only wife through the length of a year, and to have the half of your time after that." "I will not give that promise," said Finn, "to any woman of the world, and I will not give it to you," he said.

On that the young woman took a cup of white silver from under a covering, and filled it with strong drink, and she gave it to Finn. "What is this?" said Finn. "It is very strong mead," said she. Now there were bonds on Finn not to refuse anything belonging to a feast, so he took the cup and drank what was in it, and on the moment he was like one gone mad. And he turned his face towards the Fianna, and every harm and every fault and every misfortune in battle that he knew against any one of them, he sprang it on them, through the mad drunkenness the young woman had put on him.

Then the chief men of the Fianna of Ireland rose up and left the place to him, every one of them setting out for his own country, till there was no one left upon the hill but Finn and Caoilte. And Caoilte rose up and followed after them, and he said: "Fianna of Ireland," he said, "do not leave your lord and your leader through the arts and the tricks of a woman of the Sidhe." Thirteen times he went after them, bringing them back to the hill in that way. And with the end of the day and the fall of night the bitterness went from Finn's tongue; and by the time Caoilte had brought back the whole of the Fianna, his sense and his memory were come back to him, and he would sooner have fallen on his sword and got his death, than have stayed living.

And that was the hardest day's work Caoilte ever did, unless the day he brought the flock of beasts and birds to Teamhair, to ransom Finn from the High King of Ireland.

Another time Maer, wife of Bersa of Berramain, fell in love with Finn, and she made nine nuts of Segair with love charms, and sent them to Finn, and bade him eat them. "I will not," said Finn; "for they are not nuts of knowledge, but nuts of ignorance; and it is not known what they are, unless they might be an enchantment for drinking love." So he buried them a foot deep in the earth.

CHAPTER XII

The Red Woman

One time the Fianna were in Almhuin with no great work to do, and there came a very misty morning, and Finn was in dread that sluggishness would come on his men, and he rose up, and he said: "Make yourselves ready, and we will go hunting to Gleann-na-Smol."

They all said the day was too misty to go hunting; but there was no use in talking: they had to do as Finn bade them. So they made themselves ready and went on towards Gleann-na-Smol; and they were not gone far when the mist lifted and the sun came shining out.

And when they were on the edge of a little wood, they saw a strange beast coming towards them with the quickness of the wind, and a Red Woman on its track. Narrow feet the beast had, and a head like the head of a boar, and long horns on it; but the rest of it was like a deer, and there was a shining moon on each of its sides.

Finn stopped, and he said: "Fianna of Ireland," he said, "did you ever see a beast like that one until now?" "We never did indeed," said they; "and it would be right for us to let out the hounds after it." "Wait a while," said Finn, "till I speak with the Red Woman; but do not let the beast go past you," he said. They thought to keep back the beast then, going before it; but they were hardly able to hinder it at all, and it went away through them.

And when the Red Woman was come up to them, Finn asked her what was the name of the beast she was following. "I do not know that," she said, "though I am on its track since I left the borders of Loch Dearg a month ago, and I never lost sight of it since then; and the two moons that are on its two sides shine through the country all around in the night time. And I must follow it till it falls," she said, "or I will lose my own life and the lives of my three sons that are the best fighting men in the whole world." "We will take the beast for you if you have a mind," said Finn. "Do not try to do that," she said, "for I myself am swifter than you are, and I cannot come up with it." "We will not let it go till we know what sort of a beast is it," said Finn. "If you yourself or your share of men go after it, I will bind you hand and foot," said she. "It is too stiff your talk is," said Finn. "And do you not know," he said, "I am Finn, son of Cumhal; and there are fourscore fighting men along with me that were never beaten yet." "It is little heed I give to yourself or your share of men," said the Red Woman; "and if my three sons were here, they would stand up against you." "Indeed it will be a bad day," said Finn, "when the threat of a woman will put fear on myself or on the Fianna of Ireland." With that he sounded his horn, and he said: "Let us all follow now, men and dogs, after that beast that we saw."

He had no sooner said that word than the woman made a great water-worm of herself, and made an attack on Finn, and she would have killed him then and there but for Bran being with him. Bran took a grip of the worm and shook it, and then it wound itself round Bran's body, and would have crushed the life out of her, but Finn thrust his sharp sword into its throat. "Keep back your hand," said the worm then, "and you will not have the curse of a lonely woman upon you." "It is what I think," said Finn, "that you would not leave me my life if you could take it from me; but go out of my sight now," he said, "and that I may never see you again."

Then she made herself into a Red Woman again, and went away into the wood.

All the Fianna were gone on the track of the beast while Finn was talking and fighting with the Red Woman; and he did not know in what place they were, but he went following after them, himself and Bran. It was late in the evening when he came up with a share of them, and they still on the track of the beast. The darkness of the night was coming on, but the two moons in the sides of the beast gave a bright light, and they never lost it from sight. They followed it on always; and about midnight they were pressing on it, and it began to scatter blood after it, and it was not long till Finn and his men were red from head to foot. But that did not hinder them, and they followed him on till they saw him going in at the foot of Cnoc-na-righ at the breaking of day.

When they came to the foot of the hill the Red Woman was standing there before them. "You did not take the beast," she said. "We did not take it, but we know where it is," said Finn.

She took a Druid rod then, and she struck a blow on the side of the hill, and on the moment a great door opened, and they heard sweet music coming from within. "Come in now," said the Red Woman, "till you see the wonderful beast." "Our clothing is not clean," said Finn, "and we would not like to go in among a company the way we are," he said.

She put a horn to her mouth and blew it, and on the moment there came ten young men to her. "Bring water for washing," she said, "and four times twenty suits of clothes, and a beautiful suit and a crown of shining stones for Finn, son of Cumhal." The young men went away then, and they came back at the end of a minute with water and with clothing.

When the Fianna were washed and dressed, the Red Woman brought them into a great hall, where there was the brightness of the sun and of the moon on every side. From that she brought them into another great room; and although Finn and his men had seen many grand things up to that time, they had never seen any sight so grand as what they saw in this place. There was a king sitting in a golden chair, having clothes of gold and of green, and his chief people were sitting around him, and his musicians were playing. And no one could know what colour were the dresses of the musicians, for every colour of the rainbow was in them. And there was a great table in the middle of the room, having every sort of thing on it, one better than another.

The king rose up and gave a welcome to Finn and to his men, and he bade them to sit down at the table; and they ate and drank their fill, and that was wanting to them after the hunt they had made. And then the Red Woman rose up, and she said: "King of the Hill, if it is your will, Finn and his men have a mind to see the wonderful beast, for they spent a long time following after it, and that is what brought them here."

The king struck a blow then on his golden chair, and a door opened behind him, and the beast came through it and stood before the king. And it stooped down before him, and it said: "I am going on towards my own country now; and there is not in the world a runner so good as myself, and the sea is the same to me as the land. And let whoever can come up with me come now," it said, "for I am going."

With that the beast went out from the hill as quick as a blast of wind, and all the people that were in it went following after it. It was not long till Finn and his men were before the rest, in the front of the hunt, gaining on the beast.

And about midday Bran made the beast turn, and then she forced it to turn a second time, and it began to put out cries, and it was not long until its strength began to flag; and at last, just at the setting of the sun, it fell dead, and Bran was at its side when it fell.

Then Finn and his men came up, but in place of a beast it was a tall man they saw lying dead before them. And the Red Woman came up at the same time, and she said: "High King of the Fianna, that is the King of the Firbolgs you have killed; and his people will put great troubles on this country in the time to come, when you yourself, Finn, and your people will be under the sod. And I myself am going now to the Country of the Young," she said, "and I will bring you with me if you have a mind to come." "We give you our thanks for that," said Finn, "but we would not give up our own country if we were to get the whole world as an estate, and the Country of the Young along with it." "That is well," said the Red Woman; "but you are going home empty after your hunt." "It is likely we will find a deer in Gleann-na-Smol," said Finn. "There is a fine deer at the foot of that tree beyond," said the Red Woman, "and I will rouse it for you." With that she gave a cry, and the deer started out and away, and Finn and his men after it, and it never stopped till it came to Gleann-na-Smol, but they could not come up with it. Then the Red

Woman came to them, and she said: "I think you are tired now with following after the deer; and call your hounds off now," she said, "and I will let out my own little dog after it." So Finn sounded a little horn he had at his side, and on the moment the hounds came back to him. And then the Red Woman brought out a little hound as white as the snow of the mountains, and put it after the deer; and it was not long till it had come up with the deer and killed it, and then it came back and made a leap in under the cloak of the Red Woman. There was great wonder on Finn; but before he could ask a question of the Red Woman, she was gone out of sight. And as to the deer, Finn knew there was enchantment on it, and so he left it there after him. And it is tired and empty the Fianna were, going back to Almhuin that night.

CHAPTER XIII

Finn and the Phantoms

Finn went to a gathering one time at Aonach Clochair, and a great many of the men of Munster crowded to it. And the horses of the Fianna were brought there, and the horses of the men of Munster, and they ran races against one another.

And Fiachu, son of Eoghan, was in it; and when the games were over he gave good presents to Finn, a lasting black horse that won the three prizes of the gathering, and a chariot, and a horse for the chariot-driver, and a spear, having a deadly spell, and weapons of silver, and three comely hounds, Feirne and Derchaem and Dialath, having collars of yellow gold and chains of white bronze.

And Finn rose up and gave his thanks to Fiachu, son of Eoghan, and he and his people set out to the house of Cacher at Cluain-da-loch. And they stopped three days feasting in Cacher's house, and then Finn gave him the price of his feast and of his ale, fifty rings, and fifty horses and fifty cows.

And he himself and the Fianna went on from that over Luachair to the strand at Berramain. And Finn went trying his black horse on the strand, and Caoilte and Oisin went racing against him; but it was only folly for them to do that, for he gave a blow to his horse, and away with him to Traig Liath and over the Plain of Health to the Old Yew of the Old Valley, and to the inver of the Flesc and the inver of the Lemain to Loch Lein, till he came to the hill of Bairnech, and Caoilte and Oisin after him.

"Night is coming on us," said Finn then; "and go look for some place where we can sleep," he said. He looked round then at the rocks on his left hand and he saw a house, and a fire shining out from it in the valley below. "I never knew of a house in this valley," he said.

"It is best for us to go see it," said Caoilte, "for there are many things we have no knowledge of."

The three went on then to the house, and they heard screams and crying from it; and when they came to the house, the people of it were very fierce and rough; and a big grey man took hold of their horses and brought them in and shut the door of the house with iron hooks. "My welcome to you, Finn of the great name," he said then; "it is a long time you were in coming here."

They sat down then on the hard boards of a bed, and the grey man kindled a fire, and he threw logs of elderwood on it, till they went near being smothered with the smoke. They saw a hag in the house then having three heads on her lean neck; and there was on the other side a man without a head, having one eye, and it in his breast. "Rise up, you that are in the house, and make music for the King of the Fianna," said the grey man then.

With that nine bodies rose up out of the corner nearest the Fianna, and nine heads rose up on the other side of the bed, and they raised nine harsh screeches together, that no one would like to be listening to. And then the hag answered to them, and the headless man answered; and if all of that music was harsh, there was none of it that you would not wish to hear sooner than the music of the one-eyed man. And the music that was sung went near to breaking the bones of their heads; and indeed it is no sweet music that was.

Then the big grey man rose up and took the axe that was for cutting logs, and he began striking at the horses, flaying and destroying them. Then there were brought fifty pointed spits of the rowan-tree, and he put a piece of the horse's flesh on each one of the spits, and settled them on the hearth. But when he took the spits from the fire and put them before Finn, it is raw the flesh was on them yet. "Take your food away," said Finn then, "for I have never eaten meat that was raw, and I never will eat it because of being without food for one day." "If you are come into our house to refuse our food," said the grey man, "we will surely go against yourselves, Finn and Caoilte and Oisin."

With that all in the house made an attack on the three; and they were driven back into the corner, and the fire was quenched, and the fight went on through the whole night in the darkness, and but for Finn and the way he fought, they would have been put down.

And when the sun rose and lighted up the house on the morrow, a mist came into the head of each of the three, so that they fell as if dead on the floor.

But after a while they rose up again, and there was nothing to be seen of the house or of the people of the house, but they had all vanished. And their horses were there, and they took them and went on, very weak and tired, for a long way, till they came to the strand of Berramain.

And those three that fought against them were the three Shapes out of the Valley of the Yew Tree that came to avenge their sister, Cuillen of the Wide Mouth.

Now as to Cuillen, she was a daughter of the King of Munster, and her husband was the King of Ulster's son. And they had a son that was called Fear Og, the Young Man; and there was hardly in Ireland a man so good as himself in shape and in courage and in casting a spear. And one time he joined in a game with the Fianna, and he did better than them all, and Finn gave him a great reward. And after that he went out to a hunt they made, and it was by him and by none of the Fianna the first blood was got of pig or of deer. And when they came back, a heavy sickness fell on the young man through the eyes and the envy of the Fianna, and it left him without life at the end of nine days. And he was buried under a green hill, and the shining stone he used to hold in his hand, and he doing his feats, was put over his head.

And his mother, Cuillen, came to his grave keening him every day through the length of a year. And one day she died there for grief after her son, and they put her into the same green hill.

But as to Finn, he was afraid of no earthly thing, and he killed many great serpents in Loch Cuilinn and Loch Neathach, and at Beinn Edair; and Shadow-Shapes at Loch Lein and Drom Cleib and Loch Liath, and a serpent and a cat in Ath Cliath.

CHAPTER XIV

The Pigs of Angus

Angus Og, son of the Dagda, made a feast one time at Brugh na Boinne for Finn and the Fianna of the Gael. Ten hundred of them were in it, and they wearing green clothing and crimson cloaks; and as to the people of Angus' house, it is clothing of red silk they had.

And Finn was sitting beside Angus in the beautiful house, and it is long since the like of those two were seen in Ireland. And any stranger would wonder to see the way the golden cups were going from hand to hand.

And Angus said out in a loud voice that every one could hear: "It is a better life this is than to be hunting." There was anger on Finn then, and he said: "It is a worse life than hunting to be here, without hounds, without horses, without battalions, without the shouting of armies." "Why are you talking like that, Finn?" said Angus, "for as to the hounds you have," he said, "they would not kill so much as one pig." "You have not yourself," said Finn, "and the whole host of the Tuatha de Danaan have not a pig that ever went on dry land that Bran and Sceolan would not kill." "I will send you a pig," said Angus, "that will go from you and your hounds, and that will kill them in the end."

The steward of the house called out then in a loud voice: "Let every one go now to his bed, before the lightness of drunkenness comes on you." But Finn said to his people: "Let us make ready and leave this; for we are but a few," he said, "among the Men of Dea." So they set out and went westward till they came to Slieve Fuad where the Fianna were at that time.

And through the whole length of a year after that, the Tuatha de Danaan were boasting how they would get the better of the Fianna, and the Fianna were thinking how they could do best in the hunt. And at the end of that time Angus sent messengers to Finn, asking him with great respect if he was ready to keep his word. And Finn said he was, and the hounds were brought out, and he himself was holding Bran and Sceolan, one in each hand, and Caoilte had Adhnuall, and Oisin had Ablach, and merry Bran Beag had Lonn, and Diarmuid was holding Eachtach, and Osgar was holding Mac an Truim, and Garraidh was held by Faolan, and Rith Fada, of the Long Run, by hungry Conan.

And they were not long there with their hounds till they saw on the plain to the east a terrible herd of great pigs, every one of them the height of a deer. And there was one pig out in front of the rest was blacker than a smith's coal, and the bristles on its head were like a thicket of thorn-trees.

Then Caoilte let out Adhnuall, and she was the first to kill a pig of the herd. And then Bran made away from the leash that Finn was holding, and the pigs ran their best, but she came up with them, and took hold of a pig of them. And at that Angus said: "O Bran, fosterling of fair-haired Fergus, it is not a right thing you are doing, to kill my own son." But when Bran heard that, her ways changed and it was like an enemy she took hold of the pig, and did not let it go, and held her breath back and kept it for the Fianna.

And it was over Slieve Cua the hunt went, and Slieve Crot, and from Magh Cobha to Cruachan, and to Fionnabraic and to Finnias. And at evening when the hunt was over, there was not one pig of the whole herd without a hurt, and there were but a hundred and ten pigs left living. But if the hunt brought destruction on Angus, it brought losses on the Fianna as well, for there were ten hundred of their men missing besides serving-lads and dogs.

"Let us go to Brugh na Boinne and get satisfaction for our people," said Oisin then. "That is the advice of a man without sense," said Finn; "for if we leave these pigs the way they are, they will come to life again. And let us burn them," he said, "and throw their ashes in the sea."

Then the seven battalions of the Fianna made seven fires to every battalion; but for all they could do, they could not set fire to one pig. Then Bran, that had great sense and knowledge, went away, and she came back bringing three logs along with her, but no one knows what wood it was they came from. And when the logs were put on the fire they lit up like a candle, and it is with them the pigs were burned; and after that their ashes were thrown into the sea.

Then Oisin said again: "Let us go now to Brugh na Boinne and avenge the death of our people." So the whole of the Fianna set out for Brugh na Boinne, and every step they made could surely be heard through the whole of the skies.

And Angus sent out messengers to where Finn was, offering any one thing to him if he would spare his people. "I will take no gift at all from you, Angus of the slender body," said Finn, "so long as there is a room left in your house, north or east, without being burned." But Angus said: "Although you think bad of the loss of your fine people that you have the sway over, yet, O Finn, father of Oisin, it is sorrowful to me the loss of my own good son is. For as to the black pig that came before you on the plain," he said, "it was no common pig was in it, but my own son. And there fell along with him," he said, "the son of the King of the Narrow Sea, and the son of the King of the Sea of Gulls, and the son of Ilbhrec, son of Manannan, and seven score of the comely sons of kings and queens. And it is what destroyed my strength and my respect entirely, they to have been burned away from me in a far place. And it is a pity for you, sweet daring Bran," he said, "fosterling of Fergus of the thirty woods and plains, that you did not do something worth praise before killing your own foster-brother. And I will put a curse on you, Bran," he said, "beyond every hound in Ireland, that you will never see with your eyes any deer you may ever kill."

There was anger on Finn when he heard that, and he said: "If you put a curse on Bran, Angus, there will not be a room left, east or west, in the whole of your great house without being burned." "If you do that," said Angus, "I will put trees and stones in front of you in every battle; and I will know what number of men you have in your armies," he said, "looking at them through my ring."

Then Oisin, that was wise, said: "It is best for you to agree between yourselves now; and let us be helpful to one another," he said, "and pay whatever fines are due."

So they agreed to that, and they made peace, and gave children to be fostered by one another: a son of Finn's to Angus, and son of Angus Og to the Fianna.

But for all that, it is not very friendly to Finn Angus was afterwards, at the time he was following after Diarmuid and Grania through the whole length of Ireland.

CHAPTER XV

The Hunt of Slieve Cuilinn

Finn was one time out on the green of Almhuin, and he saw what had the appearance of a grey fawn running across the plain. He called and whistled to his hounds then, but neither hound nor man heard him or came to him, but only Bran and Sceolan. He set them after the fawn, and near as they kept to her, he himself kept nearer to them, till at last they reached to Slieve Cuilinn in the province of Ulster.

But they were no sooner at the hill than the fawn vanished from them, and they did not know where was she gone, and Finn went looking for her eastward, and the two hounds went towards the west.

It was not long till Finn came to a lake, and there was sitting on the brink of it a young girl, the most beautiful he had ever seen, having hair of the colour of gold, and a skin as white as lime, and eyes like the stars in time of frost; but she seemed to be some way sorrowful and downhearted. Finn asked her did she see his hounds pass that way. "I did not see them," she said; "and it is little I am thinking of your hounds or your hunting, but of the cause of my own trouble." "What is it ails you, woman of the white hands?" said Finn; "and is there any help I can give you?" he said. "It is what I am fretting after," said she, "a ring of red gold I lost off my finger in the lake. And I put you under bonds, Finn of the Fianna," she said, "to bring it back to me out of the lake."

With that Finn stripped off his clothes and went into the lake at the bidding of the woman, and he went three times round the whole lake and did not leave any part of it without searching, till he brought back the ring. He handed it up to her then out of the water, and no sooner had he done that than she gave a leap into the water and vanished.

And when Finn came up on the bank of the lake, he could not so much as reach to where his clothes were; for on the moment he, the head and the leader of the Fianna of Ireland, was but a grey old man, weak and withered.

Bran and Sceolan came up to him then, but they did not know him, and they went on round the lake, searching after their master.

In Almhuin, now, when he was missed, Caoilte began asking after him. "Where is Finn," he said, "of the gentle rule and of the spears?" But no one knew where was he gone, and there was grief on the Fianna when they could not find him. But it is what Conan said: "I never heard music pleased me better than to hear the son of Cumhal is missing. And that he may be so through the whole year," he said, "and I myself will be king over you all." And downhearted as they were, it is hardly they could keep from laughing when they heard Conan saying that.

Caoilte and the rest of the chief men of the Fianna set out then looking for Finn, and they got word of him; and at last they came to Slieve Cuilinn, and there they saw a withered old man sitting beside the lake, and they thought him to be a fisherman. "Tell us, old man," said Caoilte, "did you see a fawn go by, and two hounds after her, and a tall fair-faced man along with them?" "I did see them," he said, "and it is not long since they left me." "Tell us where are they now?" said Caoilte. But Finn made no answer, for he had not the courage to say to them that he himself was Finn their leader, being as he was an ailing, downhearted old man, without leaping, without running, without walk, grey and sorrowful.

Caoilte took out his sword from the sheath then, and he said: "It is short till you will have knowledge of death unless you will tell us what happened those three."

Then Finn told them the whole story; and when the seven battalions of the Fianna heard him, and knew it was Finn that was in it, they gave three loud sorrowful cries. And to the lake they gave the name of Loch Doghra, the Lake of Sorrow.

But Conan of the sharp tongue began abusing Finn and all the Fianna by turns. "You never gave me right praise for my deeds, Finn, son of Cumhal," he said, "and you were always the enemy of the sons of Morna; but we are living in spite of you," he said, "and I have but the one fault to find with your shape, and that is, that it was not put on the whole of the Fianna the same as on yourself." Caoilte made at him then; "Bald, senseless Conan," he said, "I will break your mouth to the bone." But Conan ran in then among the rest of the Fianna and asked protection from them, and peace was made again.

And as to Finn, they asked him was there any cure to be found for him. "There is," he said; "for I know well the enchantment was put on me by a woman of the Sidhe, Miluchradh, daughter of Cuilinn, through jealousy of her sister Aine. And bring me to the hill that belongs to Cuilinn of Cuailgne," he said, "for he is the only one can give me my shape again."

They came around him then, and raised him up gently on their shields, and brought him on their shoulders to the hill of the Sidhe in Cuailgne, but no one came out to meet them. Then the seven battalions began digging and rooting up the whole hill, and they went on digging through the length of three nights and three days. And at the end of that time Cuilinn of Cuailgne, that some say was Manannan, son of Lir, came out of the hill, holding in his hand a vessel of red gold, and he gave the vessel into Finn's hand. And no sooner did Finn drink what was in the vessel than his own shape and his appearance came back to him. But only his hair, that used to be so fair and so beautiful, like the hair of a woman, never got its own colour again, for the lake that Cuilinn's daughter had made for Finn would have turned all the men of the whole world grey if they had gone into it.

And when Finn had drunk all that was in the vessel it slipped from his hand into the earth, that was loosened with the digging, and he saw it no more. But in the place where it went into the earth, a tree grew up, and any one that would look at the branches of that tree in the morning, fasting, would have knowledge of all that was to happen on that day.

That, now, is the way Finn came by his grey hair, through the jealousy of Miluchradh of the Sidhe, because he had not given his love to her, but to her sister Aine.

BOOK V

Oisin's Children

Now as to Oisin, that was so brave and so comely, and that could overtake a deer at its greatest speed, and see a thistle thorn on the darkest night, the wife he took was Eibhir of the plaited yellow hair, that was the foreign sweetheart of the High King of Ireland.

It is beyond the sea she lived, in a very sunny place; and her father's name was Iunsa, and her sunny house was thatched with the feathers of birds, and the door-posts were of gold, and the doors of ribbed grass. And Oisin went there looking for her, and he fought for her against the High King and against an army of the Firbolgs he had helping him; and he got the better of them all, and brought away Eibhir of the yellow hair to Ireland.

And he had a daughter that married the son of Oiliol, son of Eoghan, and of Beara, daughter of the King of Spain. It was that Eoghan was driven out of Ireland one time, and it is to Spain he went for safety. And Beara, that was daughter of the King of Spain, was very shining and beautiful, and her father had a mind to know who would be her husband, and he sent for his Druid and asked the question of him. "I can tell you that," said the Druid, "for the man that is to be her husband will come to land in Spain this very night. And let your daughter go eastward to the river Eibhear," he said, "and she will find a crimson-spotted salmon in that river, having shining clothing on him from head to tail. And let her strip that clothing off him," he said, "and make with it a shining shirt for her husband."

So Beara went to the river Eibhear, and found the golden salmon as the Druid had said, and she stripped him of his crimson clothing and made a shining shirt of it.

And as to Eoghan, the waves of the shore put a welcome before him, and he came the same night to the king's house. And the king gave him a friendly welcome; and it is what all the people said, that there was never seen a comelier man than Eoghan, or a woman more beautiful than Beara, and that it was fitting for them to come together. And Eoghan's own people said they would not be sorry for being sent away out of Ireland, if only Eoghan could get her for his wife.

And after a while the king sent his Druid to ask Eoghan why he did not ask for Beara. "I will tell you that," said Eoghan; "it would not be fitting for me to be refused a wife, and I am but an exile in this country, and I have brought no treasures or goods with me out of Ireland for giving to learned men and to poets. But for all that," he said, "the king's daughter is dear to me, and I think I have the friendship of the king."

The Druid went back with that message. "That is the answer of a king," said the King of Spain; "and bid my daughter to sit at Eoghan's right hand," he said, "and I

211

will give her to him this very night." And when Beara, the king's daughter, heard that, she sent out her serving-maid to bring the shirt she had made for Eoghan, and he put it on him over his armour, and its shining was seen in every place; and it was from wearing that shirt he got the name of Eoghan the Bright.

And Oiliol was the first son they had; it was he that had his ear bitten off by Aine of the Sidhe in revenge for her brother, and it was his son married Oisin's daughter afterwards.

And as to Osgar, that was Oisin's son, of all the young men of the Fianna he was the best in battle. And when he was but a young child he was made much of by the whole of the Fianna, and it is for him they used to keep the marrow bones, and they did not like to put any hardship on him. And he grew up tall and idle, and no one thought he would turn out so strong as he did. And one day there was an attack made on a troop of the Fianna, and all that were in it went out to fight, but they left Osgar after them. And when he knew the fight was going on, he took a log of wood that was the first thing he could find, and attacked the enemy and made a great slaughter, and they gave way and ran before him. And from that out there was no battle he did not go into; and he was said to be the strongest of all the Fianna, though the people of Connacht said that Goll was the strongest. And he and Diarmuid, grandson of Duibhne, were comrades and dear friends; and it was Diarmuid taught him feats of arms and of skill, and chess-playing. And Oisin his father took great pride in him, and his grandfather Finn. And one time Finn was holding a feast at Almhuin, and he asked the chief men of the Fianna that were there what was the music they thought the best. "To be playing at games," said Conan, "that is the best music I ever heard;" for though Conan was a good hand against an enemy, there never was a man had less sense. "The music I like the best is to be talking with a woman," said Diarmuid. "My music is the outcry of my hounds, and they putting a deer to its last stand," said Lugaidh's Son. "The music of the woods is best to me," said Oisin; "the sound of the wind and of the cuckoo and the blackbird, and the sweet silence of the crane."

And then Osgar was asked, and he said: "The best music is the striking of swords in a battle." And it is likely he took after Finn in that, for in spite of all the sweet sounds he gave an account of the time he was at Conan's house, at Ceann Slieve, it used to be said by the Fianna that the music that was best with Finn was what happened.

This now is the way Osgar met with his wife.

One time Finn and his men came to Slieve Crot, and they saw a woman waiting there before them, having a crimson fringed cloak, and a gold brooch in it, and a band of yellow gold on her forehead. Finn asked her name, and where she came from. "Etain of the Fair Hair is my name," she said, "daughter of Aedh of the White Breast, of the hill of the Sidhe at Beinn Edair, son of Angus Og." "What is it brought you here, girl?" said Finn. "To ask a man of the Fianna of Ireland to run a race with me." "What sort of a runner are you?" said Diarmuid. "I am a good runner," said the girl; "for it is the same to me if the ground is long or short under my feet."

All of the Fianna that were there then set out to run with her, and they ran to the height over Badhamair and on to Ath Cliath, and from that on to the hill of the Sidhe at Beinn Edair.

And there was a good welcome before them, and they were brought meat and wine for drinking, and water for washing their feet. And after a while they saw a nice fair-haired girl in front of the vats, and a cup of white silver in her hand, and she giving out drink to every one. "It seems to me that is the girl came asking the Fianna to race against her at Slieve Crot," said Finn. "It is not," said Aedh of the White Breast, "for that is the slowest woman there is among us." "Who was it so?" said Finn. "It was Be-mannair, daughter of Ainceol, woman-messenger of the Tuatha de Danaan. And it is she that changes herself into all shapes; and she will take the shape of a fly, and of a true lover, and every one leaves their secret with her. And it was she outran you coming from the east," he said, "and not this other girl that was drinking and making merry here in the hall." "What is her name?" said Finn. "Etain of the Fair Hair," he said; "a daughter of my own, and a darling of the Tuatha de Danaan. And it is the way with her, she has a lover of the men of the Fianna." "That is well," said Finn; "and who is that lover?" "It is Osgar, son of Oisin," said Aedh; "and it is she herself sent her messenger for you," he said, "in her own shape, to Slieve Crot in the south. And the son of the High King of Ireland has offered a great bride-price to the Men of Dea for her," he said, "three hundreds of the land nearest to Bregia and to Midhe, and to put himself and his weight of gold into a balance, and to give it all to her. But we did not take it," he said, "since she had no mind or wish for it herself, and so we made no dealing or agreement about her." "Well," said Finn, "and what conditions will you ask of Osgar?" "Never to leave me for anything at all but my own fault," said the girl. "I will make that agreement with you indeed," said Osgar. "Give me sureties for it," said she; "give me the sureties of Goll for the sons of Morna, and of Finn, son of Cumhal, for the Fianna of Ireland."

So they gave those sureties, and the wedding-feast was made, and they stopped there for twenty nights. And at the end of that time Osgar asked Finn where would he bring his wife. "Bring her to wide Almhuin for the first seven years," said Finn.

But a while after that, in a great battle at Beinn Edair, Osgar got so heavy a wound that Finn and the Fianna were as if they had lost their wits. And when Etain of the Fair Hair came to the bed where Osgar was lying, and saw the way he was, and that the great kinglike shape he had was gone from him, greyness and darkness came on her, and she raised pitiful cries, and she went to her bed and her heart broke in her like a nut; and she died of grief for her husband and her first love.

Diarmuid

CHAPTER I

Birth of Diarmuid

Diarmuid, now, was son of Donn, son of Duibhne of the Fianna, and his mother was Crochnuit, that was near in blood to Finn. And at the time he was born, Donn was banished from the Fianna because of some quarrel they had with him, and Angus Og took the child from him to rear him up at Brugh na Boinne.

And after a while Crochnuit bore another son to Roc Diocain, that was Head Steward to Angus. Roc Diocain went then to Donn, and asked would he rear up his son for him, the way Angus was rearing Donn's son. But Donn said he would not take the son of a common man into his house, and it would be best for Angus to take him. So Angus took the child into Brugh na Boinne, and he and Diarmuid were reared up together.

And one day Finn was on the great Hill at Almhuin of Leinster, and no one with him but Donn and a few of the poets and learned men of the Fianna, and their hounds and dogs, and Bran Beag came in and asked did he remember there were bonds on him, not to stop in Almhuin for ten nights together. Finn asked the people about him then where would he go and be entertained for that night, and Donn said: "I will bring you to the house of Angus, son of the Dagda, where my young son is being reared."

So they went together to the house of Angus at Brugh na Boinne, and the child Diarmuid was there, and it is great love Angus had for him. And the Steward's son was with him that night, and the people of the household made as much of him as Angus made of Diarmuid; and there was great vexation on Donn when he saw that. It chanced after a while a great fight rose between two of Finn's hounds about some broken meat that was thrown to them; and the women and the common people of the place ran from them, and the others rose up to part them from one another. And in running away, the Steward's child ran between the knees of Donn, and Donn gave the child a strong squeeze between his two knees that killed him on the moment, and he threw him under the feet of the hounds. And when the Steward came after that and found his son dead, he gave a long very pitiful cry, and he said to Finn: "There is not a man in the house to-night has suffered more than myself from this uproar, for I had but one son only, and he has been killed; and what satisfaction will I get from you for that, Finn?" he said. "Try can you find the mark of a tooth or of a nail of one of the hounds on him," said Finn, "and if you can, I will give you satisfaction for him."

So they looked at the child, and there was no scratch or mark of a tooth on him at all. Then the Steward put Finn under the destroying bonds of the Druid cave of Cruachan, to give him knowledge of who it was killed his son. And Finn asked for a chess-board, and for water to be brought to him, in a basin of pale gold, and he searched, and it was shown to him truly that it was Donn had killed the Steward's son between his two knees. When Finn knew that, he said he would take the fine on himself; but the Steward would not consent to that, but forced him to tell who was it had done him the wrong. And when he knew it was Donn had killed the child, he said: "There is no man in the house it is easier to get satisfaction from than from him, for his own son is here, and I have but to put him between my two knees, and if I let him go from me safe, I will forgive the death of my son." Angus was vexed at what the Steward said, and as to Donn, he thought to strike his head off till Finn put him back from him. Then the Steward came again, having a Druid rod with him, and he struck his own son with the rod, and he made of him a wild boar, without bristle or ear or tail, and he said: "I put you under bonds to bring Diarmuid, grandson of Duibhne, to his death; and your own life will be no longer than his life," he said. With that the wild boar rose up and ran out of the open door; and he was called afterwards the Boar of Slieve Guillion, and it was by him Diarmuid came to his death at the last.

And when Diarmuid came to his full strength he was given a place among the Fianna of Ireland; and all women loved him, and he did many great deeds, fighting with the enemies of the Fianna and of Ireland; and one time he fought a wild ox through the length of seven days and seven nights on the top of the Mountain of Happiness.

CHAPTER II

How Diarmuid got his Love-Spot

Diarmuid and Conan and Goll and Osgar went one day hunting, and they went so far they could not get home in the evening, and they spent the first part of the night walking through the woods and pulling berries and eating them. And when it was about midnight they saw a light, and they went towards it, and they found a little house before them, and the light shining from it. They went in then, and they saw an old man there, and he bade them welcome, and he called them all by their names. And they saw no one in the house but the old man and a young girl and a cat. And the old man bade the girl to make food ready for the Fianna of Ireland, for there was great hunger on them.

And when the food was ready and put on the table, there came a great wether that was fastened up in the back of the house, and he rose up on the table where they were eating, and when they saw that, they looked at one another. "Rise up, Conan," said Goll, "and fasten that wether in the place it was before." Conan rose up and took hold of it, but the wether gave itself a shake that threw Conan under one of its feet. The rest were looking at that, and Goll said: "Let you rise up, Diarmuid, and fasten up the wether." So Diarmuid rose up and took hold of it, but it gave itself a shake the same way as before; and when Diarmuid was down it put one of its feet on him. Goll and Osgar looked at one another then, and shame came on them, a wether to have done so much as that. And Osgar got up, but the wether put him down under one of its feet, so that it had now the three men under him. Then Goll rose up and took hold of it and threw it down; but if he did, it rose up again in spite of him, and put Goll under his fourth foot.

"It is a great shame," said the old man then, "the like of that to be done to the Fianna of Ireland. And rise up now, cat," he said, "and tie the wether in the place where he was." The cat rose up then and took hold of the wether, and brought it over and tied it in its place at the end of the house.

The men rose up then, but they had no mind to go on eating, for there was shame on them at what the wether had done to them. "You may go on eating," said the old man; "and when you are done I will show you that now you are the bravest men of the world." So they ate their fill then, and the old man spoke to them, and it is what he said: "Goll," he said, "you are the bravest of all the men of the world, for you have wrestled with the world and you threw it down. The strength of the world is in the wether, but death will come to the world itself; and that is death," he said, showing them the cat.

They were talking together then, and they had their food eaten, and the old man said their beds were ready for them that they could go to sleep. The four of them went then into the one room, and when they were in their beds the young girl came to sleep in the same room with them, and the light of her beauty was shining on the walls like as if it was the light of a candle.

And when Conan saw her he went over to the side of the bed where she was.

Now, it was Youth the young girl was, and when she saw Conan coming to her: "Go back to your bed, Conan," she said; "I belonged to you once, and I will never belong to you again."

Conan went back to his bed then, and Osgar had a mind to go over where she was. Then she said to him: "Where are you going?" "I am going over to yourself for a while," said he.

"Go back again, Osgar," she said; "I belonged to you once, and I will never belong to you again."

Then Diarmuid rose up to go to her: "Where are you going, Diarmuid?" she said. "I am going over to yourself for a while," said he. "O Diarmuid," she said, "that cannot be; I belonged to you once, and I can never belong to you again; but come over here to me, Diarmuid," she said, "and I will put a love-spot on you, that no woman will ever see without giving you her love." So Diarmuid went over to her, and she put her hand on his forehead, and she left the love-spot there, and no woman that ever saw him after that was able to refuse him her love.

CHAPTER III

The Daughter of King Under-Wave

One snowy night of winter the Fianna were come into the house after their hunting. And about midnight they heard a knocking at the door, and there came in a woman very wild and ugly, and her hair hanging to her heels. She went to the place Finn was lying, and she asked him to let her in under the border of his covering. But when he saw her so strange and so ugly and so wild-looking he would not let her in. She gave a great cry then, and she went to where Oisin was, and asked him to let her shelter under the border of his covering. But Oisin refused her the same way. Then she gave another great scream, and she went over where Diarmuid was. "Let me in," she said, "under the border of your covering." Diarmuid looked at her, and he said: "You are strange-looking and wild and ugly, and your hair is down to your heels. But come in for all that," he said.

So she came in under the border of his covering.

"O Diarmuid," she said then, "I have been travelling over sea and ocean through the length of seven years, and in all that time I never got shelter any night till this night. And let me to the warmth of the fire now," she said. So Diarmuid brought her over to the fire, and all the Fianna that were sitting there went away from it seeing her so ugly and so dreadful to look at. And she was not long at the fire when she said: "Let me go under the warmth of the covering with you now." "It is asking too much you are," said Diarmuid; "first it was to come under the border you asked, and then to come to the fire, and now it is under the bed-covering with me you want to be. But for all that you may come," he said.

So she came in under the covering, and he turned a fold of it between them. But it was not long till he looked at her, and what he saw was a beautiful young woman beside him, and she asleep. He called to the others then to come over, and he said: "Is not this the most beautiful woman that ever was seen?" "She is that," they said, and they covered her up and did not awaken her.

But after a while she stirred, and she said: "Are you awake, Diarmuid?" "I am awake," he said. "Where would you like to see the best house built that ever was

218

built?" she said. "Up there on the hillside, if I had my choice," said he, and with that he fell asleep.

And in the morning two men of the Fianna came in, and they said they were after seeing a great house up on the hill, where there was not a house before. "Rise up, Diarmuid," said the strange woman then; "do not be lying there any longer, but go up to your house, and look out now and see it," she said. So he looked out and he saw the great house that was ready, and he said: "I will go to it, if you will come along with me." "I will do that," she said, "if you will make me a promise not to say to me three times what way I was when I came to you." "I will never say it to you for ever," said Diarmuid.

They went up then to the house, and it was ready for them, with food and servants; and everything they could wish for they had it. They stopped there for three days, and when the three days were ended, she said: "You are getting to be sorrowful because you are away from your comrades of the Fianna." "I am not sorrowful indeed," said Diarmuid. "It will be best for you to go to them; and your food and your drink will be no worse when you come back than they are now," said she. "Who will take care of my greyhound bitch and her three pups if I go?" said Diarmuid. "There is no fear for them," said she.

So when he heard that, he took leave of her and went back to the Fianna, and there was a great welcome before him. But for all that they were not well pleased but were someway envious, Diarmuid to have got that grand house and her love from the woman they themselves had turned away.

Now as to the woman, she was outside the house for a while after Diarmuid going away, and she saw Finn, son of Cumhal, coming towards her, and she bade him welcome. "You are vexed with me, Queen?" he said. "I am not indeed," she said; "and come in now and take a drink of wine from me." "I will go in if I get my request," said Finn. "What request is there that you would not get?" said she. "It is what I am asking, one of the pups of Diarmuid's greyhound bitch." "That is no great thing to ask," she said; "and whichever one you choose of them you may bring it away."

So he got the pup, and he brought it away with him.

At the fall of night Diarmuid came back to the house, and the greyhound met him at the door and gave a yell when she saw him, and he looked for the pups, and one of them was gone. There was anger on him then, and he said to the woman: "If you had brought to mind the way you were when I let you in, and your hair hanging, you would not have let the pup be brought away from me." "You ought not to say that, Diarmuid," said she. "I ask your pardon for saying it," said Diarmuid. And they forgave one another, and he spent the night in the house.

On the morrow Diarmuid went back again to his comrades, and the woman stopped at the house, and after a while she saw Oisin coming towards her. She gave him a welcome, and asked him into the house, and he said he would come if he would get his request. And what he asked was another of the pups of the greyhound.

So she gave him that, and he went away bringing the pup with him. And when Diarmuid came back that night the greyhound met him, and she cried out twice. And he knew that another of the pups was gone, and he said to the greyhound, and the woman standing there: "If she had remembered the way she was when she came to me, she would not have let the pup be brought away."

The next day he went back again to the Fianna, and when he was gone, the woman saw Caoilte coming towards her, and he would not come in to take a drink from her till he had got the promise of one of the pups the same as the others.

And when Diarmuid came back that night the greyhound met him and gave three yells, the most terrible that ever were heard. There was great anger on him then, when he saw all the pups gone, and he said the third time: "If this woman remembered the way she was when I found her, and her hair down to her heels, she would not have let the pup go." "O Diarmuid, what is it you are after saying?" she said. He asked forgiveness of her then, and he thought to go into the house, but it was gone and the woman was gone on the moment, and it was on the bare ground he awoke on the morrow. There was great sorrow on him then, and he said he would search in every place till he would find her again.

So he set out through the lonely valleys, and the first thing he saw was the greyhound lying dead, and he put her on his shoulder and would not leave her because of the love he had for her. And after a while he met with a cowherd, and he asked him did he see a woman going the way. "I saw a woman early in the morning of yesterday, and she walking hard," said the cowherd. "What way was she going?" said Diarmuid. "Down that path below to the strand, and I saw her no more after that," he said.

So he followed the path she took down to the strand till he could go no farther, and then he saw a ship, and he leaned on the handle of his spear and made a light leap on to the ship, and it went on till it came to land, and then he got out and lay down on the side of a hill and fell asleep, and when he awoke there was no ship to be seen. "It is a pity for me to be here," he said, "for I see no way of getting from it again."

But after a while he saw a boat coming, and a man in the boat rowing it, and he went down and got into the boat, and brought the greyhound with him. And the boat went out over the sea, and then down below it; and Diarmuid, when he went down, found himself on a plain. And he went walking along it, and it was not long before he met with a drop of blood. He took it up and put it in a napkin. "It is the greyhound lost this," he said. And after a while he met with another drop of blood, and then with a third, and he put them in the napkin. And after that again he saw a woman, and she gathering rushes as if she had lost her wits.

He went towards her and asked her what news had she. "I cannot tell it till I gather the rushes," she said. "Be telling it while you are gathering them," said Diarmuid. "There is great haste on me," she said. "What is this place where we are?" said Diarmuid. "It is Land-under-Wave," said she. "And what use have you for the rushes when they are gathered?" "The daughter of King Under-Wave is come home," she said, "and she was for seven years under enchantment, and there is sickness on her now, and all the physicians are gathered together and none of them can do her any good, and a bed of rushes is what she finds the wholesomest." "Will you show me where the king's daughter is?" said Diarmuid. "I will do that," said the woman; "I will put you in the sheaf of rushes, and I will put the rushes under you and over you, and I will carry you to her on my back." "That is a thing you cannot do," said Diarmuid. But she put the rushes about him, and lifted him on her back, and when she got to the room she let down the bundle. "O come here to me," said the daughter of King Under-Wave, and Diarmuid went over to her, and they took one another's hands, and were very joyful at that meeting. "Three parts of my sickness is gone from me now," she said then; "but I am not well yet, and I never will be, for every time I thought of you, Diarmuid, on my journey, I lost a drop of the blood of my heart." "I have got those three drops here in this napkin," said Diarmuid, "and take them now in a drink and you will be healed of your sickness." "They would do nothing for me," she said, "since I have not the one thing in the world that I want, and that is the thing I will never get," she said. "What things is that?" said Diarmuid. "It is the thing you will never get, nor any man in the world," she said, "for it is a long time they have failed to get it." "If it is in any place on the whole ridge of the world I will get it," said Diarmuid. "It is three draughts from the cup of the King of Magh an Ionganaidh, the Plain of Wonder," she said, "and no man ever got it or ever will get it." "Tell me where that cup is to be found," said Diarmuid, "for there are not as many men as will keep it from me on the whole ridge of the world." "That country is not far from the boundary of my father's country," she said; "but there is a little river between, and you would be sailing on that river in a ship, having the wind behind it, for a year and a day before you would reach to the Plain of Wonder."

Diarmuid set out then, and he came to the little river, and he was a good while walking beside it, and he saw no way to cross it. But at last he saw a low-sized, reddish man that was standing in the middle of the river. "You are in straits, Diarmuid, grandson of Duibhne," he said; "and come here and put your foot in the palm of my hand and I will bring you through." Diarmuid did as he bade him, and put his foot in the red man's palm, and he brought him across the river. "It is going to the King of the Plain of Wonder you are," he said, "to bring away his cup from him; and I myself will go with you."

They went on then till they came to the king's dun, and Diarmuid called out that the cup should be sent out to him, or else champions to fight with him should be sent out. It was not the cup was sent out, but twice eight hundred fighting men; and in three hours there was not one of them left to stand against him. Then twice

221

nine hundred better fighters again were sent out against him, and within four hours there was not one of them left to stand against him. Then the king himself came out, and he stood in the great door, and he said: "Where did the man come from that has brought destruction on the whole of my kingdom?" "I will tell you that," said he; "I am Diarmuid, a man of the Fianna of Ireland." "It is a pity you not to have sent a messenger telling me that," said the king, "and I would not have spent my men upon you; for seven years before you were born it was put in the prophecy that you would come to destroy them. And what is it you are asking now?" he said. "It is the cup of healing from your own hand I am asking," said Diarmuid. "No man ever got that cup from me but yourself," said the king, "but it is easy for me to give it to you, whether or not there is healing in it."

Then the King of the Plain of Wonder gave Diarmuid the cup, and they parted from one another; and Diarmuid went on till he came to the river, and it was then he thought of the red man, that he had given no thought to while he was at the king's house. But he was there before him, and took his foot in the palm of his hand and brought him over the river. "I know where it is you are going, Diarmuid," he said then; "it is to heal the daughter of King Under-Wave that you have given your love to. And it is to a well I will give you the signs of you should go," he said, "and bring a share of the water of that well with you. And when you come where the woman is, it is what you have to do, to put that water in the cup, and one of the drops of blood in it, and she will drink it, and the same with the second drop and the third, and her sickness will be gone from her from that time. But there is another thing will be gone along with it," he said, "and that is the love you have for her."

"That will not go from me," said Diarmuid. "It will go from you," said the man; "and it will be best for you make no secret of it, for she will know, and the king will know, that you think no more of her then than of any other woman. And King Under-Wave will come to you," he said, "and will offer you great riches for healing his daughter. But take nothing from him," he said, "but ask only a ship to bring you home again to Ireland. And do you know who am I myself?" he said. "I do not know," said Diarmuid. "I am the messenger from beyond the world," he said; "and I came to your help because your own heart is hot to come to the help of another."

So Diarmuid did as he bade him, and he brought the water and the cup and the drops of blood to the woman, and she drank them, and at the third draught she was healed. And no sooner was she healed than the love he had for her was gone, and he turned away from her. "O Diarmuid," she said, "your love is gone from me." "O, it is gone indeed," said he.

Then there was music made in the whole place, and the lamenting was stopped, because of the healing of the king's daughter. And as to Diarmuid, he would take no reward and he would not stop there, but he asked for a ship to bring him home to Ireland, to Finn and the Fianna. And when he came where they were, there was a joyful welcome before him.

CHAPTER IV

The Hard Servant

The Fianna went hunting one time in the two proud provinces of Munster. They went out from Almhuin by the nearest paths till they came to the Brosna river in Slieve Bladhma, and from there to the twelve mountains of Eiblinne, and on to Aine Cliach, the harp of Aine.

They scattered themselves then and hunted through the borders of the forest that is called Magh Breogain, through blind trackless places and through broken lands, over beautiful level plains and the high hills of Desmumum, under pleasant Slieve Crot and smooth Slieve na Muc, along the level banks of the blue Siuir and over the green plain of Feman and the rough plain of Eithne, and the dark woods of Belach Gabrain.

And Finn was at the side of a hill, and the chief men of the Fianna along with him, to watch the hunting; for they liked to be listening to the outcry of the hounds and the hurried cries of the boys, and the noise and the whistling and the shouts of the strong men.

Finn asked then which of the men that were with him would go and keep watch on the side of the hill where they were. And Finnbane, son of Bresel, said he would go. And he went on to the top of the hill, where he could see about him on all sides. And he was not long there till he saw coming from the east a very big man, ugly and gloomy and deformed; and it is how he was, a dark-coloured shield on his back, a wide sword on his crooked left thigh, two spears on his shoulder, a torn loose cloak over his limbs, that were as black as a quenched coal. A sulky horse he had with him that had no good appearance, bony and thin as to body, and weak in the legs, and he leading it with a rough iron halter; and it was a great wonder the head was not pulled from the horse's body, or the arms pulled out of his owner, with the sudden stands and stops and the jerks it made. And the big man was striking blows on the horse with an iron cudgel to try and knock some going out of him, and the sound of the blows was like the breaking of strong waves.

And when Finnbane saw all that, he thought to himself it would not be right to let the like of that stranger go up unknown to Finn and the Fianna, and he ran back in haste to where they were and told them all he had seen.

And when he had told his story, they saw the big man coming towards them;

but as short as he was from them he was long in coming, from the badness of his walk and his going.

And when he came into Finn's presence he saluted him, and bowed his head and bent his knee, making signs of humility.

Finn raised his hand over his head then, and asked news of him, and if he was of the noble or of the mean blood of the great world. He answered that he had no knowledge who he came from, but only that he was a man of the Fomor, travelling in search of wages to the kings of the earth, "and I heard," he said, "that Finn never refused wages to any man." "I never did indeed," said Finn, "and I will not refuse you. But why is it," he said, "you are without a boy to mind your horse?" "I have a good reason for that," said the big man; "there is nothing in the world is worse to me than a boy to be with me; for it is a hundred men's share of food," he said, "that serves me for one day, and it is little enough I think it, and I would begrudge a boy to be sharing it with me." "What is the name you have?" said Finn. "The name I have is the Gilla Decair, the Hard Servant," said he. "Why did you get that name?" said Finn. "There is a good reason for that," said the big man, "for there is nothing in the world is harder to me than to do anything at all for my master, or whatever person I am with. And tell me this, Conan, son of Morna," he said, "who gets the best wages, a horseman or a man afoot?" "A horseman gets twice as much," said Conan. "Then I call you to witness, Conan," he said, "that I am a horseman, and that it was as a horseman I came to the Fianna. And give me your guarantee now, Finn, son of Cumhal, and the guarantee of the Fianna, and I will turn out my horse with your horses." "Let him out then," said Finn.

The big man pulled off the iron halter then from his horse, and it made off as hard as it could go, till it came where the horses of the Fianna were; and it began to tear and to kick and to bite at them, killing and maiming. "Take your horse out of that, big man," said Conan; "and by the earth and the sky," he said, "only it was on the guarantee of Finn and the Fianna you took the halter off him, I would let out his brains through the windows of his head; and many as is the bad prize Finn has found in Ireland," he said, "he never got one as bad as yourself." "And I swear by earth and sky as well as yourself," said the big man, "I will never bring him out of that; for I have no serving-boy to do it for me, and it is not work for me to be leading my horse by the hand."

Conan, son of Morna, rose up then and took the halter and put it on the horse, and led it back to where Finn was, and held it with his hand. "You would never have done a horse-boy's service, Conan," said Finn, "to any one of the Fianna, however far he might be beyond this Fomor. And if you will do what I advise," he said, "you will get up on the horse now, and search out with him all the hills and hollows and flowery plains of Ireland, till his heart is broken in his body in payment for the way he destroyed the horses of the Fianna."

Conan made a leap then on to the horse, and struck his heels hard into him, but with all that the horse would not stir. "I know what ails him," said Finn, "he will not stir till he has the same weight of horsemen on him as the weight of the big man."

On that thirteen men of the Fianna went up behind Conan, and the horse lay down with them and rose up again. "I think that you are mocking at my horse and at myself," said the big man; "and it is a pity for me to be spending the rest of the year with you, after all the humbugging I saw in you to-day, Finn. And I know well," he said, "that all I heard about you was nothing but lies, and there was no cause for the great name you have through the world. And I will quit you now, Finn," he said.

With that he went from them, slow and weak, dragging himself along till he had put a little hill between himself and the Fianna. And as soon as he was on the other side of it, he tucked up his cloak to his waist, and away with him, as if with the quickness of a swallow or a deer, and the rush of his going was like a blast of loud wind going over plains and mountains in spring-time.

When the horse saw his master going from him, he could not bear with it, but great as his load was he set out at full gallop following after him. And when Finn and the Fianna saw the thirteen men behind Conan, son of Morna, on the horse, and he starting off, they shouted with mocking laughter.

And when Conan found that he was not able to come down off the horse, he screeched and shouted to them not to let him be brought away with the big man they knew nothing of, and he began abusing and reproaching them. "A cloud of death over water on you, Finn," he said, "and that some son of a slave or a robber of the bad blood, one that is a worse son of a father and mother even than yourself, may take all that might protect your life, and your head along with that, unless you follow us to whatever place or island the big man will carry us to, and unless you bring us back to Ireland again."

Finn and the Fianna rose up then, and they followed the Gilla Decair over every bald hill, and through every valley and every river, on to pleasant Slieve Luachra, into the borders of Corca Duibhne; and the big man, that was up on the horse then along with Conan and the rest, faced towards the deep sea. And Liagan Luath of Luachar took hold of the horse's tail with his two hands, thinking to drag him back by the hair of it; but the horse gave a great tug, and away with him over the sea, and Liagan along with him, holding on to his tail.

It was a heavy care to Finn, those fourteen men of his people to be brought away from him, and he himself under bonds to bring them back. "What can we do now?" Oisin asked him. "What should we do, but to follow our people to whatever place or island the big man has brought them, and, whatever way we do it, to bring them back to Ireland again." "What can we do, having neither a ship or any kind of boat?" said Oisin. "We have this," said Finn, "the Tuatha de Danaan left as a gift to the children of the Gael, that whoever might have to leave Ireland for a while, had but to go to Beinn Edair, and however many would go along with him, they would find a ship that would hold them all." Finn looked towards the sea then, and he saw two strong armed men coming towards him. The first one had on his back a shield ribbed and of many colours, having shapes of strange, wonderful beasts engraved on it, and a heavy sword at his side, and two thick spears on his shoulders; a cloak of lasting crimson about him, with a gold brooch on the breast; a band of white bronze on his head, gold under each of his feet; and the other was dressed in the same way. They made no delay till they came to where Finn was, and they bowed their heads and bent their knees before him, and Finn raised his hand over their heads, and bade them to give an account of themselves. "We are sons of the King of the Eastern World," they said, "and we are come to Ireland asking to be taken into the service of Finn; for we heard there was not a man in all Ireland," they said, "would be better than yourself to judge of the skill we have." "What is your name, and what skill is that?" said Finn. "My name is Feradach, the Very Brave," he said; "and I have a carpenter's axe and a sling, and if there were so many as thirty hundred of the men of Ireland along with me in one spot, with three blows of the axe on the sling-stick I could get a ship that would hold them all. And I would ask no more help of them," he said, "than to bow down their heads while I was striking those three blows." "That is a good art," said Finn. "And tell me now," he said, "what can the other man do?" "I can do this," he said, "I can follow the track of the teal over nine ridges and nine furrows until I come on her in her bed; and it is the same to me to do it on sea as on land," he said. "That is a good art," said Finn; "and it would be a good help to us if you would come following a track with us now." "What is gone from you?" said one of the men. Finn told them then the whole story of the Hard Servant.

Then Feradach, the Very Brave, struck three blows on his sling-stick with the axe that he had, and the whole of the Fianna bowed their heads, and on the moment the whole of the bay and of the harbour was filled with ships and with fast boats. "What will we do with that many ships?" said Finn. "We will do away with all you make no use of," he said.

Caoilte rose up then and let out three great shouts, and all the Fianna of Ireland, in whatever places they were, heard them, and they thought Finn and his people to be in some kind of danger from men from beyond the sea.

They came then in small companies as they chanced to be, till they came to the stepping-stones of the Cat's Head in the western part of Corca Duibhne. And they asked news of Finn, what had happened that he called them away from their hunting, and Finn told them all that had happened. Then Finn and Oisin went into council together, and it is what they agreed; that as but fifteen of his people were brought away from Finn, he himself with fifteen others would go on their track; Oisin to be left at the head of the Fianna to guard Ireland.

And they said farewell to one another, and a grand ship was made ready for Finn and his people, and there was food put in it for using and gold for giving away. The young men and the heroes took to their seats then, and took hold of the oars, and they set out over the restless hills and the dark valleys of the great sea.

And the sea rose up and bellowed, and there was madness on the broken green waters; but to Finn and his people it was a call in the morning and a sleepy time at night to be listening to the roaring and the crooning that was ever and always about the sides of the ship.

They went on like that for three days and three nights, and saw no country or island. But at the end of that time a man of them went up into the head of the ship, and he saw out before them a great, rough grey cliff. They went on towards it then, and they saw on the edge of the cliff a high rock, round-shaped, having sides more slippery than an eel's back. And they found the track of the Hard Servant as far as to the foot of the rock.

Fergus of the True Lips said then to Diarmuid: "It is no brave thing you are doing, Diarmuid, grandson of Duibhne, to hold back like this, for it was with Manannan the Powerful, son of Lir, you were reared and got your learning, in the Land of Promise and in the coasts of the harbours, and with Angus Og, the Dagda's son. And are you without any share of their skill and their daring now," he said, "that would bring him and his people up this rock?"

Diarmuid's face reddened when he heard those words, and he took hold of Manannan's staves of power that were with him, and he reddened again, and he rose on the staves and gave a leap, and got a standing-place for his two feet on the overhanging rock. He looked down from that on Finn and his people, but whatever wish he had to bring them up to where he was, he was not able to do it.

He left the rock behind him then, and he was not gone far when he saw a wild tangled place before him, with thick woods that were of all he had ever walked the most leafy and the fullest of the sounds of wind and streams and birds, and of the humming of bees.

He went on walking the plain, and as he was looking about him, he saw a great tree with many twigs and branches, and a rock beside it, and a smooth-pointed drinking-horn on it, and a beautiful fresh well at its foot. And there was a great drouth on Diarmuid after the sea-journey, and he had a mind to drink a hornful of the water. But when he stopped to it he heard a great noise coming towards him, and he knew then there was enchantment in the water.

"I will drink my fill of it for all that," he said. And it was not long after that till he saw a Man of Enchantments coming towards him armed, having no friendly look. And it was in no friendly way he spoke to Diarmuid when he came up to him, but he gave him great abuse. "It is no right thing," he said, "to be walking through my thickets and to be drinking up my share of water." With that they faced one another angrily, and they fought till the end of the day.

The Enchanter thought it well to leave off fighting then, and he made a leap into the bottom of the well away from him, but there was vexation on Diarmuid to be left like that.

He looked around him then, and he saw a herd of deer coming through the scrub, and he went towards them, and threw a spear that went through the nearest stag and drove the bowels out of him. He kindled a fire then, and he cut thin bits of the flesh and put them on spits of white hazel, and that night he had his fill of meat and of the water of the well.

He rose up early on the morrow, and he found the Enchanter at the well before him. "It seems to me, Grandson of Duibhne," he said, "that it is not enough for you to be walking my scrub and my woods without killing my deer as well." With that they started again, giving one another blow for blow, thrust for thrust, and wound for wound till the end of the day came on them. And Diarmuid killed another great deer that night, and in the morning the fight began again. But in the evening, when the Enchanter was making his leap into the well, Diarmuid threw his arms about his neck, thinking to stop him, but it is what happened, he fell in himself. And when he was at the bottom of the well the Enchanter left him.

Diarmuid went then following after the Enchanter, and he found before him a beautiful wide flowery plain, and a comely royal city in the plain, and on the green before the dun he saw a great army; and when they saw Diarmuid following after the Enchanter, they left a way and a royal road for the Enchanter to pass through till he got inside the dun. And then they shut the gates, and the whole army turned on Diarmuid.

But that put no fear or cowardice on him, but he went through them and over them like a hawk would go through little birds, or a wild dog through a flock of sheep, killing all before him, till some of them made away to the woods and wastes, and another share of them through the gates of the dun, and they shut them, and the gates of the city after them. And Diarmuid, all full of hurts and wounds after the hard fight, lay down on the plain. A very strong daring champion came then and kicked at him from behind, and at that Diarmuid roused himself up, and put out his brave ready hand for his weapons.

"Wait a while, Grandson of Duibhne," the champion said then; "it is not to do you any hurt or harm I am come, but to say to you it is a bad sleeping-place for you to have, and it on your ill-wisher's lawn. And come now with me," he said, "and I will give you a better resting-place."

Diarmuid followed him then, and they went a long, long way from that, till they came to a high-topped city, and three times fifty brave champions in it, three times fifty modest women, and another young woman on a bench, with blushes in her cheeks, and delicate hands, and having a silken cloak about her, and a dress sewed with gold threads, and on her head the flowing veil of a queen.

There was a good welcome before Diarmuid for his own sake and the sake of his people, and he was put in a house of healing that was in the city, and good herbs were put to his hurts till he was smooth and sound again.

And a feast was made then, and the tables and the benches were set, and no high person was put in the place of the mean, or mean in the place of the high, but every one in his own place, according to his nobility, or his descent, or his art. Plenty of good food was brought to them then, and well-tasting strong drinks, and they spent the first part of the night in drinking, and the second part with music and delight and rejoicing of the mind, and the third part in sound sleep that lasted till the sun rose over the heavy sodded earth on the morrow.

Three days and three nights Diarmuid stopped in that city, and the best feast he ever found was given to him all through. And at the end of that time he asked what was the place he was in, and who was head of it. And the champion that brought him there told him it was Land-Under-Wave, and that the man that had fought with him was its king. "And he is an enemy of the Red Hand to me," he said. "And as to myself," he said, "I was one time getting wages from Finn, son of Cumhal, in Ireland, and I never put a year over me that pleased me better. And tell me now," he said, "what is the journey or the work that is before you?"

And Diarmuid told him the story of the Hard Servant then from beginning to end.

Now, as to Finn and his people, when they thought Diarmuid was too long away from them, they made ladders of the cords of the ship and put them against the rock, looking for him.

And after a while they found the leavings of the meat he had eaten, for Diarmuid never ate meat without leaving some after him.

Finn looked then on every side, and he saw a rider coming towards him over the plain on a dark-coloured beautiful horse, having a bridle of red gold. Finn saluted him when he came up, and the rider stooped his head and gave Finn three kisses, and asked him to go with him. They went on a long way till they came to a wide, large dwelling-place full of arms, and a great troop of armed men on the green before the fort. Three nights and three days Finn and his people stopped in the dun, and the best feast they ever got was served out to them.

At the end of that time Finn asked what country was he in, and the man that brought him there told him it was the land of Sorcha, and that he himself was its king. "And I was with yourself one time, Finn, son of Cumhal," he said, "taking your wages through the length of a year in Ireland."

Then Finn and the King of Sorcha called a great gathering of the people and a great meeting. And when it was going on they saw a woman-messenger coming to them through the crowd, and the king asked news of her. "I have news indeed," she said; "the whole of the bay and the harbour is full of ships and of boats, and there are armies all through the country robbing all before them." "I know well," said the king, "it is the High King of Greece is in it, for he has a mind to put the entire world under him, and to get hold of this country like every other." The King of Sorcha looked at Finn then, and Finn understood it was help from him he was asking, and it is what he said: "I take the protection of this country on myself so long as I am in it." He and his people rose up then, and the King of Sorcha along with them, and they went looking for the strange army. And when they came up with it they made great slaughter of its champions, and those they did not kill ran before them, and made no better stand than a flock of frightened birds, till there were hardly enough of them left to tell the story.

The High King spoke then, and it is what he said: "Who is it has done this great slaughter of my people? And I never heard before," he said, "any talk of the courage or of the doings of the men of Ireland either at this time or in the old times. But from this out," he said, "I will banish the Sons of the Gael for ever to the very ends of the earth."

But Finn and the King of Sorcha raised a green tent in view of the ships of the Greeks.

The King of the Greeks called then for help against Finn and the King of Sorcha, to get satisfaction for the shame that was put on his people. And the sons of kings of the eastern and southern world came to his help, but they could make no stand against Finn and Osgar and Oisin and Goll, son of Morna. And at the last the King of Greece brought all his people back home, the way no more of them would be put an end to.

And then Finn and the King of Sorcha called another great gathering. And while it was going on, they saw coming towards them a great troop of champions, bearing flags of many-coloured silk, and grey swords at their sides and high spears reared up over their heads. And in the front of them was Diarmuid, grandson of Duibhne.

When Finn saw him, he sent Fergus of the True Lips to ask news of him, and they told one another all that had happened.

And it would take too long to tell, and it would tire the hearers, how Finn made the Hard Servant bring home his fifteen men that he had brought away. And when he had brought them back to Ireland, the whole of the Fianna were watching to see him ride away again, himself and his long-legged horse. But while they were watching him, he vanished from them, and all they could see was a mist, and it stretching out towards the sea.

And that is the story of the Hard Servant, and of Diarmuid's adventures on the island Under-Wave.

CHAPTER V

The House of the Quicken Trees

And it is often the Fianna would have been badly off without the help of Diarmuid. It was he came to their help the time Miodac, the son of the King of Lochlann, brought them into the enchanted House of the Quicken Trees.

It was by treachery he brought them in, giving himself out to be a poet, and making poems for Finn to make out the meaning of. A verse he made about a great army that he saw riding over the plains to victory, and robbing all before it, and the riders of it having no horses but plants and branches. "I understand that," said Finn, "it was an army of bees you saw, that was gathering riches from the flowers as it went." And another verse Miodac made was about a woman in Ireland that was swifter than the swiftest horse. "I know that," said Finn, "that woman is the River Boinn; and if she goes slow itself, she is swifter in the end than the swiftest horse, for her going never stops." And other verses he made about Angus' house at Brugh na Boinn, but Finn made them all out.

And after that he said he had a feast ready for them, and he bade them go into his House of the Quicken Trees till he would bring it. And they did that, and went in, and it was a beautiful house, having walls of every colour, and foreign coverings of every colour on the floor, and a fire that gave out a very pleasant smoke. And they sat down there, and after a while Finn said: "It is a wonder such a beautiful house to be here." "There is a greater wonder than that," said Goll; "that fire that was so pleasant when we came in is giving out now the worst stench in the world." "There is a greater wonder than that," said Glas; "the walls that were of all colours are now but rough boards joined together." "There is a greater wonder than that," said Fiacha; "where there were seven high doors to the house there is now but one little door, and it shut." "Indeed, there is a more wonderful thing than that," said Conan; "for we sat down on beautiful coverings, and now there is nothing between us and the bare ground, and it as cold as the snow of one night." And he tried to rise up, but he could not stir, or any of the rest of them, for there was enchantment that kept them where they were.

And it was the treachery of Miodac, and the spells of the Three Kings of the Island of the Floods that had brought them into that danger. And Finn knew by his divination that their enemies were gathering to make an end of them, and he said to his people there was no use in making complaints, but to sound the music of the Dord Fiann.

And some of the Fianna that were waiting for him not far off heard that sorrowful music, and came fighting against Miodac and his armies, and they fought well, but they could not stand against them. And at the last it was Diarmuid, grandson of Duibhne, that made an end of Miodac that was so treacherous, and of the Three Kings of the Island of the Floods, and took the enchantment off the floor of the House of the Rowan Trees with their blood.

And when he was freeing the Fianna, Conan called out, asking him to bring him a share of the feast Miodac had made ready for his own friends, for there was hunger on him. And when Diarmuid took no heed of him, he said: "If it was a comely woman was speaking to you, Diarmuid, you would not refuse to listen."

For if many women loved Diarmuid, there were many he himself gave his love to; and if he was often called Diarmuid the brave, or the hardy, or the comely, or the Hawk of Ess Ruadh, it is often he was called as well the friend and the coaxer of women, Diarmuid-na-man.

BOOK VII

Diarmuid and Grania

CHAPTER I

The Flight from Teamhair

Finn rose up one morning early in Almhuin of Leinster, and he sat out alone on the green lawn without a boy or a servant being with him. And Oisin followed him there, and Diorraing the Druid. "What is the cause of your early rising, Finn?" said Oisin. "It is not without cause, indeed, I rise early," said Finn, "for I am without a wife or a companion since Maighneis, daughter of Black Garraidh, died from me; for quiet sleep is not used to come to a man that is without a fitting wife." "Why would you be like that?" said Oisin, "for there is not a woman in all green Ireland you would throw a look on but we would bring her to you, willing or unwilling." "I myself could find a wife would be fitting for you," said Diorraing. "Who is that?" said Finn. "It is Grania, daughter of the High King of Ireland," said Diorraing; "and she is the woman of the best make and shape and the best speech of the women of the whole world." "By my word, Diorraing," said Finn, "there is strife and disagreement between the High King and myself this long time, and it would not be pleasing to me to get a refusal from him. And it is best for you two to go together," he said, "and to ask his daughter for me in marriage; the way that if he gives a refusal, it will be to you and not to myself he will give it." "We will go," said Oisin, "even if it is little profit we will get by it. And let no one at all know of our going," he said, "until such time as we are come back again."

After that the two bade farewell to Finn, and set out, and it is not told what they did till they came to Teamhair. The King of Ireland was holding a gathering at that time on the green of Teamhair, and the chief nobles of his people were with him. And there was a friendly welcome given to Oisin and to Diorraing, and the king put off the gathering till the next day, for he was sure it was some pressing thing had brought these two men of the Fianna to Teamhair. And Oisin went aside with him, and told him it was to ask his daughter Grania in marriage they were come from Finn, Head of the Fianna of Ireland.

The king spoke, and it is what he said: "There is not a son of a king or of a great prince, there is not a champion in Ireland my daughter has not given a refusal to, and it is on me they all lay the blame of that. And I will give you no answer at all," he said, "till you go to herself; for it is better for you to get her own answer, than to be displeased with me."

So they went together to the sunny house of the women, and the king sat down at the head of the high seat beside Grania, and he said: "Here, Grania, are two of the people of Finn, son of Cumhal, come to ask you as a wife for him, and what answer have you a mind to give them?" And it is what Grania said: "If he is a fitting son-in-law for you, why would he not be a fitting husband for me?"

They were satisfied then, and there was a feast made for them that night in Grania's sunny house, and the king settled for a meeting a fortnight from that time between himself and Finn at Teamhair.

So Oisin and Diorraing went back again to Almhuin, and told Finn their story from beginning to end. And as everything wears away, so did that time of delay.

And then Finn gathered together the seven battalions of the Fianna from every part where they were to Almhuin. And they set out in great bands and troops till they came to Teamhair.

The king was out on the green before them, and the great people of the men of Ireland, and there was a great welcome before Finn and the Fianna.

But when Grania saw grey-haired Finn, she said: "It is a great wonder it was not for Oisin Finn asked me, for he would be more fitting for me than a man that is older than my father."

But they talked together for a while, and Finn was putting questions to Grania, for she had the name of being very quick with answers. "What is whiter than snow?" he said. "The truth," said Grania. "What is the best colour?" said Finn. "The colour of childhood," said she. "What is hotter than fire?" "The face of a hospitable man when he sees a stranger coming in, and the house empty." "What has a taste more bitter than poison?" "The reproach of an enemy." "What is best for a champion?" "His doings to be high, and his pride to be low." "What is the best of jewels?" "A knife." "What is sharper than a sword?" "The wit of a woman between two men." "What is quicker than the wind?" said Finn then. "A woman's mind," said Grania. And indeed she was telling no lie when she said that. And for all their talk together she had no liking for Finn, and she felt the blood in her heart to be rising against him.

And the wedding-feast was made ready then, and they all went into the king's feasting-house in the Middle Court. And the king sat down to take his share of drinking and pleasure, and his wife at his left side, and Grania beside her again; and Finn, son of Cumhal, at the right hand of the king, and Oisin at the other side, and every other one according to his nobility and his birth.

Then Daire of the poems stood up before Grania, and sang the songs and good poems of her fathers to her. And there was sitting near to Grania a knowledgable man, a Druid of Finn's people, and it was not long until they began to talk together. "Tell me now," said Grania, "who is that man on the right hand of

Oisin?" "That is Goll, son of Morna," said the Druid, "the ready fighter." "Who is that beside Goll?" said Grania. "Osgar, son of Oisin," said the Druid. "And who is that thin-legged man beside Osgar?" "That is Caoilte, son of Ronan." "Who is that proud, hasty man beside Caoilte?" "Lugaidh's Son of the Strong Hand." "Who is that sweet-worded man," she said then, "with the dark hair, and cheeks like the rowan berry, on the left side of Oisin, son of Finn?" "That is Diarmuid, grandson of Duibhne," said the Druid, "that is the best lover of women in the whole world." "That is a good company," said Grania.

And after the feast had gone on a while, their own feast was made for the dogs outside. And the dogs began to fight with one another, and the noise was heard in the hall, and the chief men of the Fianna went to drive them away from one another.

Now Diarmuid was used to keep his cap always over the love-spot the woman had left on his forehead, for no woman could see that spot but she would give him her love. And it chanced, while he was driving the dogs apart, the cap fell from him, and Grania was looking out at him as it fell, and great love for him came on her there and then. And she called her serving-maid to her, and bade her bring the great golden cup that held drink for nine times nine men from the sunny house. And when the serving-maid brought the cup, she filled it with wine that had enchantment in it, and she said: "Give the cup first to Finn, and bid him take a drink from it, and tell him it is I myself sent it to him." So the serving-maid did that, and Finn took the cup and drank out of it, and no sooner did he drink than he fell into a deep sleep. And then the cup was given to the king, and the queen, and the sons of kings, and the whole company, but only Oisin and Osgar and Caoilte and Diarmuid, and Diorraing the Druid. And all that drank of it fell into the same heavy sleep.

And when they were all in their sleep, Grania rose up softly from the seat where she was, and she turned her face to Diarmuid, and she said: "Will you take my love, Diarmuid, son of Duibhne, and will you bring me away out of this house to-night?"

"I will not," said Diarmuid; "I will not meddle with the woman that is promised to Finn." "If that is so," said Grania, "I put you under Druid bonds, to bring me out of this house to-night before the awaking of Finn and of the King of Ireland from their sleep."

"It is under bad bonds you are putting me, Grania," said Diarmuid. "And why is it," he said, "that you put them on me more than on the great men and sons of kings that are in the Middle Court to-night? for there is not one of them all but is as well worthy of a woman's love as myself." "By my hand, Diarmuid, it is not without cause I laid those bonds on you," said Grania; "for I was at the door a while ago when you were parting the dogs," she said, "and my eyes fell on you, and I gave you the love there and then that I never gave to any other, and never will give for ever."

"It is a wonder you to give that love to me, and not to Finn," said Diarmuid, "for there is not in Ireland a man is a better lover of a woman than himself. And do you know this, Grania," he said, "the night Finn is in Teamhair it is he himself is the keeper of its gates. And as that is so, we cannot leave the town." "There is a side door of escape at my sunny house," said Grania, "and we will go out by it." "It is a thing I will never do," said Diarmuid, "to go out by any side door of escape at all." "That may be so," said Grania, "but I heard it said that every fighting man has leave to pass over the walls of any dun and of any strong place at all by the shafts of his spears. And I will go out through the door," she said, "and let you follow me like that."

With that she went out, and Diarmuid spoke to his people, and it is what he said, "O Oisin, son of Finn, what must I do with these bonds that are laid on me?" "You are not guilty if the bonds were laid on you," said Oisin; "and I tell you to follow Grania, and to keep yourself well out of the hands of Finn." "Osgar, son of Oisin," he said then, "what must I do with these bonds that are put on me?" "I tell you to follow Grania," said Osgar, "for it is a pitiful man that would break his bonds." "What advice do you give me, Caoilte?" said Diarmuid. "It is what I say," said Caoilte, "that I myself have a fitting wife; and that it would be better to me than all the riches of the world Grania to have given me that love." "What advice do you give me, Diorraing?" "I tell you to follow Grania," said Diorraing, "although you will get your death by it, and that is bad to me." "Is that the advice you all give me?" said Diarmuid. "It is," said Oisin, and all the rest with him. With that Diarmuid stood up and stretched out his hand for his weapons, and he said farewell to Oisin and the others, and every tear he shed was of the size of a mountain berry. He went out then to the wall of the dun, and he put the shafts of his two spears under him, and he rose with a light leap and he came down on the grassy earth outside, and Grania met him there. Then Diarmuid said: "It is a bad journey you are come on, Grania. For it would be better for you to have Finn, son of Cumhal, as a lover than myself, for I do not know any part or any western corner of Ireland that will hide you. And if I do bring you with me," he said, "it is not as a wife I will bring you, but I will keep my faith to Finn. And turn back now to the town," he said, "and Finn will never get news of what you are after doing." "It is certain I will not turn back," said Grania, "and I will never part with you till death parts us." "If that is so, let us go on, Grania," said Diarmuid.

They went on then, and they were not gone far out from the town when Grania said: "I am getting tired, indeed." "It is a good time to be tired," said Diarmuid, "and go now back again to your own house. For I swear by the word of a true champion," he said, "I will never carry yourself or any other woman to the end of life and time." "That is not what you have to do," said Grania, "for my father's horses are in a grass field by themselves, and chariots with them; and turn back now, and bring two horses of them, and I will wait in this place till you come to me again."

Diarmuid went back then for the horses, and we have no knowledge of their journey till they reached to the ford on the Sionnan, that is called now Ath-luain.

And Diarmuid said then to Grania: "It is easier to Finn to follow our track, the horses being with us." "If that is so," said Grania: "leave the horses here, and I will go on foot from this out."

Diarmuid went down to the river then, and he brought a horse with him over the ford, and left the other horse the far side of the river. And he himself and Grania went a good way with the stream westward, and they went to land at the side of the province of Connacht. And wherever they went, Diarmuid left unbroken bread after him, as a sign to Finn he had kept his faith with him.

And from that they went on to Doire-da-Bhoth, the Wood of the Two Huts. And Diarmuid cut down the wood round about them, and he made a fence having seven doors of woven twigs, and he set out a bed of soft rushes and of the tops of the birch-tree for Grania in the very middle of the wood.

CHAPTER II

The Pursuit

And as to Finn, son of Cumhal, I will tell out his story now.

All that were in Teamhair rose up early in the morning of the morrow, and they found Diarmuid and Grania were wanting from them, and there came a scorching jealousy and a weakness on Finn. He sent out his trackers then on the plain, and bade them to follow Diarmuid and Grania. And they followed the track as far as the ford on the Sionnan, and Finn and the Fianna followed after them, but they were not able to carry the track across the ford. And Finn gave them his word that unless they would find the track again without delay, he would hang them on each side of the ford.

Then the sons of Neamhuin went up against the stream, and they found a horse on each side of it, and then they went on with the stream westward, and they found the track going along the side of the Province of Connacht, and Finn and the Fianna of Ireland followed it on. And Finn said: "I know well where we will find Diarmuid and Grania now; it is in Doire-da-Bhoth they are." Oisin and Osgar and Caoilte and Diorraing were listening when Finn said those words. And Osgar spoke to the others, and it is what he said: "There is danger they might be there, and it would be right for us to give them some warning; and look now, Osgar, where is Bran the hound, for Finn himself is no dearer to him than Diarmuid, and bid him go now with a warning to him."

So Osgar told Bran, and Bran understood him well, and she went to the rear of the whole troop the way Finn would not see her, and she followed on the track of Diarmuid and Grania till she came to Doire-da-Bhoth, and she put her head into Diarmuid's bosom, and he in his sleep.

Diarmuid started up out of his sleep then, and he awoke Grania, and said to her: "Here is Bran, Finn's hound, and she is come with a warning to tell us Finn himself is coming." "Let us take that warning, then," said Grania, "and make your escape." "I will not take it," said Diarmuid, "for if I cannot escape Finn, I would as soon he took me now as at any other time." When Grania heard that, great fear came on her.

Bran went away from them then, and when Oisin saw her coming back, he said: "I am in dread Bran found no chance to get to Diarmuid, and we should send him some other warning. And look where is Fearghoin," he said, "Caoilte's serving-man." Now it was the way with Fearghoin, every shout he would give would be heard in the three nearest hundreds to him. So they made him give out three shouts the way Diarmuid would hear him. And Diarmuid heard him, and he said to Grania: "I hear Caoilte's serving-man, and it is with Caoilte he is, and it is along with Finn Caoilte is, and those shouts were sent as a warning to me." "Take that warning," said Grania. "I will not take it," said Diarmuid, "for Finn and the Fianna will come up with us before we leave the wood." And fear and great dread came on Grania when she heard him say that.

As for Finn, he did not leave off following the track till he came to Doire-da-Bhoth, and he sent the sons of Neamhuin to search through the wood, and they saw Diarmuid, and the woman along with him. They came back then where Finn was, and he asked them were Diarmuid and Grania in the wood? "Diarmuid is in it," they said, "and there is some woman with him, but we knew Diarmuid, and we do not know Grania." "May no good come to the friends of Diarmuid for his sake," said Finn, "and he will not quit that wood till he has given me satisfaction for everything he has done to me."

"It is jealousy has put you astray, Finn," said Oisin; "you to think Diarmuid would stop here on the plain of Maen Mhagh, and no close place in it but Doire-da-Bhoth, and you following after him." "Saying that will do you no good," said Finn, "for I knew well when I heard the three shouts Caoilte's serving-man gave out, it was you sent them to Diarmuid as a warning. And another thing," he said, "it was you sent my own hound Bran to him. But none of those things you have done will serve you, for he will not leave Doire-da-Bhoth till he gives me satisfaction for everything he has done to me, and every disgrace he has put on me." "It is great foolishness for you, Finn," said Osgar then, "to be thinking Diarmuid would stop in the middle of this plain and you waiting here to strike the head off him." "Who but himself cut the wood this way," said Finn, "and made this close sheltered place with seven woven narrow doors to it. And O Diarmuid," he said out then, "which of us is the truth with, myself or Oisin?" "You never failed from your good judgment, Finn," said Diarmuid, "and indeed I myself and Grania are here." Then Finn called to his men to go around Diarmuid and Grania, and to take them.

Now it was shown at this time to Angus Og, at Brugh na Boinne, the great danger Diarmuid was in, that was his pupil at one time, and his dear foster-son. He set out then with the clear cold wind, and did not stop in any place till he came to Doire-da-Bhoth. And he went unknown to Finn or the Fianna into the place where Diarmuid and Grania were, and he spoke kind words to Diarmuid, and he said: "What is the thing you have done, grandson of Duibhne?" "It is," said Diarmuid, "the daughter of the King of Ireland that has made her escape with me from her father and from Finn, and it is not by my will she came." "Let each of you come under a border of my cloak, so," said Angus, "and I will bring you out of the place where you are without knowledge of Finn or his people." "Bring Grania with you," said Diarmuid, "but I will never go with you; but if I am alive I will follow you before long. And if I do not," he said, "give Grania to her father, and he will do well or ill to her."

With that Angus put Grania under the border of his cloak, and brought her out unknown to Finn or the Fianna, and there is no news told of them till they came to Ros-da-Shoileach, the Headland of the Two Sallows.

And as to Diarmuid, after Angus and Grania going from him, he stood up as straight as a pillar and put on his armour and his arms, and after that he went to a door of the seven doors he had made, and he asked who was at it. "There is no enemy to you here," they said, "for there are here Oisin and Osgar and the best men of the sons of Baiscne along with us. And come out to us now, and no one will have the daring to do any harm or hurt on you." "I will not go out to you," said Diarmuid, "till I see at what door Finn himself is." He went then to another door of the seven and asked who was at it. "Caoilte, son of Ronan, and the rest of the sons of Ronan along with him; and come out to us now, and we will give ourselves for your sake." "I will not go out to you," said Diarmuid, "for I will not put you under Finn's anger for any well-doing to myself." He went on to another door then and asked who was at it. "There is Conan, son of Morna, and the rest of the sons of Morna along with him; and it is enemies to Finn we are, and you are a great deal more to us than he is, and you may come out and no one will dare lay a hand on you." "I will not indeed," said Diarmuid, "for Finn would be better pleased to see the death of every one of you than to let me escape." He went then to another door and asked who was at it. "A friend and a comrade of your own, Fionn, son of Cuadan, head of the Fianna of Munster, and his men along with him; and we are of the one country and the one soil, and we will give our bodies and our lives for your sake." "I will not go out to you," said Diarmuid, "for I would not like Finn to have a grudge against you for any good you did to me." He went then to another door and asked who was at it. "It is Fionn, son of Glor, head of the Fianna of Ulster, and his men along with him; and come out now to us and there is no one will dare hurt or harm you." "I will not go out to you," said Diarmuid, "for you are a friend to me, and your father along with you, and I would not like the unfriendliness of Finn to be put on you for my sake." He went then to another door, and he asked who was at it. "There is no friend of yours here," they said, "for there is here Aodh Beag the Little from Eamhuin, and Aodh Fada the Long from Eamhuin, and Caol Crodha the Fierce, and Goineach the Wounder, and Gothan the White-fingered, and Aoife his daughter, and Cuadan the Tracker from Eamhuin; and we are unfriendly people to you, and if you come out to us we will not spare you at all, but will make an end of you." "It is a bad troop is in it," said Diarmuid; "you of the lies and of the tracking and of the one shoe, and it is not fear of your hands is upon me, but because I am your enemy I will not go out."

He went then to the last of the seven doors and asked who was at it. "No friend of yours," they said, "but it is Finn, son of Cumhal, and four hundred paid fighting men along with him; and if you will come out to us we will make opened marrow of you." "I give you my word, Finn," said Diarmuid, "that the door you are at yourself is the first door I will pass out of."

When Finn heard that, he warned his battalions on pain of lasting death not to let Diarmuid past them unknown. But when Diarmuid heard what he said, he rose on the staves of his spears and he went with a very high, light leap on far beyond Finn and his people, without their knowledge. He looked back at them then, and called out that he had gone past them, and he put his shield on his back and went straight on towards the west, and it was not long before he was out of sight of Finn and the Fianna. Then when he did not see any one coming after him, he turned back to where he saw Angus and Grania going out of the wood, and he followed on their track till he came to Ros-da-Shoileach.

He found Angus and Grania there in a sheltered, well-lighted cabin, and a great blazing fire kindled in it, and the half of a wild boar on spits. Diarmuid greeted them, and the life of Grania all to went out of her with joy before him.

Diarmuid told them his news from beginning to end, and they ate their share that night, and they went to sleep till the coming of the day and of the full light on the morrow. And Angus rose up early, and he said to Diarmuid: "I am going from you now, grandson of Duibhne; and I leave this advice with you," he said, "not to go into a tree with one trunk, and you flying before Finn, and not to be going into a cave of the earth that has but one door, and not to be going to an island of the sea that has but one harbour. And in whatever place you cook your share of food," he said, "do not eat it there; and in whatever place you eat it, do not lie down there; and in whatever place you lie down, do not rise up there on the morrow." He said farewell to them after that, and went his way.

CHAPTER III

The Green Champions

Then Diarmuid and Grania went along the right bank of the Sionnan westward till they came to Garbh-abhana-Fiann, the rough river of the Fianna. And Diarmuid killed a salmon on the brink of the river, and put it to the fire on a spit. Then he himself and Grania went across the stream to eat it, as Angus bade them; and then they went westward to sleep.

They rose up early on the morrow, and they travelled straight westward till they came to the marsh of Finnliath.

And on the marsh they met with a young man, having a good shape and appearance, but without fitting dress or arms. Diarmuid greeted the young man, and asked news of him. "A fighting lad I am, looking for a master," he said, "and Muadhan is my name." "What would you do for me, young man?" said Diarmuid. "I would be a servant to you in the day, and watch for you in the night," he said. "I tell you to keep that young man," said Grania, "for you cannot be always without people."

Then they made an agreement with him, and bound one another, and they went on together westward till they reached the Carrthach river. And then Muadhan bade Diarmuid and Grania to go up on his back till he would carry them over the stream.

"That would be a big load for you," said Grania. But he put them upon his back and carried them over. Then they went on till they came to the Beith, and Muadhan brought them over on his back the same way. And they went into a cave at the side of Currach Cinn Adhmuid, the Woody Headland of the Bog, over Tonn Toime, and Muadhan made ready beds of soft rushes and tops of the birch for them in the far end of the cave. And he went himself into the scrub that was near, and took a straight long rod of a quicken-tree, and he put a hair and a hook on the rod, and a holly berry on the hook, and he went up the stream, and he took a salmon with the first cast. Then he put on a second berry and killed another fish, and he put on a third berry and killed the third fish. Then he put the hook and the hair under his belt, and struck the rod into the earth, and he brought the three salmon where Diarmuid and Grania were, and put them on spits. When they were done, Muadhan said: "I give the dividing of the fish to you, Diarmuid." "I would sooner you to divide it than myself," said Diarmuid. "I will give the dividing of the fish to you, so, Grania," said he. "I am better satisfied you to divide it," said Grania. "If it was you that divided the fish, Diarmuid," said Muadhan, "you would have given the best share to Grania; and if it was Grania divided it, she would have given you the best share; and as it is myself is dividing it, let you have the biggest fish, Diarmuid, and let Grania have the second biggest, and I myself will have the one is smallest."

They spent the night there, and Diarmuid and Grania slept in the far part of the cave, and Muadhan kept watch for them until the rising of the day and the full light of the morrow.

Diarmuid rose up early, and he bade Grania keep watch for Muadhan, and that he himself would go and take a walk around the country. He went out then, and he went up on a hill that was near, and he was looking about him, east and west, north and south. He was not long there till he saw a great fleet of ships coming from the west, straight to the bottom of the hill where he was. And when they were come to land, nine times nine of the chief men of the ships came on shore, and Diarmuid went down and greeted them, and asked news of them, and to what country they belonged.

"Three kings we are of the Green Champions of Muirna-locht," said they; "and Finn, son of Cumhal, sent looking for us by cause of a thief of the woods, and an enemy of his own that has gone hiding from him; and it is to hinder him we are come. And we are twenty hundred good fighting men, and every one of us is a match for a hundred, and besides that," he said, "we have three deadly hounds with us; fire will not burn them, and water will not drown them, and arms will not redden on them, and we will lay them on his track, and it will be short till we get news of him. And tell us who you are yourself?" they said, "and have you any word of the grandson of Duibhne?" "I saw him yesterday," said Diarmuid; "and I myself," he said, "am but a fighting man, walking the world by the strength of my hand and by the hardness of my sword. And by my word," he said, "you will know Diarmuid's hand when you will meet it." "Well, we found no one up to this," said they. "What are your own names?" said Diarmuid. "Dubh-chosach, the Black-footed, Fionn-chosach, the Fair-footed, and Treun-chosach, the Strong-footed," they said.

"Is there wine in your ships?" said Diarmuid. "There is," said they. "If you have a mind to bring out a tun of wine," said Diarmuid, "I will do a trick for you." They sent men to get the tun, and when it came Diarmuid took it between his two hands and drank a drink out of it, and the others drank what was left of it. Diarmuid took up the tun after that, and brought it to the top of the hill, and he went up himself on the tun, and let it go down the steep of the hill till it was at the bottom. And then he brought the tun up the hill again, and he himself on it coming and going, and he did that trick three times before the strangers. But they said he was a man had never seen a good trick when he called that a trick; and with that a man of them went up on the tun, but Diarmuid gave a stroke of his foot at it and the young man fell from it before it began to move, and it rolled over him and crushed him, that he died. And another man went on it, and another after him again, till fifty of them were killed trying to do Diarmuid's trick, and as many of them as were not killed went back to their ships that night.

Diarmuid went back then to where he left Grania; and Muadhan put the hair and the hook on the rod till he killed three salmon; and they ate their meal that night, and he kept watch for them the same way he did before.

Diarmuid went out early the next day again to the hill, and it was not long till he saw the three strangers coming towards him, and he asked them would they like to see any more tricks. They said they would sooner get news of the grandson of Duibhne. "I saw a man that saw him yesterday," said Diarmuid. And with that he put off his arms and his clothes, all but the shirt that was next his skin, and he struck the Crann Buidhe, the spear of Manannan, into the earth with the point upwards. And then he rose with a leap and lit on the point of the spear as light as a bird, and came down off it again without a wound on him. Then a young man of the Green Champions said: "It is a man has never seen feats that would call that a feat"; and he put off his clothing and made a leap, and if he did he came down heavily on the point of the spear, and it went through his heart, and he fell to the ground. The next day Diarmuid came again, and he brought two forked poles out of the wood and put them standing upright on the hill, and he put the sword of Angus Og, the Mor-alltach, the Big-fierce one, between the two forks on its edge. Then he raised himself lightly over it, and walked on the sword three times from the hilt to the point, and he came down and asked was there a man of them could do that feat.

"That is a foolish question," said a man of them then, "for there was never any feat done in Ireland but a man of our own would do it." And with that he rose up to walk on the sword; but it is what happened, he came down heavily on it the way he was cut in two halves.

The rest of the champions bade him take away his sword then, before any more of their people would fall by it; and they asked him had he any word of the grandson of Duibhne. "I saw a man that saw him today," said Diarmuid, "and I will go ask news of him to-night."

He went back then to where Grania was, and Muadhan killed three salmon for their supper, and kept a watch for them through the night. And Diarmuid rose up at the early break of day, and he put his battle clothes on him, that no weapon could go through, and he took the sword of Angus, that left no leavings after it, at his left side, and his two thick-handled spears, the Gae Buidhe and the Gae Dearg, the Yellow and the Red, that gave wounds there was no healing for. And then he wakened Grania, and he bade her to keep watch for Muadhan, and he himself would go out and take a look around.

When Grania saw him looking so brave, and dressed in his clothes of anger and of battle, great fear took hold of her, and she asked what was he going to do. "It is for fear of meeting my enemies I am like this," said he. That quieted Grania, and then Diarmuid went out to meet the Green Champions.

They came to land then, and they asked had he news of the grandson of Duibhne. "I saw him not long ago," said Diarmuid. "If that is so, let us know where is he," said they, "till we bring his head to Finn, son of Cumhal." "I would be keeping bad watch for him if I did that," said Diarmuid, "for his life and his body are under the protection of my valour, and by reason of that I will do no treachery on him." "Is that true?" said they. "It is true indeed," said Diarmuid. "Let you yourself quit this place, so," they said, "or we will bring your head to Finn since you are an enemy to him." "It is in bonds I would be," said Diarmuid, "the time I would leave my head with you." And with that he drew his sword the Mor-alltach out of its sheath, and he made a fierce blow at the head nearest him that put it in two halves. Then he made an attack on the whole host of the Green Champions, and began to destroy them, cutting through the beautiful shining armour of the men of Muir-na-locht till there was hardly a man but got shortening of life and the sorrow of death, or that could go back to give news of the fight, but only the three kings and a few of their people that made their escape back to their ships. Diarmuid turned back then without wound or hurt on him, and he went to where Grania and Muadhan were. They bade him welcome, and Grania asked him did he hear any news of Finn and the Fianna of Ireland, and he said he did not, and they ate their food and spent the night there.

He rose up again with the early light of the morrow and went back to the hill, and when he got there he struck a great blow on his shield that set the strand shaking with the sound. And Dubh-chosach heard it, and he said he himself would go fight with Diarmuid, and he went on shore there and then.

And he and Diarmuid threw the arms out of their hands and rushed on one another like wrestlers, straining their arms and their sinews, knotting their hands on one another's backs, fighting like bulls in madness, or like two daring hawks on the edge of a cliff. But at the last Diarmuid raised up Dubh-chosach on his shoulder and threw his body to the ground, and bound him fast and firm on the spot. And Fionn-chosach and Treun-chosach came one after the other to fight with him then, and he put the same binding on them; and he said he would strike the heads off them, only he thought it a worse punishment to leave them in those bonds. "For there is no one can free you," he said. And he left them there, worn out and sorrowful.

The next morning after that, Diarmuid told Grania the whole story of the strangers from beginning to end, and of all he had done to them, and how on the fifth day he had put their kings in bonds. "And they have three fierce hounds in a chain ready to hunt me," he said. "Did you take the heads off those three kings?" said Grania. "I did not," said Diarmuid, "for there is no man of the heroes of Ireland can loosen those bonds but four only, Oisin, son of Finn, and Osgar, son of Oisin, and Lugaidh's Son of the Strong Hand, and Conan, son of Morna; and I know well," he said, "none of those four will do it. But all the same, it is short till Finn will get news of them, and it is best for us to be going from this cave, or Finn and the three hounds might come on us."

After that they left the cave, and they went on till they came to the bog of Finnliath. Grania began to fall behind them, and Muadhan put her on his back and carried her till they came to the great Slieve Luachra. Then Diarmuid sat down on the brink of the stream that was flowing through the heart of the mountain, and Grania was washing her hands, and she asked his knife from him to cut her nails with.

As to the strangers, as many of them as were alive yet, they came to the hill where their three leaders were bound, and they thought to loose them; but it is the way those bonds were, all they did by meddling with them was to draw them tighter.

And they were not long there till they saw a woman coming towards them with the quickness of a swallow or a weasel or a blast of wind over bare mountain-tops. And she asked them who was it had done that great slaughter on them. "Who are you that is asking that?" said they. "I am the Woman of the Black Mountain, the woman-messenger of Finn, son of Cumhal," she said; "and it is looking for you Finn sent me." "Indeed we do not know who it was did this slaughter," they said, "but we will tell you his appearance. A young man he was, having dark curling hair and ruddy cheeks. And it is worse again to us," they said, "our three leaders to be bound this way, and we not able to loose them." "What way did that young man go from you?" said the woman. "It was late last night he left us," they said, "and we do not know where is he gone." "I give you my word," she said, "it was Diarmuid himself that was in it; and take your hounds now and lay them on his track, and I will send Finn and the Fianna of Ireland to you."

They left a woman-Druid then attending on the three champions that were bound, and they brought their three hounds out of the ship and laid them on Diarmuid's track, and followed them till they came to the opening of the cave, and they went into the far part of it and found the beds where Diarmuid and Grania had slept. Then they went on westward till they came to the Carrthach river, and to the bog of Finnliath, and so on to the great Slieve Luachra.

But Diarmuid did not know they were after him till he got sight of them with their banners of soft silk and their three wicked hounds in the front of the troop and three strong champions holding them in chains. And when he saw them coming like that he was filled with great hatred of them.

There was one of them had a well-coloured green cloak on him, and he came out far beyond the others, and Grania gave the knife back to Diarmuid. "I think you have not much love for that young man of the green cloak, Grania," said Diarmuid. "I have not indeed," said Grania; "and it would be better if I had never given love to any man at all to this day." Diarmuid put the knife in the sheath then, and went on; and Muadhan put Grania on his back and carried her on into the mountain.

It was not long till a hound of the three hounds was loosed after Diarmuid, and Muadhan said to him to follow Grania, and he himself would check the hound. Then Muadhan turned back, and he took a whelp out of his belt, and put it on the flat of his hand. And when the whelp saw the hound rushing towards him, and its jaws open, he rose up and made a leap from Muadhan's hand into the throat of the hound, and came out of its side, bringing the heart with it, and he leaped back again to Muadhan's hand, and left the hound dead after him.

Muadhan went on then after Diarmuid and Grania, and he took up Grania again and carried her a bit of the way into the mountain. Then another hound was loosened after them, and Diarmuid said to Muadhan: "I often heard there is nothing can stand against weapons of Druid wounding, and the throat of no beast can be made safe from them. And will you stand now," he said, "till I put the Gae Dearg, the Red Spear, through that hound."

Then Muadhan and Grania stopped to see the cast. And Diarmuid made a cast at the hound, and the spear went through its body and brought out its bowels; and he took up the spear again, and they went forward.

It was not long after that the third hound was loosed. And Grania said then: "This is the one is fiercest of them, and there is great fear on me, and mind yourself now, Diarmuid."

It was not long till the hound overtook them, and the place he overtook them was Lic Dhubhain, the flag-stone of Dubhan, on Slieve Luachra. He rose with a light leap over Diarmuid, as if he had a mind to seize on Grania, but Diarmuid took him by the two hind legs, and struck a blow of his carcase against the side of the rock was nearest, till he had let out his brains through the openings of his head and of his ears. And then Diarmuid took up his arms and his battle clothes, and put his narrow-topped finger into the silken string of the Gae Dearg, and he made a good cast at the young man of the green cloak that was at the head of the troop that killed him. Then he made another cast at the second man and killed him, and the third man in the same way. And as it is not the custom to stand after leaders are fallen, the strangers when they saw what had happened took to flight.

And Diarmuid followed after them, killing and scattering, so that unless any man of them got away over the forests, or into the green earth, or under the waters, there was not a man or messenger of them left to tell the news, but only the Woman-messenger of the Black Mountain, that kept moving around about when Diarmuid was putting down the strangers.

And it was not long till Finn saw her coming towards him where he was, her legs failing, and her tongue muttering, and her eyes drooping, and he asked news of her. "It is very bad news I have to tell you," she said; "and it is what I think, that it is a person without a lord I am." Then she told Finn the whole story from beginning to end, of the destruction Diarmuid had done, and how the three deadly hounds had fallen by him. "And it is hardly I myself got away," she said.

"What place did the grandson of Duibhne go to?" said Finn. "I do not know that," she said.

And when Finn heard of the Kings of the Green Champions that were bound by Diarmuid, he called his men to him, and they went by every short way and every straight path till they reached the hill, and it was torment to the heart of Finn to see the way they were. Then he said: "Oisin," he said, "loosen those three kings for me." "I will not loosen them," said Oisin, "for Diarmuid put bonds on me not to loosen any man he would bind." "Loosen them, Osgar," said Finn then. "I give my word," said Osgar, "it is more bonds I would wish to put on them sooner than to loosen them." Neither would Conan help them, or Lugaidh's Son. And any way, they were not long talking about it till the three kings died under the hardness of the bonds that were on them.

Then Finn made three wide-sodded graves for them, and a flag-stone was put over them, and another stone raised over that again, and their names were written in branching Ogham, and it is tired and heavy-hearted Finn was after that; and he and his people went back to Almhuin of Leinster.

CHAPTER IV

The Wood of Dubhros

And as to Diarmuid and Grania and Muadhan, they went on through Ui Chonaill Gabhra, and left-hand ways to Ros-da-Shoileach, and Diarmuid killed a wild deer that night, and they had their fill of meat and of pure water, and they slept till the morning of the morrow. And Muadhan rose up early, and spoke to Diarmuid, and it is what he said, that he himself was going away. "It is not right for you to do that," said Diarmuid, "for everything I promised you I fulfilled it, without any dispute."

But he could not hinder him, and Muadhan said farewell to them and left them there and then, and it is sorrowful and downhearted Diarmuid and Grania were after him.

After that they travelled on straight to the north, to Slieve Echtge, and from that to the hundred of Ui Fiachrach; and when they got there Grania was tired out, but she took courage and went on walking beside Diarmuid till they came to the wood of Dubhros.

Now, there was a wonderful quicken-tree in that wood, and the way it came to be there is this:

There rose a dispute one time between two women of the Tuatha de Danaan, Aine and Aoife, daughters of Manannan, son of Lir, for Aoife had given her love to Lugaidh's Son, and Aine had given her love to a man of her own race, and each

246

of them said her own man was a better hurler than the other. And it came from that dispute that there was a great hurling match settled between the Men of Dea and the Fianna of Ireland, and the place it was to be played was on a beautiful plain near Loch Lein.

They all came together there, and the highest men and the most daring of the Tuatha de Danaan were there, the three Garbhs of Slieve Mis, and the three Mases of Slieve Luachra, and the three yellow-haired Murchadhs, and the three Eochaidhs of Aine, and the three Fionns of the White House, and the three Sgals of Brugh na Boinne, and the three Ronans of Ath na Riogh, and the Suirgheach Suairc, the Pleasant Wooer from Lionan, and the Man of Sweet Speech from the Boinn, and Ilbrec, the Many-Coloured, son of Manannan, and Neamhanach, son of Angus Og, and Bodb Dearg, son of the Dagda, and Manannan, son of Lir.

They themselves and the Fianna were playing the match through the length of three days and three nights, from Leamhain to the valley of the Fleisg, that is called the Crooked Valley of the Fianna, and neither of them winning a goal. And when the Tuatha de Danaan that were watching the game on each side of Leamhain saw it was so hard for their hurlers to win a goal against the Fianna, they thought it as well to go away again without playing out the game.

Now the provision the Men of Dea had brought with them from the Land of Promise was crimson nuts, and apples, and sweet-smelling rowan berries. And as they were passing through the district of Ui Fiachrach by the Muaidh, a berry of the rowan berries fell from them, and a tree grew up from it. And there was virtue in its berries, and no sickness or disease would ever come on any person that would eat them, and those that would eat them would feel the liveliness of wine and the satisfaction of mead in them, and any old person of a hundred years that would eat them would go back to be young again, and any young girl that would eat them would grow to be a flower of beauty.

And it happened one time after the tree was grown, there were messengers of the Tuatha de Danaan going through the wood of Dubhros. And they heard a great noise of birds and of bees, and they went where the noise was, and they saw the beautiful Druid tree. They went back then and told what they had seen, and all the chief men of the Tuatha de Danaan when they heard it knew the tree must have grown from a berry of the Land of the Ever-Living Living Ones. And they enquired among all their people, till they knew it was a young man of them, that was a musician, had dropped the berry.

And it is what they agreed, to send him in search of a man of Lochlann that would guard the tree by day and sleep in it by night. And the women of the Sidhe were very downhearted to see him going from them, for there was no harper could play half so sweetly on his harp as he could play on an ivy leaf.

He went on then till he came to Lochlann, and he sat down on a bank and sleep came on him. And he slept till the rising of the sun on the morrow; and when he awoke he saw a very big man coming towards him, that asked him who was he. "I am a messenger from the Men of Dea," he said; "and I am come looking for some very strong man that would be willing to guard a Druid tree that is in the wood of Dubhros. And here are some of the berries he will be eating from morning to night," he said.

And when the big man had tasted the berries, he said: "I will go and guard all the trees of the wood to get those berries."

And his name was the Searbhan Lochlannach, the Surly One of Lochlann. Very black and ugly he was, having crooked teeth, and one eye only in the middle of his forehead. And he had a thick collar of iron around his body, and it was in the prophecy that he would never die till there would be three strokes of the iron club he had, struck upon himself. And he slept in the tree by night and stopped near it in the daytime, and he made a wilderness of the whole district about him, and none of the Fianna dared go hunt there because of the dread of him that was on them.

But when Diarmuid came to the wood of Dubhros, he went into it to where the Surly One was, and he made bonds of agreement with him, and got leave from him to go hunting in the wood, so long as he would not touch the berries of the tree. And he made a cabin then for himself and for Grania in the wood.

As for Finn and his people, they were not long at Almhuin till they saw fifty armed men coming towards them, and two that were taller and handsomer than the rest in the front of them. Finn asked did any of his people know them. "We do not know them," they said, "but maybe you yourself know them, Finn." "I do not," he said; "but it seems to be they are enemies to myself." The troop of armed men came up to them then and they greeted him, and Finn asked news of them, and from what country they came. "I am Aonghus, son of Art Og of the children of Morna," one of them said, "and this is Aodh, son of Andela; and we are enemies of your own, and our fathers were at the killing of your father, and they themselves died for that deed. And it is to ask peace we are come now to you," they said. "Where were you the time my father was killed?" "In our mothers' wombs," said they; "and our mothers were two women of the Tuatha de Danaan, and it is time for us now to get our father's place among the Fianna." "I will give you that," said Finn, "but I must put a fine on you first in satisfaction for my father's death." "We have neither gold or silver or goods or cattle to give you, Finn," said they. "Do not put a fine on them, Finn," said Oisin, "beyond the death of their fathers for your father." "It is what I think," said Finn, "if any one killed myself, Oisin, it would be easy to pay the fine you would ask. And there will no one come among the Fianna," he said, "without giving what I ask in satisfaction for my father's death." "What is it you are asking of us?" said Aonghus, son of Art Og. "I am asking but the head of a champion, or the full of a fist of the berries of the quicken-tree at Dubhros." "I will give you a good advice, children of Morna," said Oisin, "to go back to the place you were reared, and not to ask peace of Finn through the length of your lives. For it is not an easy thing Finn is asking of you;

and do you know whose head he is asking you to bring him?" "We do not," said they. "The head of Diarmuid, grandson of Duibhne, is the head he is asking of you. And if you were twenty hundred men in their full strength, Diarmuid would not let you take that head." "And what are the berries Finn is asking of us?" they said then. "There is nothing is harder for you to get than those berries," said Oisin.

He told them then the whole story of the tree, and of the Searbhan, the Surly One of Lochlann, that was put to mind it by the Tuatha de Danaan. But Aodh, son of Andela, spoke then, and it is what he said, that he would sooner get his death looking for those berries than to go home again to his mother's country. And he said to Oisin to care his people till he would come back again, and if anything should happen himself and his brother in their journey, to send them back again to the Land of Promise. And the two said farewell then to Oisin and to the chief men of the Fianna, and they went forward till they reached Dubhros. And they went along the wood till they found a track, and they followed it to the door of the hunting-cabin where Diarmuid and Grania were.

Diarmuid heard them coming, and he put his hand on his weapons and asked who was at the door. "We are of the children of Morna," they said, "Aodh, son of Andela, and Aonghus, son of Art Og." "What brings you to this wood?" said Diarmuid. "Finn, son of Cumhal, that put us looking for your head, if you are Diarmuid, grandson of Duibhne," said they. "I am indeed," said Diarmuid. "If that is so," they said, "Finn will take nothing from us but your head, or a fistful of the berries of the quicken-tree of Dubhros as satisfaction for the death of his father." "It is not easy for you to get either of those things," said Diarmuid, "and it is a pity for any one to be under the power of that man. And besides that," he said, "I know it was he himself made an end of your fathers, and that was enough satisfaction for him to get; and if you do bring him what he asks, it is likely he will not make peace with you in the end." "Is it not enough for you," said Aodh, "to have brought his wife away from Finn without speaking ill of him?" "It is not for the sake of speaking ill of him I said that," said Diarmuid, "but to save yourselves from the danger he has sent you into."

"What are those berries Finn is asking?" said Grania, "that they cannot be got for him?"

Diarmuid told her then the whole story of the berry the Tuatha de Danaan had lost, and of the tree that had sprung up from it, and of the man of Lochlann that was keeping the tree. "And at the time Finn sent me hiding here and became my enemy," he said, "I got leave from the Surly One to hunt, but he bade me never to meddle with the berries. And now, sons of Morna," he said, "there is your choice, to fight with me for my head, or to go asking the berries of the Surly One." "I swear by the blood of my people," said each of them, "I will fight with yourself first."

With that the two young men made ready for the fight. And it is what they chose, to fight with the strength of their hands alone. And Diarmuid put them down and bound the two of them there and then. "That is a good fight you made," said Grania. "But, by my word," she said, "although the children of Morna do not go looking for those berries, I will not lie in a bed for ever till I get a share of them; and I will not live if I do not get them," she said. "Do not make me break my peace with the Surly One," said Diarmuid, "for he will not let me take them." "Loose these tyings from us," said the two young men, "and we will go with you, and we will give ourselves for your sake." "You must not come with me," said Diarmuid; "for if you got the full of your eyes of that terrible one, you would be more likely to die than to live." "Well, do us this kindness," they said then; "loosen these bonds on us, and give us time to go by ourselves and see the fight before you strike off our heads." So Diarmuid did that for them.

Then Diarmuid went to the Surly One, and he chanced to be asleep before him, and he gave him a stroke of his foot the way he lifted his head and looked up at him, and he said: "Have you a mind to break our peace, Grandson of Duibhne?" "That is not what I want," said Diarmuid; "but it is Grania, daughter of the High King," he said, "has a desire to taste those berries, and it is to ask a handful of them I am come." "I give my word," said he, "if she is to die for it, she will never taste a berry of those berries." "I would not do treachery on you," said Diarmuid; "and so I tell you, willing or unwilling, I will take those berries from you."

When the Surly One heard that, he rose up on his feet and lifted his club and struck three great blows on Diarmuid, that gave him some little hurt in spite of his shield. But when Diarmuid saw him not minding himself, he threw down his weapons, and made a great leap and took hold of the club with his two hands. And when he had a hold of the club he struck three great blows on him that put his brains out through his head. And the two young men of the sons of Morna were looking at the whole fight; and when they saw the Surly One was killed they came out. And Diarmuid sat down, for he was spent with the dint of the fight, and he bid the young men to bury the body under the thickets of the wood, the way Grania would not see it. "And after that," he said, "let you go back to her and bring her here." So they dragged away the body and buried it, and they went then for Grania and brought her to Diarmuid.

"There are the berries you were asking, Grania," he said, "and you may take what you like of them now." "I give my word," said Grania, "I will not taste a berry of those berries but the one your own hand will pluck, Diarmuid." Diarmuid rose up then and plucked the berries for Grania, and for the children of Morna, and they ate their fill of them. And he said then to the young men: "Take all you can of these berries, and bring them with you to Finn, and tell him it was yourselves made an end of the Surly One of Lochlann." "We give you our word," said they, "we begrudge giving any of them to Finn."

But Diarmuid plucked a load of the berries for them, and they gave him great thanks for all he had done; and they went back to where Finn was with the

Fianna. And Diarmuid and Grania went up into the top of the tree where the bed of the Surly One was. And the berries below were but bitter berries beside the ones above in the tree. And when the two young men came to Finn, he asked news of them. "We have killed the Surly One of Lochlann," they said; "and we have brought you berries from the quicken-tree of Dubhros, in satisfaction for your father, that we may get peace from you." They gave the berries then into Finn's hand, and he knew them, and he said to the young men: "I give you my word," he said, "it was Diarmuid himself plucked those berries, for I know the smell of his hand on them; and I know well it was he killed the Surly One, and I will go now and see is he himself alive at the quicken-tree."

After that he called for the seven battalions of the Fianna, and he set out and went forward to Dubhros. And they followed the track of Diarmuid to the foot of the quicken-tree, and they found the berries without protection, so they ate their fill of them. And the great heat of the day came on them, and Finn said they would stop where they were till the heat would be past; "for I know well," he said, "Diarmuid is up in the quicken-tree." "It is a great sign of jealousy in you, Finn," said Oisin, "to think that Diarmuid would stop there up in the quicken-tree and he knowing you are wanting to kill him."

Finn asked for a chess-board after that, and he said to Oisin: "I will play a game with you now on this." They sat down then, Oisin and Osgar and Lugaidh's Son and Diorraing on the one side of the board, and Finn on the other side.

And they were playing that game with great skill and knowledge, and Finn pressed Oisin so hard that he had no move to make but the one, and Finn said: "There is one move would win the game for you, Oisin, and I defy all that are with you to show you that move." Then Diarmuid said up in the tree where he was, and no one heard him but Grania: "It is a pity you be in straits, and without myself to show you that move." "It is worse off you are yourself," said Grania, "to be in the bed of the Surly One of Lochlann in the top of the quicken-tree, and the seven battalions of the Fianna round about it to take your life."

But Diarmuid took a berry of the tree, and aimed at the one of the chessmen that ought to be moved, and Oisin moved it and turned the game against Finn by that move. It was not long before the game was going against Oisin the second time, and when Diarmuid saw that he threw another berry at the chessman it was right to move, and Oisin moved it and turned the game against Finn in the same way. And the third time Finn was getting the game from Oisin, and Diarmuid threw the third berry on the man that would give the game to Oisin, and the Fianna gave a great shout when the game was won. Finn spoke then, and it is what he said: "It is no wonder you to win the game, Oisin, and you having the help of Osgar, and the watchfulness of Diorraing, and the skill of Lugaidh's Son, and the teaching of the grandson of Duibhne with you." "That is a great sign of jealousy in you, Finn," said Osgar, "to think Diarmuid would stop in this tree, and you so near him." "Which of us has the truth, Diarmuid, grandson of Duibhne,"

Finn said out then, "myself or Osgar?" "You never lost your good judgment, Finn," said Diarmuid then; "and I myself and Grania are here, in the bed of the Surly One of Lochlann." Then Diarmuid rose up and gave three kisses to Grania in the sight of Finn and the Fianna. And a scorching jealousy and a weakness came on Finn when he saw that, and he said: "It was worse to me, Diarmuid, the seven battalions of the Fianna to see what you did at Teamhair, taking away Grania the night you were yourself my guard. But for all that," he said, "you will give your head for the sake of those three kisses."

With that Finn called to the four hundred paid fighting men that were with him that they might make an end of Diarmuid; and he put their hands into one another's hands around that quicken-tree, and bade them, if they would not lose their lives, not to let Diarmuid pass out through them. And he said that to whatever man would take Diarmuid, he would give his arms and his armour, and a place among the Fianna of Ireland.

Then one of the Fianna, Garbh of Slieve Cua, said it was Diarmuid had killed his own father, and he would avenge him now, and he went up the quicken-tree to make an end of him.

Now, about that time it was made known to Angus Og, in Brugh na Boinne, the danger Diarmuid was in, and he came to his help, unknown to the Fianna. And when Garbh of Slieve Cua was coming up the tree, Diarmuid gave him a kick of his foot, and he fell down among the hired men, and they struck off his head, for Angus Og had put the appearance of Diarmuid on him. But after he was killed, his own shape came on him again, and the Fianna knew that it was Garbh was killed.

Then Garbh of Slieve Crot said it was Diarmuid had killed his father, and he went up to avenge him, and the same thing happened. And in the end all the nine Garbhs, of Slieve Guaire, and Slieve Muice, and Slieve Mor, and Slieve Lugha, and Ath Fraoch, and Slieve Mis and Drom-mor, went trying to take Diarmuid's life and lost their own lives, every one of them having the shape and appearance of Diarmuid when he died. And Finn was very sorry and discouraged when he saw that these nine men had come to their death.

Then Angus said he would bring away Grania with him. "Do so," said Diarmuid; "and if I am living at evening I will follow you. Then Angus said farewell to Diarmuid, and he put his Druid cloak about Grania and about himself, and they went away in the safety of the cloak, unknown to Finn and the Fianna, till they came to Brugh na Boinne.

Then Diarmuid, grandson of Duibhne, spoke, and it is what he said: "I will come down to you, Finn, and to the Fianna. And I will do death and destruction on you and on your people, for I am certain your mind is made up to give me no rest, but to bring me to my death in some place. And I have nowhere to go from this danger," he said, "for I have no friend or comrade under whose protection I could go in any far part of the great world, for it is often I fought against the men of the great world for love of you. For there never came battle or fight, danger or trouble on you, but I would go into it for your sake and the sake of the Fianna; and not only that, but I would fight before you and after you. And I give my word, Finn," he said, "you will pay hard for me, and you will not get me as a free gift." "It is the truth Diarmuid is speaking," said Osgar, "and give him forgiveness now, and peace." "I will not do that," said Finn, "to the end of life and time; and he will not get peace or rest for ever till I get satisfaction from him for every reproach he has put on me." "It is a great shame and a great sign of jealousy you to say that," said Osgar. "And I give the word of a true champion," he said, "that unless the skies come down upon me, or the earth opens under my feet, I will not let you or any one of the Fianna of Ireland give him cut or wound; and I take his body and his life under the protection of my valour, and I will keep him safe against all the men of Ireland." "Those are big words you have, Osgar," said Goll then, "to say you would bring a man away in spite of all the men of Ireland." "It is not you will raise them up against me, Goll," said Osgar, "for none of them would mind what you would say." "If that is what you are saying, you champion of great fights," said Goll, "let us see now what you can do." "You will have to go through with the fight you have taken on yourself," said Corrioll, son of Goll, in a loud voice. And Osgar answered him fiercely: "If I do I will shorten your bones, and your father's bones along with them. And come down now, Diarmuid," he said, "since Finn has no mind to leave you in peace, and I promise on my body and my life there will no harm be done to you to-day."

Then Diarmuid stood up on a high bough of the boughs of the tree, and he rose with a light leap by the shaft of his spear, and lit on the grass far beyond Finn and the Fianna. And he himself and Osgar went towards one another, in spite of the Fianna that went between them, and Diarmuid struck down those that were in his way; and as to Osgar, the throwing of his spears as he scattered the Fianna was like the sound of the wind going through a valley, or water falling over flag-stones. And Conan, that was always bitter, said: "Let the sons of Baiscne go on killing one another." But Finn, when he saw Diarmuid was gone from him, bade them put their weapons up, and turn back again to Almhuin.

And he sent those of his men that could be healed to places of healing, and the nine Garbhs, and the others of his men that were killed, he put into wide-sodded graves. And it is tired and downhearted and sorrowful he was after that, and he made an oath he would take no great rest till he would have avenged on Diarmuid all that he had done.

CHAPTER V

The Quarrel

And as to Osgar and Diarmuid, they went on, and no cut or wound on them, to where Angus and Grania were at Brugh na Boinne; and there was a good welcome before them, and Diarmuid told them the whole story from beginning to end, and it is much that Grania did not die then and there, hearing all he had gone through.

And then she and Diarmuid set out again, and they went and stopped for a while in a cave that was near the sea.

And one night while they were there a great storm came on, so that they went into the far part of the cave. But bad as the night was, a man of the Fomor, Ciach, the Fierce One, his name was, came over the western ocean in a currach, with two oars, and he drew it into the cave for shelter. And Diarmuid bade him welcome, and they sat down to play chess together. And he got the best of the game, and what he asked as his winnings was Grania to be his wife, and he put his arms about her as if to bring her away. And Grania said: "I am this long time going with the third best man of the Fianna, and he never came as near as that to me."

And Diarmuid took his sword to kill Ciach, and there was anger on Grania when she saw that, and she had a knife in her hand and she struck it into Diarmuid's thigh. And Diarmuid made an end of the Fomor, and he said no word to Grania, but ran out and away through the storm.

And Grania went following after him, and calling to him, but there was great anger on him and he would not answer her. And at last at the break of day she overtook him, and after a while they heard the cry of a heron, and she asked him what was it made the heron cry out.

"Tell me that," she said, "Grandson of Duibhne, to whom I gave my love." And Diarmuid said: "O Grania, daughter of the High King, woman who never took a step aright, it is because she was frozen to the rocks she gave that cry." And Grania was asking forgiveness of him, and he was reproaching her, and it is what he said: "O Grania of the beautiful hair, though you are more beautiful than the green tree under blossom, your love passes away as quickly as the cold cloud at break of day. And you are asking a hard thing of me now," he said, "and it is a pity what you said to me, Grania, for it was you brought me away from the house of my lord, that I am banished from it to this day; and now I am troubled through the night, fretting after its delight in every place.

"I am like a wild deer, or a beast that is astray, going ever and always through the long valleys; there is great longing on me to see one of my kindred from the host.

"I left my own people that were brighter than lime or snow; their heart was full of generosity to me, like the sun that is high above us; but now they follow me angrily, to every harbour and every strand.

"I lost my people by you, and my lord, and my large bright ships on every sea; I lost my treasure and my gold; it is hunger you gave me through your love.

"I lost my country and my kindred; my men that were used to serve me; I lost quietness and affection; I lost the men of Ireland and the Fianna entirely.

"I lost delight and music; I lost my own right doing and my honour; I lost the Fianna of Ireland, my great kinsmen, for the sake of the love you gave me.

"O Grania, white as snow, it would have been a better choice for you to have given hatred to me, or gentleness to the Head of the Fianna."

And Grania said: "O Diarmuid of the face like snow, or like the down of the mountains, the sound of your voice was dearer to me than all the riches of the leader of the Fianna.

"Your blue eye is dearer to me than his strength, and his gold and his great hall; the love-spot on your forehead is better to me than honey in streams; the time I first looked on it, it was more to me than the whole host of the King of Ireland.

"My heart fell down there and then before your high beauty; when you came beside me, it was like the whole of life in one day.

"O Diarmuid of the beautiful hands, take me now the same as before; it was with me the fault was entirely; give me your promise not to leave me."

But Diarmuid said: "How can I take you again, you are a woman too fond of words; one day you give up the Head of the Fianna, and the next day myself, and no lie in it.

"It is you parted me from Finn, the way I fell under sorrow and grief; and then you left me yourself, the time I was full of affection."

And Grania said: "Do not leave me now this way, and my love for you ever growing like the fresh branches of the tree with the kind long heat of the day."

But Diarmuid would not give in to her, and he said: "You are a woman full of words, and it is you have put me under sorrow. I took you with myself, and you struck at me for the sake of the man of the Fomor."

They came then to a place where there was a cave, and water running by it, and they stopped to rest; and Grania said: "Have you a mind to eat bread and meat now, Diarmuid?"

"I would eat it indeed if I had it," said Diarmuid.

"Give me a knife, so," she said, "till I cut it." "Look for the knife in the sheath where you put it yourself," said Diarmuid.

She saw then that the knife was in his thigh where she had struck it, for he would not draw it out himself. So she drew it out then; and that was the greatest shame that ever came upon her.

They stopped then in the cave. And the next day when they went on again, Diarmuid did not leave unbroken bread like he had left every other day as a sign to Finn that he had kept his faith with him, but it was broken bread he left after him.

CHAPTER VI

The Wanderers

And they went on wandering after that, all through Ireland, hiding from Finn in every place, sleeping under the cromlechs, or with no shelter at all, and there was no place they would dare to stop long in. And wherever they went Finn would follow them, for he knew by his divination where they went. But one time he made out they were on a mountain, for he saw them with heather under them; and it was beside the sea they were, asleep on heather that Diarmuid had brought down from the hills for their bed; and so he went searching the hills and did not find them.

And Grania would be watching over Diarmuid while he slept, and she would make a sleepy song for him, and it is what she would be saying:

"Sleep a little, a little little, for there is nothing at all to fear, Diarmuid, grandson of Duibhne; sleep here soundly, soundly, Diarmuid, to whom I have given my love.

"It is I will keep watch for you, grandchild of shapely Duibhne; sleep a little, a blessing on you, beside the well of the strong field; my lamb from above the lake, from the banks of the strong streams.

"Let your sleep be like the sleep in the South, of Dedidach of the high poets, the time he took away old Morann's daughter, for all Conall could do against him.

"Let your sleep be like the sleep in the North, of fair comely Fionnchadh of Ess Ruadh, the time he took Slaine with bravery as we think, in spite of Failbhe of the Hard Head.

"Let your sleep be like the sleep in the West, of Aine, daughter of Gailian, the time she went on a journey in the night with Dubhthach from Doirinis, by the light of torches.

"Let your sleep be like the sleep in the East, of Deaghadh the proud, the brave fighter, the time he took Coincheann, daughter of Binn, in spite of fierce Decheall of Duibhreann.

"O heart of the valour of the lands to the west of Greece, my heart will go near to breaking if I do not see you every day. The parting of us two will be the parting of two children of the one house; it will be the parting of life from the body, Diarmuid, hero of the bright lake of Carman."

And then to rouse him she would make another song, and it is what she would say: "Caoinche will be loosed on your track; it is not slow the running of Caoilte will be; do not let death reach to you, do not give yourself to sleep for ever.

"The stag to the east is not asleep, he does not cease from bellowing; though he is in the woods of the black-birds, sleep is not in his mind; the hornless doe is not asleep, crying after her speckled fawn; she is going over the bushes, she does not sleep in her home.

"The cuckoo is not asleep, the thrush is not asleep, the tops of the trees are a noisy place; the duck is not asleep, she is made ready for good swimming; the bog lark is not asleep to-night on the high stormy bogs; the sound of her clear voice is sweet; she is not sleeping between the streams."

One time they were in a cave of Beinn Edair, and there was an old woman befriending them and helping them to keep a watch. And one day she chanced to go up to the top of Beinn Edair, and she saw an armed man coming towards her, and she did now know him to be Finn; and when he was come near she asked what was he looking for. "It is looking for a woman I am come," he said, "and for a woman's love. And will you do all I will ask you?" he said.

"I will do that," she said; for she thought it was her own love he was asking.

"Tell me then," he said, "where is Diarmuid, grandson of Duibhne?"

So she told him where he was hiding, and he bade her to keep him in the cave till such time as he would come back with his men.

The old woman went back then, and it is what she did, she dipped her cloak in the sea-water before she went into the cave; and Diarmuid asked her why was her cloak so wet. "It is," she said, "that I never saw or never heard of the like of this day for cold and for storms. There is frost on every hillside," she said, "and there is not a smooth plain in all Elga where there is not a long rushing river between every two ridges. And there is not a deer or a crow in the whole of Ireland can find a shelter in any place." And she was shaking the wet off her cloak, and she was making a complaint against the cold, and it is what she said:

"Cold, cold, cold to-night is the wide plain of Lurg; the snow is higher than the mountains, the deer cannot get at their share of food.

"Cold for ever; the storm is spread over all; every furrow on the hillside is a river, every ford is a full pool, every full loch is a great sea; every pool is a full loch; horses cannot go through the ford of Ross any more than a man on his two feet.

"The fishes of Inisfail are going astray; there is no strand or no pen against the waves; there are no dwellings in the country, there is no bell heard, no crane is calling.

"The hounds of the wood of Cuan find no rest or no sleep in their dwelling-place; the little wren cannot find shelter in her nest on the slope of Lon.

"A sharp wind and cold ice have come on the little company of birds; the blackbird cannot get a ridge to her liking or shelter for her side in the woods of Cuan.

"It is steady our great pot hangs from its hook; it is broken the cabin is on the

257

slope of Lon; the snow has made the woods smooth, it is hard to climb to the ridge of Bennait Bo.

"The ancient bird of Glen Ride gets grief from the bitter wind; it is great is her misery and her pain, the ice will be in her mouth.

"Mind well not to rise up from coverings and from down, mind this well; there would be no good sense in it. Ice is heaped up in every ford; it is for that I am saying and ever saying 'Cold.' "

The old woman went out after that, and when she was gone, Grania took hold of the cloak she had left there and she put her tongue to it, and found the taste of salt water on it. "My grief, Diarmuid," she said then, "the old woman has betrayed us. And rise up now," she said, "and put your fighting suit upon you."

So Diarmuid did that, and he went out, and Grania along with him. And no sooner were they outside than they saw Finn and the Fianna of Ireland coming towards them. Then Diarmuid looked around him and he saw a little boat at hand in the shelter of the harbour, and he himself and Grania went into it. And there was a man before them in the boat having beautiful clothes on him, and a wide embroidered golden-yellow cloak over his shoulders behind. And they knew it was Angus was in it, that had come again to help them to escape from Finn, and they went back with him for a while to Brugh na Boinne, and Osgar came to them there.

CHAPTER VII

Fighting and Peace

And after a while Finn bade his people to make his ship ready, and to put a store of food and of drink in it. They did that, and he himself and a thousand of his men went into the ship; and they were nine days between sailing and rowing till they came to harbour in the north of Alban.

They bound the ship to the posts of the harbour then, and Finn with five of his people went to the dun of the King of Alban, and Finn struck a blow with the hand-wood on the door, and the door-keeper asked who was in it, and they told him it was Finn, son of Cumhal. "Let him in," said the king.

Then Finn and his people went in, and the king made them welcome, and he bade Finn to sit down in his own place, and they were given strong pleasant drinks, and the king sent for the rest of Finn's people and bade them welcome to the dun.

Then Finn told what it was brought him there, and that it was to ask help and advice against the grandson of Duibhne he was come.

"And you have a right to give me your help," he said, "for it was he that killed your father and your two brothers, and many of your best men along with them."

"That is true," said the king; "and I will give you my own two sons and a thousand men with each of them." Finn was glad when he heard that, and he and his men took leave of the king and of his household, and left wishes for life and health with them, and the king did the same by them.

And it was near Brugh na Boinne Finn and his people came to land, and Finn sent messengers to the house of Angus to give out a challenge of battle against Diarmuid, grandson of Duibhne.

"What should I do about this, Osgar?" said Diarmuid.

"We will both go out and make a stand against them, and we will not let a serving-man of them escape, but we will make an end of them all," said Osgar.

So they rose up on the morning of the morrow and they put their suits of battle on their comely bodies; and it would be a pity for those, be they many or few, that would meet those two men, and their anger on them. And they bound the rims of their shields together the way they would not be parted from one another in the fight. And the sons of the King of Alban said that they themselves and their people would go first to meet them. So they came to shore, and made a rush to meet Diarmuid and Osgar. But the two fought so well that they beat them back and scattered them, and made a great slaughter, and put great terror on them, so that at the last there was not a man left to stand against them.

And after that, Finn went out again on the sea, and his people with him, and there is no word of them till they came to the Land of Promise where Finn's nurse was. And when she saw Finn coming she was very joyful before him. And Finn told her the whole story from beginning to end, and the cause of his quarrel with Diarmuid; and he said it was to ask an advice from her he was come, and that it was not possible to put him down by any strength of an army, unless enchantment would put him down. "I will go with you," said the old woman, "and I will do enchantment on him." Finn was very glad when he heard that, and he stopped there that night, and they set out for Ireland on the morrow.

And when they came to Brugh na Boinne, the nurse put a Druid mist around Finn and the Fianna, the way no one could know they were there. Now the day before that, Osgar had parted from Diarmuid, and Diarmuid was out hunting by himself. That was shown to the hag, and she took a drowned leaf having a hole in it, like the quern of a mill, and she rose with that by her enchantments on a blast of Druid wind over Diarmuid, and began to aim at him through the hole with deadly spears, till she had done him great harm, for all his arms and his clothing, and he could not make away he was so hard pressed. And every danger he was ever in was little beside that danger. And it is what he thought, that unless he could strike the old woman through the hole that was in the leaf, she would give him his death there and then. And he lay down on his back, and the Gae Dearg, the Red Spear, in his hand, and he made a great cast of the spear, that it went through the hole, and the hag fell dead on the spot. And he struck off her head and brought it back with him to Angus Og.

And the next morning early, Angus rose up, and he went where Finn was, and he asked would he make peace with Diarmuid, and Finn said he would. And then he went to the King of Ireland to ask peace for Diarmuid, and he said he would agree to it.

And then he went back to where Diarmuid and Grania were, and asked him would he make peace with the High King and with Finn. "I am willing," said Diarmuid, "if they will give the conditions I will ask." "What conditions are those?" said Angus.

"The district my father had," said Diarmuid, "that is, the district of Ui Duibhne, without right of hunting to Finn, and without rent or tribute to the King of Ireland, and with that the district of Dumhais in Leinster, for they are the best in Ireland, and the district of Ceis Corainn from the King of Ireland as a marriage portion with his daughter; and those are the conditions on which I will make peace with them." "Would you be peaceable if you got those conditions?" said Angus. "It would go easier with me to make peace if I got them," said Diarmuid.

Then Angus went with that news to where the King of Ireland was with Finn. And they gave him all those conditions, and they forgave him all he had done through the whole of the time he had been in his hiding, that was sixteen years.

And the place Diarmuid and Grania settled in was Rath Grania, in the district of Ceis Corainn, far away from Finn and from Teamhair. And Grania bore him children there, four sons and one daughter. And they lived there in peace, and the people used to be saying there was not a man living at the same time was richer as to gold and to silver, as to cattle and to sheep, than Diarmuid.

CHAPTER VIII

The Boar of Beinn Gulbain

But at last one day Grania spoke to Diarmuid, and it is what she said, that it was a shame on them, with all the people and the household they had, and all their riches, the two best men in Ireland never to have come to the house, the High King, her father, and Finn, son of Cumhal. "Why do you say that, Grania," said Diarmuid, "and they being enemies to me?"

"It is what I would wish," said Grania, "to give them a feast, the way you would get their affection." "I give leave for that," said Diarmuid.

So Grania was making ready a great feast through the length of a year, and messengers were sent for the High King of Ireland, and for Finn and the seven battalions of the Fianna; and they came, and they were using the feast from day to day through the length of a year.

And on the last night of the year, Diarmuid was in his sleep at Rath Grania; and in the night he heard the voice of hounds through his sleep, and he started up, and Grania caught him and put her two arms about him, and asked what had startled him. "The voice of a hound I heard," said he; "and it is a wonder to me to hear that in the night." "Safe keeping on you," said Grania, "for it is the Tuatha de Danaan are doing that on you, on account of Angus of Brugh na Boinn, and lie down on the bed again." But for all that no sleep came to him, and he heard the voice of the hound again, and he started up a second time to follow after it. But Grania caught hold of him the second time and bade him to lie down, and she said it was no fitting thing to go after the voice of a hound in the night. So he lay down again, and he fell asleep, but the voice of the hound awakened him the third time. And the day was come with its full light that time, and he said: "I will go after the voice of the hound now, since the day is here." "If that is so," said Grania, "bring the Mor-alltach, the Great Fierce One, the sword of Manannan, with you, and the Gae Dearg." "I will not," he said; "but I will take the Beag-alltach, the Little Fierce One, and the Gae Buidhe in the one hand, and the hound Mac an Chuill, the Son of the Hazel, in the other hand."

Then Diarmuid went out of Rath Grania, and made no delay till he came to the top of Beinn Gulbain, and he found Finn before him there, without any one at all in his company. Diarmuid gave him no greeting, but asked him was it he was making that hunt. Finn said it was not a hunt he was making, but that he and some of the Fianna had gone out after midnight; "and one of our hounds that was loose beside us, came on the track of a wild boar," he said, "and they were not able to bring him back yet. And there is no use following that boar he is after," he said, "for it is many a time the Fianna hunted him, and he went away from them every time till now, and he has killed thirty of them this morning. And he is coming up the mountain towards us," he said, "and let us leave this hill to him now."

"I will not leave the hill through fear of him," said Diarmuid. "It would be best for you, Diarmuid," said Finn, "for it is the earless Green Boar of Beinn Gulbain is in it, and it is by him you will come to your death, and Angus knew that well when he put bonds on you not to go hunting pigs." "I never knew of those bonds," said Diarmuid; "but however it is, I will not quit this through fear of him. And let you leave Bran with me now," he said, "along with Mac an Chuill." "I will not," said Finn, "for it is often he met this boar before and could do nothing against him." He went away then and left Diarmuid alone on the top of the hill. "I give my word," said Diarmuid, "you made this hunt for my death, Finn; and if it is here I am to find my death," he said, "I have no use in going aside from it now."

The boar came up the face of the mountain then, and the Fianna after him. Diarmuid loosed Mac an Chuill from his leash then, but that did not serve him, for he did not wait for the boar, but ran from him. "It is a pity not to follow the advice of a good woman," said Diarmuid, "for Grania bade me this morning to bring the Mor-alltach and the Gae Dearg with me." Then he put his finger into the silken string of the Gae Buidhe, and took a straight aim at the boar and hit him full in the face; but if he did, the spear did not so much as give him a scratch. Diarmuid was discouraged by that, but he drew the Beag-alltach, and made a full stroke at the back of the boar, but neither did that make a wound on him, but it made two halves of the sword. Then the boar made a brave charge at Diarmuid, that cut the sod from under his feet and brought him down; but Diarmuid caught hold of the boar on rising, and held on to him, having one of his legs on each side of him, and his face to his hinder parts. And the boar made away headlong down the hill, but he could not rid himself of Diarmuid; and he went on after that to Ess Ruadh, and when he came to the red stream he gave three high leaps over it, backwards and forwards, but he could not put him from his back, and he went back by the same path till he went up the height of the mountain again. And at last on the top of the mountain he freed himself, and Diarmuid fell on the ground. And then the boar made a rush at him, and ripped him open, that his bowels came out about his feet. But if he did, Diarmuid made a cast at him with the hilt of his sword that was in his hand yet, and dashed out his brains, so that he fell dead there and then. And Rath na h-Amhrann, the Rath of the Sword Hilt, is the name of that place to this day.

It was not long till Finn and the Fianna of Ireland came to the place, and the pains of death were coming on Diarmuid at that time. "It is well pleased I am to see you that way, Diarmuid," said Finn; "and it is a pity all the women of Ireland not to be looking at you now, for your great beauty is turned to ugliness, and your comely shape to uncomeliness." "For all that, you have power to heal me, Finn," said Diarmuid, "if you had a mind to do it." "What way could I heal you?" said Finn. "Easy enough," said Diarmuid, "for the time you were given the great gift of knowledge at the Boinn, you got this gift with it, that any one you would give a drink to out of the palms of your hands would be young and well again from any sickness after it." "You are not deserving of that drink from me," said Finn. "That is not true," said Diarmuid; "it is well I deserve it from you; for the time you went to the house of Dearc, son of Donnarthadh, and your chief men with you for a feast, your enemies came round the house, and gave out three great shouts against you, and threw fire and firebrands into it. And you rose up and would have gone out, but I bade you to stop there at drinking and pleasure, for that I myself would go out and put them down. And I went out, and put out the flames, and made three red rushes round the house, and I killed fifty in every rush, and I came in again without a wound. And it is glad and merry and in good courage you were that night, Finn," he said, "and if it was that night I had asked a drink of you, you would have given it; and it would be right for you to give it to me now." "That is not so," said Finn; "it is badly you have earned a drink or any good thing from me; for the night you went to Teamhair with me, you took Grania away from me in the presence of all the men of Ireland, and you being my own guard over her that night."

"Do not blame me for that, Finn," said Diarmuid, "for what did I ever do against you, east or west, but that one thing; and you know well Grania put bonds on me, and I would not fail in my bonds for the gold of the whole world. And you will know it is well I have earned a drink from you, if you bring to mind the night the feast was made in the House of the Quicken Tree, and how you and all your men were bound there till I heard of it, and came fighting and joyful, and loosed you with my own blood, and with the blood of the Three Kings of the Island of the Floods; and if I had asked a drink of you that night, Finn, you would not have refused it. And I was with you in the smiting of Lon, son of Liobhan, and you are the man that should not forsake me beyond any other man. And many is the strait has overtaken yourself and the Fianna of Ireland since I came among you, and I was ready every time to put my body and my life in danger for your sake, and you ought not to do this unkindness on me now. And besides that," he said, "there has many a good champion fallen through the things you yourself have done, and there is not an end of them yet; and there will soon come great misfortunes on the Fianna, and it is few of their seed will be left after them. And it is not for yourself I am fretting, Finn," he said, "but for Oisin and Osgar, and the rest of my dear comrades, and as for you, Oisin, you will be left lamenting after the Fianna. And it is greatly you will feel the want of me yet, Finn," he said; "and if the women of the Fianna knew I was lying in my wounds on this ridge, it is sorrowful their faces would be at this time."

And Osgar said then: "Although I am nearer in blood to you, Finn, than to Diarmuid, grandson of Duibhne, I will not let you refuse him this drink; and by my word," he said, "if any prince in the world would do the same unkindness to Diarmuid that you have done, it is only the one of us that has the strongest hand would escape alive. And give him a drink now without delay," he said.

"I do not know of any well at all on this mountain," said Finn. "That is not so," said Diarmuid, "for there is not nine footsteps from you the well that has the best fresh water that can be found in the world."

Then Finn went to the well, and he took the full of his two hands of the water. But when he was no more than half-way back, the thought of Grania came on him, and he let the water slip through his hands, and he said he was not able to bring it. "I give my word," said Diarmuid, "it was of your own will you let it from you." Then Finn went back the second time to get the water, but coming back he let it through his hands again at the thought of Grania. And Diarmuid gave a pitiful sigh of anguish when he saw that. "I swear by my sword and by my spear," said Osgar, "that if you do not bring the water without any more delay, Finn, there will not leave this hill but yourself or myself." Finn went back the third time to the well after what Osgar said, and he brought the water to Diarmuid, but as he reached him the life went out of his body. Then the whole company of the Fianna that were there gave three great heavy shouts, keening for Diarmuid.

And Osgar looked very fiercely at Finn, and it is what he said, that it was a greater pity Diarmuid to be dead than if he himself had died. And the Fianna of Ireland had lost their yoke of battle by him, he said. "Let us leave this hill," said Finn then, "before Angus and the Tuatha de Danaan come upon us, for although we have no share in the death of Diarmuid, he would not believe the truth from us." "I give my word," said Osgar, "if I had thought it was against Diarmuid you made the hunt of Beinn Gulbain, you would never have made it."

Then Finn and the Fianna went away from the hill, and Finn leading Diarmuid's hound Mac an Chuill. But Oisin and Osgar and Caoilte and Lugaidh's Son turned back again and put their four cloaks over Diarmuid, and then they went after the rest of the Fianna.

And when they came to the Rath, Grania was out on the wall looking for news of Diarmuid; and she saw Finn and the Fianna of Ireland coming towards her. Then she said: "If Diarmuid was living, it is not led by Finn that Mac an Chuill would be coming home." And she was at that time heavy with child, and her strength went from her and she fell down from the wall. And when Oisin saw the way she was he bade Finn and the others to go on from her, but she lifted up her head and she asked Finn to leave Mac an Chuill with her. And he said he would not, and that he did not think it too much for him to inherit from Diarmuid, grandson of Duibhne.

When Oisin heard that, he snatched the hound out of Finn's hand and gave it to Grania, and then he followed after his people.

Then when Grania was certain of Diarmuid's death she gave out a long very pitiful cry that was heard through the whole place, and her women and her people came to her, and asked what ailed her to give a cry like that. And she told them how Diarmuid had come to his death by the Boar of Beinn Gulbain in the hunt Finn had made. "And there is grief in my very heart," she said, "I not to be able to fight myself with Finn, and I would not have let him go safe out of this place."

When her people heard of the death of Diarmuid they gave three great heavy cries in the same way, that were heard in the clouds and the waste places of the sky. And then Grania bade the five hundred that she had for household to go to Beinn Gulbain for the body of Diarmuid.

And when they were bringing it back, she went out to meet them, and they put down the body of Diarmuid, and it is what she said:

"I am your wife, beautiful Diarmuid, the man I would do no hurt to; it is sorrowful I am after you to-night.

"I am looking at the hawk and the hound my secret love used to be hunting with; she that loved the three, let her be put in the grave with Diarmuid.

"Let us be glad to-night, let us make all welcome to-night, let us be open-handed to-night, since we are sitting by the body of a king.

"And O Diarmuid," she said, "it is a hard bed Finn has given you, to be lying on the stones and to be wet with the rain. Ochone!" she said, "your blue eyes to be without sight, you that were friendly and generous and pursuing. O love! O Diarmuid! it is a pity it is he sent you to your death.

"You were a champion of the men of Ireland, their prop in the middle of the fight; you were the head of every battle; your ways were glad and pleasant.

"It is sorrowful I am, without mirth, without light, but only sadness and grief and long dying; your harp used to be sweet to me, it wakened my heart to gladness. Now my courage is fallen down, I not to hear you but to be always remembering your ways. Och! my grief is going through me.

"A thousand curses on the day when Grania gave you her love, that put Finn of the princes from his wits; it is a sorrowful story your death is to-day.

"Many heroes were great and strong about me in the beautiful plain; their hands were good at wrestling and at battle; Ochone! that I did not follow them.

"You were the man was best of the Fianna, beautiful Diarmuid, that women loved. It is dark your dwelling place is under the sod, it is mournful and cold your bed is; it is pleasant your laugh was to-day; you were my happiness, Diarmuid."

And she went back then into the Rath, and bade her people to bring the body to her there.

Now just at this time, it was showed to Angus at Brugh na Boinne that Diarmuid was dead on Beinn Gulbain, for he had kept no watch over him the night before.

And he went on the cold wind towards Beinn Gulbain, and his people with him, and on the way they met with Grania's people that were bringing the body to the Rath.

And when they saw him they held out the wrong sides of their shields as a sign of peace, and Angus knew them; and he and his people gave three great terrible cries over the body of Diarmuid.

And Angus spoke then, and it is what he said: "I was never one night since the time I brought you to Brugh na Boinne, being nine months old, without keeping watch and protection over you till last night, Diarmuid, grandson of Duibhne; and now your blood has been shed and you have been cut off sharply, and the Boar of Beinn Gulbain has put you down, Diarmuid of the bright face and the bright sword. And it is a pity Finn to have done this treachery," he said, "and you at peace with him.

"And lift up his body now," he said, "and bring it to the Brugh in the lasting rocks. And if I cannot bring him back to life," he said, "I will put life into him the way he can be talking with me every day."

Then they put his body on a golden bier, and his spears over it pointed upwards, and they went on till they came to Brugh na Boinne.

And Grania's people went to her and told her how Angus would not let them bring the body into the Rath, but brought it away himself to Brugh na Boinne. And Grania said she had no power over him.

And she sent out then for her four sons that were being reared in the district of Corca Ui Duibhne. And when they came she gave them a loving welcome, and they came into the Rath and sat down there according to their age. And Grania spoke to them with a very loud, clear voice, and it is what she said: "My dear children, your father has been killed by Finn, son of Cumhal, against his own bond and agreement of peace, and let you avenge it well upon him. And here is your share of the inheritance of your father," she said, "his arms and his armour, and his feats of valour and power; and I will share these arms among you myself," she said, "and that they may bring you victory in every battle. Here is the sword for Donnchadh," she said, "the best son Diarmuid had; and the Gae Dearg for Eochaidh; and here is the armour for Ollann, for it will keep the body it is put on in safety; and the shield for Connla. And make no delay now," she said, "but go and learn every sort of skill in fighting, till such time as you will come to your full strength to avenge your father."

So they took leave of her then, and of their household.

And some of their people said: "What must we do now, since our lords will be going into danger against Finn and the Fianna of Ireland?" And Donnchadh, son of Diarmuid, bade them stop in their own places; "for if we make peace with Finn," he said, "there need be no fear on you, and if not, you can make your choice between ourselves and him." And with that they set out on their journey.

But after a while Finn went secretly and unknown to the Fianna to the place where Grania was, and he got to see her in spite of all her high talk, and he spoke gently to her. And she would not listen to him, but bade him to get out of her sight, and whatever hard thing her tongue could say, she said it. But all the same, he went on giving her gentle talk and loving words, till in the end he brought her to his own will.

And there is no news told of them, until such time as they came to where the seven battalions of the Fianna were waiting for Finn. And when they saw him coming, and Grania with him, like any new wife with her husband, they gave a great shout of laughter and of mockery, and Grania bowed down her head with shame. "By my word, Finn," said Oisin, "you will keep a good watch on Grania from this out."

And some said the change had come on her because the mind of a woman changes like the water of a running stream; but some said it was Finn that had put enchantment on her.

And as to the sons of Diarmuid, they came back at the end of seven years, after learning all that was to be learned of valour in the far countries of the world. And when they came back to Rath Grania they were told their mother was gone away with Finn, son of Cumhal, without leaving any word for themselves or for the King of Ireland. And they said if that was so, there was nothing for them to do.

But after that they said they would make an attack on Finn, and they went forward to Almhuin, and they would take no offers, but made a great slaughter of every troop that came out against them.

But at last Grania made an agreement of peace between themselves and Finn, and they got their father's place among the Fianna; and that was little good to them, for they lost their lives with the rest in the battle of Gabhra. And as to Finn and Grania, they stopped with one another to the end.

BOOK VIII

Cnoc-an-Air

CHAPTER I

Tailc, Son of Treon

One time the Fianna were all gathered together doing feats and casting stones. And after a while the Druid of Teamhair that was with them said: "I am in dread, Finn of the Fianna, that there is some trouble near at hand; and look now at those dark clouds of blood," he said, "that are threatening us side by side overhead. And there is fear on me," he said, "that there is some destruction coming on the Fianna."

Finn looked up then, and he saw the great cloud of blood, and he called Osgar to look at it. "That need not knock a start from you," said Osgar, "with all the strength there is in your arms, and in the men that are with you." Then all the Fianna looked up at the cloud, and some of them were glad and cheerful and some were downhearted.

Then the Druid bade Finn to call all his battalions together and to divide them into two halves, that they could be watching for the coming of the enemy.

So Finn sounded the Dord Fiann, and they answered with a shout, every one hurrying to be the first. And Finn bade Osgar and Goll and Faolan to keep watch through the night, and he bade Conan the Bald to stop in the darkness of the cave of Liath Ard. "For it is you can shout loudest," he said, "to warn us if you see the enemy coming." "That I may be pierced through the middle of my body," said Conan, "if I will go watching for troubles or for armies alone, without some more of the Fianna being with me." "It is not fitting for you to refuse Finn," said Lugaidh's Son; "and it is you can shout the loudest," he said, "if the enemies come near the height." "Do not be speaking to me any more," said Conan, "for I will not go there alone, through the length of my days, for Finn and the whole of the Fianna." "Go then, Conan," said Osgar, "and Aodh Beag will go with you, and you can bring dogs with you, Bran and Sceolan and Fuaim and Fearagan; and let you go now without begrudging it," he said.

So Conan went then to Liath Ard, and Aodh Beag and Finn's hounds along with him. And as to Finn, he lay down to sleep, and it was not long till he saw through his sleep Aodh Beag his son, and he without his head. And after that he saw Goll fighting with a very strong man. And he awoke from his sleep, and called the Druid of the Fianna to him, and asked him the meaning of what he saw. "I am in dread there is some destruction coming on the Fianna," said the Druid; "but Aodh Beag will not be wounded in the fight, or Goll," he said.

And it was not long till Finn heard a great shout, and he sounded the Dord Fiann, and then he saw Conan running, and the hounds after him. And Finn sounded the Dord Fiann again before Conan came up, and when he came, Osgar asked him where was Aodh Beag. "He was at the door of the cave when I left it," said Conan, "but I did not look behind me since then," he said; "and it was not Aodh Beag was troubling me." "What was troubling you then?" said Osgar. "Nothing troubles me but myself," said Conan; "although I am well pleased at any good that comes to you," he said.

Osgar went then running hard, till he came to the cave, and there he found Aodh Beag with no fear or trouble on him at all, stopping there till he would hear the noise of the shields. And Osgar brought him back to where the Fianna were, and they saw a great army coming as if in search of them.

And a beautiful woman, having a crimson cloak, came to them over the plain, and she spoke to Finn, and her voice was as sweet as music. And Finn asked her who was she, and who did she come looking for. "I am the daughter of Garraidh, son of Dolar Dian, the Fierce," she said; "and my curse upon the King of Greece that bound me to the man that is following after me, and that I am going from, Tailc, son of Treon." "Tell me why are you shunning him, and I will protect you in spite of him," said Finn. "It is not without reason I hate him," said she, "for he has no good appearance, and his skin is of the colour of coal, and he has the head and the tail of a cat. And I have walked the world three times," she said, "and I did not leave a king or a great man without asking help from him, and I never got it yet." "I will give you protection," said Finn, "or the seven battalions of the Fianna will fall for your sake."

With that they saw the big strange man, Tailc, son of Treon, coming towards them, and he said no word at all of greeting to Finn, but he called for a battle on account of his wife.

So a thousand of the Fianna went out to meet him and his men; and if they did they all fell, and not one of them came back again. And then another thousand of the best men of the Fianna, having blue and green shields, went out under Caoilte, son of Ronan, and they were worsted by Tailc and his people. And then Osgar asked leave of Finn to go out and fight the big man. "I will give you leave," said Finn, "although I am sure you will fall by him." So Osgar went out, and he himself and Tailc, son of Treon, were fighting through the length of five days and five nights without food or drink or sleep. And at the end of that time, Osgar made an end of Tailc, and struck his head off. And when the Fianna saw that, they gave a shout of lamentation for those they had lost of the Fianna, and two shouts of joy for the death of Tailc.

And as to the young woman, when she saw all the slaughter that had been done on account of her, shame reddened her face, and she fell dead there and then. And to see her die like that, after all she had gone through, preyed more on the Fianna than any other thing.

CHAPTER II

Meargach's Wife

And while the Fianna were gathered yet on the hill where Tailc, son of Treon, had been put down, they saw a very great champion coming towards them, having an army behind him. He took no notice of any one more than another, but he asked in a very rough voice where was Finn, the Head of the Fianna. And Aodh Beag, that had a quiet heart, asked him who was he, and what was he come for. "I will tell you nothing at all, child," said the big man, "for it is short your years are, and I will tell nothing at all to any one but Finn." So Aodh Beag brought him to where Finn was, and Finn asked him his name. "Meargach of the Green Spears is my name," he said; "and arms were never reddened yet on my body, and no one ever boasted of driving me backwards. And was it you, Finn," he said, "put down Tailc, son of Treon?" "It was not by me he fell," said Finn, "but by Osgar of the strong hand." "Was it not a great shame for you, Finn," said Meargach then, "to let the queen-woman that had such a great name come to her death by the Fianna?" "It was not by myself or by any of the Fianna she got her death," said Finn; "it was seeing the army lost that brought her to her death. But if it is satisfaction for her death or the death of Tailc you want," he said, "you can get it from a man of the Fianna, or you can go quietly from this place." Then Meargach said he would fight with any man they would bring against him, to avenge Tailc, son of Treon.

And it was Osgar stood up against him, and they fought a very hard fight through the length of three days, and at one time the Fianna thought it was Osgar was worsted, and they gave a great sorrowful shout. But in the end Osgar put down Meargach and struck his head off, and at that the seven battalions of the Fianna gave a shout of victory, and the army of Meargach keened him very sorrowfully. And after that, the two sons of Meargach, Ciardan the Swift and Liagan the Nimble, came up and asked who would come against them, hand to hand, that they might get satisfaction for their father.

And it was Goll stood up against Ciardan, and it was not long till he put him down; and Conan came out against Liagan, and Liagan mocked at him and said:

"It is foolishness your coming is, bald man!" But Conan made a quick blow and struck his head off before the fight was begun at all.

And Faolan said that was a shameful thing to do, not to stand his ground and make a fair fight. But Conan said: "If I could make an end of the whole army by one blow, I would do it, and I would not be ashamed, and the whole of the Fianna could not shelter them from me."

Then the two armies came towards each other, and they were making ready for the attack. And they saw a beautiful golden-haired woman coming towards them, and she crying and ever crying, and the battle was given up on both sides, waiting for her to come; and the army of Meargach knew it was their queen, Ailne of the Bright Face, and they raised a great cry of grief; and the Fianna were looking at her, and said no word.

And she asked where was her husband, and where were her two sons. "High Queen," said Finn then, "for all they were so complete and quick and strong, the three you are asking for fell in fight."

And when the queen-woman heard that, she cried out aloud, and she went to the place where her husband and her two sons were lying, and she stood over their bodies, and her golden hair hanging, and she keened them there. And her own people raised a sharp lamentation listening to her, and the Fianna themselves were under grief.

And it is what she said: "O Meargach," she said, "of the sharp green spears, it is many a fight and many a heavy battle your hard hand fought in the gathering of the armies or alone.

"I never knew any wound to be on your body after them; and it is full sure I am, it was not strength but treachery got the upper hand of you now.

"It is long your journey was from far off, from your own kind country to Inisfail, to come to Finn and the Fianna, that put my three to death through treachery.

"My grief! to have lost my husband, my head, by the treachery of the Fianna; my two sons, my two men that were rough in the fight.

"My grief! my food and my drink; my grief! my teaching everywhere; my grief! my journey from far off, and I to have lost my high heroes.

"My grief! my house thrown down; my grief! my shelter and my shield; my grief! Meargach and Ciardan; my grief! Liagan of the wide chest.

"My grief! my protection and my shelter; my grief! my strength and my power; my grief! there is darkness come from this thing; my grief to-night you to be in your weakness.

"My grief! my gladness and my pleasure; my grief! my desire in every place; my grief! my courage is gone and my strength; my grief from this night out for ever.

"My grief! my guide and my going; my grief! my desire to the day of my death; my grief! my store and my sway; my grief! my heroes that were open-handed.

"My grief! my bed and my sleep; my grief! my journey and my coming; my grief! my teacher and my share; my sorrowful grief! my three men.

"My grief! my beauty and my ornaments; my grief! my jewels and my riches; my grief! my treasures and my goods; my grief! my three Candles of Valour.

"My grief! my friends and my kindred; my grief! my people and my friends. My grief! my father and my mother; my grief and my trouble! you to be dead.

"My grief! my portion and my welcome; my grief! my health at every time; my grief! my increase and my light; my sore trouble, you to be without strength.

"My grief! your spear and your sword; my grief! your gentleness and your love; my grief! your country and your home; my grief! you to be parted from my reach.

"My grief! my coasts and my harbours; my grief! my wealth and my prosperity; my grief! my greatness and my kingdom; my grief and my crying are until death.

"My grief! my luck altogether; my grief for you in time of battle; my grief! my gathering of armies; my grief! my three proud lions.

"My grief! my games and my drinking; my grief! my music and my delight; my grief! my sunny house and my women; my crying grief, you to be under defeat.

"My grief! my lands and my hunting; my grief! my three sure fighters; Och! my grief! they are my sorrow, to fall far off by the Fianna.

"I knew by the great host of the Sidhe that were fighting over the dun, giving battle to one another in the valleys of the air, that destruction would put down my three.

"I knew by the noise of the voices of the Sidhe coming into my ears, that a story of new sorrow was not far from me; it is your death it was foretelling.

"I knew at the beginning of the day when my three good men went from me, when I saw tears of blood on their cheeks, that they would not come back to me as winners.

"I knew by the voice of the battle-crow over your dun every evening, since you went from me comely and terrible, that misfortune and grief were at hand.

"It is well I remember, my three strong ones, how often I used to be telling you that if you would go to Ireland, I would not see the joy of victory on your faces.

"I knew by the voice of the raven every morning since you went from me, that your fall was sure and certain; that you would never come back to your own country.

"I knew, my three great ones, by your forgetting the thongs of your hounds, that you would not gain the day or escape from the treachery of the Fianna.

"I knew, Candles of Valour, by the stream near the dun turning to blood when you set out, that there would be treachery in Finn.

"I knew by the eagle coming every evening over the dun, that it would not be long till I would hear a story of bad news of my three.

"I knew by the withering of the tree before the dun, that you would never come back as conquerors from the treachery of Finn, son of Cumhal."

When Grania, now, heard what the woman was saying, there was anger on her, and she said: "Do not be speaking against Finn or the Fianna, Queen, for it was not by any treachery or any deceit your three men were brought to their end."

But Ailne made her no answer and gave no heed to her, but she went on with her complaint, and she crying and ever crying.

"I knew, looking after you the day you went out from the dun, by the flight of the raven before you, there was no good sign of your coming back again.

"I knew by Ciardan's hounds that were howling mournfully every evening, that it would not be long till I would have bad news of you.

"I knew by my sleep that went from me, by my tears through every lasting night, that there was no luck before you.

"I knew by the sorrowful vision that showed myself in danger, my head and my hands cut off, that it was yourselves were without sway.

"I knew by the voice of Uaithnin, the hound that is dearest to Liagan, howling early every morning, that death was certain for my three.

"I knew when I saw in a vision a lake of blood in the place of the dun, that my three were put down by the deceit that was always with Finn."

"Do not be faulting Finn," said Grania then, "however vexed your heart may be. And leave off now," she said, "speaking against the Fianna and against himself; for if your men had stopped in their own country," she said, "without coming to avenge the son of Treon, there would no harm have happened them." "I would not put any reproach on the Fianna, Grania," said Ailne, "if my three men had been put down in fair battle, but they are not living to bear witness to me," she said; "and it is likely they were put under Druid spells at the first, or they would never have given in." "If they were living, Queen," said Grania, "they would not be running down the Fianna, but they would tell you it was by bravery and the strong hand they fell." "I do not believe you or the Fianna when you say that," said Ailne; "for no one that came to meet them ever got the sway over them by the right of the sword." "If you do not believe what I am saying, beautiful Ailne," said Grania, "I tell you more of your great army will fall by the Fianna, and that not by treachery." "That is not so," said Ailne, "but I have good hopes that my own army will do destruction on the Fianna, for the sake of the men that are dead." "Well, Ailne," said Grania, "I know it is a far journey you have come. And come now and eat and drink," she said, "with myself and with the Fianna."

But Ailne would not do that, but she said it would not be fitting for her to take food from people that did such deeds, and what she wanted was satisfaction for the death of her husband and her two sons.

And first it was settled for two men of each side to go out against one another; and then Ailne said that there should be thirty men on each side, and then she said she would not be satisfied to go back to her own country till she brought the head of Finn with her, or till the last of his men had fallen. And there was a great battle fought in the end, and it is seldom the Fianna fought so hard a battle as that.

And it would be too long to tell, and it would tire the hearers, how many good men were killed on each side. But in the end Ailne of the Bright Face was worsted, and she went back with what were left of her men to their own country, and no one knew where they went.

And the hill in the west those battles were fought on got the name of Cnoc-an-Air, the Hill of Slaughter.

CHAPTER III

Ailne's Revenge

One day Finn and his people were hunting on Slieve Fuad, and a stag stood against them for a while and fought with his great rough horns, and then he turned and ran, and the Fianna followed after him till they came to the green hill of Liadhas, and from that to rocky Cairgin. And there they lost him again for a while, till Sceolan started him again, and he went back towards Slieve Fuad, and the Fianna after him.

But Finn and Daire of the Songs, that were together, went astray and lost the rest of their people, and they did not know was it east or west they were going.

Finn sounded the Dord Fiann then, and Daire played some sorrowful music to let their people know where they were. But when the Fianna heard the music, it seemed to be a long way off; and sometimes they thought it was in the north it was, and sometimes in the east, and then it changed to the west, the way they did not know in the wide world where was it coming from.

And as to Finn and Daire, a Druid mist came about them, and they did not know what way they were going.

And after a while they met with a young woman, comely and pleasant, and they asked who was she, and what brought her there. "Glanluadh is my name," she said, "and my husband is Lobharan; and we were travelling over the plain together a while ago, and we heard the cry of hounds, and he left me and went after the hunt, and I do not know where is he, or what way did he go." "Come on then with us," said Finn, "and we will take care of you, for we ourselves do not know what way the hunt is gone, east or west." So they went on, and before long they came to a hill, and they heard sleepy music of the Sidhe beside them. And after that there came shouts and noises, and then the music began again, and heavy sleep came on Finn and Daire. And when they awoke from their sleep they saw a very large lighted house before them, and a stormy blue sea around it. Then they saw a very big grey man coming through the waves, and he took hold of Finn and of Daire, and all their strength went from them, and he brought them across the waves and into the house, and he shut the door of the house with iron hooks.

"My welcome to you, Finn of the great name," he said then in a very harsh voice; "it is long we are waiting here for you."

They sat down then on the hard side of a bed, and the woman of the house came to them, and they knew her to be Ailne, wife of Meargach. "It is long I am looking for you, Finn," she said, "to get satisfaction for the treachery you did on Meargach and on my two comely young sons, and on Tailc, son of Treon, and all his people. And do you remember that, Finn?" she said. "I remember well," said Finn, "that they fell by the swords of the Fianna, not by treachery but in fighting." "It was by treachery they fell," said the Grey Man then; "and it is our witness to it, pleasant Ailne to be the way she is, and many a strong army under grief on account of her." "What is Ailne to you, man of the rough voice?" said Finn. "I am her own brother," said the man.

With that he put bonds on the three, Finn and Daire and Glanluadh, and he put them down into some deep shut place.

They were very sorrowful then, and they stopped there to the end of five days and five nights, without food, without drink, without music.

And Ailne went to see them then, and Finn said to her: "O Ailne," he said, "bring to mind the time you come to Cnoc-an-Air, and the way the Fianna treated you with generosity; and it is not fitting for you," he said, "to keep us now under shame and weakness and in danger of death." "I know well I got kind treatment from Grania," said Ailne in a sorrowful voice; "but for all that, Finn," she said, "if all the Fianna were in that prison along with you under hard bonds, it would please me well, and I would not pity their case. And what is it set you following after Finn," she said then to Glanluadh, "for that is not a fitting thing for you to do, and his own kind wife living yet."

Then Glanluadh told her the whole story, and how she was walking the plain with Lobharan her husband, and he followed the hunt, and the mist came about her that she did not know east from west, and how she met then with Finn that she never saw before that time. "If that is so," said Ailne, "it is not right for you to be under punishment without cause."

She called then to her brother the Grey Man, and bade him take the spells off Glanluadh. And when she was set free it is sorry she was to leave Daire in bonds, and Finn. And when she had bidden them farewell she went out with Ailne, and there was food brought to her, but a cloud of weakness came on her of a sudden, that it was a pity to see the way she was.

And when Ailne saw that, she brought out an enchanted cup of the Sidhe and gave her a drink from it. And no sooner did Glanluadh drink from the cup than her strength and her own appearance came back to her again; but for all that, she was fretting after Finn and Daire in their bonds. "It seems to me, Glanluadh, you are fretting after those two men," said Ailne. "I am sorry indeed," said Glanluadh, "the like of those men to be shut up without food or drink." "If it is pleasing to you to give them food you may give it," said Ailne, "for I will not make an end of them till I see can I get the rest of the Fianna into bonds along with them." The two women brought food and drink then to Finn, and to Daire; and Glanluadh gave her blessing to Finn, and she cried when she saw the way he was; but as to Ailne, she had no pity at all for the King of the Fianna.

Now as to the Grey Man, he heard them talking of the Fianna, and they were saying that Daire had a great name for the sweetness of his music. "I have a mind to hear that sweet music," said he. So he went to the place where they were, and he bade Daire to let him hear what sort of music he could make. "My music pleased the Fianna well," said Daire; "but I think it likely it would not please you." "Play it for me now, till I know if the report I heard of you is true," said the Grey Man. "Indeed, I have no mind for music," said Daire, "being weak and downhearted the way I am, through your spells that put down my courage." "I will take my spells off you for so long as you play for me," said the Grey Man. "I could never make music seeing Finn in bonds the way he is," said Daire; "for it is worse to me, he to be under trouble than myself." "I will take the power of my spells off Finn till you play for me," said the Grey Man.

He weakened the spells then, and gave them food and drink, and it pleased him greatly the way Daire played the music, and he called to Glanluadh and to Ailne to come and to listen to the sweetness of it. And they were well pleased with it, and it is glad Glanluadh was, seeing them not so discouraged as they were.

Now as to the Fianna, they were searching for Finn and for Daire in every place they had ever stopped in. And when they came to this place they could hear Daire's sweet music; and at first they were glad when they heard it, and then when they knew the way he himself and Finn were, they made an attack on Ailne's dun to release them.

But the Grey Man heard their shouts, and he put the full power of his spells again on Finn and on Daire. And the Fianna heard the music as if stammering, and then they heard a great noise like the loud roaring of waves, and when they heard that, there was not one of them but fell into a sleep and clouds of death, under those sorrowful spells.

And then the Grey Man and Ailne came out quietly from where they were, and they brought the whole of the men of the Fianna that were there into the dun. And they put hard bonds on them, and put them where Finn and Daire were. And there was great grief on Finn and Daire when they saw them, and they were all left there together for a while.

Then Glanluadh said to the Grey Man: "If Daire's music is pleasing to you, let him play it to us now." "If you have a mind for music," said the Grey Man, "Daire must play it for us, and for Finn and his army as well."

They went then to where they were, and bade Daire to play. "I could never play sweet music," said Daire, "the time the Fianna are in any trouble; for when they are in trouble, I myself am in trouble, and I could not sound any sweet string," he said, "while there is trouble on any man of them." The Grey Man weakened the spells then on them all, and Daire played first the strings of sweetness, and of the noise of shouting, and then he sang his own grief and the grief of all the Fianna. And at that the Grey Man said it would not be long before he would put the whole of the Fianna to death; and then Daire played a tune of heavy shouts of lamentation. And then at Finn's bidding he played the music of sweet strings for the Fianna.

They were kept, now, a long time in that prison, and they got very hard treatment; and sometimes Ailne's brother would come in and strike the heads off some of them, for none of them could rise up from the seats they were sitting on through his enchantments. But one time he was going to strike the bald head off Conan, and Conan made a great leap from the seat; but if he did, he left strips of his skin hanging to it, that his back was left bare. And then he came round the Grey Man with his pitiful words: "Stop your hand now," he said, "for that is enough for this time; and do not send me to my death yet awhile, and heal me of my wounds first," he said, "before you make an end of me." And the reason he said that was because he knew Ailne to have an enchanted cup in the dun, that had cured Glanluadh.

And the Grey Man took pity on his case, and he brought him out and bade Ailne to bring the cup to him and to cure his wounds. "I will not bring it," said Ailne, "for it would be best give no time at all to him or to the Fianna, but to make an end of them." "It is not to be saved from death I am asking, bright-faced Ailne," said Conan, "but only not to go to my death stripped bare the way I am." When Ailne heard that, she brought a sheepskin and she put it on Conan's back, and it fitted and grew to him, and covered his wounds. "I will not put you to death, Conan," said the Grey Man then, "but you can stop with myself to the end of your life." "You will never be without grief and danger and the fear of treachery if you keep him with you," said Ailne; "for there is treachery in his heart the same as there is in the rest of them." "There is no fear of that," said her brother, "for I will make no delay until I put the whole of the Fianna to death." And with that he brought Conan to where the enchanted cup was, and he put it in his hand. And just at that moment they heard Daire playing very sweet sorrowful music, and the Grey Man went to listen to it, very quick and proud. And Conan followed him there, and after a while the Grey Man asked him what did he do with the enchanted cup. "I left it where I found it, full of power," said Conan.

The Grey Man hurried back then to the place where the treasures of the dun were. But no sooner was he gone than Conan took out the cup that he had hidden, and he gave a drink from it to Finn and to Osgar and to the rest of the Fianna. And they that were withered and shaking, without strength, without courage, got back their own appearance and their strength again on the moment.

And when the Grey Man came back from looking for the cup, and saw what had happened, he took his sword and made a stroke at Conan. But Conan called to Osgar to defend him, and Osgar attacked the Grey Man, and it was not long till he made him acquainted with death.

And when Ailne saw that, with the grief and the dread that came on her, she fell dead then and there.

Then all the Fianna made a feast with what they found of food and of drink, and they were very joyful and merry. But when they rose up in the morning, there was no trace or tidings of the dun, but it was on the bare grass they were lying.

But as to Conan, the sheepskin never left him; and the wool used to grow on it every year, the same as it would on any other skin.

BOOK XI

The Wearing Away of the Fianna

CHAPTER I

The Quarrel with the Sons of Morna

One time when the Fianna were gone here and there hunting, Black Garraidh and Caoilte were sitting beside Finn, and they were talking of the battle where Finn's father was killed. And Finn said then to Garraidh: "Tell me now, since you were there yourself, what way was it you brought my father Cumhal to his death?" "I will tell you that since you ask me," said Garraidh; "it was my own hand and the hands of the rest of the sons of Morna that made an end of him." "That is cold friendship from my followers the sons of Morna," said Finn. "If it is cold friendship," said Garraidh, "put away the liking you are letting on to have for us, and show us the hatred you have for us all the while." "If I were to lift my hand against you now, sons of Morna," said Finn, "I would be well able for you all without the help of any man." "It was by his arts Cumhal got the upper hand of us," said Garraidh; "and when he got power over us," he said, "he banished us to every far country; a share of us he sent to Alban, and a share of us to dark Lochlann, and a share of us to bright Greece, parting us from one another; and for sixteen years we were away from Ireland, and it was no small thing to us to be without seeing one another through that time. And the first day we came back to Ireland," he said, "we killed sixteen hundred men, and no lie in it, and not a man of them but would be keened by a hundred. And we took their duns after that," he said, "and we went on till we were all around one house in Munster of the red walls. But so great was the bravery of the man in that house, that was your father, that it was easier to find him than to kill him. And we killed all that were of his race out on the hill, and then we made a quick rush at the house where Cumhal was, and every man of us made a wound on his body with his spear. And I myself was in it, and it was I gave him the first wound. And avenge it on me now, Finn, if you have a mind to," he said.

It was not long after that, Finn gave a feast at Almhuin for all his chief men, and there came to it two sons of the King of Alban, and sons of the kings of the great world. And when they were all sitting at the least, the serving-men rose up and took drinking-horns worked by skilled men, and having shining stones in them, and they poured out strong drink for the champions; and it is then mirth rose up in their young men, and courage in their fighting men, and kindness and gentleness in their women, and knowledge and foreknowledge in their poets.

And then a crier rose up and shook a rough iron chain to silence the clowns and the common lads and idlers and then he shook a chain of old silver to silence the high lords and chief men of the Fianna, and the learned men, and they all listened and were silent.

And Fergus of the True Lips rose up and sang before Finn the songs and the good poems of his forefathers; and Finn and Oisin and Lugaidh's Son rewarded him with every good thing. And then he went on to Goll, son of Morna, and told the fights and the destructions and the cattle-drivings and the courtings of his fathers; and it is well-pleased and high-minded the sons of Morna were, listening to that.

And Goll said then: "Where is my woman-messenger?" "I am here, King of the Fianna," said she. "Have you brought me my hand-tribute from the men of Lochlann?" "I have brought it surely," said she. And with that she rose up and laid on the floor of the hall before Goll a load of pure gold, the size of a good pig, and that would be a heavy load for a strong man. And Goll loosened the covering that was about it, and he gave Fergus a good reward from it as he was used to do; for there never was a wise, sharp-worded poet, or a sweet harp-player, or any learned man of Ireland or of Alban, but Goll would give him gold or silver or some good thing.

And when Finn saw that, he said: "How long is it, Goll, you have this rent on the men of Lochlann, and my own rent being on them always with it, and one of my own men, Ciaran son of Latharne, and ten hundred men of his household, guarding it and guarding my right of hunting?" And Goll saw there was anger on Finn, and he said: "It is a long time, Finn, I have that rent on the men of Lochlann, from the time your father put war and quarrels on me, and the King of Ireland joined with him, and I was made to quit Ireland by them. And I went into Britain," he said, "and I took the country and killed the king himself and did destruction on his people, but Cumhal put me out of it; and from that I went to Fionnlochlann, and the king fell by me, and his household, and Cumhal put me out of it; and I went from that to the country of the Saxons, and the king and his household fell by me, and Cumhal put me out of it. But I came back then to Ireland, and I fought a battle against your father, and he fell by me there. And it was at that time I put this rent upon the men of Lochlann. And, Finn," he said, "it is not a rent of the strong hand you have put on them, but it is a tribute for having the protection of the Fianna of Ireland, and I do not lessen that. And you need not begrudge that tribute to me," he said, "for if I had more than that again, it is to you and to the men of Ireland I would give it."

There was great anger on Finn then, and he said: "You tell me, Goll," he said, "by your own story, that you came from the city of Beirbhe to fight against my father, and that you killed him in the battle; and it is a bold thing you to tell that to me." "By your own hand," said Goll, "if you were to give me the same treatment your father gave me, I would pay you the same way as I paid him." "It would be hard for you to do that," said Finn, "for there are a hundred men in my household against every man there is in your household." "That was the same with your father," said Goll, "and I avenged my disgrace on him; and I would do the same on yourself if you earned it," he said.

Then Cairell of the White Skin, son of Finn, said: "It is many a man of Finn's household you have put down, Goll!" And Bald Conan when he heard that said: "I swear by my arms, Goll was never without having a hundred men in his household, every one of them able to get the better of yourself." "And is it to them you belong, crooked-speaking, bare-headed Conan?" said Cairell. "It is to them I belong, you black, feeble, nail-scratching, rough-skinned Cairell; and I will make you know it was Finn was in the wrong," said Conan.

With that Cairell rose up and gave a furious blow of his fist to Conan, and Conan took it with no great patience, but gave him back a blow in his teeth, and from that they went on to worse blows again. And the two sons of Goll rose up to help Conan, and Osgar went to the help of Cairell, and it was not long till many of the chief men of the Fianna were fighting on the one side or the other, on the side of Finn or on the side of the sons of Morna.

But then Fergus of the True Lips rose up, and the rest of the poets of the Fianna along with him, and they sang their songs and their poems to check and to quiet them. And they left off their fighting at the sound of the poets' songs, and they let their weapons fall on the floor, and the poets took them up, and made peace between the fighters; and they put bonds on Finn and on Goll to keep the peace for a while, till they could ask for a judgment from the High King of Ireland. And that was the end for that time of the little quarrel at Almhuin.

But it broke out again, one time there was a falling out between Finn and Goll as to the dividing of a pig of the pigs of Manannan. And at Daire Tardha, the Oak Wood of Bulls, in the province of Connacht, there was a great fight between Finn's men and the sons of Morna. And the sons of Morna were worsted, and fifteen of their men were killed; and they made their mind up that from that time they would set themselves against any friends of Finn or of his people. And it was Conan the Bald gave them that advice, for he was always bitter, and a maker of quarrels and of mischief in every place.

And they kept to their word, and spared no one. There was a yellow-haired queen that Finn loved, Berach Brec her name was, and she was wise and comely and worthy of any good man, and she had her house full of treasures, and never refused the asking of any. And any one that came to her house at Samhain time might stay till Beltaine, and have his choice then to go or to stay. And the sons of

Morna had fostered her, and they went where she was and bade her to give up Finn and she need be in no dread of them. But she said she would not give up her kind lover to please them; and she was going away from them to her ship, and Art, son of Morna, made a cast of his spear that went through her body, that she died, and her people brought her up from the strand and buried her.

And as to Goll, he took a little hound that Finn thought a great deal of, Conbeg its name was, and he drowned it in the sea; and its body was brought up to shore by a wave afterwards, and it was buried under a little green hill by the Fianna. And Caoilte made a complaint over it, and he said how swift the little hound was after deer, or wild pigs, and how good at killing them, and that it was a pity it to have died, out on the cold green waves. And about that time, nine women of the Tuatha de Danaan came to meet with nine men of the Fianna, and the sons of Morna saw them coming and made an end of them.

And when Caoilte met with Goll, he made a cast of his spear at him that struck the golden helmet off his head and a piece of his flesh along with it. But Goll took it very proudly, and put on the helmet again and took up his weapons, and called out to his brothers that he was no way ashamed.

And Finn went looking for the sons of Morna in every place to do vengeance on them. They were doing robbery and destruction one time in Slieve Echtge, that got its name from Echtge, daughter of Nuada of the Silver Hand, and Finn and the Fianna were to the west, Slieve Cairn in the district of Corcomruadh. And Finn was in doubt if the sons of Morna were gone southward into Munster or north into Connacht. So he sent Aedan and Cahal, two sons of the King of Ulster, and two hundred fighting men with them, into the beautiful pleasant province of Connacht, and every day they used to go looking for the sons of Morna from place to place. But after a while the three battalions of the Fianna that were in Corcomruadh saw the track of a troop of men, and they thought it to be the track of the sons of Morna; and they closed round them at night, and made an end of them all. But when the full light came on the morrow, they knew them to be their own people, that were with the King of Ulster's sons, and they gave three great heavy cries, keening the friends they had killed in mistake.

And Caoilte and Oisin went to Rath Medba and brought a great stone and put it over the king's sons, and it was called Lia an Imracail, the Stone of the Mistake. And the place where Goll brought his men the time he parted from Finn in anger got the name of Druimscarha, the Parting Hill of Heroes.

CHAPTER II

Death of Goll

And at last it chanced that Goll and Cairell, son of Finn, met with one another, and said sharp words, and they fought in the sea near the strand, and Cairell got his death by Goll. And there was great anger and great grief on Finn, seeing his son, that was so strong and comely, lying dead and grey, like a blighted branch.

And as to Goll, he went away to a cave that was in a point stretching out into the sea; and he thought to stop there till Finn's anger would have passed.

And Osgar knew where he was, and he went to see him, that had been his comrade in so many battles. But Goll thought it was as an enemy he came, and he made a cast of his spear at him, and though Osgar got no wound by it, it struck his shield and crushed it. And Finn took notice of the way the shield was, and when he knew that Goll had made a cast at Osgar there was greater anger again on him. And he sent out his men and bade them to watch every path and every gap that led to the cave where Goll was, the way they would make an end of him.

And when Goll knew Finn to be watching for his life that way, he made no attempt to escape, but stopped where he was, without food, without drink, and he blinded with the sand that was blowing into his eyes.

And his wife came to a rock where she could speak with him, and she called to him to come to her. "Come over to me," she said; "and it is a pity you to be blinded where you are, on the rocks of the waste sea, with no drink but the salt water, a man that was first in every fight. And come now to be sleeping beside me," she said; "and in place of the hard sea-water I will nourish you from my own breast, and it is I will do your healing. And the gold of your hair is my desire for ever," she said, "and do not stop withering there like an herb in the winter-time, and my heart black with grief within me."

But Goll would not leave the spot where he was for all she could say. "It is best as it is," he said, "and I never took the advice of a woman east or west, and I never will take it. And O sweet-voiced queen," he said, "what ails you to be fretting after me; and remember now your silver and your gold, and your silks and stuffs, and remember the seven hounds I gave you at Cruadh Ceirrge, and every one of them without slackness till he has killed the deer. And do not be crying tears after me, queen with the white hands," he said; "but remember your constant lover, Aodh, the son of the best woman of the world, that came out from Spain asking for you, and that I fought at Corcar-an-Deirg; and go to him now," he said, "for it is bad when a woman is in want of a good man."

And he lay down on the rocks, and at the end of twelve days he died. And his wife keened him there, and made a great lamentation for her husband that had such a great name, and that was the second best of the Fianna of Ireland.

And when Conan heard of the death of Goll his brother, there was great anger on him, and he went to Garraidh, and asked him to go with him to Finn to ask satisfaction for Goll. "I am not willing to go," said Garraidh, "since we could get no satisfaction for the great son of Morna." "Whether you have a mind to go or not, I will go," said Conan; "and I will make an end of every man I meet with, for the sake of yellow-haired Goll; I will have the life of Oisin, Finn's great son, and of Osgar and of Caoilte and of Daire of the Songs; I will have no forgiveness for them; we must show no respect for Finn, although we may die in the fight, having no help from Goll. And let us take that work in hand, and make no delay," he said; "for if Finn is there, his strength will be there, until we put him under his flag-stone."
But it is not likely Garraidh went with him, and he after speaking such foolish words.

And what happened Conan in the end is not known. But there is a cairn of stones on a hill of Burren, near to Corcomruadh, and the people of Connacht say it is there he is buried, and that there was a stone found there one time, having on it in the old writing: "Conan the swift-footed, the bare-footed." But the Munster people say it is on their own side of Burren he is buried.

CHAPTER III

The Battle of Gabhra

Now, with one thing and another, the High King of Ireland had got to be some-way bitter against Finn and the Fianna; and one time that he had a gathering of his people he spoke out to them, and he bade them to remember all the harm that had been done them through the Fianna, and all their pride, and the tribute they asked. "And as to myself," he said, "I would sooner die fighting the Fianna, if I could bring them down along with me, than live with Ireland under them the way it is now."
All his people were of the same mind, and they said they would make no delay, but would attack the Fianna and make an end of them. "And we will have good days of joy and of feasting," they said, "when once Almhuin is clear of them."
And the High King began to make plans against Finn; and he sent to all the men of Ireland to come and help him. And when all was ready, he sent and bade Osgar to come to a feast he was making at Teamhair.

And Osgar, that never was afraid before any enemy, set out for Teamhair, and three hundred of his men with him. And on the way they saw a woman of the Sidhe washing clothes at a river, and there was the colour of blood on the water where she was washing them. And Osgar said to her: "There is red on the clothes you are washing; and it is for the dead you are washing them." And the woman answered him, and it is what she said: "It is not long till the ravens will be croaking over your own head after the battle." "Is there any weakness in our eyes," said Osgar, "that a little story like that would set us crying? And do another foretelling for us now," he said, "and tell us will any man of our enemies fall by us before we ourselves are made an end of?"

"There will nine hundred fall by yourself," she said; "and the High King himself will get his death-wound from you."

Osgar and his men went on then to the king's house at Teamhair, and they got good treatment, and the feast was made ready, and they were three days at pleasure and at drinking.

And on the last day of the drinking, the High King called out with a loud voice, and he asked Osgar would he make an exchange of spears with him. "Why do you ask that exchange," said Osgar, "when I myself and my spear were often with yourself in time of battle? And you would not ask it of me," he said, "if Finn and the Fianna were with me now." "I would ask it from any fighting man among you," said the king, "and for rent and tribute along with it." "Any gold or any treasure you might ask of us, we would give it to you," said Osgar, "but it is not right for you to ask my spear." There were very high words between them then, and they threatened one another, and at the last the High King said: "I will put my spear of the seven spells out through your body." "And I give my word against that," said Osgar, "I will put my spear of the nine spells between the meeting of your hair and your beard."

With that he and his men rose up and went out of Teamhair, and they stopped to rest beside a river, and there they heard the sound of a very sorrowful tune, that was like keening, played on a harp. And there was great anger on Osgar when he heard that, and he rose up and took his arms and roused his people, and they went on again to where Finn was. And there came after them a messenger from the High King, and the message he brought was this, that he never would pay tribute to the Fianna or bear with them at all from that time.

And when Finn heard that, he sent a challenge of battle, and he gathered together all the Fianna that were left to him. But as to the sons of Morna, it was to the High King of Ireland they gathered.

And it was at the hill of Gabhra the two armies met, and there were twenty men with the King of Ireland for every man that was with Finn.

And it is a very hard battle was fought that day, and there were great deeds done on both sides; and there never was a greater battle fought in Ireland than that one.

And as to Osgar, it would be hard to tell all he killed on that day; five score of the Sons of the Gael, and five score fighting men from the Country of Snow, and seven score of the Men of Green Swords that never went a step backward, and four hundred from the Country of the Lion, and five score of the sons of kings; and the shame was for the King of Ireland.

But as to Osgar himself, that began the day so swift and so strong, at the last he was like leaves on a strong wind, or like an aspen-tree that is falling. But when he saw the High King near him, he made for him like a wave breaking on the strand; and the king saw him coming, and shook his greedy spear, and made a cast of it, and it went through his body and brought him down on his right knee, and that was the first grief of the Fianna. But Osgar himself was no way daunted, but he made a cast of his spear of the nine spells that went into the High King at the meeting of the hair and the beard, and gave him his death. And when the men nearest to the High King saw that, they put the king's helmet up on a pillar, the way his people would think he was living yet. But Osgar saw it, and he lifted a thin bit of a slab-stone that was on the ground beside him, and he made a cast of it that broke the helmet where it was; and then he himself fell like a king.

And there fell in that battle the seven sons of Caoilte, and the son of the King of Lochlann that had come to give them his help, and it would be hard to count the number of the Fianna that fell in that battle.

And when it was ended, those that were left of them went looking for their dead. And Caoilte stooped down over his seven brave sons, and every living man of the Fianna stooped over his own dear friends. And it was a lasting grief to see all that were stretched in that place, but the Fianna would not have taken it to heart the way they did, but for being as they were, a beaten race.

And as to Oisin, he went looking for Osgar, and it is the way he found him, lying stretched, and resting on his left arm and his broken shield beside him, and his sword in his hand yet, and his blood about him on every side. And he put out his hand to Oisin, and Oisin took it and gave out a very hard cry. And Osgar said: "It is glad I am to see you safe, my father." And Oisin had no answer to give him. And just then Caoilte came where they were, and he looked at Osgar. "What way are you now, my darling?" he said. "The way you would like me to be," said Osgar.

Then Caoilte searched the wound, and when he saw how the spear had torn its way through to the back, he cried out, and a cloud came over him and his strength failed him. "O Osgar," he said, "you are parted from the Fianna, and they themselves must be parted from battle from this out," he said, "and they must pay their tribute to the King of Ireland."

Then Caoilte and Oisin raised up Osgar on their shields and brought him to a smooth green hill till they would take his dress off. And there was not a handsbreadth of his white body that was without a wound.

And when the rest of the Fianna saw what way Osgar was, there was not a man of them that keened his own son or his brother, but every one of them came keening Osgar.

And after a while, at noonday, they saw Finn coming towards them, and what was left of the Sun-banner raised on a spear-shaft. All of them saluted Finn then, but he made no answer, and he came up to the hill where Osgar was. And when Osgar saw him coming he saluted him, and he said: "I have got my desire in death, Finn of the sharp arms." And Finn said: "It is worse the way you were, my son, on the day of the battle at Beinn Edair when the wild geese could swim on your breast, and it was my hand that gave you healing." "There can no healing be done for me now for ever," said Osgar, "since the King of Ireland put the spear of seven spells through my body." And Finn said: "It is a pity it was not I myself fell in sunny scarce Gabhra, and you going east and west at the head of the Fianna." "And if it was yourself fell in the battle," said Osgar, "you would not hear me keening after you; for no man ever knew any heart in me," he said, "but a heart of twisted horn, and it covered with iron. But the howling of the dogs beside me," he said, "and the keening of the old fighting men, and the crying of the women one after another, those are the things that are vexing me." And Finn said: "Child of my child, calf of my calf, white and slender, it is a pity the way you are. And my heart is starting like a deer," he said, "and I am weak after you and after the Fianna of Ireland. And misfortune has followed us," he said; "and farewell now to battles and to a great name, and farewell to taking tributes; for every good thing I ever had is gone from me now," he said.

And when Osgar heard those words he stretched out his hands, and his eyelids closed. And Finn turned away from the rest, and he cried tears down; and he never shed a tear through the whole length of his lifetime but only for Osgar and for Bran.

And all that were left of the Fianna gave three sorrowful cries after Osgar, for there was not one of the Fianna beyond him, unless it might be Finn or Oisin.

And it is many of the Fianna were left dead in Gabhra, and graves were made for them. And as to Lugaidh's Son, that was so tall a man and so good a fighter, they made a very wide grave for him, as was fitting for a king. And the whole length of the rath at Gabhra, from end to end, it is that was the grave of Osgar, son of Oisin, son of Finn.

And as to Finn himself, he never had peace or pleasure again from that day.

BOOK X

The End of the Fianna

CHAPTER I

Death of Bran

One day Finn was hunting, and Bran went following after a fawn. And they were coming towards Finn, and the fawn called out, and it said: "If I go into the sea below I will never come back again; and if I go up into the air above me, it will not save me from Bran." For Bran would overtake the wild geese, she was that swift.

"Go out through my legs," said Finn then. So the fawn did that, and Bran followed her; and as Bran went under him, Finn squeezed his two knees on her, that she died on the moment.

And there was great grief on him after that, and he cried tears down the same as he did when Osgar died.

And some said it was Finn's mother the fawn was, and that it was to save his mother he killed Bran. But that is not likely, for his mother was beautiful Muirne, daughter of Tadg, son of Nuada of the Tuatha de Danaan, and it was never heard that she was changed into a fawn. It is more likely it was Oisin's mother was in it.

But some say Bran and Sceolan are still seen to start at night out of the thicket on the hill of Almhuin.

CHAPTER II

The Call of Oisin

One misty morning, what were left of the Fianna were gathered together to Finn, and it is sorrowful and downhearted they were after the loss of so many of their comrades.

And they went hunting near the borders of Loch Lein, where the bushes were in blossom and the birds were singing; and they were waking up the deer that were as joyful as the leaves of a tree in summer-time.

And it was not long till they saw coming towards them from the west a beautiful young woman, riding on a very fast slender white horse. A queen's crown she
had on her head, and a dark cloak of silk down to the ground, having stars of red
gold on it; and her eyes were blue and as clear as the dew on the grass, and a gold
ring hanging down from every golden lock of her hair; and her cheeks redder than
the rose, and her skin whiter than the swan upon the wave, and her lips as sweet
as honey that is mixed through red wine.

And in her hand she was holding a bridle having a golden bit, and there was a
saddle worked with red gold under her. And as to the horse, he had a wide smooth
cloak over him, and a silver crown on the back of his head, and he was shod with
shining gold.

She came to where Finn was, and she spoke with a very kind, gentle voice, and
she said: "It is long my journey was, King of the Fianna." And Finn asked who
was she, and what was her country and the cause of her coming. "Niamh of the
Golden Head is my name," she said; "and I have a name beyond all the women of
the world, for I am the daughter of the King of the Country of the Young." "What
was it brought you to us from over the sea, Queen?" said Finn then. "Is it that
your husband is gone from you, or what is the trouble that is on you?" "My
husband is not gone from me," she said, "for I never went yet to any man. But O
King of the Fianna," she said, "I have given my love and my affection to your own
son, Oisin of the strong hands." "Why did you give your love to him beyond all
the troops of high princes that are under the sun?" said Finn. "It was by reason of
his great name, and of the report I heard of his bravery and of his comeliness," she
said. "And though there is many a king's son and high prince gave me his love, I
never consented to any till I set my love on Oisin."

When Oisin heard what she was saying, there was not a limb of his body that
was not in love with beautiful Niamh; and he took her hand in his hand, and he
said: "A true welcome before you to this country, young queen. It is you are the
shining one," he said; "it is you are the nicest and the comeliest; it is you are better
to me than any other woman; it is you are my star and my choice beyond the
women of the entire world." "I put on you the bonds of a true hero," said Niamh
then, "you to come away with me now to the Country of the Young." And it is
what she said:

"It is the country is most delightful of all that are under the sun; the trees are
stooping down with fruit and with leaves and with blossom.

"Honey and wine are plentiful there, and everything the eye has ever seen; no
wasting will come on you with the wasting away of time; you will never see death
or lessening.

"You will get feasts, playing and drinking; you will get sweet music on the
strings; you will get silver and gold and many jewels.

"You will get, and no lie in it, a hundred swords; a hundred cloaks of the
dearest silk; a hundred horses, the quickest in battle; a hundred willing hounds.

"You will get the royal crown of the King of the Young that he never gave to any one under the sun. It will be a shelter to you night and day in every rough fight and in every battle.

"You will get a right suit of armour; a sword, goldhilted, apt for striking; no one that ever saw it got away alive from it.

"A hundred coats of armour and shirts of satin; a hundred cows and a hundred calves; a hundred sheep having golden fleeces; a hundred jewels that are not of this world.

"A hundred glad young girls shining like the sun, their voices sweeter than the music of birds; a hundred armed men strong in battle, apt at feats, waiting on you, if you will come with me to the Country of the Young.

"You will get everything I have said to you, and delights beyond them, that I have no leave to tell; you will get beauty, strength and power, and I myself will be with you as a wife."

And after she had made that song, Oisin said: "O pleasant golden-haired queen, you are my choice beyond the women of the world; and I will go with you willingly," he said.

And with that he kissed Finn his father and bade him farewell, and he bade farewell to the rest of the Fianna, and he went up then on the horse with Niamh.

And the horse set out gladly, and when he came to the strand he shook himself and he neighed three times, and then he made for the sea. And when Finn and the Fianna saw Oisin facing the wide sea, they gave three great sorrowful shouts. And as to Finn, he said: "It is my grief to see you going from me; and I am without a hope," he said, "ever to see you coming back to me again."

CHAPTER III

The Last of the Great Men

And indeed that was the last time Finn and Oisin and the rest of the Fianna of Ireland were gathered together, for hunting, for battle, for chess-playing, for drinking or for music; for they all wore away after that, one after another.

As to Caoilte, that was old and had lost his sons, he used to be fretting and lonesome after the old times. And one day that there was very heavy snow on the ground, he made this complaint:—

"It is cold the winter is; the wind is risen; the fierce high-couraged stag rises up; it is cold the whole mountain is to-night, yet the fierce stag is calling. The deer of Slievecarn of the gatherings does not lay his side to the ground; he no less than the stag of the top of cold Echtge hears the music of the wolves.

"I, Caoilte, and brown-haired Diarmuid and pleasant light-footed Osgar, we used to be listening to the music of the wolves through the end of the cold night. It is well the brown deer sleeps with its hide to the hollow, hidden as if in the earth, through the end of the cold night.

"To-day I am in my age, and I know but a few men; I used to shake my spear bravely in the ice-cold morning. It is often I put silence on a great army that is very cold to-night."

And after a while he went into a hill of the Sidhe to be healed of his old wounds. And whether he came back from there or not is not known; and there are some that say he used to be talking with Patrick of the Bells the same time Oisin was with him. But that is not likely, or Oisin would not have made complaints about his loneliness the way he did.

But a long time after that again, there was a king of Ireland making a journey. And he and his people missed their way, and when night-time came on, they were in a dark wood, and no path before them.

And there came to them a very tall man, that was shining like a burning flame, and he took hold of the bridle of the king's horse, and led him through the wood till they came to the right road. And the King of Ireland asked him who was he, and first he said: "I am your candlestick"; and then he said: "I was with Finn one time." And the king knew it was Caoilte, son of Ronan, was in it.

And three times nine of the rest of the Fianna came out of the west one time to Teamhair. And they took notice that now they were wanting their full strength and their great name, no one took notice of them or came to speak with them at all. And when they saw that, they lay down on the side of the hill at Teamhair, and put their lips to the earth and died.

And for three days and a month and a year from the time of the destruction of the Fianna of Ireland, Loch Dearg was under mists.

And as to Finn, there are some say he died by the hand of a fisherman; but it is likely that is not true, for that would be no death for so great a man as Finn, son of Cumhal. And there are some say he never died, but is alive in some place yet.

And one time a smith made his way into a cave he saw, that had a door to it, and he made a key that opened it. And when he went in he saw a very wide place, and very big men lying on the floor. And one that was bigger than the rest was lying in the middle, and the Dord Fiann beside him; and he knew it was Finn and the Fianna were in it.

And the smith took hold of the Dord Fiann, and it is hardly he could lift it to his mouth, and he blew a very strong blast on it, and the sound it made was so great, it is much the rocks did not come down on him. And at the sound, the big men lying on the ground shook from head to foot. He gave another blast then, and they all turned on their elbows.

And great dread came on him when he saw that, and he threw down the Dord Fiann and ran from the cave and locked the door after him, and threw the key into the lake. And he heard them crying after him, "You left us worse than you found us." And the cave was not found again since that time.

But some say the day will come when the Dord Fiann will be sounded three times, and that at the sound of it the Fianna will rise up as strong and as well as ever they were. And there are some say Finn, son of Cumhal, has been on the earth now and again since the old times, in the shape of one of the heroes of Ireland.

And as to the great things he and his men did when they were together, it is well they have been kept in mind through the poets of Ireland and of Alban. And one night there were two men minding sheep in a valley, and they were saying the poems of the Fianna while they were there. And they saw two very tall shapes on the two hills on each side of the valley, and one of the tall shapes said to the other: "Do you hear that man down below? I was the second doorpost of battle at Gabhra, and that man knows all about it better than myself."

BOOK XI

Oisin and Patrick

CHAPTER I

Oisin's Story

As to Oisin, it was a long time after he was brought away by Niamh that he came back again to Ireland. Some say it was hundreds of years he was in the Country of the Young, and some say it was thousands of years he was in it; but whatever time it was, it seemed short to him.

And whatever happened him through the time he was away, it is a withered old man he was found after coming back to Ireland, and his white horse going away from him, and he lying on the ground.

And it was S. Patrick had power at that time, and it was to him Oisin was brought; and he kept him in his house, and used to be teaching him and questioning him. And Oisin was no way pleased with the way Ireland was then, but he used to be talking of the old times, and fretting after the Fianna.

And Patrick bade him to tell what happened him the time he left Finn and the Fianna and went away with Niamh. And it is the story Oisin told:—"The time I went away with golden-haired Niamh, we turned our backs to the land, and our faces westward, and the sea was going away before us, and filling up in waves after us. And we saw wonderful things on our journey," he said, "cities and courts and duns and lime-white houses, and shining sunny-houses and palaces. And one time we saw beside us a hornless deer running hard, and an eager white red-eared hound following after it. And another time we saw a young girl on a horse and having a golden apple in her right hand, and she going over the tops of the waves; and there was following after her a young man riding a white horse, and having a crimson cloak and a gold-hilted sword in his right hand."

"Follow on with your story, pleasant Oisin," said Patrick, "for you did not tell us yet what was the country you went to."

"The Country of the Young, the Country of Victory, it was," said Oisin. "And O Patrick," he said, "there is no lie in that name; and if there are grandeurs in your Heaven the same as there are there, I would give my friendship to God.

"We turned our backs then to the dun," he said, "and the horse under us was quicker than the spring wind on the backs of the mountains. And it was not long till the sky darkened, and the wind rose in every part, and the sea was as if on fire, and there was nothing to be seen of the sun.

"But after we were looking at the clouds and the stars for a while the wind went down, and the storm, and the sun brightened. And we saw before us a very delightful country under full blossom, and smooth plains in it, and a king's dun that was very grand, and that had every colour in it, and sunny-houses beside it, and palaces of shining stones, made by skilled men. And we saw coming out to meet us three fifties of armed men, very lively and handsome. And I asked Niamh was this the Country of the Young, and she said it was. 'And indeed, Oisin,' she said, 'I told you no lie about it, and you will see all I promised you before you for ever.'

"And there came out after that a hundred beautiful young girls, having cloaks of silk worked with gold, and they gave me a welcome to their own country. And after that there came a great shining army, and with it a strong beautiful king, having a shirt of yellow silk and a golden cloak over it, and a very bright crown on his head. And there was following after him a young queen, and fifty young girls along with her.

"And when all were come to the one spot, the king took me by the hand, and he said out before them all: 'A hundred thousand welcomes before you, Oisin, son of Finn. And as to this country you are come to,' he said, 'I will tell you news of it without a lie. It is long and lasting your life will be in it, and you yourself will be young for ever. And there is no delight the heart ever thought of,' he said, 'but it is here against your coming. And you can believe my words, Oisin,' he said, 'for I myself am the King of the Country of the Young, and this is its comely queen, and it was golden-headed Niamh our daughter that went over the sea looking for you to be her husband for ever.' I gave thanks to him then, and I stooped myself down before the queen, and we went forward to the royal house, and all the high nobles came out to meet us, both men and women, and there was a great feast made there through the length of ten days and ten nights.

"And that is the way I married Niamh of the Golden Hair, and that is the way I went to the Country of the Young, although it is sorrowful to me to be telling it now, O Patrick from Rome," said Oisin.

"Follow on with your story, Oisin of the destroying arms," said Patrick, "and tell me what way did you leave the Country of the Young, for it is long to me till I hear that; and tell us now had you any children by Niamh, and was it long you were in that place."

"Two beautiful children I had by Niamh," said Oisin, "two young sons and a comely daughter. And Niamh gave the two sons the name of Finn and of Osgar, and the name I gave to the daughter was The Flower.

"And I did not feel the time passing, and it was a long time I stopped there," he said, "till the desire came on me to see Finn and my comrades again. And I asked leave of the king and of Niamh to go back to Ireland. 'You will get leave from me,' said Niamh; 'but for all that,' she said, 'it is bad news you are giving me, for I am in dread you will never come back here again through the length of your days.' But I bade her have no fear, since the white horse would bring me safe back again from Ireland. 'Bear this in mind, Oisin,' she said then, 'if you once get off the horse while you are away, or if you once put your foot to ground, you will never come back here again. And O Oisin,' she said, 'I tell it to you now for the third time, if you once get down from the horse, you will be an old man, blind and withered, without liveliness, without mirth, without running, without leaping. And it is a grief to me, Oisin,' she said, 'you ever to go back to green Ireland; and it is not now as it used to be, and you will not see Finn and his people, for there is not now in the whole of Ireland but a Father of Orders and armies of saints; and here is my kiss for you, pleasant Oisin,' she said, 'for you will never come back any more to the Country of the Young.'

"And that is my story, Patrick, and I have told you no lie in it," said Oisin. "And O Patrick," he said, "if I was the same the day I came here as I was that day, I would have made an end of all your clerks, and there would not be a head left on a neck after me."

"Go on with your story," said Patrick, "and you will get the same good treatment from me you got from Finn, for the sound of your voice is pleasing to me."

So Oisin went on with his story, and it is what he said: "I have nothing to tell of my journey till I came back into green Ireland, and I looked about me then on all sides, but there were no tidings to be got of Finn. And it was not long till I saw a great troop of riders, men and women, coming towards me from the west. And when they came near they wished me good health; and there was wonder on them all when they looked at me, seeing me so unlike themselves, and so big and so tall.

"I asked them then did they hear if Finn was still living, or any other one of the Fianna, or what had happened them. 'We often heard of Finn that lived long ago,' said they, 'and that there never was his equal for strength or bravery or a great name; and there is many a book written down,' they said, 'by the sweet poets of the Gael, about his doings and the doings of the Fianna, and it would be hard for us to tell you all of them. And we heard Finn had a son,' they said, 'that was beautiful and shining, and that there came a young girl looking for him, and he went away with her to the Country of the Young.'

"And when I knew by their talk that Finn was not living or any of the Fianna, it is downhearted I was, and tired, and very sorrowful after them. And I made no delay, but I turned my face and went on to Almhuin of Leinster. And there was great wonder on me when I came there to see no sign at all of Finn's great dun, and his great hall, and nothing in the place where it was but weeds and nettles."

And there was grief on Oisin then, and he said: "Och, Patrick! Och, ochone, my grief! It is a bad journey that was to me; and to be without tidings of Finn or the Fianna has left me under pain through my lifetime."

"Leave off fretting, Oisin," said Patrick, "and shed your tears to the God of grace. Finn and the Fianna are slack enough now, and they will get no help for ever." "It is a great pity that would be," said Oisin, "Finn to be in pain for ever; and who was it gained the victory over him, when his own hand had made an end of so many a hard fighter?"

"It is God gained the victory over Finn," said Patrick, "and not the strong hand of an enemy; and as to the Fianna, they are condemned to hell along with him, and tormented for ever."

"O Patrick," said Oisin, "show me the place where Finn and his people are, and there is not a hell or a heaven there but I will put it down. And if Osgar, my own son, is there," he said, "the hero that was bravest in heavy battles, there is not in hell or in the Heaven of God a troop so great that he could not destroy it."

"Let us leave off quarrelling on each side now," said Patrick; "and go on, Oisin, with your story. What happened you after you knew the Fianna to be at an end?"

"I will tell you that, Patrick," said Oisin. "I was turning to go away, and I saw the stone trough that the Fianna used to be putting their hands in, and it full of water. And when I saw it I had such a wish and such a feeling for it that I forgot what I was told, and I got off the horse. And in the minute all the years came on me, and I was lying on the ground, and the horse took fright and went away and left me there, an old man, weak and spent, without sight, without shape, without comeliness, without strength or understanding, without respect.

"There, Patrick, is my story for you now," said Oisin, "and no lie in it, of all that happened me going away and coming back again from the Country of the Young."

CHAPTER II

Oisin in Patrick's House

And Oisin stopped on with S. Patrick, but he was not very well content with the way he was treated. And one time he said: "They say I am getting food, but God knows I am not, or drink; and I Oisin, son of Finn, under a yoke, drawing stones." "It is my opinion you are getting enough," said S. Patrick then, "and you getting a quarter of beef and a churn of butter and a griddle of bread every day." "I often saw a quarter of a blackbird bigger than your quarter of beef," said Oisin, "and a rowan berry as big as your churn of butter, and an ivy leaf as big as your griddle of bread." S. Patrick was vexed when he heard that, and he said to Oisin that he had told a lie.

There was great anger on Oisin then, and he went where there was a litter of pups, and he bade a serving-boy to nail up the hide of a freshly killed bullock to the wall, and to throw the pups against it one by one. And every one that he threw fell down from the hide till it came to the last, and he held on to it with his teeth and his nails. "Rear that one," said Oisin, "and drown all the rest."

Then he bade the boy to keep the pup in a dark place, and to care it well, and never to let it taste blood or see the daylight. And at the end of a year, Oisin was so well pleased with the pup, that he gave it the name of Bran Og, young Bran.

And one day he called to the serving-boy to come on a journey with him, and to bring the pup in a chain. And they set out and passed by Slieve-nam-ban, where the witches of the Sidhe do be spinning with their spinning-wheels; and then they turned eastward into Gleann-na-Smol. And Oisin raised a rock that was there, and he bade the lad take from under it three things, a great sounding horn of the Fianna, and a ball of iron they had for throwing, and a very sharp sword. And when Oisin saw those things, he took them in his hands, and he said: "My thousand farewells to the day when you were put here!" He bade the lad to clean them well then; and when he had done that, he bade him to sound a blast on the horn. So the boy did that, and Oisin asked him did he see anything strange. "I did not," said the boy. "Sound it again as loud as you can," said Oisin. "That is as hard as I can sound it, and I can see nothing yet," said the boy when he had done that. Then Oisin took the horn himself, and he put it to his mouth, and blew three great blasts on it. "What do you see now?" he said. "I see three great clouds coming," he said, "and they are settling down in the valley; and the first cloud is a flight of very big birds, and the second cloud is a flight of birds that are bigger again, and the third flight is of the biggest and the blackest birds the world ever saw." "What is the dog doing?" said Oisin. "The eyes are starting from his head, and there is not a rib of hair on him but is standing up." "Let him loose now," said Oisin.

The dog rushed down to the valley then, and he made an attack on one of the birds, that was the biggest of all, and that had a shadow like a cloud. And they fought a very fierce fight, but at last Bran Og made an end of the big bird, and lapped its blood. But if he did, madness came on him, and he came rushing back towards Oisin, his jaws open and his eyes like fire. "There is dread on me, Oisin," said the boy, "for the dog is making for us, mad and raging." "Take this iron ball and make a cast at him when he comes near," said Oisin. "I am in dread to do that," said the boy. "Put it in my hand, and turn it towards him," said Oisin. The boy did that, and Oisin made a cast of the ball that went into the mouth and the throat of the dog, and choked him, and he fell down the slope, twisting and foaming.

Then they went where the great bird was left dead, and Oisin bade the lad to cut a quarter off it with the sword, and he did so. And then he bade him cut open the body, and in it he found a rowan berry, the biggest he had ever seen, and an ivy leaf that was bigger than the biggest griddle.

So Oisin turned back then, and went to where S. Patrick was, and he showed him the quarter of the bird that was bigger than any quarter of a bullock, and the rowan berry that was bigger than a churning of butter, and the leaf. "And you know now, Patrick of the Bells," he said, "that I told no lie; and it is what kept us all through our lifetime," he said, "truth that was in our hearts, and strength in our arms, and fulfilment in our tongues."

"You told no lie indeed," said Patrick.

And when Oisin had no sight left at all, he used every night to put up one of the serving-men on his shoulders, and to bring him out to see how were the cattle doing. And one night the servants had no mind to go, and they agreed together to tell him it was a very bad night.

And it is what the first of them said; "It is outside there is a heavy sound with the heavy water dropping from the tops of trees; the sound of the waves is not to be heard for the loud splashing of the rain." And then the next one said: "The trees of the wood are shivering, and the birch is turning black; the snow is killing the birds; that is the story outside." And the third said: "It is to the east they have turned their face, the white snow and the dark rain; it is what is making the plain so cold is the snow that is dripping and getting hard."

But there was a serving-girl in the house, and she said: "Rise up, Oisin, and go out to the white-headed cows, since the cold wind is plucking the trees from the hills."

Oisin went out then, and the serving-man on his shoulders; but it is what the serving-man did, he brought a vessel of water and a birch broom with him, and he was dashing water in Oisin's face, the way he would think it was rain. But when they came to the pen where the cattle were, Oisin found the night was quiet, and after that he asked no more news of the weather from the servants.

CHAPTER III

The Arguments

And S. Patrick took in hand to convert Oisin, and to bring him to baptism; but it was no easy work he had to do, and everything he would say, Oisin would have an answer for it. And it is the way they used to be talking and arguing with one another, as it was put down afterwards by the poets of Ireland:—

PATRICK. "Oisin, it is long your sleep is. Rise up and listen to the Psalm. Your strength and your readiness are gone from you, though you used to be going into rough fights and battles."

OISIN. "My readiness and my strength are gone from me since Finn has no armies living; I have no liking for clerks, their music is not sweet to me after his."

298

PATRICK. "You never heard music so good from the beginning of the world to this day; it is well you would serve an army on a hill, you that are old and silly and grey."

OISIN. "I used to serve an army on a hill, Patrick of the closed-up mind; it is a pity you to be faulting me; there was never shame put on me till now.

"I have heard music was sweeter than your music, however much you are praising your clerks: the song of the blackbird in Leiter Laoi, and the sound of the Dord Fiann; the very sweet thrush of the Valley of the Shadow, or the sound of the boats striking the strand. The cry of the hounds was better to me than the noise of your schools, Patrick.

"Little Nut, little Nut of my heart, the little dwarf that was with Finn, when he would make tunes and songs he would put us all into deep sleep.

"The twelve hounds that belonged to Finn, the time they would be let loose facing out from the Siuir, their cry was sweeter than harps and than pipes.

"I have a little story about Finn; we were but fifteen men; we took the King of the Saxons of the feats, and we won a battle against the King of Greece.

"We fought nine battles in Spain, and nine times twenty battles in Ireland; from Lochlann and from the eastern world there was a share of gold coming to Finn.

"My grief! I to be stopping after him, and without delight in games or in music; to be withering away after my comrades; my grief it is to be living. I and the clerks of the Mass books are two that can never agree.

"If Finn and the Fianna were living, I would leave the clerks and the bells; I would follow the deer through the valleys, I would like to be close on his track.

"Ask Heaven of God, Patrick, for Finn of the Fianna and his race; make prayers for the great man; you never heard of his like."

PATRICK. "I will not ask Heaven for Finn, man of good wit that my anger is rising against, since his delight was to be living in valleys with the noise of hunts."

OISIN. "If you had been in company with the Fianna, Patrick of the joyless clerks and of the bells, you would not be attending on schools or giving heed to God."

PATRICK. "I would not part from the Son of God for all that have lived east or west; O Oisin, O shaking poet, there will harm come on you in satisfaction for the priests."

OISIN. "It was a delight to Finn the cry of his hounds on the mountains, the wild dogs leaving their harbours, the pride of his armies, those were his delights."

PATRICK. "There was many a thing Finn took delight in, and there is not much heed given to it after him; Finn and his hounds are not living now, and you yourself will not always be living, Oisin."

OISIN. "There is a greater story of Finn than of us, or of any that have lived in our time; all that are gone and all that are living, Finn was better to give out gold than themselves."

PATRICK. "All the gold you and Finn used to be giving out, it is little it does for you now; he is in Hell in bonds because he did treachery and oppression."

OISIN. "It is little I believe of your truth, man from Rome with the white books, Finn the open-handed head of the Fianna to be in the hands of devils or demons."

PATRICK. "Finn is in bonds in Hell, the pleasant man that gave out gold; in satisfaction for his disrespect to God, he is under grief in the house of pain."

OISIN. "If the sons of Morna were within it, or the strong men of the sons of Baiscne, they would take Finn out of it, or they would have the house for themselves."

PATRICK. "If the five provinces of Ireland were within it, or the strong seven battalions of the Fianna, they would not be able to bring Finn out of it, however great their strength might be."

OISIN. "If Faolan and Goll were living, and brown-haired Diarmuid and brave Osgar, Finn of the Fianna could not be held in any house that was made by God or devils."

PATRICK. "If Faolan and Goll were living, and all the Fianna that ever were, they could not bring out Finn from the house where he is in pain."

OISIN. "What did Finn do against God but to be attending on schools and on armies? Giving gold through a great part of his time, and for another while trying his hounds."

PATRICK. "In payment for thinking of his hounds and for serving the schools of the poets, and because he gave no heed to God, Finn of the Fianna is held down."

OISIN. "You say, Patrick of the Psalms, that the Fianna could not take out Finn, or the five provinces of Ireland along with them.

"I have a little story about Finn. We were but fifteen men when we took the King of Britain of the feasts by the strength of our spears and our own strength.

"We took Magnus the great, the son of the King of Lochlann of the speckled ships; we came back no way sorry or tired, we put our rent on far places.

"O Patrick, the story is pitiful, the King of the Fianna to be under locks; a heart without envy, without hatred, a heart hard in earning victory.

"It is an injustice, God to be unwilling to give food and riches; Finn never refused strong or poor, although cold Hell is now his dwelling-place.

"It is what Finn had a mind for, to be listening to the sound of Druim Dearg; to sleep at the stream of Ess Ruadh, to be hunting the deer of Gallimh of the bays.

"The cries of the blackbird of Leiter Laoi, the wave of Rudraighe beating the strand, the bellowing of the ox of Magh Maoin, the lowing of the calf of Gleann da Mhail.

"The noise of the hunt on Slieve Crot, the sound of the fawns round Slieve Cua, the scream of the sea-gulls there beyond on Iorrus, the screech of the crows over the battle.

"The waves vexing the breasts of the boats, the howling of the hounds at Druim Lis; the voice of Bran on Cnoc-an-Air, the outcry of the streams about Slieve Mis.

"The call of Osgar going to the hunt; the voice of the hounds on the road of the Fianna, to be listening to them and to the poets, that was always his desire.

"A desire of the desires of Osgar was to listen to the striking of shields; to be hacking at bones in a battle, it is what he had a mind for always.

"We went westward one time to hunt at Formaid of the Fianna, to see the first running of our hounds.

"It was Finn was holding Bran, and it is with myself Sceolan was; Diarmuid of the Women had Fearan, and Osgar had lucky Adhnuall.

"Conan the Bald had Searc; Caoilte, son of Ronan, had Daol; Lugaidh's Son and Goll were holding Fuaim and Fothran.

"That was the first day we loosed out a share of our hounds to a hunting; and Och! Patrick, of all that were in it, there is not one left living but myself.

"O Patrick, it is a pity the way I am now, a spent old man without sway, without quickness, without strength, going to Mass at the altar.

"Without the great deer of Slieve Luchra; without the hares of Slieve Cuilinn; without going into fights with Finn; without listening to the poets.

"Without battles, without taking of spoils; without playing at nimble feats; without going courting or hunting, two trades that were my delight."

PATRICK. "Leave off, old man, leave your foolishness; let what you have done be enough for you from this out. Think on the pains that are before you; the Fianna are gone, and you yourself will be going."

OISIN. "If I go, may yourself not be left after me, Patrick of the hindering heart; if Conan, the least of the Fianna, were living, your buzzing would not be left long to you.

"Or if this was the day I gave ten hundred cows to the headless woman that came to the Valley of the Two Oxen; the birds of the air brought away the ring I gave her, I never knew where she went herself from me."

PATRICK. "That is little to trouble you, Oisin; it was but for a while she was with you; it is better for you to be as you are than to be among them again."

OISIN. "O Son of Calphurn of the friendly talk, it is a pity for him that gives respect to clerks and bells; I and Caoilte my friend, we were not poor when we were together.

"The music that put Finn to his sleep was the cackling of the ducks from the lake of the Three Narrows; the scolding talk of the blackbird of Doire an Cairn, the bellowing of the ox from the Valley of the Berries.

"The whistle of the eagle from the Valley of Victories, or from the rough branches of the ridge by the stream; the grouse of the heather of Cruachan; the call of the otter of Druim-re-Coir.

"The song of the blackbird of Doire an Cairn indeed I never heard sweeter music, if I could be under its nest.

"My grief that I ever took baptism; it is little credit I got by it, being without food, without drink, doing fasting and praying."

PATRICK. "In my opinion it did not harm you, old man; you will get nine score cakes of bread, wine and meat to put a taste on it; it is bad talk you are giving."

OISIN. "This mouth that is talking with you, may it never confess to a priest, if I would not sooner have the leavings of Finn's house than a share of your own meals."

PATRICK. "He got but what he gathered from the banks, or whatever he could kill on the rough hills; he got hell at the last because of his unbelief."

OISIN. "That was not the way with us at all, but our fill of wine and of meat; justice and a right beginning at the feasts, sweet drinks and every one drinking them.

"It is fretting after Diarmuid and Goll I am, and after Fergus of the True Lips, the time you will not let me be speaking of them, O new Patrick from Rome."

PATRICK. "We would give you leave to be speaking of them, but first you should give heed to God. Since you are now at the end of your days, leave your foolishness, weak old man."

OISIN. "O Patrick, tell me as a secret, since it is you have the best knowledge, will my dog or my hound be let in with me to the court of the King of Grace?"

PATRICK. "Old man in your foolishness that I cannot put any bounds to, your dog or your hound will not be let in with you to the court of the King of Power."

OISIN. "If I had acquaintance with God, and my hound to be at hand, I would make whoever gave food to myself give a share to my hound as well.

"One strong champion that was with the Fianna of Ireland would be better than the Lord of Piety, and than you yourself, Patrick."

PATRICK. "O Oisin of the sharp blades, it is mad words you are saying. God is better for one day than the whole of the Fianna of Ireland."

OISIN. "Though I am now without sway and my life is spent to the end, do not put abuse, Patrick, on the great men of the sons of Baiscne.

"If I had Conan with me, the man that used to be running down the Fianna, it is he would break your head within among your clerks and your priests."

PATRICK. "It is a silly thing, old man, to be talking always of the Fianna; remember your end is come, and take the Son of God to help you."

OISIN. "I used to sleep out on the mountain under the grey dew; I was never used to go to bed without food, while there was a deer on the hill beyond."

PATRICK. "You are astray at the end of your life between the straight way and the crooked. Keep out from the crooked path of pains, and the angels of God will come beneath your head."

OISIN. "If myself and open-handed Fergus and Diarmuid were together now on this spot, we would go in every path we ever went in, and ask no leave of the priests."

PATRICK. "Leave off, Oisin; do not be speaking against the priests that are telling the word of God in every place. Unless you leave off your daring talk, it is great pain you will have in the end."

OISIN. "When myself and the leader of the Fianna were looking for a boar in a valley, it was worse to me not to see it than all your clerks to be without their heads."

PATRICK. "It is pitiful seeing you without sense; that is worse to you than your blindness; if you were to get sight within you, it is great your desire would be for Heaven."

OISIN. "It is little good it would be to me to be sitting in that city, without Caoilte, without Osgar, without my father being with me.

"The leap of the buck would be better to me, or the sight of badgers between two valleys, than all your mouth is promising me, and all the delights I could get in Heaven."

PATRICK. "Your thoughts are foolish, they will come to nothing; your pleasure and your mirth are gone. Unless you will take my advice to-night, you will not get leave on this side or that."

OISIN. "If myself and the Fianna were on the top of a hill to-day drawing our spear-heads, we would have our choice of being here or there in spite of books and priests and bells."

PATRICK. "You were like the smoke of a wisp, or like a stream in a valley, or like a whirling wind on the top of a hill, every tribe of you that ever lived."

OISIN. "If I was in company with the people of strong arms, the way I was at Bearna da Coill, I would sooner be looking at them than at this troop of the crooked croziers.

"If I had Scolb Sceine with me, or Osgar, that was smart in battles, I would not be without meat to-night at the sound of the bell of the seven tolls."

PATRICK. "Oisin, since your wits are gone from you be glad at what I say; it is certain to me you will leave the Fianna and that you will receive the God of the stars."

OISIN. "There is wonder on me at your hasty talk, priest that has travelled in every part, to say that I would part from the Fianna, a generous people, never niggardly."

PATRICK. "If you saw the people of God, the way they are settled at feasts, every good thing is more plentiful with them than with Finn's people, however great their name was.

"Finn and the Fianna are lying now very sorrowful on the flag-stone of pain; take the Son of God in their place; make your repentance and do not lose Heaven."

OISIN. "I do not believe your talk now, O Patrick of the crooked staves, Finn and the Fianna to be there within, unless they find pleasure being in it."

PATRICK. "Make right repentance now, before you know when your end is coming; God is better for one hour than the whole of the Fianna of Ireland."

OISIN. "That is a daring answer to make to me, Patrick of the crooked crozier; your crozier would be in little bits if I had Osgar with me now.

"If my son Osgar and God were hand to hand on the Hill of the Fianna, if I saw my son put down, I would say that God was a strong man.

"How could it be that God or his priests could be better men than Finn, the King of the Fianna, a generous man without crookedness.

"If there was a place above or below better than the Heaven of God, it is there Finn would go, and all that are with him of his people.

"You say that a generous man never goes to the hell of pain; there was not one among the Fianna that was not generous to all.

"Ask of God, Patrick, does He remember when the Fianna were alive, or has He seen east or west any man better than themselves in their fighting.

"The Fianna used not to be saying treachery; we never had the name of telling lies. By truth and the strength of our hands we came safe out of every battle.

"There never sat a priest in a church, though you think it sweet to be singing psalms, was better to his word than the Fianna, or more generous than Finn himself.

"If my comrades were living to-night, I would take no pleasure in your crooning in the church; as they are not living now, the rough voice of the bells has deafened me.

"Och! in the place of battles and heavy fights, where I used to have my place and to take my pleasure, the crozier of Patrick being carried, and his clerks at their quarrelling.

"Och! slothful, cheerless Conan, it is great abuse I used to be giving you; why do you not come to see me now? you would get leave for making fun and reviling through the whole of the niggardly clerks.

"Och! where are the strong men gone that they do not come together to help me! O Osgar of the sharp sword of victory, come and free your father from his bonds!

"Where is the strong son of Lugaidh? Och! Diarmuid of all the women! Och! Caoilte, son of Ronan, think of our love, and travel to me!"

PATRICK. "Stop your talk, you withered, witless old man; it is my King that made the Heavens, it is He that gives blossom to the trees, it is He made the moon and the sun, the fields and the grass."

OISIN. "It was not in shaping fields and grass that my king took his delight, but in overthrowing fighting men, and defending countries, and bringing his name into every part.

"In courting, in playing, in hunting, in baring his banner at the first of a fight; in playing at chess, at swimming, in looking around him at the drinking-hall.

"O Patrick, where was your God when the two came over the sea that brought away the queen of Lochlann of the Ships? Where was He when Dearg came, the son of the King of Lochlann of the golden shields? Why did not the King of Heaven protect them from the blows of the big man?

"Or when Tailc, son of Treon, came, the man that did great slaughter on the Fianna; it was not by God that champion fell, but by Osgar, in the sight of all.

"Many a battle and many a victory was gained by the Fianna of Ireland; I never heard any great deed was done by the King of Saints, or that He ever reddened His hand.

"It would be a great shame for God not to take the locks of pain off Finn; if God Himself were in bonds, my king would fight for His sake.

"Finn left no one in pain or in danger without freeing him by silver or gold, or by fighting till he got the victory.

"For the strength of your love, Patrick, do not forsake the great men; bring in the Fianna unknown to the King of Heaven.

"It is a good claim I have on your God, to be among his clerks the way I am; without food, without clothing, without music, without giving rewards to poets.

"Without the cry of the hounds or the horns, without guarding coasts, without courting generous women; for all that I have suffered by the want of food, I forgive the King of Heaven in my will."

Oisin said: "My story is sorrowful. The sound of your voice is not pleasant to me. I will cry my fill, but not for God, but because Finn and the Fianna are not living."

CHAPTER IV

Oisin's Laments

And Oisin used to be making laments, and sometimes he would be making praises of the old times and of Finn; and these are some of them that are remembered yet:—

I saw the household of Finn; it was not the household of a soft race; I had a vision of that man yesterday.

I saw the household of the High King, he with the brown, sweet-voiced son; I never saw a better man.

I saw the household of Finn; no one saw it as I saw it; I saw Finn with the sword, Mac an Luin. Och! it was sorrowful to see it.

I cannot tell out every harm that is on my head; free us from our trouble for ever; I have seen the household of Finn.

It is a week from yesterday I last saw Finn; I never saw a braver man. A king of heavy blows; my law, my adviser, my sense and my wisdom, prince and poet, braver than kings, King of the Fianna, brave in all countries; golden salmon of the sea, clean hawk of the air, rightly taught, avoiding lies; strong in his doings, a right judge, ready in courage, a high messenger in bravery and in music.

His skin lime-white, his hair golden; ready to work, gentle to women. His great green vessels full of rough sharp wine, it is rich the king was, the head of his people.

Seven sides Finn's house had, and seven score shields on every side. Fifty fighting men he had about him having woollen cloaks; ten bright drinking-cups in his hall; ten blue vessels, ten golden horns.

It is a good household Finn had, without grudging, without lust, without vain boasting, without chattering, without any slur on any one of the Fianna.

Finn never refused any man; he never put away any one that came to his house. If the brown leaves falling in the woods were gold, if the white waves were silver, Finn would have given away the whole of it.

Blackbird of Doire an Chairn, your voice is sweet; I never heard on any height of the world music was sweeter than your voice, and you at the foot of your nest.

The music is sweetest in the world, it is a pity not to be listening to it for a while, O son of Calphurn of the sweet bells, and you would overtake your nones again.

If you knew the story of the bird the way I know it, you would be crying lasting tears, and you would give no heed to your God for a while.

In the country of Lochlann of the blue streams, Finn, son of Cumhal, of the red-gold cups, found that bird you hear now; I will tell you its story truly.

Doire an Chairn, that wood there to the west, where the Fianna used to be delaying, it is there they put the blackbird, in the beauty of the pleasant trees.

The stag of the heather of quiet Cruachan, the sorrowful croak from the ridge of the Two Lakes; the voice of the eagle of the Valley of the Shapes, the voice of the cuckoo on the Hill of Brambles.

The voice of the hounds in the pleasant valley; the scream of the eagle on the edge of the wood; the early outcry of the hounds going over the Strand of the Red Stones.

The time Finn lived and the Fianna, it was sweet to them to be listening to the whistle of the blackbird; the voice of the bells would not have been sweet to them.

There was no one of the Fianna without his fine silken shirt and his soft coat, without bright armour, without shining stones on his head, two spears in his hand, and a shield that brought victory.

If you were to search the world you would not find a harder man, best of blood, best in battle; no one got the upper hand of him. When he went out trying his white hound, which of us could be put beside Finn?

One time we went hunting on Slieve-nam-ban; the sun was beautiful overhead, the voice of the hounds went east and west, from hill to hill. Finn and Bran sat for a while on the hill, every man was jealous for the hunt. We let out three thousand hounds from their golden chains; every hound of them brought down two deer.

Patrick of the true crozier, did you ever see, east or west, a greater hunt than that hunt of Finn and the Fianna? O son of Calphurn of the bells, that day was better to me than to be listening to your lamentations in the church.

There is no strength in my hands to-night, there is no power within me; it is no wonder I to be sorrowful, being thrown down in the sorrow of old age.

Everything is a grief to me beyond any other man on the face of the earth, to be dragging stones along to the church and the hill of the priests.

I have a little story of our people. One time Finn had a mind to make a dun on the bald hill of Cuailgne, and he put it on the Fianna of Ireland to bring stones for building it; a third on the sons of Morna, a third on myself, and a third on the sons of Baiscne.

I gave an answer to Finn, son of Cumhal; I said I would be under his sway no longer, and that I would obey him no more.

When Finn heard that, he was silent a long time, the man without a lie, without fear. And he said to me then: "You yourself will be dragging stones before your death comes to you."

I rose up then with anger on me, and there followed me the fourth of the brave battalions of the Fianna. I gave my own judgments, there were many of the Fianna with me.

Now my strength is gone from me, I that was adviser to the Fianna; my whole body is tired to-night, my hands, my feet, and my head, tired, tired, tired.

It is bad the way I am after Finn of the Fianna; since he is gone away, every good is behind me.

Without great people, without mannerly ways; it is sorrowful I am after our king that is gone.

I am a shaking tree, my leaves gone from me; an empty nut, a horse without a bridle; a people without a dwelling-place, I Oisin, son of Finn.

It is long the clouds are over me to-night! it is long last night was; although this day is long, yesterday was longer again to me; every day that comes is long to me!

That is not the way I used to be, without fighting, without battles, without learning feats, without young girls, without music, without harps, without bruising bones, without great deeds; without increase of learning, without generosity, without drinking at feasts, without courting, without hunting, the two trades I was used to; without going out to battle, Ochone! the want of them is sorrowful to me.

No hunting of deer or stag, it is not like that I would wish to be; no leashes for our hounds, no hounds; it is long the clouds are over me to-night!

Without rising up to do bravery as we were used, without playing as we had a mind; without swimming of our fighting men in the lake; it is long the clouds are over me to-night!

There is no one at all in the world the way I am; it is a pity the way I am; an old man dragging stones; it is long the clouds are over me to-night!

I am the last of the Fianna, great Oisin, son of Finn, listening to the voice of bells; it is long the clouds are over me to-night!

NOTES

I. THE APOLOGY

The Irish text of the greater number of the stories in this book has been published, and from this text I have worked, making my own translation as far as my scholarship goes, and when it fails, taking the meaning given by better scholars. In some cases the Irish text has not been printed, and I have had to work by comparing and piecing together various translations. I have had to put a connecting sentence of my own here and there, and I have fused different versions together, and condensed many passages, and I have left out many, using the choice that is a perpetual refusing, in trying to get some clear outline of the doings of the heroes.

I have found it more natural to tell the stories in the manner of the thatched houses, where I have heard so many legends of Finn and his friends, and Oisin and Patrick, and the Ever-Living Ones, and the Country of the Young, rather than in the manner of the slated houses, where I have not heard them.

Four years ago, Dr Atkinson, a Professor of Trinity College, Dublin, in his evidence before the Commission of Intermediate Education, said of the old literature of Ireland:—"It has scarcely been touched by the movements of the great literatures; it is the untrained popular feeling. Therefore it is almost intolerably low in tone—I do not mean naughty, but low; and every now and then, when the circumstance occasions it, it goes down lower than low . . . If I read the books in the Greek, the Latin or the French course, in almost every one of them there is something with an ideal ring about it—something that I can read with positive pleasure—something that has what the child might take with him as a κτῆμα εἰς ἀεί—a perpetual treasure; but if I read the Irish books, I see nothing ideal in them, and my astonishment is that through the whole range of Irish literature that I have read (and I have read an enormous range of it), the smallness of the element of idealism is most noticeable. . . . And as there is very little idealism there is very little imagination. . . . The Irish tales as a rule are devoid of it fundamentally."

Dr Atkinson is an Englishman, but unfortunately not only fellow-professors in Trinity but undergraduates there have been influenced by his opinion, that Irish literature is a thing to be despised. I do not quote his words to draw attention to a battle that is still being fought, but to explain my own object in working, as I have worked ever since that evidence was given, to make a part of Irish literature accessible to many, especially among my young countrymen, who have not opportunity to read the translations of the chief scholars, scattered here and there in learned periodicals, or patience and time to disentangle overlapping and contradictory versions, that they may judge for themselves as to its "lowness" and "want of imagination," and the other well-known charges brought against it before the same Commission.

I believe that those who have once learned to care for the story of Cuchulain of Muirthemne, and of Finn and Lugh and Etain, and to recognise the enduring belief in an invisible world and an immortal life behind the visible and the mortal, will not be content with my redaction, but will go, first to the fuller versions of the best scholars, and then to the manuscripts themselves. I believe the forty students of old Irish lately called together by Professor Kuno Meyer will not rest satisfied until they have explored the scores and scores of uncatalogued and untranslated manuscripts in Trinity College Library, and that the enthusiasm which the Gaelic League has given birth to will lead to much fine scholarship.

A day or two ago I had a letter from one of the best Greek scholars and translators in England, who says of my "Cuchulain": "It opened up a great world of beautiful legend which, though accounting myself as an Irishman, I had never known at all. I am sending out copies to Irish friends in Australia who, I am sure, will receive the same sort of impression, almost an impression of pride in the beauty of the Irish mind, as I received myself." And President Roosevelt wrote to me a little time ago that after he had read "Cuchulain of Muirthemne," he had sent for all the other translations from the Irish he could get, to take on his journey to the Western States.

I give these appreciative words not, I think, from vanity, for they are not for me but for my material, to show the effect our old literature has on those who come fresh to it, and that they do not complain of its "want of imagination." I am, of course, very proud and glad in having had the opportunity of helping to make it known, and the task has been pleasant, although toilsome. Just now, indeed, on the 6th October, I am tired enough, and I think with sympathy of the old Highland piper, who complained that he was "withered with yelping the seven Fenian battalions."

II. THE AGE AND ORIGIN OF THE STORIES OF THE FIANNA

Mr Alfred Nutt says in *Ossian and the Ossianic Literature*, No. 3 of his excellent series of sixpenny pamphlets, *Popular Studies in Mythology, Romance, and Folklore:*—

"The body of Gaelic literature connected with the name of Ossian is of very considerable extent and of respectable antiquity. The oldest texts, prose for the most part, but also in verse, are preserved in Irish MSS of the eleventh and twelfth centuries, and go back to a period from one hundred and fifty to two hundred and fifty years older at least. The bulk of Ossianic literature is, however, of later date as far as the form under which it has come down to us is concerned. A number of important texts, prose for the most part, are preserved in MSS of the fourteenth century, but were probably redacted in the thirteenth and twelfth centuries. But by far the largest mass consists of narrative poems, as a rule dramatic in structure. These have come down to us in MSS written in Scotland from the end of the fifteenth to the middle of the seventeenth century, in Ireland from the sixteenth down to the middle of the nineteenth century. The Gaelic-speaking peasantry, alike in Ireland and Scotland, have preserved orally a large number of these ballads, as also a great mass of prose narratives, the heroes of which are Ossian and his comrades.

"Were all Ossianic texts preserved in MSS older than the present century to be printed, they would fill some eight to ten thousand octavo pages. The mere bulk of the literature, even if we allow for considerable repetition of incident, arrests attention. If we further recall that for the last five hundred years this body of romance has formed the chief imaginative recreation of Gaeldom, alike in Ireland and Scotland, and that a peasantry unable to read or write has yet preserved it almost entire, its claims to consideration and study will appear manifest."

He then goes on to discuss how far the incidents in the stories can be accepted as they were accepted by Irish historical writers of the eleventh century as authentic history:—

"Fortunately there is little need for me to discuss the credibility or otherwise of the historic records concerning Finn, his family, and his band of warriors. They may be accepted or rejected according to individual bent of mind without really modifying our view of the literature. For when we turn to the romances, whether in prose or verse, we find that, although the history is professedly the same as that of the Annals, firstly, we are transported to a world entirely romantic, in which divine and semi-divine beings, ungainly monsters and giants, play a prominent part, in which men and women change shapes with animals, in which the lives of the heroes are miraculously prolonged—in short, we find ourselves in a land of Faery; secondly, we find that the historic conditions in which the heroes are represented as living do not, for the most part, answer to anything we know or can surmise of the third century. For Finn and his warriors are perpetually on the watch to guard Ireland against the attacks of over-sea raiders, styled Lochlannac by the narrators, and by them undoubtedly thought of as Norsemen. But the latter, as is well known, only came to Ireland at the close of the eighth century, and the heroic period of their invasions extended for about a century, from 825 to 925; to be followed by a period of comparative settlement during the tenth century, until at the opening of the eleventh century the battle of Clontarf, fought by Brian, the great South Irish chieftain, marked the break-up of the separate

Teutonic organisations and the absorption of the Teutons into the fabric of Irish life. In these pages then we may disregard the otherwise interesting question of historic credibility in the Ossianic romances: firstly, because they have their being in a land unaffected by fact; secondly, because if they ever did reflect the history of the third century the reflection was distorted in after-times, and a pseudo-history based upon events of the ninth and tenth centuries was substituted for it. What the historian seeks for in legend is far more a picture of the society in which it took rise than a record of the events which it commemorates."

In a later part of the pamphlet Mr Nutt discusses such questions as whether we may look for examples of third-century customs in the stories, what part of the stories first found their way into writing, whether the Oisin and Patrick dialogues were written under the influence of actual Pagan feeling persisting from Pagan times, or whether "a change came over the feeling of Gaeldom during the fourteenth and fifteenth centuries," when the Oisin and Patrick dialogues in their present form began to be written. His final summing-up is that "well-nigh the same stories that were told of Finn and his warrior braves by the Gael of the eleventh century are told in well-nigh the same way by his descendant to-day." Mr Nutt does not enquire how long the stories may have been told before the first story was written down. Larminie, however, whose early death was the first great loss of our intellectual movement, pushes them backward for untold ages in the introduction to his *West Irish Folk Tales and Romances*. He builds up a detailed and careful argument, for which I must refer readers to his book, to prove that the Scottish Highlands and Ireland have received their folk-lore both from "Aryan and Non-Aryan sources," and that in the Highlands there is more non-Aryan influence and more non-Aryan blood than in Ireland. He argues that nothing is more improbable than that all folk-tales are Aryan, as has sometimes been supposed, and sums up as follows:—

"They bear the stamp of the genius of more than one race. The pure and placid but often cold imagination of the Aryan has been at work on some. In others we trace the more picturesque fancy, the fierceness and sensuality, the greater sense of artistic elegance belonging to races whom the Aryan, in spite of his occasional faults of hardness and coarseness, has, on the whole, left behind him. But as the greatest results in the realm of the highest art have always been achieved in the case of certain blends of Aryan with other blood, I should hardly deem it extravagant if it were asserted that in the humbler regions of the folk-tale we might trace the working of the same law. The process which has gone on may in part have been as follows:—Every race which has acquired very definite characteristics must have been for a long time isolated. The Aryans during their period of isolation probably developed many of their folk-germs into their larger myths, owing to the greater constructiveness of their imagination, and thus, in a way, they used up part of their material. Afterwards, when they became blended with other races less advanced, they acquired fresh material to work on. We have in

Ireland an instance to hand, of which a brief discussion may help to illustrate the whole race theory.

"The larger Irish legendary literature divides itself into three cycles—the divine, the heroic, the Fenian. Of these three the last is so well-known orally in Scotland that it has been a matter of dispute to which country it really belongs. It belongs, in fact, to both. Here, however, comes in a strange contrast with the other cycles. The first is, so far as I am aware, wholly unknown in Scotland, the second comparatively unknown. What is the explanation? Professor Zimmer not having established his late-historical view as regards Finn, and the general opinion among scholars having tended of recent years towards the mythical view, we want to know why there is so much more community in one case than in the other. Mr O'Grady long since seeing this difficulty, and then believing Finn to be historical, was induced to place the latter in point of time before Cuchulain and his compeers. But this view is of course inadmissible when Finn is seen not to be historical at all. There remains but one explanation. The various bodies of legend in question are, so far as Ireland is concerned, only earlier or later, as they came into the island with the various races to which they belonged. The wider prevalence, then, of the Finn Saga would indicate that it belonged to an early race occupying both Ireland and Scotland. Then entered the Aryan Gael, and for him henceforth, as the ruler of the island, his own gods and heroes were sung by his own bards. His legends became the subject of what I may call the court poetry, the aristocratic literature. When he conquered Scotland, he took with him his own gods and heroes; but in the latter country the bardic system never became established, and hence we find but feeble echoes of the heroic cycle among the mountains of the North. That this is the explanation is shown by what took place in Ireland. Here the heroic cycle has been handed down in remembrance almost solely by the bardic literature. The popular memory retains but few traces of it. Its essentially aristocratic character is shown by the fact that the people have all but forgotten it, if they ever knew it. But the Fenian cycle has not been forgotten. Prevailing everywhere, still cherished by the conquered peoples, it held its ground in Scotland and Ireland alike, forcing its way in the latter country even into the written literature, and so securing a twofold lease of existence. . . . The Fenian cycle, in a word, is non-Aryan folk-literature partially subjected to Aryan treatment."

The whole problem is extremely complex, and several other writers have written upon it. Mr Borlase, for instance, has argued in his big book on the Dolmens that the cromlechs, and presumably the Diarmuid and Grania legend, is connected with old religious rites of an erotic nature coming down from a very primitive state of society.

I have come to my own conclusion not so much because of any weight of argument, as because I found it impossible to arrange the stories in a coherent form so long as I considered them a part of history. I tried to work on the foundation of the Annalists, and fit the Fianna into a definite historical epoch, but the whole story seemed trivial and incoherent until I began to think of them as almost contemporaneous with the battle of Magh Tuireadh, which even the Annalists put back into mythical ages. In this I have only followed some of the story-tellers, who have made the mother of Lugh of the Long Hand the grandmother of Finn, and given him a shield soaked with the blood of Balor. I cannot think of any of the stories as having had a modern origin, or that the century in which each was written down gives any evidence as to its age. "How Diarmuid got his Love-Spot," for instance, which was taken down only a few years ago from some old man's recitation by Dr Hyde, may well be as old as "Finn and the Phantoms," which is in one of the earliest manuscripts. It seems to me that one cannot choose any definite period either from the vast living mass of folk-lore in the country or from the written text, and that there is as good evidence of Finn being of the blood of the gods as of his being, as some of the people tell me, "the son of an O'Shaughnessy who lived at Kiltartan Cross."

Dr Douglas Hyde, although he placed the Fenian after the Cuchulain cycle in his *History of Irish Literature*, has allowed me to print this note:—

"While believing in the real objective existence of the Fenians as a body of Janissaries who actually lived, ruled, and hunted in King Cormac's time, I think it equally certain that hundreds of stories, traits, and legends far older and more primitive than any to which they themselves could have given rise, have clustered about them. There is probably as large a bulk of primitive mythology to be found in the Finn legend as in that of the Red Branch itself. The story of the Fenians was a kind of nucleus to which a vast amount of the flotsam and jetsam of a far older period attached itself, and has thus been preserved."

As I found it impossible to give that historical date to the stories, I, while not adding in anything to support my theory, left out such names as those of Cormac and Art, and such more or less historical personages, substituting "the High King." And in the "Battle of the White Strand," I left out the name of Caelur, Tadg's wife, because I had already followed another chronicler in giving him Ethlinn for a wife. In the earlier part I have given back to Angus Og the name of "The Disturber," which had, as I believe, strayed from him to the Saint of the same name.

III. THE AUTHORITIES

The following is a list of the authorities I have been chiefly helped by in putting these stories together and in translation of the text. But I cannot make it quite accurate, for I have sometimes transferred a mere phrase, sometimes a whole passage from one story to another, where it seemed to fit better. I have sometimes, in the second part of the book, used stories preserved in the Scottish Gaelic, as will be seen by my references. I am obliged to write these notes away from libraries, and cannot verify them, but I think they are fairly correct.

PART ONE. BOOKS ONE, TWO, AND THREE

THE COMING OF THE TUATHA DE DANAAN, AND LUGH OF THE LONG HAND, AND THE COMING OF THE GAEL.—O'Curry, *Manners and Customs of the Ancient Irish; MSS. Materials; Atlantis;* De Jubainville, *Cycle Mythologique;* Hennessy, *Chronicum Scotorum;* Atkinson, *Book of Leinster; Annals of the Four Masters;* Nennius, *Hist. Brit.* (Irish Version); Zimmer, *Glossae Hibernacae;* Whitley Stokes, *Three Irish Glossaries; Revue Celtique* and *Irische Texte; Gaedelica;* Nutt, *Voyage of Bran; Proceedings Ossianic Society;* O'Beirne Crowe, *Amra Columcille;* Dean of Lismore's Book; Windisch, *Irische Texte;* Hennessy and others in *Revue Celtique; Kilkenny Archæological Journal;* Keatinge's *History; Ogyia;* Curtin's *Folk Tales; Proceedings Royal Irish Academy,* MSS. Series; Dr Sigerson, *Bards of Gael and Gall;* Miscellanies, *Celtic Society.*

BOOK FOUR

THE EVER-LIVING LIVING ONES

I have used many of the above, and for separate stories, I may give these authorities:—

MIDHIR AND ETAIN.—O'Curry, *Manners and Customs;* Whitley Stokes, *Dinnsenchus;* Müller, *Revue Celtique;* Nutt, *Voyage of Bran;* De Jubainville, *Epopée Celtique;* Standish Hayes O'Grady, MS. lent me by him.

MANANNAN AT PLAY.—S. Hayes O'Grady, *Silva Gaedelica.*

HIS CALL TO BRAN.—Professor Kuno Meyer in Nutt's *Voyage of Bran;* S. Hayes O'Grady, *Silva Gaedelica;* De Jubainville, *Cycle Mythologique.*

HIS THREE CALLS TO CORMAC.—Whitley Stokes, *Irische Texte.*

CLIODNA'S WAVE.—S. Hayes O'Grady, *Silva Gaedelica;* Whitley Stokes, *Dinnsenchus.*

HIS CALL TO CONNLA.—O'Beirne Crowe, *Kilkenny Arch. Journal;* Windisch, *Irische Texte.*

TADG IN THE ISLANDS.—S. Hayes O'Grady, *Silva Gaedelica.*

LAEGAIRE IN THE HAPPY PLAIN.—S. H. O'Grady, *Silva Gaedelica*; Kuno Meyer in Nutt's *Voyage of Bran*.

FATE OF THE CHILDREN OF LIR.—O'Curry, *Atlantis*.

PART TWO. THE FIANNA

THE COMING OF FINN, AND FINN'S HOUSEHOLD.—*Proceedings Ossianic Society;* Kuno Meyer, *Four Songs of Summer and Winter; Revue Celtique;* S. Hayes O'Grady, *Silva Gaedelica;* Curtin's *Folk Tales*.

BIRTH OF BRAN.—*Proc. Ossianic Society*.

OISIN'S MOTHER.—Kennedy, *Legendary Fictions Irish Celts*; Mac Innis; *Leabhar na Feinne*.

BEST MEN OF THE FIANNA.—Dean of Lismore's Book; *Silva Gaedelica; Leabhar na Feinne*.

LAD OF THE SKINS.—*Waifs and Strays of Celtic Tradition;* Larminie's *Folk Tales;* Curtin's *Tales*.

THE HOUND.—*Silva Gaedelica;* Whitley Stokes, *Dinnsenchus*.

RED RIDGE.—*Silva Gaedelica*.

BATTLE OF THE WHITE STRAND.—Kuno Meyer, *Anec. Oxonienses;* Hanmer's *Chronicle;* Dean of Lismore; Curtin's *Tales; Silva Gaedelica*.

KING OF BRITAIN'S SON.—*Silva Gaedelica*.

THE CAVE OF CEISCORAN.—*Silva Gaedelica*.

DONN, SON OF MIDHIR.—*Silva Gaedelica*.

HOSPITALITY OF CUANNA'S HOUSE.—*Proc. Ossianic Society*.

CAT-HEADS AND DOG-HEADS.—Dean of Lismore; *Leabhar na Feinne*; Campbell's *Popular Tales of the Western Highlands*.

LOMNA'S HEAD.—O'Curry, *Orc. Treith*, O'Donovan, ed. Stokes.

ILBREC OF ESS RUADH.—*Silva Gaedelica*.

CAVE OF CRUACHAN.—Stokes, *Irische Texte*.

WEDDING AT CEANN SLIEVE.—*Proc. Ossianic Society*.

THE SHADOWY ONE.—O'Curry.

FINN'S MADNESS.—*Silva Gaedelica.*

THE RED WOMAN.—Hyde, *Sgealuidhe Gaedhealach.*

FINN AND THE PHANTOMS.—*Kuno Meyer, Revue Celtique.*

THE PIGS OF ANGUS.—*Proc. Ossianic Society.*

HUNT OF SLIEVE CUILINN.—*Proc. Ossianic Society.*

OISIN'S CHILDREN.—O'Curry; *Leabhar na Feinne*; Campbell's *Popular Tales of the Western Highlands*; Stokes, *Irische Texte*; Dean of Lismore; *Celtic Magazine*; *Waifs and Strays of Celtic Tradition.*

BIRTH OF DIARMUID.—*Pursuit of Diarmuid and Grania* (Society for Preservation of the Irish Language); Campbell's *Popular Tales.*

HOW DIARMUID GOT HIS LOVE-SPOT.—Hyde, *Sgealuidhe Gaedhealach.*

DAUGHTER OF KING UNDER-WAVE.—Campbell's *Popular Tales.*

THE HARD SERVANT.—*Silva Gaedelica.*

HOUSE OF THE QUICKEN TREES.—MSS. in Royal Irish Academy, and in Dr Hyde's possession.

DIARMUID AND GRANIA.—Text Published by S. Hayes O'Grady, *Proc. Ossianic Society* and re-edited by N. O'Duffey for Society for Preservation of the Irish Language; Kuno Meyer, *Revue Celtique*, and *Four Songs*; *Leabhar na Feinne*; Campbell's *Popular Tales*; *Kilkenny Arch. Journal*; *Folk Lore*, vol. vii., 1896; Dean of Lismore; Nutt, *Waifs and Strays of Celtic Tradition.*

CNOC-AN-AIR, ETC.—*Proc. Ossianic Society.*

WEARING AWAY OF THE FIANNA.—*Silva Gaedelica*; Dean of Lismore; *Leabhar na Feinne*; Campbell's *Popular Tales*; *Proc. Ossianic Society*; O'Curry; *Waifs and Strays of Celtic Tradition*; Stokes, *Irische Texte.*

THE END OF THE FIANNA.—Hyde, *Sgealuidhe Gaedhealach*; *Proc. Ossianic Society*; *Silva Gaedelica*; Miss Brooke's *Reliques*; *Annals of the Four Masters*; *Celtic Magazine.*

OISIN AND PATRICK, AND OISIN'S LAMENTS.—*Proc. Ossianic Society*: Dean of Lismore; *Kilkenny Arch. Journal*; Curtin's *Tales.*

I have taken Grania's sleepy song, and the description of Finn's shield and of Cumhal's treasure-bag, and the fact of Finn's descent from Ethlinn, from *Duanaire Finn*, now being edited for the Irish Texts Society by Mr John MacNeill, the proofs of which I have been kindly allowed to see. And I have used sometimes

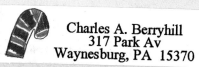

parts of stories, or comments on them gathered directly from the people, who have kept these heroes so much in mind. The story of Caoilte coming to the help of the King of Ireland in a dark wood is the only one I have given without either a literary or a folk ancestry. It was heard or read by Mr Yeats, he cannot remember where, but he had, with it in his mind, written of "Caoilte's burning hair" in one of his poems.

I and my readers owe special thanks to those good workers in the discovery of Irish literature, Professor Kuno Meyer and Mr Whitley Stokes, translators of so many manuscripts; and to my friend and kinsman Standish Hayes O'Grady, for what I have taken from that wonderful treasure-house, his *Silva Gaedelica*.

IV. THE PRONUNCIATION

This is the approximate pronunciation of some of the more difficult names:

Adhnuall	Ai-noo-al.
Ailbhe	Alva.
Almhuin	All-oon, *or* Alvin
Aobh	Aev, *or* Eev.
Aodh	Ae (rhyming to "day").
Aoibhill	Evill.
Aoife	Eefa.
Badb	Bibe.
Beltaine, or Bealtaine	Bal-tinna.
Bladhma	Bly-ma.
Bodb Dearg	Bove Darrig.
Caoilte	Cweeltia.
Carn Ruidhe	Corn Rwee.
Ciabhan	Kee-a-van.
Cliodna	Cleevna.
Coincheann	Kun-Kann.
Crann Buidhe	Cran bwee.
Credhe	Crae-a.
Cumhal	Coo-al.
Deaghadh	D'ya-a.
Dubhthach	Duffách.
Duibhreann	Dhiv-răn.
Duibhrium	Dhiv-rinn.
Dun	Doon.

Eimher	Aevir.
Emhain	Avvin.
Eochaid	Eohee.
Eoghan	Owen.
Fionnchad	Finn-ăch-a.
Fodhla	Fóla.
Fodla	Fola.
Gallimh	Gol-yiv.
Glas Gaibhnenn	Glos Gov-nan.
Leith Laeig	Lĕh Laeg.
Loch Dairbhreach	Loch Darvragh.
Lugaidh	Loo-ee, or Lewy.
Lugh	Loo.
Magh an Ionganaidh	Moy-in-eean-ee.
Magh Cuillean	Moy Cullin.
Magh Feabhail	Moy Fowl.
Magh Macraimhe	Moy Mucrivva.
Magh Mell	Moy Mal.
Magh Rein	Moy Raen.
Magh Tuireadh	Moytirra.
Manannan	Mānanaun.
Midhe	Mee.
Midhna	Mee-na.
Mochaomhog	Mo-cweev-ōg.
Muadhan	Moo-aun.
Murchadh	Murachu.
Nemhnain	Now-nin.
Niamh	Nee-av.
Og	Ōg.
Rath Medba, or Meadhbha	Ra Maev-a.
Rudraighe	Rury.
Samhain	Sow-in.
Scathniamh	Scau-nee-av.
Sceolan	Skolaun.
Searbhan	Sharavaun.
Sidhe	Shee.
Slieve Echtge	Sleev Acht-ga.
Tadg	Teig.
Teamhair	T'yower, or Tavvir.
Tuatha de Danaan	Too-ă-hă dae. Donnan.
Tuathmumhain	Too-moon.

319

LADY GREGORY

I have not followed a fixed rule as to the spelling of Irish names; I have taken the spelling I give from various good authorities, but they vary so much that, complete accuracy not being easy, I sometimes look to custom and convenience. I use, for instance, "Slieve" for "Sliabh," because it comes so often, and a mispronunciation would spoil so many names. I have treated "Inbhir" (a river mouth) in the same way, spelling it "Inver," and even adopting it as an English word, because it is so useful. The forty scholars of the New School of Old Irish will do us good service if they work at the question both of spelling and of pronunciation of the old names and settle them as far as is possible.

V. THE PLACE NAMES

Accuill	Achill, Co. Mayo.
Aine Cliach	Cnoc Aine, Co. Limerick.
Almhuin	Near Kildare.
Ath Cliath	Dublin.
Athluain	Athlone.
Ath na Riogh	Athenry.
Badhamain	Cahir, Co. Tipperary.
Baile Cronin	Barony of Imokilty, Co. Cork.
Banna	The Bann.
Beare	Berehaven.
Bearna na Eadargana	Roscommon.
Bearnas Mor	Co. Donegal.
Beinn Gulbain	Benbulban, Co. Sligo.
Beire do Bhunadas	Berehaven.
Bel-atha Senaig	Ballyshannon.
Belgata	In Connemara.
Benna Boirde	Source of the Bann and Mourne Mountains.
Berramain	Near Tralee.
Bhas	River Bush.
Boinn	River Boyne.
Bri Leith	Co. Longford.
Cairbre	Carbury.
Cairgin	Three miles south of Londonderry.
Carrthach River	River Carra, near

	Dunkerrin Mountains.
Ceanntaile	Kinsale.
Ceiscorainn	Co. Sligo.
Cill Dolun	Killaloe, Co. Clare.
Cliodna's Wave	At Glandore, Co. Cork.
Cluantarbh	Clontarf.
Cnoc Aine	Co. Limerick.
Cnoc-an-Air	Co. Kerry.
Cnoc na righ	Co. Sligo.
Corca Duibhne	Corcaguiny, Co. Kerry.
Corrslieve	Carlow Mountains.
Crotta Cliach	Galtee Mountains.
Cruachan	Co. Roscommon.
Cruachan Aigle	Croagh Patrick.
Doire a Cairn	Derrycarn, Co. Meath.
Doire-da-Bhoth	In Slieve Echtge.
Druim Cleibh	Co. Sligo.
Druim Lis	Near Loch Gill.
Druimscarha	Near River Arighis, Co. Cork.
Dun Sobairce	Dunsevenh, Co. Antrim.
Durlas	Thurles.
Ess Dara	Near Sligo.
Ess Ruadh	Assaroe, Co. Donegal.
Fidh Gaible	Fergill, Co. Sligo.
Finntraighe	Ventry.
Fionn	The Finn.
Fionnabraic	Kilfenna, Co. Clare.
Fionntutach	Co. Limerick.
Fleisge	Co. Kerry.
Gabhra	Near Tara.
Gaibh atha na Fiann	River Leamhar, flows from Killarney.
Gairech and Ilgairech	Hills near Mullingar.
Gallimh	Galway.
Gleann na Caor	Co. Cork.

Gullach Dollairb	Barony of Rathconrath.
Hill of Bairnech	Near Killarney.
Hill of Uisnech	Co. Westmeath.
Inver Cechmaine	East coast of Ulster.
Inver Colpa	Drogheda.
Inver Slane	N. E. of Leinster.
Irrus Domnann	Erris, Co. Mayo.
Island of Toraig	Tory Island, Co. Donegal.
Laoi	River Lee.
Leith Laoi	Leitrim.
Linn Feic	Near Slaney.
Loch Bel Sead	Co. Tipperary.
Loch Cé	Co. Roscommon.
Loch Dairbhreach	Loch Derryvaragh, Co. Westmeath.
Loch Deirg Dheirc	Loch Derg on the Shannon.
Loch Eirne	Loch Erne.
Loch Featbhail	Loch Foyle.
Loch Lein	Killarney.
Loch Orbson	Loch Corrib.
Loch na-n Ean	In Co. Roscommon.
Lough Neatach	Loch Neagh.
Luimneach	Limerick.
Maev Mhagh	Plain about Loughrea.
Magh Cobha	Iveagh, Co. Down.
Magh Cuilenn	Moycullen, Co. Galway.
Magh Femen	Co. Tipperary.
Magh Larg	Co. Roscommon.
Magh Leine	King's County.
Magh Luirg	Co. Roscommon.
Magh Maini	Co. Wexford.
Magh Mucraimhe	Near Athenry.
Magh Nia	Same as Magh Tuireadh.
Magh Rein	Co. Leitrim.
Magh Tuireadh	Moytura near Sligo, scene of great battle,

	and Moytura, near Cong, scene of first battle.
March of Finnliath	River Lee, near Tralee.
Midhe	Meath, west of Ardagh.
Mis Geadh	In Bay of Erris.
Muaid	River Moy.
Muc-inis	Muckinish, off Connemara.
Nas	Naas.
Nem	The Nem.
Oenach Clochan	Morristown, Co. Limerick.
Osraige	Ossory.
Paps of Dana	Co. Kerry.
Portlairge	Waterford.
River Maigh	Co. Limerick.
Ros da Shioleach	Limerick.
Ruirlech	Liffey.
Samair	R. Cumhair, runs through Bruff.
Sionnan	River Shannon.
Siuir	River Suir, Co. Tipperary.
Siuir and Beoir and Berba	Suir and Nore and Barrow.
Slieve Baisne	Co. Roscommon.
Slieve Bladmai	Slieve Bloom.
Slieve Buane	Slieve Banne, Co. Roscommon.
Slieve Conaill	Border of Leitrim and Donegal.
Slieve Crot	Co. Tipperary.
Slieve Cua	Co. Waterford.
Slieve Cua and Slieve Crot	In Galtee Mountains.
Slieve Cuailgne	Co. Louth.
Slieve Echtge	Co. Galway.
Slieve Fuad	Co. Armagh.
Slieve Guaire	Co. Cavan.
Slieve Luchra	Co. Kerry.

Slieve Lugha	Co. Mayo.
Slieve Mis	Co. Kerry.
Slieve Muice	Co. Tipperary.
Slieve-nam-Ban	Co. Tipperary.
Sligach	Sligo.
Srub Bruin	In West Kerry.
Sruth na Maoile	Mull of Cantire.
Tailltin	Telltown.
Teamhair	Tara, Co. Meath.
Teunhair Luchra	Near Castle Island, Co. Kerry.
The Beith	River Behy, Barony of Dunkerrin.
The Beoir	The Berba.
The Islands of Mod	In Clew Bay.
The Lemain	River Laune, Co. Kerry.
The Muaidh	River Moy, Co. Sligo.
Tonn Toime	Toines, near Killarney.
Traigh Eothaile	Near Ballisodare.
Tuathmumain	Thomond.
Ui Chonaill Gabhra	Co. Limerick.
Ui Fiachraih, Fiachraig	Co. Mayo.
Wave of Rudraighe	Bay of Dundrum.

CUCHULAIN OF MUIRTHEMNE

THE HISTORY OF THE MEN OF THE RED
BRANCH OF ULSTER, ARRANGED AND
PUT INTO ENGLISH BY LADY GREGORY.
WITH A PREFACE BY W.B. YEATS

"Deiṗim an ṁóiḋ ḋo ḃeiṗ mo ṁuinntiṗ," aṗ Cú-
culain, "ʒo mḃéiḋ tṗáċt aʒuṗ iomṗáḋ ḟóṗ aṗ mo
ʒníoṁaṗtaiḃ-ṗe ameaṗʒ na n-áṗḋ-ʒníoṁ ḋo ṗinne na
ʒaiṗʒiḋiʒ iṗ tṗéine."

"I swear by the oath of my people," said Cuchulain, "I will
make my doings be spoken of among the great doings of
heroes in their strength."

Dedication of the Irish Edition

to the People of Kiltartan

My Dear Friends,

When I began to gather these stories together, it is of you I was thinking, that you would like to have them and to be reading them. For although you have not to go far to get stories of Finn and Goll and Oisin from any old person in the place, there is very little of the history of Cuchulain and his friends left in the memory of the people, but only that they were brave men and good fighters, and that Deirdre was beautiful.

When I went looking for the stories in the old writings, I found that the Irish in them is too hard for any person to read that has not made a long study of it. Some scholars have worked well at them, Irishmen and Germans and Frenchmen, but they have printed them in the old cramped Irish, with translations into German and French or English, and these are not easy for you to get, or to understand, and the stories themselves are confused, every one giving a different account from the others in some small thing, the way there is not much pleasure in reading them. It is what I have tried to do, to take the best of the stories, or whatever part of each will fit best to one another, and in that way give a fair account of Chuchulain's life and death. I left out a good deal I thought you would not care about for one reason or another, but I put in nothing of my own that could be helped, only a sentence or two now and again to link the different parts together. I have told the whole story in plain and simple words, in the same way my old nurse Mary Sheridan used to be telling stories from the Irish long ago, and I a child at Roxborough.

And indeed if there was more respect for Irish things among the learned men that live in the college at Dublin, where so many of these old writings are stored, this work would not have been left to a woman of the house, that has to be minding the place, and listening to complaints, and dividing the share of food.

My friend and your friend the *Craoibhin Aoibhin* has put Irish of today on some of these stories that I have set in order, for I am sure you will like to have the history of the heroes of Ireland told in the language of Ireland. And I am very glad to have something that is worth offering you, for you have been very kind to me ever since I came over to you from Kilchrist, two and twenty years ago.

AUGUSTA GREGORY.

March 1902.

PREFACE

I

I think this book is the best that has come out of Ireland in my time. Perhaps I should say that it is the best book that has ever come out of Ireland; for the stories which it tells are a chief part of Ireland's gift to the imagination of the world—and it tells them perfectly for the first time. Translators from the Irish have hitherto retold one story or the other from some one version, and not often with any fine understanding of English, of those changes of rhythm for instance that are changes in the sense. They have translated the best and fullest manuscripts they knew, as accurately as they could, and that is all we have the right to expect from the first translators of a difficult and old literature. But few of the stories really begin to exist as great works of imagination until somebody has taken the best bits out of many manuscripts. Sometimes, as in Lady Gregory's version of Deirdre, a dozen manuscripts have to give their best before the beads are ready for the necklace. It has been as necessary also to leave out as to add, for generations of copyists, who had often but little sympathy for the stories they copied, have mixed versions together in a clumsy fashion, often repeating one incident several times, and every century has ornamented what was once a simple story with its own often extravagant ornament. One does not perhaps exaggerate when one says that no story has come down to us in the form it had when the story-teller told it in the winter evenings. Lady Gregory has done her work of compression and selection at once so firmly and so reverently that I cannot believe that anybody, except now and then for scientific purpose, will need another text than this, or than the version of it the Gaelic League has begun to publish in Modern Irish. When she has added her translations from other cycles, she will have given Ireland its Mabinogion, its Morte D'Arthur, its Nibelungenlied. She has already put a great mass of stories, in which the ancient heart of Ireland still lives, into a shape at once harmonious and characteristic; and without writing more than a very few sentences of her own to link together incidents or thoughts taken from different manuscripts, without adding more indeed than the story-teller must often have added to amend the hesitation of a moment. Perhaps more than all she has discovered a fitting dialect to tell them in. Some years ago I wrote some stories of mediæval Irish life, and as I wrote I was sometimes made wretched by the thought

331

that I knew of no kind of English that fitted them as the language of Morris' prose stories—the most beautiful language I have ever read—fitted his journeys to woods and wells beyond the world. I knew of no language to write about Ireland in but raw modern English; but now Lady Gregory has discovered a speech as beautiful as that of Morris, and a living speech in the bargain.

As she moved about among her people she learned to love the beautiful speech of those who think in Irish, and to understand that it is as true a dialect of English as the dialect that Burns wrote in. It is some hundreds of years old, and age gives language authority. One finds in it the vocabulary of the translators of the Bible, joined to an idiom which makes it tender, compassionate, and complaisant, like the Irish language itself. It is certainly well suited to clothe a literature which never ceases to be folk-lore even when it was recited in the Courts of Kings.

II

Lady Gregory could with less trouble have made a book that would have better pleased the hasty reader. She could have plucked away details, smoothed out characteristics till she had left nothing but the bare stories; but a book of that kind would never have called up the past, or stirred the imagination of a painter or a poet, and would be as little thought of in a few years as if it had been a popular novel.

The abundance of what may seem at first irrelevant invention in a story like the death of Conaire, is essential if we are to recall the time when people were in love with a story, and gave themselves up to imagination as if to a lover. One may think there are too many lyrical outbursts, or too many enigmatical symbols here and there in some other story, but delight will always overtake in the end. One comes to accept without reserve an art that is half epical, half lyrical, like that of the historical parts of the Bible, the art of a time when perhaps men passed more readily than they do now from one mood to another, and found it harder than we do to keep to the mood in which one tots up figures or banters a friend.

III

The Church when it was most powerful created an imaginative unity, for it taught learned and unlearned to climb, as it were, to the great moral realities through hierarchies of Cherubim and Seraphim, through clouds of Saints and Angels who had their precise duties and privileges. The story-tellers of Ireland, perhaps of every primitive country, created a like unity, only it was to the great æsthetic realities that they taught people to climb. They created for learned and unlearned alike, a communion of heroes, a cloud of stalwart witnesses; but because they were as much excited as a monk over his prayers, they did not think sufficiently about the shape of the poem or the story. One has to get a little weary or a little distrustful of one's subject, perhaps, before one can lie awake thinking how one will make the most of it. They were more anxious to describe energetic characters, and to invent beautiful stories, than to express themselves with perfect dramatic logic or perfectly-ordered words. They shared their characters and their stories, their very images, with one another, and handed them down from generation to generation; for nobody, even when he had added some new trait, or some new incident, thought of claiming for himself what so obviously lived its own merry or mournful life. The wood-carver who first put a sword into St Michael's hand would have as soon claimed as his own a thought which was perhaps put into his mind by St Michael himself. The Irish poets had also, it may be, what seemed a supernatural sanction, for a chief poet had to understand not only innumerable kinds of poetry, but how to keep himself for nine days in a trance. They certainly believed in the historical reality of even their wildest imaginations. And so soon as Christianity made their hearers desire a chronology that would run side by side with that of the Bible, they delighted in arranging their Kings and Queens, the shadows of forgotten mythologies, in long lines that ascended to Adam and his Garden. Those who listened to them must have felt as if the living were like rabbits digging their burrows under walls that had been built by Gods or Giants, or like swallows building their nests in the stone mouths of immense images, carved by nobody knows who. It is no wonder that one sometimes hears about men who saw in a vision ivy-leaves that were greater than shields, and blackbirds whose thighs were like the thighs of oxen. The fruit of all these stories, unless indeed the finest activities of the mind are but a pastime, is the quick intelligence, the abundant imagination, the courtly manners of the Irish country people.

IV

William Morris came to Dublin when I was a boy, and I had some talk with him about these old stories. He had intended to lecture upon them, but "the ladies and gentlemen"—he put a communistic flavour of hatred into that phrase—knew nothing about them. He spoke of the Irish account of the battle of Clontarf, and of the Norse account, and said, that one saw the Norse and Irish tempers in the two accounts. The Norseman was interested in the way things are done, but the Irishman turned aside, evidently well pleased to be out of so dull a business, to describe the beautiful supernatural events. He was thinking, I suppose, of the young man who came from Aebhen of the Grey Rock, giving up immortal love and youth, that he might fight and die by Murrugh's side. He said that the Norseman had the dramatic temper, and the Irishman had the lyrical. I think I should have said epical and romantic rather than dramatic and lyrical, but his words, which have so much greater authority than mine, mark the distinction very well, and not only between Irish and Norse, but between Irish and other un-Celtic literatures. The Irish story-teller could not interest himself with an unbroken interest in the way men like himself burned a house, or won wives no more wonderful than themselves. His mind constantly escaped out of daily circumstances, as a bough that has been held down by a weak hand suddenly straightens itself out. His imagination was always running off to Tir-nan-oge, to the Land of Promise, which is as near to the country-people of today, as it was to Cuchulain and his companions. His belief in its nearness, cherished in its turn the lyrical temper, which is always athirst for an emotion, a beauty which cannot be found in its perfection upon earth, or only for a moment. His imagination, which had not been able to believe in Cuchulain's greatness, until it had brought the Great Queen, the red eye-browed goddess to woo him upon the battlefield, could not be satisfied with a friendship less romantic and lyrical than that of Cuchulain and Ferdiad, who kissed one another after the day's fighting, or with a love less romantic and lyrical than that of Baile or Aillinn, who died at the report of one another's death, and married in Tir-nan-oge. His art, too, is often at its greatest when it is most extravagant, for he only feels himself among solid things, among things with fixed laws and satisfying purposes, when he has reshaped the world according to his heart's desire. He understands as well as Blake that the ruins of time build mansions in eternity, and he never allows anything, that we can see and handle, to remain long unchanged. The characters must remain the same, but the strength of Fergus may change so greatly, that he, who a moment before was merely a strong man among many, becomes the master of Three Blows that would destroy an army, did they not cut off the heads of three little hills instead, and his sword, which a fool had been able to steal out of its sheath, has of a sudden the likeness of a rainbow. A wandering lyric moon must knead and kindle perpetually that moving world of cloaks made out of the fleeces of Manannan; of armed men who change themselves into sea-birds; of goddesses who become crows; of trees that bear fruit and flower at the same time. The great emotions of love, terror, and friendship must alone remain untroubled by the moon in that world, which is still the world of the Irish country-people, who do not open their eyes very wide at the most miraculous change, at the most sudden enlightenment. Its events, and things, and people are wild, and are like unbroken horses, that are so much more beautiful than horses that have learned to run between shafts. One thinks of actual life, when one reads those Norse stories, which were already in decadence, so necessary were the proportions of actual life to their efforts, when a dying man remembered his heroism enough to look down at his wound and say, "Those broad spears are coming into fashion"; but the Irish stories make one understand why the Greeks called myths the activities of the dæmons. The great virtues, the great joys, the great privations come in the myths, and, as it were, take mankind between their naked arms, and without putting off their divinity. Poets have taken their themes more often from stories that are all, or half, mythological, than from history or stories that give one the sensation of history, understanding, as I think, that the imagination which remembers the proportions of life is but a long wooing, and that it has to forget them before it becomes the torch and the marriage-bed.

V

One finds, as one expects, in the work of men who were not troubled about any probabilities or necessities but those of emotion itself, an immense variety of incident and character and of ways of expressing emotion. Cuchulain fights man after man during the quest of the Brown Bull, and not one of those fights is like another, and not one is lacking in emotion or strangeness; and when one thinks imagination can do no more, the story of the Two Bulls, emblematic of all contests, suddenly lifts romance into prophecy. The characters too have a distinctness one does not find among the people of the Morte D'Arthur. One knows one will be long forgetting Cuchulain, whose life is vehement and full of pleasure, as though he always remembered that it was to be soon over; or the dreamy Fergus who betrays the sons of Usnach for a feast, without ceasing to be noble; or Conall who is fierce and friendly and trustworthy, but has not the sap of divinity that makes Cuchulain mysterious to men, and beloved of women. Women indeed, with their lamentations for lovers and husbands and sons, and for fallen rooftrees and lost wealth, give the stories their most beautiful sentences; and after Cuchulain, one thinks most of certain great queens—of angry Maeve, with her long pale face; of Findabair, her daughter, who dies of shame and of pity; of Deirdre who might be some mild modern housewife but for her prophetic wisdom. If one does not set Deirdre's lamentations among the greatest lyric poems of the world, I think one may be certain that the wine-press of the poets has been trodden for one in vain; and yet I think it may be proud Emer, Cuchulain's fitting wife, who will linger longest in the memory. What a pure flame burns in her always, whether she is the newly-married wife fighting for independence, fierce as some beautiful bird, or the confident housewife, who would awaken her husband from his magic sleep with mocking words; or the great queen who would get him out of the tightening net of his doom, by sending him into the Valley of the Deaf, with Niamh, his mistress, because he will be more obedient to her; or the woman whom sorrow has set with Helen and Iseult and Brunnhilda, and Deirdre, to share their immortality in the rosary of the poets.

" 'And oh! my love!' she said, 'we were often in one another's company, and it was happy for us; for if the world had been searched from the rising of the sun to sunset, the like would never be found in one place, of the Black Sainglain and the Grey of Macha, and Laeg the chariot-driver, and myself and Cuchulain.'

" 'And after that Emer bade Conall to make a wide, very deep grave for Cuchulain; and she laid herself down beside her gentle comrade, and she put her mouth to his mouth, and she said: 'Love of my life, my friend, my sweetheart, my one choice of the men of the earth, many is the women, wed or unwed, envied me until to-day; and now I will not stay living after you.' "

VI

To us Irish these personages should be more important than all others, for they lived in the places where we ride and go marketing, and sometimes they have met one another on the hills that cast their shadows upon our doors at evening. If we but tell these stories to our children the Land will begin again to be a Holy Land, as it was before men gave their hearts to Greece and Rome and Judea. When I was a child I had only to climb the hill behind the house to see long, blue, ragged hills flowing along the southern horizon. What beauty was lost to me, what depth of emotion is still perhaps lacking in me, because nobody told me, not even the merchant captains who knew everything, that Cruachan of the Enchantments lay behind those long, blue, ragged hills!

W. B. YEATS

March 1902.

CONTENTS

CHAPTER I

Birth of Cuchulain

In the time long ago, Conchubar, son of Ness, was King of Ulster, and he held his court in the palace of Emain Macha. And this is the way he came to be king. He was but a young lad, and his father was not living, and Fergus son of Rogh, who was at that time King of Ulster, asked his mother Ness in marriage.

Now Ness, that was at one time the quietest and kindest of the women of Ireland, had got to be unkind and treacherous because of an unkindness that had been done to her, and she planned to get the kingdom away from Fergus for her own son. So she said to Fergus: "Let Conchubar hold the kingdom for a year, so that his children after him may be called the children of a king; and that is the marriage portion I will ask of you."

"You may do that," the men of Ulster said to him; "for even though Conchubar gets the name of being king, it is yourself that will be our king all the time." So Fergus agreed to it, and he took Ness as his wife, and her son Conchubar was made king in his place.

But all through the year, Ness was working to keep the kingdom for him, and she gave great presents to the chief men of Ulster to get them on her side. And though Conchubar was but a young lad at that time, he was wise in his judgments, and brave in battle, and good in shape and in form, and they liked him well. And at the end of the year, when Fergus asked to have the kingship back again, they consulted together; and it is what they agreed, that Conchubar was to keep it. And they said; "It is little Fergus thinks about us, when he was so ready to give up his rule over us for a year; and let Conchubar keep the kingship," they said, "and let Fergus keep the wife he has got."

Now it happened one day that Conchubar was making a feast at Emain Macha for the marriage of his sister Dechtire with Sualtim son of Roig. And at the feast Dechtire was thirsty, and they gave her a cup of wine, and as she was drinking it, a mayfly flew into the cup, and she drank it down with the wine. And presently she went into her sunny parlour, and her fifty maidens along with her, and she fell into a deep sleep. And in her sleep, Lugh of the Long Hand appeared to her, and he said: "It is I myself was the mayfly that came to you in the cup, and it is with me you must come away now, and your fifty maidens along with you." And he put on them the appearance of a flock of birds, and they went with him southward till they came to Brugh na Boinne, the dwelling-place of the Sidhe. And no one at Emain Macha could get tale or tidings of them, or know where they had gone, or what had happened them.

It was about a year after that time, there was another feast in Emain, and Conchubar and his chief men were sitting at the feast. And suddenly they saw from the window a great flock of birds, that lit on the ground and began to eat up everything before them, so that not so much as a blade of grass was left.

The men of Ulster were vexed when they saw the birds destroying all before them, and they yoked nine of their chariots to follow after them. Conchubar was in his own chariot, and there were following with him Fergus son of Rogh, and Laegaire Buadach, the Battle-Winner, and Celthair son of Uithecar and many others, and Bricriu of the bitter tongue was along with them.

They followed after the birds across the whole country southward, across Slieve Fuad, by Ath Lethan, by Ath Garach and Magh Gossa, between Fir Rois and Fir Ardae; and the birds before them always. They were the most beautiful that had ever been seen; nine flocks of them there were, linked together two and two with a chain of silver, and at the head of every flock there were two birds of different colours, linked together with a chain of gold; and there were three birds that flew by themselves, and they all went before the chariots, to the far end of the country, until the fall of night, and then there was no more seen of them.

And when the dark night was coming on, Conchubar said to his people: "It is best for us to unyoke the chariots now, and to look for some place where we can spend the night."

Then Fergus went forward to look for some place, and what he came to was a very small poor-looking house. A man and a woman were in it, and when they saw him they said: "Bring your companions here along with you, and they will be welcome." Fergus went back to his companions and told them what he had seen. But Bricriu said; "Where is the use of going into a house like that, with neither room nor provisions nor coverings in it; it is not worth our while to be going there."

Then Bricriu went on himself to the place where the house was. But when he came to it, what he saw was a grand, new, well-lighted house; and at the door there was a young man wearing armour, very tall and handsome and shining. And he said: "Come into the house, Bricriu; why are you looking about you?" And there was a young woman beside him, fine and noble, and with curled hair, and she said: "Surely there is a welcome before you from me." "Why does she welcome me?" said Bricriu. "It is on account of her that I myself welcome you," said the young man. "And is there no one missing from you at Emain?" he said. "There is surely," said Bricriu. "We are missing fifty young girls for the length of a year." "Would you know them again if you saw them?" said the young man. "If I would not know them," said Bricriu, "it is because a year might make a change in them, so that I would not be sure." "Try and know them again," said the man, "for the fifty young girls are in this house, and this woman beside me is their mistress, Dechtire. It was they themselves, changed into birds, that went to Emain Macha to bring you here." Then Dechtire gave Bricriu a purple cloak with gold fringes; and he went back to find his companions. But while he was going he thought to himself: "Conchubar would give great treasure to find these fifty young girls again, and his sister along with them. I will not tell him I have found them. I will only say I have found a house with beautiful women in it, and no more than that."

When Conchubar saw Bricriu, he asked news of him. "What news do you bring back with you, Bricriu?" he said. "I came to a fine well-lighted house," said Bricriu; "I saw a queen, noble, kind, with royal looks, with curled hair; I saw a troop of women, beautiful, well-dressed; I saw the man of the house, tall and open-handed and shining." "Let us go there for the night," said Conchubar. So they brought their chariots and their horses and their arms; and they were hardly in the house when every sort of food and of drink, some they knew and some they did not know, was put before them, so that they never spent a better night. And when they had eaten and drunk and began to be satisfied, Conchubar said to the young man: "Where is the mistress of the house that she does not come to bid us welcome?" "You cannot see her to-night," said he, "for she is in the pains of childbirth."

So they rested there that night, and in the morning Conchubar was the first to rise up; but he saw no more of the man of the house, and what he heard was the cry of a child. And he went to the room it came from, and there he saw Dechtire, and her maidens about her, and a young child beside her. And she bade Conchubar welcome, and she told him all that had happened here, and that she had called him there to bring herself and the child back to Emain Macha. And Conchubar said: "It is well you have done by me, Dechtire; you gave shelter to me and to my chariots; you kept the cold from my horses; you gave food to me and my people, and now you have given us this good gift. And let our sister, Finchoem, bring up the child," he said. "No, it is not for her to bring him up, it is for me," said Sencha son of Ailell, chief judge and chief poet of Ulster. "For I am skilled; I am good in disputes; I am not forgetful; I speak before any one at all in the presence of the king; I watch over what he says; I give judgment in the quarrels of kings; I am judge of the men of Ulster; no one has a right to dispute my claim, but only Conchubar."

"If the child is given to me to bring up," said Blai, the distributor, "he will not suffer from want of care or from forgetfulness. It is my messages that do the will of Conchubar; I call up the fighting men from all Ireland; I am well able to provide for them for a week, or even for ten days; I settle their business and their disputes; I support their honour; I get satisfaction for their insults."

"You think too much of yourself," said Fergus. "It is I that will bring up the child; I am strong; I have knowledge; I am the king's messenger; no one can stand up against me in honour or riches; I am hardened to war and battles; I am a good craftsman; I am worthy to bring up a child. I am the protector of all the unhappy; the strong are afraid of me; I am the helper of the weak."

"If you will listen to me at last, now you are quiet," said Amergin, "I am able to bring up a child like a king. The people praise my honour, my bravery, my courage, my wisdom; they praise my good luck, my age, my speaking, my name, my courage, and my race. Though I am a fighter, I am a poet; I am worthy of the king's favour; I overcome all the men who fight from their chariots; I owe thanks to no one except Conchubar; I obey no one but the king."

Then Sencha said: "Let Finchoem keep the child until we come to Emain, and Morann, the judge, will settle the question when we are there."

So the men of Ulster set out for Emain, Finchoem having the child with her. And when they came there Morann gave his judgment. "It is for Conchubar," he said, "to help the child to a good name, for he is next of kin to him; let Sencha teach him words and speaking; let Fergus hold him on his knees; let Amergin be his tutor." And he said: "This child will be praised by all, by chariot drivers and fighters, by kings and by wise men; he shall be loved by many men; he will avenge all your wrongs; he will defend your fords; he will fight all your battles."

And so it was settled. And the child was left until he should come to sensible years, with his mother Dechtire and with her husband Sualtim. And they brought him up upon the plain of Muirthemne, and the name he was known by was Setanta, son of Sualtim.

CHAPTER II

Boy Deeds of Cuchulain

It chanced one day, when Setanta was about seven years old, that he heard some of the people of his mother's house talking about King Conchubar's court at Emain Macha, and of the sons of kings and nobles that lived there, and that spent a great part of their time at games and at hurling. "Let me go and play with them there," he said to his mother. "It is too soon for you to do that," she said, "but wait till such time as you are able to travel so far, and till I can put you in charge of some one going to the court, that will put you under Conchubar's protection." "It would be too long for me to wait for that,' he said, "but I will go there by myself if you will tell me the road." It is too far for you," said Dechtire, "for it is beyond Slieve Fuad, Emain Macha is." "Is it east or west of Slieve Fuad?" he asked. And when she had answered him that, he set out there and then, and nothing with him but his hurling stick, and his silver ball, and his little dart and spear; and to shorten the road for himself he would give a blow to the ball and drive it from him, and then he would throw his hurling stick after it, and the dart after that again, and then he would make a run and catch them all in his hand before one of them would have reached the ground.

So he went on until he came to the lawn at Emain Macha, and there he saw three fifties of kings' sons hurling and learning feats of war. He went in among them, and when the ball came near him he got it between his feet, and drove it along in spite of them till he had sent it beyond the goal. There was great surprise and anger on them when they saw what he had done, and Follaman, King Conchubar's son, that was chief among them, cried out to them to come together and drive out this stranger and make an end of him. "For he has no right," he said, "to come into our game without asking leave, and without putting his life under our protection. And you may be sure," he said, "that he is the son of some common fighting man, and it is not for him to come into our game at all." With that they all made an attack on him, and began to throw their hurling sticks at him, and their balls and darts, but he escaped them all, and then he rushed at them, and began to throw some of them to the ground. Fergus came out just then from the palace, and when he saw what a good defence the little lad was making, he brought him in to where Conchubar was playing chess, and told him all that had happened. "This is no gentle game you have been playing," he said. "It is on themselves the fault is," said the boy; "I came as a stranger, and I did not get a stranger's welcome." "You did not know then," said Conchubar, "that no one can play among the boy troop of Emain unless he gets their leave and their protection." "I did not know that, or I would have asked it of them," he said. "What is your name and your family?" said Conchubar. "My name is Setanta, son of Sualtim and of Dechtire," he said. When Conchubar knew that he was his sister's son, he gave him a great welcome, and he bade the the boy troop to let him go safe among them. "We will do that," they said. But when they went out to play, Setanta began to break through them, and to overthrow them, so that they could not stand against him. "What are you wanting of them now?" said Conchubar. "I swear by the gods my people swear by," said the boy, "I will not lighten my hand of them till they have come under my protection the same way I have come under theirs." Then they all agreed to give in to this; and Setanta stayed in the king's house at Emain Macha, and all the chief men of Ulster had a hand in bringing him up.

There was a great smith in Ulster of the name of Culain, who made a feast at that time for Conchubar and for his people. When Conchubar was setting out to the feast, he passed by the lawn where the boy troop were at their games, and he watched them awhile, and he saw how the son of Dechtire was winning the goal from them all. "That little lad will serve Ulster yet," said Conchubar; "and call him to me now," he said, "and let him come with me to the smith's feast." "I cannot go with you now," said Setanta, when they had called to him, "for these boys have not had enough of play yet." "It would be too long for me to wait for you," said the king. "There is no need for you to wait; I will follow the track of the chariots," said Setanta.

So Conchubar went on to the smith's house, and there was a welcome before him, and fresh rushes were laid down, and there were poems and songs and recitals of laws, and the feast was brought in, and they began to be merry. And then Culain said to the king: "Will there be any one else of your people coming after you to-night?" "There will not," said Conchubar, for he forgot that he had told the little lad to follow him. "But why do you ask me that?" he said. "I have a great fierce hound," said the smith, "and when I take the chain off him, he lets no one come into the one district with himself, and he will obey no one but myself, and he has in him the strength of a hundred." "Loose him out," said Conchubar, "until he keeps a watch on the place." So Culain loosed him out, and the dog made a course round the whole district, and then he came back to the place where he was used to lie and to watch the house, and every one was in dread of him, he was so fierce and so cruel and so savage.

Now, as to the boys at Emain, when they were done playing, every one went to his father's house, or to whoever was in charge of him. But Setanta set out on the track of the chariots, shortening the way for himself as he was used to do with his hurling stick and his ball. When he came to the lawn before the smith's house, the hound heard him coming, and began such a fierce yelling that he might have been heard through all Ulster, and he sprang at him as if he had a mind not to stop and tear him up at all, but to swallow him at the one mouthful. The little fellow had no weapon but his stick and his ball, but when he saw the hound coming at him, he struck the ball with such force that it went down his throat, and through his body. Then he seized him by the hind legs and dashed him against a rock until there was no life left in him.

When the men feasting within heard the outcry of the hound, Conchubar started up and said: "It is no good luck brought us on this journey, for that is surely my sister's son that was coming after me, and that has got his death by the hound." On that all the men rushed out, not waiting to go through the door, but over walls and barriers as they could. But Fergus was the first to get to where the boy was, and he took him up and lifted him on his shoulder, and brought him in safe and sound to Conchubar, and there was great joy on them all.

But Culain the smith went out with them, and when he saw his great hound lying dead and broken there was great grief in his heart, and he came in and said to Setanta: "There is no good welcome for you here." "What have you against the little lad?" said Conchubar.

"It was no good luck that brought him here, or that made me prepare this feast for yourself, King," he said; "for from this out, my hound being gone, my substance will be wasted, and my way of living will be gone astray. And little boy," he said, "that was a good member of my family you took from me, for he was the protector of my goods and my flocks and my herds and of all that I had." "Do not be vexed on account of that," said the boy, "and I myself will make up to you for what I have done." "How will you do that?" said Conchubar. "This is how I will do it: if there is a whelp of the same breed to be had in Ireland, I will rear him and train him until he is as good a hound as the one killed; and until that time,

Culain," he said, "I myself will be your watch-dog, to guard your goods and your cattle and your house." "You have made a fair offer," said Conchubar. "I could have given no better award myself," said Cathbad the Druid. "And from this out," he said, "your name will be Cuchulain, the Hound of Culain." "I am better pleased with my own name of Setanta, son of Sualtim," said the boy. "Do not say that," said Cathbad, "for all the men in the whole world will some day have the name of Cuchulain in their mouths." "If that is so, I am content to keep it," said the boy. And this is how he came by the name Cuchulain.

It was a good while after that, Cathbad the Druid was one day teaching the pupils in his house to the north-east of Emain. There were eight boys along with him that day, and one of them asked him: "Do your signs tell of any special thing this day is favourable to?" "If any young man should take arms to-day," said Cathbad, "his name will be greater than any other name in Ireland. But his span of life will be short," he said.

Cuchulain was outside at play, but he heard what Cathbad said, and there and then he put off his playing suit, and he went straight to Conchubar's sleeping-room, and said: "All good be with you, King!" "What is it you are wanting?" said Conchubar. "What I want is to take arms to-day." "Who put that into your head?" "Cathbad the Druid," said Cuchulain. "If that is so, I will not deny you," said Conchubar. Then he gave him his choice of arms, and the boy tried his strength on them, and there were none that pleased him or that were strong enough for him but Conchubar's own. So he gave him his own two spears, and his sword and his shield.

Just then Cathbad the Druid came in, and there was wonder on him, and he said: "Is it taking arms this young boy is?" "He is indeed," said the king. "It is sorry I would be to see his mother's son take arms on this day," said Cathbad. "Was it not yourself bade him do it?" said the king. "I did not surely," he said. "Then you have lied to me, boy," said Conchubar. "I told no lie King," said Cuchulain, "for it was he indeed put it in my mind when he was teaching the others, for when one of them asked him if there was any special virtue in this day, he said that whoever would for the first time take arms to-day, his name would be greater than any other in Ireland, and he did not say any harm would come on him, but that his life would be short." "And what I said is true," said Cathbad, "there will be fame on you and a great name, but your lifetime will not be long." "It is little I would care," said Cuchulain, "if my life were to last one day and one night only, so long as my name and the story of what I had done would live after me." Then Cathbad said: "Well, get into a chariot now, and let us see if it was the truth I spoke."

Then Cuchulain got into a chariot and tried its strength, and broke it to pieces, and he broke in the same way the seventeen chariots that Conchubar kept for the boy troop at Emain, and he said: "These chariots are no use, Conchubar, they are not worthy of me." "Where is Jubair, son of Riangabra?" said Conchubar. "Here I am," he answered. "Make ready my own chariot, and yoke my own horses to it for this boy to try," said Conchubar. So he tried the king's chariot and shook it and strained it, and it bore him. "This is the chariot that suits me," he said. "Now, little one," said Jubair, "let us take out the horses and turn them out to graze." "It is too early for that, Jubair; let us drive on to where the boy troop are, that they may wish me good luck on the day of my taking arms?" So they drove on, and all the lads shouted when they saw him—"Have you taken arms?" "I have indeed," said Cuchulain. "That you may do well in wounding and in first killing and in spoil-winning," they said; "but it is a pity for us, you to have left playing."

"Let the horses go graze now," said Jubair. "It is too soon yet," said Cuchulain, "and tell me where does that great road that goes by Emain lead to?" "It leads to Ath-an-Foraire, the watchers' ford in Slieve Fuad," said Jubair. "Why is it called the watchers' ford?" "It is easy to tell that; it is because some choice champion of the men of Ulster keeps watch there every day to do battle for the province with any stranger that might come to the boundary with a challenge." "Do you know who is in it to-day?" said Cuchulain. "I know well it is Conall Cearnach, the Victorious, the chief champion of the young men of Ulster and of all Ireland." "We will go on then to the ford," said Cuchulain. So they went on across the plain, and at the water's edge they found Conall, and he said: "And are those arms you have taken to-day, little boy?" "They are indeed," Jubair said for him. "May they bring him triumph and victory and shedding of first blood," said Conall. "But I think, little Hound," he said, "that you are too ready to take them; for you are not fit as yet to do a champion's work." "What is it you are doing here, Conall?" said the boy. "I am keeping watch and guard for the province." "Rise out of it, Conall," he said, "and for this one day let me keep the watch." "Do not ask that, little one," said Conall; "for you are not able yet to stand against trained fighting men." "Then I will go down to the shallows of Loch Echtra and see if I can redden my arms on either friend or enemy." "Then I will go with you myself," said Conall, "to take care of you and to protect you, that no harm may happen you." "Do not," said Cuchulain. "I will indeed," said Conall, "for if I let you go into a strange country alone, all Ulster would avenge it on me."

So Conall's horses were yoked to his chariot, and he set out to follow Cuchulain, for he had waited for no leave, but had set out by himself. When Cuchulain saw Conall coming up with him he thought to himself, "If I get a chance of doing some great thing, Conall will never let me do it." So he picked up a stone, the size of his fist, from the ground, and made a good cast at the yoke of Conall's chariot, so that he broke it, and the chariot came down, and Conall himself was thrown to the ground sideways. "What did you do that for?" he said. "It was to see could I throw straight, and if there was the making of a good champion in me." "Bad luck on your throwing and on yourself," said Conall. "And any one that likes may strike your head off now, for I will go with you no farther." "That is just what I wanted," said Cuchulain. And with that, Conall went back to his place at the ford.

As for the lad, he went on towards Lough Echtra in the south. Then Jubair said: "If you will listen to me, little one, I would like that we would go back now to Emain; for at this time the carving of the food is beginning there, and it is all very well for you that have your place kept for you, between Conchubar's knees. But as to myself," he said, "it is among the chariot-drivers and the jesters and the messengers I am, and I must take a place and fight for myself where I can." "What is that mountain before us?" said Cuchulain. "That is Slieve Mourne, and that is Finncairn, the white cairn, on its top." "Let us go to it," said Cuchulain. "We would be too long going there," said Jubair. "You are a lazy fellow," said Cuchulain; "and this is my first adventure, and the first journey you have made with me." "And that it may be my last," said Jubair, "if ever I get back to Emain again." They went on then to the cairn. "Good Jubair," said the boy, "show me now all that we can see of Ulster, for I do not know my way about the country yet." So Jubair showed him from the cairn all there was to see of Ulster, the hills and the plains and the duns on every side. "What is that sloping square plain before us to the south?" "That is Magh Breagh, the fine meadow." "Show me the duns and strong places of that plain." So Jubair showed him Teamhair and Tailte, Cleathra and Cnobhach and the Brugh of Angus on the Boyne, and the dun of Nechtan Sceine's sons. "Are those the sons of Nechtan that say in their boasting they have killed as many Ulstermen as there are living in Ulster to-day?" "They are the same," said Jubair. "On with us then to that dun," said Cuchulain. "No good will come to you through saying that," said Jubair; "and whoever may go there I will not go," he said. "Alive or dead, you must go there for all that," said Cuchulain. "Then if so, it is alive I will go there," said Jubair, "and it is dead I will be before I leave it."

They went on then to the dun of Nechtan's sons, and when they came to the green lawn, Cuchulain got out of the chariot, and there was a pillar stone on the lawn, and an iron collar about it, and there was Ogham writing on it that said no man that came there, and he carrying arms, should leave the place without giving a challenge to some one of the people of the dun. When Cuchulain had read the Ogham, he put his arms round the stone and threw it into the water that was there at hand. "I don't see it is any better there than where it was before," said Jubair; "and it is likely this time you will get what you are looking for, and that is a quick death." "Good Jubair," said the boy, "spread out the coverings of the chariot now for me, until I sleep for a while." "It is no good thing you are going to do," said Jubair, "to be going to sleep in an enemy's country." He put out the coverings then, and Cuchulain lay down and fell asleep.

It was just at that time, Foill, son of Nechtan Sceine, came out, and when he saw the chariot, he called out to Jubair, "Let you not unyoke these horses." "I was not going to unyoke them," said Jubair; "the reins are yet in my hands." "What horses are they?" "They are Conchubar's two speckled horses." "So I thought when I saw them," said Foill. "And who is it has brought them across our boundaries?" "A young little lad," said Jubair, "that has taken arms to-day for luck, and it is to show himself off he has come across Magh Breagh." "May he never have good luck," said Foill, "And if he were a fighting man, it is not alive but dead he would go back to Emain to-day." "Indeed he is not able to fight, or it could not be expected of him," said Jubair, "and he but a child that should be in his father's house." At that the boy lifted his head from the ground, and it is red his face was, and his whole body, at hearing so great an insult put on him, and he said: "I am indeed well able to fight." But Foill said: "I am more inclined to think you are not," "You will soon know what to think," said the boy, "and let us go down now to the ford. But go first and get your armour," he said, "for I would not like to kill an unarmed man." There was anger on Foill then, and he went running to get his arms. "You must have a care now," said Jubair, "for that is Foill, son of Nechtan, and neither point of spear or edge of sword can harm him." "That suits me very well," said the boy. With that out came Foill again, and Cuchulain stood up to him, and took his iron ball in his hand, and hurled it at his head, and it went through the forehead and out at the back of his head, and his brains along with it, so that the air could pass through the hole it made. And then Cuchulain struck off his head.

Then Tuachel, the second son of Nechtan, came out on the lawn. "It is likely you are making a great boast of what you are after doing," he said. "I see nothing to boast of in that," said Cuchulain, "a single man to have fallen by me." "You will not have long to boast of it," said Tuachel, "for I myself am going to make an end of you on the moment." "Then go back and bring your arms," said Cuchulain, "for it is only a coward would come out without arms." He went back into the house then, and Jubair said: "You must have a care now, for that is Tuachel, son of Nechtan, and if he is not killed by the first stroke, or the first cast, or the first thrust, he cannot be killed at all, for there is no way of getting at him after that." "You need not be telling me that, Jubair," said Cuchulain, "for it is Conchubar's great spear, the Venomous, I will take in my hand, and that is the last thrust that will be made at him, for after that, there is no physician will heal his wounds for ever."

Then Tuachel came out on the lawn, and Cuchulain took hold of the great spear, and made a cast at him, that went through his shield and broke three of his ribs, and made a hole through his heart. And then he struck his head off, before the body reached the ground.

Then Fainnle, the youngest of the three sons of Nechtan, came out. "Those were foolish fellows," he said, "to come at you the way they did. But come out now, after me," he said, "into the water where your feet will not touch bottom," and with that he made a plunge into the water. "Mind yourself well now," said Jubair, "for that is Fainnle, the Swallow, and it is why that name was put on him, he travels across water with the swiftness of a swallow, and there is not one of the swimmers of the whole world can come near him." "It is not to me you should be saying that," said Cuchulain, "for you know the river Callan that runs through Emain, and it is what I used to do," he said, "when the boy troop would break off from their games and plunge into the river to swim, I used to take a boy of them on each shoulder and a boy on each hand, and I would bring them through the river without so much as to wet my back." With that he made a leap into the water, where it was very deep, and himself and Fainnle wrestled together, and then he got a grip of him, and gave him a blow of Conchubar's sword, and struck his head off, and he let his body go away down the stream.

Then he and Jubair went into the house and destroyed what was in it, and they set fire to it, and left it burning, and turned back towards Slieve Fuad, and they brought the heads of the three sons of Nechtan along with them. Presently they saw a herd of wild deer before them. "What sort of cattle are those?" said the boy. "They are not cattle, but the wild deer of the dark places of Slieve Fuad." "Make the horses go faster," said Cuchulain, "until we can see them better." But with all their galloping the horses could not come up with the wild deer. Then Cuchulain got down from the chariot and raced and ran after them until two stags lay moaning and panting from the hardness of their run through the wet bog, and he bound them to the back of the chariot with the throngs of it. Then they went on till they came to the plain of Emain, and there they saw a flock of white swans that were whiter than the swans of Conchubar's lake, and Cuchulain asked where they came from. "They are wild swans," said Jubair, "that are come from the rocks and the islands of the great sea to feed on the low levels of the country." "Would it be best to take them alive or to kill them?" "It would be best to take them alive," said Jubair, "for many a one kills them, and many a one makes casts at them, but you would hardly find any one at all would bring them in alive." With that Cuchulain put a little stone in his sling and made a cast, and brought down eight birds of them, and then he put a bigger stone in, and with it he brought down sixteen more. "Get out now, Jubair," he said, "and bring me the birds here." "I will not," said Jubair, "for it would not be easy to stop the horses the way they are going now, and if I leap out, the iron wheels of the chariot will cut through me, or the horns of the stags will make a hole in me." "You are no good of a warrior, Jubair; but give me the reins and I will quiet the horses and the stags." So then Jubair went and brought in the swans, and tied them, and they alive, to the chariot and to the harness. And it is like that they went on till they came to Emain.

It was Levarcham daughter of Aedh, the conversation woman and messenger to the king, that was there at that time, and was sometimes away in the hills, was the first to see them coming. "There is a chariot-fighter coming, Conchubar," she said, "and he is coming in anger. He has the bleeding heads of his enemies with him in the chariot, and wild stags are bound to it, and white birds are bearing him company. By the oath of my people!" she said, "if he comes on us with his anger still upon him, the best of the men of Ulster will fall by his hand." "I know that chariot-fighter," said Conchubar. "It is the young lad, the son of Dechtire, that went over the boundaries this very day. He has surely reddened his hand, and if his anger cannot be cooled, the young men of Emain will be in danger from him," he said.

Then they all consulted together, and it is what they agreed, to send out three fifties of the women of Emain to meet him, and they having their breasts uncovered. When the boy saw the women coming, there was shame on him, and he leaned down his head into the cushions of the chariot, and hid his face from them. And the wildness went out of him, and his feasting clothes were brought, and water for washing; and there was a great welcome before him.

This is the story of the boy deeds of Cuchulain, as it was told by Fergus to Ailell and to Maeve at the time of the war for the Brown Bull of Cuailgne.

CHAPTER III

The Courting of Emer

When Cuchulain was growing out of his boyhood at Emain Macha, all the women of Ulster loved him for his skill in feats, for the lightness of his leap, for the weight of his wisdom, for the sweetness of his speech, for all the beauty of his face, for the loveliness of his looks, for all his gifts. He had the gift of caution in fighting, until such time as his anger would come on him, and the hero light would shine about his head; the gift of feats, the gift of chess-playing, the gift of draught-playing, the gift of counting, the gift of divining, the gift of right judgment, the gift of beauty. And all the faults they could find in him were three, that he was too young and smooth-faced, so that young men who did not know him would be laughing at him, that he was too daring, and that he was too beautiful.

The men of Ulster took counsel together then about Cuchulain, for their women and their maidens loved him greatly, and it is what they settled among themselves, that they would seek out a young girl that would be a fitting wife for him, the way that their own wives and their daughters would not be making so much of him. And besides that they were afraid he might die young, and leave no heir after him.

So Conchubar sent out nine men into each of the provinces of Ireland to look for a wife for Cuchulain, to see if in any dun or in any chief place, they could find the daughter of a king or of an owner of land or a householder, who would be pleasing to him, that he might ask her in marriage.

All the messengers came back at the end of a year, but not one of them had found a young girl that would please Cuchulain. And then he himself went out to court a young girl he knew in Luglochta Loga, the Garden of Lugh, Emer, the daughter of Forgall Manach, the Wily.

He set out in his chariot, that all the chariots of Ulster could not follow by reason of its swiftness, and of the chariot chief who sat in it. And he found the young girl on her playing field, with her companions about her, daughters of the landowners that lived near Forgall's dun, and they learning needlework and fine embroidery from Emer. And of all the young girls of Ireland, she was the one Cuchulain thought worth courting; for she had the six gifts—the gift of beauty, the gift of voice, the gift of sweet speech, the gift of needlework, the gift of wisdom, the gift of chastity. And Cuchulain had said that no woman should marry him but one that was his equal in age, in appearance, and in race, in skill and handiness; and one who was the best worker with her needle of the young girls of Ireland, for that would be the only one would be a fitting wife for him. And that is why it was Emer he went to ask above all others.

And it was in his rich clothes he went out that day, his crimson five-folded tunic, and his brooch of inlaid gold, and his white hooded shirt, that was embroidered with red gold. And as the younger girls were sitting together on their bench on the lawn, they heard coming towards them the clatter of hoofs, the creaking of a chariot, the cracking of straps, the grating of wheels, the rushing of horses, the clanking of arms. "Let one of you see," said Emer, "what is it that is coming towards us." And Fiall, daughter of Forgall, went out and met him, and he came with her to the place where Emer and her companions were, and he wished a blessing to them. Then Emer lifted up her lovely face and saw Cuchulain, and she said, "May the gods make smooth the path before you." "And you," he said, "may you be safe from every harm." "Where are you come from?" she asked him. And he answered her in riddles, that her companions might not understand him, and he said, "From Intide Emna." "Where did you sleep?" "We slept," he said, "in the house of the man that tends the cattle of the plain of Tethra." "What was your food there?" "The ruin of a chariot was cooked for us," he said. "Which way did you come?" "Between the two mountains of the wood." "Which way did you take after that?" "That is not hard to tell," he said. 'From the Cover of the Sea, over the Great Secret of the Tuatha De Danaan, and the Foam of the horses of Emain, over the Morrigu's Garden, and the Great Sow's back; over the Valley of the Great Dam, between the God and his Druid; over the Marrow of the Woman, between the Boar and his Dam; over the Washing-place of the horses of Dea; between the King of Ana and his servant, to Mandchuile of the Four Courners of the World; over Great Crime and the Remnants of the Great Feast; between the Vat and the Little Vat, to the Gardens of Lugh, to the daughters of Tethra, the nephew of the King of the Fomor." "And what account have you to give of yourself?" said Emer. "I am the nephew of the man that disappears in another in the wood of Badb," said Cuchulain.

"And now, maiden," he said, "what account have you to give of yourself?" "That is not hard to tell," said Emer, "for what should a maiden be but Teamhair upon the hills, a watcher that sees no one, an eel hiding in the water, a rush out of reach. The daughter of a king should be a flame of hospitality, a road that cannot be entered. And I have champions that follow me," she said, "to keep me from whoever would bring me away against their will, and against the will and the knowledge of Forgall, the dark king."

"Who are the champions that follow you, maiden?" said Cuchulain.

"It is not hard to tell you that," said Emer. "Two of the name of Lui; two Luaths; Luath and Lath Goible, sons of Tethra; Traith and Trescath; Brion and Bolor; Bas, son of Omnach; the eight Condla, and Cond, son of Forgall. Every man of them has the strength of a hundred and the feats of nine. And it would be hard for me," she said, "to tell of all the many powers Forgall has himself. He is stronger than any labouring man, more learned than any Druid, more quick of mind than any poet. You will have more than your games to do when you fight against Forgall, for many have told of his power and the strength of his doings."

"Why do you not count me as a strong man as good as those others?" said Cuchulain. "Why would I not indeed, if your doings had been spoken of like theirs?" she said. "I swear by the oath of my people," said Cuchulain, "that I will make my doings be spoken of among the great doings of heroes in their strength." "What is your strength, then?" said Emer. "That is easily told; when my strength in fighting is weakest I defend twenty; a third part of my strength is enough for thirty; in my full strength I fight alone against forty; and a hundred are safe under my protection. For dread of me, fighting men avoid fords and battles; armies and armed men go backward from the fear of my face."

"That is a good account for a young boy," said Emer, "but you have not reached yet to the strength of chariot chiefs." "But, indeed," said Cuchulain, "it is well I have been reared by Conchubar, my dear foster-father. It is not as a countryman strives to bring up his children, between the flags and the kneading trough, between the fire and the wall, on the floor of the one room, that Conchubar has brought me up; but it is among chariot chiefs and heroes, among jesters and Druids, among poets and learned men, among landowners and farmers of Ulster I have been reared, so that I have all their manners and their gifts."

"Who are these men, then, that have brought you up to do the things you are boasting of?" said Emer.

"That is easily told," he said. "Fair-speaking Sencha taught me wisdom and right judgment; Blai, lord of lands, my kinsman, took me to his house, so that I have entertained the men of Conchubar's province; Fergus brought me up to fights and to battles, so that I am able to use my strength. I stood by the knee of Amergin the poet, he was my tutor, so that I can stand up to any man, I can make praises for the doings of a king. Finchoem helped to rear me, so that Conall Cearnach is my foster-brother. Cathbad of the Gentle Face taught me, for the sake of Dechtire, so that I understand the arts of the Druids, and I have learned all the goodness of knowledge. All the men of Ulster have had a hand in bringing me up, chariot-drivers and chiefs of chariots, kings and chief poets, so that I am the darling of the whole army, so that I fight for the honour of all alike. And as to yourself, Emer," he said, "what way have you been reared in the Garden of Lugh?"

"It is easy to tell you that," said Emer. "I was brought up," she said, "in ancient virtues, in lawful behaviour, in the keeping of chastity, in stateliness of form, in the rank of a queen, in all the noble ways among the women of Ireland." "These are good virtues indeed," said Cuchulain. "And why, then, would it not be right for us two to become one? For up to this time," he said, "I have never found a young girl able to hold talk with me the way you have done." "Have you no wife already?" said Emer. "I have not, indeed." "I may not marry before my sister is married," she said then, "for she is older than myself." "Truly, it is not with your sister, but with yourself, I have fallen in love," said Cuchulain.

While they were talking like this, Cuchulain saw the breasts of the maiden over the bosom of her dress, and he said: "Fair is this plain, the plain of the noble yoke." And Emer said, "No one comes to this plain who does not overcome as many as a hundred on each ford, from the ford at Ailbine to Banchuig Arcait."

"Fair is the plain, the plain of the noble yoke," said Cuchulain. "No one comes to this plain," said she, "who does not go out in safety from Samhain to Oilmell, and from Oilmell to Beltaine, and again from Beltaine to Bron Trogain."

"Everything you have commanded, so it will be done by me," said Cuchulain.

"And the offer you have made me, it is accepted, it is taken, it is granted," said Emer.

With that Cuchulain left the place, and they talked no more with one another on that day.

When he was driving across the plain of Bregia, Laeg, his chariot-driver, asked him, "What, now, was the meaning of the words you and the maiden Emer were speaking together?" "Do you not know," said Cuchulain, "that I came to court Emer? And it is for this reason we put a cloak on our words, that the young girls with her might not understand what I had come for. For if Forgall knew it, he would not consent to it, but to you, Laeg," he said, "I will tell the meaning of our talk.

" 'Where did you come from,' said she. 'From Intide Emna,' said I, and I meant by that, from Emain Macha. For it took its name from Macha, daughter of Aed the Red, one of the three kings of Ireland. When he died Macha asked for the kingship, but the sons of Dithorba said they would not give kingship to a woman. So she fought against them and routed them, and they went as exiles to the wild places of Connaught. And after a while she went in search of them, and she took them by treachery, and brought them all in one chain to Ulster. The men of Ulster wanted to kill them, but she said, 'No, for that would be a disgrace on my good government. But let them be my servants,' she said, 'and let them dig a rath for me, that shall be the chief seat of Ulster for ever.' Then she marked out the rath for them with the gold pin on her neck, and its name came from that; a brooch in the neck of Macha.

"The man, in whose house we slept, is Ronca, the fisherman of Cuchubar. 'A man that tends cattle,' I said. For he catches fish on his line under the sea, and the fish are the cattle of the sea, and the sea is the plain of Tethra, a king of the kings of the Fomor.

" 'Our food was the ruin of a chariot,' I said. For a foal was cooked for us on the hearth, and it is the horse that holds up the chariot.

" 'Between the two mountains of the wood,' I said. These are the two mountains between which we came, Slieve Fuad to the west, and Slieve Cuilinn to the east of us, and we were in Oircil between them, the wood that is between the two.

" 'The road,' I said, 'from the Cover of the Sea.' That is from the plain of Muirthemne. And it is from this it got its name; there was at one time a magic sea on it, with a sea turtle in it that was used to suck men down, until the Dagda came with his club of anger and sang these words, so that it ebbed away on the moment:—

> 'Silence on your hollow head;
> Silence on your dark body;
> Silence on your dark brow.'

" 'Over the Great Secret of the men of Dea,' I said. That is a wonderful secret and a wonderful whisper, because it was there that the gathering to the battle of Magh Tuireadh was first whispered of by the Tuatha De Danaan.

" 'Over the horses of Emain,' I said. When Ema Nemed, son of Nama, reigned over the Gael, he had his two horses reared for him in Sidhe Ercman of the Tuatha De Danaan, and when those horses were let loose from the Sidhe, a bright stream burst out after them, and the foam spread over the land for a great length of time, and was there to the end of a year, so that the water was called Uanib, that is, foam on the water, and it is Uanib to-day.

" 'The Back of the Great Sow,' I said. That is Drimne Breg, the Ridge of Bregin. For the shape of a sow appeared to the sons of Milid on every hill and on every height in Ireland, when they came over the sea, and wanted to land by force, after a spell had been cast on it by the Tuatha De Danaan.

" 'The Valley of the Great Dam,' I said, 'between the God and his Druid.' That is, between Angus Og of the Sidhe of the Brugh and his Druid, to the west of the Brugh, and between them was the one woman, the wife of the Smith. That is the way I went, between the hill of the Sidhe of the Brugh where Angus is, and the Sidhe of Bresal, the Druid.

" 'Over the Marrow of the Woman,' I said. That is the Bruinne, and it gets its name from Boann, the wife of Nechtan, son of Labraid. She went down to the hidden well at the bottom of the dun with the three cup-bearers of Nechtan, Flex and Lex and Luam. No one came back from that well without blemish unless the three cup-bearers went with him. But the queen went out of pride and overbearing to the well, and it is what she said, that nothing would spoil her shape or put a blemish on her. She passed left-hand-wise round the well, to mock at its powers. Then three waves broke over her and bruised her two knees and her right hand and one of her eyes, and she ran out of the dun to escape until she came to the sea, and wherever she ran, the water followed after her. Segain was its name on the dun; the River Segsa from the dun to the Pool of Mochua; the hand of the wife of Nechtan and the knee of the wife of Nechtan after that; the Boinne in Meath; Arcait it is called from the Finda to the Troma; the Marrow of the Woman from the Troma to the sea.

" 'The Boar,' I said, 'and his Dam.' That is, between Cleitech and Fessi. For Cleitech is the name for a boar, but it is also the name for a king, the leader of great hosts, and Fessi is the name for the great sow of a farmer's house.

" 'The King of Ana,' I said, 'and his servant.' That is Cerna, through which we passed, and that is its name since Enna Aignech put Cerna, king of Ana, to death on that hill, and he put his steward to death in the east of that place.

" 'The Washing of the Horses of Dea,' I said. That is Ange, for in it the men of Dea washed their horses when they came from the battle of Magh Tuireadh. And it as called Ange, because the Tuatha De Danaan washed their horses in it.

" 'The Four-cornered Mandchuile,' I said. That is Muincille. It is there Mann, the farmer, was, and there he made spells in his great four-cornered chambers underground, to keep off the plague from the cattle of Ireland in the time of Bresel Brec, king of Leinster.

" 'Great Crime,' I said. That is Ailbine. There was a king here in Ireland, Ruad, son of Rigdond of Munster. He had an appointment of meeting with foreigners, and he set out for the meeting round the south of Alban with three ships, and thirty men were in each ship. But the ships were stopped, and were held from below in the middle of the sea, and throwing jewels and precious things into the sea did not get them off. Then lots were cast among them who should go into the sea and find out what was holding them. The lot fell on the king himself, Ruad, son of Rigdond, and he leaped into the sea, and it closed over him. He lit upon a large plain, where nine beautiful women met him, and they confessed that it was they themselves had stopped the ships, the way that he might come to them. And he stopped with them nine days, and they gave him nine vessels of gold; and through the length of that time his men were not able to go on, through the power of the women. When he was going away, a woman of them said she would bear him a son, and that he must come back to them and bring away his son, when he would be coming from the east.

"Then he joined his men, and they went on their voyage, and they stopped away seven years, and then they came back by a different way, and they did not go near the same spot. They landed in the bay, and the sea-women came up to them there, and the men heard them playing music in their brazen ship. And then the women came to the shore, and they put the boy out of the ship on the land where the men were. And the harbour was stony and rocky, and the boy slipped and fell on one of the rocks, so that he died there. And the women saw it, and they cried all together, 'Olbine, Olbine,' that is 'Great Crime.' And it is from that it is called Ailbine.

"The Remnants of the Great Feast,' I said. That is Tailne. It was there the great feast was given to Lugh, son of Ethlenn, to comfort him after the battle of Magh Tuireadh, for that was his wedding feast of kingship.

" 'In the Garden of Lugh, to the daughters of Tethra's nephew,' I said; for Forgall Manach is sister's son of Tethra, king of the Fomor.

"As to the account of myself I gave her, there are two rivers in the land of Ross; Conchubar is the name of one of them, and it mixes with the other; and I am the nephew of Conchubar; and as to the plague that comes on dogs, it is wild fierceness, and truly I am a strong fighter of that plague, for I am wild and fierce in battles and in fights. And the Wood of Badb, that is the land of Ross, the wood of the Morrigu, the Battle Crow, the Goddess of Battle.

"And when she said that no man should come to the plain of her breasts until he had killed three times nine men with one blow, and yet had saved one man from each nine, it is what she meant, that three brothers of her own will be guarding her, Ibur and Seibur and Catt, and a company of nine with each of them. And it is what I must do, I must strike a blow on each nine, from which eight will die, but no stroke will reach any of her brothers among them; and I must carry her and her foster sister, with their share of gold and silver, out of the dun of Forgall.

" 'Go out from Samhain to Oimell,' she said. That is, that I shall fight without harm to myself from Samhain, the end of summer, to Oimell, the beginning of spring; and from the beginning of spring to Beltaine, and from that to Bron Trogain. For Oi, in the language of poetry, is a name for sheep, and Oimell is the time when the sheep come out and are milked, and Suain is a gentle sound, and it is at Samhain that gentle voices sound; and Beltaine is a favouring fire; for it is at that time the Druids used to make fires with spells and to drive the cattle between them against the plagues every year. And Bron Trogain, that is the beginning of autumn, for it is then the earth is in labour, that is, the earth under fruit, Bron Trogain, the trouble of the earth."

Then Cuchulain went on his way, and he slept that night in Emain Macha.

When Forgall came back to his dun, and his lords of land with him, their daughters were telling them of the young man that had come in a splendid chariot, and how himself and Emer had been talking together, and they could not understand their talk with one another. The lords of land told this to Forgall, and it is what he said, "You may be sure it is the mad boy from Emain Macha has been here, and he and the girl have fallen in love with one another. But they will gain nothing by that," he said; "for it is I will hinder them."

With that Forgall went out to Emain, with the appearance of a foreigner on him, and he gave out that he was sent by the king of the Gall, to speak with Conchubar, and to bring him a present of golden treasures, and wine of the Gall, and many other things. And he brought some of his men with him, and there was a great welcome before them.

And on the third day, Cuchulain and Conall and other chariot chiefs of Ulster were praised before him, and he said it was right for them to be praised, and that they did wonderful feats, and Cuchulain above them all. But he said that if Cuchulain would go to Scathach, the woman-warrior that lived in the east of Alban, his skill would be more wonderful still, for he could not have perfect knowledge of the feats of a warrior without that.

But his reason for saying this was that he thought if Cuchulain set out, he would never come back again, through the dangers he would put around him on the journey, and through the wildness and the fierceness of the people about Scathach.

So then Forgall went home, and Cuchulain rose up in the morning, and made ready to set out for Alban, and Laegair Buadach, the Battle Winner, and Conall Cearnach said they would go with him. But first Cuchulain went across the plain of Bregia to visit Emer, and to talk with her before going in the ship. And she told him how it was Forgall had gone to Emain, and had advised him to go and learn warriors' feats, the way they two might not meet again. Then each of them promised to be true to the other till they would meet again, unless death should come between them, and they said farewell to one another, and Cuchulain turned towards Alban.

When they came there, they stopped for a while at the forge of Donall, the smith, and then they set out to go to the east of Alban. But before they had gone far, a vision came before their eyes of Emain Macha, and Laegaire and Conall were not able to pass by it, and they turned back. It was Forgall raised that vision, to draw them away from Cuchulain, that he might be in the more danger, being alone. Then Cuchulain went on by himself on a strange road, and he was sad and tired and down-hearted for the loss of his comrades, but he held to his word that he would not go back to Emain without finding Scathach, even if he should die in the attempt.

But now he was astray and ignorant, and not knowing which way to take, and he saw a terrible great beast like a lion coming towards him, and it watching him, but it did not try to harm him. Whatever way he went, the beast went before him, and then it stopped and turned its side to him. So he made a leap and was on its back, and he did not guide it, but went whatever way it chose. They travelled like that through four days, till they came to the end of the bounds of men, and to an island where lads were rowing in a small loch; and the lads began to laugh when they saw a beast of that sort, and a man riding it. And then Cuchulain leaped off, and the beast left him, and he bade it farewell.

He passed on till he came to a large house in a deep valley, and a comely young girl in it, and she spoke to him, and bade him welcome. "A welcome before you, Cuchulain," said said. He asked her how did she know him, and she said, "I was a foster child of Wulfkin, the Saxon, the time you came there to learn sweet speech from him." And she gave him meat and drink, and he went away from her. Then he met with a young man, and he gave him the same welcome, and he said his name was Eochu, and they talked together, and Cuchulain asked him what was the way to Scathach's dun. The young man told him the way, across the Plain of Ill-Luck, that lay before him, and he said that on the near side of the plain the feet of men would stick fast, and on the far side every blade of grass would rise and hold them fast on its points. And he gave him a wheel, and bade him to follow its track across the one half of the plain. And he gave him an apple along with that, and bade him to throw it, and to follow the way it went, till he would reach the end of the plain. And he told him many other things that would happen him, and how he would win a great name at the last. And then each of them wished a blessing to the other, and Cuchulain did as he bade him, and so he got across the plain and went on his journey. And then, as the young man had told him, he came to a valley, and it full of monsters, sent there by Forgall to destroy him, and only one narrow path through it, but he went through it safely. And after that his road led through a terrible, wild, mountain. Then he came to the place where Scathach's scholars were, and among them he saw Ferdiad, son of Daman, and Naoise, Ainnle, and Ardan, the three sons of Usnach, and when they knew that he was from Ireland they welcomed him with kisses, and asked for news of their own country. He asked them where was Scathach. "In that island beyond," they said. 'What way must I take to reach her?" he asked. "By the bridge of the cliff," they said, "and no man can cross it till he has proved himself a champion, and many a king's son has got his death there."

And this is the way the bridge was: the two ends of it were low, and the middle was high, and whenever any one would leap on it, the first time it would narrow till it was as narrow as the hair of a man's head, and the second time it would shorten till it was as short as an inch, and the third time it would get slippery till it was as slippery as an eel of the river, and the fourth time it would rise up on high against you till it was as tall as the mast of a ship.

All the warriors and people on the lawn came down to see Cuchulain making his attempt to cross the bridge, and he tried three times to do it, and he could not, and the others were laughing at him, that he should think he could cross it, and he so young. Then is anger came on him, and the hero light shone round his head, and it was not the appearance of a man that was on him, but the appearance of a god; and he leaped upon the end of the bridge and made the hero's salmon leap, so that he landed on the middle of it, and he reached the other end of the bridge before it could raise itself fully up, and threw himself from it, and was on the ground of the island where Scathach's sunny house was, and it having seven great doors, and seven great windows between every two doors, and seven great windows between every two doors, and three times fifty couches between every two windows, and three times fifty young girls, with scarlet cloaks and beautiful blue clothing on them, waiting on Scathach.

And Scathach's daughter, Uactach, was sitting by a window, and when she saw the young man, and he a stranger, and comeliest of the men of Ireland, making his attempt to cross the bridge, she loved him, and her face and her colour began to change continually, so that now she would be as white as a little flower, and then again she would grow crimson red. And in her needlework that she was doing, she would put the gold thread where the silver thread should be, and the silver thread in the place where the gold thread should be. And when Scathach saw that, she said: "I think this young man has pleased you." And Uactach said: "There would be great grief on me indeed, were he not to return alive to his own people, in whatever part of the world they may be, for I know there is surely some one to whom it would be great anguish to know the way he is now."

Then, when Cuchulain had crossed the bridge, he went up to the house, and struck the door with the shaft of his spear, so that it went through it. And when Scathach was told that, she said, "Truly this must be some one who has finished his training in some other place." Then Uacthach opened the door for him, and when he asked for Scathach, and Uacthach told him where she was, and what he had best do when he found her. So he went out to the place where she was teaching her two sons, Cuar and Cett, under the great yew-tree; and he took his sword and put its point between her breasts, and he threatened her with a dreadful death if she would not take him as her pupil, and if she would not teach him all her own skill in arms. So she promised him she would do that.

Now it was while Cuchulain was with Scathach that a great king in Munster, Lugaid, son of Ros, went northward with twelve chariot chiefs to look for a wife among the daughters of the men of Mac Rossa, but they had all been promised before.

And when Forgall Manach heard this, he went to Emain, and he told Lugaid that the best of the maidens of Ireland, both as to form and behaviour and handiwork, was in his house unwed. Lugaid said he was well pleased, and Forgall promised him his daughter Emer in marriage. And to the twelve chariot chiefs that were with him, he promised twelve daughters of twelve lords of land in Bregia, and Lugaid went back with him to his dun for the wedding.

But when Emer was brought to Lugaid to sit by his side, she laid one of her hands on each side of his face, and she said on the truth of her good name and of her life, that it was Cuchulain she loved, although her father was against him, and that no one that was an honourable man should force her to be his wife.

Then Lugaid did not dare take her, for he was in dread of Cuchulain, and so he returned home again.

As to Cuchulain, after he had been a good time with Scathach, a war began between herself and Aoife, queen of the tribes that were round about. The armies were going out to fight, but Cuchulain was not with them, for Scathach had given him a sleeping-drink that would keep him safe and quiet till the fight would be over, for she was afraid some harm would come to him if he met Aoife, for she was the greatest woman-warrior in the world, and she understood enchantments and witchcraft. But after one hour, Cuchulain started up out of his sleep, for the sleeping-drink that would have held any other man for a day and a night, held him for only that length of time. And he followed after the army, and he met with the two sons of Scathach, and they three went against the three sons of Ilsuanach, three of the best warriors of Aoife, and it was by Cuchulain they were killed, one after the other.

On the morning of the morrow the fight was begun again, and the two sons of Scathach were going up the path of feats to fight against three others of the best champions of Aoife, Cire, Bire, and Blaicne, sons of Ess Enchenn. When Scathach saw them going up she gave a sigh, for she was afraid for her two sons, but just then Cuchulain came up with them, and he leaped before them on to the path of feats, and met the three champions, and all three fell by him.

When Aoife saw that her best champions were after being killed, she challenged Scathach to fight against herself, but Cuchulain went out in her place. And before he went, he asked Scathach, "What things does Aoife think most of in all the world?" "Her two horses and her chariot and her chariot-driver," said Scathach.

So then Cuchulain and Aoife attacked one another and began a fierce fight, and she broke Cuchulain's spear in pieces, and his sword she broke off at the hilt. Then Cuchulain called out, "Look, the chariot and the horses and the driver of Aoife are fallen down into the valley and are lost!" At that Aoife looked about her, and Cuchulain took a sudden hold of her, and lifted her on his shoulders, and brought her down to where the army was, and laid her on the ground, and held his sword to her breast, and she begged for her life, and he gave it to her. And after that she made peace with Scathach, and bound herself by sureties not to go against her again. And she gave her love to Cuchulain; and out of that love great sorrow came afterwards.

And as Cuchulain was going home by the narrow path, he met an old hag, and she blind of the left eye. She asked him to leave room for her to pass by, but he said there was no room on that path, unless he would throw himself down the great sea cliff that was on the one side of it. But she asked him again to leave the road to her, and he would not refuse, and he dropped down the cliff, with only his one hand keeping a hold of the path. Then she came up, and as she passed him, she gave a hit of her foot at his hand, the way he would leave his hold and drop into the sea. But at that, he gave a leap up again on the path, and struck off the hag's head. For she was Ess Enchenn, the mother of the last three warriors that had fallen by him, and it was to destroy him she had come out to meet him, for she knew that under his rules of championship, he would make way for her when she asked it.

After that, he stayed for another while with Scathach, until he had learned all the arts of war and all the feats of a champion; and then a message came to him to come back to his own country, and he bade her farewell. And Scathach told him what would happen him in the time to come, for she had the Druid gift; and she told him there were great dangers before him, and that he would have to fight against great armies, and he alone; and that he would scatter his enemies, so that his name would come again to Alban; but that his life would not be long, for he would die in his full strength.

Then Cuchulain went on board his ship to set out for Ireland and in the same ship with him were Lugaid and Luan, the two sons of Loch, and Ferbaeth and Larin and Ferdiad, and Durst, son of Derb.

On the night of Samhain they came to the island of Rechrainn, and Cuchulain left his ship and came to the strand. And there he heard a sound of crying, and he saw a beautiful young girl, and she sitting there alone. He asked her who she was, and what ailed her, and she said she was Devorgill, daughter of the king of Rechrainn, and that every year he was forced to pay a heavy tax to the Fomor, and this year, when he could not pay it, they made him leave her there near the sea, till they would come and bring her away in place of it.

"Where do these men come from?" said Cuchulain. "From that far country over there," she said, "and let you not stop here or they will see you when they come." But Cuchulain would not leave her, and presently three fierce men of the Fomor landed in the bay, and made straight for the spot where the girl was. But before they had time to lay a hand on her, Cuchulain leaped on them and he killed the three of them, one after the other. The last man wounded him in the arm, and the girl tore a strip from her dress, and gave it to him to bind round the wound. And then she ran to her father's house and told him all that had happened. After that Cuchulain came to the king's house, like any other guest, and his companions with him, and Conall Cearnach and Laegaire Buadach were there before them, where they had been sent from Emain Macha to collect tribute. For at that time a tribute was paid to Ulster from the islands of the Galls.

And they were all talking about the escape Devorgill had, and some were boasting that it was they themselves had saved her, for she could not be sure who it was had come to her, because of the dusk of the evening. Then there was water brought for them all to wash before they would go to the feat; and when it came to Cuchulain's turn to bare his arms, she knew by the strip of her dress that was bound about it, that it was he had saved her. "I will give the girl to you as your wife," said the king, "and I myself will pay her wedding portion." "Not so," said Cuchulain, "for I must make no delay in going back to Ireland."

So then he made his way back to Emain Macha, and he told his whole story and all that had happened him. And as soon as he had rested from the journey, he set out to look for Emer at her father's house. But Forgall and his sons had heard he was come home again, and they had made the place so strong, and they kept so good a watch round it, that for the whole length of a year he could not get so much as a sight of her.

It was one day at that time he went down to the shore of Lough Cuan with Laeg, his chariot-driver, and with Lugaid. And when they were there, they saw two birds coming over the sea. Cuchulain put a stone in his sling, and made a cast at the birds, and hit one of them. And when they came to where the birds were, they found in their place two women, and one of them the most beautiful in the world and they were Devorgill, daughter of the king of Rechrainn, that had come from her own country to find Cuchulain, and her serving-maid along with her; and it was Devorgill that Cuchulain had hit with the stone. "It is a bad thing you have done, Cuchulain," she said, "for it was to find you I came, and now you have wounded me." Then Cuchulain put his mouth to the wound and sucked out the stone and the blood along with it. And he said, "You cannot be my wife, for I have drunk your blood. But I will give you to my comrade," he said, "to Lugaid of the Red Stripes." And so it was done, and Lugaid gave her his love all through her life, and when she died he died of the grief that was on him after her.

After that, Cuchulain got his scythe chariot made ready, and he set out again for Forgall's dun. And when he got there, he leaped with his hero leap over the three walls, so that he was inside the court, and there he made three attacks, so that eight men fell from each attack, but one escaped in every troop of nine; that is the three brothers of Emer, Seibur and Ibur and Catt. And Forgall made a leap from the wall of the court to escape Cuchulain, and he fell in the leap and got his death from the fall.

And then Cuchulain went out again, and brought Emer with him and her foster sister, and their two loads of gold and silver.

And then they heard cries all around them, and Scenmend, Forgall's sister, came following them with her men, and came up with them at the ford; and Cuchulain killed her in the fight, and it is from that it is called the Ford of Scenmend. And her men came up with them again at the next ford, and he killed a hundred of them there. "It is a great thing you have done," said Emer. 'You have killed a hundred strong armed men; and Glondath, the Ford of Deeds, is the name that shall be on it for ever." Then they came to Raeban, the white field, and he gave three great angry blows to his enemies there, so that streams of blood went over it on every side. "This white hill is a hill of red sods to-day, through your work, Cuchulain," said Emer. And from that time it has been called the Ford of the Sods.

Then they were overtaken again at another ford on the Boinne, and Emer quitted the chariot, and Cuchulain followed his enemies along the banks, so that the sods were flying from the feet of the horses across the ford northward; and then he turned and followed them northward, so that the sods flew over the ford southward. And from that it is called Ath na Imfuait, the Ford of the Two Clods. And at each of these fords Cuchulain killed a hundred, and so he kept his word to Emer, and he came safely out of it all, and they came to Emain Mancha, toward the fall of night.

And then Cuchulain was given the headship of the young men of Ulster, of the warriors, the poets, the trumpeters, the musicians, the three pipers, the three jesters to say sharp words; the three distributors of fame. It is of them the poet spoke, and set out their names, and it is what he said:—"The young men of Ireland, when they were in the Red Branch, it is they were the fairest of all hosts." And of Cuchulain he said, "He is as hard as steel and as bright, Cuchulain, the victorious son of Dechtire."

And then Cuchulain took Emer for his wife, after that long courting, and all the hardships he had gone through. And he brought her into the House of the Red Branch, and Conchubar and all the chief men of Ulster gave her a great welcome.

It was at Emain Macha, that was sometimes called Macha of the Spears, Conchubar, the High King, had the Eachrais Uladh, the Assembly House of Ulster, and it was there he had his chief palace.

A fine palace it was, having three houses in it, the Royal House, and the Speckled House, and the House of the Red Branch.

In the Royal House there were three times fifty rooms, and the walls were made of red yew, with copper rivets. And Conchubar's own room was on the ground, and the walls of it faced with bronze, and silver up above, with gold birds on it, and their heads set with shining carbuncles; and there were nine partitions from the fire to the wall, and thirty feet the height of each partition. And there was a silver rod before Conchubar with three golden apples on it, and when he shook the rod or struck it, all in the house would be silent.

It was in the House of the Red Branch were kept the heads and the weapons of beaten enemies, and in the Speckled House were kept the swords and the shields and the spears of the heroes of Ulster. And it was called the Speckled House because of the brightness and the colours of the hilts of the swords, and the bright spears, green or grey, with rings and bands of silver and gold about them, and the gold and silver that were on the rims and the bosses of the shields, and the brightness of the drinking-cups and the horns.

It was the custom with the men of the Red Branch, if one of them heard a word of insult, to get satisfaction for it on the moment. He would get up in the feasting hall itself, and make his attack; and it was to prevent that, the arms were kept together in one place. Conchubar's shield, the Ochain, that is the Moaning One, was hanging there; whenever Conchubar would be in danger, it would moan, and all the shields of Ulster would moan in answer to it. And Conall Cearnach's Lam-tapaid, the Quick Hand, was in it. And Fergus's Leochain, and Dubthach's

Uathach, and Laegaire's Nithach; and Sencha's Sciath-arglan and Celthair's Comla Catha, the Gate of Battle, and a great many others along with these.

And Cuchulain's shield was there, and the way he got it was this.

There was a law made by the men of the Red Branch that the carved device on every shield should be different from every other. And the name of the man that used to make the shields was Mac Enge. Cuchulain went to him after coming back from Scathach, and bade him make a shield, and put some new device on it. "I cannot do that," said Mac Enge, "for all I can do I have done already on the shields of the men of Ulster." There was anger on Cuchulain then, and he threatened Mac Enge with death, was he, or was he not, under Conchubar's protection.

Mac Enge was greatly put out at what had happened, and he was thinking what was best for him to do, when he saw a man coming towards him. "There is some trouble on you," he said. "There is, indeed," said the shield-maker, "for I am in danger of death unless I make a shield for Cuchulain." "Clear out your work-shop," said the strange man, "and spread ashes a foot deep on the floor."

And when this was done, Mac Enge saw the man coming over the outer wall to him again, and a fork in his hand, and it having two prongs. And he put one of the prongs in the ashes, and with the other he made the pattern that was to be cut on Cuchulain's shield. And so Cuchulain got it, and the name it had was Dubhan, the Black One.

And as to Cuchulain's sword that was hanging alone with the shield, its name was the Cruaidin Cailidcheann; that is, the Hard, Hard Headed. And it had a hilt of gold with ornaments of silver, and if the point of the sword would be bent back to its hilt, it would come as straight as a rod back again. It would cut a hair on the water, or it would cut a hair off the head without touching the skin, or it would cut a man in two, and the one half of him would not miss the other for some time after.

And as to Cuchulain's spear, the Gae Bulg, whether it was or was not kept in the Speckled House, this is the way he came by it. There were two monsters fighting in the sea one time, the Curruid and the Coinchenn their names were, and at the last the Coinchenn made for the strand to escape, but the other followed him and killed him there.

Then Bolg, son of Buan, a champion of the eastern part of the world, found the bones of the Coinchennm on the strand, and he made a spear with them. And he gave it to a great fighting man, the son of Jubar, and it went from one to another till it came to the woman-champion, Aoife. And Aoife gave it to Cuchulain, and he brought it to Ireland. And it was with it he killed his own son, and his friend Ferdiad afterwards.

There were three hundred and sixty-five men belonging to Cuchulain's house-hold; and one among them served the supper every night, and when the year came round, he would take his turn again. And it is not a small thing that supper was:

beef and pork and beer for every man. But the three days before and the three days after Samhain, the chief men of Ulster used to come together, and to eat together in Conchubar's palace, and Conchubar himself took charge of the supper at that feast; for every man that did not come on Samhain night, his wits would go from him, and it was as well to make his grave and to put his memorial stone over him the next day.

And there were a great many poets and learned men used to come to Conchubar's court, for they were made welcome there when they were driven out of other places. Cathbad, the Druid, was among them, and his son, bright-faced Geanann, and Sencha, and Ferceirtne, that was very learned, and Morann, that could not give a wrong judgment, for if he did, the collar round his neck would tighten; and many others.

Adhna was the chief poet there at one time, and after he died Athairne was made chief poet of Ulster in his place. But Neidhe, Adhna's son, came back from Alban, expecting to be made chief poet. And it was the waves of the sea, breaking on the strand where he was, that told him of his father's death. And when he got to Emain, he went into the palace and sat down in the chief poet's chair, that he found empty, and put the chief poet's cloak about him, that was lying there, and that was ornamented with beautiful birds' feathers. And then Athairne came in and found him there, and they began an argument with one another in the language of poetry, and Conchubar and all the chief men of Ulster came in to listen to them, and some of the other poets joined in the argument.

And Neidhe proved himself to be the best, but if he did, as soon as it was given in his favour, he came down from the chair, and took off the cloak and put it about Athairne, and said that, his father being dead, he would take him for his master.

So Athairne was chief poet, but no one had any great liking for him, for he was too fond of riches, and was no way hospitable or open-handed. It was he went to Midhir, and brought away secretly his three cranes of churlishness and denial, the way none of the men of Ireland would get a good reception if they would come to ask anything at his house. "Do not come, do not come," the first crane would say. "Get away, get away," the second would say. "Go past the house, past the house," the third would say to any one that came near it.

It was after that argument between Athairne and Neidhe, king Conchubar made a change in the laws. For it had been a law that no one that was not a poet could be a judge. But the language of the poets was hard to understand, and the king was vexed when he could understand but a small part of their argument. So he said that from that time out, any fitting man might be made judge, was he or was he not a poet. And all the people agreed to that, and the new law turned out very well in the end.

And the twelve chief heroes of Conchubar's Red Branch were these: Fergus, son of Rogh; Conall Cearnach, the Victorious; Laegaire Buadach, the Battle-Winner;

Cuchulain, son of Sualtim; Eoghan, son of Durthact, chief of Fernmaige; Celthair, son of Uthecar; Dubthach Doel Uladh, the Beetle of Ulster; Muinremar, son of Geirgind; Cethern, son of Findtain; and Naoise, Ainnle, and Ardan, the three sons of Usnach.

CHAPTER IV

Bricriu's Feast, and the War of Words of the Women of Ulster

Bricriu of the Bitter Tongue made a great feast one time for Conchubar, son of Ness, and for all the chief men of Ulster. He was the length of a year getting the feast ready, and he built a great house to hold it in at Dun-Rudraige. He built it in the likeness of the House of the Red Branch in Emain, but it was entirely beyond all the buildings of that time in shape and in substance, in plan and in ornament, in pillars and in facings, in doors and in carvings, so that it was spoken of in all parts. It was on the plan of the drinking-hall at Emain it was made inside, and it having nine divisions from hearth to wall, and every division faced with bronze that was overlaid with gold, thirty feet high. In the front part of the hall there was a royal seat made for Conchubar, high above all the other seats of the house. It was set with carbuncles and other precious stones of all colours, that shone like gold and silver, so that they made the night the same as the day; and round about it were the twelve seats of the twelve heroes of Ulster.

Good as the material was, the work done on it was as good. It took six horses to bring home every beam, and the strength of six men to fix every pole, and thirty of the best skilled men in Ireland were ordering it and directing it.

Then Bricriu made a sunny parlour for himself, on a level with Conchubar's seat and the seats of the heroes of valour, and it had every sort of ornament, and windows of glass were put on every side of it, the way he could see the hall from his seat, for he knew the men of Ulster would not let him stop inside.

When he had finished building the hall and the sunny parlour, and had furnished them with quilts and coverings, beds and pillows, and with a full supply of meat and drink, so that nothing was wanting, he set out for Emain Macha to see Conchubar and the chief men of Ulster.

It happened that day they were all gathered together at Emain Macha, and they made him welcome, and they put him to sit beside Conchubar, and he said to Conchubar and to them all, "Come with me to a feast I have made ready." "I am willing to go," said Conchubar, "if the men of Ulster are willing."

But Fergus, son of Rogh, and the others, said: "We will not go, for if we do, our dead will be more than our living, after Bricriu has set us to quarrel with one another." "It will be worse for you if you do not come," said Bricriu. "What will you do if they do not go with you?" said Conchubar. "I will stir up strife," said Bricriu, "between the kings and the leaders, and the heroes of valour, and the swordsmen, till every one makes an end of the other, if they will not come with me to use my feast." "We will not go for the sake of pleasing you," said Conchubar. "I will stir up anger between father and son, so that they will be the death of one another," said Bricriu; "if I fail in doing that, I will make a quarrel between mother and daughter; if that fails, I will set the women of Ulster one against the other, so that they will come to deadly blows, and be striking one another on the breast." "It is better for us to go," said Fergus. "Let us consult with the chief men of Ulster," said Sencha, son of Ailell. "Some harm will come of it," said Conchubar, "if we do not consult together against this man."

On that, all the chief men met together in council, and it is what Sencha advised. "It is best for you to get securities from Bricriu, as you have to go along with him; and put eight swordsmen around him, to make him leave the house as soon as he has laid out the feast for you." So Ferbenn Ferbeson, son of Conchubar, brought the answer to Bricriu. "I am satisfied to do that," said Bricriu. With that the men of Ulster set out from Emain, host, troop, and company under king, chief, and leader, and it was a good march they all made together to Dun-Rudraige.

Then Bricriu set himself to think how with the securities that were given for him, he could best manage to set the men of Ulster one against the other. After he had been thinking a while, he went over to Laegaire Buadach, son of Connad, son of Iliath. "All good be with you, Laegaire, Winner of Battles, you mighty mallet of Bregia, you hot hammer of Meath, you flame-red thunderbolt, what hinders you from getting the championship of Ireland for ever?" "If I want it I can get it," said Laegaire. "You will be head of all the champions of Ireland," said Bricriu, "if you do as I advise." "I will do that, indeed," said Laegaire.

"Well," said Bricriu, "if you can get the Champion's Portion at the feast in my house, the championship of Ireland will be yours for ever. And the Champion's Portion of my house is worth fighting for," he said, "for it is not the portion of a fool's house. There goes with it a vat of good wine, with room enough in it to hold three of the brave men of Ulster; with that a seven-year-old boar, that has been fed since it was born on no other thing but fresh milk, and fine meal in spring-time, curds and sweet milk in summer, the kernel of nuts and wheat in harvest, beef and broth in the winter; with that a seven-year-old bullock that never had in its mouth, since it was a sucking calf, either heather or twig tops, but only sweet milk and herbs, meadow hay and corn; along with that, five-score wheaten cakes made with honey. That is the Champion's Portion of my house. And since you are yourself the best hero among the men of Ulster," he said, "it is but right to give it to you; and that is my wish, you to get it. And at the end of the day, when the feast is spread out, let your chariot-driver rise up, and it is to him the Champion's Portion will be given." "There will be dead men if that is not done," said Laegaire. Then Bricriu laughed, for he liked to hear that.

When he had done stirring up Laegaire Buadach, he went on till he met with Conall Cearnach. "May good be with you, Conall," he said. "It is you are the hero of fights and of battles; it is many victories you have won up to this over the heroes of Ulster. By the time the men of Ulster cross the boundary of a strange country, it is three days and three nights in advance of them you are, over many a ford and river; it is you who protect their rear coming back again, so that no enemy can get past you or through you, or over you. What would hinder you from being given the Champion's Portion of Emain to hold for ever?" Great as was his treachery with Laegaire, he showed twice as much in what he said to Conall Cearnach.

When he had satisfied himself that Conall was stirred up to a quarrel, he went on to Cuchulain. "May all good be with you, Cuchulain, conqueror of Bregia, bright banner of the Lifé, darling of Emain, beloved by wives and by maidens, Cuchulain is no nickname for you to-day, for you are the champion of the men of Ulster: it is you keep off their great quarrels and disputes; it is you get justice for every man of them; it is you have what all the men of Ulster are wanting in; all the men of Ulster acknowledge that your bravery, your valour, and your deeds are beyond their own. Why, then, would you leave the Champion's Portion for some other one of the men of Ulster, when not one of them would be able to keep it from you?" "By the god of my people," said Cuchulain, "whoever comes to try and keep it from me will lose his head." With that Bricriu left them and followed after the army, as if he had done nothing to stir up a quarrel at all.

After that they came to the feasting-house and went in, and every one took his place—king, prince, landowner, swordsman, and young fighting man. One half of the house was set apart for Conchubar and his following, and the other half was kept for the wives of the heroes of Ulster.

And there were attending on Conchubar in the front part of the house Fergus, son of Rogh; Celthair, son of Uthecar; Eoghan, son of Durthact; the two sons of the king, Fiacha and Fiachaig; Fergus, son of Leti; Cuscraid, the Stutterer of Macha; Sencha, son of Ailell; the three sons of Fiachach, that is Rus and Dare and Imchad; Muinremar, son of Geirgind; Errge Echbel; Amergin, son of Ecit; Mend, son of Slchah; Dubthach Doel Uladh, the Beetle of Ulster; Feradach Find Fectnach; Fedelmid, son of Ilair Cheting; Furbaide Ferbende; Rochad, son of Atheon; Laegaire Buadach; Conall Cearnach; Cuchulain; Conrad, son of Mornai; Erc, son of Fedelmid; Iollan, son of Fergus; Fintan, son of Nial; Cethern, son of Fintan; Factna, son of Sencad; Conla the False; Ailell the Honey-Tongued; the chief men of Ulster, with the young men and the song-makers.

While the feast was being spread out, the musicians and players made music for them. As soon as Bricriu had spread the feast with its well-tasting, savoury meats, he was ordered by his sureties to leave the hall on the moment; and they rose up with their drawn swords in their hands to put him out. So he and his followers went out, and when he was on the threshold of the house he turned and called out, "The Champion's Portion of my house is not the portion of a fool's house; let it be given to whoever you think the best hero of Ulster." And with that he left them.

Then the distributers rose up to divide the food, and the chariot-driver of Laegaire Buadach, Sedlang, son of Riangabra, rose up and said to them, "Let you give the Champion's Portion to Laegaire, for he has the best right to it of all the young heroes of Ulster."

Then Id, son of Riangabra, chariot-driver to Conall Cearnach, rose up, and bade them to give it to his master. But Laeg, son of Riangabra, said, "It is to Cuchulain it must be brought; and it is no disgrace for all the men of Ulster to give it to him, for it is he is the bravest of you all." "That is not true," said Conall, and Laegaire said the same.

With that they got up upon the floor, and put on their shields and took hold of their swords, and they attacked and struck at one another till the one half of the hall was as if on fire with the clashing of swords and spears, and the other half was as white as chalk with the whiteness of the shields. There was fear on the whole gathering; all the men were put from their places, and there was great anger on Conchubar himself and on Fergus, son of Rogh, to see the injustice and the hardship of two men fighting against one, Conall and Laegaire both together attacking Cuchulain; but there was no one among the men of Ulster dared part them till Sencha spoke to Conchubar. "It is time for you to part these men," he said.

With that, Conchubar and Fergus came between them, and the fighters let their hands drop to their sides. "Will you do as I advise?" said Sencha. "We will do it," they said. "Then my advice is," said Sencha,"for this night to divide the Champion's Portion among the whole gathering, and after that to let it be settled according to the judgment of Ailell, king of Connaught, for it will be better for the men of Ulster, this business to be settled in Cruachan."

So with that they sat down to the feast again, and gathered round the fire and drank and made merry.

All this time Bricriu and his wife were in their upper room, and from there he had seen how things were going on in the great hall. And he began to search his mind how he could best stir up the women to quarrel with one another as he had stirred up the men. When he had done searching his mind, it just chanced as he could have wished, that Fedelm of the Fresh Heart came from the hall with fifty women after her, laughing and merry. Bricriu went to meet her. "All good be with you to-night, wife to Laegaire Buadach. Fedelm of the Fresh Heart is no nickname for you, with respect to your appearance and your wisdom and your family. Conchubar, king of Ulster, is of your kindred; Laegaire Buadach is your husband.

I would not think well of it that any of the women of Ulster should go before you into the hall, for it is at your heel that all the other women of Ulster should walk. If you go first into the hall to-night, you will be queen over them all for ever and ever."

Fedelm went on after that, the length of three ridges from the hall.

After that there came out Lendabair, the Favourite, daughter of Eoghan, son of Durthact, wife of Conall Cearnach.

Bricriu came over to her, and he said, "Good be with you, Lendabair; and that is no nickname, for you are the favourite and the darling of the men of the whole world, because of the brightness of your beauty. As far as your husband is beyond the whole world in bravery and in comeliness, so far are you before the women of Ulster." Great as his deceit was in what he said to Fedelm, it was twice as great in what he said to Lendabair.

Then Emer came out and fifty women after her. "Health be with you, Emer, daughter of Forgall Manach, wife of the best man in Ireland! Emer of the Beautiful Hair is no nickname for you; the kings and princes of Ireland are quarrelling with one another about you. So far as the sun outshines the stars of heaven, so far do you outshine the women of the whole world in form, and shape, and birth, in youth, and beauty, and nicety, in good name, and wisdom, and speech." However great his deceit was towards the other women, it was twice as much towards Emer.

The three women went on then till they met at one spot, three ridges from the house, but none of them knew that Bricriu had been speaking to the other. They set out then to go back to the house. Their walk was even and quiet and easy on the first ridge; hardly did one of them put her foot before the other. But on the next ridge their steps were closer and quicker; and when they came to the ridge next the house, it was hardly one of them could keep up with the other, so that they took up their skirts nearly to their knees, each one trying to get first into the hall, because of what Bricriu had said to them, that whoever would be first to enter the house, would be queen of the whole province. And such was the noise they made in their race, that it was like the noise of forty chariots coming. The whole palace shook, and all the men started up for their arms, striking against one another.

"Stop," said Sencha, "it is not enemies that are coming, it is Bricriu has set the women quarrelling. By the god of my people!" he said, "unless the hall is shut against them, those that are dead among us will be more than those that are living." With that the doorkeepers shut the doors. But Emer was quicker than the other women, and outran them, and put her back against the door, and called to the doorkeepers before the other women came up, so that the men rose up, each of them to open the door before his own wife, so that she might be the first to come within.

"It is a bad night this will be," said Conchubar; and he struck the silver rod he had in his hand against the bronze post of the hall, and they all sat down. "Quiet yourselves," said Sencha; "it is not a war of arms we are going to have here, it is a war of words." Each women then put herself under the protection of her husband outside, and then there followed the war of words of the women of Ulster.

Fedelm of the Fresh Heart was the first to speak, and it is what she said:

"The mother who bore me was free, noble, equal to my father in rank and in race; the blood that is in me is royal; I was brought up like one of royal blood. I am counted beautiful in form and in shape and in appearance; I was brought up to good behaviour, to courage, to mannerly ways. Look at Laegaire, my husband, and what his red hand does for Ulster. It was by himself alone its boundaries were kept from the enemies that were as strong as all Ulster put together; he is a defence and a protection against wounds; he is beyond all the heroes; his victories are greater than their victories. Why should not I, Fedelm, the beautiful, the lovely, the joyful, be the first to step into the drinking-hall to-night?"

Then Lendabair spoke, and it is what she said:

"I myself have beauty too, and good sense and good carriage; it is I should walk into the hall with free, even steps before all the women of Ulster.

"For my husband is pleasant Conall of the great shield, the Victorious; he is proud, going with brave steps up to the spears of the fight; he is proud coming back to me after it, with the heads of his enemies in his hands.

"He brings his hard sword into the battle for Ulster; he defends every ford or he destroys it to keep out the enemy; he is a hero will have a stone raised over him.

"The son of noble Amergin, who can speak against his courage or his deeds? It is Conall who leads the heroes.

"All eyes look on the glory of Lendabair; why would she not go first into the hall of the king?"

Then Emer spoke, and it is what she said:

"There is no woman comes up to me in appearance, in shape, in wisdom, there is no one comes up to me for goodness of form, or brightness of eye, or good sense, or kindness, or good behaviour.

"No one has the joy of loving or the strength of loving that I have; all Ulster desires me; surely I am a nut of the heart. If I were a light woman, there would not be a husband left to any of you to-morrow.

"And my husband is Cuchulain. It is he is not a bound that is weak; there is blood on his spear, there is blood on his sword, his white body is black with blood, his soft skin is furrowed with sword cuts, there are many wounds on his thigh.

"But the flame of his eye is turned westward; he is the strong protector; his chariot is red, its cushions are red; he fights from over the ears of horses, from over the breath of men; he leaps in the air like a salmon when he makes his hero leap; he does strange feats, the dark feat, the blind feat, the feat of nine; he breaks down armies in the hard fight; he saves the life of proud armies; he finds joy in the terror of the ignorant.

"Your fine heroes of Ulster are not worth a stalk of grass compared with my husband, Cuchulain, letting on to have a woman's sickness on them; he is like the clear red blood, they are like the scum and the leavings, worth no more than a stalk of grass.

"Your fine women of Ulster, they are shaped like cows and led like cows, when they are put beside the wife of Cuchulain."

When the men in the hall heard what the women said, Laegaire and Conall made a rush at the wall, and broke a plank out of it at their own height, to let their own wives in. But Cuchulain raised up that part of the house that was opposite to his place, so that the stars and the sky could be seen through the wall. By that opening Emer came in with the fifty women that waited on her, and with them the women that waited on the other two. None of the other women could be compared at all with Emer, and no one at all could be compared with her husband. And then Cuchulain let the wall he had lifted fall suddenly again, so that seven feet of it went into the ground, and the whole house shook, and Bricriu's upper room was laid flat in such a way that Bricriu himself and his wife were thrown into the dirt among the dogs. "My grief," cried Bricriu, "enemies are come in!" And he got up quickly and took a turn round, and he saw that the hall was now crooked and leaning entirely to one side. He clapped his hands together and went inside, but he was so covered with dirt that none of the Ulster people could know him, it was only by his way of speaking they made out who he was.

Then he said, from the middle of the floor, "It is a pity I ever made a feast for you, men of Ulster. My house is more to me than everything else I have. I put *geasa*, that is, bonds, on you, not to drink or to eat or to sleep till you leave my house the same way as you found it." At that, all the men of Ulster went out and tried to pull the house straight, but they did not raise it by so much as a hand's breadth.

"What are we to do?" they said. "There is nothing for you to do," said Sencha, "but to ask the man that pulled it crooked to set it straight again."

Upon that they bid Cuchulain to put the wall up straight again, and Bricriu said, "O king of the heroes of Ireland, unless you can set it up straight, there is no man in the world can do it." And all the men of Ulster begged and prayed of Cuchulain to settle the matter. And that they might not have to go without food or drink, Cuchulain rose up and tried to lift the house with a tug, and he failed. Anger came on him then, and the hero light shone about him, and he put out all his strength, and strained himself till a man's foot could find place between each of his ribs, and he lifted the house up till it was a straight as it was before. After that they enjoyed the feast, with the chief men on the one side round about Conchubar, High King of Ulster, and their wives on the other side—Fedelm of the Nine Shapes (nine shapes she could take on, and each shape more beautiful than the other), and Findchaem, daughter of Cathbad, wife of Amergin of the Iron Jaw, and Devorgill, wife of Lugaid of the Red Stripes, besides Emer, and Fedelm of the

Fresh Heart, and Lendabair; and it would be too long to count and to tell of all the other noble women besides.

There was soon a buzzing of words in the hall again, with the women praising their men, as if to stir up another quarrel between them. Then Sencha, son of Ailell, got up and shook his bell branch, and they all stopped to listen to him, and then to quiet the women he said:

"Have done with this word-fighting, lest you drive the men of Ulster to grow white-faced in the anger and the pride of battle with one another.

"It is through the fault of women the shields of men are broken, heroes go out to fight and struggle with one another in their anger.

"It is the folly of women brings men to do these things, to bruise what they cannot bind up again, to strike down what they cannot raise up again. Wives of heroes, keep yourself from this."

But Emer answered him, and it is what she said:

"It is right for me to speak, Sencha, and I the wife of the comely, pleasant hero, who is beyond all others in beauty, in wisdom, in speaking, since the learning that was easy to him is done with.

"No one can do his feats, the over-breath feat, the apple feat, the ghost feat, the screw feat, the cat feat, the red-whirling feat, the barbed-spear feat, the quick stroke, the fire of the mouth, the hero's cry, the wheel feat, the sword-edge feat; no one can throw himself against hard-spiked places the way he does.

"There is no one is his equal in youth, in form, in brightness, in birth, in mind, in voice, in bravery, in boldness, in fire, in skill; no one is his equal in hunting, in running, in strength, in victories, in greatness. There is no man to be found who can be put beside Cuchulain."

"If it is truth you are speaking, Emer," said Conall Caernach, "let this lad of feats stand up, that we may see them."

"I will not," said Cuchulain. "I am tired and broken to-day, I will do no more till after I have had food and sleep." It was true what he said for it was on that morning he had met with the Grey of Macha by the side of the grey lake at Slieve Fuad. When it came out of the lake, Cuchulain slipped his hands round the neck of the horse, and the two of them struggled and wrestled with one another, and in that way they went all round Ireland, till late in the day he brought the horse home to Emain. It was in the same way he got the Black Sanglain from the black lake of Sainglen.

And Cuchulain said: "To-day myself and the Grey of Macha have gone through the great plains of Ireland, Bregia of Meath, the seashore marsh of Muirthemne Macha, through Moy Medba, Currech Cleitech Cerna, Lia of Linn Locharn, Fer Femen Fergna, Curros Dommand, Ros Roigne, and Eo. And now I would sooner eat and sleep than do any other thing. But I swear by the gods my people swear by," he said, "I would be ready to fight with any man of you if I had but my fill of food and of sleep." "Well," said Bricriu, "this has gone on long enough. Let food and drink be brought, and let the women's war be put a stop to till the feast is done."

They did so, and it was a pleasant time they had till the end of three days and three nights.

CHAPTER V

The Championship of Ulster

After they were gone back to Emain after Bricriu's feast, a quarrel began between Conall and Laegaire and Cuchulain about the Champion's Portion, and Conchubar and the chief men of Ulster came between them to settle it. And Conchubar bade them to go to Cruachan in Connaught, to have the matter judged by Ailell and by Maeve. "And if that fails you," he said, "what you have to do is to go to Curoi, son of Daire, at Slieve Mis, in Munster. And it is a true judgment he will give, for he is just and fair-minded, his house is open to guests, his hand is good in battle, in leading he is a king. He will give you a right judgment, but it is only a brave man will ask it from him, for he is wise in all sorts of enchantments, and can do things that no other man can do."

"We will go first to Cruachan," said Cuchulain. "I agree to that," said Laegaire. "Let us go, then," said Conall Cearnach. "Let horses be brought, and your chariot yoked, Conall," said Cuchulain; "and go on the first." "I do not like that," said Conall. "That is no wonder," said Cuchulain, "for every one knows the awkwardness of your horses, and the unsteadiness of your chariot; it is so heavy that each of the wheels raises the sod on each side wherever it goes, the way that for the length of a year it is easy for the men of Ulster to know the track it has left after it."

"Do you hear that, Laegaire?" said Conall. "It is for you to go first." "Do not begin to mock at me," said Laegaire, "for I am good at crossing fords, and I am ready to go up and face a storm of spears before any man. But do not put me beside chariot kings till I practise going through hard and narrow places, and racing against single chariots, till the champion of a single chariot will be afraid to pass me."

With that Laegaire had his chariot yoked, and leaped into it. He drove over Magh da Gabal, the Plain of the Two Forks, over Bernaid na Foraire, the Gap of the Watch, over the Ford of Carpat Fergus, over the Ford of the Morrigu, to Caerthund Cluana da Dam, the Rowan Meadow of the Two Oxen, in the Fews of Firbuide; by the four ways, past Dundealgan, across Magh Slicech, the Peeled Plain, westward by Bregia. And it was not long till Conall Cearnach followed after him, and many of the chief men of Ulster with them.

374

But Cuchulain stayed behind the others, amusing the women of Ulster with his feats. He did nine feats with apples, nine with spears, and nine with knives, without ever letting one touch the other. And he took three times fifty needles from the women, and threw them up, one after the other, so that each needle went into the eye of the other, and in that way they were all joined together. Then he gave every woman her needle back into her own hand.

But Laeg, son of Riangabra, went to look for him, and reproached him, and said: "You pitiful splinter, your courage has gone from you! The Champion's Portion is lost to you, the men of Ulster have got to Cruachan before this." "I never thought of it, my Laeg," said Cuchulain; "but yoke the chariot for me now." So Laeg yoked it, and they set out on their journey. By that time the men of Ulster were come to Matgh Breagh, the Fine Meadow; but Cuchulain, after he was roused up by Laeg, travelled so fast, and the Grey of Macha and the Black Sainglen went racing in such a way with his chariot across the whole province of Conchubar, across Slieve Faud and the Plain of Bregia, that he came up with the others before they came to Cruachan.

The noise the whole troop made was so great, going at such speed as they did, that a great shaking came on Cruachan, and the arms·fell from the racks to the ground, and the whole of the dun began to shake, so that every man was trembling like a rush in a stream. On that Maeve said: "Since the day I first came to Cruachan I never before heard thunder, there being no clouds in the sky." Then Findabair of the Fair Eyebrows, daughter of Ailell and of Maeve, went up, for she had a bird's sight, to her sunny parlour over the great door of the fort, to tell them what was coming. "Dear mother," she said, "I see a chariot coming over the plain." "Tell me what is its appearance," said Maeve, "and the colour of its horses, and the appearance of the man that sits in it." "I see well," said Findabair, "the two horses that are in the chariot. Two fiery dappled greys, of the one colour, shape and goodness, having the one speed, keeping the one pace; their ears pricked, their heads high, their nostrils broad, foreheads broad, manes and tails curled, thin-sided, wide-chested, galloping together. The chariot is made of fine wood with wicker-work newly polished, the yoke curved, with silver ornaments on it; it has two black wheels, soft looped yellow reins. I see in the chariot a big stout man, with reddish yellow hair, with long forked beard. He has a soft purple coat about him, and it striped with bright gold. His bronze shield is edged with gold; there is a five-pronged javelin at his wrist, a cover of strange birds' feathers over his head."

"I know well who that man is," said Maeve, and it is what she said: "A companion of kings, an old bestower of victories, a storm of war, a flame of judgment, a long knife of victory that will cut us to pieces, mighty Laegaire of the Red Hand. His sword cuts through men as a knife cuts through a leek; his stroke is the back stroke of the wave to the land. And I swear by the gods my people swear by," she said, "if it is in anger, and for fighting Laegaire Buadach is coming at us, that as leeks are cut close to the ground with a sharp knife, the same way we will be cut down, as many of us as are in Cruachan, unless we smooth down his anger by giving in to everything he asks."

"Good mother," said Findabair, "I see another chariot as good as the first coming over the plain." "Tell me what is its appearance," said Maeve.

"I see," she said, "yoked to the chariot, on the one side a red horse, taking strong, high strides across fords and splashes, over banks and gaps, over plains and hollows, with the quickness of birds that the quick eye loses in following. On the other side a bay horse of great strength; it is at full speed he races over the plain, between stones and hard places; he finds no hindrance in the land of oaks, hurrying on his way. A chariot of fine wood with wicker-work, on two wheels of bright bronze; its pole bright with silver, its frame very high and creaking, having a curved, firm yoke, with looped yellow reins.

"In the chariot a fair man, with wavy, hanging hair; his face white and red, his vest clean and white, his cloak blue and crimson, his shield brown with yellow bosses, its edge worked with bronze. In his hand a bright spear; a cover of the feathers of strange birds over the wicker frame of his chariot."

"I know who that man is," said Maeve, and she said then: "The growing of a lion; a flame that can cut like a sharpened stone; he heaps head on head, battle on battle. As a trout is cut upon red sandstone, so would the son of Finchoem cut us if he came on us in anger.

"For, by the oath of my people," she said, "as a speckled fish is beaten upon a shining red stone with iron rods, so would we be broken by Conall Cearnach, if he came against us."

"I see another chariot coming over the plain," said Findabair. "Tell me what its appearance is," said Maeve. "I see two horses of the one size and beauty, the one fierceness and speed, with ears pricked, heads high, spirited and powerful, with fine nostrils, wide foreheads, mane and tail curled, leaping together. The one grey, handsome, with broad thighs, eager, leaping, thundering and trampling. As he goes, his fierce hoofs throw up sods of earth like a flock of swift birds after him. As he gallops on his way, he breathes out a blast of hot breath, a fire comes from his curbed jaws. The other, dark, small-headed, well-shaped, broad-hoofed, thin-sided, high-couraged, broad-backed, sure-footed spirited; he takes long strides in the race; he leaps over streams, he throws off heaviness, he crosses the plains of the middle valley. They come together with fast, joyful steps, moving over the plain like a swift mountain mist, or like the speed of a hill hind, or like a hare on level ground, or like the rushing of a loud wind in winter.

"The chariot is of fine wood with wicker-work, having two iron wheels, a bright silver pole with bronze ornaments, a frame very high and creaking streng-thened with iron, a curved yoke overlaid with gold, two soft looped yellow reins.

"I see in the chariot a dark, sad man, comeliest of the men of Ireland. A pleated crimson tunic about him, fastened at the breast with a brooch of inlaid gold; a long-sleeved linen cloak on him with a white hood embroidered with flame-red gold. His eyebrows as black as the blackness of a spit, seven lights in his eyes, seven colours about his head, love and fire in his look. Across his knees there lies a gold-hilted sword, there is a blood-red spear ready to his hand, a sharp-tempered blade with a shaft of wood. Over his shoulders a crimson shield with a rim of silver, overlaid with shapes of beasts in gold.

"There is before him in the chariot a driver, a very thin, tall, freckled man; very bright red hair, kept back from his face with a golden thread, a cup of gold at each side of his head. A short cloak about him with sleeves opening at the two elbows; in his hand a goad of red gold to guide his horses."

"That is truly a drop before a downpour," said Maeve. "I know well who that man is." And it is what she said: "Like the sound of an angry sea, like a great moving wave, with the madness of a wild beast that is vexed, he leaps through his enemies in the crash of battle, they hear their death in his shout. He heaps deed upon deed, head upon head; he is a name to be put in songs. As fresh malt is ground in the mill, so shall we be ground by Cuchulain.

"For I swear by the oath of my people," she said, "that as a mill of ten spokes grinds very hard malt, so he, with only himself, would grind us to dust and to gravel, if we had the whole province with us, unless his anger and his heat go down.

"And what way are the rest of the men of Ulster coming?" she said. And Findabair answered her, and it is what she said: "Hand to hand, arm to arm, side to side, shoulder to shoulder, wheel to wheel, axle to axle, that is the way they are coming. Their horses are coming on us like thunder on the roof, like heavy waves stirred by the storm; the trampling of their feet makes the earth shake under them."

And Maeve said, "Let our women be ready before them with vats of cold water; let the beds be made ready, bring the best of food, the best of ale. Open the courtyard, have a welcome before them, and surely they will not harm us."

Then Maeve went out by the high door of the dun into the courtyard, and three times fifty young girls attending her, with three vats of cold water to cool the heat of the three heroes in front of the rest. And she gave them their choice, would each man have a house for himself, or would they have one house for the three? "A house for each to himself," said Cuchulain. And when the rest of the men of Ulster came, Ailell and Maeve with their whole household went out and bade them welcome. "We are well pleased with the welcome," said Sencha for them.

After that, they all came into the fort and into the palace. They went round from one door to the other and there was room for them all, and the musicians were playing music while everything was being made ready. And Conchubar, and Fergus, son of Rogh, were in Ailell's division, with nine others along with them, and there was a great feast made ready then, and they stopped there the length of three days and three nights.

At the end of that time Ailell asked Conchubar what was the business that had brought them there. And Sencha told him the whole story, about the quarrel of the women as to who should walk first, and the quarrel of their husbands for the Champion's Portion. "And they were not satisfied to be judged by any one but yourself," he said. Ailell did not seem to be well pleased at that. "Indeed, it was no friend of mine that left this judgment on me," he said. "There is no better judge than yourself," said Sencha. "Well," said Ailell, "you must give me time to think upon it." "Do not make too much delay," said Sencha, "for we cannot spare our heroes long from us." "Three days and three nights will be enough for me," said Ailell. "That much will not break friendship," said Sencha.

With that the men of Ulster went home to Emain, leaving Laegaire and Conall and Cuchulain to be judged by Ailell, and they left their blessing with Ailell and with Maeve, and their curse with Bricriu, because it was he had first started the quarrel.

That night the three heroes were given as good a feast as before, but they were put to eat it in a room by themselves. When night came on, three enchanted monsters, with the shape of cats, were let out from the cave that was in the hill of the Sidhe at Cruachan, to attack them. When Conall and Laegaire saw them, they got up into the rafters, leaving their food after them, and there they stayed till morning. Cuchulain did not leave his place, but when one of the monsters came to attack him, he gave a blow of his sword at its head; but the sword slipped off as if from a stone. Then the monster stayed quiet, and Cuchulain sat there through the night watching it. With the break of day the cats were gone, and Ailell came in and saw what way the three heroes were. "Are you not satisfied to give the Championship to Cuchulain, after this?" he said. "We are not," said Conall and Laegaire; "it is not against beasts we are used to fight, but against men."

Then Maeve said to them, "Go and spend the night with my foster-father, Ercol, and his wife Garmna. So they went, but first they were given their choice of food for their horses. Conall and Laegaire chose oats two years old for theirs, but Cuchulain chose barley grain for his. Then they set out, racing all the way, and Cuchulain winning the race.

Ercol and Garmna bade them welcome, and they knew it was to try them they had been sent there, so they sent them out that night, one after the other, to fight with the witches of the valley.

Laegaire went first, but he could not stand against them, and he came back, and left his arms and his clothes with them.

Then Conall went, and he was driven back, and left his spear with them, but he brought his sword that was his best weapon away with him.

Then Cuchulain went down into the valley and the witches screamed at him and attacked him, and he and they fought together till his spear was in splinters, his shield broken and his clothes torn off him. The witches were beating him and getting the better of him, but Laeg saw it, and he called out. "O Cuchulain," he said, "you poor coward, you squinting clown! Your courage is gone from you, witches to be beating you!" Then great anger came on Cuchulain, and he turned on the witches and cut and gashed them till the valley was filled with their blood, and he brought away their cloaks of battle with him, and went back to the house where his comrades were. And Garmna and her daughter Buan made much of him and bade him welcome.

They slept there that night, and the next day Ercol challenged them to come one by one, each man with his horse, to fight against himself and his horse. Laegaire was the first to go against him, and his horse was killed by Ercol's horse, and he himself was overcome by Ercol, so that he took to flight, and did not stop till he got back to Cruachan, and he brought the story there that both his companions had been killed by Ercol. Conall was the next to run away, after his horse being killed by Ercol's horse; and his servant Rathand was drowned in the river as he ran, and it takes its name after him, Snam Rathand, from that day.

But the Grey of Macha killed Ercol's horse, and Cuchulain put down Ercol and tied him behind his chariot and set out for Cruachan. And Buan, Garmna's daughter, ran out after the chariot for love of Cuchulain to follow him. And she knew the track of his chariot, for it was no roundabout track it used to take, but to be breaking through gaps or going over them; and in following it at last she gave a great leap and fell, and her forehead struck against a rock, and she died; and it is from this the place was given the name of Buan's Grave.

And when Conall and Cuchulain get back to Cruachan, they found the people of the dun keening them, for by the report Laegaire brought, they were sure they had been killed.

Then Ailell went to his inner room, and leaned his back against the wall, for he was not quiet in his mind, and he knew there was danger in whatever judgment he might give; and he had not eaten or slept for three days and three nights. Then Maeve said to him, "It is a coward you are, and if you do not settle this matter I will settle it myself." "It is hard for me to give judgment," said Ailell, "it is a misfortune for any one to have to do it." "It is easy enough," said Maeve, "for Laegaire and Conall Cearnach are as different as bronze and silver, and Conall Cearnach and Cuchulain are as different as silver and red gold."

After a while, when Maeve had searched her mind, Laegaire Buadach was called to her. "Welcome, Laegaire Buadach," she said, "it is right for you to have the Champion's Portion. We give you the headship of the heroes of Ireland from this out, and the Champion's Portion, and along with that this cup of bronze, having a bird in raised silver on the bottom. Take it with you as a token of the judgment, but let no one see it till you come to Conchubar and his Red Branch at the end of the day. When the Champion's Portion is set out, then, bring out your cup in the presence of all the great men of Ulster, and not one of them will dispute it with you any more, for they will know by this token that the Championship has been given to you." With that, the cup was given to him with its full of rich wine, and he drank it off at a draught. "Now you have the Championship," said Maeve; "and I wish you may enjoy it a hundred years at the head of all Ulster."

So Laegaire left her, and Conall Cearnach was called up to the queen. "Welcome, Conall Cearnach," she said; "it is right for us to give you the Champion's Portion, and a silver cup along with it, having a bird on the bottom in raised gold." And she said the same to him as she had said to Laegaire before.

Then Conall went away, and a messenger was sent to bring Cuchulain. "Come up to speak with the king and queen," said the messenger.

Cuchulain was playing chess at the time with Laeg, his chariot-driver. "I am not a fool to be mocked at," he said, and he hurled one of the chessmen at the messenger, and hit him between the eyes, so that it is hardly he could get back to Ailell and Maeve.

"By my word," said Maeve, "this Cuchulain is hard to deal with." And then she came down herself to Cuchulain, and put her two arms round his neck. "Give your flattery to some other one," said Cuchulain.

But Maeve said, "Great son of Ulster, flame of the heroes of Ireland, there is no flattery in our mind when it is you we have to do with. For if all the heroes of Ireland should come here, it is to you we would give the Champion's Portion, for as to bravery and a great name, and as to youth and great deeds, it is well-known that you are far beyond all the men of Ireland."

Cuchulain rose up then, and went with Maeve into the palace, and Ailell gave him a great welcome. And he was given a gold cup full of wine, and it having on the bottom of it a bird in precious stones. "Now, you have the Championship," said Maeve, "and it is my wish you may enjoy it a hundred years at the head of all the heroes of Ulster." "And besides that," Ailell and Maeve said, "it is our judgment, that as much as you are beyond the heroes of Ulster, so far is your wife beyond their wives. And we think it right that she should walk before all the women of Ulster when they go together into the drinking-hall."

Then Cuchulain drank at one draught the full of the cup, and bade farewell to the king and the queen and the whole household. And he went till he came to Emain Macha at the end of the day. And there was no one among the men of Ulster would venture to ask news of any of the three until the time came to eat and to drink in the great hall.

When the feast was laid out, they all stopped their arguing and their talking, and gave themselves up to eating and to enjoyment. It was Sualtim, son of Roig, father of Cuchulain, was attending the feast that night, and Conchubar's great vat had been filled for it. The distributers began serving out the meat, but at first they kept back the Champion's Portion. Then Dubthach of the Chafter Tongue said, "Why is not the Champion's Portion given to one of these three heroes that are come back from Cruachan? They must surely have brought some token with them, that we may know which one is to have it."

Upon that, Laegaire Buadach rose up and held out the bronze cup with the silver bird on it. "The Champion's Portion is mine," he said, "and no one can dispute it with me."

"That is not so," said Conall Cearnach; "here is my token. Yours is a bronze cup but mine is a silver cup. You see by the difference in them it is to me the Champion's Portion belongs."

"It belongs to neither of you," said Cuchulain, and he rose up and he said, "It was only to deceive you and to keep up the quarrel between us, the king and queen we went to gave you those. It is to me the Champion's Portion belongs, for you see my token, that it is far above the others."

With that he lifted high up the cup of red gold, with the bird on it of precious stones, and all the men in the feasting-hall saw it. "It is I myself that will get the Championship," he said, "if I get fair play." "It is yours indeed," said Conchubar, and Fergus, and all the chief men. "It is yours by the judgment of Ailell and Maeve." "I swear by the oath of my people," said Laegaire, "that the cup you have with you was not given to you, but bought. You gave riches and treasures for it to Ailell and Maeve, the way the Championship would not go to any other person; but by my hand of valour," he said, "that judgment shall not stand."

Then, with their swords drawn, they sprang at one another, but Conchubar went between them, and then they let down their hands and sheathed their swords. "It is best," said Sencha, "for you to go to Curoi for judgment." "We agree to that," said they.

So on the morning of the morrow, the three—Cuchulain, Conall, and Laegaire—set out for Curoi's dun. At the gate of the dun they unyoked their chariots, and they went into the courtyard, and Blanad, daughter of Mind, Curoi's wife, gave them a good welcome. Curoi was not at home that night, but knowing, by his enchantments, they would come, he had left instructions with his wife how to entertain them; and she did according to his wish, giving them water for washing, and drinks for refreshing, and beds of the best, so that they were well satisfied.

When bedtime came, Blanad told them they were each to take a night to watch the fort, till Curoi would come back. "And it is what he said, that you should take your turn according to age."

Now in whatever part of the world Curoi was, he made a spell every night over the dun, so that it went round like a mill, and no entrance could be found in it after the setting of the sun.

The first night Laegaire Buadach took the watch, for he was the oldest of the three. As he was keeping watch, towards the end of the night he saw a great shadow coming towards him from the sea westward. Very huge and ugly and terrible he thought it, and it took the shape of a giant and reached up to the sky, and the shining of the sea could be seen between its legs. It is how it came, its hands full of what had the appearance of stripped oaks, and each of them enough for a load for six horses; and he hurled one of them at Laegaire, but it went past him. He did this two or three times, but the beam did not reach either the skin or the shield of Laegaire. Then Laegaire hurled a spear at him, and it did not hit him.

He stretched out his hand then to Laegaire, and the length of it reached across the three ridges that were between them while they were throwing at one another, and he gripped hold of him. Big and strong as Laegaire was, he fitted like a child of a year old into his hand. The giant turned him round between his two palms as a chessman is turned in a groove, and then he threw him half dead over the wall of the fort, into a heap of mud. There was no opening there, and the people inside the dun thought he had leaped over from outside, as a challenge to the others to do the same.

There they stayed until the end of the day, and at the fall of night Conall went out to take the watch, as he was older than Cuchulain. Everything happened as it did to Laegaire the first night. And when the third night came, Cuchulain went into the seat of the watch.

When midnight was come he heard a noise, and by the light of the cold moon he saw nine grey shapes coming towards him over the marsh. "Stop," said Cuchulain, "who is there? If they are friends, let them not stir; if they are enemies, let them come on." Then they raised a great shout at him, and Cuchulain rushed at them and attacked them, so that the nine fell dead to the ground, and he cut their heads off and made a heap of them, and sat down again to keep the watch. Another nine and then another shouted at him, but he made an end of the three nines, and made one heap of their heads and their arms.

While he was watching on through the night, tired and down-hearted, he heard a sound rising from the lake, like the sound of a very heavy sea. However tired he was, his mind would not let him keep quiet, without going to see what was the cause of that great noise he heard. Then he saw a great worm coming up from the lake, and it raised itself into the air over him and made for the dun, and opened its mouth, and it seemed to him that one of the houses would fit into its gullet.

Then Cuchulain with one leap reached its head and put his arm round its neck, and stretched his hand across its gullet, and tore the monster's heart out and threw it to the ground. Then the beast fell down, and Cuchulain hacked it with his sword, and made little bits of it, and brought the head along with him to the heap of skulls.

He was sitting there, towards the break of day, worn out and discouraged, and he saw the great shadow shaped like a giant coming to him westward from the sea. "This is a bad night," he said. "It will be worse for you yet," said Cuchulain. Then he threw one of the beams at Cuchulain, but it passed by him, and he did that two or three times, but it did not reach either his shield or his skin. Then he stretched out his hand to grip Cuchulain as he did the others, but Cuchulain leaped his salmon leap at the head of the monster, with his drawn sword, and brought him down. "Life for life, Cuchulain," he said, and with that he vanished and was no more seen.

Then Cuchulain wondered to himself how his fellows had made their leap over the fort, for the wall was big and broad and high, and twice he tried it and failed. Then anger came on him, and he went a good way back and made a run, and with the dint of the anger that was on him, and the courage of his heart and of his mind, he hardly took the dew off the tips of the grass in the run, and he made one leap over the wall, and lit in the middle, at the door of the house. Then he went in through the door and gave a sigh. And Blanad, wife of Curoi, said, "That is not the sigh of a beaten man, but a conqueror's sigh of triumph." For the daughter of the king of the Isle of the Men of Falga knew well all Cuchulain had gone through that night.

"The Champion's Portion must go now to Cuchulain," she said to the others; "for you see by this that you are not equal to him." "We do not agree to that," said they; "for we know it was one of his friends among the Sidhe came to put us down and to put us out of the Championship. We will not give up for that," they said.

Then she gave them a message she had from Curoi, that the three champions were to go back to Emain, until he would bring his judgment there himself. So they bade her farewell, and went back to the Red Branch.

It was a good while after this, as the men of Ulster were in Emain, tired after the gathering and the games, Conchubar and Fergus, son of Rogh, with the chief men, went from the field of sports outside, and sat down in the house of the Red Branch; but Cuchulain was not there that night, or Conall Cearnach, but all the rest of the chief heroes were in it.

As they were sitting there towards evening, and the day wearing to its close, they saw a big awkward fellow, very ugly, coming to them into the hall. It seemed to them as if none of the men of Ulster could reach to half his height. He was frightful to look at, next his skin he had an old cow's hide, and a grey cloak around him, and over him he had a great spreading branch the size of a winter shed under which thirty cattle could find shelter. Ravenous yellow eyes he had and in his right hand an axe weighing fifty cauldrons of melted metal, its sharpness such that it would cut through hairs, if the wind would blow them against its edge.

He went over and leaned against the branched beam that was beside the fire.

"Who are you at all?" said Dubthach of the Chafer Tongue. "Is there no other place for you in the hall that you come up here? Is it to be candlestick to the house you want, or is it to set the house on fire you want?"

"Uath, the Stranger, is my name," said he; "and neither of those things is the thing I want. The thing I want is the thing I cannot find, and I after going through the whole of Ireland and the whole world looking for it, and that is a man that will keep his word and will hold to his agreement with me."

"What agreement is that?" said Fergus. "Here is this axe," he said, "and the man into whose hands it is put is to cut off my head to-day, I to cut his head off to-morrow. And as you men of Ulster have a name beyond the men of all other countries for strength and skill, for courage, for greatness, for highmindedness, for behaviour, for truth and generosity, for worthiness, let you find one among you that will hold to his word and keep to his bargain. Conchubar I put aside because of his kingship, and Fergus, son of Rogh, for the same reason. But outside these two, come, whichever of you will venture, he to cut off my head to-night, I to cut off his head to-morrow night."

"It is not right for dishonour to be put on a whole province," said Fergus, "for the want of one man that will keep his word." "Sure there is no champion here after these two are left out," said Dubthach. "By my word, there will be one this moment," said Laegaire, and he leaped out on the floor of the hall. "Stoop down, clown, that I may cut off your head to-night, you to cut off mine to-morrow night." "By the oath of my people," said Dubthach, "it is no good prospect you have if the man killed to-night comes to kill you to-morrow."

Then Uath put spells on the edge of the axe and laid his neck down on a block, and Laegaire struck a blow across it with the axe, till it went into the block underneath, and the head fell on the floor and the house was filled with the blood. But presently Uath rose up and gathered his head, and his axe to his breast and went out from the hall, his neck streaming with blood, so that there was terror on all the people in the house.

"I swear," said Dubthach, "if the stranger, being killed, comes back to-morrow night, he will not leave a man alive in Ulster."

Back he came the next night to have his agreement kept. But Laegaire's heart failed him, and he was nowhere to be found. But Conall Cearnach was in the hall, and he said he would make a new agreement with him. So all happened the same as the night before, but when Uath came the next day, it was the same with Conall as with Laegaire, his heart failed him when it came to the keeping of his bargain.

Cuchulain was there that night when Uath came in and began to reproach and to mock at them all. "And for you, men of Ulster," he said, "all your courage and your daring is gone from you; you covet a great name, but you are not able to earn it. Where is that poor squinting fellow that is called Cuchulain," he said, "till I see if his word is any better than the word of the others?" "I will keep my word without any agreement," said Cuchulain. "That is likely, you miserable fly, it is in great fear of death you are."

On that, Cuchulain made a leap towards him and gave him a blow with the axe, and hurled his head to the top rafter of the hall, so that the whole house shook.

On the morrow the men of Ulster were watching Cuchulain to see if he would break his word to the stranger, as the others had done. As Cuchulain sat there waiting for him, they saw that he was very down-hearted, and they made sure that his life was at its end, and that they might as well begin keening him. And then Cuchulain said to Conchubar, and there was hanging of the head on him, "Do not go from this till my agreement is fulfilled, for death is coming to me, but I would sooner have death than break my word."

They were there till the close of day, and then they saw Uath coming. "Where is Cuchulain?" he said. "Here I am," he answered. "It is dull your speech to-night," said the stranger; "it is in great fear of death you are. But however great your fear, you have not failed me."

Then Cuchulain went to him and laid his head on the block. "Stretch out your head better," said he. "You are keeping me in torment," said Cuchulain, "put an end to me quickly. For last night," he said, "by my oath, I made no delay with you." Then he stretched out his neck, and Uath raised his axe till it reached the rafters of the hall, and the creaking of the old hide that was about him, and the crashing of the axe through the rafters, was like the loud noise of a wood in a stormy night. But when the axe came down, it was with its blunt side, and it was the floor it struck, so that Cuchulain was not touched at all. And all the chief men of Ulster were standing around looking on, and they saw on the moment that it was no strange clown was in it, but Curoi, son of Daire, that had come to try the heroes through his enchantments.

"Rise up, Cuchulain," he said. "Of all the heroes of Ulster, whatever may be their daring, there is not one to compare with you in courage and in bravery and in truth. The Championship of the heroes of Ireland is yours from this out, and the Champion's Portion with it, and to your wife the first place among all the women of Ulster. And whoever tried to put himself before you after this," he said, "I swear by the oath my people swear by, his own life will be in danger."

With that he left them. And this was the end of the Women's War of Words, and of the quarrel among the heroes for the Championship of Ulster.

CHAPTER VI

The High King of Ireland

There was a king over Ireland before this time whose name was Eochaid Feidlech, and it is he who was Grandfather to Conaire the great.

He was going one time over the fair green of Brithe Leith, and he saw at the side of a well a woman, with a bright comb of silver and gold, and she was washing in a silver basin, having four golden birds on it, and little bright purple stones set in the rim of the basin. A beautiful purple cloak she had, and silver fringes to it, and a gold brooch; and she had on her a dress of green silk with a long hood embroidered in red gold, and wonderful clasps of gold and silver on her breasts and on her shoulders. The sunlight was falling on her, so that the gold and the green silk were shining out. Two plaits of hair she had, four locks in each plait, and a bead at the point of every lock, and the colour of her hair was like yellow flags in summer, or like gold after it is rubbed.

There she was, letting down her hair to wash it, and her arms out through the sleeve-holes of her shift. Her soft hands were as white as the snow of a single night, and her eyes as blue as any blue flower, and her lips as red as the berries of the rowan-tree, and her body as white as the foam of a wave. The bright light of the moon was in her face, the highness of pride in her eyebrows, a dimple of delight in each of her cheeks, the light of wooing in her eyes, and when she walked she had a step that was steady and even, like the walk of a queen.

Of all the women of the world she was the best and the nicest and the most beautiful that had ever been seen, and it is what King Eochaid and his people thought, that she was from the hills of the Sidhe. It is of her it was said, "All are dear and all are shapely till they are put beside Etain."

Then Eochaid sent his people to bring her to him, and when she came, he said, "Who are you yourself, and where do you come from?" "It is easy to say that," she said; "I am Etain, daughter of Etar, king of the Riders of the Sidhe. And I have been in this place ever since I was born, twenty years ago, in a hill of the Sidhe, and kings and great men among them have been asking my love, but they got nothing from me, for since the time I could first speak I have loved yourself, and given you a child's love, because of the great talk I heard of your grandeur. And when I saw you now I knew you by all I had heard of you; and so I have reached to you at last."

"It is no bad friend you have been looking for," said Eochaid, "but there will be a welcome before you, and I will leave every other woman for you, and it is with yourself I will live from this out, so long as you keep good behaviour."

Then he gave her the bride price, and she lived with him till he died. But one time she was brought away from him by Midhir, and Eochaid brought her back by force, and the Sidhe had no good will towards him after that, but brought a revenge on his house, and on his grandson, Conaire.

They had one daughter, that was called by the same name as her mother, Etain, and that was married to Cormac, king of Ulster. And, like her mother, she had but the one daughter, and there was vexation on Cormac when she had no son, and he bade two of his serving-men to bring the child away out of his sight, and to do away with her. So they brought her to a pit, but when they were putting her in, she smiled a laughing smile at them, and they had not the heart to harm her. So they brought her to a calf-shed belonging to the herds that minded the cattle of Eterscel, great-grandson of Iar, king of Teamhair; and they cared her well there, and there was not a king's daughter in Ireland was nicer than herself. And they made a little house of wicker-work for her, with no door, but only a window high up in it.

King Eterscel's people thought it was provisions the herds used to keep in that house. But one day a man of them got up and looked in through the window, and what he saw was the nicest and the most beautiful young girl of the whole world.

When King Eterscel heard that, he sent his people to break into the house and to bring her away, and ask no leave of the cowherds. For he had no child, and it is what his Druids had foretold, that it was a women of unknown race would bear him a son; and he was sure this was the woman that had been foretold for him.

But before the king's messengers reached the house in the morning, Etain saw a bird coming in at the window. And when it came in, it left its birdskin on the floor, and what she saw was a man before her. And he said, "The king is sending messengers to bring you to him, that he may have a son. But it is to me you will bear a son, and no bird must ever be killed by him. And his name will be Conaire, son of Mess Buachall, that is, son of the cowherd's foster-child."

Then she was brought away to the king, and the herds that had fostered her went with her, and they all got good treatment. And it is what she asked, when her son Conaire was born, that he might be brought up between three households, the household of her own fosters, and of the two honey-worded Maines, and her own. And she said that if any of the men of Ireland had a mind to give help in his bringing up, they should give it to those three households.

So it was like that the boy was reared, and there were five other boys reared along with him, Ferger, Fergel, Ferogain, Ferobain, and Lomna Druth the Fool, of the house of Dond Dessa, the champion of the army from Muclesi. And they all used the same food, and their clothing and their armour and the colour of their horses were the same.

And after a while King Eterscel died, and there was a bull feast made ready at Teamhair, as the custom was, to find out by it the best man for the kingship.

It is this way the bull feast was made. A white bull was killed, and one man would eat his fill of the meat and of the broth, and in his sleep after that meal, a charm of truth would be said over him by four Druids. And whoever he would see in his sleep would be king, and he would tell them his appearance; and if he told what was not true, his lips would perish. And what the dreamer saw in his sleep this time was a young man, and he naked, and having a stone in his sling, passing the road to Teamhair.

Now just at that time Conaire was out playing games near the Lifé River with his foster brothers, and the cowherds that had reared him came and bid him go up to Teamhair to attend the bull feast that was going on there.

So he left his foster-brothers at their games, and turned his chariot and went on till he came to Ath Cliath. And there he saw great white speckled birds, the best in size and appearance he had ever seen, and he followed after them till his horses were tired, but he could not come up with them, for they always kept just out of his reach. Then he got down from his chariot and took his sling and followed them to the strand, and they went into the sea and were swimming on the waves, and he went after them to take hold of them. Then they left their birdskins, and it was men he saw before him, and they turning to face him with spears and swords.

But one of them took him under his protection and said, "I am Nemglan, king of your father's birds, and there was a command put on you never to make a cast at birds, for there is not one here but should be dear to you." "I never knew of that command till this day," said Conaire. Then Nemglan said, "What you have to do is to go to Teamhair to-night, to the bull feast, and it is through it you will be made king, for it is a man that will go naked, and having a sling and a stone in his hand, along one of the roads to Teamhair, towards the end of the night, that will be king.

"And your bird reign will be great," he said. "But there is *geasa*, that is a bond, on you not to do these things.

"Do not go righthandwise round Teamhair, and lefthandwise round Bregia; do not hunt the evil beasts of Cerna; do not go out beyond Teamhair every ninth night; do not settle the quarrel of two of your own people; let no robbery be done in your reign; do not sleep in a house you can see the firelight shining from after sunset; do not let one woman or one man come into the house where you are after sunset; do not let three Reds go before you to the House of Red."

Then Conaire set out for Teamhair, naked, and having a stone in his sling. And on every one of the four roads to Teamhair there were three kings waiting, and having clothing with them, for the king that was foretold. And when the three kings on Conaire's road saw him coming, they met him, and put royal clothes on him, and brought him in a chariot to Teamhair. But the people of Teamhair said when they saw him: "Our bull feast and our charm of truth were not worth much, when it is only a young, beardless lad they have brought us!"

"That is no matter," said Conaire, "for it is no disgrace for you to have a young king, when my father and my grandfather held the same place." "That is true," they all said then, and they gave him the kingship, and he said, "I will learn of wise men, that I myself may be wise."

Now there was great plenty in Ireland through his reign; seven ships coming at the one time to Inver Colptha, and corn and nuts up to the knees in every harvest, and the trees bending from the weight of fruit, and the Buais and the Boinne full of fish every summer, and that much law and peace and good-will among the people, that each one thought the other's voice as sweet as the strings of harps. And the wolves themselves were held by hostages not to kill more than one calf in every pen. There was no thunder or storm in his reign, and from spring to harvest there was not as much wind as would stir a cow's tail, and the cattle were without keepers because of the greatness of peace. And in his reign there were the three crowns in Ireland, the crown of flowers, and the crown of acorns, and the crown of wheatears.

But after a while there began to be discontent on the sons of Donn Dessa, because they were hindered from the robbery and killing there used to be in the old time. And to vex the king, and to see what would he do, they stole three things, a pig and a bullock and a cow, from the same man every year for three years. And every year the countryman would come to the king to make his complaint, and every year the king would say, "It is to the sons of Donn Dessa you should go, for it is they took the beasts." But whenever he would go and speak to them, they would go near to kill him, and he would not go back to the king for fear he might be vexed.

So the sons of Donn Dessa went on with their robbery, and three times fifty other young men joined with them, sons of the great men of Ireland.

But one time they went doing their bad work in Connaught, and they followed a swineherd that ran from them, and he called out for help, and the people gathered to him, and the robbers were taken and brought back to Teamhair.

King Conaire was asked to give judgment then, and it is what he said, "Let every father of a robber put his own son to death, but let my foster-brothers be spared." "Give us leave," said all the people, "and we will put them to death for you." "I will not consent to that, indeed," said Conaire. "Their life must be spared. But if they must do robbery," he said, "let them go across the sea, and do it on the men of Alban."

So the sons of Donn Dessa and their men were driven out of the country, and some of the Maines went with them, the sons of Ailell and Maeve, and three great fighting men of Leinster, that were called the Three Red Hounds of Cualu, and they brought a troop of wild restless men with them.

They set out then in their ships and when they were out on the rough sea, they met with the ship of Ingcel, the One-Eyed, grandson of Cormac of Britain. They were going to make an attack on him, but Ingcel said, "It would be best for us to come to an agreement together, for you have been driven out of Ireland, and I myself have been driven out from Britain. Let us make this agreement," he said. "Let you come and spoil the people of my country, and then I will go back with you and spoil the people of your country."

So they agreed to that, and they cast lots as to where they would go first, and it is how the lot fell, that they should go first to Britain with Ingcel. And when they got there it chanced that the father and mother and the seven brothers of Ingcel, had been sent for to the house of the king of the district, and Ingcel and his comrades made an attack on them, and killed them all in the one night.

Then they made for Alban, and there they did every sort of destruction and robbery. And at last they turned back again to Ireland, that Ingcel might spoil their people the same way as they had spoiled his.

Now just at that time peace was after being broken in Ireland by the two Carbres that were at war with one another in Tuathmumain of Munster, and no one was able to put an end to their quarrel till Conaire himself went there to make peace. And he did that, although by doing it he broke two of the bonds put on him by the Man of the Waves. And on his way back to Teamhair, when he was passing Usnach in Meath, he and his people thought they saw fighting from east to west, and from north to south, and armies of naked men, and the country of the Ua Neills like a cloud of fire around them.

"What is that?" said Conaire. "It is easy to know that," said his people. "The king's law has broken down, and the country is on fire." "What way had we best go?" said Conaire. "To the north-west," said his people.

So then they went righthandways round Teamhair, and lefthandways round Bregia, and that was another breaking of his bonds, and they met with beasts and hunted them, and he did not know till afterwards that they were the evil beasts of Cerna.

And it was the Sidhe had made that Druid mist of smoke about him, because he had begun to break his bonds.

Great fear came on Conaire then, and he did not know what way would be best to go, and they went on by the sea coast, towards the south, by the road of Cualu. And then Conaire said, "Where shall we go to spend the night?"

"I can say this truly," said Mac Cecht, one of his fighting men, he that kept three of the Fomor as hostages at the king's court, the way their people would not spoil corn or milk in Ireland through his reign; "it is oftener the men of Ireland have been quarrelling to have you in the house, than you have been straying about, looking for a lodging." "I have a friend not far from this," said Conaire, "if we but knew the way to his house." "What is his name?" said Mac Cecht. "Da Derga of Leinster, that keeps the great Inn," said Conaire. "He came to ask a gift of me, and it is not a refusal he met with. I gave him a hundred head of cattle, I gave him a hundred fat swine, I gave him a hundred cloaks of fine cloth, I gave him a hundred swords and spears, I gave him a hundred red-gilded brooches, I gave him ten vats of good brown ale, I gave him three times nine white hounds in silver chains, I gave him a hundred swift horses. I would give him the same if he would come again. He will make a return to me to-night, for it would be a strange thing, he to begrudge me anything when I come to his house."

"When I knew his house," said Mac Cecht, "the road we are in now led straight to it. Seven doorways there are in it, and seven sleep-rooms between every two doorways." "We will go to the house with all our people," said Conaire. "If that is so," said Mac Cecht, "I will go on first till I light a fire in the house before you."

They went on then towards Ath Cliath, and presently a man with hair cut short, with a dreadful appearance, with but one hand and one foot and one eye, overtook them. A forked pole of black iron he had in his hand, and on his back a black-bristled singed pig, and it squealing; and there was a woman coming after him, ugly and big-mouthed. "Welcome to you, my master, Conaire," he said. "It is long we have known of your coming." "Who gives that welcome?" said Conaire. "Fer Coille, the Man of the Wood," he said, "and his black pig with him, that you may not be fasting to-night, for you are the best king that ever came into the world." "Leave me for to-night," said Conaire, "and I will go to you any other night that pleases you." "We will not," said he; "but we will go to the place you will be in to-night, O fair little master, Conaire."

So he went on towards the inn, and his wife behind him, and his black pig squealing on his back.

After that Conaire saw before him three horsemen going towards the Inn. Red cloaks they had, and red shields, and red spears in their hands, and they riding on red horses.

"What men are these before me," said Conaire. "It is in my bonds not to let them go before me; three Reds to the House of Red, that is, of Derga. Who will follow them and bid them to come back and to follow after me?" "I will follow them," said Lefriflaith, Conaire's son.

So he struck his horse and went after them, but he could not come up with them. So he called to them to turn back, and not to go on before the king. And he did this three times, and the third time one of the three men turned his head and said, "There is great news before us, my son; wetting of swords, destroying of life, shields with broken bosses, after the fall of night. Our horses are tired; we are riding the horses of the Sidhe; although we are alive we are dead." And with that they went from him, and he went back to his father.

"You did not keep back the men," said Conaire. "It was not my fault, indeed," said Lefriflaith. Then he told the answer they had given him, and Conaire and his people were not well pleased to hear that, and uneasiness came on them. "All my bonds are ended to-night," said Conaire, "and those three Reds before me are sent by the Sidhe."

Now while he and his people were in the road of Cualu going towards the Inn, Ingcel and the outlaws of Ireland were come in their ships to the coast of Bregia against Etair. And the sons of Donn Dessa said, "Strike the sails now, and let some light-footed messenger go on shore and see can we keep our bargain with Ingcel, and give him a spoil for the spoil he gave us." "Let some man go," said Ingcel, "that has the gift of hearing and of far sight and of judgment."

"I have the gift of hearing," said Maine Milscothach. "I have the gift of far sight and of judgment," said Maine Andoe. "It is as well for you to go, so," said the others.

So they landed and went on till they came to Beinn Etair, and they stopped there to try what they might see and hear. "Be quiet now," said Maine Milscothach, "and listen." "What do you hear?" said Maine Andoe. "I hear the coming of a king," he said, "and look now and tell me what you see." "I see," he said, "a great company of men, travelling over hills and rivers. Clothes of every colour they have, and grey spears over their chariots, and swords with ivory hilts beside them, and silver shields; and I swear by the oath my people swear by," he said, "the horses they have with them are the horses of some good lord. And it is my opinion that it is Conaire, son of Eterscel, and a good share of the men of Ireland with him, that is travelling the road."

With that they went back and told their comrades what they had heard and seen. And when they heard it they brought the boats to shore and landed on the strand of Furbuithe. And it was just at the same moment Mac Cecht was striking a spark to kindle a fire at the Inn before the High King.

Then Conaire came to the lawn of the Inn, and he went in, and his people, and they took their seats, and the three Red Men sat down along with them, and the Man of the Wood with his squealing pig.

And Da Derga came to them with three times fifty fighting men, every one of them having a long head of hair and a short cloak and a great blackthorn stick with bands of iron in his hand. "Welcome, my master, Conaire," said Da Derga, "and if you were to bring the whole of the men of Ireland with you, there would be a welcome before them all."

After the fall of evening they saw a lone woman coming to the door of the Inn; long hair she had, and a grey woollen cloak, and her mouth was drawn to one side of her head. She came and leaned up against the doorpost, and she threw an evil eye on the king and the young men about him. "Well, woman," said Conaire, "if you have the Druid sight, what is it you see for us?" "It is what I see for you," she said, "that nothing of your skin or of your flesh will escape from the place you are in, except what the birds will bring away in their claws. And let me come into the house now," she said. "There are bonds on me," said Conaire, "not to let one woman come by herself into the house after the setting of the sun. And bring her out," he said, "a good share of food from my own table, but let her stop for the night in some other place."

"If the king's hospitality is gone from him," she said, "and if it is the way with him not to have room in his house for one lone woman to be fed and lodged, I will go and get food and lodging from some better man." "Let her in, in spite of my bonds," said Conaire, when he heard that. So they let her in, but none of them felt easy in their minds after what she had said.

Now all this time the outlaws were on their way to the Inn, and they stopped at Leccaibcend Slebe. And when they saw the great light that was shining from the inn through the wheels of the chariots that were outside the doors, Ingcel said to Ferogain, "What is that great light beyond?" "It is what I think," said Ferogain, "that it is the fire of Conaire, the High King. And I would be glad he not to be there to-night, for it would be a pity if harm would come on him, or his life be shortened, for he is a branch in its blossom."

"It is good luck for me," said Ingcel, "if he is there. Spoil for spoil. It is no worse for you than it was for me when I gave up my father and mother and my seven brothers and the king of my country into your hands." "That is true, that is true," said all the others.

Then every man of them brought up a stone from the strand to make a cairn, as they were used to do before they would make an attack on any place, to know by it afterwards how many men they had lost. For every man that would come from the fight would take his stone from the cairn, and the stones of all that would be killed would be left there.

After that they held a council, and it is what they agreed, that one man should go and spy out what way things were at the Inn. And it was Ingcel himself went to do that, and he was a good while looking in by the seven doors of the house, but at least some one of the men inside caught sight of him, and he made his way back to his comrades, where they were all sitting down, and their leaders in the middle, waiting to hear his news.

"Did you see the house, Ingcel?" said Ferogain. "I did see it," said Ingcel; "and whether or not there is a king in it, it is a royal house, and I will take it as my share when the time comes." "You may do that," said Conaire's foster-brothers. "But we will not go against it before we know who is in it."

"The first I saw," said Ingcel, "was a large man, of good race, with bright eyes, with hair like flax; his face open, wide above and narrow below; with modest looks, and having no beard. A five-barbed spear in his hand, and a shield with five gold circles on it. Nine men he had about him, all beautiful and all alike, so that you would think they had the one father and mother. Who were those men, Ferogain?" he said.

"It is easy to say that," said Ferogain. "That was Cormac Conloingeas, son of Conchubar, the best fighter behind a shield in all Ireland, but he is modest with all that. And those were his nine comrades about him; they have never put men to death because of their poverty, or spared them because of their riches. He is a good leader they have with them. I swear by the gods my people swear by, it is no small slaughter they will make before the Inn to-night."

"It is a pity for him that will make the attack," said Lomna Druth, the Fool, "Because of that man only, Cormac Conloingeas. And if I had my way," he said, "the attack would not be made, for the sake of that man alone and his beauty and his goodness."

"You will not be able to hinder it, Lomna," said Ingcel. "You are no good of a fighter; I know you well, there are clouds of weakness coming on you. No one, whether old man or story-teller, will be able to say I drew back from this fight before I had gone through with it."

"It is well enough for you, Ingcel," said Lomna; "you will escape after the fight, and you will bring away the head of a strange king with you, but as for myself," he said, "it is my head will be the first to be tossed to and fro to-night."

"What did you see after that?" said Ferogain.

"I saw a room with three soft young boys in it and they wearing cloaks of silk with gold brooches. Long yellow hair they had, as curly as a ram's head; a golden shield and a candle of a king's house over each of them, and every one in the house humours them. Who were those, Ferogain?" he said.

But Ferogain was crying tears down, so that the front of his cloak was wet, and it was a long time before he could bring out his voice. "O little ones," he said then, "I have good reason for crying. Those are the three sons of the king, Oball and Obline and Corpre Findmor."

"There is grief on us if that story is true," said the other sons of Donn Dessa; "for it is good those three are. They are as mannerly as young girls, and they have the hearts of brothers, and the courage of lions. Whoever has been with them and parts from them, it is little he sleeps or eats till the end of nine days, fretting after their company. It is a pity for him that will destroy them."

"I saw after that," said Ingcel, "a very fair man, having a golden bush of hair, the size of a reaping basket. A long, heavy three-edged sword in his hand, a red shield speckled with rivets of white bronze between plates of gold."

"That man is known to all the men of Ireland," said Ferogain. "It is Conall Cearnach, son of Amergin, and he is the man Conaire thinks most of in the world; and that shield in his hand is the Lam-tapaid. There are seven doorways in that inn, and when the attack is made, Conall Cearnach will be at every one of them. What did you see after that, Ingcel?" he said.

"I saw," he said, "a brown big man, with short brown hair and a red speckled cloak, and a black shield with clasps of gold; and with him two chief men, in their first greyness, and black swords at their sides. And one of them had in his hand a great spear, with fifty rivets through it, and he shook it over his head, and struck the haft against the palm of his hand three times, and then he plunged it into a great pot that stood before them, with some black thing in it, and when he was putting it in there were flames on the shaft. Who were those men, Ferogain?"

"That brown man is Muinremar, son of Geirgind, one of the champions of the Red Branch. And another is Sencha, the beautiful son of Ailell; and the man with the spear is Dubthach, the Beetle of Ulster, and the spear in his hand is Celthair's Luin, that was in the battle of Magh Tuireadh, and that was brought from the east by the three children of Tuireann, and when a battle is coming near, it flames up of itself, and it must be kept quenched in a vessel, or it will go through whoever has it in his hand."

"I saw after that," said Ingcel, "a room with nine men in it, fair-haired and beautiful, with speckled cloaks, and above them were nine bagpipes, and light was shining from the ornaments that were on them."

"Those are the nine pipers that came to Conaire out of the hill of the Sidhe at Bregia," said Ferogain, "because of the great stories about him. The best pipers they are in the whole world. And they are good fighters, but to fight with them is to fight with a shadow, for they kill but cannot be killed, because they are from the Sidhe."

"I saw after that," said Ingcel, "three very big men, with terrible looks. A dress of rough hair they had, and a club of iron with chains on it in every man's hand.

There was sadness on them, and they standing alone, and every one in the house avoiding them. Who were those, Ferogain?"

Ferogain was silent for a while, and he said then, "I do not know of any such men in the world, unless they might be the three giants Cuchulain spared the time he took them from the men of Falga; he would not let them be killed because of their strangeness. Conaire bought them from Cuchulain after that, so it is along with him they are."

"I saw nine men in the north side of the house," said Ingcel, "with very yellow manes of hair, and short linen dresses, and purple cloaks without brooches; broad spears, and red curved shields."

"I know those men," said Ferogain; "three royal princes of Britain that are with the king, Oswald and his two foster-brothers, Osbrit of the Long Hand and his two foster-brothers, Lindas and his two foster-brothers."

"Three red men I saw after that," said Ingcel; "red shields above them, red spears in their hands, their three red horses in their bridles in front of the Inn."

"Those are the three champions that did deceit and falsehood among the Sidhe," said Ferogain, "and it is the punishment was put on them by the king of Sidhe, to be three times destroyed by the king of Teamhair; and Conaire is the last king through whom they will be destroyed; yet they will not be killed, nor will they kill any one. It is to work out their own destruction they are come."

"I saw after that," said Ingcel, "a big man, and his hair white, and the shame of baldness on him, and gold earrings in his ears. Nine swords he had in his hand, and nine silver shields, and nine golden apples. He was throwing each of them upwards, and not one would fall on the ground, but each of them rising and falling past each other like bees on a sunny day. But as I looked at him, he let all fall to the ground, and the people about him cried out, and the king that was sitting there said to him, 'We have been together since I was a little boy, and your tricks never failed till to-night.'

" 'My grief' he said. 'Fair master, Conaire, I have good cause for it; an unfriendly eye looked at me; there is some bad thing in front of the Inn.' "

"And when the king heart that, it is what he said. 'I had a dream in my sleep a while ago, of the howling of my dog Ossar, of wounded men, of a wind of terror, of keening that overcame laughter.' "

"That was Taulchinne, Conaire's juggler," said Ferogain. "And tell me now," he said, "what was the appearance of the king?"

"Of all the men I ever saw in the world," said Ingcel, "he is the best in shape, and the most beautiful; young he is, and wise and kinglike. The colour of his hair was like the shining of purified gold; the cloak about him was like the mist of a May morning, changing from colour to colour, every colour more beautiful than another; a wheel brooch of gold reaching from his chin to his waist; his golden-hilted sword within his reach."

"That was Conaire, the High King, indeed," said Ferogain; "and it is he is the greatest and the best and the comeliest of the kings of the whole world, and there is no fault in him, either as to wisdom or bravery or knowledge or words or worthiness. Tender he is, a sleepy, simple man, till he chances on some deed of courage, but when his anger is awaked, the champions of Ireland and Scotland will not win their battle so long as he is against them. And I swear by the oath my people swear by, unless drink should fail him, or the like, that man alone would hold the Inn till help would gather to him from the Wave of Cliodna in the south, to the Wave of Assaroe in the north."

"It is time for us to rise up," said Ingcel then, "and to get on to the house."

So with that the outlaws rose up and went on to the Inn, and the noise of their voices was heard about it.

"Be quiet now and listen," said Conaire. "What is that we hear?"

"Fighting men about the house," said Conall Cearnach. "There are fighting men to meet them here," said Conaire. "They will be wanted to-night," said Conall.

Then Lomna Druth, the Fool, broke in first to the house, and the doorkeepers struck off his head, and it was tossed three times in and out of the Inn, just as he himself had foretold.

Then they all attacked one another, and Conaire himself went out with his people and killed a great many of the outlaws outside. And three times the Inn was set on fire, and three times it was put out again. And Conaire got to his arms then, for he had not got them in the first attack, and he went out and again and made a great slaughter, so that the outlaws were driven back. "I told you," said Ferogain, "that all the men of Ireland and of Alban could not take the house till Conaire's rage would be quenched." "It is short his time will be," said the Druids that were along with the outlaws. And what they put on him by their enchantments was a great thirst, so that he went back to the house and called for a drink. "A drink to me, Mac Cecht," he said. "That is not the order you are used to give me," said Mac Cecht. "What I have to do is to keep you from the men that are attacking you all round the house; ask a drink of your steward and of your cup-bearers," he said.

Then Conaire called to his cup-bearers for a drink. "There is none," they said, "for every drop in the house was thrown on the fire to put it out." "Get me a drink, Mac Cecht," he said again then; "for if I am to die, it is all the same to me by what death I die."

Then Mac Cecht gave a choice to the champions of Ireland that were in the house, would they go out and look for a drink for Conaire, or would they stop in the house and defend him. And Conall Cearnach called out: "Leave the defence of the king to us, and go you and look for the drink, for it was of you it was asked." And he was vexed with Mac Cecht for putting the choice to them, and there was never a very friendly feeling between them afterwards.

Then Mac Cecht went to look for a drink, and he brought Conaire's great golden cup with him, and an iron spit, the cauldron spit, in his other hand.

He burst out on the outlaws, and attacked them with blows of the spit, so that many got their death; and then he took his shield and made a round with his sword above his head, and cut down all before him, and got through the whole band.

And it would be too long to tell, and it would tire the hearers, all that happened after that; the people of the Inn coming out and making attacks, and some of them getting their death, and the most part making their escape. And at last there were none left in the Inn with Conaire but Conall, and Sencha, and Dubthach.

Now from the rage that was on Conaire, and the greatness of the fight he had fought, a great drouth came on him again, and such a fever of thirst, and no drink to get, that he died of it in the end.

Then the other three, when they saw the High King was dead, went out and cut their way through their enemies, and got away with their lives, but if they did, they were wounded, and hurt, and broken.

And Conall Cearnach, after he got away, went on to his father's house, and but half his shield left in his hand, and a few bits left of his two spears. And he found Amergin, his father, out before his dun in Tailltin.

"Those are fierce wolves that have hunted you, my son," said he. "It was not wolves that wounded me, but a sharp fight with fighting-men," said Conall. "Have you news from Da Derga's Inn?" said Amergin. "Is your lord living?" "He is not living," said Conall. "I swear by the gods the great tribes of Ulster swear by, the man is a coward that came out alive, leaving his lord dead among his enemies," said Amergin. "My own wounds are not white, old hero," said Conall. And with that he showed him his right arm, that was full of wounds. "That arm fought there, my son," said Amergin. "That is true," said Conall. "There are many in front of the Inn now, it gave drinks of death to last night."

Now, as to Mac Cecht, after he got away from the Inn, he went on to the well of Casair, that was near him in Crith Cualann, but he could not find so much as the full of the cup of water in it. Then he went on through the night, from lake to lake, and from river to river, but he could not find the full of the cup of water in any one of them. But at last he came to Uaran Garad on Magh Ai, and it could not hide itself from him, and he filled the cup, and went back again, and reached Da Derga's Inn before morning. And when he got there, he saw two men, and they striking off Conaire's head; and Mac Cecht struck off the head of one of them, and then the other man was going away with the king's head, and he took up a stone and threw it at him, that it broke his back.

Then Mac Cecht stooped down and poured the water into Conaire's mouth and his throat. And after that he dragged his body with him on his back to Teamhair, and buried him there, as some say. And he himself went to his own country, into Connaught. And the place he stopped in was called, from his sharp grief, Mag Bron-gear.

And there was no High King chosen to rule over Ireland for a good many years after that.

CHAPTER VII

Fate of the Children of Usnach

Now it was one Fedlimid, son of Doll, was harper to King Conchubar, and he had but one child, and this is the story of her birth.

Cathbad, the Druid, was at Fedlimid's house one day. "Have you got knowledge of the future?" said Fedlimid. "I have a little," said Cathbad. "What is it you are wanting to know?" "I was not asking to know anything," said Fedlimid, "but if you know of anything that may be going to happen me, it is as well for you to tell me."

Cathbad went out of the house for a while, and when he came back he said: "Had you ever any children?" "I never had," said Fedlimid, "and the wife I have had none, and we have no hope ever to have any; there is no one with us but only myself and my wife." "That puts wonder on me," said Cathbad, "for I see by Druid signs that it is on account of a daughter belonging to you, that more blood will be shed than ever was shed in Ireland since time and race began. And great heroes and bright candles of the Gael will lose their lives because of her." "Is that the foretelling you have made for me?" said Fedlimid, and there was anger on him, for he thought the Druid was mocking him; "if that is all you can say, you can keep it for yourself; it is little I think of your share of knowledge." "For all that," said Cathbad, "I am certain of its truth, for I can see it all clearly in my own mind."

The Druid went away, but he was not long gone when Fedlimid's wife was found to be with child. And as her time went on, his vexation went on growing, that he had not asked more questions of Cathbad, at the time he was talking to him, and he was under a smouldering care by day and by night, for it is what he was thinking, that neither his own sense and understanding, or the share of friends he had, would be able to save him, or to make a back against the world, if this misfortune should come upon him, that would bring such great shedding of blood upon the earth; and it is the thought that came, that if this child should be born, what he had to do was to put her far away, where no eye would see her, and no ear hear word of her.

The time of the delivery of Fedlimid's wife came on, and it was a girl-child she gave birth to. Fedlimid did not allow any living person to come to the house or to see his wife, but himself alone.

But just after the child was born, Cathbad, the Druid, came in again, and there was shame on Fedlimid when he saw him, and when he remembered how he would not believe his words. But the Druid looked at the child and he said: "Let Deirdre be her name; harm will come through her.

"She will be fair, comely, bright-haired; heroes will fight for her, and kings go seeking for her."

And then he took the child in his arms, and it is what he said: "O Deirdre, on whose account many shall weep, on whose account many women shall be envious, there will be trouble on Ulster for you sake, O fair daughter of Fedlimid.

"Many will be jealous of your face, O flame of beauty; for your sake heroes shall go to exile. For your sake deeds of anger shall be done in Emain; there is harm in your face, for it will bring banishment and death on the sons of kings.

"In your fate, O beautiful child, are wounds, and ill-doings, and shedding of blood.

"You will have a little grave apart to yourself; you will be a tale of wonder for ever, Deirdre."

Cathbad went away then, and he sent Levarcham, daughter of Aedh, to the house; and Fedlimid asked her would she take the venture of bringing up the child, far away where no eye would see her, and no ear hear of her. Levarcham said she would do that, and that she would do her best to keep her the way he wished.

So Fedlimid got his men, and brought them away with him to a mountain, wide and waste, and there he bade them to make a little house, by the side of a round green hillock, and to make a garden of apple-trees behind it, with a wall about it. And he bade them put a roof of green sods over the house, the way a little company might live in it, without notice being taken of them.

Then he sent Levarcham and the child there, that no eye might see, and no ear hear of Deirdre. He put all in good order before them, and he gave them provisions, and he told Levarcham that food and all she wanted would be sent from year to year as long as she lived.

And so Deirdre and her foster-mother lived in the lonely place among the hills without the knowledge or the notice of any strange person, until Deirdre was fourteen years of age. And Deirdre grew straight and clean like a rush on the bog, and she was comely beyond comparison of all the women of the world, and her movements were like the swan on the wave, or the deer on the hill. She was the young girl of the greatest beauty and of the gentlest nature of all the women of Ireland.

Levarcham, that had charge of her, used to be giving Deirdre every knowledge and skill that she had herself. There was not a blade of grass growing from root, or a bird singing in the wood, or a star shining from heaven, but Deirdre had the name of it. But there was one thing she would not have her know, she would not let her have friendship with any living person of the rest of the world outside their own house.

But one dark night of winter, with black clouds overhead, a hunter came walking the hills, and it is what happened, he missed the track of the hunt, and lost his way and his comrades.

And a heaviness came upon him, and he lay down on the side of the green hillock by Deirdre's house. He was weak with hunger and going, and perished with cold, and a deep sleep came upon him. While he was lying there a dream came to the hunter, and he thought that he was near the warmth of a house of the Sidhe, and the Sidhe inside making music, and he called out in his dream, "If there is any one inside, let them bring me in, in the name of the Sun and the Moon." Deirdre heard the voice, and she said to Levarcham, "Mother, mother, what is that?" But Levarcham said, "It is nothing that matters; it is the birds of the air gone astray, and trying to find one another. But let them go back to the branches of the wood." Another troubled dream came on the hunter, and he cried out a second time. "What is that?" asked Deirdre again. "It is nothing that matters," said Levarcham. "The birds of the air are looking for one another; let them go past to the branches of the wood." Then a third dream came to the hunter, and he cried out a third time, if there was any one in the hill to let him in for the sake of the Elements, for he was perished with cold and overcome with hunger. "Oh! what is that, Levarcham?" said Deirdre. "There is nothing there for you to see, my child, but only the birds of the air, and they lost to one another, but let them go past us to the branches of the wood. There is no place or shelter for them here to-night." "Oh, mother," said Deirdre, "the bird asked to come in for the sake of the Sun and the Moon, and it is what you yourself told me, that anything that is asked like that, it is right for us to give it. If you will not let in the bird that is perished with cold and overcome with hunger, I myself will let it in." So Deirdre rose up and drew the bolt from the leaf of the door, and let in the hunter. She put a seat in the place for sitting, food in the place for eating, and drink in the place for drinking, for the man who had come into the house. "Come now and eat food, for you are in want of it," said Deirdre. "Indeed it is I was in want of food and drink and warmth when I came into this house; but by my word, I have forgotten that since I saw yourself," said the hunter. "How little you are able to curb your tongue," said Levarcham. "It is not a great thing for you to keep your tongue quiet when you get the shelter of a house and the warmth of a hearth on a dark winter night." "That is so," said the hunter, "I may do that much, to keep my mouth shut; but I swear by the oath my people swear by, if some others of the people of the world saw this great beauty that is hidden away here, they would not leave her long with you." "What people are those?" said Deirdre. "I will tell you that," said the hunter; "they are Naoise, son of Usnach, and Ainnle and Ardan, his two brothers." "What is the appearance of these men, if we should ever see them?" said Deirdre. "This is the appearance that is on those three men," said the hunter: "the colour of the raven is on their hair, their skin is like the swan on the wave, their cheeks like the blood of the speckled red calf, and their swiftness and their leap are like the salmon of the stream and like the deer of the grey mountain; and the head and shoulders of Naoise are above all the other men of Ireland." "However they may be," said Levarcham, "get you out from here, and take another road; and by my word, little is my thankfulness to yourself, or to her that let you in." "You need not send him out for telling me that," said Deirdre, "for as to those three men, I myself saw them last night in a dream, and they hunting upon a hill."

The hunter went away, but in a little time after he began to think to himself how Conchubar, High King of Ulster, was used to lie down at night and to rise up on the morning by himself, without a wife or any one to speak to; and that if he could see this great beauty it was likely he would bring her home to Emain, and that he himself would get the good-will of the king for telling him there was such a queen to be found on the face of the world.

So he went straight to King Conchubar at Emain Macha, and he sent word in to the king that he had news for him, if he would hear it. The king sent for him to come in. "What is the reason of your journey?" he said. "It is what I have to tell you, king," said the hunter, "that I have seen the greatest beauty that ever was born in Ireland, and I am come to tell you of it." "Who is this great beauty, and in what place is she to be seen, when she was never seen before you saw her, if you did see her?" "I did see her, indeed," said the hunter, "but no other man can see her, unless he knows from me the place where she is living." "Will you bring me to the place where she is, and you will have a good reward?" said the king. "I will bring you there," said the hunter. "Let you stay with my household to-night," said Conchubar, "and I myself and my people will go with you early on the morning of to-morrow." "I will stay," said the hunter, and he stayed that night in the household of King Conchubar.

Then Conchubar sent to Fergus and to the other chief men of Ulster, and he told them of what he was about to do. Though it was early when the songs and the music of the birds began in the woods, it was earlier yet when Conchubar, king of Ulster, rose up with his little company of near friends, in the fresh spring morning of the fresh and pleasant month of May, and the dew was heavy on every bush and flower as they went out towards the green hill where Deirdre was living.

But many a young man of them that had a light, glad, leaping step when they set out, had but a tired, slow, failing step before the end, because of the length and the roughness of the way. "It is down there below," said the hunter, "in the house in that valley, the woman is living, but I myself will not go nearer it than this."

Conchubar and his troop went down then to the green hillock where Deirdre was, and they knocked at the door of the house. Levarcham called out that neither answer nor opening would be given to any one at all, and that she did not want disturbance put on herself or her house. "Open," said Conchubar, "in the name of the High King of Ulster." When Levarcham heard Conchubar's voice, she knew there was no use trying to keep Deirdre out of sight any longer, and she rose up in haste and let in the king, and as many of his people as could follow him.

When the king saw Deirdre before him, he thought in himself that he never saw

401

in the course of the day, or in the dreams of the night, a creature so beautiful, and he gave her his full heart's weight of love there and then. It is what he did; he put Deirdre up on the shoulders of his men, and she herself and Levarcham were brought away to Emain Macha.

With the love that Conchubar had for Deirdre, he wanted to marry her with no delay, but when her leave was asked, she would not give it, for she was young yet, and she had no knowledge of the duties of a wife, or the ways of a king's house. And when Conchubar was pressing her hard, she asked him to give her a delay of a year and a day. He said he would give her that, though it was hard for him, if she would give him her certain promise to marry him at the year's end. She did that, and Conchubar got a woman teacher for her, and nice, fine, pleasant, modest maidens to be with her at her lying down and at her rising up, to be companions to her. And Deirdre grew wise in the works of a young girl, and in the understanding of a woman; and if any one at all looked at her face, whatever colour she was before that, she would blush crimson red. And it is what Conchubar thought, that he never saw with the eyes of his body a creature that pleased him so well.

One day Deirdre and her companions were out on a hill near Emain Macha, looking around them in the pleasant sunshine, and they saw three men walking together. Deirdre was looking at the men and wondering at them, and when they came near, she remembered the talk of the hunter, and the three men she saw in her dream, and she thought to herself that these were the three sons of Usnach, and that this was Naoise, that had his head and shoulders above all the men of Ireland. The three brothers went by without turning their eyes at all upon the young girls on the hillside, and they were singing as they went, and whoever heard the low singing of the sons of Usnach, it was enchantment and music to them, and every cow that was being milked and heard it, gave two-thirds more of milk. And it is what happened, that love for Naoise came into the heart of Deirdre, so that she could not but follow him. She gathered up her skirt and went after the three men that had gone past the foot of the hill, leaving her companions there after her.

But Ainnle and Ardan had heard talk of the young girl that was at Conchubar's Court, and it is what they thought, that if Naoise their brother would see her, it is for himself he would have her, for she was not yet married to the king. So when they saw Deirdre coming after them, they said to one another to hasten their steps, for they had a long road to travel, and the dusk of night coming on. They did so, and Deirdre saw it, and she cried out after them, "Naoise, son of Usnach, are you going to leave me?" "What cry was that came to my ears, that it is not well for me to answer, and not easy for me to refuse?" said Naoise. "It was nothing but the cry of Conchubar's wild ducks," said his brothers; "but let us quicken our steps and hasten our feet, for we have a long road to travel, and the dusk of the evening coming on." They did so, and they were widening the distance between themselves and her. Then Deirdre cried, "Naoise! Naoise! son of Usnach, are you going to leave me?" "What cry was it that came to my ears and struck my heart, that it is not well for me to answer, or easy for me to refuse?" said Naoise. "Nothing but the cry of Conchubar's wild geese," said his brothers; "but let us quicken our steps and hasten our feet, the darkness of night is coming on." They did so, and were widening the distance between themselves and her. Then Deirdre cried the third time, "Naoise! Naoise! Naoise! son of Usnach, are you going to leave me?" "What sharp, clear cry was that, the sweetest that ever came to my ears, and the sharpest that ever struck my heart, of all the cries I ever heard," said Naoise. "What is it but the scream of Conchubar's lake swans," said his brothers. "That was the third cry of some person beyond there," said Naoise, "and I swear by my hand of valour," he said, "I will go no further until I see where the cry comes from." So Naoise turned back and met Deirdre, and Deirdre and Naoise kissed one another three times, and she gave a kiss to each of his brothers. And with the confusion that was on her, a blaze of red fire came upon her, and her colour came and went as quickly as the aspen by the stream. And it is what Naoise thought to himself that he never saw a woman so beautiful in his life; and he gave Deirdre, there and then, the love that he never gave to living thing, to vision, or to creature, but to herself alone.

Then he lifted her high on his shoulder, and he said to his brothers to hasten their steps; and they hastened them.

"Harm will come of this," said the young men. "Although there should harm come," said Naoise, "I am willing to be in disgrace while I live. We will go with her to another province, and there is not in Ireland a king who will not give us a welcome." So they called their people, and that night they set out with three times fifty men, and three times fifty women, and three times fifty greyhounds, and Deirdre in their midst.

They were a long time after that shifting from one place to another all around Ireland, from Esro in the south, to Beinn Etair north-east again, and it is often they were in danger of being destroyed by Conchubar's devices. And one time the Druids raised a wood before them, but Naoise and his brothers cut their way through it. But at last they got out of Ulster and sailed to the country of Alban, and settled in a lonely place; and when hunting on the mountains failed them, they fell upon the cattle of the men of Alban, so that these gathered together to make an end of them. But the sons of Usnach called to the king of Scotland, and he took them into his friendship, and they gave him their help when he went out into battles or to war.

But all this time they had never spoken to the king of Deirdre, and they kept her with themselves, not to let any one see her, for they were afraid they might get their death on account of her, she being so beautiful.

But it chanced very early one morning, the king's steward came to visit them, and he found his way into the house where Naoise and Deirdre were, and there he saw them asleep beside one another. He went back then to the king, and he said: "Up to this time there has never been found a woman that would be a fitting wife for you; but there is a woman on the shore of Loch Ness now, is well worthy of you, king of the East. And what you have to do is to make an end of Naoise, for it is of his wife I am speaking." "I will not do that," said the king; "but go to her," he said, "and bid her to come and see me secretly." The steward brought her that message, but Deirdre sent him away, and all that he had said to her, she told it to Naoise afterwards. Then when she would not come to him, the king sent the sons of Usnach into every hard fight, hoping they would get their death, but they won every battle, and came back safe again. And after a while they went to Loch Eitche, near the sea, and they were left to themselves there for a while in peace and quietness. And they settled and made a dwelling house for themselves by the side of Loch Ness, and they could kill the salmon of the stream from out their own door, and the deer of the grey hills from out their window. But when Naoise went to the court of the king, his clothes were splendid among the great men of the army of Scotland, a cloak of bright purple, rightly shaped, with a fringe of bright gold; a coat of satin with fifty hooks of silver; a brooch on which were a hundred polished gems; a gold-hilted sword in his hand, two blue-green spears of bright points, a dagger with the colour of yellow gold on it, and a hilt of silver. But the two children they had, Gaiar and Aebgreine, they gave into the care of Manannan, son of the sea. And he cared them well in Emhain of the Apple Trees, and he brought Bobaris the poet to give learning to Gaiar. And Aebgreine of the Sunny Face, he gave in marriage afterwards to Rinn, son of Eochaidh Juil of the Land of Promise.

Now it happened after a time that a very great feast was made by Conchubar, in Emain Macha, for all the great among his nobles, so that the whole company were easy and pleasant together. The musicians stood up to play their songs and to give poems, and they gave out the branches of relationship and of kindred. These are the names of the poets who were in Emain at that time, Cathbad, the Druid, son of Conall, son of Rudraige; and Geanann of the bright Face, son of Cathbad; and Ferceirtne, and Geanann Black-Knee, and many others, and Sencha, son of Ailell.

They were all drinking and making merry until Conchubar, the king, raised his voice and spoke aloud, and it is what he said: "I desire to know from you, did you ever see a better house than this house of Emain, or a hearth better than my hearth in any place you were ever in?" "We did not," they said. "If that is so," said Conchubar, "do you know of anything at all that is wanting to you?" "We know of nothing," said they. "That is not so with me," said Conchubar. "I know of a great want that is on you, the want of the three best candles of the Gael, the three noble sons of Usnach, that ought not to be away from us for the sake of any woman in the world, Naoise, Ainnle, and Ardan; for surely they are the sons of a king, and they would defend the High Kingship against the best men of Ireland." "If we had dared," said they, "it is long ago we would have said it, and more than

that the province of Ulster would be equal to any other province in Ireland, if
there was no Ulsterman in it but those three alone, for it is lions they are in
hardness and in bravery." "If that is so," said Conchubar, "let us send word by a
messenger to Alban, and to the dwelling-place of the sons of Usnach, to ask them
back again." "Who will go there with the message?" said they all. "I cannot know
that," said Conchubar, "for there is *geasa*, that is bonds, on Naoise not to come
back with any man only one of the three, Conall Cearnach, or Fergus, or Cuch-
alain, and I will know now," said he, "which one of those three loves me best."
Then he called Conall to one side, and he asked him, "What would you do with
me if I should send you for the sons of Usnach, and if they were destroyed
through me – a thing I do not mean to do." "As I am not going to undertake it,"
said Conall, "I will say that it is not one alone I would kill, but any Ulsterman I
would lay hold of that had harmed them would get shortening of life from me,
and the sorrow of death." "I see well," said Conchubar, "you are no friend of
mine," and he put Conall away from him. Then he called Cuchulain to him, and
asked him the same as he did the other. "I give my word, as I am not going," said
Cuchulain, "if you want that of me, and that you think to kill them when they
come, it is not one person alone that would die for it, but every Ulsterman I could
lay hold of would get shortening of life from me and the sorrow of death." "I see
well," said Conchubar, "that you are no friend of mine." And he put Cuchulain
from him. And then he called Fergus to him and asked him the same question, and
Fergus said, "Whatever may happen, I promise your blood will be safe from me,
but besides yourself there is no Ulsterman that would try to harm them, and that I
would lay hold of, but I would give him shortening of life and the sorrow of
death." "I see well," said Conchubar, "it is yourself must go for them, and it is to-
morrow you must set out, for it is with you they will come, and when you are
coming back to us westward, I put you under bonds to go first to the fort of
Borach, son of Cainte, and give me your word now that as soon as you get there,
you will send on the sons of Usnach to Emain, whether it be day or night at the
time." After that the two of them went in together, and Fergus told all
the company how it was under his charge they were to be put.

Then Conchubar went to Borach and asked had he a feast ready prepared for
him. "I have," said Borach, "but although I was able to make it ready, I was not
able to bring it to Emain." "If that is so," said Conchubar, "give it to Fergus when
he comes back to Ireland, for it is *geasa* on him not to refuse your feast." Borach
promised he would do that, and so they wore away that night.

So Fergus set out in the morning, and he brought no guard nor helpers with
him, but himself and his two sons, Fair-Haired Iollan, and Rough-Red Buinne,
and Cuillean, the shield-bearer, and the shield itself. They went on till they got to
the dwelling-place of the sons of Usnach, and to Loch Eitche in Alba. It is how the
sons of Usnach lived; they had three houses, and the house where they made ready

the food, it is not there they would eat it, and the house where they would eat it, it is not there they would sleep.

When Fergus came to the harbour he let a great shout out of him. And it is how Naoise and Deirdre were, they had a chessboard between them, and they playing on it. Naoise heard the shout, and he said, "That is the shout of a man of Ireland." "It is not, but the cry of a man of Alban," said Deirdre. She knew at the first it was Fergus gave the shout, but she denied it. Then Fergus let another shout out of him. "That is an Irish shout," said Naoise again. "It is not, indeed," said Deirdre, "let us go on playing." Then Fergus gave the third shout, and the sons of Usnach knew this time it was the shout of Fergus, and Naoise said to Ardan to go out and meet him. Then Deirdre told him that she herself knew at the first shout that it was Fergus. "Why did you deny it, then, Queen?" said Naoise. "Because of a vision I saw last night," said Deirdre. "Three birds I saw coming to us from Emain Macha, and three drops of honey in their mouths, and they left them with us, and three drops of our blood they brought away with them." "What meaning do you put on that, Queen?" said Naoise. "It is," said Deirdre, "Fergus that is coming to us with a message of peace from Conchubar, for honey is not sweeter than a message of peace sent by a lying man." "Let that pass," said Naoise. "Is there anything in it but troubled sleep and the melancholy of woman? And it is a long time Fergus is in the harbour. Rise up, Ardan, to be before him, and bring him with you here." And Ardan went down to meet him, and gave a fond kiss to himself and to his two sons. And it is what he said: "My love to you, dear comrades." After that he asked news of Ireland, and they gave it to him, and then they came to where Naoise and Ainnle and Deirdre were, and they kissed Fergus and his two sons, and they asked news of Ireland from them. "It is the best news I have for you," said Fergus, "that Conchubar, king of Ulster, has sworn by the earth beneath him, by the high heaven above him, and by the sun that travels to the west, that he will have no rest by day nor sleep by night, if the sons of Usnach, his own foster-brothers, will not come back to the land of their home and the country of their birth; and he has sent us to ask you there." "It is better for them to stop here," said Deirdre, "for they have a greater sway in Scotland than Conchubar himself has in Ireland." "One's own country is better than any other thing," said Fergus, "for no man can have any pleasure, however great his good luck and his way of living, if he does not see his own country every day." "That is true," said Naoise, "for Ireland is dearer to myself than Alban, though I would get more in Alban than in Ireland." "It will be safe indeed," said Naoise, "and we will go with you to Ireland; and though there were no trouble beneath the sun, but a man to be far from his own land, there is little delight in peace and a long sleep to a man that is an exile. It is a pity for the man that is an exile; it is little his honour, it is great his grief, for it is he will have his share of wandering."

It was not with Deirdre's will Naoise said that, and she was greatly against going with Fergus. And she said: "I had a dream last night of the three sons of

Usnach, and they bound and put in the grave by Conchubar of the Red branch."
But Naoise said: "Lay down your dream, Deirdre, on the heights of the hills, lay
down your dream on the sailors of the sea, lay down your dream on the rough
grey stones, for we will give peace and we will get it from the king of the world
and from Conchubar." But Deirdre spoke again, and it is what she said: "There is
the howling of dogs in my ears; a vision of the night is before my eyes, I see Fergus
away from us, I see Conchubar without mercy in his dun; I see Naoise without
strength in battle; I see Ainnle without his loud sounding shield; I see Ardan
without shield or breastplate, and the Hill of Atha without delight. I see Conchubar asking for blood; I see Fergus caught with hidden lies; I see Deirdre crying
with tears, I see Deirdre crying with tears."

"A thing that is unpleasing to me, and that I would never give in to," said
Fergus, "is to listen to the howling of dogs, and to the dreams of women; and
since Conchubar, the High King, has sent a message of friendship, it would not be
right for you to refuse it." "It would not be right, indeed," said Naoise, "and we
will go with you to-morrow." And Fergus gave his word, and he said, "If all the
men of Ireland were against you, it would not profit them, for neither shield nor
sword or a helmet itself would be any help or protection to them against you, and
I myself to be with you." "That is true," said Naoise, "and we will go with you to
Ireland."

They spent the night there until morning, and then they went where the ships
were, and they went on the sea, and a good many of their people with them, and
Deirdre looked back on the land of Alban, and it is what she said: "My love to
you, O land to the east, and it goes ill with me to leave you; for it is pleasant are
your bays and your harbours and your wide flower plains and your green-sided
hills; and little need was there for us to leave you." And she made this complaint:
"Dear to me is that land, that land to the east, Alban, with its wonders; I would
not have come from it hither but that I came with Naoise.

"Dear to me, Dun Fiodhaigh and Dun Fionn; dear is the dun above them; dear
to me Inis Droignach, dear to me Dun Suibhne.

"O Coill Cuan! ohone! Coill Cuan! where Ainnle used to come. My grief it was
short I thought his stay there with Naoise in Western Alban. Glen Laoi, O Glen
Laoi, where I used to sleep under soft coverings; fish and venison and badgers'
flesh, that was my portion in Glen Laoi.

"Glen Masan, my grief Glen Masan! high its hart's-tongue, bright its stalks; we
were rocked to pleasant sleep over the wooded harbour of Masan.

"Glen Archan, my grief Glen Archan, the straight valley of the pleasant ridge;
never was there a young man more light-hearted than my Naoise used to be in
Glen Archan.

"Glen Eitche, my grief Glen Eitche, it was there I built my first house; beautiful
were the woods on our rising; the home of the sun is Glen Eitche.

"Glen-da-Rua, my grief Glen-da-Rua, my love to every man that belongs to it;

sweet is the voice of the cuckoo on the bending branch on the hill above Glen-da-Rua.

"Dear to me is Droighin over the fierce strand, dear are its waters over the clean sand; I would never have come out from it at all but that I came with my beloved!"

After she had made that complaint they came to Dun Borach, and Borach gave three fond kisses to Fergus and to the sons of Usnach along with him. It was then Borach said he had a feast laid out for Fergus, and that it was *geasa* for him to leave it until he would have eaten it. But Fergus reddened with anger from head to foot, and it is what he said: "It is a bad thing you have done, Borach, laying out a feast for me, and Conchubar to have made me give my word that as soon as I would come to Ireland, whether it would be by day or in the night-time, I would send on the sons of Usnach to Emain Macha." "I hold you under *geasa*," said Borach, "to stop and use the feast."

Then Fergus asked Naoise what should he do about the feast. "You must choose," said Deirdre, "whether you will forsake the children of Usnach or the feast, and it would be better for you to refuse the feast than to forsake the sons of Usnach." "I will not forsake them," said he, "for I will send my two sons, Fair-Haired Iollan and Rough-Red Buinne, with them, to Emain Macha." "On my word," said Naoise, "that is a great deal to do for us; for up to this no other person ever protected us but ourselves." And he went out of the place in great anger; and Ainnle, and Ardan, and Deirdre, and the two sons of Fergus followed him, and they left Fergus dark and sorrowful after them. But for all that, Fergus was full sure that if all the provinces of Ireland would go into one council, they would not consent to break the pledge he had given.

As for the sons of Usnach, they went on their way by every short road, and Deirdre said to them, "I will give you a good advice, Sons of Usnach, though you may not follow it." "What is that advice, Queen?" said Naoise. "It is, said she, "to go to Rechrainn, between Ireland and Scotland, and to wait there until Fergus has done with the feast; and that will be the keeping of his word to Fergus, and it will be the lengthening of your lives to you." "We will not follow that advice," said Naoise; and the children of Fergus said it was little trust she had in them, when she thought they would not protect her, though their hands might not be so strong as the hands of the sons of Usnach; and besides that, Fergus had given them his word. "Alas! it is sorrow came on us with the word of Fergus," said Deirdre, "and he to forsake us for a feast," and she made this complaint: "It is grief to me that ever I came from the east on the word of the unthinking son of Rogh. It is only lamentations I will make. Och! it is very sorrowful my heart is!

"My heart is heaped up with sorrow; it is to-night my great hurt is. My grief my dear companions, the end of your days is come."

And it is what Naoise answered her: "Do not say that in your haste, Deirdre, more beautiful than the sun. Fergus would never have come for us eastward to bring us back to be destroyed."

And Deirdre said, "My grief I think it too far for you, beautiful sons of Usnach, to have come from Alban of the rough grass; it is lasting will be its life-long sorrow."

After that they went forward to Finncairn of the watch-tower on sharp-peaked Slieve Fuad, and Deirdre stayed after them in the valley, and sleep fell on her there.

When Naoise saw that Deirdre was left after them, he turned back as she was rising out of her sleep, and he said, "What made you wait after us, Queen?" "Sleep that was on me," said Deirdre; "and I saw a vision in it." "What vision was that?" said Naoise. "It was," she said, "Fair-Haired Iollan that I saw without his head on him, and Rough-Red Buinne with his head on him; and it is without help of Rough-Red Buinne you were, and it is with the help of Fair-Haired Iollan you were." And she made this complaint:

"It is a sad vision has been shown to me, of my four tall, fair, bright companions; the head of each has been taken from him, and no help to be had one from another."

But when Naoise heard this he reproached her, and said, "O fair, beautiful woman, nothing does your mouth speak but evil. Do not let the sharpness and the great misfortune that come from it fall on your friends." And Deirdre answered him with kind, gentle words, and it is what she said: "It would be better to me to see harm come on any other person than upon any one of you three, with whom I have travelled over the seas and over the wide plains; but when I look on you, it is only Buinne I can see whole and untouched and I know by that his life will be longest among you; and indeed it is I that am sorrowful to-night."

After that they came forward to the high willows, and it was then Deirdre said, "I see a cloud in the air, and it is a cloud of blood; and I would give you a good advice, sons of Usnach," she said. "What is that advice?" said Naoise. "To go to Dundealgan where Cuchulain is, until Fergus has done with the feast, and to be under the protection of Cuchulain, for fear of the treachery of Conchubar." "Since there is no fear on us, we will not follow that advice," said Naoise. And Deirdre complained, and it is what she said: "O Naoise, look at the cloud I see above us in the air; I see a cloud over green Macha, cold and deep red like blood. I am startled by the cloud that I see here in the air; a thin, dreadful cloud that is like a clot of blood. I give a right advice to the beautiful sons of Usnach not to go to Emain to-night, because of the danger that is over them.

"We will go to Dundealgan, where the Hound of the Smith is; we will come to-morrow from the south along with the Hound, Cuchulain."

But Naoise said in his anger to Deirdre, "Since there is no fear on us, we will not follow your advice." And Deirdre turned to the grandsons of Rogh, and it is what she said: "It is seldom until now Naoise, that yourself and myself were not of the one mind. And I say to you, Naoise, that you would not have gone against me like this, the day Manannan gave me the cup in the time of his great victory."

After that they went on to Emain Macha. "Sons of Usnach," said Deirdre, "I have a sign by which you will know if Conchubar is going to do treachery on you." "What sign is that?" said Naoise. "If you are let come into the house where Conchubar is, and the nobles of Ulster, then Conchubar is not going to do treachery on you. But if it is in the House of the Red Branch you are put, then he is going to do treachery on you."

After that they came to Emain Macha, and they took the handwood and struck the door, and the doorkeeper asked who was there. They told him that it was the sons of Usnach, and Deirdre, and the two sons of Fergus were there.

When Conchubar heard that, he called his stewards and serving men to him, and he asked them how was the House of the Red Branch for food and drink. They said that if all the seven armies of Ulster would come there, they would find what would satisfy them. "If that is so," said Conchubar, "bring the sons of Usnach into it."

It was then Deirdre said, "It would have been better for you to follow my advice, and never to have come to Emain, and it would be right for you to leave it, even at this time." "We will not," said Fair-Haired Iollan, "for it is not fear or cowardliness was ever seen on us, but we will go to the house." So they went on to the House of the Red Branch, and the stewards and the serving-men with them, and well-tasting food was served to them, and pleasant drinks, till they were all glad and merry, except only Deirdre and the sons of Usnach; for they did not use much food or drink, because of the length and the greatness of their journey from Dun Borach to Emain Macha. Then Naoise said, "Give the chessboard to us till we go playing." So they gave them the chessboard and they began to play.

It was just at that time Conchubar was asking, "Who will I send that will bring me word of Deirdre, and that will tell me if she has the same appearance and the same shape she had before, for if she has, there is not a woman in the world has a more beautiful shape or appearance than she has, and I will bring her out with edge of blade and point of sword in spite of the sons of Usnach, good though they be. But if not, let Naoise have her for himself." "I myself will go there," said Levarcham, "and I will bring you word of that." And it is how it was, Deirdre was dearer to her than any other person in the world; for it was often she went through the world looking for Deirdre and bringing news to her and from her. So Levarcham went over to the House of the Red Branch, and near it she saw a great troop of armed men, and she spoke to them, but they made her no answer, and she knew by that it was none of the men of Ulster were in it, but men from some strange country that Conchubar's messengers had brought to Emain.

And then she went in where Naoise and Deirdre were, and it is how she found them, the polished chessboard between them, and they playing on it; and she gave them fond kisses, and she said: "You are not doing well to be playing; and it is to bring Conchubar word if Deirdre has the same shape and appearance she used to have that he sent me here now; and there is grief on me for the deed that will be done in Emain to-night, treachery that will be done, and the killing of kindred, and the three bright candles of the Gael to be quenched, and Emain will not be the better of it to the end of life and time," and she made this complaint sadly and wearily.

"Sad is my heart for the treachery that is being done in Emain this night; on account of this treachery, Emain will never be at peace from this out.

"The three that are most king-like today under the sun; the three best of all that live on the earth, it is grief to me to-night they to die for the sake of any woman. Naoise and Ainnle whose deeds are known, and Ardan, their brother; treachery is to be done on the young, bright-faced three; it is not I that am not sorrowful to-night."

When she had made this complaint, Levarcham said to the sons of Usnach and to the children of Fergus to shut close the doors and the windows of the house and to do bravery. "And, oh, sons of Fergus," she said, "defend your charge and your care bravely till Fergus comes, and you will have praise and a blessing for it." And she cried with many tears, and she went back to where Conchubar was, and he asked news of Deirdre of her. And Levarcham said, "It is good news and bad news I have for you." "What news is that?" said Conchubar. "It is the good news," she said, "the three sons of Usnach to have come to you and to be over there, and they are the three that are bravest and mightiest in form and in looks and in countenance, of all in the world; and Ireland will be yours from this out, since the sons of Usnach are with you; and the news that is worst with me is, the woman that was best of the women of the world in form and in looks, going out of Emain, is without the form and without the appearance she used to have."

When Conchubar heard that, much of his jealousy went backward, and he was drinking and making merry for a while, until he thought on Deirdre again the second time, and on that he asked, "Who will I get to bring me word of Deirdre?" But he did not find any one would go there. And then he said to Gelban, the merry, pleasant son of the king of Lochlann: "Go over and bring me word if Deirdre has the same shape and the same appearance she used to have, for if she has, there is not on the ridge of the world or on the waves of the earth, a woman more beautiful than herself."

So Gelban went to the House of the Red Branch, and he found the doors and the windows of the fort shut, and fear came on him. And it is what he said: "It is not an easy road for any one that would get to the sons of Usnach, for I think there is very great anger on them." And after that he found a window that was left open by forgetfulness in the house, and he was looking in. Then Deirdre saw him through the window, and when she saw him looking at her, she went into a red blaze of blushes, and Naoise knew that some one was looking at her from the window, and she told him that she saw a young man looking in at them. It is how

Naoise was at that time, with a man of the chessmen in his hand, and he made a fair throw over his shoulder at the young man, that put the eye out of his head. The young man went back to where Conchubar was. "You were merry and pleasant going out," said Conchubar, "but you are sad and cheerless coming back." And then Gelban told him the story from beginning to end. "I see well," said Conchubar, "the man that made that throw will be king of the world, unless he has his life shortened. And what appearance is there on Deirdre?" he said. "It is this," said Gelban, "although Naoise put out my eye, I would have wished to stay there looking at her with the other eye, but for the haste you put on me; for there is not in the world a woman is better of shape or of form than herself."

When Conchubar heard that, he was filled with jealousy and with envy, and he bade the men of his army that were with him, and that had been drinking at the feast, to go and attack the place where the sons of Usnach were. So they went forward to the House of the Red Branch, and they gave three great shouts around it, and they put fires and red flames to it. When the sons of Usnach heard the shouts, they asked who those men were that were about the house. "Conchubar and the men of Ulster," they all said together. "Is it the pledge of Fergus you would break?" said Fair-Haired Iollan. "On my word," said Conchubar, "there will be regret on the sons of Usnach, Deirdre to be with them." "That is true," said Deirdre, "Fergus had deceived you." "By my oath," said Rough-Red Buinne, "if he betrayed, we will not betray." It was then Buinne went out and killed three-fifths of the fighting men outside, and put great disturbance on the rest; and Conchubar asked who was there, and who was doing destruction on his men like that. "It is I, myself, Rough-Red Buinne, son of Fergus," said he. "I will give you a good gift if you will leave off," said Conchubar. "What gift is that?" said Rough-Red Buinne. "A hundred of land," said Conchubar. "What besides?" said Rough-Red Buinne. "My own friendship and my counsel," said Conchubar. "I will take that," said Rough-Red Buinne. It was a good mountain that was given him as a reward, but it turned barren in the same night, and no green grew on it again for ever, and it used to be called the Mountain of the Share of Buinne.

Deirdre heard what they were saying. "By my word," she said, "Rough-Red Buinne has forsaken you, and in my opinion, it is like the father the son is." "I give my word," said Fair-Haired Iollan, "that is not so with me; as long as this narrow, straight sword stays in my hand, I will not forsake the sons of Usnach."

After that, Fair-Haired Iollan went out, and made three courses around the house, and killed three-fifths of heroes outside, and he came in again where Naoise was, and he playing chess, and Ainnle with him. So Iollan went out the second time, and made three other courses round the fort, and he brought a lighted torch with him on the lawn, and he went destroying the hosts, so that they dared not come to attack the house. And he was a good son, Fair-Haired Iollan, for he never refused any person on the ridge of the world anything that he had, and he never took wages from any person but only Fergus.

It was then Conchubar said: "What place is my own son, Fiacra, the Fair?" "I am here, High Prince," said Fiacra. "By my word," said Conchubar, "it is on the one night yourself and Iollan were born, and as it is the arms of his father he has with him, let you take my arms with you, that is, my shield, the Ochain, my two spears, and my great sword, the Gorm Glas, the Blue Green—and do bravery and great deeds with them."

Then Fiacra took Conchubar's arms, and he and Fair-Haired Iollan attacked one another, and they made a stout fight, one against the other. But however it was, Fair-Haired Iollan put down Fiacra, so that he made him lie under the shelter of his shield, till it roared for the greatness of the strait he was in; for it was the way with the Ochain, the shield of Conchubar, to roar when the person on whom it would be was in danger; and the three chief waves of Ireland, the Wave of Tuagh, the Wave of Cliodna, and the Wave of Rudraige, roared in answer to it.

It was at that time Conall Cearnach was at Dun Sobairce, and he heard the Wave of Tuagh. "True it is," said Conall, "Conchubar is in some danger, and it is not right for me to be here listening to him."

Conall rose up on that, and he put his arms and his armour on him, and came forward to where Conchubar was at Emain Macha, and he found the fight going on on the lawn, and Fiacra, the son of Conchubar, greatly pressed by Fair-Haired Iollan, and neither the king of Ulster nor any other person dared to go between them. But Conall went aside, behind Fair-Haired Iollan and thrust his sword through him. "Who is it has wounded me behind my back?" said Fair-Haired Iollan. "Whoever did it, by my hand of valour, he would have got a fair fight, face to face, from myself." "Who are you yourself?" said Conall. "I am Iollan, son of Fergus, and are you yourself Conall?" "It is I," said Conall. "It is evil and it is heavy the work you have done," said Iollan, "and the sons of Usnach under my protection." "Is that true?" said Conall. "It is true, indeed," said Iollan. "By my hand of valour," said Conall, "Conchubar will not get his own son alive from me to avenge it," and he gave a stroke of the sword to Fiacra, so that he struck his head off, and he left them so. The cloud of death came upon Fair-Haired Iollan then, and he threw his arms towards the fortress, and called out to Naoise to do bravery, and after that he died.

It is then Conchubar himself came out and nineteen hundred men with him, and Conall said to him: "Go up now to the doorway of the fort, and see where your sister's children are lying on a bed of trouble." And when Conchubar saw them he said: "You are not sister's children to me; it is not the deed of sister's children you have done me, but you have done harm to me with treachery in the sight of all the men of Ireland." And it is what Ainnle said to him: "Although we took well-shaped, soft-handed Deirdre from you, yet we did a little kindness to you at another time, and this is the time to remember it. That day your ship was breaking up on the sea, and it full of gold and silver, we gave you up our own ship, and ourselves went swimming to the harbour." But Conchubar said: "If you did fifty good deeds to me, surely this would be my thanks; I would not give you peace, and you in distress, but every great want I could put on you."

And then Ardan said: "We did another little kindness to you, and this is the time to remember it; the day the speckled horse failed you on the green of Dundealgan, it was we gave you the grey horse that would bring you fast on your road."

But Conchubar said: "If you had done fifty good deeds to me, surely this would be my thanks; I would not give you peace, and you in distress, but every great want I could put on you."

And then Naoise said: "We did you another good deed, and this is the time to remember it; we have put you under many benefits; it is strong our right is to your protection.

"The time when Murcael, son of Brian, fought the seven battles at Beinn Etair, we brought you, without fail, the heads of the sons of the king of the South-East."

But Conchubar said: "If you had done me fifty good deeds, surely this is my thanks; I would not give you peace in your distress, but every great want I could put upon you.

"Your death is not a death to me now, young sons of Usnach, since he that was innocent fell by you, the third best of the horsemen of Ireland."

Then Deirdre said: "Rise up, Naoise, take your sword, good son of a king, mind yourself well, for it is not long that life will be left in your fair body."

It is then all Conchubar's men came about the house and they put fires and burning to it. Ardan went out then, and his men, and put out the fires, and killed three hundred men. And Ainnle went out in the third part of the night, and he killed three hundred, and did slaughter and destruction on them.

And Naoise went out in the last quarter of the night and drove away all the army from the house.

He came into the house after that, and it is then Deirdre rose up and said to him: "By my word, it is well you won your way; and do bravery and valour from this out, and it was bad advice you took when you ever trusted Conchubar."

As for the sons of Usnach, after that they made a good protection with their shields, and they put Deirdre in the middle and linked the shields around her, and they gave three leaps out over the walls of Emain, and they killed three hundred men in that sally.

When Conchubar saw that, he went to Cathbad, the Druid, and said to him: "Go, Cathbad, to the sons of Usnach, and work enchantment on them; for unless they are hindered they will destroy the men of Ulster for ever if they go away in spite of them; and I give the word of a true hero, they will get no harm from me, but let them only make agreement with me." When Cathbad heard that, he agreed, believing him, and he went to the end of his arts and his knowledge to hinder the sons of Usnach, and he worked enchantment on them, so that he put the likeness of a dark sea about them, with hindering waves. And when Naoise saw the waves rising he put up Deirdre on his shoulder, and it is how the sons of

Usnach were, swimming on the ground as they were going out of Emain; yet the men of Ulster did not dare to come near them until their swords had fallen from their hands. But after their swords fell from their hands, the sons of Usnach were taken. And when they were taken, Conchubar asked of the children of Durthacht to kill them. But the children of Durthacht said they would not do that. There was a young man with Conchubar whose name was Maine, and his surname Rough-Hand, son of the king of the fair Norwegians, and it is Naoise had killed his father and his two brothers; Athrac and Triathrach were their names. And he said he himself would kill the sons of Usnach. "If that is so," said Ardan, "kill me the first, for I am younger than my brothers, so that I will not see my brothers killed. "Let him not be killed but myself," said Ainnle. "Let that not be done," said Naoise, "for I have a sword that Manannan, son of Lir, gave me, and the stroke of it leaves nothing after it, track nor trace; and strike the three of us together, and we will die at the one time." "That is well," said they all, "and let you lay down your heads," they said. They did that, and Maine gave a strong quick blow of the sword on the three necks together on the block, and struck the three heads off them with one stroke; and the men of Ulster gave three loud sorrowful shouts, and cried aloud about them there.

As for Deirdre, she cried pitifully, wearily, and tore her fair hair, and she was talking on the sons of Usnach and on Alban, and it is what she said:

"A blessing eastward to Alban from me; good is the sight of her bays and valleys, pleasant was it to sit on the slopes of her hills, where the sons of Usnach used to be hunting.

"One day, when the nobles of Scotland were drinking with the sons of Usnach, to whom they owed their affection, Naoise gave a kiss secretly to the daughter of the lord of Duntreon. He sent her a frightened deer, wild and a fawn at its foot; and he went to visit her coming home from the host of Inverness. When myself heard that, my head filled full of jealousy; I put my boat on the waves, it was the same to me to live or to die. They followed me swimming, Ainnle and Ardan, that never said a lie; they turned me back again, two that would give battle to a hundred; Naoise gave me his true word, he swore three times with his arms as witness, he would never put vexation on me again, until he would go from me to the hosts of the dead.

"Och! if she knew to-night, Naoise to be under a covering of clay, it is she would cry her fill, and it is I would cry along with her."

After she had made this complaint, seeing they were all taken up with one another, Deirdre came forward on the lawn, and she was running round and round, up and down, from one to another, and Cuchulain met her, and she told him the story from first to last, how it had happened to the sons of Usnach. It is sorrowful Cuchulain was for that, for there was not in the world a man was dearer to him than Naoise. And he asked who killed him. "Maine Rough-Hand," said Deirdre. Then Cuchulain went away, sad and sorrowful, to Dundealgan.

After that Deirdre lay down by the grave, and they were digging earth from it, and she made this lament after the sons of Usnach:

"Long is the day without the sons of Usnach; it was never wearisome to be in their company; sons of a king that entertained exiles; three lions of the Hill of the Cave.

"Three darlings of the women of Britain; three hawks of Slieve Cuilenn; sons of a king served by valour, to whom warriors did obedience. The three mighty bears; three lions of the fort of Conrach; three sons of a king who thought well of their praise; three nurslings of the men of Ulster.

"Three heroes not good at homage; their fall is a cause of sorrow; three sons of the sister of a king; three props of the army of Cuailgne.

"Three dragons of Dun Monad, the three valiant men from the Red Branch; I myself will not be living after them, the three that broke hard battles.

"Three that were brought up by Aoife, to whom lands were under tribute; three pillars in the breach of battle; three pupils that were with Scathach.

"Three pupils that were with Uathach; three champions that were lasting in might; three shining sons of Usnach; it is weariness to be without them.

"The High King of Ulster, my first betrothed, I forsook for love of Naoise; short my life will be after him; I will make keening at their burial.

"That I would live after Naoise let no one think on the earth; I will not go on living after Ainnle and after Ardan.

"After them I myself will not live; three that would leap through the midst of battle; since my beloved is gone from me I will cry my fill over his grave.

"Oh, young man, digging the new grave, do not make the grave narrow; I will be along with them in the grave, making lamentation and ochones!

"Many the hardship I met with along with the three heroes; I suffered want of house, want of fire, it is myself that used not to be troubled.

"Their three shields and their spears made a bed for me often. Oh, young man put their three swords close over their grave.

"Their three hounds, their three hawks, will be from this time without huntsmen; three aids of every battle; three pupils of Conall Cearnach.

"The three leashes of those three hounds have brought a sigh from my heart; it is I had the care of them, the sight of them is a cause of grief.

"I was never one day alone to the day of the making of this grave, though it is often that myself and yourselves were in loneliness.

"My sight is gone from me with looking at the grave of Naoise; it is short till my life will leave me, and those who would have keened me do not live.

"Since it is through me they were betrayed I will be tired out with sorrow; it is a pity I was not in the earth before the sons of Usnach were killed.

"Sorrowful was my journey with Fergus, betraying me to the Red Branch; we were deceived all together with his sweet, flowery words. I left the delights of

Ulster for the three heroes that were bravest; my life will not be long, I myself am alone after them.

"I am Deirdre without gladness, and I at the end of my life; since it is grief to be without them, I myself will not be long after them."

After that complaint Deirdre loosed out her hair, and threw herself on the body of Naoise before it was put in the grave and gave three kisses to him, and when her mouth touched his blood the colour of burning sods came into her cheeks, and she rose up like one that had lost her wits, and she went on through the night till she came to where the waves were breaking on the strand. And a fisherman was there and his wife, and they brought her into their cabin and sheltered her, and she neither smiled nor laughed, nor took food, drink, or sleep, nor raised her head from her knees, but crying always after the sons of Usnach.

But when she could not be found at Emain, Conchubar sent Levarcham to look for her, and to bring her back to his palace, that he might make her his wife. And Levarcham found her in the fisherman's cabin, and she bade her come back to Emain, where she would have protection and riches and all that she would ask. And she gave her this message she brought from Conchubar: "Come up to my house, O branch with the dark eye-lashes, and there need be no fear on your fair face, of hatred or of jealousy or of reproach." And Deirdre said: "I will not go up to his house, for it is not land or earth or food I am wanting, or gold or silver or horses, but leave to go to the grave where the sons of Usnach are lying, till I give the three honey kisses to their three white, beautiful bodies." And she made this complaint:

"Make keening for the heroes that were killed on their coming to Ireland; stately they used to be, coming to the house, the three great sons of Usnach.

"The sons of Usnach fell in the fight like three branches that were growing straight and nice, and they destroyed in a heavy storm that left neither bud nor twig of them.

"Naoise, my gentle, well-learned comrade, made no delay in crying him with me; cry for Ardan that killed the wild boars, cry for Ainnle whose strength was great.

"It was Naoise that would kiss my lips, my first man and my first sweetheart; it was Ainnle would pour out my drink, and it was Ardan would lay my pillow.

"Though sweet to you is the mead that is drunk by the soft-living son of Ness, the food of the sons of Usnach was sweeter to me all through my lifetime.

"Whenever Naoise would go out to hunt through the woods or the wide plains, all the meat he would bring back was better to me than honey.

"Though sweet to you are the sounds of pipes and of trumpets, it is truly I say to the king, I have heard music that is sweeter.

"Delightful to Conchubar, the king, are pipes and trumpets; but the singing of the sons of Usnach was more delightful to me.

"It was Naoise had the deep sound of the waves in his voice; it was the song of Ardan that was good, and the voice of Ainnle towards their green dwelling-place.

"Their birth was beautiful and their blossoming, as they grew to the strength of manhood; sad is the end to-day, the sons of Usnach to be cut down.

"Dear were their pleasant words, dear their young, high strength; in their going through the plains of Ireland there was a welcome before the coming of their strength.

"Dear their grey eyes that were loved by women, many looked on them as they went; when they went freely searching through the woods, their steps were pleasant on the dark mountain.

"I do not sleep at any time, and the colour is gone from my face; there is no sound can give me delight since the sons of Usnach do not come.

"I do not sleep through the night; my senses are scattered away from me, I do not care for food or drink. I have no welcome to-day for the pleasant drink of nobles, or ease, or comfort, or delight, or a great house, or the palace of a king.

"Do not break the strings of my heart as you took hold of my young youth, Conchubar; though my darling is dead, my love is strong to live. What is country to me, or land, or lordship? What are swift horses? What are jewels and gold? Och! it is I will be lying to-night on the strand like the beautiful sons of Usnach."

So Levarcham went back to Conchubar to tell him what way Deirdre was, and that she would not come with her to Emain Macha.

And when she was gone, Deirdre went out on the strand, and she found a carpenter making an oar for a boat, and making a mast for it, clean and straight, to put up a sail to the wind. And when she saw him making it, she said: "It is a sharp knife you have, to cut the oar so clean and so straight, and if you will give it to me," she said, "I will give you a ring of the best gold in Ireland for it, the ring that belonged to Naoise, and that was with him through the battle and through the fight; he thought much of it in his lifetime; it is pure gold, through and through." So the carpenter took the ring in his hand, and the knife in the other hand, and he looked at them together, and he gave her the knife for the ring, and for her asking and her tears. Then Deirdre went close to the waves, and she said: "Since the other is not with me now, I will spend no more of my lifetime without him." And with that she drove the black knife into her side, but she drew it out again and threw it in the sea to her right hand, the way no one would be blamed for her death.

Then Conchubar came down to the strand and five hundred men along with him, to bring Deirdre away to Emain Macha, but all he found before him was her white body on the ground, and it without life. And it is what he said:

"A thousand deaths on the time I brought death on my sister's children; now I am myself without Deirdre, and they themselves are without life.

"They were my sister's children, the three brothers I vexed with blows, Naoise, and Ainnle, and Ardan; they have died along with Deirdre."

And they took her white, beautiful body, and laid it in a grave, and a flagstone was raised over her grave, and over the grave of the sons of Usnach, and their names were written in Ogham, and keening was made for their burial.

And as to Fergus, son of Rogh, he came on the day after the children of Usnach were killed, to Emain Macha. And when he found they had been killed and his pledge to them broken, he himself, and Cormac Conloingeas, Conchubar's own son, and Dubthach, the Beetle of Ulster, with their men, made an attack on Conchubar's house and men, and a great many were killed by them, and Emain Macha was burned and destroyed.

And after doing that, they went into Connaught, to Ailell and to Maeve at Cruachan, and they were made welcome there, and they took service with them and fought with them against Ulster because of the treachery that was done by Conchubar. And that is the way Fergus and the others came to be on the side of the men of Connaught in the war for the Brown Bull of Cuailgne.

And Cathbad laid a curse on Emain Macha, on account of that great wrong. And it is what he said that none of the race of Conchubar should have the kingdom, to the end of life and time.

And that came true, for the most of Conchubar's sons died in his own lifetime, and when he was near his death, he bade the men of Ulster bring back Cormac Conloingeas out of Cruachan, and give him the kingdom.

So they sent messengers to Cormac, and he set out and his three troops of men with him, and he left his blessing with Ailell and with Maeve, and he promised them a good return for all the kind treatment they had given him. And they crossed the river at Athluain, and there they saw a red woman at the edge of the ford, and she washing her chariot and her harness. And after that they met a young girl coming towards them, and a light green cloak about her, and a brooch of precious stones at her breast. And Cormac asked her was she coming with them, and she said she was not, and it would be better for himself to turn back, for the ruin of his life was come.

And he stopped for the night at the House of the Two Smiths on the hill of Bruighean Mor, the great dwelling-place.

But a troop of the men of Connaught came about the house in the night, for they were on the way home after destroying and robbing a district of Ulster, and they thought to make an end of Cormac before he would get to Emain.

And it chanced there was a great harper, Craiftine, living close by, and his wife, Sceanb, daughter of Scethern, a Druid of Connaught, loved Cormac. Conloingeas, and three times she had gone to meet him at Athluain, and she planted three trees there—Grief, and Dark, and Dumbness.

And there was great hatred and jealousy of Cormac on Craiftine, so when he knew the men of Connaught were going to make an attack on him, he went outside the house with his harp, and played a soft sleepy tune to him, the way he had not the strength to rouse himself up, and himself and the most of his people were killed. And Amergin, that had gone with the message to him, made his grave and his mound, and the place is called Cluain Duma, the Lawn of the Mound.

CHAPTER VIII

The Dream of Angus

Angus, son of the Dagda, was asleep in his bed one night, and he saw what he thought was a young girl standing near him at the top of the bed, and she the most beautiful he had ever seen in Ireland. He put out his hand to take her hand, but she vanished on the moment, and in the morning when he awoke there were no trace or tidings of her.

He got no rest that day thinking of her, and that she had gone away before he could speak to her. And the next night he saw her again, and this time she brought a little harp in her hand, the sweetest he ever heard, and she played a song to him, so that he fell asleep and slept till morning. And the same thing happened every night for a year. She would come to his bedside and be playing on the harp to him, but she would be gone before he could speak with her. And at the end of the year she came no more, and Angus began to pine away with love of her and with fretting after her; and he would take no food, but lay upon the bed, and no one knew what it was ailed him. And all the physicians of Ireland came together, but they could not put a name on his sickness or find any cure for him.

But at last Fergne, the physician of Conn, was brought to him, and as soon as he looked at him he knew it was not on his body the sickness was, but on his mind. And he sent every one away out of the room, and he said: "I think it is for the love of some woman that you are wasting away like this." "That is true, indeed," said Angus; "and it is my sickness has betrayed me." And then he told him how the woman with the most beautiful appearance of any woman in Ireland, used to come and to be playing the harp to him through the night, and how she had vanished away.

Then Fergne went and spoke with Boann, Angus's mother, and he told her all that happened, and he bade her to send and search all through Ireland if she could find a young girl of the same appearance as the one Angus had seen in his sleep. And then he left him in his mother's care, and she had all Ireland searched for a year, but no young girl of that appearance could be found.

At the end of the year, Boann sent for Fergne to come again, and she said: "We have not got any help from our search up to this." And Fergne said: "Send for the Dagda, that he may come and speak to his son." So they sent for the Dagda, and when he came, he said: "What have I been called for?" "To give an advice to your son," said Fergne, "and to help him, for he is lying sick on account of a young girl that appeared to him in his sleep, and that cannot be found; and it would be a pity for him to die." "What use will it be, I to speak to him?" said the Dagda, "for my knowledge is no higher than your own." "By the word," said Fergne, "you are the king of all the Sidhe of Ireland, and what you have to do is to go to Bodb, the king of the Sidhe of Munster, for he has a name for knowledge all through Ireland." So messengers were sent to Bodb, at his house in Sidhe Femain, and he bade them welcome. "A welcome before you, messenger of the Dagda," he said, "and what is the message you have brought?" "This is the message," they said, "Angus, son of the Dagda, is wasting away these two years with love of a woman he saw in his dreams, and we have not been able to find her in any place. And this is an order to you," they said, "from the Dagda, to search out through Ireland a young girl of the same form and appearance as the one he saw." "The search will be made," said Bodb, "if it lasts me a year."

And at the end of a year he sent messengers to the Dagda. "Is it a good message you have brought?" said the Dagda. "It is, indeed," they said; "and this is the message Bodb bade us give you, 'I have searched all Ireland until I found the young girl with the same form and appearance that you said, at Loch Beul Draguin, at the Harp of Cliach.' And now," they said, "he bids Angus to come with us, till he sees if it is the same woman that appeared to him in his dream."

So Angus set out in his chariot to Sidhe Femain, and Bodb bade him welcome, and made a great feast for him, that lasted three days and three nights. And at the end of that time he said: "Come out now with me, and see if this is the same woman as came to you."

So they set out together till they came to the sea, and there they saw three times fifty young girls, and the one they were looking for among them; and she was far beyond them all. And there was a silver chain between every two of them, but about her own neck there was a necklace of shining gold. And Bodb said: "Do you see that woman you were looking for?" "I see her, indeed," said Angus. "But tell me who she is, and what her name is." "Her name is Caer Ormaith, daughter of Ethal Anbual, from Sidhe Uaman, in the province of Connaught. But you cannot bring her away with you this time," said Bodb.

Then Angus went to visit his father, the Dagda, and his mother, Boann, at Brugh na Boinne; and Bodb went with him, and they told how they had seen the girl, and they had heard her own name, and her father's name. "What had we best do now?" said the Dagda. "The best thing for you to do," said Bodb, "is to go to Ailell and Maeve, for it is in their district she lives, and you had best ask their help."

So the Dagda set out until he came into the province of Connaught, and sixty chariots with him; and Ailell and Maeve made a great feast for him. And after they had been feasting and drinking for the length of a week, Ailell asked the reason of their journey. And the Dagda said: "It is by reason of a young girl in your district, for my son has sickness upon him on account of her, and I am come to ask if you will give her to him." "Who is she?" said Ailell. "She is Caer Ormaith, daughter of Ethal Anbual." "We have no power over her that we could give her to him," said Ailell and Maeve. "The best thing for you to do," said the Dagda, "would be to call her father here to you."

So Ailell sent his steward to Ethal Anbual, and he said: "I am come to bid you to go and speak with Ailell and with Maeve." "I will not go," he said; "I will not give my daughter to the son of the Dagda." So the steward went back and told this to Ailell. "He will not come," he said, "and he knows the reason you want him for."

Then there was anger on Ailell and on the Dagda, and they went out, and their armed men with them, and they destroyed the whole place of Ethal Anbual, and he was brought before them. And Ailell said to him: "Give your daughter now to the son of the Dagda." "That is what I cannot do," he said, "for there is a power over her that is greater than mine." "What power is that?" said Ailell. "It is an enchantment," he said, "that is on her, she to be in the shape of a bird for one year, and in her own shape the next year." "Which shape is on her at this time?" said Ailell. "I would not like to say that," said her father. "Your head from you if you will not tell it," Said Ailell. "Well," said he, "I will tell you this much; she will be in the shape of a swan next month at Loch Beul Draguin, and three fifties of beautiful birds will be along with her, and if you will go there, you will see her."

So then Ethal was set free, and he made friends again with Ailell and Maeve; and the Dagda went home and told Angus all that had happened, and he said: "Go next summer to Loch Beul Draguin, and call her to you there."

So when the time came Angus Og went to the loch, and he saw the three times fifty white birds there, with their silver chains about their necks. And Angus stood in a man's shape at the edge of the loch, and he called to the girl: "Come and speak with me, O Caer!" "Who is calling me?" said Caer. "Angus calls you," he said, "and if you come, I swear by my word, I will not hinder you from going into the loch again." "I will come," she said. So she came to him, and he laid his two hands on her, and then, to hold to his word, he took the shape of a swan on himself, and they went into the loch together, and they went around it three times. And then they spread their wings and rose up from the loch, and went in that shape till they were at Brugh na Boinne. And as they were going, the music they made was so sweet that all the people that heard it fell asleep for three days and three nights.

And Caer stopped there with him ever afterwards, and from that time there was friendship between Angus Og and Ailell and Maeve. And it was on account of that friendship, Angus gave them his help at the time of the war for the Brown Bull of Cuailgne.

CHAPTER IX

Cruachan

Now as to Cruachan, the home of Ailell and of Maeve, it is on the plain of Magh Ai it was, in the province of Connaught.

And this is the way the plain came by its name. In the time long ago, there was a king whose name was Conn, that had the Druid power, so that when the Sidhe themselves came against him, he was able to defend himself with enchantments as good as their own. And one time he went out against them, and broke up their houses, and carried away their cattle, and then, to hinder them from following after him, he covered the whole province with a deep snow.

The Sidhe went then to consult with Dalach, the king's brother, that had the Druid knowledge even better than himself; and it is what he told them to do, to kill three hundred white cows with red ears, and to spread out their livers on a certain plain. And when they had done this, he made spells on them, and the heat the livers gave out melted the snow over the whole plain and the whole province, and after that the plain was given the name of Magh Ai, the Plain of the Livers.

Ailell was son of Ross Ruadh, king of Leinster, and Maeve was daughter of Eochaid, king of Ireland, and her brothers were the Three Fair Twins that rose up against their father, and fought against him at Druim Criadh. And they were beaten in the fight, and went back over the Sionnan, and they were overtaken and their heads were cut off, and brought back to their father, and he fretted after them to the end of his life.

Seven sons Ailell and Maeve had, and the name of every one of them was Maine. There was Maine Mathremail, like his mother, and Maine Athremail, like his father, and Maine Mo Epert, the Talker, and Maine Milscothach, the Honey-Worded, and Maine Andoe the Quick, and Maine Mingor, the Gently Dutiful, and Maine Morgor, the Very Dutiful. Their own people they had, and their own place of living.

This now was the appearance of Cruachan, the Royal house of Ailell and of Maeve, that some called Cruachan of the poets; there were seven divisions in the house, with couches in them, from the hearth to the wall; a front of bronze to every division, and of red yew with carvings on it; and there were seven strips of bronze from the foundation to the roof of the house. The house was made of oak, and the roof was covered with oak shingles; sixteen windows with glass there were, and shutters of bronze on them, and a bar of bronze across every shutter. There was a raised place in the middle of the house for Ailell and Maeve, with silver fronts and strips of bronze around it, and four bronze pillars on it, and a silver rod beside it, the way Ailell and Maeve could strike the middle beam and check their people.

And outside the royal house was the dun, with the walls about it that were built by Brocc, son of Blar, and the great gate; and it is there the houses were for strangers to be lodged.

And besides this, there was at Cruachan the Hill of the Sidhe, or, as some called it, the Cave of Cruachan. It was there Midhir brought Etain one time, and it is there the people of the Sidhe lived; but it is seldom any living person had the power to see them.

It is out of that hill a flock of white birds came one time, and everything they touched in all Ireland withered up, until at last the men of Ulster killed them with their slings. And another time enchanted pigs came out of the hill, and in every place they trod, neither corn nor grass nor leaf would sprout before the end of seven years, and no sort of weapon could wound them. But if they were counted in any place, or if the people so much as tried to count them, they would not stop in that place, but they would go on to another. But however often the people of the country tried to count them, no two people could ever make out the one number, and one man would call out, "There are three pigs in it," and another, "No, but there are seven," and another that it was eleven were in it, or thirteen, and so the count would be lost. One time Maeve and Ailell themselves tried to count them on the plain, but while they were doing it, one of the pigs made a leap over Maeve's chariot, and she in it. Every one called out, "A pig has gone over you, Maeve!" "It has not," she said, and with that she caught hold of the pig by the shank, but if she did, its skin opened at the head, and it made its escape. And it is from that the place was called Magh-mucrimha, the plain of swine-counting.

Another time Fraech, son of Idath, of the men of Connaught, that was son of Boann's sister, Befind, from the Sidhe, came to Cruachan. He was the most beautiful of the men of Ireland or of Alban, but his life was not long. It was to ask Findabair for his wife he came, and before he set out his people said: "Send a message to your mother's people, the way they will send you clothing of the Sidhe." So he went to Boann, that was at Magh Breagh, and he brought away fifty blue cloaks with four black ears on each cloak, and a brooch of red gold with each, and pale while shirts with loop beasts of gold around them; and fifty silver shields with edges, and a candle of a king's house in the hand of each of the men, knobs of carbuncle under them, and their points of precious stones. They used to light up the night as if they were sun's rays.

And he had with him seven trumpeters with gold and silver trumpets, with many coloured clothing, with golden, silken, heads of hair, with coloured cloaks; and three harpers with the appearance of a king on each of them, every harper having the white skin of a deer about him and a cloak of white linen, and a harp bag of the skins of water-dogs.

The watchman saw them from the dun when they had come into the Plain of

Cruachan. "I see a great crowd," he said, "coming towards us. Since Ailell was king and Maeve was queen, there never came and there never will come a grander or a more beautiful crowd than this one. It is like as if I had my head in a vat of wine, with the breeze that goes over them."

Then Fraech's people let out their hounds, and the hounds found seven deer and seven foxes and seven hares and seven wild boars, and hunted them to Rath Cruachan, and there they were killed on the lawn of the dun.

Then Ailell and Maeve gave them a welcome, and they were brought into the house, and while food was being made ready, Maeve sat down to play a game of chess with Fraech. It was a beautiful chess-board they had, all of white bronze, and the chessmen of gold and silver, and a candle of precious stones lighting them.

Then Ailell said: "Let your harpers play for us while the feast is being made ready." "Let them play, indeed," said Fraech.

So the harpers began to play, and it was much that the people of the house did not die with crying and with sadness. And the music they played was the Three Cries of Uaithne. It was Uaithne, the harp of the Dagda, that first played those cries the time Boann's sons were born. The first was a song of sorrow for the hardness of her pains, and the second was a song of smiling and joy for the birth of her sons, and the third was a sleeping song after the birth.

And with the music of the harpers, and with the light that shone from the precious stones in the house, they did not know the night was on them, till at last Maeve started up, and she said: "We have done a great deed to keep these young men without food." It is more you think of chess-playing than of providing for them," said Ailell; "and now, let them stop from the music," he said, "till the food is given out."

Then the food was divided. It was Lothar used to be sitting on the floor of the house, dividing the food with his cleaver, and he not eating himself, and from the time he began dividing, food never failed under his hand.

After that, Fraech was brought into the conversation-house, and they asked him what was it he wanted.

"A visit to yourselves," he said, but he said nothing of Findabair. So they told him he was welcome, and he stopped with them for a while, and every day they went out hunting, and all the people of Connaught used to come and to be looking at them.

But all this time Fraech got no chance of speaking with Findabair, until one morning at daybreak, he went down to the river for washing, and Findabair and her young girls had gone there before him. And he took her hand, and he said: "Stay here and talk with me, for it is for your sake I am come, and would you go away with me secretly?" "I will not go secretly," she said, "for I am the daughter of a king and of a queen."

So she went from him then, but she left him a ring to remember her by. It was a ring her mother had given her.

Then Fraech went to the conversation-house to Ailell and to Maeve. "Will you give your daughter to me?" he said. "We will give her if you will give the marriage portion we ask," said Ailell, "and that is, sixty black-grey horses with golden bits, and twelve milch cows, and a white red-eared calf with each of them; and you to come with us with all your strength and all your musicians at whatever time we go to war in Ulster." "I swear by my shield and my sword, I would not give that for Maeve herself," he said; and he went away out of the house.

But Ailell had taken notice of Findabair's ring with Fraech, and he said to Maeve: "If he brings our daughter away with him, we will lose the help of many of the kings of Ireland. Let us go after him and make an end of him before he has time to harm us." "That would be a pity," said Maeve, "and it would be a reproach on us." "It will be no reproach on us, the way I will manage it," said he. And Maeve agreed to it, for there was vexation on her that it was Findabair that Fraech wanted, and not herself. So they went into the palace, and Ailell said: "Let us go and see the hounds hunting until mid-day." So they did so, and at mid-day they were tired, and they all went to bathe in the river. And Fraech was swimming in the river, and Ailell said to him: "Do not come back till you bring me a branch of the rowan-tree there beyond, with the beautiful berries." For he knew there was a prophecy that it was in a river Fraech would get his death.

So he went and broke a branch off the tree and brought it back over the water, and it is beautiful he looked over the black water, his body without fault, and his face so nice, and his eyes very grey, and the branch with the red berries between the throat and the white face. And then he threw the branch to them out of the water. "It is ripe and beautiful the berries are," said Ailell; "bring us more of them."

So he went off again to the tree, and the water-worm that guarded the tree caught a hold of him. "Let me have a sword," he called out, but there was not a man on the land would dare to give it to him, through fear of Ailell and of Maeve. But Findabair made a leap to go into the water with a gold knife she had in her hand, but Ailell threw a sharp-pointed spear from above, through her plaited hair, that held her; but she threw the knife to Fraech, and he cut off the head of the monster, and brought it with him to the land, but he himself had got a deep wound. Then Ailell and Maeve went back to the house. "It is a great deed we have done," said Maeve. "It is a pity, indeed, what we have done to the man," said Ailell. "And let a healing-bath be made for him now," he said, "of the marrow of pigs and of a heifer." Fraech was put in the bath then, and pleasant music was played by the trumpeters, and a bed was made for him.

Then a sorrowful crying was heard on Cruachan, and they saw three times fifty women with purple gowns, with green head-dresses, and pins of silver on their wrists, and a messenger went and asked them who was it they were crying for. "For Fraech, son of Idath," they said, "boy darling of the king of the Sidhe of Ireland."

Then Fraech heard their crying, and he said: "Lift me out of this, for that is the cry of my mother, and of the women of Boann." So they lifted him out, and the women came round him and brought him away into the Hill of Cruachan.

And the next day he came out, and he whole and sound, and fifty women with him, and they with the appearance of women of the Sidhe. And at the door of the dun they left him, and they gave out their cry again, so that all the people that heard it could not but feel sorrowful. It is from this the musicians of Ireland learned the sorrowful cry of the women of the Sidhe.

And when he went into the house, the whole household rose up before him and bade him welcome, as if it was from another world he was come. And there was shame and repentance on Ailell and on Maeve for trying to harm him, and peace was made, and he went away to his own place.

And it was after that he came to help Ailell and Maeve, and that he got his death in a river as was foretold, at the beginning of the war for the Brown Bull of Cuailgne.

And one time the Hill was robbed by the men of Cruachan, and this is the way it happened.

One night at Samhain, Ailell and Maeve were in Cruachan with their whole household, and the food was being made ready.

Two prisoners had been hanged by them the day before, and Ailell said: "Whoever will put a gad round the foot of either of the two men on the gallows, will get a prize from me."

It was a very dark night, and bad things would always appear on that night of Samhain, and every man that went out to try came back very quickly into the house. "I will go if I will get a prize," said Nera, then. "I will give you this gold-hilted sword," said Ailell.

So Nera went out and he put a gad round the foot of one of the men that had been hanged. Then the man spoke to him. "It is good courage you have," he said, "and bring me with you where I can get a drink, for I was very thirsty when I was hanged." So Nera brought him where he would get a drink, and then he put him on the gallows again, and went back to Cruachan.

But what he saw was the whole of the palace as if on fire before him, and the heads of the people of it lying on the ground, and then he thought he saw an army going into the Hill of Cruachan, and he followed after the army. "There is a man on our track," the last man said. "The track is the heavier," said the next to him, and each said that word to the other from the last to the first. Then they went into the Hill of Cruachan. And they said to their king: "What shall be done to the man that is come in?" "Let him come here till I speak with him," said the king. So Nera came, and the king asked him who it was had brought him in. "I came in with your army," said Nera. "Go to that house beyond," said the king: "there is a woman there will make you welcome. Tell her it is I myself sent you to her. And come every day," he said, "to this house with a load of firing."

So Nera went where he was told, and the woman said: "A welcome before you, if it is the king sent you." So he stopped there, and took the woman for his wife. And every day for three days he brought a load of firing to the king's house, and on each day he saw a blind man, and a lame man on his back, coming out of the house before him. They would go on till they were at the brink of a well before the Hill. "Is it there?" the blind man would say. "It is, indeed," the lame man would say. "Let us go away," the lame man would say then.

And at the end of three days, as he thought, Nera asked the woman about this. "Why do the blind man and the lame man go every day to the well?" he said. "They go to know is the crown safe that is in the well. It is there the king's crown is kept." "Why do these two go?" said Nera, "It is easy to tell that," she said; "they are trusted by the king to visit the crown, and one of them was blinded by him, and the other was lamed. And another thing," she said, "go now and give a warning to your people to mind themselves next Samhain night, unless they will come to attack the hill, for it is only at Samhain," she said, "the army of the Sidhe can go out, for it is at that time all the hills of the Sidhe of Ireland are opened. But if they will come, I will promise them this, the crown of Briun to be carried off by Ailell and by Maeve."

"How can I give them that message," said Nera, "when I saw the whole dun of Cruachan burned and destroyed, and all the people destroyed with it?" "You did not see that, indeed," she said. "It was the host of the Sidhe came and put that appearance before your eyes. And go back to them now," she said, "and you will find them sitting round the same great pot, and the meat has not yet been taken off the fire."

"How will it be believed that I have gone into the Hill?" said Nera. "Bring flowers of summer with you," said the woman. So he brought wild garlic with him, and primroses and golden fern.

So he went back to the palace, and he found his people round the same great pot, and he told them all that had happened him, and the sword was given to him, and he stopped with his people to the end of a year.

At the end of the year Ailell said to Nera: "We are going now against the Hill of the Sidhe, and let you go back," he said, "if you have anything to bring out of it." So he went back to see the woman, and she bade him welcome. "Go now," she said, "and bring in a load of firing to the king, for I went in myself every day for the last year with the load on my back, and I said there was sickness on you." So he did that.

Then the men of Connaught and the black host of the exiles of Ulster went into the Hill and robbed it and brought away the crown of Briun, son of Smetra, that was made by the smith of Angus, son of Umor, and that was kept in the well at Cruachan, to save it from the Morrigu. And Nera was left with his people in the hill, and he has not come out till now, and he will not come out till the end of life and time.

Now one time the Morrigu brought away a cow from the Hill of Cruachan to the Brown Bull of Cuailgne, and after she brought it back again its calf was born. And one day it went out of the Hill, and it bellowed three times. At that time Ailell and Fergus were playing draughts, for it was after Fergus had come as an exile from Ulster, because of the death of the sons of Usnach, and they heard the bellowing of the bull-calf in the plain. Then Fergus said: "I do not like the sound of the calf bellowing. There will be calves without cows," he said, "when the king goes on his march."

But now Ailell's bull, Finbanach, the White-Horned, met the calf in the plain of Cruachan, and they fought together, and the calf was beaten and it bellowed. "What did the calf bellow?" Maeve asked her cow-herd Buaigle. "I know that, my master, Fergus," said Bricriu. "It is the song that you were singing a while ago." On that Fergus turned and struck with his fist at his head, so that the five men of the chessmen that were in his hand went into Bricriu's head, and it was a lasting hurt to him. "Tell me now, Buaigle, what did the calf bellow?" said Maeve. "It said indeed," said Buaigle, "that if its father the Brown of Cuailgne would come to fight with the White-Horned, he would not be seen any more in Ai, he would be beaten through the whole plain of Ai on every side." And it is what Maeve said: "I swear by the gods my people swear by, I will not lie down on feathers, or drink red or white ale, till I see those two bulls fighting before my face."

CHAPTER X

The Wedding of Maine Morgor

When Maine Morgor, the Very Dutiful, the son of Ailell and of Maeve, set out for his wedding with Ferb, daughter of Gerg of Rath Ini, in Ulster, he brought three troops of young men with him, and fifty men in each troop, and this is the appearance that was on the first two troops. Shining white shirts they had, striped with purple down the sides; gold shields on their backs with borders of white silver, with figures engraved on them, and with edges of white bronze as sharp as knives. Great two-edged swords with silver hilts at their belts; chains of white silver round their necks. And there were neither helmets on their heads, or shoes on their feet.

And as to the third troop, the one Maine himself was in, there were fifty reddish-brown horses in it, and fifty white horses with red ears, with long manes and tails coloured purple, and bridles on them, with a ball of red gold on the one side, and a ball of white silver on the other side, and a gold or a silver bit to every one of them. A collar of gold with bells from it on the neck of every horse, and when the horses would be moving, the sound of these bells would be as sweet as the strings of a harp when the player strikes it with his hand. There was a chariot of white bronze ribbed with gold and silver to every two of the horses; purple cushions sewed with gold bound to every chariot; fifty fair slender young men in these fifty chariots, and not one among them but was the son of a king and a queen, and was a hero and a brave man of Connaught, and they wearing purple cloaks about them, that had borders ornamented with gold and silver, and a clasp of pure red gold to every cloak; fine silk coats fastened with hooks of gold close to their white bodies; fifty silver shields on their backs with gold rims studded with carbuncles and other precious stones of every colour; two candles of valour were the two shining spears on the hand of every man of them; fifty rivets of bronze and of gold in every spear, and if any man of them had a debt of a bushel of silver or gold, one rivet from his spear would pay it. And there were precious stones on their spears that would flame in the night like the rays of the sun. At their belts they had long, gold-hilted swords with silver sheaths; goads in their hands of white bronze with silver crooks. And as to the young men themselves, they were very handsome and stately, and large and shining; curled yellow hair on them, hanging down on their shoulders; proud, clear, blue eyes; their cheeks like the flowers of the woods in May, or like the foxglove of the mountains. There were seven greyhounds following Maine's chariot in chains of silver, and apples of gold on every chain. There were seven trumpeters with gold and silver trumpets, wearing clothes of many colours, and having all of them light yellow hair. And three Druids went in front of them, and they having bands of silver on their heads, and speckled cloaks on them, and carrying shields of bronze with ornaments of red copper. And there were three harpers with them, that had the appearance of kings.

It is like that they gathered at the royal house of Cruachan, and they went three times round the lawn before the house. And they said farewell to Maeve and to Ailell, and then they set out for Rath Ini.

"It is a fine setting out you are having," said Bricriu; "but maybe the coming back will not be so fine." "It is a journey that will be heard of in every place," said Maine. "I suppose," said Bricriu, "it is but a day visit you will make there, for you will hardly stop to feast through the night in a district that is under Conchubar." "I give my word," said Maine, "we will not turn back to Cruachan till we have feasted three days and three nights in Gerg's house." He did not waste any more time talking, but set out on the journey.

When the messengers they sent before them came to Gerg's house at Rath Ini, the people there began to make all ready before them, and they laid down green-leaved birch branches and fresh green rushes in the house. Then Ferb sent her foster-sister, Findchoem, daughter of Erg, and bade her go a part of the way with the messengers, and bring her back word what appearance was on Maine and on his companions. She was not long away, and as soon as she came back she went with her report to the sunny parlour where Ferb was, and it is what she said: "I never saw since Conchubar was in Emain, and I never will see till the end of life and time, a finer, or grander, or a more beautiful troop, than the troop that is coming now over the plain. It was the same as if I was in a sweet apple-garden, from the sweetness that came to me when the light wind passed over them and stirred their clothes."

With that, the men of Connaught came to the dun, and the people within pressed upon one another to look at them. And the gates were set open, and their chariots unyoked, and baths of pure water were made ready for them. And then they were brought into the hall of heroes in the middle of the house, and they were given every sort of food and of drink that is to be found on the whole ridge of the world.

But as they were using the feast and making merry, there came a sudden blast of wind that shook the whole place, so that the hall they were in trembled, and the shields fell from their hooks and the spears from their places, and the tables fell like leaves in an oak wood. All the young men were astonished, and Gerg asked Maine's Druids what meaning they could put on that blast. And Ollgaeth, Maine's chief Druid, said: "I think it is no good sign for those who are come to-night to this wedding. A blast of wind," he said; "a sorrowful sound; it is the man that will conquer.

"A shield struck out of a white hand; the bodies of dead men laid under stones; a high stone over stiff bodies; the story is sorrowful!

"And if you will take my advice," he said, "you will quit this feast this very night."

But he got a sharp rebuke from Maine for saying that, and Gerg said: "There is no cause for any uneasiness, for the men of Ulster are not gathered at Emain at this time. And if they were itself," he said, "I and my two sons would be ready to go out and fight against Conchubar along with you."

They hung up their arms then again, and gave no more heed to what the Druid had said.

Now on the morning of this very day, when Conchubar was lying in his sleep at Emain, he saw in a dream a beautiful woman coming to his bedside, and she having the appearance of a queen. Yellow plaited hair she had, and folds of silk over her white skin, and a cloak of green silk from her shoulders, and two sandals of white bronze between her soft feet and the ground. "All good be with you, Conchubar," she said. "What is the reason of your coming?" said Conchubar. "It is not long from this time," she said, "that Ulster will be attacked and will be robbed, and the Brown Bull of Cuailgne will be driven away. And the son of the man that will do this thing," she said, "Maine Morgor, son of Ailell and Maeve, is coming this very night to his wedding with Ferb, daughter of Gerg of Rath Ini, and three times fifty young men with him. Rise up now," she said, "there are but three times fifty men against you, and the victory will be with you."

Then Conchubar sprang up, and sent for Cathbad, the Druid, and told him his vision. "It is likely enough," he said, "that it is meant to warn us against the men of Connaught. And you may be sure," he said, "that if we stop here quietly, they will be doing their robbery. And let me have the truth from you now, and tell me what is best to do, for there is not the like of you among the Druids."

And Cathbad said: "It is what your vision means, that many men will get their death, and Maine of Connaught, he that is above all disgrace, along with them; and he and his companions will never go back again to beautiful Cruachan. But you yourself will come back safe," he said, "with fame and victory."

Then Conchubar set out, and there went with him Cathrach Catuchenn, a queen with a great name, that had come to Emain from the country of Spain for love of Cuchulain; and she went out now with Conchubar's army. And there went with him as well, the three outlaws of the race of the Fomor, Siabarcha, son of Suilremar, and Berngal Brec, and Buri of the Rough Word. And Facen, son of Dublongsech of the old stock of Ulster came, and Fabric Fiacail from Great Asia, and Forais Fingalach from the Isle of Man. So Conchubar set out, and three times fifty men with him, but he brought none of the men of Ulster with him, but himself and his chariot-driver Brod, and Imrinn the Druid, Cathbad's son. And none of them brought a servant with him, except only Conchubar, but their shields on their backs, and their bright green spears in their hands, and their heavy swords in their belts. And if they were not many in number, the pride of their minds was great.

When they were come within sight of Rath Ini, they saw a great heavy cloud over it, the one end of it black and the middle red, and the other end green. And Conchubar asked Imrinn the Druid, "What is this cloud over the house a token of?" "Truly," said Imrinn, "it is a sign there will be fighting to-night, and the sorrow of death will be on the house like a cloud, and it is for a young man the death darkness is made ready."

Then Conchubar went on towards the dun, and just at that time the great vat that belonged to the house and that got afterwards the name of the Ol Guala, was brought into the feasting hall, and it full of wine. But whoever went to draw it let the silver vessel fall into the vat, so that the wine flowed over the edges in three waves. "My grief," said Ollgaeth the Druid, "it is not long before these vessels will be with strangers. He is not a happy son born of a mother that is in this house to-night."

Then Conchubar came to the door, and the strangers that were with him gave their shout of attack around the dun, as their custom was. At that Gerg rose up, and his two sons with him, Con Coscorach and Cobthach Cnesgel, and they took hold of their arms. And Gerg said to Maine: "Let this be fought out now between us men of Ulster till you see which of us is the bravest. And we are all answerable for you, and it is best for you that we should fight together. But if we fall, then let you hold the place if you can."

And then Gerg went out and his two sons along with him and their people. And they held the place, and fought Conchubar outside; and for a long time they did not let any one go past them. And Gerg stood outside the door, and a hewing and cutting was aimed at him on every side, and five men of the Fomor fell by him, and Imrinn the Druid, along with them, and he cut his head off and brought it to the door with him.

Then Cathrach Catuchenn came between him and the door, and she made a sharp attack on him, and Gerg struck her head off, and brought it back with him into the house, for he had got a hard wound. And he threw the heads down before Maine, and he sat down on a bed, and gave a heavy sigh and asked for a drink. And then Conchubar and his people came up to the wall, and they were holding their shields over their heads with their left hands, and tearing down the wall with their right hands, till they were able to make their way through it.

Then Brod, Conchubar's chariot-driver, threw one of the spears he had in his hand into the house, and it went through Gerg's body, and through the body of Airisdech his servant that was behind him, so that the two of them fell together. And Conchubar attacked Gerg's people in the house, so that thirty of them fell, and he killed Conn, Gerg's son, by his own hand, and many of his own people got their death as well.

Then Nuagal, Gerg's wife, rose up, and she gave three great angry cries of grief, and she took the head of her husband into her bosom. "By my word," she said, "it is a fine servant's deed, Brod to have killed Gerg in his own house. But there are many," she said, "that will keen you, and as you have fallen on account of your daughter, many women shall have sorrow on account of you." And she made this complaint:

"It is a good fight Gerg made, that is lying here now, the fair-haired champion with the red sword; he that was proud, open-handed, brave, wise, beautiful.

"Where is there a better hero than Gerg? Where is the man that has not anger on him. Where is the army that does not keen for your death?

"It is grief to me to see you on your bed of death, O beautiful fair-haired Gerg! It is a pity for me, you to be dead.

"Before you here in Rath Ini, and at Loch Ane and at Irard, and in the valleys of the south, there were many women who gave you their love.

"You were the friend of every army; every one gave you full obedience; your friendly word was dear to every one; surely it is you were the good adviser.

"It is great indeed your deeds were, it is stately your assemblies were; you were a king among great lords.

"Your house was great, it was well-known, the house within which harm came to you; it was there Brod killed you in the hall of kings.

"It was a great harm and a great curse Brod put on us, he to kill a king of Ireland before his time; he has killed him; he has killed all of us along with him."

Then Gerg's two sons said they would hold the place and they were not without killing many in the fight. Then Maine could not hold in his strength any longer, and he went out to avenge his father-in-law. And his three times fifty companions rose up along with him, and it was not easy to stand against them. There was great pride in the mind, and great courage in the heart of every one of them, and there was great desire and longing on them to do high deeds.

And as to Maine, the king's son, he was stately, kind, mannerly, and although he was hardly out of his boyhood, he was braver in the fight than any other. He was gentle in the drinking-house, and he was hard in battle, and he was mindful of his enemies, and he was pitiful in wounding, and a spender of treasure, and a stone of anger, and a wave of justice; and he was the head in the gatherings of the three Connaughts, and their hand in spending, and their fitting king.

He thought it would be dishonour on him, ever to be overcome in equal fight by any men in the world, or the place to be taken that he was defending. And he went out and drove the Fomor away from the house, and it is not a hand of healing Maine had that time; and nine of the Fomor fell by his first attack. Then the outlaw of Great Asia, Fabric Fiacail, came up to the threshold, and began destroying the men before him, and no one stood against him till he came to the place where Maine was. And then they two set their shields one against the other, and they were fighting together till after midnight; and Fabric gave Maine three deep wounds, and when they were tired out with the fight, Maine struck off his head. Then Conchubar came, and thirty of Gerg's men were killed by him, and the two armies fell upon one another, and it is much that even the toes of their feet did not make an attack of their own. And the blood that was in the dun was as high as a man's knees, and in all the district round nothing could be heard but the striking of blows on shields, and the clinking of spears, and the clash of swords against one another, and the roar of beaten men.

And Maine, when he had overcome the Fomor, came where Facen, son of Dublongsech was, and they fought together a good while, and then Facen was killed. Then Maine and Cobthach were driven up into the house after their people were put down, and they held it bravely till morning, and no one was able to make a way in.

In this same night, the same woman that had brought news to Conchubar, went to where Maeve was lying in her sleep at Cruachan, and said to her: "If you had the Druid sight, Maeve," she said, "you would not be in your sleep now." "What has happened?" said Maeve. "Conchubar is at this very moment," said the strange woman, "getting the upper hand of Maine, and he is on the point of putting him to death. Rise up now, and gather your men together," she said, "and go out and avenge him."

With that Maeve wakened out of her sleep, and she called to Ailell and told him the vision, and told it to her people as well. "There is no truth in it," said Bricriu.

But when Fiannamail, the innkeeper's son at Cruachan, heard it, he waited for no one and made no delay, but set out for the place where Maine was, for Maine was his foster-brother. And Maeve chose out seven hundred armed men, the best that were to be found in Cruachan at that time. And then Donall Dearg came, that was the best fighter in the province, and that was another of Maine's foster-brothers. And he set out in the same way, before the others, and thirty fighting men with him, and the name of every one of them was Donall. And then Maeve set out after them on her journey.

But as to Maine, he held the house till the bright rising of the sun on the morrow, and it was not pleasant rest this night brought to either side. When they could see each other by the light of day, each remembered the other to his hurt, and Conchubar began to rouse up his people. "If it was the men of Ulster I had with me now," he said, "they would not be dragging on with this battle, the way the Fomor are doing." When the Fomor heard that sharp reproach, their courage rose up in them, and they pressed on hard in the fight, and never left off till they were through the door of the house. The house they came into had a great name for grandeur, but it was bad work that was done in it now. There were a hundred tables of white silver in it, and three hundred of brass, and three hundred of white bronze. And there were thirty vessels with pure silver from Spain on their rims, and two hundred cowhorns ornamented with gold or silver, and thirty silver cups, and thirty brass cups, and on the walls there were hangings of white linen with wonderful figures worked on them.

Then the two armies met one another in the middle of the house, and a great many were killed there. And Cobthach, Gerg's son, after he had killed many of the Fomor, came to where Berngal Brec was hewing the heads off the men of Connaught, and they fought together, and Berngal was worsted in the end.

And as to Maine, he killed Buri of the Rough Word, and after that he went mad and raging through the house, and thirty other men fell by him. But when Conchubar saw the madness that was on Maine, he turned to him, and Maine waited for him, and they fought a long while, and Maine threw his casting spear so strong and straight, that it went through Conchubar's body; and while Conchubar was striving to draw out that spear, Maine wounded him with the long spear that was in his hand. Then Brod came to help Conchubar, and Maine gave him three heavy wounds, so that he was able to fight no more. But then Conchubar attacked him with blows on every side, until he laid him dead before him.

And after he had killed Maine, he began to attack the crowd about him, so that they fell, foot to foot, and neck to neck, all through the house. And at the end, there was not one of Maine's people left living, and of the three times fifty men that came with Conchubar, there was not one left living but himself and Brod, and if they were itself, they did not come whole out of it.

Then Conchubar drove Cobthach, Gerg's son, out of the house; and while he was following him over the plain, Ferb came with her foster-sister to the place where Maine was lying, and she cried and lamented over him, and she said: "My grief, you are alone now, you that spent so many nights in company." And she made this complaint:—

'O young man, it is red your bed is! It is bad the signs were, and you coming into the house, a foretelling of tears to all your people.

"O son of Maeve! O branch of high honour! O son of Ailell who is not weak! It is a pity it is for my heart and my body, you to be lying there for ever!

"O young man, the best I ever saw; a rod of gold, and you lying on the pillow; whenever you and an enemy met together, that was the last meeting there was between you.

"There is grief on me, you to be lying there, young man, son of Maeve; your face was ruddy, your hand was rough in battle; it is grief that has been put into my heart that was waiting for you.

"It is seldom you were without arms up to this, until you were struck down, lying dead. The shining spear pierced you, the hard sword wounded you, till blood was dropping down on your cheeks.

"Och! What were you to me, and I not to have seen your death, my darling, my choice among men, he that was worth good treasure.

"He is my husband for all my days, great Maine, Ailell's son; I will die for the want of him, and he not able to come and care me.

"His purple cloak is grief to me, and himself lying there on the floor of the house, and his hand that was struck off after he fell, and his head in the hand of Conchubar;

"And his sword that was strong, heavy in striking, Conchubar has carried it far away; and his shield there where he fell, and he defending his people.

"He himself a hero, and no lie in it; it is he divided much riches; it is not a little thing he did to die like that, and he defending his people.

"The fair young man of Connaught to be lying there cold, and the best of his troop along with him; it is a pity for his people that died defending him; it is a pity for me, his unmarried wife.

"There is nothing I can do for you, Maine; it is on myself the hurt is come; my heart is broken with it, and I looking at you, Maine."

Then Fiannamail, the innkeeper's son from Cruachan, came to the house, and Ferb saw him, and she said: "Here is Fiannamail come to visit us, but whatever companions he has left at home, he will find none before him here." "That is rough news you are giving me, Ferb," said Fiannamail; "and indeed I am parted from my companions, if it is they that are lying here," he said. "They are your companions indeed," said Ferb; "they overcame others, and now they are overcome themselves."

And Fiannamail said: "And Maine, is he living? my comrade, my dear friend, my prince at home!" And Ferb said: "It is bitter to me, you to ask this, for I know you did not think it was Maine's last bed you would find here."

And then she told Fiannamail all that had happened. And Fiannamail said:

"When this news of the thing the people of Ulster have done goes out, they will be attacked in the west and in the east as long as there is a man living in Connaught." But Ferb said: "There are not left of the army of Ulster but Conchubar himself and Brod his chariot-driver, and the both of them were wounded by Maine before Conchubar killed him at the last."

Then Fiannamail went out to follow after Conchubar, to get satisfaction for Maine's death. And he met with Niall of the Fair Head, Conchubar's son, and a hundred men with him, and they looking for Conchubar; and for all they were so many, he fought a hot battle with them, till he fell dead.

And after he left Ferb, she was looking at the young men of Connaught, and she made this complaint:—

"A pity it is, young men of Connaught, that there is not soft down in your pillows under you; you that took the defence and would not give it up. What troop was there better than yourselves, and now you are lying like a loosened thread.

"It is a heavy hand was laid on your eyes; you were given the sour drink of beaten men; your story is hard, it will be a cause of battles; it will be a foretelling of many tears.

"It is a pity there is no help for me to bring you, but only to be keening and crying over you; it would be better for me to go with you, and my ashes to be scattered abroad.

"You were the best of the armies of Ireland, young men of Connaught, and I keening you; many women will cry Och! Och! after your proud ways.

"It is proud you were coming into the house; it is not common men you had for your fathers. O beautiful young men of Connaught, it is a pity it is the way you are now!"

Then Donall Dearg came to the lawn before the dun. And Ferb's foster-sister saw him, and she said: "It is a pity he was not here and Maine living, for he would have given him good help." And when Ferb heard he was there, she went out to him and she said: "Well, Donall, hawk of valour, here is a thing for you to do, to avenge your foster-brother that has got his death." And it is what Donall said: "If Maine has fallen, the man has fallen that was above all his companions, in courage, in wisdom, and in gentleness." And Ferb said: "It is not the work of a hero, you to be sighing and keening and crying Ochone! But since Maine will not come back for that, it is better for you to go out against his enemies." And Donall said: "I will go; I will destroy Conchubar, I will destroy his two sons in revenge for Maine." And Ferb said: "If it had been yourself, Donall Dearg, that had got your death from the men of Ulster on account of me, the story of the great vengeance Maine did for it would be told in every place." Then Donall said: "And as it is Maine Morgor himself has got his death, I will never go home westward so long as there is a man left living in Ulster."

So Donall went out, and he had not long to wait till he saw a great troop coming towards him, and Feradach of the Long Hand, Conchubar's son, with them. And Donall and his men attacked them, but they were outnumbered, and all his men fell. And he himself wounded Feradach twice, but then his men came at him, and Feradach struck his head off, and let out his shout of victory, and his people shouted along with him.

And Ferb was gone into the house again, and she was looking at Maine. "There is no good appearance on you now, the way you are, Maine," she said; "and my father got his death through you, and my father's son; but even so, I will die with the fret of losing you." And it is what she said: "There are many women and many young girls will be lonely after you, you to be the only one to fail them.

"It is beautiful you were up to this, proud and tall, going out with your young hounds to the hunting; it is spoiled your body is now, it is pale your hands are.

"It is bad the news is that will travel westward to Findabair of the Fair Eyebrows; the story of her brother that failed Ferb; it is not I that have not my fill of sorrow."

Then Maeve and her men came up to where Conchubar was, and his two sons that had joined him, and they faced one another, and the fight began; and Maeve broke through the army of Ulster to get satisfaction for her son and for her people, and she killed Conchubar's two sons. But Conchubar stood out and faced her in spite of his wounds, and in spite of being tired out; for his hurts were healed by the greatness of his anger after his two sons being killed.

Then Maeve was driven back and lost the battle; and the Druids brought her away as was their custom; and Conchubar followed after them till they had passed Magh Ini. And then he turned back to spoil Gerg's dun, and he carried away with him all he could find of treasures; and he took away the great brass vat that was in the house, and brought it to Emain. And when it was filled with beer, all the province of Ulster used to drink from it; and it got the name of the Champion's Drinking Vat.

And Ferb died with grief for Maine, and Nuagal died with grief for her husband and for her two sons. And a grave was made for them, and a stone put over it, and their names were written in Ogham; and Rath Ini got the name of Duma Ferb, Ferb's Mound, after that.

And this was the first blood shed in Ulster on the account of the Brown Bull of Cuailgne.

CHAPTER XI

The War For The Bull of Cuailgne

It happened one time when Maeve and Ailell rose up from their royal bed in Cruachan, they began to talk to one another. "It is what I am thinking," said Ailell, "it is a true saying, 'Good is the wife of a good man.'" "A true saying, indeed," said Maeve, "but why do you bring it to mind at this time?" "I bring it to mind now because you are better to-day than the day I married you." "I was good before I ever had to do with you," said Maeve. "How well we never heard of that and never knew it until now," said Ailell, "but only that you stopped at home like any other woman, while the enemies at your boundaries were slaughtering and destroying and driving all before them, and you not able to hinder them." "That is not the way it was at all," said Maeve, "but of the six daughters of my father Eochaid, King of Ireland, I was the best and the one that was thought most of. As to dividing gifts and giving wages, I was the best of them, and as to battle feats and arms and fighting, I was the best of them. It was I had fifteen hundred paid soldiers, and fifteen hundred more that were the sons of chief men. And I had these," she said, "for my own household; and along with that my father gave me one of the provinces of Ireland, the province of Cruachan; so that Maeve of Cruachan is the name that was given to me.

"And as to being asked in marriage," she said, "messengers came to me from your own brother, Finn, son of Ross Ruadh, king of Leinster, and I gave him a refusal; and after that there came messengers from Cairbre Naifer, son of Rossa, king of Tara; and from Conchubar, son of Ness, king of Ulster; and after that again from Eochu Beag, son of Luchta, and I refused them all. For it is not a common marriage portion would have satisfied me, the same as is asked by the other women of Ireland," she said; "but it is what I asked as a marriage portion, a man without stinginess, without jealousy, without fear. For it would not be fitting for me to be with a man that would be close-handed, for my own hand is open in wage-paying and in free-giving; and it would be a reproach on my husband, I to be a better wage-payer than himself. And it would not be fitting for me to be with a man that would be cowardly, for I myself go into struggles and fights and battles and gain the victory; and it would be a reproach to my husband, his wife to be braver than himself. And it would not be fitting for me to be with a husband that would be jealous, for I would never hold myself to be bound to one man only. Now I have got such a husband as I looked for in yourself, Ailell, son of Ross Ruadh, king of Leinster, for you are not close-handed or jealous or cowardly. And I gave you good wedding gifts," she said, "suits of clothing enough for twelve men; a chariot that was worth three times seven serving-maids; the width of your face in red gold, the round of your arm in a bracelet of white bronze. And the fine or the tribute you can ask of your enemies is no more than the fine or the tribute I have a right to ask, for you are nothing of yourself, but it is in the pay of a woman you are," she said. "That is not so," said Ailell, "for I am a king's son, and I have two brothers that are kings Finn, king of Leinster, and Cairbre, king of Tara, and I would have been king in their places but that they are older than myself. And as to giving of wages and dividing of gifts," he said, "you are no better than myself; and if this province is under the rule of a woman, it is the only province in Ireland that is so: and it is not through your right I took the kingship of it, but through the right of my mother, Mata of Murrisk, daughter of Magach. And if I took the daughter of the chief king of Ireland for my wife, it was because I thought she was a fitting wife for me." "You know well," said Maeve, "the riches that belong to me are greater than the riches that belong to you." "There is no truth in that," said Ailell, "for there is no one in Ireland has a better store of jewels and riches and treasure than myself and you know well there is not."

"Let our goods and our riches be put beside one another, and let a value be put on them," said Maeve, "and you will know which of us owns most." "I am content to do that," said Ailell.

With that, orders were given to their people to bring out their goods and to count them, and to put a value on them. They did so, and the first things they brought out were their drinking vessels, their vats, their iron vessels, and all the things belonging to their households, and they were found to be equal. Then their rings were brought out, and their bracelets and chains and brooches, their clothing of crimson and blue and black and green and yellow and saffron and speckled silks, and these were found to be equal. Then their great flocks of sheep were driven from the green plains of the open country and were counted, and they were found to be equal; and if there was a ram among Maeve's flock that was the equal of a serving-maid in value, Ailell had one that was as good. And their horses were brought in from the meadows, and their herds of swine out of the woods and the valleys, and they were equal one to another. And the last thing that was done was to bring in the herds of cattle from the forest and the wild places of the province, and when they were put beside one another they were found to be equal, but for one thing only. It happened a bull had been calved in Maeve's herd, and his name was Fionnbanach, the "White-horned." But he would not stop in Maeve's herds, for he did not think it fitting to be under the rule of a woman, and he had gone into Ailell's herds and stopped there; and now he was the best bull in the whole province of Connaught. And when Maeve saw him, and knew he was better than any bull of her own, there was great vexation on her, and it was as bad to her as if she did not own one head of cattle at all. So she called Mac Roth, the herald, to her, and bade him to find out where there was a bull as good as the White-horned to be got in any province of the provinces of Ireland.

"You know that well yourself," said Mac Roth, "for there is a bull that is twice as good as himself at the house of Daire, son of Fachtna, in the district of Cuailgne, and that is Donn Cuailgne, the Brown Bull of Cuailgne." "Rise up, then," said Maeve, "and make no delay, but go to Daire from me, and ask the loan of that bull for a year, and I will return him at the end of the year, and fifty heifers along with him, as fee for the loan. And there is another thing for you to say, Mac Roth; if the people of Daire's district and country think bad of him for sending away that wonderful jewel the Donn of Cuailgne, let Daire himself come along with him, and I will give him the equal of his own lands on the smooth plain of Ai, and a chariot that is worth three times seven serving-maids, and my own close friendship along with that."

So Mac Roth set out on his journey, and nine men along with him, and when they came to Daire's house there was a good welcome before them, as there should be, for Mac Roth was the chief herald of all Ireland.

Daire asked him then what was the reason of his journey, and Mac Roth told him the whole story of the quarrel between Maeve and Ailell, and of the counting of their herds, and of the great rewards Maeve offered if he would give her the loan for one year of the Brown Bull of Cuailgne. Daire was so well pleased when he heard this, that he started up and said: "By my hand of valour, I will send him to Maeve into Connaught, with no delay, whether the men of Ulster like it or do not like it." Mac Roth was well content with what he said, and then he and his men were attended to, and fresh rushes were spread, and a feast was put before them, with every sort of food and of drink, so that after a while they were not so clear in their wits as they were before.

Two of them began talking to one another then, and one said: "This is a good man in whose house we are." "He is good indeed," said the other. "Is there any man in Ulster better than himself?" said the first. "There is, surely," said the other, "for Conchubar the High King is a better man, and it is no shame for all the men of Ulster to gather to him." "It is a wonder," said the first, "Daire to have given up to us what it would have taken the strength of the four provinces of Ireland to bring away by force." "That I may see the mouth that spoke those words filled with blood," said another of the men; "for if Daire had refused to give it willingly, the strength of Ailell and of Maeve, and the knowledge of Fergus, son of Rogh, would have brought it from him against his will."

Just as they were talking, the chief steward of Daire's house came in, and servants along with him bringing meat and drink; and he heard what the men of Connaught said, and great anger came on him, and he bade the servants put down the food for them, but he never told them to use it or not to use it, but he went to where Daire was and said: "Was it you, Daire, promised the Brown Bull of Cuailgne to these messengers?" "It was myself indeed," said Daire. "Then what they have said is true?" "What is that?" said Daire. "They say that you knew if you did not give him willingly, you would have had to give him against your will

by the strength of Aillel and Maeve and by the guidance of Fergus, son of Rogh."
"If they say that," said Daire, "I swear by the gods my people swear by, that they
will not take him away till they take him by force."

On the morning of the morrow the messengers rose up and went into the house
where Daire was. "Show us now," they said, "the place where the bull is." "I will
not indeed," said Daire; "but if it was a habit with me," he said, "to do treachery
to messengers or to travellers or to men on their road, not one of you would go
back alive to Cruachan." "What reason have you for this change?" said Mac
Roth. "I have a good reason for it, for you were saying last night that if I did not
give the bull willingly, I would be forced to give it against my will by Ailell and by
Maeve and by Fergus." "If that was said, it was the talk of common messengers,
and they after eating and drinking," said Mac Roth, "and it is not fitting for you
to take notice of a thing like that."

"It may be so," said Daire; "but for all that," he said, "I will not give the bull
this time."

They went back then to Cruachan, and Maeve asked news of them, and Mac
Roth told her the whole story, how Daire gave them the promise of the bull at
first, and refused it afterwards. "What was the reason of that?" she asked. And
when it was told her she said: "This riddle is not hard to guess; they did not intend
to let us get the bull at all; but now we will take him from them by force," she said.

And this was the cause of the great war for the Brown Bull of Cuailgne.

Then Maeve sent messengers to the six Maines, her sons, to come to Cruachan,
the brothers of Maine Morgor that got his death at Dun Gerg. And she sent
messengers to the sons of Magach; and they came with thirty hundred armed
men, and to Cormac Conloingeas, son of King Conchubar, and to Fergus, son of
Rogh; and they came, and thirty hundred armed men with them.

This is the appearance that was on the first troop. They had black heads of hair,
and green cloaks about them, held with silver brooches, and on their bodies shirts
of gold thread, embroidered with red gold, and they had swords with white
sheaths and hilts of silver.

As to the second troop, they had short-cut hair, and grey cloaks about them,
and on their bodies pure white shirts; and they had swords with knobbed hilts of
gold, and sheaths of silver. Every one asked: "Is that Cormac among them?" "It is
not indeed," said Maeve.

As to the last troop, they had gold-yellow hair, falling loose like manes, and
crimson cloaks, well ornamented, about them, and gold brooches with jewels at
their breasts, and long silk shirts coming down to their ankles. And as they
walked they lifted up their feet and put them down again all together. "Is that
Cormac among them?" every one asked. "It is, surely," said Maeve.

So they made their camp there, and between the four fords of Ai, Athmaga,

Athslisen, Athberena, and Athcoltna, there were red fires blazing through the night. And they stopped a fortnight there at Cruachan, eating, drinking, and resting themselves, that they might be the better able for the journey and the marching.

Then Maeve bade her chariot-driver to yoke her horses, that she might go and consult with her Druid and ask a prophecy from him, to foretell for her if the army she was bringing out would get the victory, and would come back safely. And she said to the Druid: "There are many that will part here to-day from their companions and their friends, from their country and their lands, from their father and their mother. And if it happens that the whole of them do not come back again safe and sound, it is on me the complaints and the curses will fall. And besides that," she said, "there is no none that goes out or that stops behind, that is dearer to us than we are to ourselves. So find out for us now whether we shall return, or not return." And the Druid said: "Whoever returns or does not return, you yourself will return."

Her chariot was turned then, and she went back again homeward. But presently she saw a thing she wondered at, a woman sitting on the shaft of the chariot, facing her, and this is how she was: a sword of white bronze in her hand, with seven rings of red gold on it, and she seemed to be weaving a web with it; a speckled green cloak about her, fastened at the breast with a brooch of red gold; a ruddy, pleasant face she had, her eyes grey, and her mouth like red berries, and when she spoke her voice was sweeter than the strings of a curved harp, and her skin showed through her clothes like the snow of a single night. Long feet she had, very white, and the nails on them pink and even; her hair gold-yellow, three locks of it wound about her head, and another that fell down loose below her knee.

Maeve looked at her, and she said: "What are you doing here, young girl?" "It is looking into the future for you I am," she said, "to see what will be your chances and your fortunes, now you are gathering the provinces of Ireland to the war for the Brown Bull of Cuailgne." "And why would you be doing this for me?" said Maeve. "There is good reason for it," she said, "for I am a serving-maid of your own people." "Which of my people do you belong to?" said Maeve. "I am Fedelm of the Sidhe, of Rath Cruachan." "It is well, Fedelm of the Sidhe; tell me what way you see our hosts." "I see crimson on them, I see red." "Yet Conchubar is lying in his weakness at Emain; my messengers are come back from there, and we need not be in dread of anything from Ulster," said Maeve. "But look again, Fedelm of the Sidhe, and tell me the truth of the matter." "I see crimson on them, I see red," said the girl. "Yet Eoghan, son of Durthacht, is in his weakness at Rathairthir; my messengers are come back from him; we need not be afraid of anything from Ulster. Look again, Fedelm of the Sidhe; how do you see our hosts?" "I see them all crimson, I see them all red." "Celtchair, son of Uthecar, is lying in his weakness within his fort; my messengers are come back from him. Tell me again, Fedelm of the Sidhe, how do you see our hosts?" "I see crimson on them, I see red." "There may be no harm in what you see," said Maeve, "for when all the men of Ireland are gathered together in one place, there will surely be quarrels and fights among them, about going first or last over fords and rivers, or about the first wounding of some stag or boar, or such like. Tell me truly now, Fedelm of the Sidhe, what way do you see our hosts?" "I see crimson on them, I see red. And I see," she said, "a low-sized man doing many deeds of arms; there are many wounds on his smooth skin; there is a light about his head, there is victory on his forehead; he is young and beautiful, and modest towards women; but he is like a dragon in the battle. His appearance and his courage are like the appearance and the courage of Cuchulain of Muirthemne; and who that Hound from Muirthemne may be I do not know; but I know this much well, that all this host will be reddened by him. He is setting out for the battle; he will make your dead lie thickly; the memory of the blood shed by him will be lasting; women will be keening over the bodies brought low by the Hound of the Forge that I see before me."

This is the foretelling that was made for Maeve by Fedelm of the Sidhe, before the setting out of the hosts at Cruachan for Ulster.

Now, when Maeve told Fedelm of the Sidhe that there need be no fear of the men of Ulster coming out to attack the army, for they were lying in their weakness, she meant that they were under the curse and the enchantment that was put on them one time by a woman they had ill-treated. And the story of it is this:-

There was a man of the name of Crunden, son of Agnoman, that lived in a lonely part of Ulster, among the mountains, and he had a good way of living; but his wife had died, and he had the care of all his children on him. One day he was sitting in the house, and he saw a woman come in at the door, tall and handsome, and with good clothes on her, and she did not say a word, but she sat down by the hearth and began to make up the fire. And then she went to where the meal was, and took it out and mixed it, and baked a cake. And when the evening was drawing on, she took a vessel and went out and milked the cows, but all the time she never spoke a word. Then she came back into the house, and took a turn to the right, and was the last to stop up and to cover over the fire.

She stayed on there, and Crunden, the man of the house, married her, and she tended him and his sons, and everything he had prospered.

It happened one day, there was to be a great gathering of the men of Ulster, for games and races and all sorts of amusements, and all that could go, both of men and women, used to go to that gathering. "I will go there to-day," said Crunden, "the same as every other man is going." "Do not," said his wife, "for if you so much as say my name there at the fair," she said, "I will be lost to you for ever." "Then indeed I will not speak of you at all," said Crunden. So he set out with the others to the fair, and there was every sort of amusement there, and all the people of the country were at it.

At the ninth hour, the royal chariot was brought on the ground, and the king's horses won the day. Then the bards and poets, and the Druids, and the servants of the king, and the whole gathering, began to praise the king and the queen and their horses, and they cried out: "There were never seen such horses as these; there are no better runners in all Ireland." "My wife is a better runner than those horses," said Crunden. When the king was told of that he said: "Take hold of the man, and keep him until his wife can be brought to try her chance and to run against the horses."

So they took hold of him, and kept him, and messengers were sent from the king to the woman. She bade the messengers welcome, and asked what brought them. "We are come by the king's order," they said, "to bring you to the fair, to see if you will run faster than the king's horses; for your husband boasted that you would, and he is kept prisoner now until you will come and release him." "It is foolish my husband was to speak like that," she said; "and as for myself I am not fit to go, for I am soon going to give birth to a child." "That is a pity," said the messengers, "for if you do not come, your husband will be put to death." "If that is so, I must go, whatever happens," she said.

So with that she set out for the gathering, and when she got there all the people were crowding about her to see her. "It is not fitting I to be looked at, and I the way I am," she said; "and what have I been brought here for?" "To run against the two horses of the king," the people called out. "Ochone!" she said, "do not ask me, for I am close upon my hour." "Take out your swords and put the man to death," said the king. "Give me your help," she said to the people, "for every one of you has been born of a mother." And then she said to the king: "Give me even a delay until my child is born." "I will give no delay," said the king. "Then the shame that is on you will be greater than the shame that is on me," she said. "And because you have showed no pity and no respect to me," she said, "it is a heavier punishment will fall on you then has fallen upon me. And bring out the horses beside me now." Then they started, and the woman outran the horses and gained the race; and at the goal the pains of childbirth came on her, and she bore two children, a boy and a girl, and she gave a great cry in her pain.

And a weakness came suddenly on all that heard the cry, so that they had no more strength than the woman as she lay there. And it is what she said: "From this out, and till the ninth generation, the shame that you have put on me will fall on you; and at whatever time you most want your strength, at the time your enemies are closing on you, that is the time the weaknesses of a woman in childbirth will come upon all the men of the province of Ulster."

And so it happened; and of all the men of Ulster that were born after that day, there was no one escaped that curse and that enchantment but only Cuchulain.

When the men of Connaught set out from Cruachan for the north, they stopped toward evening at Cuilsilinne, and there they made their encampment for the night. Ailell took his place in the middle of the camp, and on his right was Fergus, son of Rogh, and Cormac Conloingeas next to him again, and their people on the same side; and on Ailell's left there was a place made for Maeve, and Findabair her daughter. But Maeve stopped behind until the whole of the army had come up, and then she went in her chariot to see if all was in order, and after that she came and took her seat at Ailell's right hand. "Which of the troops do you think the best?" said Ailell. "None of them are any good at all," said Maeve, "compared with the men of Leinster, the Gailiana." "What have they done beyond all the others that you praise them so much?" said Ailell. "There is reason for praising them," said Maeve; "for while the others were choosing a place for themselves, the Gailiana had their huts and their shelters made, and while the others were making their shelters, they had their share of food and drink cooked and set out, and while the others were making ready their food they had theirs eaten, and while the others were eating, they were laid down and sleeping. And as their servants have been better than the servants of the men of Ireland," she said, "so will their young men and their fighting men be better than the young men of Ireland on this march." "I am well pleased to hear that," said Ailell, "for it was with me they came, and they are of my own province." "Then you need not be so well pleased," said Maeve, "for they shall march no further with you, for I will not have them boasted of, before me or to me." "Let them stop in this camp, then," said Ailell. "They shall not do that either," said Maeve. "What must they do, then?" said Findabair, "if they are neither to go on nor to stop in the camp?" "They will get death and destruction from myself," said Maeve. "It is a pity you to say that," said Ailell, "and they only just after joining us." "If you think to harm them," said Fergus, "you will have to fight with me as well as with them; for by the oath of my people," he said, "it is only over my body and the bodies of the men of Ulster that are with me, you can come at their death." "Do not speak that way, Fergus," said Maeve; "for if you were to join with these strangers against me, I would have the six Maines and their men on my side, and the sons of Magach and their men, and my own troops along with them. And I think we would be well able for you," she said. "It is not right for you to say that," said Fergus, "for there are no men in Ireland better than the young men of Ulster that came to Connaught with me, and they have been a good help to you up to this. But I will tell you another thing to do," he said: "let the men of Leinster be divided through all the other troops of the men of Ireland, the way there will not be more than five of them together in any one place." "I will agree to that," said Maeve, "for I know there would be nothing but fighting and jealousy if they were left together the way they are now."

On the morning of the morrow, they made ready to set out again, but the chief men among them consulted together first, what way they could best keep the peace between so many troops and tribes and families; and it is what they settled, to put every troop under its own leader, and to let it, great or small, take a road of its own. And besides that, they consulted who would be the best man to put over the whole army, to lead them and to show them the way. And they all said Fergus would be the best, for he had been king of Ulster seventeen years, until Conchubar put him out of the kingship, and he had stopped on in Ulster after that until the time Conchubar killed the sons of Usnach in spite of the guarantee he had given them.

So Fergus was made leader of the whole army; but as they went on, a great love for his own province and his home came on him, and instead of going on northward he turned to the south. And while he was delaying the army like that, he sent messengers into Ulster to give warning and news of their coming. But Maeve was keeping a watch on him, and when she saw what had happened, she went to him and said: "Why is it, Fergus, that we have turned again to the south?" Then Fergus knew it was no use to try and deceive her, and they turned again, but they did not go far, but only to the place they had left in the morning, Cuilsilinne.

Then Fergus called to mind that they were coming near the borders of Ulster, and that it was likely it would not be long before they would meet with Cuchulain; and he gave a warning to the army and bade them mind themselves well, lest the Hound of Muirthemne should fall on them and destroy them.

And then the men of Connaught set out again eastward, and when they came to Monecolthan, they saw before them eight-score deer, in the one herd, and the whole army surrounded them, and all the deer were killed; but if they were, it was the Gailiana, scattered as they were, that killed all the deer but five, and those five were all that were killed by the rest of the men of Ireland.

It was on that same day Cuchulain and his father, Sualtim, came to the pillarstone at Ardcullin, for they had got the warning Fergus had sent, and there they let their horses graze, and Sualtim's horses cropped the grass to the north of the pillar-stone to the earth, but Cuchulain's horses, at the south side, cropped it to the bare flags.

"It is in my mind, Sualtim," said Cuchulain, "that the army of Connaught is not far away from us now. Go now, then," he said, "and bring a warning to the men of Ulster, and tell them not to stop in the open plains, but to go into the woods and the valleys of the province, that the men of Ireland may not come upon them." "And you yourself, little son, what will you do?" said Sualtim. "I must go," said Cuchulain, "southward to Teamhair, for I promised to go there to-day, to see a young girl of the household of Fedelm of the Fair Shape, Laegaire's wife." "It is a pity for you to go for a thing like that," said Sualtim, "and you leaving Ulster under the feet of enemies and strangers." "I must go, indeed," said Cuchulain, "for if I break my word to a woman, it will be said from this out that a woman's word is better than a man's."

So Sualtim set out then, to give a warning to the men of Ulster, and Cuchulain went into the oak woods and cut down an oak sapling, and twisted it into a ring, and cut a message on it in Ogham. And then he forced the ring over the top of the pillar-stone, and down to the thick part of it. And then he went on to keep his appointment at Teamhair.

As to the men of Ireland, they went on till they came to Ardcullin, and the whole country of Ulster lay there before them. And then they saw the pillar-stone and the oak ring that was on it; and Ailell took it off, and gave it to Fergus, and bade him read the Ogham. And what he read on it was Cuchulain's name, and the warning on it that the men of Ulster should not pass the pillar-stone that night, for if they did, he would do a great revenge on them at the sunrise of the morrow.

"It would be a pity," said Maeve, "that the first blood to be shed after going into the province should be the blood of our own people: it would be best for us to draw blood first on the people of Ulster." "I agree to that," said Ailell, "for I am loth to go against this ring or the man that twisted it; but let us go into the wood and make our camp there for the night." So they went into the wood, and cut a way for the chariots with their swords as they went, and it is from that the place is called Sleact na Gearbat, "the cut way of the chariots," until this time. And a great snow fell that night, so that it made one plain of the five provinces of Ireland, and they could make no shelter or prepare food, and none of the men in the camp knew though the whole night was it friend or enemy was near him, until the clear light of the sun fell on the snow in the morning. And then they left that place, and went on into Ulster.

As to Cuchulain, he did not rise very early that morning, and when he did, there was food made ready for him, and a bath of pure water. Then he bade Laeg to make his chariot ready, and they set out; and after a while they came to the track of the army of Ireland where it had gone over the border into Ulster. "Well, Laeg," said Cuchulain, "I have not much luck out of my appointment that I kept last night; for it is expected of one that is watching the borders that the least he should do is to raise a cry or give a warning of the enemy that is coming, and I have missed doing this, so that the men of Ireland have slipped by without news or notice into Ulster." "I told you, Cuchulain," said Laeg, "that if you kept to your meeting last night, some vexation like this would fall on you." "Well, Laeg," said Cuchulain, "let you follow their track now, and count them, and see what number of the men of Ireland are come over the border." Laeg did this, and he came back and told their number, as he had counted them. "There is a mistake in your counting," said Cuchulain. "I will count them myself this time." Then he told their number. "It is with yourself the mistake is, Cuchulain," said Laeg. "It is not," he said, "but there are eighteen divisions have passed the border, but the eighteenth is broken up and distributed among the others, so that no sure reckoning can be made of it." This, now, was one of the three best estimates ever made in Ireland, and the other two were made by Lugh of the Long Hand, and by Angus at Brugh na Boinne.

"But now, Laeg," he said, "turn the chariot towards the army, and hurry on the horses; for unless I can make an end of some of them to-day," he said, "I will not live through the night myself."

So they went on to the place that is called now Athgowla, northward from Knowth.

There they met with two young men, the sons of Neara, that were sent out in front of Maeve's army, to see was there any hindrance before it, and Cuchulain struck off their heads and the heads of their chariot-drivers.

And he cut down a tree with his sword, and it having four branches, and he lopped them short, and cleared the tree; and he stood up in his chariot, and with one cast he drove the tree into the ground that it stood deep and firm, and he set the four heads he had struck off on the four lopped branches of it. And then he turned back their horses in their chariots towards the army.

Now it is the way Maeve used to be going, she in a chariot by herself, and two chariots on each side of her, and behind her and before her, the way no sod from the feet of the horses of the army, or foam from their mouths, would touch her clothing. And when she saw the two chariots coming back, and the bodies in them without heads, she stopped to see what had happened. "What are these?" she said. "They are the chariots and the bodies of the two sons of Neara that went on before us," said her chariot-driver.

Then she held a council with her chief men, and it is what they agreed, that it must be some part of the army of Ulster was there before them at the ford they were drawing near, and that it was best to send out Cormac Conloingeas and his men to see who was in it, for the men of Ulster would not be willing to harm the son of their High King.

So Cormac and his troop went on to the ford, but when he got there all he saw was a lopped tree and four heads on it, and the blood dripping down from them, and the track of one chariot only, going eastward out of the ford. Then the rest of the army came with the other chief men. "There is wonder on me," said Ailell; "our four men to have been made an end of so easily as this." "You may wonder as well," said Fergus, "at the way this pole was driven into the ground by one man, and it will be hard for you to find a man of your army will drag it out again." "Do it yourself, Fergus," said Maeve, "for you are of my army." So Fergus called for a chariot, and stood up in it, and gave such a strong pull at the pole, that the chariot broke under him. "Give me another chariot," he said. And when he had broken seventeen of the war-chariots of Connaught one after another, and had not so much as loosened the pole, Maeve said: "Leave off now, Fergus, from breaking my people's chariots; and if you yourself had not been with us on this march," she said, "we would have been up with the men of Ulster before now, and we would have taken men and cattle. And I know well why you did this; it was to give the men of Ulster time to get over their weakness and their pains, and to come out against us to defend their bull and their cattle." "Give me my own chariot, then," said Fergus. So they gave him his own chariot, and he got up in it and gave a great pull at the pole; but neither the frame nor the wheels of his chariot started or strained like the others, and he pulled up the pole and gave it into Ailell's hand, and Ailell looked at it and said: "There is dread on me, of the man that set that pole there; do you think, Fergus," he said, "was it Conchubar the High King that did it?" "It was not," said Fergus, "for if Conchubar had come here, his army would have come along with him, and all the men of Ulster, and he would not have been so near to you without offering you battle, and by this time whichever got the better would be boasting of it." "Do you think was it Cuscraid, Conchubar's son?" said Ailell; "or Eoghan, son of Durthacht, king of Fernmaighe; of Celthair, son of Uthecar?" "I do not," said Fergus, "but it is what I think, that it was my own foster-son and Conchubar's that was here, Cuchulain, son of Sualtim." "We heard you often talking at Cruachan about that young man, and what is his age at this time?" "His age is of no great matter," said Fergus, "for he did great deeds, when he was but a soft child." "He is young enough yet," said Maeve, "and I think it will not be hard to find some one of our own men that will get the better of this wild Hound, for he has but the one body to wound or to put to flight." "You will get no one," said Fergus, "among your fighting men and your young men and your champions that will be able to put down Cuchulain."

They stopped there then and made their camp, and rested that night, with food and with music.

And it was in that night Fergus gave Maeve and Ailell the whole story of the boy deeds of Cuchulain and how he used to have a stone for a pillow, and no one dared to wake him, lest he might chance to give them a blow of the stone in his anger. And he told of one night when he was asleep, and Conchubar was attacked and was beaten by Eoghan, son of Durthacht. And Cuchulain was awakened by the cries of the beaten men that were running away, and he went out in the darkness of the night to look for Conchubar; and where the battle had been, he saw a man with the half of a man's body on his back, and he called to Cuchulain to help him, and threw the half-body to him, and Cuchulain threw it back again, and they fought, and he struck off the man's head. And then he found Conchubar lying in a grave, and he dug him out of that, and as they went home, they met Cuscraid that was wounded, and Cuchulain brought him home to Emain on his back. And another time he went into a wood and saw a terrible-looking man having a wild boar in one hand, and his weapon in the other hand, and he killed him, and brought home the boar. And another time when the men of Ulster were in their weakness, three times nine sea-robbers came to Emain, and the women ran shrieking to the palace when they saw them, and when the boys that were at play on the lawn knew what they were running from, they ran along with them. But Cuchulain went out and killed nine of the sea-robbers and wounded the rest of them, so that he drove them all back. And he told them many other stories of his doings beside these.

The next day, the army marched on eastward beyond the mountain. But there was a narrow place they had to pass through, and Cuchulain cut down a great oak tree, and laid it across the gap, and wrote an Ogham on it; and when the men of Ireland came up to it, it hindered them, and they could not move it, and they made their camp there that night. And early in the morning they sent the young man Fraech, son of Idath, to get the hindrance cleared away. But Fraech went on beyond it, till he came to a river, and there he found Cuchulain bathing. And they attacked one another in the water, and Fraech was beaten, and Cuchulain went away and left his body on the bank.

And when the men of Ireland found his body they began to keen him. And then they saw a great band of women of the Sidhe, with green dresses on them, coming for his body, and they gave out a great cry over him and brought him away to the hill of the Sidhe. And Findabair cried after him, and went to see the green bank where he was lying.

And they knew that Cuchulain was not far from them, for presently Maeve's little dog, Baiscne, got his death by a stone from a sling. There was anger on Maeve then, and she urged her men to follow after Cuchulain, so that they broke the poles of their chariots in their hurry.

The next day Cuchulain was going through the wood, and he heard the sound of blows on the trees. "It is too bold the men of Ulster are, Laeg," he said, "to be cutting down trees like this, with the men of Ireland coming on them; and stop here," he said, "till I find out who is it that is in the wood."

He went on till he met with a young man of Connaught, that was chariot-driver to Orlam, son of Maeve and Ailell. "What is it you are doing there, young man?" he asked. "I am cutting holly poles," said the young man, "for we have broken our chariots hunting that notable deer, Cuchulain. And now, good friend," he said, "lend me a hand with these poles, lest that same notable Cuchulain should come upon me here." "Your choice, boy; shall I cut the holly poles, or shall I trim them for you?" "Let you do the trimming," said he. So Cuchulain took them and trimmed them straight and smooth, that a fly could not have kept his footing on them. The chariot-driver looked at the poles, and he said: "I am thinking this is not the work you have a right to be put to. And who are you at all?" he said. "I am that notable Cuchulain you were speaking of just now." "That is bad news for me," said the driver, "for surely I am a dead man." "There need be no fear on you," said Cuchulain, "for I do not fight against drivers or messengers or unarmed men. But where is your master?" he said. "He is out before you on the plain." "Go to him, then, and give him this warning, that I am here, and that if we meet, he will surely get his death from me." With that the young man went to look for his master, but quick as he went, Cuchulain was quicker, and as soon as he came up with Orlam he struck off his head, and held it up and shook it before the men of Ireland.

After that, the three sons of Garach came out and made an attack on him, but he overcame them, and struck off their heads, and he killed their chariot-drivers as well, that they had armed against him. And Lethan and his chariot-driver came against him, and he killed them in the same way.

At that time the harpers of Cainbile came to Maeve's camp, and played on their magic harps; but the men of Ireland thought it might be as spies they came, and they drove them out of the camp, and followed after them till they came to the great stone of Lecmore. But when they thought to overtake them there, the harpers took on themselves the shape of wild deer, and went away. And it was on the same day that Cuchulain, with two casts of a sling stone, killed the squirrel and the pet bird that were sitting on Maeve's two shoulders.

Then the men of Ireland came into Magh Breagh and Muirthemne, and carried off and destroyed all before them. And Fergus warned them that Cuchulain was not far off, and that he would do a great vengeance on them, since they had spoiled Muirthemne. And it was at that time Lugaid, son of Nois, that had gone into Connaught with Fergus, went secretly to Cuchulain and told him of all that was going on in the camp, and of the dread of him that was on all the men of Ireland, so that they did not dare to stir out alone, and that he himself was true to him yet.

And now that the army was coming so near to Cuailgne, the War-goddess, the Battle Crow, the Morrigu, came and sat on a pillar-stone at Teamhair, and gave a warning to the Brown Bull of Cuailgne, and it is what she said: "Have a care, and keep a good watch, my poor bull, or the men of Ireland will come on you and will drive you away to their camp." And when the bull heard the warning, he brought fifty of his heifers with him, and went away to a valley of Slieve Cuilinn.

And the men of Ireland came on, bringing the herds of cattle they took on the way, where there was no one to defend them. And they stopped for the night at Conaille Muirthemne, and there Maeve bade one of her women go down to the stream for water. And the woman was wearing Maeve's golden covering on her head, and Cuchulain saw her, and he thought it was Maeve herself that was in it, and he made a cast of a stone and killed her, and the gold covering was broken in pieces.

And they were delayed there for a while, for the river was in flood, and when they tried to cross it, the chariots that went in were swept away to the sea; and one of Maeve's best men, Uala, that she sent to try the depth of it, was swept along with them. And while they were stopping here, Cuchulain killed Raen and Rae, that were come to tell the story of the war, and a hundred men along with them.

Then Maeve said: "Some man of you must go out and stand against Cuchulain to save the army." "It is not I that will go," said one of them. "It is not I," said all the others, "for Cuchulain is no easy man to stand against." Then when none of them would go out, Maeve made them cut a way through the mountain before them, that it might be left as a lasting disgrace to Ulster. So they did this, and it is called Berna Ulaid, the Gap of Ulster, to this day.

Now, when they were setting out to cross the mountain, Maeve gave orders that the army was to be divided in two parts, each with its own share of cattle, and of all other things, and she said, that she herself and Fergus would go with the one part, by the Gap of Ulster, and that Ailell should go with the other part, by the road of Midluachair.

So Ailell set out, and his chariot-driver, Ferloga, with him, and that was the same Ferloga that made a bargain with Conchubar, the High King, one time; and this is the way it happened. It was at the time Mac Datho of Leinster had stirred up a fight between the men of Ulster and the men of Connaught, about the dividing of a pig at a feast he made, the same way Bricriu had stirred up a fight about the Championship, and Conchubar was following after the men of Connaught over the plain of Fearbile; and all of a sudden Ferloga, that had been left behind by Ailell, and that was hiding himself, made a leap to the back of Conchubar's chariot, and took a hold of his neck between his two hands. "What will you give me to let you loose, king?" he said. "What is it you are asking?" said Conchubar. "Indeed it is no great gift I am asking," said Ferloga, "but only you to bring me along with you to Emain Macha, and the young women and the young girls of Ulster to sing a song around me every evening, and every one of them to say, 'Ferloga is my favourite.'" Conchubar agreed to that, and Ferloga went with him to Emain; but at the end of a year they sent him back, and presents with him, to Ailell and to Maeve.

At that time, a suspicion came on Ailell, that there was some understanding between Maeve and Fergus, and he bade Ferloga to keep a watch on them. After a while, Ferloga saw that Maeve and Fergus had stopped in a wood behind the rest of the army, and he followed after them quietly, the way they would not hear him, and there he found Fergus's sword lying on the ground. So he took the sword out of the sheath, and he cut a wooden sword and shaped it, and put it into the sheath in its place, and he brought Fergus's sword back to Ailell, and told him how he had found it, and Ailell bade him hide it in his chariot. When Fergus saw that his sword was gone and a wooden one was put in its place, there was great confusion on him; but Ailell said nothing of it when they met, but asked him to come and play a game of chess with him. And at the game they quarrelled, and Ailell said sharp words of blame to Fergus and to Maeve, and they answered him back, and Fergus bade him give him up his sword. But Ailell said he would never give it to him until the day of the great battle would come, between the men of Ireland and the men of Ulster.

Then Cuchulain came there and stood on a height, and shook his spears and his sword before them, so that great dread came on them.

After that, Maeve sent Fiacha, son of Firaba, to talk with Cuchulain, and to try could he win him over. "What will you offer him?" said Fiacha. "I will give him full payment for all that has been spoiled of his goods, and a good place for himself in Cruachan Ai, and my own protection and Ailell's, if he will give up

Conchubar's service and come into ours. And indeed that would be better for him," she said, "than to stop under a little king like Conchubar."

So Fiacha went to speak with Cuchulain, and he gave him a good welcome. And Fiacha told him the message he had brought from Maeve, and the offer she had made if he would quit Conchubar's service. "I will not do that," said Cuchulain; "I will not betray my mother's brother for the sake of any strange king. But I will consent to go myself to-morrow," he said, "to speak with Maeve and Ailell and with Fergus." So Fiacha bade him farewell, and went back to the army.

On the morning of the morrow Cuchulain went to Glen Ochain, and Maeve and Fergus came to meet him; and Maeve looked at him and she said: "Is this the same Cuchulain you put such a great name on, Fergus? I see that he has not yet grown out of his boyhood." Then she spoke with Cuchulain and made her offer again, and he refused it, and they left the place with great anger on them one against the other. And that night, and the two nights after it, the men of Ireland were afraid either to eat or to sleep or to make music; for Cuchulain killed so many of their men before the clear light of every morning, that it was as if the whole army was melting away. "Some one must go and make him another offer," said Maeve, and this time she sent Mac Roth, the herald. "Where will I find him?" said Mac Roth. "It is likely," said Fergus, "he will be between Ochain and the sea, letting the sun shine and the wind blow upon him after so many nights spent without sleep."

It was there he found him sure enough, and Laeg keeping a watch a good way off. "There is an armed man coming towards us, Cuchulain," said Laeg. "What sort of a man is he?" said Cuchulain. "A brown-haired, broad-faced, handsome young man; a fine brown cloak on him; a bright bronze spear-like brooch fastening his cloak; a well-fitting shirt next his skin; two strong shoes between his feet and the ground. There is a white hazel rod in one hand, and a sword with a sea-horse tooth for a hilt in the other." "Well, Laeg," said Cuchulain, "let him come, for these are the tokens of a herald."

Mac Roth came up to him then and asked, "Who are you serving under, young man?" "We are serving under Conchubar, High King of Ulster." "Can you tell me where can I find Cuchulain, that has killed so many of the men of Ireland?" "Whatever you would say to him, you may say to me," said Cuchulain. Then Mac Roth told him all the new offers he had brought from Maeve, and Cuchulain said: "I am Cuchulain that you are looking for, and I refuse all your offers." So Mac Roth went back to the camp. "Did you find Cuchulain?" said Maeve. "I found," he said, "an angry boy between Ochain and the sea, and I do not know if it was Cuchulain." "Did he take your offer?" said Maeve. "He did not," said Mac Roth. "It is Cuchulain he was talking to," said Fergus. "You must go to him again," said Maeve, "and make new offers." So Mac Roth went out again to make some terms with Cuchulain, but he refused all his offers. "And another thing," he said, "I would never consent to give in to a woman, or to be under a woman's rule." "Is there any bargain you would make?" said Mac Roth. "If there is," said Cuchulain, "you must find it out for yourselves, and there is one in the camp can tell of it," he said; "and if he himself comes to me, I will speak with him, but if any other man comes to me again with offers, that will be the last day of his life."

So Mac Roth went back again and told all this to Maeve. "And I will not go near him again, myself," he said, "for all that any king in Ireland could give me." Then Maeve said to Fergus: "Have you any knowledge of the terms Cuchulain would take?" "I have not," said Fergus. But after she had questioned him a while, he said: "It is what he wants, that one man of the men of Ireland should meet him and fight alone with him every day. And while that fight is going on, he will put no hindrance on the rest of the army, but it may march on. But so soon as he has killed the man set against him, the army must stop, and make its camp until the morning of the morrow." "I will agree to that," said Maeve, "for it is better to lose one man every day than a hundred every night. And who will go and make this agreement with him?" "Fergus must go," they all said. "I will not go," said Fergus. "Why so?" said Ailell. "I will not go," he said, "unless you bind yourselves on your oath to keep to your agreement with him." "We will do that," they said; and so Fergus bound them on their oath, and his horses were yoked to his chariot.

Then a young lad, Etarcomal by name, foster-son of Maeve and of Ailell, made ready his own chariot. "What side are you going, Etarcomal?" said Fergus. "I am going with you," he said, "the way I will get a sight of Cuchulain." "If you take my advice, you will not make that journey," said Fergus. "Why so?" "Because if your pride and his pride meet together, some misfortune will surely happen." "I give my word not to anger him in any way," said Etarcomal.

They went on then to where Cuchulain was, between Ochain and the sea, and himself and Laeg were playing a game with their casting spears. "There is an armed man coming to us," said Laeg. "What sort of man is he?" said Cuchulain. "He is large and proud, and he standing in a high chariot, and the waving yellow hair about his head gives him the appearance of the top of a tall tree that stands on a green lawn," said Laeg. "He has a crimson cloak about him with a deep border of gold thread, and an inlaid gold brooch in the cloak; a broad green spear in his hand; a shield with a boss of red gold over him; a long sword in a toothed sheath across his knees." "It is Fergus that is in it," said Cuchulain. Then Fergus came where he was and got out of his chariot, and Cuchulain gave him a great welcome. "Do you welcome me indeed?" said Fergus. "I do surely," said Cuchulain; "but if it is to look for a feast from me you are come, the white birds are on the side of the cliffs, and the fish are in the stream, and the wild deer on the hills." "It is not to look for a feast I am come," said Fergus, "for I know well it is not easy for you to get your own share of food. But I am come for the men of Ireland, to agree to your conditions. And from this out they will send one of their best men to fight with you alone every day." "I agree to keep to my part of the bargain," said Cuchulain, "and let us not stop talking here any more," he said, "or the men of Ireland will be thinking you are doing some treachery on them."

So Fergus went back to the camp, but Etarcomal stopped for a while looking at Cuchulain. "What are you looking at?" said Cuchulain. "I am looking at yourself," he said. "Then take your eyes off me, and go after Fergus; and maybe you think yourself a better fighting man than the one you are looking at," said Cuchulain. "You look to me as good a fighter as I ever saw for one of your age," said Etarcomal, "but you would not be thought much of among trained fighters and grown men." "It is well for you," said Cuchulain, "it is under Fergus's protection you came, or I swear, by the gods my people swear by, you would not go back safe and sound to the camp." "You have no right to say that," said Etarcomal; "and what you want of the men of Ireland, I will give it to you," he said, "for you ask for one champion at a time to fight with, and I myself will be the first to come to you to-morrow." "Come, then," said Cuchulain, "and however early you may come in the morning, you will find me here before you."

So Etarcomal set out, and he began to tell his chariot-driver all he had said, and how he had promised to go out and fight with Cuchulain on the morrow. "Did you make that promise?" said his driver. "I did," said Etarcomal, "and I have given my word I will go—and I do not know," he said, "would it be better for me to wait till to-morrow, or to go back and fight with him to-day." "You will not get the better of him to-morrow," said his driver, "and it would be just as well for you to be beaten to-night." "Turn the chariot and let us go back," said Etarcomal, "for I swear by the oath of my people, I will not go back to the camp without bringing Cuchulain's head in my hand." So they turned back again towards the sea.

Then Laeg said: "That chariot that was here a while ago has turned back again to us, Cuchulain." "It is Etarcomal coming back to challenge me, and it is not I that will fall in this fight," said Cuchulain. "But bring me my arms," he said, "for it would not be right for me not to be ready to meet him." So he went to meet him, and took his sword out of the sheath, and said: "What are you come back for?" "I am come to fight with you." "I am loth to fight with you," said Cuchulain, "for it was under the protection of Fergus you came here."

And with that he gave a blow of his sword that cut the sod clean away from under the soles of Etarcomal's feet, so that he fell on his back. "Go back now," he said, "for you have had a warning." "I will not go back until I have fought with you." Then Cuchulain gave another stroke with the edge of his sword that cut the hair close off his head, but drew no blood. "You may go back now, at least," he said. "I will not go," said Etarcomal, "until I have made an end of you, or you have made an end of me." "Well," said Cuchulain, "if you are set upon that, it is I must make an end of you." With that he made a cross blow at him that cut him through and through, so that he fell dead.

Fergus, now, had seen nothing of all this, for it was his custom, when he was travelling, never to look back, but always to be looking before him; and presently,

Etarcomal's chariot-driver came up with him, and he said: "Where have you left your master?" "Cuchulain is after attacking and making an end of him on the plain," said the man. "It was not right of him to do that," said Fergus, "to any one that came under my protection. Turn my chariot about now," he said, "until I go back and talk with him." And when he came to where Cuchulain was, he said: "It was not right of you, my own foster-son, to kill one that came under my protection." "Ask his chariot-driver," said Cuchulain, "on which of us the blame should be laid." Then the chariot-driver told the whole story, and when Fergus heard it, he said: "There is no blame on you, Cuchulain." Then he bound the body of Etarcomal to his chariot, so that it was dragged after it along the road and through the camp to the door of Ailell and Maeve. "There is the young man you sent out," he said, "and this is the treatment Cuchulain will give to every other man that goes out against him." And Maeve came out of the door and spoke high, angry, loud words: "I had put great hopes in that young man," she said, "and I did not think it was under bad protection he was going, when he went under the protection of Fergus." And Fergus said: "What business had he going out at all, to meddle with Cuchulain? And if I went there myself," he said, "it is well pleased I was to get back again safely."

The next day, the men of Ireland consulted together as to who should go against Cuchulain, and they agreed that it was best to send Natchrantal, that was a great fighting man.

So he set out, but he would bring no arms with him but three times nine holly rods, and they having hardened points.

Cuchulain was at that time following after a flock of wild birds, to bring some of them down for the evening's food, and he took no notice of Natchrantal, but went on following after the birds. But Natchrantal thought it was afraid of him he was, and he went back to the door of Maeve's tent and gave a loud shout, and he said: "That great Cuchulain there is so much talk about, is running away now after the challenge I gave him." "I would hardly believe that," said Maeve, "for he has stood against many good fighting men before now, and why would he not stand against you." Fergus heard what was said, and it vexed him, any man to say Cuchulain had run before him; and he sent Fiacha, son of Firaba, to reproach him, for letting such a thing be said, and Cuchulain bade him welcome. "I am come from Fergus," said Fiacha, "and it is what he says, that it would have been more fitting for you to spill the blood of the man that was sent against you, than to run from him." "Who did I run from?" said Cuchulain. "Tell me who makes that boast." "It is Natchrantal," said Fiacha. "What would Fergus have me do?" said Cuchulain; "would he have me kill an unarmed man? For he brought nothing with him but wooden rods, and it is not my custom to wound chariot-drivers or messengers or unarmed men. But let him come out armed to meet me," he said, "on the morning of to-morrow."

So Fiacha went back to the camp, and the day seemed long to Natchrantal till he could meet Cuchulain. But when he went out in the morning and came to the plain he said to Cormac Conloingeas: "Where is Cuchulain?" "He is there before you," said he. "That is not the appearance that was on him yesterday," said Natchrantal; for Cuchulain's anger had come on him so that the appearance he had was changed, and he was leaning against a pillar-stone, and in the strength of his anger, as he was throwing his cloak about him, he broke off the pillar-stone, and he never noticed that it was wrapped between the cloak and himself; and Natchrantal threw his sword at him, and it broke to pieces against the pillar-stone, and then Cuchulain gave him a blow over the top of his shield that struck off his head.

While this fight was going on, Maeve, having a third part of the army with her, set out Northward to Dun-Sobairce, to look for the Brown Bull. And Cuchulain followed after her for a while; but then he turned back to defend his own country. And he saw before him Buac, son of Bainblai, that was the man Maeve trusted better than any other, and twenty-four men along with him, and they driving the Brown Bull before them, and fifteen of his heifers that they had brought out of Glen-na-masc in Slieve Cuilinn. "Where are you bringing these cattle from?" said Cuchulain. "Out of that mountain beyond." "What is your name?" he said. "If I tell it, it is not either through love of you or through fear of you," he said. "I am Buac, son of Bainblai, from Ailell's country and Maeve's." "Take this from me, then," said Cuchulain, and with that he threw his spear at him so that it went through his body, and he fell dead. But while he was doing this, the rest of the men drove way the Bull with great haste to the camp of the men of Ireland; and this was the greatest affront that was put on Cuchulain through the whole of the war for the Brown Bull of Cuailgne.

Then the men of Ireland began saying to one another that Cuchulain would not have the mastery over them but for the bronze spear he had, and that there must be enchantment on it, for none of them could stand against it. And they said to Maeve that she should send Rae, the satirist, to ask it of him, for he could not refuse a satirist; so Rae went and asked it of him. "Give me your spear," he said. "I will not give you that indeed," said Cuchulain, "but I will give you other things." "I will not take any other thing," said Rae, "and I will put a bad name on you, if you refuse me the spear." "Take it, then," said Cuchulain, and with that he threw it with all his force at his head. "That is a weighty present," said the satirist, and he dropped dead.

Then Cur, son of Daltach, was sent out, for the men of Ireland thought he would be able to rid them of Cuchulain. But it was hard to persuade Cur, because he thought it was not worth his while to go and fight with a young, beardless boy. And when he went out in the morning Cuchulain was practising all his feats that he had learned, and Cur was for a while trying to get near enough to come at him with his weapons, but he could not; and Cuchulain was so taken up with doing his feats that he never noticed him at all. Then Laeg saw him and said: "Have a care, Cuchulain; there is an armed man making ready to attack you." Cuchulain was doing his apple feat at that time, keeping nine apples, and his shield, and his sword in the air, that none of them fell to the ground. And when he saw Cur, he threw the apple that was in his hand straight at his forehead, and it went through, and brought out a share of his brains the size of itself, at the other side.

And after that, other fighting men were sent out every day through a week, and he killed them all. And one day he said: "Go, Laeg, to the camp, to my friend Lugaid, and say you are come from me, and ask him which of the men of Ireland is to be sent against me to-morrow." So Laeg went, and when he came back he said: "It is your own comrade and fellow-pupil with Scathach, Ferbaeth, your blood-friend, is coming against you; for he has only lately joined the army, and he has brought four-fifths of his men with him, and Maeve has promised him her daughter Findabair, and he has drunk from her cup, and been fed by her hand." "I am sorry to hear that," said Cuchulain, "for I think worse of a comrade of my own coming against me, than of any other man." And when Ferbaeth came out to fight against him in the morning, Cuchulain did his best to make him give up the fight, for the sake of the old friendship between them, but Ferbaeth would not listen to him. Cuchulain turned from him then in anger, and to loosen the blood-bond between them, he struck the sole of his own foot with a spear, that it drew blood, and then he threw his spear at Ferbaeth, but he did not look to see did it hit him or not. But the spear went through his head and out of his mouth, and this is the way Ferbaeth came to his death.

Then Ailell made up a plan by which he thought to make Cuchulain give up the stand he was making against the army, and his plan was to offer Findabair to him if he would give his word to leave off attacking the men of Ireland, and he sent Lugaid to make the offer to him. Cuchulain was not very well pleased with the message, and he thought there might be some treachery in it, but he agreed that he would meet Ailell and Findabair, and speak with them. But when the time came, Ailell made his fool put on his clothes, and wear his gold circle on his head, and go with Findabair; and he bade him stop as far back as he could, the way Cuchulain would not know it was not the king that was in it; and then Findabair was to bind him over to their side, not to fight any more against the men of Ireland, and when that was done, she herself and the fool were to hurry back to the camp together. But when Cuchulain saw them, he knew the fool, and he sent a stone out of his sling and killed him. And because Findabair had taken a share in the treachery, he cut off her two plaits of hair and took them away. And after a while Ailell and Maeve came to see what had happened them, and there they found Findabair beside the dead body of the fool. And they brought her home and said nothing of it, but all the same the story was talked of in the camp.

Then Cuchulain sent Laeg into the camp again to ask news of Lugaid. And it is what Lugaid told him that the next to be sent against him was his own brother Larine, that Maeve had persuaded with wine, and with the promise of Findabair, to go against him. "And it is what they think," said Lugaid, "that if Cuchulain should kill my brother, I myself would have to go and get satisfaction for his death; and tell Cuchulain," he said, "not to make an end of Larine, but only to give him some punishment he will not forget." So when Larine came out, at the breaking of the day, Cuchulain came to meet him without any weapons; but he took him in his two hands and shook him, and left him there with the life still in him. But he was never the better of the shaking he got to the end of his life.

As Cuchulain lay in his sleep one night a great cry from the North came to him, so that he started up and fell from his bed to the ground like a sack. He went out of his tent, and there he saw Laeg yoking the horses to the chariot. "Why are you doing that?" he said. "Because of a great cry I heard from the plain to the north-west," said Laeg. "Let us go there then," said Cuchulain. So they went on till they met with a chariot, and a red horse yoked to it, and a woman sitting in it, with red eyebrows, and a red dress on her, and a long red cloak that fell on to the ground between the two wheels of the chariot, and on her back she had a grey spear. "What is your name, and what is it you are wanting?" said Cuchulain. "I am the daughter of King Buan," she said, "and what I am come for is to find you and to offer you my love, for I have heard of all the great deeds you have done." "It is a bad time you have chosen for coming," said Cuchulain, "for I am wasted and worn out with the hardship of the war, and I have no mind to be speaking with women." "You will have my help in everything you do," she said, "and it is protecting you I was up to this, and I will protect you from this out." "It is not trusting to a woman's protection I am in this work I have in my hands," said Cuchulain. "Then if you will not take my help," she said, "I will turn it against you; and at the time when you will be fighting with some man as good as yourself, I will come against you in all shapes, by water and by land, till you are beaten." There was anger on Cuchulain then, and he took his sword, and made a leap at the chariot. But on the moment, the chariot and the horse and the woman had disappeared, and all he saw was a black crow, and it sitting on a branch; and by that he knew it was the Morrigu had been talking with him.

After that, Loch, son of Mofebis, was sent for to Maeve, and she asked him would he go out to the next day's fight. "I will not go," he said, "for it would not be fitting for me to go out against a young boy, whose beard is not grown; but I have one to meet him," he said, "and that is my brother Long, son of Emonis, and you can make an agreement with him." So then Long was sent for, and Maeve promised him a great reward, suits of armour for twelve men, and a chariot, and Findabair for a wife, and the right of coming to every feast at Cruachan. Then Long went out to the fight, but Cuchulain killed him.

Then Maeve said to her women: "Go now to Cuchulain, and tell him to put some likeness of a beard on himself, and say to him there is no good warrior in the camp thinks it fitting to go out and fight him, he being young and beardless."

When Cuchulain heard that, he took blackberries and smeared the juice on his face, the way he would have the appearance of a beard, and then he came out on the hill and showed himself to the men of Ireland. When Loch, son of Mofebis, saw him, he said: "Is that a beard on Cuchulain?" "That is certainly what I see," said Maeve. "Then I will go out and meet him," said Loch. So they met beside the ford, where Long had got his death. "Come to the ford that is higher up," said Loch, for he would not fight at the ford where his brother died. So they fought at the upper ford, and while they were fighting, the Morrigu came against Cuchulain with the appearance of a white, red-eared heifer, and fifty other heifers along with her, and a chain of white bronze between every two of them, and they made a rush into the ford. But Cuchulain made a cast at her, and wounded one of her eyes. Then she came down the stream in the shape of a black eel, and wound herself about Cuchulain's legs in the water; and while he was getting himself free of her, and bruising her against a green stone of the ford, Loch wounded his body. Then she took the appearance of a grey wolf, and took hold of his right arm, and while he was getting free of her, Loch wounded him again. Then great anger came on him, and he took the spear Aoife had given him, the Gae Bulg, and gave him a deadly wound. "I ask one thing for the sake of your great name, Cuchulain," he called out. "What thing is that?" "It is not to spare my life I am asking you," said Loch, "but let me rise up, the way I may fall on my face, and not backwards towards the men of Ireland, so that none of them can say it was in running away or in going backward I fell." "I will surely give that leave," said Cuchulain, "for the thing you ask is a right gift for a fighting man." And after that he went back to his own camping-place.

Now, on that day above any other, a very downhearted feeling came on Cuchulain, he to be fighting alone against the four provinces of Ireland. And he bade Laeg to go to Conchubar and to the men of Ulster, and to say to them that he, the son of Dechtire, was tired with fighting every day, and with the wounds he had got, and not one of his people or his friends coming to help him.

After that Maeve sent out six all together against him, three men and three women that understood enchantments; but he destroyed them all. And now that Maeve had broken her agreement with him, not to send more than one against him at a time, he did not spare her men any longer, but from where he was he used his sling so well that in the whole army there was neither dog, horse, or man, that dared turn his face towards Cuchulain.

It was one day at that time the Morrigu came to try and get healing of her wounds from him, for it was only by his own hand the wounds he gave could be healed. She took the appearance of an old woman on her, and she milking a cow with three teats. Cuchulain was passing by, and there was thirst on him, and he asked a drink, and she gave him the milk of one teat. "May this be to the good of the giver," he said, and with that her eye that was wounded was healed. Then she gave him milk from another teat, and he said the same words; then she gave him the milk from the third teat. "The full blessing of the gods, and of the people of the plough, on you," he said. And with that, all the wounds of the Great Queen were healed.

Then the men of the four great provinces of Ireland made their camp, and put up walls at the place called the Great Breach, on the plain of Mirthemne; but they sent the cattle they had with them southward. And Cuchulain took his place on a hill; and in the evening Laeg made a fire for him there, and the flame flashed on the bright shining weapons of the men of Ireland. And when Cuchulain saw so many of them, and they so near him, great anger came on him, and he took his spears and his shield and his sword and shook them, and he gave out his loud hero cry, and it was such a great cry he gave that the Bocanachs and Bananachs and the witches of the valley answered it from all parts.

And when the men in the camp heard these great cries, they thought it was an attack that was being made upon them, and they ran against one another, and fought one another in their fright, so that a hundred of them were killed in that night.

Then Laeg saw a man coming through the camp from the north-east. "There is a man coming towards us, little Hound," he said. "What is the appearance on him?" said Cuchulain. "He is very tall and handsome and shining, and he has a green cloak about him, fastened with a silver brooch; a shirt of silk that is embroidered with red gold, falling to his knees; a black shield in his hand, with a border of white bronze, and a spear with five prongs. And it is a strange thing," he said, "that no one in the whole camp seems to see him or to take any heed of him." "That is so," said Cuchulain; "and the men of Ireland take no heed of him because they cannot see him; and I know well it is one of my friends among the Sidhe that is coming to give me help and relief; for they know it is hard for me to be standing alone against the four provinces of Ireland."

Then the man of the Sidhe, that was Lugh of the Long Hand, came and spoke with Cuchulain, and it is what he said, that he knew he was tired out and in want of sleep. "And sleep now, Cuchulain," he said, "by the grave in the Lerga, and I myself will keep watch over you till the end of three days and three nights. So Cuchulain fell asleep there and then by the grave that is in the Lerga, and no wonder in that, for he had been fighting since before the feast of Samhain without sleep, but all the while killing and attacking and destroying the men of Ireland— unless he might sleep a little while beside his spear in the middle of the day, his head on his hand, and his hand on his spear, and his spear on his knee. And while he was lying in his heavy sleep, the man of the Sidhe put Druid herbs on his wounds, so that they were all healed. So he slept for three days and three nights, and at the end of that time he rose up and passed his hand over his face, and he blushed red from head to foot with the strengthening of his courage that he felt in him, and he would have been ready to go there and then into any great gathering or feasting hall in all Ireland. "How long have I been in my sleep?" he asked the man. "Three days and three nights." "Then you have done me a bad turn indeed," he said, "for the men of Ireland have been left in quiet all that time." "They were not indeed," said the man. "Who was it stood up to them then?" said Cuchulain. "It was the boy troop came from the North, from Emain Macha," he said; "three times fifty sons of the chief men of Ulster, and they attacked the army three times, and they killed three times their own number, but they themselves were all killed in the end. And Follaman, son of Conchubar, was leading them, and he had made a boast that he would never go home again unless he could bring Ailell's head along with him, and the gold crown that was on it. But two foster-sons of Ailell, the two sons of Betchach, son of Baen, fell on him and wounded him, so that he got his death." "My grief, and oh! my grief that I was not there," said Cuchulain; "for if I had been in it, the boy troop would never have been destroyed, and Conchubar's son would not have come to his death." "Do not be fretting, little Hound," said the strange man; "there is no reproach on your name by it." "Stop here with me to-night," said Cuchulain, "and the two of us together will avenge the boy troop." "I will not indeed," said he; "but let you yourself play the game out now with the men of Ireland, for it is not they that have power over your life at this time."

With that he went away, and Cuchulain said to Laeg, "Yoke the scythed chariot for me now, if you have the things belonging to it." Then Laeg rose up and got ready the chariot, and he put on his light dress of deerskins, that was spotted and striped and close-fitting, so that his arms were left free. And over that he put his raven-black cloak, and his shining helmet on his head; and on his forehead he put the narrow band of gold that chariot-drivers were used to wear. And then he threw over the horses the cloths that covered them all over, and that were studded with little blades, and spikes, and points, so that every time the chariot moved, it brought some sharp point against those that were near it, so that every point and every head of the chariot would cut its sure path; and he gathered the reins in his hand, and the goad, and the long whip.

And then Cuchulain put on his armour, and took his spears, and his sword, and his shield that had a rim so sharp it would cut a hair against the stream, and his cloak that was made of the precious fleeces of the land of the Sidhe, that had been brought to him by Manannan, from the Kings of Sorcha. He went out then against the men of Ireland, and attacked them, and his anger came on him, so that it was not his own appearance he had on him, but the appearance of a god. And after that he turned back and left them, and there was no wound on himself, or on the horses, or on Laeg that day. And he made a round of the whole army, mowing them down on every side, in revenge for the boy troop of Emain.

But the next day he was standing on the hill, young, and comely, and shining, and the cloud of his anger had gone from him. Then the women and the young girls in the camp, and the poets and the singers, came out to look at him; but Maeve hid her face behind a shelter of shields, thinking he might make a cast at her with his sling. And there was wonder on these women to see him so quiet and so gentle to-day, and he such a terror to the whole army yesterday; and they bade the men lift them up on their shields to the height of their shoulders, the way they could have a good sight of him.

But Dubthach, the Beetle of Ulster, saw his own wife climbing up with the other women to look at Cuchulain, and great anger and jealousy came on him; and he said to the chief men of the army that it would be best for them to surround Cuchulain secretly on all sides, and then to let on to be fighting among themselves, so as to lead him down where he could not escape them. But when Fergus was told this, he gave a great kick of his foot to Dubthach, that sent him from where he was. And he spoke angry words against Dubthach, and he told him he would be well paid for the harm he had planned, whenever the men of Ulster would get up from their weakness, and come out to help Cuchulain.

And that night the army of Ireland made their camp at the great stone in the country of Ross; and then Maeve asked which of them would go out and fight with Cuchulain on the morrow. But every one of the men of Ulster said: "It is not I that will go." "It is not one of my family that should be sent to his death." Then Maeve asked Fergus to go out and fight him. "It is not right for you," said Fergus, "to ask me to go against a young boy, and he my own pupil and my foster-son." But Maeve pressed him so hard that he could not but take the work in hand; and early in the morning he went out to the ford of fighting where Cuchulain was. When Cuchulain saw him coming he said: "Truly, my master, it is not safe for you to come and fight, and you without a sword," for Ailell had not given him back his own sword yet. "It is no matter," he said, "for if I had a sword in my sheath, it is not on you I would use it. And now, Cuchulain," he said, "for the sake of all I did for you, and all Conchubar and the whole of Ulster did for you in your bringing-up, let you give way before me to-day, in the sight of the men of Ireland." "Indeed I am loth to give way before any man in this war," said Cuchulain. "You need not mind that," said Fergus, "for I will do the same for you when the great last battle of this war is fought; it is then I will turn and run before you, when you are covered with wounds and with blood. And if I run then," he said, "all the men of Ireland will run along with me." So Cuchulain agreed to do that, because it would be for the profit of Ulster. And he bade Laeg make ready his chariot; and presently, as if he had been beaten by Fergus, he gave way to him in the sight of the men of Ireland. When they saw it, they called out: "He is running before you, Fergus." And Maeve called out: "Follow him, Fergus—make haste, the way he will not escape you." "I will not indeed," said Fergus, "I will follow him no farther; and if you think I did not make him run far enough," he said, "I did more than all the rest of the men that went against him up to this; and I will make no other attack on him," he said, "until all the men of Ireland have fought with him, one by one."

So that was the end of the fight between Fergus and Cuchulain.

There was a man of Connaught at that time whose name was Ferchu, and he had been at war with Ailell and Maeve from the time they got the kingdom, and he used to be robbing the country and destroying it, so that he was made an outlaw. And some of his men heard that the whole army of Connaught was being vexed and hindered by one man; and when they told it to Ferchu, he said: "It would be a good chance for us to go and attack that man, and to bring his head with us to Ailell and Maeve, for if we do that," he said, "they will forgive us all the harm we have done their country."

So he himself and his twelve men went forward to where Cuchulain was, and they attacked him all together. But Cuchulain was not long in making an end of them, and he struck off their heads, and put them on twelve stones; and he put Ferchu's head on a stone by itself.

Then the men of Ireland consulted together again who they would send out to fight on the next day; and it is what they all said, that it was Calatin and his twenty-seven sons and his sister's son, Glas, son of Delga, should go out. Now it is the way they were, every man of them had poison in himself and in his weapons; and there was not one of them ever made a cast of a spear or a stone that missed, and there was no one that would be wounded by them but he would die, either on the spot or within the week. So great rewards were promised them, if they would go out against Cuchulain. And Fergus was there at the time the business was knotted. "And surely," every one said, "they are only one man, for they are all members of Calatin's body." After that, Fergus went into his tent, to his people, and he gave a deep groan of trouble, and he said: "My grief for the thing that is to be done to-morrow." "What thing is that?" said they all. "Cuchulain to be killed," he said. "Who would kill him?" said they. "Calatin and his sons," he said, "and if there is any one of you would go and watch the fight and bring me word what happens, I would give him a good reward, and my blessing." "I will go," said Fiacha, son of Firaba.

So in the morning Calatin, with his sons and his sister's son, rose up and went to where Cuchulain was, and Fiacha, son of Firaba, went along with them. And as soon as they came near him, they threw their twenty-nine spears at him all together, in one cast, and not one of them drew blood, for he caught them all on his shield. Then Cuchulain drew his sword from the sheath to hack off the spears and to lighten his shield; but while he was doing that, they all ran at him as one man, and put their twenty-nine right hands on his head, and forced his face down to the gravel and the sand of the ford. And he gave out his great hero cry, and the cry of a man in unequal fight, and there was not a man in the camp, and he not dead or asleep, but heard it.

Then Fiacha, son of Firaba, came up, and when he saw what had happened, the love of his own countryman came over him, and he pulled out his sword and hit the nine-and-twenty hands off Calatin and his sons, with one blow. Cuchulain raised up his head then, and gave a deep sigh of relief, and he saw who it was had come to his help. "That was done quiet and easy, my good comrade," he said.

"You may think it is quiet and easy I was," said Fiacha, "but if what I did is heard of in the camp, the reward that will fall on me will not be quiet and easy. For if the men of the children of Rudraige should hear of the stroke I made for you, it is with sword and spear my reward will be paid." "I give you my word," said Cuchulain, "that now I have lifted my head and got my breath again, unless you tell tales on yourself, none of these men will tell tales on you."

With that he made an attack on Calatin and his sons, and he began to hack and to cut at them till there was nothing left of them but limbs and little pieces eastward and westward over the whole face of the ford. Only one man of them, Glas, son of Delga, got away and ran, but Cuchulain rushed after him and gave him a great blow. But he got as far as Ailell and Maeve's tent, and all he could say was, "Fiacha! Fiacha!" before he fell dead.

Fergus and Maeve said: "What debts are those he called out about?"—for Fiacha is the word for debts in Irish. "I do not know indeed," said Fergus, "unless it might be that some one in the camp owed him a debt, and that it was on his mind." "That must have been so," said Ailell. "By my word," said Fergus, "however it was, all his debts are paid now."

And at the ford where Calatin and his sons got their death, there is a stone with the marks of their sword-hilts, and the butt-ends of their spears on it to this day.

Then it was settled by the men of Ireland that it was Ferdiad, son of Daire, the great champion of the men of Domnand, should go out and meet Cuchulain the next day. For they had the same way of fighting, and it was with the same teachers they had learned the knowledge of arms, with Scathach and with Uathach and with Aoife; and neither of them had an advantage over the other, except that Cuchulain had the feat of the Gae Bulg. But Ferdiad had good armour to protect him against any man he would fight with.

So they sent messengers to bring Ferdiad, but he refused and would not come, for he knew it was what they wanted of him, to fight against his friend, his companion and his fellow-pupil, Cuchulain.

Then Maeve sent the Druids and the satirists to him, that they might make three hurtful satires and three hilltop satires on him, if he would not come with them, that would raise three blisters on his face, shame and blemish and reproach, so that if he did not die on the moment, he would be dead before the end of nine days.

Then Ferdiad came with them for the sake of his good name, for he thought it better to fall by spears than by satires. And when he came he was received with honour and attendance, and he was served with pleasant drinks, so that he grew merry, and his mind was confused. And great rewards were offered him if he would go out against Cuchulain; clothes of all colours for his men, and speckled satins, and silver and gold, and the equal of his own lands of the level plains of Magh Ai, without rent or disturbance, secure to his son and to his grandson and to their children to the end of life and time.

And it is what Maeve said: "It is a great reward I am giving you, Ferdiad, and why would you not accept it?" And Ferdiad was making excuses. "I will not take your reward without good pledges," he said, "for it is a heavy fight is before me; he that has the name of Cuchulain is surely a good Hound." "I will give you a champion's pledge," said Maeve; "you will not be bound to come to our gatherings, you will get horses and bridles; I will call you my friend above all other men." "I will not go to this fight," said Ferdiad, "without some other securities, for this is a fight will be heard of till the end of life and time." "Take all you want," said Maeve. "There is no delay except with yourself. Bind us till you are satisfied by the right hand of kings and of princes; there is nothing I will refuse you." "I must have six securities and no less," said Ferdiad, "before I will go out and be destroyed by Cuchulain, and all the whole army looking on." "I will give you whatever securities you want," said Maeve, "however hard it may be to come at them; Domnall in his chariot; Niaman of the Slaughter, both of them protectors of bards; bind Morann if you want sure payment; bind Carpre Min of Manand, he that has a string of knowledge in his harp; bind your own two sons." "O Maeve, it is a bitter woman you are," said Ferdiad. "And it is not a gentle wife to a husband you are, but it is a fit queen you are for Cruachan of the Swords, with your high talk and your fierce strength. But in spite of all the words you are stirring me up with," he said, "if you would offer me the land and the sea, I would not take them, without the sun and the moon along with them." "You need not wait longer than to-day and to-morrow," said Maeve, "before you will get your fill of all sorts of the jewels of the earth. And here is my brooch with its hooked pin," she said; "and more than all that, Ferdiad, so soon as you have killed this Hound of feats, I will give you Findabair of the champions, queen of the west of Elga."

Ferdiad gave in to her then, and he bound her on the sureties of the aforesaid six for the fulfilment of her promises of the reward; and she bound him to fight with Cuchulain on the morrow.

Then Fergus got his horses harnessed and his chariot yoked, and he went out to where Cuchulain was, to tell him of all that had happened. "My welcome before you, my master Fergus," said Cuchulain. "I am glad of that welcome, my pupil," said Fergus. "But what I am come for is to tell you who it is that is coming to fight at the early hour of the morning of to-morrow." "I will listen to that," said Cuchulain. "Your own friend and companion, and fellow-pupil, the man that learned the use of arms with you, Ferdiad, son of Daire, the hero of the men of Domnand." "I give my word," said Cuchulain, "it is not my wish, my friend to come out against me." "And now," said Fergus, "you must be careful, and ready more than any other time, for there was not the like of Ferdiad among any of the men who have fought you up to this." "I am here," said Cuchulain, "hindering and delaying the four great provinces of Ireland, from the beginning of the winter to the beginning of spring, and I have not drawn back one foot before any man in that time, and I think it likely I will not draw back before him." "Neither has

Ferdiad any fear on him before you, now his anger is stirred up," said Fergus, "and besides that, he has good armour to protect him." "Be quiet now, Fergus, and do not let me hear any more of that story," said Cuchulain. "I was always well able to stand against him in any place, or on any ground." "It is not easy to get the better of him," said Fergus, "for he is fierce in fighting, and he has the strength of a hundred." "There will be a sharp fight when myself and Ferdiad come to the ford," said Cuchulain; "it will not be without being told in stories." "O Cuchulain of the red sword," said Fergus, "it would be better to me than a great reward, you to carry proud Ferdiad's purple cloak eastward." "I give my word and my oath," said Cuchulain, "it is I myself will get the victory over Ferdiad." Then Fergus went back to the encampment.

At the same time Ferdiad went to his tent and to his people, and told them how he was bound by Maeve to fight with Cuchulain on the morrow, and he told how he had bound Maeve by six sureties for the fulfilment of her promises, if Cuchulain should fall by him.

It is not happy in their minds the people of Ferdiad's tent were that night, but gloomy and heavy-hearted; for they were sure that wherever Cuchulain and Ferdiad would meet, it was there one of them would get his death, and they were sure that one would be their own master; for no one at all had been able to stand against Cuchulain since the beginning of the war.

Ferdiad slept through the early part of the night very heavily, and when the latter end of the night came, his sleep went from him, and his drunkenness had passed away, and the thought of the fight was pressing on him. And he bade his driver to harness the horses, and to yoke his chariot. But the driver tried to turn him from it. "It would be better for you to stop here than to go," he said, "for my liking of it is not more than my disliking."

"Be silent, boy," said Ferdiad, "for I will not be turned from this journey by any young lad; but I will go to the ford, a ford the ravens will be croaking over; I will fight with Cuchulain till I wound his strong body, till I crush the courage out of him the way that he will die."

"It would be better for you to stop here," said the driver, "for it is not gentle your threats are; your parting will be sorrowful; there is one to whom it will be a sickness; grief will come of that meeting with Cuchulain; it is long it will be remembered; it is a pity for him who goes that journey." "It is not right what you are saying," said Ferdiad; "it is not for a brave man to refuse—it is not in our race. I will delay no longer, courage is better than fear; let us set out now to the ford."

Then Ferdiad's horses were harnessed, and his chariot was yoked, and he went forward to the ford, and the day with its full light came upon him there. "Now, boy," he said, "spread out the skins and the cushions of my chariot under me here, until I get some sleep and rest, for I got no sleep at the end of the night, with the care of the fight upon me."

So his servant unharnessed the horses, and settled the skins and cushions of the chariot under him, and the heavy rest of sleep came upon him.

But as to Cuchulain, he did not rise up at all till the day had come with its full light, the way the men of Ireland would not say it was fear that was on him that made him rise. And when the day came: "It would be as well, Laeg," he said, "to yoke the chariot, for it is an early-rising man that is coming to meet us to-day."

"The horses are harnessed, and the chariot is yoked," said Laeg; "let you get into it, and there will be no hindrance to your courage."

With that the ready-handed, battle-winning son of Sualtim leaped into the chariot, and there shouted around him the Bocanachs and Bananachs, and witches of the valley. For the Sidhe were used to set up their shouts around him, the way the fear and the wonder would be great before him in every fight he would go into.

And it was not long until Ferdiad's driver heard the noise coming near, the straining of the harness, the creaking of the chariot, the ringing of the armour and of the shield, the trampling of the horses, and joyful coming of Cuchulain to the ford.

The driver came and laid his hand on his master. "Good Ferdiad," he said, "rise up; here they are coming. I hear," he said, "the creaking of a chariot; it has come over Breg Ross, over Braine; it has come over the highway by the foot of Baile-in-Bile; he is a mighty Hound that urges it; he is a good driver that yokes it; he is a free hawk that hurries his horses towards the south. It is not he who will be slow in the fight. It is a pity for him that is on the height waiting for the Hound of valour. It is a year ago I foretold there would come a Hound, the Hound of Emain, a Hound with all colours about him—the Hound of Ulster, the Hound of Battle; I hear him—I have heard him coming."

"Good servant," said Ferdiad, "why is it you have been praising that man ever since you came out from the house? It is likely you are not without wages for your great praise of him. Yet it has been foretold to me by Ailell and by Maeve, it is he that will fall by me. And it is a time to help me," he said; "and let you be silent, and give up praising him, that your foretelling may not come true. It is not for you to give up on the brink of the fight; surely I will soon have the reward."

And the driver said: "He is coming, not slowly, but quick as the wind, or as water from a high cliff, or like swift thunder." "Surely you have taken wages for these great praises you put upon him," said Ferdiad; "it is not against him you are, but praising him, and putting a great name on him."

It was not long then until Ferdiad saw Cuchulain coming towards him in his chariot, and it is how his two horses were going, like a hawk sweeping from a cliff on a day of hard wind, or like a sweeping gust of the spring wind on a March day over a smooth plain, or like the swiftness of a wild stag when he is first started by the hounds in his first field; as if they were on fiery flagstones, so that the earth was shaking and trembling with the quickness of their going.

So Cuchulain reached the ford, and Ferdiad came to the south side, and Cuchulain drew up on the north side, and Ferdiad bade Cuchulain welcome. "I am happy at your coming, Cuchulain," he said. "I would have been glad of that welcome up to this time," said Cuchulain, "but to-day I do not take it as the welcome of a friend. And Ferdiad," he said, "it would be fitter for me to welcome you than for you to welcome me, for it is you have come to me in the country and province where I am, and it is not right for you to come to fight with me, but it is I should go to fight with you, for it is out before you are the women and the children, the young men and the horses, the flocks, the herds, and the cattle of the province of Ulster."

"Good Cuchulain," said Ferdiad, "what has brought you to fight with me at all? For when we were with Scathach and with Uathach and with Aoife, you were my serving-boy, to tie up my spears and to make ready my bed." "That is true indeed," said Cuchulain; "but it was as less in age than you I was used to do so; but that is not the story that will be told of us after this day, for there is not a man in the whole world I would not fight to-day."

And it is then each of them spoke sharp, unfriendly words against the other; and it is what Ferdiad said: "What has brought you, O Hound, to fight with a strong fighter? It is red your blood will be, flowing over the harness of your horses; it is a pity for your journey; it is long it will be spoken of; you will be in much want of healing if you ever get back to your own house," he said.

"I have fought with heroes, with chiefs of armies, with troops, with hundreds before now," said Cuchulain, "and what I have to do to-day is to make an end of you, to bring you down in our first path of battle."

"You have met now with a man that will put reproach on you," said Ferdiad, "for it is I myself will do that. It is well the loss of the men of Ulster will be remembered," he said, "their champion to be put down, and they looking on."

"What way shall we meet one another?" said Cuchulain. "Is it in our chariots we had best fight, or is it with my sword and spear I am to overthrow you, if the time has come?" And Ferdiad said: "Before the setting of the sun to-night, you will be fighting as if with a mountain, and it is not white that battle will be. The men of Ulster will be shouting for you," he said, "till you grow overbold; but it is sorrowful they will be, when your ghost passes over them and through them." "You are fallen into the gap of danger, Ferdiad," said Cuchulain; "the end of your life has come, not by treachery, but by sharp weapons. You may think much of yourself till we meet one another, but you will never fight in a battle again, from this day to the end of time." "Leave off now from your boastings," said Ferdiad; "it is you are the greatest boaster in the world. I know well you are no fighter at all, you heart of a bird in a cage; you are but a giggling fellow, without courage, without strength." But Cuchulain said: "When we were together with Scathach, we used to be practising together, we used to go to every battle together, because of our bravery that was equal. You were my heart companion, you were my people, you were my family—I never found one was dearer; it is sorrowful your death would be to me."

"Where is the use of all this talk?" said Ferdiad; "your great name will be lost, your head will be on a stake before the crowing of the cock. Madness and grief are taking hold of you, Cuchulain," he said, "and it is bad treatment you will get from me, because it is on yourself the fault is."

"Good Ferdiad," Cuchulain said then, "it was not right for you to come out against me, through the stirring up and the meddling of Ailell and of Maeve; and none of those who came before you got victory or success, but they all fell by me, and you will fall along with them. And, O Ferdiad, strong fighter," he said, "do not come against me; the meeting will bring sorrow to many, and what is worse than sorrow to you. Have you not been bought with many presents? A purple belt, a suit of armour? But, Ferdiad," he said, "the woman for whom you are come to this fight, Findabair, daughter of Maeve, however comely she may be, will never be given to you; for she has been offered to many before you," he said, "and many like you have been wounded for her sake.

"Do not break your oath not to fight with me; do not break friendship. Do not break the word you gave me, do not come against me.

"The woman has been promised to fifty others; it was a heavy gift for them; it is by me they were sent to their grave; it is by me they got the end that was fitting for them.

"Though Ferbaeth was boastful, he who had a houseful of brave men, it is short the time was till I quieted his rage; I killed him by the one cast.

"The striking down of Srub Daire's courage was bitter to him; it is he held the secrets of a hundred women; he had a great name at one time; it is not silver thread but gold thread was in his clothes.

"If it were to me the woman was promised on whom the kings of the fair province smile, I would not bring the red blood on your body for it, south or north, east or west.

"And good Ferdiad," he said, "this is why it is not right for you to come to this fight. When we were with Scathach, it is together we used to go to every battle, to every wild place, through every darkness and every hardship. We were heart companions; we were comrades in gatherings; we shared the one bed where we used to sleep sound sleep. We used to practise together, in many far countries; we used to go to hard fights; we used to go through every forest together."

"O Cuchulain of the wonderful feats," said Ferdiad, "although we learned knowledge together, and although I know the bonds friendship put upon us, it is I that will give you your first wounds; do not be remembering our companionship, for it will not protect you. And it is too long we are delaying like this," he said; "and what arms shall we use to-day, Cuchulain?"

"It is you have the choice of arms to-day," said Cuchulain, "for it is you were the first to reach the ford." "Do you remember at all," said Ferdiad, "the casting spears we used to practise with Scathach and with Uacthach and with Aoife?" "I remember them indeed," said Cuchulain. "If you remember, let us begin with them," said Ferdiad.

So they began with their casting weapons, and they took their protecting shields, and their round-handled spears, and their little quill spears, and their ivory-hilted knives, and their ivory-hafted spears, eight of each of them they had. And these were flying from them and to them like bees on the wing on a fine summer day; there was no cast that did not hit, and each one went on shooting at the other with those weapons from the twilight of the early morning to the full midday, until all their weapons were blunted against the faces and the bosses of the shields. And as good as the throwing was, the defence was so good that neither of them drew blood from the other through that time.

"Let us leave these weapons now, Cuchulain," said Ferdiad, "for it is not by the like of them our fight will be settled." "Let us leave them indeed if the time is come," said Cuchulain.

They stopped then, and threw their darts into the hands of their chariot-drivers. "What weapons shall we use now, Cuchulain?" said Ferdiad. "The choice of weapons is yours till night," said Cuchulain. "Let us then," said Ferdiad, "take to our straight spears, with the flaxen strings in them." "Let us now indeed," said Cuchulain. And then they took two stout shields, and they took to their spears.

Each of them went on throwing at the other with the spears from the middle of mid-day until the fall of evening. And good as the defence was, yet the throwing was so good that each of them wounded the other in that time.

"Let us leave this now," said Ferdiad. "Let us leave it indeed if the time has come," said Cuchulain.

So they left off, and they threw their spears away from them into the hands of their chariot-drivers. Each of them came to the other then, and each put his hands round the neck of the other, and gave him three kisses. Their horses were in the one enclosure that night, and their chariot-drivers at the one fire; and their chariot-drivers spread beds of green rushes for them, with wounded men's pillows on them. The men that had knowledge of healing came then, and put herbs of healing to their wounds. And of every herb and plant that was put to Cuchulain's wounds, he would send an equal share from him westward over the ford to Ferdiad, the way the men of Ireland might not say if Ferdiad should fall by him, that it was by better means of cure he was able to overcome him.

And of every kind of food and of drink that was sent by the men of Ireland to Ferdiad, he would send a fair share over the ford northward to Cuchulain; because the providers of Ferdiad were more than the providers of Cuchulain. All the men of Ireland were providers to Ferdiad for beating off Cuchulain from them, but only the Bregians were providers to Cuchulain. They used to come and to be talking with him at the dusk of every night.

They rested there that night, and they rose up early on the morrow, and came forward to the ford of battle.

"What weapons shall we use to-day, Ferdiad?" said Cuchulain. "It is you have the choice of weapons until night," said Ferdiad, "because I had my choice of them the last day." "Let us then," said Chuchulain, "take to our great broad spears to-day; for we shall be nearer to the end of our battle by the thrusting to-day than we were by the throwing yesterday."

Each of them continued to cut, and to wound, and to redden the other, from the twilight of the early morning till the fall of the evening. If it were the custom for birds in their flight to pass through the bodies of men, they could have passed through their bodies on that day, and they could have carried pieces of flesh and blood through their stabs and cuts, into the clouds and the sky all around. And when the fall of evening came, their horses were tired, and their chariot-drivers were down-hearted, and they were tired themselves as well.

"Let us stop from this now, Ferdiad," said Cuchulain, "for our horses are tired, and our chariot-drivers are down-hearted; and when they are tired, why would not we be tired as well? And we are not bound to go on for ever," he said, "as is the custom with the Fomor. Let us put the quarrel away for a while, now the noise of the fighting is over." "Let us leave off indeed if the time is come," said Ferdiad.

They threw their spears from them then into the hands of their chariot-drivers, and each of them came towards the other. Each of them put his hand round the neck of the other and gave him three kisses. Their horses were in the one enclosure that night, and their chariot-drivers at the one fire.

Their chariot-drivers made beds of green rushes for them, with wounded men's pillows on them, and the men that had knowledge of healing came to examine them that night, but they could do nothing more for them, because of the deepness of their many wounds, but to use charms and spells on them, to staunch their blood. Every charm and every spell that was used on the wounds of Cuchulain, he sent a full share of them over the ford westward to Ferdiad. And of every sort of food and of drink that was sent to Ferdiad, he sent a share of them over the ford northward to Cuchulain.

They rested there that night, and they rose up early on the morrow, and they came forward to the ford of battle. Cuchulain saw a sort of a dark look on Ferdiad that day. "It is bad you are looking to-day, Ferdiad," he said; "there is a darkness on your face, and a heaviness on your eyes, and your own appearance is gone from you." "It is not from fear or dread of you I am like this to-day," said Ferdiad; "for there is not a champion in Ireland to-day I could not put down." And Cuchulain was fretted to see him that way, and it is what he said: "O Ferdiad, if it is you yourself, I am sure you are a miserable man, to have come at the bidding of a woman to fight against your own companion." But Ferdiad said: "O Cuchulain, giver of wounds, true hero, every man must come in the end to the sod where his last grave shall be."

"As to Findabair, daughter of Maeve," said Cuchulain, "whatever her beauty may be, it is not for love of you she was given to you, but only for the sake of your great strength." "O Hound of the gentle sway," said Ferdiad, "it is long ago my strength was tried; but I never heard of any man braver in fight than yourself; I never met so brave a man until to-day." "It is your own fault what has happened," said Cuchulain; "you to have come at the bidding of a woman to try your sword against your fellow." "If I had gone back," said Ferdiad, "without doing battle with you, it is little my name and my word would be thought of by Ailell and by Maeve of Cruachan." "No one has ever put food to his lips," said Cuchulain, "and no one has ever been born in honour of a king or queen, for whose sake I would have harmed you." "O Cuchulain, winner of battles," said Ferdiad; "it was not you but Maeve that betrayed me; let you take the victory and the fame, for it is not on you the blame is."

And Cuchulain said: "My faithful heart is like a clot of blood; my life is nearly gone from me; I have no strength for high deeds, fighting with you, Ferdiad." "Much as you are complaining over me now," said Ferdiad, "what arms shall we use to-day?" "It is you have the choice to-day," said Cuchulain, "because it was I had it yesterday." "Let us then," said Ferdiad, "take to our swords to-day, for we will be nearer the end of our battle by the hewing to-day, than we were by the thrusting yesterday." "Let us do so indeed," said Cuchulain.

And then they put two long wide shields on them, and they took to their swords, and each of them continued to hack at the other, from the dawn of the early morning till the time of the fall of evening. "Let us leave off from this now," said Cuchulain. So they left off.

They threw their swords from them into the hands of their chariot-drivers, and it was the parting, mournful, sorrowful, down-hearted, of two men that night.

Their horses were not in the one enclosure that night, their chariot-drivers were not at the one fire. They rested that night there.

And Ferdiad rose up early next morning, and went forward by himself to the ford. For he knew that day would decide the fight, and he knew one of them would fall on that day there, or they would both fall.

And then he put on his battle suit, before the coming of Cuchulain to him. He put on his shirt of striped silk, with its border of speckled gold, next to his white skin. He put on his coat of brown leather, well sewed, over the outside. He put on his apron of purified iron, through dread of the Gae Bulg that day. He put his crested helmet of battle on his head, on which were forty gems, carbuncles, in each division, and it was studded with crystal and with shining rubies of the eastern world. He took his strong spear into his right hand, and his curved sword upon his left side, with its golden hilt, and its knobs of red gold, and his great, large, bossed shield on his back.

And then he began to show off many changing, wonderful feats, that he had never learned with any other person, neither with nurse or with tutor, or with

Scathach or with Uacthach, or with Aoife, but that were made up that day by himself against Cuchulain.

Then Cuchulain came to the ford, and when he saw all Ferdiad was doing: "I see, my friend Laeg," he said, "all those feats will be tried on me one after another; and because of that," he said, "if it is I that begin to give in to-day, it is for you to reproach me, and to speak hard words to me, the way that the strength of my anger may grow the more on me. But if I am getting the better of him, then you are to praise me, and make much of me, that my courage may be the greater." "I will do that indeed, my master Cuchulain," said Laeg.

And then Cuchulain put on his battle suit, and he said: "What arms shall we take to-day, Ferdiad?" "The choice is yours to-day," said Ferdiad. "Let us try the ford feat then," said Cuchulain. "Let us indeed," said Ferdiad. But though Ferdiad agreed to it, it is sorry he was to say those words, for he knew Cuchulain was used to put an end to every fighter than was against him in the feat of the ford.

It was great work, now, that was done on that day at the ford; the two champions of western Europe, the two gift-giving and wage-giving hands of the northwest of the world; the two pillars and the two keys of the courage of the Gael; to be brought from far off, to fight one against the other, through the stirring up and the meddling of Ailell and Maeve. Each of them began to throw his weapons at the other, from the dawn of early morning to the middle of mid-day. And when mid-day came, the anger of the men grew hotter, and each of them drew nearer to the other. And then it was that Cuchulain leaped on to the boss of Ferdiad's shield, to strike at his head over the rim of the shield. But Ferdiad gave the shield a blow of the left elbow, and threw Cuchulain from him like a bird on the brink of the ford. Cuchulain leaped up again to the boss of the shield, but Ferdiad gave it a stroke of his left knee, and threw Cuchulain from him like a little child.

Laeg saw that done. "My grief indeed," he said, "the fighter that is against you, Cuchulain, casts you away as a light woman would cast her child. He throws you as foam is thrown by the river; he grinds you as a mill would grind fresh malt; he cuts through you as the axe cuts through the oak; he binds you as the woodbine binds the tree; he darts on you as the hawk darts on little birds; and from this out, you have no call nor claim to courage or a brave name to the end of life and time, you little fairy fighter," said Laeg.

It is then Cuchulain leaped up with the quickness of the wind, and with the readiness of the swallow, and with the fierceness of the lion, towards the troubled clouds of the air the third time, until he lit on the boss of Ferdiad's shield, to strike at his head from above. And Ferdiad gave his shield a shake and cast Cuchulain from him, the same as if he had never been cast off before at all.

And it is then Cuchulain's anger came on him, and the flames of the hero light began to shine about his head, like a red thorn bush in a gap, or like the sparks of a fire, and he lost the appearance of a man, and what was on him was the appearance of a god.

So close was the fight they made now, that their heads met above and their feet below, and their hands in the middle, over the rims and bosses of their shields. So close was the fight, that they broke and loosened their shields from the rim to the middle. So close was the fight, that they turned and bent and shattered their spears from the points to the hilts. So close was the fight, that the Bocanachs and Bananachs and the witches of the valley screamed from the rims of their shields and from the hilts of their swords, and from the handles of their spears. So close was the fight, that they drove the river out of its bed and out of its course, so that it might have been a place for a king or a queen to rest in, so that there was not a drop of water in it, unless it dropped into it by the trampling and the hewing the two champions made in the middle of the ford.

So great was the fight, that the horses of the men of Ireland broke away in fright and shyness, with fury and madness, breaking their chains and their yokes, their ropes and their traces; and the women and the young lads and the children and the followers of the men of Ireland broke out of the camp to the south-west.

They were using the edge of their swords through that time; and it was then Ferdiad found a time when Cuchulain was off his guard, and he gave him a stroke of the sword, and hid it in his body, and the ford was reddened with Cuchulain's blood, and Ferdiad kept on making great strokes at him. And Cuchulain could not bear with this, and he called to Laeg for the Gae Bulg, and it was sent down the stream to him, and he caught it with his foot. And when Ferdiad heard the name of the Gae Bulg, he made a stroke of his shield down to protect his body. But Cuchulain made a straight cast of the spear, the Gae Bulg, off the middle of his hand, over the rim of the shield, and it passed through his armour and went out through his body, so that its sharp end could be seen.

Ferdiad gave a stroke of his shield up to protect the upper part of his body, though it was "the relief after danger," as the saying is. "That is enough," said Ferdiad; "I die by that. And I may say, indeed, you have left me sick after you, and it was not right that I should fall by your hand. O Hound of the beautiful feats, it was not right, you to kill me; the fault of my death is yours, it is on you my blood is. A foolish man does not escape when he goes into the gap of danger; my grief I am going away, my end is come. My ribs will not hold my heart, my heart is all turned to blood. I have not done well in the battle; you have killed me, Cuchulain."

Cuchulain ran towards him after that, and put his two arms about him, and lifted him across the ford northwards, so that his body should be by the ford on the north, and not on the west of the ford with the men of Ireland.

He laid him down then, and a cloud and a weakness came on him as he stood over Ferdiad. Laeg saw that, and he saw that all the men of Ireland were rising up to come towards him. "Good Cuchulain," said Laeg, "rise up now, for the men of Ireland are coming towards us, and it is not one man they will put to fight against us, now that Ferdiad has fallen by you." "What use is it to me to rise up now, and he after falling by me?" said Cuchulain. But Laeg said: "Rise up, O chained Hound of Emain; it is glad and shouting you have a right to be now, since Ferdiad of the hosts has fallen by you." "What are joy and shouting to me now?" said Cuchulain; "it is madness and to grief I am driven after the thing I have done, and the body I wounded so hard." "It is not right for you to be lamenting him," said Laeg. "It is making rejoicing over him should be. It was at you he aimed his spears." But Cuchulain said: "Even if he had cut one arm and one leg from me, it is my grief Ferdiad not to be riding his horses through the long days of his lifetime." And Laeg said: "It is better pleased the women of the Red Branch will be, he to have died and you to be living. They know it is not few but many you have sent away for ever; for from the day you came out of Cuailgne to meet Maeve of the great name, it is a grief to her all you have killed of her people and of her fighting men. You have not taken quiet sleep since the spoiling of your country began; though there were few along with you, many were the mornings you rose up early."

Then Cuchulain began to keen and to lament for Ferdiad there, and it is what he said: "Well, Ferdiad, it is a pity for you it was not one of the men that knew my courage you asked an advice of before you came to meet me in the fight that was too hard for you. It is a pity it was not Laeg, son of Riangabra, you asked how we stood one to another. It is a pity you did not ask a true advice of Fergus. It is a pity it was not pleasant comely Conall you asked which of us would put down the other.

"And these men know well," he said, "there will never be born one among the men of Connaught who will do deeds equal to yours, to the end of life and time. And they know that if they looked among the places, the gatherings, the swearings, the false promises of the fair-haired women of Connaught, or in the playing with targets and shields, the playing with shields and swords, the playing backgammon and chess, the playing with horses and chariots, there will not be found the hand of a man that will wound like Ferdiad's hand, or a man to bring the red-mouthed birds croaking over the speckled battle, nor one that will fight for Cruachan, that will be your equal to the end of life and time, O red-cheeked son of Daman." And then he rose up and stood over Ferdiad. "Well, Ferdiad," he said, "it is great wrong and treachery was played on you by the men of Ireland, to bring you out to fight with me. For it has not been easy to stand against me in the war for the Bull of Cuailgne." And he made this complaint:—

"O Ferdiad, you were betrayed to your death; your last end was sorrowful; you to die, I to be living; our parting for ever is a grief for ever.

"When we were far away, with Scathach the victorious, we gave our word that to the end of time we would never go against one another.

"Dear to me was your beautiful ruddiness; dear to me your comely form; dear to me your clear grey eye; dear to me your wisdom and your talk.

"There has not come to the battle, there has not been made angry in the fight, there had not held up shield on the field of spears, the like of you, O red son of Daman.

"Findabair, the daughter of Maeve, with all her great beauty, it was putting a gad on the sand, or on the sun, for you to think to get her, Ferdiad."

Then Cuchulain was still looking down on Ferdiad, "Well, my friend Laeg," he said, "strip Ferdiad now, and take his armour and his clothes off him, until I see the brooch for the sake of which he undertook the fight."

Laeg stripped Ferdiad then, and when Cuchulain saw the brooch, he began to lament and complain over him again, and it is what he said:

"My grief, O gold brooch! O Ferdiad of the poets, O strong striker of many blows, it is brave your arm was.

"Your yellow hair, curled, well-loved; your soft, leaf-like belt about you until death.

"Dear was our fellowship, dear the brightness of your eyes; your shield with its rim of gold; your chessboard that was worth riches.

"It was not right, you to fall by my hand; it was not a friendly ending. My grief, O gold brooch, my grief

"Well, my friend Laeg," he said then, "come now and take the Gae Bulg out of him, for I cannot afford to be without my spear." So Laeg took the Gae Bulg out of him, and when Cuchulain saw his reddened spear lying beside Ferdiad, he said: "O Ferdiad, it is a sorrowful story to me, that I should see you so red and so pale, I with my spear reddened, and you in a bed of blood.

"When we were over in the east with Scathach, there would not have been angry words between us, or destroying weapons.

"Scathach spoke fiery words to us, 'Go all of you to the battle that will be fought by Germain the terrible.'

"I said to Ferdiad and to Lugaid, the always generous, and to the son of Baetan the fair, 'Let us all go against Germain.'

"We all of us came to the battle-ground on the shore of the lake of Lind Formait; we brought four hundred out with us from the islands of the Athisech.

"As I and brave Ferdiad were together in the door of Germain's dun, I killed Rind, the son of Niul, I killed Ruad, son of Finnial.

"Ferdiad killed upon the shore Blath, son of Calba of the red swords. Lugaid killed Mugarne of the Torrian Sea, a surly, fierce man.

"We spoiled the dun of Germain the crafty; we brought him with us alive over the wide sea of speckled waters; we brought him to Scathach of the broad shield.

"She, our teacher, whose name was well known, bound us to friendship together, the way our anger would not turn against one another among the fair tribes of Elga.

"Sorrowful the morning when the strength was taken from the son of Daman. My grief I loved the friend to whom I have given a drink of red blood.

"It is a sorrowful thing has happened to us the pupils of Scathach—I myself red and wounded; you yourself not driving your chariot.

"It is a sorrowful thing has happened to us the pupils of Scathach—I myself hard with blood; you yourself entirely dead.

"It is a sorrowful thing has happened to us the pupils of Scathach—yourself to have died, myself to be alive and strong; it is angry we were in the battle."

"Good Cuchulain," said Laeg, "let us leave this ford now; it is too long we are here." "Let us leave it now indeed, my friend Laeg," said Cuchulain. "But every other fight I ever made was as a game and a sport beside the fight with Ferdiad." And it is what he said:

"Each fight was a game, each one was a sport, until Ferdiad came to the ford; we got the same teaching, we got the same rewards; our teacher was kind to us both alike, setting us both above all the others.

"Each was as a game, each was as a sport, until Ferdiad came to the ford; we had the same ways, we used to do the same deeds; it was at the one time Scathach gave a shield to me, and a shield to Ferdiad.

"Each was a game, each was a sport, until Ferdiad came to the ford; dear to me was the pillar of gold that I broke down on the ford; he who, when he attacked the tribes, was braver than any other.

"Each was a game, each was a sport, until Ferdiad came to the ford, like a proud swelling wave, threatening to destroy all before him.

"Each was a game, each was a sport, until Ferdiad came to the ford; this thing will hang over me for ever. Yesterday he was larger than a mountain; to-day there is nothing of him but a shadow."

CHAPTER XII

The Awakening of Ulster

Then some of the men of Ulster came to comfort Cuchulain, and among them were Senoll Uathach and the two sons of Gege, Muredach and Cotreb. They brought him away to the five streams of Conaille Muirthemne, to wash his hurts in them. And the Sidhe threw all sorts of herbs and plants into the streams for his healing, so that they were all strewed over with green leaves.

Then when Ailell and Maeve heard there were men beginning to come from Ulster, they sent Mac Roth, the herald, to watch at Slieve Fuad, and to warn them if he could see any one coming. And after a while he came back, and Ailell asked news of him. "I saw," he said, "one chariot only, to the north of Slieve Fuad, and it coming straight on, and the man that was in it naked, and without armour or weapons, but only an iron spit in his hand, and he goading on the horses as if he would never get to the army alive." "Who do you think was that man, Fergus?" said Ailell. "I think," said Fergus, "it was Cethern, son of Fintan, from the North, and he will soon be upon us." With that, Cethern came bursting into the camp, and he attacked everyone he met with his spit, and he himself got many wounds back again, so that he had to hold up the board of the chariot to his body to keep his bowels from falling out; and at last he made his escape, and came to the place where Cuchulain was lying. Then Cuchulain said to Laeg: "Rise up now, and go into the camp, and bring some of Ailell's physicians to cure Cethern; for I give my word, if they do not come before this time to-morrow, I will bring death and destruction on them." So Laeg went, and he brought back the physicians with him, and it was only the dread of Cuchulain that made them come. Then Cethern showed the first one of them his wounds, and it is what he said, that he could not be cured. Then Cethern gave him a blow that sent him out of the house. And the same thing happened with all the rest, fifteen there were of them altogether. Then he asked Cuchulain would he get him another physician, for those of the men of Ireland had done him no good. "Rise up, Laeg," said Cuchulain; "go to Slieve Fuad, to Fingan, the Druid physician of Conchubar, and bid him to come here and to heal Cethern." Now, Fingan was the greatest physician in all Ireland, and it was said of him that he could tell what a person's sickness was by looking at the smoke of the house he was in; and he knew by looking at a wound what sort the person was that gave it. Then he came, and Cethern showed him his wounds. "Look at this wound for me, good Fingan," he said. "There came at me two young men, with clear noble looks, with strange foreign clothes on them, and each of them threw a spear into me, and I threw my spear into each of them." "I know those two very well," said Cuchulain; "they are two choice men of Norway, and they were sent against you by Ailell and Maeve." "Look at this wound for me, Fingan," said Cethern. Fingan looked at it. "That is the work of two brothers," he said. "That is true indeed," said Cethern. "Two young men came at me, and they were like one another; but one had curling brown hair, and the other had curling yellow hair. Two green cloaks about them, with brooches of bright silver; two soft shirts of yellow silk; bright swords in their belts they had, and shields with bright silver fastenings, and spears with veins of silver on their handles." "I know those two very well," said Cuchulain; "they are Maine Athremail and Maine Mathremail, two sons of Ailell and Maeve."

"Look at this wound for me, good Fingan," said Cethern. Fingan looked at the wound, and he said: "It was a father and a son made that together." "That is true," said Cethern; "there came at me two large men with flaming eyes, and they having gold bands on their heads, and the dress of kings, and gold swords at their sides." "I know those two very well," said Cuchulain; "it was Ailell and his son Maine Andoe that gave you that wound." "Look at this wound, good Fingan," said Cethern. Fingan looked at the wound. "That is the work of a proud woman," he said. "That is true," said Cethern; "there came at me a beautiful, pale, long-faced woman, with long, flowing yellow hair on her, a crimson cloak with a brooch of gold over her breast, and a straight spear shining red in her hand. It was she gave me that wound, and she got a little wound from me." "I know that woman well," said Cuchulain. "She is Maeve, daughter of the High King of Ireland, and Queen of Connaught. She would have thought it a great victory and a great triumph, you to have fallen by her hand." "Good Fingan," said Cethern then, "tell me now, what do you think of the way I am, and what can you do for me?" "It is what I think," said Fingan, "you will hardly see the calves that are following your cows at this time grow to be yearlings; or if you do itself," he said, "it will not be much use your life will be to you." "That is what all the others said to me," said Cethern, "and it is not much profit or credit they got by it, and it is not much you yourself will get"; and with that he made a kick at him, to drive him out of the house. But in spite of that treatment, Fingan gave him his choice of two things: the first to be a long time on his bed, so that he would see the men of Ulster coming in the end to avenge him; or to be made well enough at the end of three days to go out himself and spend what he had of strength on his enemies.

"I will choose that," he said, "for I would not like to leave my enemies after me; and who is there better than myself to get satisfaction from them?" So then Fingan bade Cuchulain to make a healing bath that would ease Cethern. So Cuchulain went down to the camp, and he brought away with him all that he met of the cattle of the men of Ireland. Then their flesh was cut up with their bones and their skins to make a Druid bath, and Cethern was put in it for the length of three days and three nights. And at the end of that time he rose up and got into his chariot, to do vengeance on the men of Ireland. And his wife Ionda, daughter of Eochaid, came to him from the North, and brought him his sword that he had forgotten in his hurry at his first setting out.

But it happened that one of the physicians he had driven out with a blow had fallen down outside the tent, and lay there, not able to stir from that. But when Cethern was making ready to set out, he rose up and made his way back to the camp, and he said to the men of Ireland: "Cethern is after being cured by Fingan, the Druid, and he is coming at you now, and do you lay some trap for him." So it is what they did: they took Ailell's cloak and his shirt, and they put them about the pillar-stone, at the boundary of Ross, and his crown on top of it, and left them there. Cethern came rushing on them, and when he saw the pillar-stone, he thought it was Ailell was standing there, and he made at it, and gave a great blow of his sword, that it broke in pieces against the stone.

Then he saw what it was, and he said: "This is some trick they have played on me. And by the oath of my people," he said, "I will not stop my hand from killing, until such time as I have killed some man having a dress like this."

When Maine Andoe heard that, he put on his father's armour, and came out to meet him. And Cethern saw him, and made for him, and threw his shield at him, so that he was cut through and through the body by the rim of the shield.

And when the men of Ireland saw that, they pressed on Cethern from all sides and made an end of him. And his wife Ionda, daughter of Eochaid, came and cried over him there.

And then Fintan, Cethern's father, came with three times fifty men to get satisfaction for his son, and he made three attacks on the army, and killed a great many of Ailell's men; but Fintan lost a good many of his own men, and his son Crimthan was made prisoner. And the men of Ireland were afraid their army would be too much weakened by little fights of this sort before the great last battle that was foretold would come, and they made an agreement with Fintan to give him back his son, and to fall back themselves a day's march; and he gave his word not to vex them again until the time of the last battle. And they found, where the fight had been, one of Fintan's men and one of Ailell's men lying dead together, and they with their teeth fixed into one another. And it is from this the fight was given the name of Fintan's Tooth-fight.

Then Rochad, son of Fatheman, came to help Cuchulain, and three times fifty men with him. Now Findabair loved him, and when she heard he was coming, she told her secret, and she said to her mother: "That is my love and my choice out of all the men of Ireland." And when Maeve heard that, she made a plan to draw him off, and she said to Findabair: "Go now and meet him secretly, and bid him to go back with his men until the day of the great battle, and I will give you to him for his wife." So Findabair went and gave him the message, and he went back north-wards with his men. But this was heard of in the camp, and the twelve kings of Munster that were in Maeve's army began speaking with one another; and it is what they all said, that Maeve had secretly promised Findabair as a wife to each one of them as a reward, if he would join in the war. "And the best thing we can do now," they said, "is to go and avenge ourselves on Maeve's men, and on Rochad, for the treachery that was done on us."

So they went out and made an attack on them, and Ailell and Maeve's men and Rochad made ready to defend themselves; but Fergus went out and tried to make them leave off, and to make peace between them, and before he could do that, seven hundred men had got their death.

And it was told to Findabair how these seven hundred men had got their death on account of her, and how Maeve had promised her in marriage to every one of the twelve kings of Munster. And when she heard that, her heart broke with the shame and the pity that came on her, and she fell dead there and then, and they buried her.

Now at that time Iliach, son of Cas, of the race of Rudraige, was living in the North with his son's son, Laegaire Buadach. And it was told him how the four provinces of Ireland were plundering and destroying the people of Ulster since the day before Samhain, and driving off their cattle and their goods, and all that they had. So he consulted with his people, and it is what he said, that he would go out himself and make an attack on the men of Ireland, and let loose his strength on them, and destroy what he could of them, and do what he could for Ulster. "For as to myself," he said, "if I come out of it, or do not come out of it, is all one to me." Then his two old spent horses, that had been let loose for life, were brought from where they were on the shore by the dun, and yoked to his old chariot, that had neither cushions nor skins in it. And he took his rough, dark, iron shield, with its hard rim of silver, over his shoulder, and his rough, grey, heavy sword at his left side. And he put in the chariot his two rusty, blunt spears, and his people gave him a store of stones and bits of rocks in a heap about him; and that is the way he went out against the army, and no armour on him at all.

When the men of Ireland saw him coming like that, they began mocking and laughing at him, but it is what Maeve said: "I would be glad indeed all the men of Ulster to come and meet us like that." Then Doche, son of Magach, chanced to meet him, and bade him welcome. "Who is it bids me welcome?" said Iliach. "The comrade and friend of Laegaire Buadach," said he; "Doche, son of Magach." "I am glad of that welcome," said Iliach, "and for the sake of it, let you come to me when I have spent my rage on the army, and when my strength is going, and when my hand is tried, and let you, and no other of the men of Ireland, make an end of me. And keep my sword," he said, "for your friend, Laegaire Buadach."

Then he made an attack on the men of Ireland, and when his spears were all broken in pieces, he began hitting and throwing with the stones he had. And when they were out, he attacked the men that were near him with the strength of his own hands, so that he made an end of some of them. And when all he could do was done, he saw Doche, son of Magach, near him, and he said: "Come to me now, Doche, and strike my head off, and take charge of my sword for Laegaire Buadach." And Doche did as he told him, but he brought his head to Ailell and to Maeve.

At this time Sualtim, son of Becaltach, was told that Cuchulain had fought with Calatin and his sons, and with Ferdiad, and of the hard fight he had made, and the wounds he had got. And it is what Sualtim said: "Is it the sky bursting I hear, or is it the sea going backward, or the earth breaking up, or is it the groaning of my son in his weakness?" With that he set out to visit him, and he found him covered with hurts and wounds, and he began to cry over him. But that did not please Cuchulain, and he knew Sualtim would do no good by stopping there, for he was not the man to avenge him, for he was no great hero, not that he was a coward, but just like any other good fighting man. And Cuchulain said to him: "Well, Sualtim, stop your crying over me, and rise up and go to Emain, and tell the men of Ulster they must come themselves and follow on with the war from this out, for I am not able to defend them any more; for after all I went through, not one of them comes to help me or to comfort me. And tell them," he said, "what way you found me, that I cannot bear to have my clothing next my skin, but it is with crooks of hazel I have to hold it off me, and it is grass that is laid over my wounds; for there is not the place of the point of a needle on me from head to foot but has some hurt on it, except my left hand that was holding my shield; and tell them to make no delay in coming," he said.

Then Sualtim set out on the Grey of Macha to give his message; and when he got close to Emain he called out: "Men are being killed, women brought away, cattle driven off in Ulster," but he got no word of answer. Then he went up to the very wall, and he cried again: "Men are being killed, women brought away, cattle brought away in Ulster"; but the second time he got no answer. Then he went on to the Stone of the Hostages at Emain, and he called out the same words the third time. Then Cathbad, the Druid, asked: "Who are taken, and who is it is taking them?" "It is Ailell and Maeve that are robbing you and destroying you," said Sualtim; "they are bringing away your women, your little boys, your cattle and your horses, and there is only Cuchulain to delay and to hinder the four great provinces of Ireland in the gaps and the passes of Conaille Muirthemne." But Cathbad was vexed at being waked out of his sleep, and he said: "Any man that comes to scold at the king this way has a right to be put to death." But Conchubar, the king, said: "It is true what Sualtim is saying." "It is true indeed," said all the men of Ulster.

Then anger came on Sualtim that he got no better answer than that, and he turned sharply, and the Grey of Macha reared up, the way the sharp edge of Sualtim's shield came against his own head, and cut it clean off. Then the Grey turned again to Emain; and the shield dragged after him by its thongs, and Sualtim's head in the hollow of it, and the head said the same words as before: "Men are being killed, women brought away, cattle brought away in Ulster." Then Conchubar said: "The sky is over our heads, the earth is under our feet, the sea is round about us; and unless the sky with all its shower of stars comes down on earth, or the earth breaks open under our feet, or the blue sea goes over the whole face of the world, I swear that I will bring back every cow to its own shed, and every woman to her own dwelling-house."

Then he called to one of his messengers, Finnched, son of Troiglethan, that chanced to be there, and he bade him to go and to call out the men of Ulster. But with the sleep that was on him still, and the weakness, he bade him go and call those of his people that were dead, as well as those that were living.

It was easy work Finnched had to do now, for the men of Ulster were rising from out of their weakness, and they all made ready to come out with Conchubar, and as for those that were to the south and to the west of Emain, they did not wait for Conchubar at all, but met out on the track of the army of Ireland.

Then Conchubar and his men set out from Emain, and the first day they went as far as Irard Cuillenn, and there they made a halt. "What are we stopping here for?" said Conchubar. "We are waiting for your own two sons," his men said, "Fiachna and Fiacha, that are gone to meet your grandson Erc, son of Fedelm, and of Cairbre, king of Teamhair, to bring him with us." "By my word," said Conchubar, "I will not make any more delay here, for fear the men of Ireland might hear I am risen from my weakness; for they do not know it up to this," he said, "or even if I am alive at all."

So he himself and Celthair, and thirty hundred fierce chariot-fighters, went on, and it was not long before they came on eight times twenty strong men belonging to Ailell and to Maeve, and each of them bringing away a woman of the women of Ulster with him. And Conchubar and Celthair struck their heads off, and set the women free; and then they went back to Irard Cuillenn.

Now, as to the men of Ireland, they spent that night at Sleamhain of Meath. And in the night Cormac Conlingeas started up out of his sleep, and he called out that there had a warning dream come to him, and that there was a terrible battle before them. And after a while Dubthach, the Beetle of Ulster, started up out of his sleep, and called out the same thing, that there had a warning dream come to him, and that it would not be long till there would be a great clashing of shields. And with these dreams and foretellings, great fear came on the men of Ireland, and it was an uneasy night they spent at Sleamhain that time.

And in the morning Ailell said: "We have been harrying Ulster and Cuailgne this long time, and we have taken the women and the cattle and the goods of the men of Ulster, and we have cut down hills behind us; and now," he said, "it is time for us to turn back to Magh Ai, and they can follow us and fight with us there if they have a mind to. But before that," he said, "I will send a messenger to look out across the great plain of Meath, to see if any of them are coming against us; and if they are," he said, "I will not go from this without giving battle to them, for he would not be a good king that would be good at running away."

So he sent out Mac Roth, the herald. And he had not long to wait before he heard a noise that was like the falling of the sky, or the breaking in of the sea over the land, or the falling of trees on one another in a great storm. And he saw the plain covered with wild creatures that had broken away out of the woods. Then he went back to Ailell and to Maeve, and told them his story, and they asked him what had he seen; and he said: "I thought I saw a grey mist far away across the plain, and then I saw something like falling snow, and then through the mist I saw something shining like sparks from a fire, or like the stars on a very frosty night." "What was it he saw, Fergus?" said Ailell. And Fergus said: "The mist he saw was the dust that went up from the march of the men of Ulster, and the flakes of snow were the foam flakes from the bits of their horses; and what he saw shining like sparks from the fire, or like stars on a frosty night, was the angry light of their eyes shining under their helmets."

"It is little I care for that," said Maeve; "we have good fighting men to meet them." "It is a pity for you to think that," said Fergus; "for there is neither in Alban nor in Ireland an army that can put down the men of Ulster when once their weakness is gone from them and their anger is kindled."

That night the men of Ireland made their camp in Clartha, and they put Mac Roth and another man to keep a good watch, the way the men of Ulster would not fall on them without warning. Now Conchubar and Celtchair, with their thirty hundred men, had followed them to Slieve Sleamhain, and when they found them gone from there they followed on to Clartha, for they thought to get the start of the rest of Ulster in reddening their hands upon the men of Ireland. So Mac Roth was not long waiting when he saw men and horses coming from the north-east, and he went back into the camp. "Well, Mac Roth," said Ailell, "have you seen any of the men of Ulster on our track?" "I saw men and horses coming," he said. "What is the number of them?" said Ailell. "Not less than thirty hundred chariots." "Those are the men of Ulster coming with Conchubar," said Ailell; "and what did you mean a while ago, Fergus, threatening us with the dust of a great army in the plain, when a little troop like that is all that can be brought against us?" "You are too quick in complaining of that," said Fergus, "and you will soon know what their number is."

"Let us make some good plan now," said Maeve, "for I am sure it is that hot, rude man, Conchubar, king of Ulster, that is coming to attack us. Let us make a pen before him," she said, "of all the army standing round on three sides, and thirty hundred men ready to shut the mouth of it on him when he comes in. For we must take these fellows alive and not kill them, for it would be unworthy of our name to do more than make prisoners of them, and they so few." Now this was one of the most laughable things that was said in the whole course of the war, Conchubar and his thirty hundred of the best men of Ulster to be taken alive. And when Conchubar's son, Cormac Conlingeas, heard this, there was great anger on him, and it is what he thought: "If I do not get satisfaction now at once from Maeve for this boast of hers, I will never get it again." So he rose up with his three thousand men to make an attack on her, and on Ailell; and they rose up as well, and their sons the Maines along with them, and the sons of Magach. But then the Gailiana, and the men of Munster, and of Teamhair, came between them, and made peace, and persuaded them to lay down their arms. But for all that, Maeve did make a pen of the army of Ireland to shut up Conchubar, and she had men ready to close it up when once he would be in. But it is what Conchubar did, he never so much as looked for an opening, but when he saw the army before him, he went straight through it, and he broke open a gap of two hundred on the right hand, and a gap of two hundred on the left, and went through them all, and cut them down in the very middle, so that eight hundred men of them were killed.

And then he went away from them, back to Slieve Sleamhain, to join the army of Ulster.

Then the men of Ulster began to gather upon the plain in their full strength, and when Ailell heard it, he said: "Let some one go up and watch them coming, and bring us a report of the appearance that is on them, and of the chief men that are leading them." "Let Mac Roth go," said Fergus.

So Mac Roth went out and took a post on the plain from the early light of the morning till the fall of evening, and through all that time the men of Ulster were coming, so that the ground was not naked under them, every division under its own chief man, and every troop under its own lord, and each one of them apart from the others, and they came on till they had covered the Hill of Sleamhain.

And when evening came, Mac Roth came back to Ailell and to Maeve, and they questioned him and said: "What sort were the men of Ulster as they came across the plain?" And Mac Roth said: "The first troop I saw coming had three thousand men in it, and as soon as they got to the hill, they took their armour off, and they began to dig and to make a seat of sods and of earth on the highest part of the hill, for their leader to sit on until the rest of the army would come.

"He had the appearance of a tall, proud man, used to giving orders, and he had yellow, curling hair on him, and a yellow forked beard, and a red, pleasant face, and blue eyes you would be afraid of. A five-folded crimson cloak he had on him, and a gold pin over his breast, and a white shirt with threads of gold woven into it next his body." "Who was that man, Fergus?" said Ailell. "He was Conchubar, son of Fachtna and of Ness, High-King of Ulster." "There was a man stood beside him," said Mac Roth, "with scattered white hair, and a purple cloak, and a shield with bosses of red brass, and a long iron sword of foreign make. And he looked up to the sky, and threw his hand upwards, and with that the crowds seemed like as if they were rushing at one another, and fire came from them towards the men of Ireland." "That was Cathbad, the Druid," said Fergus, "and he trying by his enchantments to know how the battle would go to-morrow."

"I saw another man with Conchubar," said Mac Roth, "and he was having a smooth, dark face, and white eyes in his head; a long bronze rod in his hand, and a little bell beside him, and when he touched it with his rod, all the people near him began to laugh." "Who is that man?" said Ailell. "It is easy to know that," said Fergus; "that is Rocmid, the king's fool. There was never trouble or tiredness on any man of Ulster that he would not forget if he saw Rocmid." "There came another troop then," said Mac Roth, "and it is what I thought, that the leader they had was the handsomest and the most comely of all the men of Ireland, tall and well formed. Deep red-yellow hair he had, his face wide at the top and narrow below; thin, red lips, and grey eyes that were laughing. A red and white cloak on him, that the wind stirred as he walked, a white shield with gold fastenings at his shoulder, a long, dark green spear in his hand." "Who was that man, Fergus?" said Ailell. "That man is himself half an army, Rochad, son of Fatheman, from Rachlainn, in the North," said Fergus. Now this was the same Rochad that Findabair had loved. "There was another troop came then," said Mac Roth, "and a quiet, grey-haired man at the head of it. A dark-green, long-woolled cloak he had about him, and a white shirt, and a silver belt around his waist, and a bell branch at his shoulder. He sat before King Conchubar when he came to the hill, and his whole company sat about him. And the sound of his voice when he spoke before the king, and when he was advising him, was sweeter than a three-cornered harp in the player's hand." "Who was that man, Fergus?" said Ailell. "That was

Sencha, the orator, the best-spoken of all the men of the whole world, and the peace-maker of the army of Ulster," said Fergus; "and the whole of the men of the world, from the rising to the setting of the sun, he would pacify with his three fair words. But by my word, it is no cowardly or no peaceful counsel that man will give his king to-day, but counsel of courage, and of strength, and of battle."

"There came another troop," said Mac Roth, "and a man at the head of them, and it would not be easy to find a man with a better appearance, or with hair more like gold than what he has. There was a sword with an ivory hilt in his hand, and he throwing it up and catching it in his hand again, just when it was coming on the heads of the people near him." "That is Aithirne, the poet and satirist," said Fergus. "Covetous he is, and it is said of him that he would ask the one-eyed man for his one eye, and that the rivers and the lakes go back before him when he makes a satire on them, and rise when he praises them. And one time when the men of Ulster were fighting to protect him against the men of Leinster, that he had stirred up, and were shut up in Beinn Etair, he had plenty of cows himself in the fort, but he would not give a drop of milk to man or boy, or to a wounded man itself, but left them without food and without drink, unless they would eat the clay or drink the salt water of the sea."

"I saw another troop coming," said Mac Roth, "wild-looking, and in the middle of it a young little lad, red and freckled. He had a silk shirt on him with a border of red gold, and a shield faced with gold, with a golden rim, and a little bright gold sword at his side." "Who is that, Fergus?" said Ailell. "I do not remember leaving any such boy as that when I left Ulster," said Fergus; "but it is likely it may be Erc, son of Cairbre, that has come without leave of his father to help his grandfather, Conchubar; and the men of Teamhair with him. And if what I think is true," he said, "You will find that troop to be a drowning sea, and it is by that troop and by that little boy the battle will be won against you."

Now that was the same Erc that fought afterwards in the last battle against Cuchulain at Muirthemne, and some said it was he that made an end of Cuchulain, but others said it was only the Grey of Macha he made an end of. And Conall Cearnach killed him afterwards in his red vengeance; and his sister Acaill came to Teamhair where he was buried, and cried for him through nine days, till her heart broke like a nut inside her, and she desired that her grave and her mound should be made in a place where the grave and the mound of Erc could be seen from it. And it was made in the place that used to be called the place of the poet Maine, but that is called now the place of Acaill.

"I saw another company," said Mac Roth, "having at its head a tall, large man, with high looks, with soft brown hair in thin smooth locks on his forehead; a deep grey cloak wrapped around him, having a silver brooch in it; a soft white shirt next his skin." "I know that man," said Fergus; "he is Eoghan, son of Durthact, king of Fernmaige, one of the twelve chief heroes of the Red Branch."

"I saw another company coming," said Mac Roth, "and a great many in it; and they red with the fire of their anger, strong and eager and destroying. At their head an angry man, dreadful to look at, long-nosed, large-eared, with coarse grey hair; a striped cloak on him, an iron skewer in place of a brooch, a coarse striped shirt next his skin, a great spear in his hand."

"I know that man," said Fergus; "Celthair, son of Uthecar; a head of battle in Ulster. And the spear in his hand is the great spear, the Luin, that was brought back from the East by the three sons of Tuireann."

"I saw the troop that came last," said Mac Roth, "and it without a leader. There were thirty hundred in it, of proud, clean, ruddy men; long fair hair they had, and shining eyes, and long shining cloaks with good brooches, blue shining spears, good coverings on their heads, and shirts of striped silk. But they seemed to have some great trouble on them, and to be very down-hearted." "What men are those, Fergus?" said Ailell. "I know them well," said Fergus. "It is well for those on whose side they are, and it is a pity for those they are against; for they are able by themselves," he said, "to fight the whole army of Ireland; for they are Cuchulain's men from Muirthemne."

Now all this time Cuchulain was lying on his bed, with the dint of his wounds. But when he knew by the noise on the plain that the men of Ulster were gathering for the battle, he used all his strength and tried to rise up; and he gave a great shout, that all his own troop heard it, and all the whole army. But his people that were about him laid him down on the bed again by force, and put ropes and fastenings over him, the way he could not move from it to open his wounds again. And as he was lying there, two mocking women came from Ailell's camp, and stood beside his bed, and let on to be crying and lamenting; and it is what they told him, that the men of Ulster were beaten, and that Conchubar was killed, and that Fergus was killed along with him. And in the night the Morrigu came like a lean, grey-haired hag, shrieking from the one army to the other, hopping over the points of their weapons, to stir up anger between them, and she called out that ravens would be picking men's necks on the morrow. And with all this outcry, Cuchulain could not sleep, and when the day began to break he said to Laeg: "Look out now, and bring me word of everything that happens on his day." So Laeg looked out, and he said: "I see a little herd of cattle breaking out from the west of Ailell's camp, and there are lads following after them and trying to bring them back; and I see more lads coming out from the army of Ulster to attack them." "That little herd on the plain is the beginning of a great battle," said Cuchulain, "for it is the Brown Bull of Cuailgne and his heifers are in it, and now the young men of the east and of the west will come out against one another. And go now, Laeg," he said, "for I cannot go out myself, and call to the men of Ulster, and stir them up to the battle." So Laeg went out and called to them in Cuchulain's name to get themselves ready and to come out to the battle.

When the men of Ulster heard that message from Cuchulain, they rose up, and rushed out without stopping to put on their clothing, but only taking their weapons in their hands; and such of them as had the door of their tents facing eastward did not wait to go through it, but broke out to the west.

But Conchubar was not in such haste to bring his own men out, but he said to Sencha: "Keep them back till the right time will have come, when the sun will have lighted all the valleys and the hills."

Then Laeg went to look out again, and he saw the army of Ireland coming out to meet the men of Ulster, and there began a great fight between them, and it went on a good while without one side getting the better of the other. And when Cuchulain heard it he said: "My grief I not to be able to go among them!"

Now as to Maeve, she was sending out her men, the three Conaires from Slieve Lis, the three red Luachras, the three nimble Suibhnes, the three sky-like Eochaids, the three bards from Lough Riach, the three Fachtnas from the woods of Navan, the three sad-faced Murroughs, the three boiling Laegaires, the three dove-like Conalls, the three sons of Driscoll that fought together, the three Fintans from beside the sea. And some say that besides these there were three young men of the Sidhe in shining armour, that mixed through the army to stir up courage, and that none of the men of the army could see among them, Delbhaeth, son of Eithlin, and Cermat Honey-mouth, and Angus Og, son of the Dagda.

But when Maeve saw the battle going on, and neither side getting the victory, she called to Fergus, and she said: "It is time for you, Fergus, to go out and avenge yourself on your enemy Conchubar; and besides that," she said, "it is right for you to go and to fight for us now, after all the good treatment you got from us in Connaught." "I would go out willingly," said Fergus, "if I had my own sword again, the Caladcholg, the sword that Leite brought from the country of the Sidhe." Then Ailell said to his chariot-driver, Ferlogha: "Go now and bring Fergus's sword that I bade you to hide away." So Ferlogha brought the sword, and put it in Fergus's hand, and Fergus gave it a great welcome. "Come out now into the battle, Fergus," said Maeve, "and spare no one to-day, unless it might be some very dear friend."

Then Fergus and Maeve and Ailell went out into the battle, and three times they made the army of Ulster go back before them. And when Conchubar heard his people were being driven back, he called out to the household of the Red Branch: "Let you hold the place I am in now, till I go see who has turned back our men against us three times on the north side."

And the men of the Red Branch called back to him: "We will do that, and unless the sky should fall on us, or the earth give way under us, we will not give up one inch of ground before the men of Ireland till you come to us again, or till we get our death."

Then Conchubar went to see who it was that was driving back his army, and it was Fergus he found before him; and Fergus struck three great blows on Conchubar's shield, the Ochain, so that the shield screamed out loud, and all the shields of the army of Ulster screamed with it, and the three great waves of Ireland answered it.

Then Fergus said: "Who is it is holding his shield against me?" And Conchubar knew then who was before him, and he cried out: "It is the man, Fergus, that is greater and more comely and younger and better than yourself, the man whose father and mother were better than your own; the man that put to death the three great candles of the valour of the Gael, the three prosperous sons of Usnach, in spite of your guarantee and your protection; the man that banished you out of your own country; the man that made your house a dwelling-place for deer and foxes; the man that never left you so much as the breadth of your foot of land in Ulster; the man that drove you to the entertainment of a woman; and the man that will drive you back to-day in the presence of the men of Ireland, Conchubar, son of Fachtna Fathach, High King of Ulster, the High King of Ireland."

When Fergus heard that, he took his sword, the Caladcholg, in his two hands, and he was swinging it over his head, that it seemed to have the size and appearance of a rainbow, and he was about to give his three great strokes on the men of Ulster.

But Conchubar's son, Cormac Conloingeas, saw what he was doing, and he made a rush at Fergus, and put his arms about his knees, and he said: "Do not put out your great strength, my master Fergus, to destroy the whole army of Ulster." "Let me go," said Fergus, "for I will not live through the day unless I strike my three blows on the men of Ulster." But Cormac Conloingeas would not leave off from asking him, and then he said: "Tell Conchubar to go back to his own place in the battle, and I will spare the army." So Conchubar went back, and then Fergus struck his three blows on three little hills that were near him, and cut their tops off, and they are called "the three bare hills of Meath" to this day.

But when Cuchulain heard the scream of Conchubar's shield the time Fergus struck it, he called out to Laeg: "Who has dared to strike those three blows upon the Ochain, and I still living?" "It is Fergus, son of Rogh, struck them," said Laeg. "Where is the battle going on now?" said Cuchulain. "The armies are coming as far as Gairech," said Laeg. "By my hand of valour," said Cuchulain, "they will not have reached to Ilgairech before I will be with them." With that he put out all his strength, and he broke the ropes that were about him, and threw them off, and he scattered the grass that was on his wounds into the high air. And the two mocking women were there yet, and he dashed them one against the other, and left them there on the ground. And he looked for his arms, but he could see none of them; but only his chariot, that was broken, was lying there. And he took hold of a shaft of it, and rushed, with all his wounds, straight into the battle, till he found Fergus, and he called to him to go back before him now, as he had promised he would do. But Fergus gave him no answer. Then Cuchulain said: "Go back now, Fergus, or by the oath of my people," he said, "I will grind you to pieces as a mill grinds the malt." Then Fergus said: "Do not be giving out threats to me, for my army is well able for the army of Ulster." "You gave me your promise, Fergus," said Cuchulain, "to go back before me when we would meet in the great battle, and when I would be covered with wounds. You bound yourself to that the time I went back before you, and you without your sword."

Then Fergus, when he heard that, went back three steps, and then he turned, and his men with him, and gave way before Cuchulain. And all the men of Ireland turned when they saw that, and broke out of their ranks, and ran over the hill westward, and Cuchulain and the men of Ulster followed after them, making a great slaughter. And Cuchulain came up with Maeve, and she called out: "A gift to me, Cuchulain." "What is it you are asking of me?" he said. "Take what is left of my army under your protection, and let it pass over the great ford westward." So he agreed to do that, and what was left of the army of Ireland went over the great ford of the Sionnan at Athluain, and Maeve and Ailell and Fergus, and the Maines, and the sons of Magach stopped to the last, and drew their shields of protection behind the men of Ireland, till they had got back to Cruachan in Connaught, the place they set out from.

It was mid-day when Cuchulain came into the battle, and the sun was setting when the last of them went over the ford. And then Cuchulain took his sword that Laeg had brought him, for he had but a few splinters left of the shaft of the chariot he had used in the fight, and he made three blows at three rocks, and cut the tops off them, for an insult to Connaught for ever, the way if any one should speak of the three bare hills of Meath, the three bare rocks of Athluain would be there to give the answer.

And Fergus was watching the army of Ireland going back over the ford, and it is what he said: "This army is swept away to-day; it is wandering and going astray like a mare among her foals that goes astray in a strange place, not knowing what path to take. And it is following the lead of a woman," he said, "has brought it into this distress."

This then was the end of the battle of Gairech and Ilgairech, and the end of the war for the Brown Bull of Cuailgne.

CHAPTER XIII

The Two Bulls

This, now, is the story of the two bulls, the Brown of Cuailgne, and the White-horned of Cruachan Ai, and this is the way it was with them—for they were not right bulls, but there was enchantment on them. In the time long ago Bodb was king of the Sidhe of Munster, and it is in Femen, of Slieve-na-man he was, and Ochall Ochne was king of the Sidhe of Connaught, and it is in Cruachan he used to be. They used at one time to be fighting one against the other, but afterwards they made peace, and were good friends. Now Bodb had a swineherd, whose name was Friuch, and Ochall had a swineherd whose name was Rucht, and they were friendly with one another the same as their masters. And they had the knowledge of enchantments, and could turn themselves into every shape. And when there was a great plenty of mast in Munster, the swineherd from Connaught would bring his lean swine to the south, and in the same way, when mast was plentiful in Connaught, the swineherd would bring his swine northward, and would bring them home again fat.

But after a while some bad feeling rose up between the two, for the men of Connaught and the men of Munster began to set them one against the other. So one year when there was great mast in Munster, and Rucht brought his herd from Connaught, so soon as his comrade Friuch had bade him welcome, he said: "The people are all saying your power is greater than mine." "It is no less any way," said Ochall's herd. "We will soon know that," said Friuch. "I will put an enchantment on your swine, and even though they eat their share of mast, they will not be fat, like mine will be." And so it happened, he put an enchantment on the Connaught swine, and when Rucht went home with them they could hardly walk at all, they were so thin and so weak, and all the people were laughing at the state they were in. "It was a bad day for you, you went to the South," they said, "for your comrade has greater power than what you have." "That is not so," said he. "Wait till it is our turn to have mast, and I will play the same trick on him."

So the next year he did as he had said, and the Munster swine pined away, so that every one said their power was the same. And when Bodb's swineherd went back home to Munster with his lean swine, his master put him out of the place. And Ochall put his herd out of his place as well, because of the swine coming back in so bad a state from Munster.

One day, two full years after that, the men of Munster were gathered together near Femen, and they took notice of two ravens that were making a great cawing. "What a noise those birds have been making all through the year!" they said.

"They never stop scolding at one another." Just then Findell, Ochall's steward from Cruachan, came towards them on the hill, and they bade him welcome. "What a noise those birds are making!" he said; "any one would think them to be the same two birds we had in Cruachan last year." With that, they saw the two ravens change into the shape of men, and they knew them to be the two swineherds, and they bade them welcome. "It is not right you to welcome us," said Bodb's swineherd, "for there will be many dead bodies of friends, and much crying on account of us two." "What has happened, you all through this time?" they asked. "Nothing good," he said. "Since we went from you we have been all the time in the shape of birds, and you saw the way we were scolding at one another all through this year. And we were quarrelling in the same way the whole of last year at Cruachan, and the men of the North and of the South have seen what our power is. And now," he said, "we will go into the shape of water beasts, and be under the water for the length of two years." And with that one of them went into the Sionnan, and the other into the Suir, and they were seen for a year in the Suir, and for a year in the Sionnan, and they devouring one another. And one day the men of Connaught had a great gathering at Ednecha, on the Sionnan, and they saw these two beasts in the river; each one of them looked to be as big as the top of a hill, and they made such a furious attack on one another that fiery swords seemed to be coming from their jaws, and the people came round them on every side. They came out of the Sionnan then, and as soon as they touched the shore, they changed again into the shape of the two swineherds. Ochall bade them welcome. "Where have you been wandering?" he asked them. "Indeed it is tired we are with our wanderings," they said. "You saw what we were doing before your eyes, and that is what we were doing through these years, under seas and waters. And now we must take new shapes on us, till we try one another's strength again." And with that they went away.

It happened a good while after that there was a great gathering of the men of Connaughts at Loch Riach, for Bodb was coming on a friendly visit to Ochall. And Bodb brought a great troop with him, the most splendid ever seen; speckled horses they had, and green cloaks with silver brooches and shoes with clasps of red bronze, and every one of them had a collar of gold, with a stone worth a newly-calved cow set in it. When Ochall saw what grand clothes and horses they had, he called to his people secretly, and asked could they match Bodb's people in dress and in horses and arms, and they said they could not. Then Ochall said: "That is a pity, and our great name is lost." But just then a troop of men were seen coming from the North, and black horses with them, that you would think had been cast up by the sea, and bridle-bits of gold in their mouths. And the men had black-grey cloaks, and a gold brooch at the beast of each, and a white tunic with crimson stripes, and fifty coils of bright gold round every man. And every man of them had black hair, as smooth as if a cow had licked it. And they stopped a little way off, and then the men of Connaught stood up and gave up their place to them. There was a Druid from Britain there, and when he saw them make way he said: "From this out, to the end of life and time, the Connaught men will be under the yoke, attending on hounds and on sons of kings and queens for ever."

Then after they had been feasting for a while, Bodb asked could any Connaught man be found that would fight against his champion Rinn, that was with him, and that had a great name, but no one knew where he came from. And at first there could no one be found, but then a strange champion came out from among the men of Connaught, and he said, "I will go against him." "That is no welcome news," said Rinn. Then they fought against one another for three days and three nights, and before the end of that time the two armies began to join into the fight, and a troop came from Leinster and joined with Bodb, and another troop came from Meath and joined with Ochall. And four kings were killed there, and Ochall among them, and then Bodb went back to Slieve-na-man. But as to the two champions, they were seen no more, and it was known they were the two swine-herds. After that they were for two years with the appearance of shadows threatening one another, the way that many people died of fright after seeing them.

And after that, they were in the shape of eels, and one went into the river Cruind, in Cuailgne; and after a while a cow belonging to Daire, son of Fachna, drank it down. And the other went into the Spring of Uaran Garad, in Connaught; and one day Maeve went out to the spring, and a small bronze vessel in her hand, and she dipped it in the water, and the little eel went into it and every colour was to be seen on him. And she was a long time looking at him, she thought the colours so beautiful. Then the water went away, and the eel was alone in the vessel. "It is a pity you cannot speak to me," said Maeve. "What is it you want to know?" said the eel. "I would like to know what way it is with you in that shape of a beast," she said; "and I would like to know what will happen me after I get the sway over Connaught." "Indeed it is a tormented beast I am," he said, "and it is in many shapes I have been. And as to yourself," he said, "handsome as you are, you should take a good man to be with you in your sway." "I have no wish," said Maeve, "to let a man of Connaught get the upper hand over me," and with that she went home again.

But she married Ailell after that, and as for the eel, he was swallowed down by one of Maeve's cows that came to drink from the spring.

And it was from that cow, and from the cow that belonged to Daire, son of Fachna, the two bulls were born, the White-horned and the Brown. They were the finest ever seen in Ireland, and gold and silver were put on their horns by the men of Ulster and Connaught. In Connaught no bull dared bellow before the White-horned, and in Ulster no bull dared bellow before the Brown.

As to the Brown, he that had been Friuch, the Munster swineherd, his lowing when he would be coming home every evening to his yard was good music to the people of the whole of Cuailgne. And wherever he was, neither Bocanachs nor

Bananachs nor witches of the valley, could come into the one place with him. And it was on account of him the great war broke out.

Now, when Maeve saw at Ilgaireth that the battle was going against her, she sent eight of her own messengers to bring away the Brown Bull, and his heifers. "For whoever goes back or does not go back," she said, "the Brown Bull must go to Cruachan."

Now when the Brown Bull came into Connaught, and saw the beautiful, trackless country before him, he let three great loud bellowings out of him. As soon as the White-horned heard that, he set out for the place those bellowings came from, with his head high in the air.

Then Maeve said that the men of her army must not go to their homes till they would see the fight between the two bulls.

And they all said some one must be put to watch the fight, and to give a fair report of it afterwards. And it is what they agreed, that Bricriu should be sent to watch it, because he had not taken any side in the war; for he had been through the whole length of it under care of physicians at Cruachan, with the dint of the wound he got the day he vexed Fergus, and that Fergus drove the chess-men into his head. "I will go willingly," said Bricriu. So he went out and took his place in a gap, where he could have a good view of the fight.

As soon as the bulls caught sight of one another, they pawed the earth so furiously that they sent the sods flying, and their eyes were like balls of fire in their heads; they locked their horns together, and they ploughed up the ground under them and trampled it, and they were trying to crush and to destroy one another through the whole length of the day.

And once the White-horned went back a little way and made a rush at the Brown, and got his horn into his side, and he gave out a great bellow, and they rushed both together through the gap where Bricriu was the way he was trodden into the earth under their feet. And that is how Bricriu of the bitter tongue, son of Cairbre, got his death.

Then when the night was coming on, Cormac Conloingeas took hold of a spear-shaft, and he laid three great strokes on the Brown Bull from head to tail, and he said: "This is a great treasure to be boasting of, that cannot get the better of a calf of his own age." When the Brown Bull heard that insult, great fury came on him, and he turned on the White-horned again. And all through the night the men of Ireland were listening to the sound of their bellowing, and they going here and there, all through the country.

On the morrow, they saw the Brown Bull coming over Cruachan from the west, and he carrying what was left of the White-horned on his horns. Then Maeve's sons, the Maines, rose up to make an attack on him on account of the Connaught bull he had destroyed. "Where are those men going?" said Fergus. "They are going to kill the Brown Bull of Cuailgne." "By the oath of my people," said

Fergus, "if you do not let the Brown Bull go back to his own country in safety, all he has done to the White-horned is little to what I will do now to you."

Then the Brown Bull bellowed three times, and set out on his way. And when he came to the great ford of the Sionnan he stopped to drink, and the two loins of the White-horned fell from his horns into the water. And that place is called Ath-luain, the ford of the loin, to this day. And its liver fell in the same way into a river of Meath, and it is called Ath-Truim, the ford of the liver, to this day.

Then he went on till he came to the top of Slieve Breagh, and when he looked from it he saw his own home, the hills of Cuailgne; and at the sight of his own country, a great spirit rose up in him, and madness and fury came on him, and he rushed on, killing everyone that came in his way.

And when he got to his own place, he turned his back to a hill and he gave out a loud bellowing of victory. And with that his heart broke in his body, and blood came bursting from his mouth, and he died.

CHAPTER XIV

The Only Jealousy of Emer

It happened one time, near to the day of Samhain, the men of Ulster came together for games and for feasting upon the plain of Muirthemne.

And they were all of them there but Conall Cearnach and Lugaid of the Red Stripes. "Let the feast be begun," they said. "It shall not be begun," said Cuchulain, "till Conall and Lugaid are here."

Sencha, the poet, said then: "Let us play chess while we are waiting, and let poems be sung for us, and let games be played." And they agreed to that.

While they were doing these things, a flock of birds came down on the lake before them, and in all Ireland there were not birds to be seen that were more beautiful.

A great longing came on the women that were there to have the birds that were on the lake, and they began to quarrel with one another as to who should have them.

King Conchubar's wife said: "I must have a bird of these birds on each of my two shoulders." "We must all have the same," said the other women. "If any one is to get them, it is I that must first get them," said Eithne Inguba, who loved Cuchulain. "What shall we do?" said the women. "It is I will tell you that," said Levarcham, "for I will go to Cuchulain from you to ask him to get them."

So she went to Cuchulain and said: "The women of Ulster desire that you will get these birds for them." Cuchulain put his hand upon his sword as if to strike her, and he said: "Have the idle women of Ulster nothing better to do than to send me catching birds to-day?" "It is not for you," said Levarcham, "to be angry with them; for there are many of them are half blind to-day with looking at you, from the greatness of their love for you."

Then Cuchulain told Laeg to yoke his chariot for him, and he went in it to the lake, and he gave the birds a side stroke of his sword, so that their feet and their wings could not rise from the water.

They caught them all then, and divided them among the women, so that there was not a woman among them who did not get two birds, but Eithne Inguba only. Cuchulain came last to her. "It is vexed you seem to be," he said. "Is it because I have given the birds to the other women?" "You have good reason for that," she said, "for there is not a woman of them but would share her love and her friendship with you; while, as to me, no person shares my love but you alone."

"Do not be vexed then," said Cuchulain; "for whatever birds may come to the plain of Muirthemne, or to the Boinne, from this out, you shall have the two most beautiful among them."

It was not long after that, two other birds came on the lake, and they linked together with a chain of red gold, and they were singing soft music that went near to put sleep on the whole gathering.

Cuchulain went over towards the birds, but Laeg said to him not to go, and Eithne said: "If you would take our advice, you would not go near them, for there is enchantment behind these birds; let some other birds be got for me besides these."

"Do you think you can put me from what I have a mind to do?" said Cuchulain. And he said to Laeg: "Put a stone in that sling." Laeg took a stone and put it in a sling, and Cuchulain made a cast, but it missed. "My grief" he said. Then he took another stone, and made another cast, and it passed by them. "I am good for nothing," he said, "for since I first took arms I never made a bad cast till this day." Then he threw his heavy spear, and it went through the flying wing of one of the birds, and the two of them dived down under the water.

Cuchulain went away then with vexation on him, and he lay down with his head against a rock, and sleep came on him. And he saw two women coming towards him, one of them having a green cloak about her, and the other a five-folded crimson cloak.

The woman with the green cloak went up to him, and smiled at him, and she gave him a stroke of a rod. The other went up to him then, and smiled at him, and gave him a stroke in the same way; and they went on doing this for a long time, each of them striking him in turn, till he was more dead than alive. And then they went away and left him there.

All the men of Ulster saw that something had happened, and they asked if they would awaken him. "Do not," said Conall; "do not move him before night."

After that Cuchulain stood up in his sleep, and the men of Ulster asked him who was it had used him like that, but he could not speak with them. But after a while he said: "Bring me and lay me on my bed, not to Dundealgan, but to the Speckled House at Emain." "Let him be brought to Dundealgan, where Emer his wife is," said Laeg. "Not so," said Cuchulain, "but bring me to the Speckled House." So he was brought there, and he stopped to the end of a year in that place, without speaking to any person.

One day before the next feast of Samhain, at the end of the year, Conchubar and the men of Ulster were around him in the house; that is, Laegaire between him and the wall, and Conall Cearnach between him and the door, Lugaid of the Red Stripes beside his pillow, and Eithne Inguba at his feet.

As they were sitting like this, one who had the appearance of a man came into the house to them, and sat down on the side of the bed where Cuchulain was lying.

"What has brought you here?" said Conall. "I will tell you that," said he. "it is to speak with the man lying here on the bed I am come. And if the man lying here were in his health, he would be a protection to all the men of Ulster; but as he is, under great sickness and weakness, he is a better protection to them." And he stood up then, and it is what he said:

"If Cuchulain, son of Sualtim, would take my friendship to-day, all he has seen in his sleep would be his, with no help from his army.

"Liban, she who sits at the right hand of Labraid of the quick sword, has said that the coming of Cuchulain would bring great joy to the heart of Fand her sister.

"O Cuchulain, it is not long your sickness would be on you if they would come, the two daughters of Aedh Abrat. Here to the south, to the plain of Muirthemne, I will send Liban to cure your sickness, Cuchulain."

"Who are you yourself?" they said to him then.

"I am Angus," he said, and with that he went out; and they did not know where he came from, or where he went. And then Cuchulain sat up and spoke to them. "It is time indeed," said the men of Ulster, "for you to tell us all that has happened to you." "I saw," he said, "a vision about this time last year": and then he told them all he had seen, and of the women that had come and had struck him with their rods. "And what is to be done now, my master, Conchubar?" he said. "This must be done," said Conchubar: "you must go back till you come to the same rock."

So then Cuchulain set out, and came to the same rock, and there he saw the same woman with the green cloak coming towards him. "That is well, Cuchulain," said she. "It is not well indeed; and tell me what did you want with me when you came last year?" said Cuchulain.

"It was not to harm you, indeed, we came," said the woman, "but to ask your love; and I am come now to speak to you," she said, "from Fand, daughter of Aedh Abrat; for Manannan, son of the Sea, has left her, and her love has fallen on you; and my own name is Liban, wife of Labraid of the quick sword. And I have a message for you from him," she said, "that he will give all you can wish for, if you will give him one day's help against Senach of the crooked body, and against Eochaid Juil, and against Eoghan of Inbhir, that is Eoghan of the River's Mouth."

"My weakness is on me yet," said Cuchulain, "and I could not go out fighting against men to-day." "You will not be long so," said Liban; "you will be healed, and what is lost of your strength will be given back to you again; and you ought to do this much for Labraid," she said, "because he is the best of the heroes of the world."

"In what place is he?" said Cuchulain. "He is in Magh Mell, the Happy Plain," she said. "I will not go," said Cuchulain, "until I see Emer, my wife. And you are to go for me, Laeg," he said, "to where she is, and tell her it was the women of the Sidhe came to me from the hills and struck me; and tell her I am getting better now, and bid her come and visit me."

So Laeg went to Emer, and he told her what way Cuchulain was. And Emer said: "It is a bad servant you are, Laeg, you that are coming and going by the hills, and that cannot find a cure for your master; and it is a pity for the men of Ulster," she said, "that they do not find a certain cure for him. If it had been Conchubar that was in bonds, or Fergus that could not sleep, or Conall Cearnach that had wounds on him, it is Cuchulain that would give them relief." And it is what she said:

"My grief! son of Riangabra, you who go early and late among the hills, you are not early but late in bringing a cure for the beautiful son of Dechtire.

"It is a pity for the brave men of Ulster, with all the knowledgeable men and the learners among them, that they have not searched the whole face of the world for a cure for their friend Cuchulain.

"If it was Fergus had lost his sleep, and that any enchantment could cure him, it is the son of Dechtire would not sleep at home till he had found a Druid to do it.

"If it were Connal in the same way was suffering from wounds and from sores, it is the Hound would search the wide world till he would find one that would cure him.

"If it were Laegaire of many gifts was wounded in battle, Cuchulain would have searched through all Ireland to cure the grandson of Iliach.

"If it were on Celthair the revengeful sleep had fallen and long sickness, night and day would see the journeys of Setanta among the hills.

"If it had been Furbaigh, chief of fighters, that lay wasting in his bed, he would have searched the ridge of the world until he had found what would save him.

"The host of the hill of Truin has killed him; they have taken from him his great courage; the Hound of Muirthemne is no better than any other hound since the sleep of the hill of Bruagh came on him.

"My grief! sickness has laid hold of me for the Hound of the smith of Conchubar; it will be sickness to my heart and my body, I to fail in bringing him a cure.

"My grief! It hurts my heart, sickness to be on the rider of the plain, so that he could not come here, to the gathering at the plain of Muirthemne.

"It is why he does not come from Emain, the appearance he had is gone from him; my voice is weak and dead because of the way he is. A month and a quarter and a year without sleep, that is the way I am, and without hearing any one speak pleasant words, son of Riangabra, O son of Riangabra."

After she had made this complaint, Emer went forward to Emain Macha to attend on Cuchulain, and she sat on the side of the bed where he was, and it is what she was saying:

"Rise up, champion of Ulster, awake from your sleep, in health and happiness. Look at the well-shaped king of Macha; he will not allow your long sleep. Look at his shoulder, smooth like crystal; look at his drinking-horns and battle spoils; look at his chariots that sweep the valleys; look at the movements of his chess-men.

"Think on his heroes in their strength; think on his high, fine women; think on his kings of brave doings; think on their high noble queens.

"Think on the beginning of clear winter; think on its wonders in their turn; think in yourself of what it brings forth—its cold, its length, its want of beauty. This stupor, it is not good wholesome sleep; it is idleness and the fear of battle; long sleep is the same as drunkenness; weakness is only second to death.

"Awake from the sleep of the Sidhe you have drunk; cast it off with all your great strength. You have had your fill of sweet flowery words; rise up, O hero of Ulster."

Cuchulain rose up then, and he drew his hand across his face, and he put his stupor and his heaviness off him. Then Laeg said: "It is great idleness for a hero to give in to the sleep of a sick-bed because women from Magh Mell have appeared to you, who overcame you, who bound you, who put you within the power of idle women. Rise up out of death, you who are wounded by women of the Sidhe, for your strength has come, the strength of a hero among heroes; rise up till you go to the place of fighting men, till you do great deeds, where Labraid of the quick hand leads his men. Rise up that you may be great, and leave this idleness."

Then Cuchulain went again to the rock, and he saw Liban coming towards him, and she asked him again to go with her to her country. "What place is Labraid in at this time?" said Cuchulain. "I will tell you that," said Liban, and it is what she said:

"Labraid is at this time upon a clear lake, where companies of women come to. It is not tired you would be coming to his country, if you would but visit Labraid of the quick sword.

"A happy house ordered by a kind woman; a hundred men in it that are masters of learning; the beauty of redness is on the cheek of Labraid.

"He shakes a wolf's head before his thin red sword; he bruises the armour of rushing hosts; he breaks the shields of heroes.

"His appearance in the fight is the delight of the eye; he does his brave deeds at all points; it is he is worth more than any other man.

"The greatest of fighters, the one told of in stories, has reached the country of

Eochaid Juil; his hair is like rings of gold upon him; his coming is like the smell of wine.

"A man of many strange deeds, Labraid of the quick-hand at sword; he does not strike till he is forced; he keeps his people in quietness.

"There are bridles and collars of red gold on his horses, and this is not all his riches; the house he lives in is supported by pillars of silver and of crystal."

"I will not go on a woman's asking," said Cuchulain. "Let Laeg come with me then," said Liban, "to see and to know everything." "Let him go then," said Cuchulain.

Then Laeg went along with the woman, and they went past Magh Luada, the Racing Plain, and past the Bile Buada, the Tree of Victory, and past Oenach Emna, the gathering-place of Emain, and to Oenach Fidhga, the gathering-place of the woods; and it was there Aedh Abrat used to be with his daughters. And Liban caught Laeg by the shoulder: "You will not escape to-day, Laeg," she said, "unless you are protected by a woman." "That is not what we were much used to up to this," said Laeg, "to be under woman protection." "My grief for ever, Cuchulain not to be in your place now!" said Liban. "I would be glad indeed he to be here," said Laeg.

They went away then towards the Island of Labraid, and when they came to the lake they saw a little copper ship upon the water before them. Then they went into the ship, and they came to the island, and there they went to the door of a house. And they saw a man coming towards them, and Liban said to him: "Where is Labraid of the quick sword?" And the man said: "Labraid is putting courage into the people, and he is gathering them for battle. There will be great slaughter made there, that will fill the plain of Fidgha."

Then they went up to the house, and Laeg thought he had seen it before, and yet it was strange. And in it were beds, crimson, green, white and gold; and the great candle there was a bright precious stone. And at the western door, where the sun goes down, there was a stud of horses with grey speckled manes, and others of red-brown. And at the eastern door were three tall trees of pure crimson, with lasting flowers, and birds singing from them for the young men of the king's rath. And there was a tree at the door of the court that there was not the like for beauty, a silver tree, and when the sun was shining on it, it was like gold. And there were three times twenty other trees there, and the top of every one meeting the other, and three hundred could be fed from every tree with fruit that is different, that is always ripe. And there was a fountain in the great court, and three times fifty striped cloaks, and a shining gold pin in the ear of every cloak. And there was a vat of merry mead for dividing among the household; it is a lasting custom that it is always full, ever and always. And in the house were three times fifty women, and they all bade welcome to Laeg, and it is what they all said to him: "There is a welcome before you, Laeg, for the sake of the person with whom you come, and for the sake of him from whom you come, and for your own sake."

"What will you do now, Laeg?" said Liban. "Will you go first and speak with Fand?" "I will, if I know the place she is in," said Laeg. "I will tell you that, for she is apart in a room by herself," said Liban. So they went to speak with her, and she bade Laeg welcome in the same way as the others. And the meaning of the name Fand is a tear that passes over the fire of the eye. It was for her purity she was called that, and for her beauty; for there was nothing in life with which she could be compared besides it.

And when she had bade Laeg welcome, she said: "For what reason did Cuchulain not come?" "He had no mind to come on a woman's asking," said Laeg. "And besides that," he said, "he did not know if it was from yourself the message came." "It was from myself indeed," she said, "and let him not be long in coming, for it is on this day the battle is to be fought."

While they were there together, they heard the sound of Labraid's chariot coming to the island. "It is troubled Labraid's mind to-day," said Liban. "Let us go out before him." So they went out, and Liban bade him welcome, and it is what she said:

"Welcome, Labraid of the quick hand at sword, yourself an army, a destroyer of heroes; welcome, welcome, Labraid."

Labraid made no answer, and Liban spoke again:

"Welcome, Labraid of the quick hand at sword; his hand is open to all; his word is faithful; his justice is right; kind his sway; strong his right arm; gentle to his horses; welcome, welcome, Labraid!"

Still Labraid did not answer, and she spoke again, and it is what she said:

"Welcome, Labraid of the quick sword; lifter up of the weak; subduer of the strong; welcome, Labraid; welcome, Labraid!"

Then Labraid said: "Leave your praises, woman, for it is not pride or happiness or high thoughts of myself I have in mind to-day. A battle is near, and the striking of swords in right and left hands; the one heart of Eochaid Juil is equal to many. It is not a time for pride."

"There is good news before you," said Liban then. "Laeg, the chariot-driver of Cuchulain, is here, and he has brought a message from him that he will go into the battle with you." Then Labraid bade him welcome as the women had done, and he said : "Go back home now, and tell Cuchulain to make no delay in coming, for it is to-day the battle is to be fought."

So Laeg went away then to Emain Macha, and told his story to Cuchulain, and to all the rest, and it is what he said:

"Labraid is a king of great armies. I saw his country, bright, free, where no lies are spoken, and no bad thing. I saw the masters of music within, giving delight to the daughters of Aedh. If I had not come away quickly, they would have taken my strength from me.

"I saw all this at the hill of the Sidhe. The women there are beautiful, their gifts are beyond counting; as to Fand, the daughter of Aedh Abrat, no one could reach her beauty but the queens of the kings.

"Eithne Inghuba is a beautiful woman, but the woman I am speaking of now takes away the wits from whole armies.

"It is a pity, Cuchulain, you did not go a while ago, and every one asking you to do it, that you might see the way it is in the great house I have seen.

"If all Ireland were mine, and I king over the happy hills, I would give it, and that would be no small thing, to live for ever in the place I have been in."

"That is good," said Cuchulain. "It is good," said Laeg, "and it is right to go to reach it, and everything in that country is good."

Then Cuchulain rose up, and he passed his hand over his face, and he spoke pleasantly with Laeg, and he felt that the things the young man was telling him were a strengthening to his mind. And Laeg said: "It is time to come, for the battle is being fought to-day."

Cuchulain went along with him then to that country, and took his chariot with him till they reached the island. Labraid bade them welcome, and all the women; and Fand bade Cuchulain her own welcome.

"What is to be done here now?" said Cuchulain. "This is what we have to do," said Labraid; "to go and take a turn round the army that is against us."

They went forward then till they reached the gathering-place of the armies, and till they cast an eye over them, and it seemed as if there was no end to them. "Go you away for a while," said Cuchulain to Labraid. So Labraid went away then, and Cuchulain stayed before the armies. Then two black ravens croaked, and all the armies laughed. "It is likely," they said, "the ravens are telling of the coming of the angry man from Muirthemne." And they hunted them away.

After that Eochaid Juil went to wash his hands at the spring, and Cuchulain saw his bare shoulder through the shirt, and he threw a spear at him, and it passed through him; and then he attacked the army alone, and killed a great many. Then he was attacked by Senach Siabartha the Unearthly, and they fought very hard and Cuchulain overcame him in the end. And Labraid came then, and broke the armies before him, and he called to Cuchulain to leave off from killing. But Laeg said: "I am in dread he will spend his rage on us, since he has not had enough of fighting. And let your people go," he said, "and let them make ready three vats of water to put out his heat. The first vat he will go into will boil over; the second vat, no person could bear its heat; but the heat of the third vat will be fit to bear."

When the women saw Cuchulain coming back, it was then Fand sang before him: "Stately is the man that comes in his chariot; young he is, and without a beard; his course is splendid across the plain at evening, at Senach Fidhga, the gathering-place of the woods.

"It is not the music of the Sidhe would keep him in a bed; it is the red colour of blood that is upon him; I stand looking at the horses of his chariot; their like is not known, they are as fast as the winds of spring.

"It is Cuchulain that is coming, the young hero from Muirthemne; it is a pity for the man against whom he is angered."

Then Liban asked him what he had done in the fight. And Cuchulain said: "Fair, ruddy-faced men attacked me on every side from the back of horses, the people of Manannan, son of the sea, called there by Eochaid of Inbhir; I gave them wound for wound. I threw my spear at Eochaid Juil; it was not with the uncertain cast of a man among mists I threw it. I heard his groan, and its sound was friendly to me; if those who have spoken have told the truth, it was that throw won the battle." It was to the son, now, of this Eochaid Juil of the Land of Promise, that Aebgreine, the daughter of Naoise and Deirdre was given afterwards in marriage by Manannan.

After that, Cuchulain stopped a month in that country with Fand, and at the end of the month he bade her farewell, and she said to him: "In whatever place you tell me to go and meet you, I will go there." And the place they settled to meet at was at Ibar Cinn Tracta, the yew at the head of Baile's strand.

But when all this was told to Emer, there was great anger on her, and she had knives made ready to kill the woman with; and she came, and fifty young girls with her, to the place where they had settled to meet.

Cuchulain and Laeg were playing chess there, and they did not see the women coming. It was Fand saw them first, and she said to Laeg: "Look, Laeg, at what I see." "What is that?" said Laeg. Then he looked, and it is what Fand said: "Look behind you, Laeg; there are women listening to you, wise, with sharp, green knives in their right hands, with gold at their well-shaped breasts; they move as brave men do, going through a battle of chariots. Well does Emer, daughter of Forgall, change colour in her anger."

"No harm shall be done to you by her," said Cuchulain; "and she shall not reach to you at all. Come into the sunny seat of the chariot, opposite myself, for I will defend you against all the many women of the four points of Ulster; for though Forgall's daughter may threaten," he said, "on the strength of her companions, to do some daring thing, it is surely not against me she will dare it."

Then Cuchulain said to Emer: "It is little I mind you, woman, in spite of my affection for you, more than any other man minds a woman. The spear in your shaking hand does not wound me, nor your weak, thin knife, nor your vain, gathered anger; for it would be a pity my strength to be put down by a woman's strength."

"I ask then," said Emer, "what was it led you, Cuchulain, to dishonour me before all the women of the province, and before all the women of Ireland, and before all honourable people in the same way? For it was under your shelter I came, and on the strength of your faithfulness; for although you threaten a great quarrel in your pride, it is certain, Cuchulain, you cannot put me away, even if you would try to do it."

"I ask you, Emer," said Cuchulain, "why I may not have my turn in the company of this woman; for in the first place she is well-behaved, comely, well-mannered, worthy of a king, this woman from beyond the waves of the great sea; with form and countenance and high descent; with embroidery and handiness, with sense and quickness; for there is not anything under the skies her husband could ask, but she would do it, even if she had not given her promise. And O Emer," he said, "you will never find any brave, comely man so good as myself."

"It is certain," said Emer, "that I will not refuse this woman if you follow her. But all the same, everything red is beautiful, everything new is fair, everything high is lovely, everything common is bitter, everything we are without is thought much of; everything we know is thought little of, till all knowledge is known. And O Cuchulain," she said, "I was at one time in esteem with you, and I would be so again, if it were pleasing to you."

And grief came upon her, and overcame her. "By my word, now," said Cuchulain, "you are pleasing to me, and will be pleasing as long as I live."

"Let me be given up," said Fand. "It is better for me to be given up," said Emer. "Not so," said Fand, "it is I that will be given up in the end, and it is I that have been in danger of it all this time."

And great grief and trouble of mind came on Fand, because she was ashamed to be given up, and to have to go back to her home there and then; and the great love she had given Cuchulain troubled her; and so she was lamenting, and she made this complaint:

"It is I will go on the journey; I agree to it with great sorrow; though my father has so great a name, I would sooner stay with Cuchulain. It would be better for me to be here, to be under your rule without grief, than to go, though you may wonder at it, to the sunny house of Aedh Abrat.

"O Emer, the man is yours, and well may you wear him, for you are worthy; what my arm cannot reach, that at least I may wish well to.

"Many were the men asking for me, in the court and in country places; I never went to meet one of them, for it is myself was of right behaviour.

"A pity it is to give love to a man, and he to take no heed to it. It is better to be turned away, if you are not loved as you love.

"It was not right of you, Emer of the yellow hair, to take hold of Fand, to kill her in her misery."

Now all this was told to Manannan, that Fand, daughter of Aedh Abrat was fighting alone against the women of Ulster, and that Cuchulain was putting her away. Manannan came then from the east in search of her, and he was near them, and no one of them saw him but only Fand. And then great fear and trouble of mind came on her at seeing Manannan, and it is what she said:

"Look on the great son of the sea, from the plains of Eoghan of Inbhir; Manannan lord of the fair hills of the world; there was a time when he was dear to me.

"He may even to-day be constant; my mind is no friend to jealousy. There is a road love leads us in.

"The time I and the friend of Lugh were in the sunny palace of Dun Inbhir, we thought, without a doubt, that we should never be parted from one another.

"When Manannan the great married me, I was a wife worthy of him; he gave me a bracelet of heavy gold, as the price of my beauty.

"I see, coming over the sea, no earthly person sees him, the crested horseman of the high-maned waves; he has no need of long ships.

"As for me myself, because there is foolishness in the minds of women, the man I loved exceedingly has left me here astray.

"Farewell to you, beautiful Cuchulain; I go away from you with a kind heart. Though I do not come back again, let me have your good will; all things are good in comparison with a parting.

"It is time for me to go away; there is one to whom it is not grief, but for all that, it is a great disgrace to me, O Laeg, son of Riangabra.

"It is with my own husband I will go, because he will do as I desire. Look now at my going, that it may not be said I went away secretly."

Then Fand went over to Manannan, and Manannan bade her welcome, and he said: "Well, woman, is it after Cuchulain you will be going from this time, or is it with me you will go?" "By my word now," said she, "there is one of you I would sooner follow than the other; but it is along with you I will go, and I will not wait on Cuchulain, because he has left me; and another thing," she said, "you have not a queen that is fitting for you, and that is what Cuchulain has."

But when Cuchulain saw the woman going away from him with Manannan, he said to Laeg: "What is that?" "It is Fand," said Laeg, "that is going to Manannan, son of the sea, because she was not pleasing to you."

It is then there was great anger on Cuchulain, and he went with great leaps southward to Luachair, the place of rushes; and he stopped for a long while without drink, without food, among the mountains, and where he slept every night, was on the road of Midluachan.

And when Emer heard that, she went to visit Conchubar in Emain Macha, and she told him the way Cuchulain was.

Then Conchubar sent the poets and the skilled men and the Druids of Ulster to visit him, that they might lay hold of him, and bring him to Emain Macha along with them. But when they came to him, he would have killed them, but the Druids did enchantment on him, until they had laid hold of him, and until his wits began to come back to him. Then he asked them for a drink, and the Druids gave him a drink of forgetfulness. From the moment he drank that drink, he did not remember Fand, and all the things he had done. And they gave a drink of forgetfulness to Emer as well, that she might forget her jealousy, for the state she was in was no better than his own.

And after that, Manannan shook his cloak between Cuchulain and Fand, the way they should never meet one another again.

507

CHAPTER XV

Advice to a Prince

There was a meeting of the three provinces of Ireland held about this time in Teamhair, to try could they find some person to give the High Kingship of Ireland to; for they thought it a pity the Hill of the Lordship of Ireland, that is Teamhair, to be without the rule of a king on it, and the tribes to be without a king's government to judge their houses. For the men of Ireland had been without the government of a High King over them since the death of Conaire at Da Derga's Inn.

And the kings that met now at the court of Cairbre Niafer were Ailell and Maeve of Connaught, and Curol, and Tigernach, son of Luchta, king of Tuathmumaim, and Finn, son of Ross, king of Leinster. But they would not ask the men of Ulster to help them in choosing a king, for they were all of them against the men of Ulster.

There was a bull-feast made ready then, the same way as the time Conaire was chosen, to find out who was the best man to get the kingship.

After a while the dreamer screamed out in his sleep, and told what he saw to the kings. And what he saw this time, was a young strong man, with high looks, and with two red stripes on his body, and he sitting over the pillow of a man, that was wasting away in Emain Macha.

A message was sent then with this account to Emain Macha. The men of Ulster were gathered at that time about Cuchulain, that was on his sick-bed. The messenger told his story to Conchubar and to the chief men of Ulster.

"There is a young man of good race and good birth with us now that answers to that account," said Conchubar; "that is Lugaid of the Red Stripes, son of Clothru, daughter of Eochaid Feidlech, the pupil of Cuchulain; and he is sitting by his pillow within, caring him, for he is on his sick-bed."

And when it was told Cuchulain that messengers were come for Lugaid, to make him king in Teamhair, he rose up and began to advise him, and it is what he said:

"Do not be a frightened man in a battle; do not be light-minded, hard to reach, or proud. Do not be ungentle, or hasty, or passionate; do not be overcome with the drunkenness of great riches, like a flea that is drowned in the ale of a king's house. Do not scatter many feasts to strangers; do not visit mean people that cannot receive you as a king. Do not let wrongful possession stand because it has lasted long; but let witnesses be searched to know who is the right owner of land. Let the tellers of history tell truth before you; let the lands of brothers and their increase be set down in their lifetime; if a family has increased in its branches, is it not from the one stem they are come? Let them be called up, let the old claims be established by oaths; let the heir be left in lawful possession of the place his fathers lived in; let strangers be driven off it by force.

"Do not use too many words. Do not speak noisily; do not mock, do not give insults, do not make little of old people. Do not think ill of any one; do not ask what is hard to give. Let you have a law of lending, a law of oppression, a law of pledging. Be obedient to the advice of the wise; keep in mind the advice of the old. Be a follower of the rules of your fathers. Do not be cold-hearted to friends; be strong towards your enemies; do not give evil for evil in your battles. Do not be given to too much talking. Do not speak any harm of others. Do not waste, do not scatter, do not do away with what is your own. When you do wrong, take the blame of it; do not give up the truth for any man. Do not be trying to be first, the way you will not be jealous; do not be an idler, that you may not be weak; do not ask too much, that you may not be thought little of. Are you willing to follow this advice, my son?"

Then Lugaid answered Cuchulain, and it is what he said: "As long as all goes well, I will keep to your words, and every one will know that there is nothing wanting in me; all will be done that can be done."

Then Lugaid went away with the messengers to Teamhair, and he was made king, and he slept in Teamhair that night. And after that all the people that had gathered there went to their own homes.

CHAPTER XVI

The Sons of Doel Dermait

One time Cuchulain was gone south to Carraige, in the province of Munster, and Lugaid of the Red Stripes with him, and Laeg. And one day they saw a young girl standing on the burial-hill of Tetach. "What is it you are wanting?" said Lugaid. "I want Cuchulain, son of Sualtim," she said, "for I have set my love on him on account of his great deeds that I have heard of." "There he is, beyond," said Lugaid. Then she went over to him, and put her arms about his neck, and kissed him; and she told him she was Finnchoem, daughter of Eocho Rond, king of Hy Maine.

Then Cuchulain took her into his keeping, and they travelled northward through the night, towards Fid Manach, they saw three fires in a wood before them, and nine men at every fire; outlaws they were, that were robbing the country. And Cuchulain killed three of them at every fire.

And in the morning they saw a troop of men coming towards them on the plain, and Finnchoem's father, the king of Hy Maine, leading them, and he having on him a four-folded crimson cloak, with four borders of gold, and a shield with eight borders of white bronze, and a gold-hilted sword at his side. And he had light yellow hair falling down on each side to the flanks of his grey-black horse; and there was a gold chain of the weight of seven ounces hanging from his hair, and it was from that he took his name, Eocho Rond, that is, Eocho of the gold chain. And as soon as he saw Cuchulain, he threw his spear at him. But Cuchulain caught the spear and threw it back again, and it struck the horse in the neck, so that he reared up and threw his master. And Cuchulain lifted Eocho in his arms, and carried him as far as Cruachan, that they were near at the time, to leave him with Ailell and with Maeve. And there was great shame on the king of Hy Maine at what had happened.

And when Cuchulain was leaving him he said: "May you never have rest in sitting, or in lying down, until you find out what it was brought away the three sons of Doel Dermait, the Beetle of Forgetfulness, out of their own country."

And Cuchulain went on to Emain. But when he sat down in his place, it seemed to him the walls of the house and the ground under him to be on fire. Then he said to his people: "I think what Eocho Rond threatened me with is coming on me, and I will get my death if I do not do as he bade me."

Then he went back to his own place, Dundealgan, and out westward to Baile's strand. And there he saw a boat coming, and the king of Alban's son in it, and his people, and they bringing presents for King Conchubar, of purple and of golden drinking-cups. And when they saw the three men on the strand, Cuchulain and Lugaid and Laeg, they said to them: "It is likely if the king knew we were here, he would send us food and drink by you." "Is it a steward you would make of me?" said Cuchulain, and anger came on him, and he took the sword in his hand to strike them. "Give us our life, Cuchulain, for we did not know you," said the king's son.

"Do you know what was it drove the three sons of Doel Dermait from their own country?" said Cuchulain. "I do not know that," said the king's son. "But I have a sea charm, and I will set it for you, and I will give it to you, and you will find the knowledge you are looking for."

Then Cuchulain gave him his little spear, and scratched an Ogham on it, and said to him: "Set out now, and go and take my seat at Emain Macha."

Then they took the things out of the boat, and Cuchulain got in, and Lugaid of the Red Stripes, and Laeg; and they put up the sail, and went on for a day and a night until they came to an island. It was a fine, large, beautiful island, and it having a silver wall about it, and a paling of bronze.

Then Cuchulain landed, and he saw a house with pillars of white bronze, and three times fifty beds in the house, and a chessboard, and a draughtboard, and a harp hanging over every bed. And he saw a grey king and queen in the house, with purple cloaks on them, worked with dark-coloured gold, and three young girls of the one age, having a dress worked with gold thread on each of them.

And the king gave them a friendly welcome, and he said: "Cuchulain is welcome to us for Lugaid's sake, and Laeg is welcome for his father and his mother's sake."

Then Cuchulain asked him did he know what was it drove the three sons of Doel Dermait out of their own country. "You will soon know that," he said, "for their sister and their sister's husband are in that island there to the south."

Then three pieces of iron were put in the fire, and when they were red-hot, the three young girls took them out, and put them in three vats, and Cuchulain and Lugaid and Laeg bathed in the vats. And they were brought cups of mead. And then they heard a noise of arms and of trumpets, and they saw fifty armed men coming to the house, and every two of them bringing a pig and an ox, and every one a cup of mead of hazel nuts. And then every man of them came again, and a load of firing on his back; and then the oxen and the pigs were cooked, and a feast for hundreds was given to Cuchulain and his comrades.

And the next day they went on to the island where the daughter of Doel Dermait was, and the boat went on, steering itself, to the island. And Condla, son-in-law of Doel Dermait, was lying on the strand, and his head against a pillar at the east of the island, and his feet at the west of the island, and every time he breathed, he made a wave in the sea that turned the boat back. But then he called out to Cuchulain: "Come to land, for there is no fear of you on us; for however great your anger may be, it is not in the prophecy that it is by you this island will be destroyed." Then Cuchulain came to land, and Condla and his wife bade him welcome. And Cuchulain asked if they knew what it was had driven the three sons of Doel Dermait from their own country. "I know it," said the woman, "and I will show you where they are, for it is foretold that their healing is to come by you; and it is glad my true, warm heart would be, they to be healed." And then she said: "Go to where that wall is, and you will find Cairpre Cundail, and he will bring you to the valley where they are kept by Eocho Glas, the strong man."

So they went on to the wall, and they saw two women that were cutting rushes, and Cuchulain said to one of them: "What is the name of this country I have come to?" And the woman rose up, and it is what she said: "There are seven princes in this country, and every one of them has had seven victories; and there are seven women in this country, every one of them having a king under her feet. And every one of them has seven armies; and when a thief comes to this place, he does not go back again to tell the story of it."

Then Cuchulain struck her down with his hand, and the other woman went away to tell Cairpre Cundail what had happened.

Cairpre Cundail came out then, and he and Cuchulain fought through the day, and neither got the better of the other. But at night Cairpre said: "That is enough, Cuchulain." And they left off for the night. And next morning Cairpre brought

Cuchulain to the valley where Eocho Glas was, that he himself was always at war with. And Eocho Glas called out: "Is any one there of your miserable fighters?" "There is some one here," said Cuchulain. At that Eocho said: "That is not a voice that pleases me, for it is the voice of the angry man from Muirthemne."

Then he came out, and they fought together in the valley, and then they fought beside the sea. And in the end Cuchulain took the Gae Bulg and put it through him, and he fell, and Cuchulain struck his head off.

Then the prisoners of Eocho Glas came running from the hills on every side, east and west, and bathed themselves in his blood, for he had been doing them every sort of hurt and harm, and they all got healing.

And the three sons of Doel Dermait came with them, and were healed along with them, and they told their whole story to Cuchulain. And then they set out for their own country.

And Cuchulain went back the same way as he came; and he brought wonderful presents with him from Cairpre Cundail.

And when he got back to Ulster, he went on to Emain Macha, and his share of food and drink were waiting there for him yet. And he told his whole story to Conchubar and to the heroes of the Red Branch, and to Eocho Rond, king of Hy Maine; and that is the way he made his peace with him.

CHAPTER XVII

Battle of Rosnaree

There was a time, now, after the war for the Bull of Cuailgne, when King Conchubar got someway down-hearted, and there was a heaviness on his mind.

And the men of Ulster thought it might be lonesome he was, and fretting after Deirdre yet, and they searched about through the whole province for a wife for him.

And at last they found a beautiful young girl of good race, whose name was Luain, and they brought her to Emain Macha, and a great wedding was made, and great feasting; and the king grew to be quiet and happy in his mind. But among the men that came to the wedding were the two sons of the poet Aithirne, that had such a bad name for covetousness and for cruelty.

The two sons were poets as well, Cuingedach and Abhartach, and when they saw Luain, Conchubar's queen, and she so beautiful, the two of them fell in love with her there and then. And they stopped at Emain, and after a while each of them tried to gain her secret love. But there was great anger and displeasure on Luain at that, and she drove them from her.

They went home then to their father, Aithirne, and the three of them, to avenge themselves on Luain, made satires on her, that brought blotches out on her face. And when her face that was so beautiful was spoiled like that, she went back and hid herself in her father's house, and with the shame and the sorrow that were on her, she died there.

Then great anger and rage came on Conchubar, and he sent the men of Ulster to Aithirne's house, and they killed himself and his two sons, and they pulled his house down to the ground.

But the rest of the poets of Ulster were not well pleased that Conchubar should put such disrespect on one of themselves and do such a great vengeance on him, and they gathered together and gave Aithirne a great burial and keened him, and it was Amergin that made a lament over his grave.

And then Conchubar stopped in Emain Macha, and the cloud of trouble came on him again, and he used to be thinking of the war for the Bull of Cuailgne, and of all that Maeve's army did when he was in his weakness; and he did not sleep in the night, and there was no food that pleased him.

And then the men of Ulster bid Cathbad, the Druid, go to Conchubar, and rouse him out of his sickness.

So Cathbad went to him, and he cried tears down when he saw him, and he said: "Tell me, Conchubar, what wound it is or what sickness has weakened you and has made your face so pale?" "It is no wonder sickness to be on me," said Conchubar, "when I think of the way the four provinces of Ireland came and destroyed my forts and my duns and my walled towns and the houses of my people, and when I think how Maeve brought away cattle and gold and silver, and how she came as far as Dun Sescind and Dun Sobairce, and brought away Daire's bull out of my own province. And it is what vexes me, Maeve herself to have got away safe from the battle; and it is time for me to go and avenge that time on the men of Ireland," he said. "That is no right thing you are saying," said Cathbad, "for the men of Ulster did a good vengeance on the men of Ireland the time they gained the battle of Ilgaireth." "I do not count any battle to be a battle," said Conchubar, "unless a king or a queen has fallen in it; and I swear by the oath of my people, Cathbad," he said, "that kings and great men will be brought to their death by me, or else I myself will go to my death."

"This is my advice to you," said Cathbad, "not to set out till the winter is gone by; for at this time the winds are rough, and the roads are heavy, and the rivers are full and flooded, and every windy gap is cold. It is best to wait for the summer," he said, "till the fords are shallow and the roads are smooth, till the thick leaves on the bushes will be shelters, till every sod of grass will be a pillow, till our colts will be strong, till the nights will be short for keeping watch against an enemy. It is best to wait," he said, "till you can gather together the men of Ulster, and till you can send messengers to your friends among the Gall." "I am willing to do that," said Conchubar, "but I give my word," he said, "let them come, or let them not come, I will go myself to Teamhair to get satisfaction from Cairbre Niafer, my own son-in-law, that did not come to help me at the gathering at Ilgaireth, and to Lugaid, son of Curoi, and to Eocha, son of Luchta, and to Maeve, and to Ailell, till I throw down the stones over the graves of their chief men, till I destroy and lay waste their country, the same way as the men of Ireland destroyed my province."

So then Conchubar sent out messengers to Conall Cearnach, that was raising his tribute in the islands of Leodus, and of Cadd, and of Orc, and to the countries of the Gall, to Olaib, grandson of the king of Norway, and to Baire of the Scigger islands, and to Siugraid Soga, king of Sudiam; to the seven sons of Romra, and to the son of the king of Alban, to the king of the island of Orc.

And the first to answer the messengers, and to set out for Ulster was Conall Cearnach, for there was great anger on him when he heard of all that had happened in Ulster in the war for the Bull of Cuailgne, and he not in it. "And if I had been in it," he said, "the men of Connaught would not have taken spoil from Ulster, without an equal vengeance being measured to them again." And Olaib, grandson of the king of Norway, came with him, and Baire, of the Scigger islands, and their men with them in their ships; and they came through the green waves, and the seals and the swordfishes rising about them, towards Dundealgan, and the place where they landed was at the Strand of Baile, son of Buan.

This, now, is the story of Baile that was buried at that strand.

He was of the race of Rudraige, and although he had but little land belonging to him, he was the heir of Ulster, and every one that saw him loved him, both man and woman, because he was so sweet-spoken; and they called him Baile of the Honey Mouth. And the one that loved him best was Aillinn, daughter of Lugaidh, the king of Leinster's son. And one time she herself and Baile settled to meet one another near Dundealgan, beside the sea. Baile was the first to set out, and he came from Emain Macha, over Slieve Fuad, over Muirthemne, to the strand where they were to meet; and he stopped there, and his chariots were unyoked, and his horses were let out to graze. And while he and his people were waiting there they saw a strange, wild-looking man, coming towards them from the South, as fast as a hawk that darts from a cliff or as the wind that blows from off the green sea. "Go and meet him," said Baile to his people, "and ask him news of where he is going, and where he comes from, and what is the reason of his haste." So they asked news of him, and he said: "I am going back now to Tuagh Inbhir, from Slieve Suidhe Laighen, and this is all the news I have, that Aillinn, daughter of Lugaidh, was on her way to meet Baile, son of Buan, that she loved. And the young men of Leinster overtook her, and kept her back from going to him, and she died of the heartbreak there and then. For it was foretold by Druids that were friendly to them that they would not come together in their lifetime, but that after their death they would meet, and be happy for ever after." And with that he left them, and was gone again like a blast of wind, and they were not able to hinder him.

And when Baile heard that news, his life went out from him, and he fell dead there on the strand.

And at that time the young girl Aillinn was in her sunny parlour to the south, for she had not set out yet. And the same strange man came in to her, and she asked him where he came from. "I come from the North," he said, "from Tuagh Inbhir, and I am going past this place to Slieve Suidhe Laighen. And all the news I have," he said, "is that I saw the men of Ulster gathered together on the strand near Dundealgan, and they raising a stone, and writing on it the name of Baile, son of Buan, that died there when he was on his way to meet the woman he had given his love to; for it was not meant for them ever to reach one another alive, or that one of them should see the other alive." And when he had said that he vanished away, and as to Aillinn, her life went from her, and she died the same way that Baile had died.

And an apple-tree grew out of her grave, and a yew-tree out of Baile's grave. And it was near that yew-tree Conall Cearnach landed, and Baire, and the grandson of the king of Norway. And Cuchulain had made ready a great feast for them, and for Conchubar that had come to meet them, at bright-faced Dundealgan.

And the Hound bade them a kind, loving welcome, and he said: "Welcome to those I know, and those I do not know, to the good and the bad, the young and the old among you." And they stopped there a week, and Conchubar was well pleased to see the whole strand full of his friends that were come in their ships. And then he bade farewell to Emer, daughter of Forgall, and he said to Cuchulain: "Go now to the three fifties of old fighting men, that are resting in their age, under Irgalach, son of Macclach, and say to them to come with me to this gathering and to this war, the way I will have their help and their advice." "Let them go to it if they have a mind," said Cuchulain; "but it is not I that will go and ask it of them."

So then Conchubar himself went to the great house, where the old fighting men used to be living that had laid by their arms. And when he came in, they raised their heads from their places to look at the great king. And then they leaped up, and they said: "What has brought you to us to-day, our chief and our lord?" "Did you get no word," he said, "of the way the four provinces of Ireland came against us, and how they burned down our forts, and our houses, and how they brought their makers of poems and of stories along with them, that their deeds might be told, and our disgrace might be the greater. And I am going out against them now," he said, "to get satisfaction from them; and let you come with me, and I will have your advice." Then the hearts of the old men rose in them, and they caught their old horses and yoked their old chariots. And they went on with the king to the mouth of the Water of Luachann that night.

And the next day Conchubar set out with his own men and his friends from beyond the sea, to Slieve Breagh, that is near Rosnaree on the Boinne. And they made their camp at Cuanglas, the green harbour, and lighted their fires, and music and merry songs were made for them. But Cuchulain stopped behind in

Dundealgan to gather his own people, and to make provision for them on the march.

Now, news had been brought to Cairbre Niafer at Teamhair, that Conchubar was gathering his men to get satisfaction for all that had been done to Ulster in the war for the Bull of Cuailgne, and that it was likely he himself would be the first he would come against.

For there was some bad feeling between Caibre and the men of Ulster, since the time he drove the sons of Umor into Connaught, with the heavy rent he put on them, and that after Conall Cearnach and Cuchulain giving their own security for their good behaviour. They turned on their securities after that, and fought with them, and Conall Cool, the son of their chief, fell; and Cuchulain, and his father, and his friends, raised the heap of stones over him that is called Carn Chonaill, in the province of Connaught.

And Cairbre sent a message to Cruachan, to say to Ailel and to Maeve: "If it is towards us Conchubar and the men of Ulster are coming, let you come to our help; but if it is past us they go, into the fairheaded province of Connaught, we will go to your help." So when Conchubar came to Cuanglas, at Rosnaree, there was a good army gathered there to make a stand against him; the three troops of the children of Deagha, and a great troop of the Collamnachs, and of the men of Bregia, and of the Gailiana. And he rose up early in the morning, and he could see the moving of men and the shining of spears, and he heard the noise of a great army, and he said; "We will send some one of our men to bring us word about them."

And he sent out Feic, son of Follaman. And Feic went up to a hill beside the Boinne, and he began to look at the army and to count it, and it vexed him to see how many were in it. "If I go back now and tell this," he said, "the men of Ulster will come and will begin the battle, and there will be no better chance for me to get a great name and do great deeds than for any other man. And why would I not go and begin a fight now by myself?" And with that he crossed the river.

But the men that were in front caught sight of him, and the whole army began shouting around him, and he had not courage to go against them, but he turned to cross the river again. But he gave a false leap, just where the water was deepest, and a wave laughed over him, and he died.

It seemed a long time to Conchubar that he was away, and he said to the men of Ulster: "What is your advice to us about this battle?" "It is what we advise," they said, "to wait till our strong fighters and our chief men are come." And they had not long to wait before they saw troops coming, Cathbad with twelve hundred men, and Amergin with twelve hundred men, and Eoghan, king of Fernmaighe, and Laegaire Buadach, and the three sons of Conall Buide.

And then they saw another troop coming, and in the front of it a fierce, brown man. Rough, dark hair he had, and a big nose and hollow cheeks, and his talk was quick and hurried. A blue cloak about him, and a brooch of silver as white as a bird, a heavy sword, and a shield with iron rims. And this is who he was, Daire of Cuailgne, that was come to get satisfaction for his bull and for his herds on the men of Ireland. "What is delaying you here," he said to Conchubar. "I have good reason for delaying,' said Conchubar, "for there is a great army under Cairbre Niafer before us at Rosnaree, and there are not enough of us to go against them. And it is not refusing a battle we are, but waiting till we get our full number." "By my word," said Daire, "if you do not go out against them, it is I will go against them by myself."

Then Conchubar put on his armour, and took his many-coloured shield, and his sword, the Ochain. And all the men of Ulster gathered around him, and they raised their spears and their shields, and it was like a great river breaking from the side of a mountain, and breaking what it meets of stones and trees before it, that they went to meet the men of Leinster at Rosnaree on the Boinne.

And when Cairbre Niafer and his friends and his men saw them coming, they made ready for them, and came towards the river.

And the men of Ulster crossed the river, and the two armies met, and each of them took to hacking and destroying the other. And the Gailiana pressed heavily on the men of Ulster, and came in to the middle of them, and cut them down like trees are cut in a wood. And as for Conchubar he did not give back, where he was, and Celthair on his right hand, and Amergin the poet, on his right hand again, and Eoghan, king of Fernmaighe, on his left, and Daire of Cuailgne near him. These few stood against the Gailiana, and fought against them, stout and proud. But as to the young men and those that were never in a fight before, they turned round and burst through the battle northwards.

It was just then Conall Cearnach was coming in his chariot, and when the young men of Ulster saw the face of Conall, they came to a stop, and Conall saw that they were beaten and running from the battle, and he called out sharp words to them, for there was anger on him, they to have left the fight, and with no sign of blood or of wounds upon them.

But they were ashamed then, and content to go back to the battle, when they had Conall's hand to help them; and each one of them tore a green branch off the oak trees that were near them, and held it up, and they went with him; for they knew there would be no running away in any place where Conall's face would be seen.

And it happened just at that time Conchubar, the High King, was taking three backward steps out of the battle northward, but when he saw the face of Conall coming towards him, he called to him to stop the army from falling back. "I give my word," said Conall, "I think it easier to fight the battle by myself than to stop the rout now."

Then Conall drew his sword out of its sheath, and he played the music of his sword on the armies of Leinster, and the sound of it was heard on every side; and when the men near him heard it their faces whitened, and each one of them went back to his place in the battle. And at that time Cuchulain came into the battle, and the men of the Gailiana gave wild shouts at him, and anger came on him and he scattered them.

And strength came again into the hearts of the men of Ulster, and their anger rose, and the earth shook under their feet, and there was clashing of swords on both sides, and the shouting of young men, and the screams of old men, and the groaning of chariot-fighters, and the crying of ravens. And there were many lying in cold pools, the white soles of their feet close together, and the red lips turning grey, and the bright faces very pale, and darkness coming on their grey eyes, and confusion on their clear wits.

It is then Cuchulain met with Cairbre Niafer, and he went against him, and put his shield against his shield, and there they were face to face. And Cairbre said words of insult to Cuchulain, and Cuchulain answered him back and said: "It is all I ask of you, to fight with me now alone." "I will do that," said Cairbre Niafer, "for I am a king in my way of living, and a champion in battles."

Then each attacked the other, and it was hard for them to hold their feet firm, or to strike with their hands, in the closeness of the fight. And Cairbre broke all his weapons, but nine of his men came and kept up the fight against Cuchulain till more weapons could be brought to him. And then Cuchulain's weapons were broken, and Cairbre and nine of his men came and held up their shields before him till Laeg could bring him his own right weapons, the Dubach, the grim one, his spear, and the Cruaidin, his sword. And then they took to hitting at one another again, and at last Cuchulain took his spear into his left hand, and struck at Cairbre with it and he lowered his shield to protect his body. And then Cuchulain changed it to his right hand, and struck at him over the rim of his shield, and it went through his heart; and before his body could reach the ground, Cuchulain made a spring and struck his head off. And then he held up the head, and shook it before the two armies.

Then Sencha, son of Ailell, rose up and shook the branch of peace, and the men of Ulster stood still. As to the men of Leinster, when they saw their king was killed, they fell back; but Iriel of the Great Knees, the son of Conall Cearnach, followed after them, and did a great slaughter on the Gailiana and on the rest of the army till they reached to the Rye of Leinster.

And then the men of Ulster went back to their homes. And as to Conchubar, he went back to Emain, and it was not till a good while after that he got the wound in his head that Fintan sewed up with gold thread, to match the colour of his hair, and that brought him to his death in the end.

CHAPTER XVIII

The Only Son of Aoife

The time Cuchulain came back from Alban, after he had learned the used of arms under Scathach, he left Aoife, the queen he had overcome in battle, with child.

And when he was leaving her, he told her what name to give the child, and he gave her a gold ring, and bade her keep it safe till the child grew to be a lad, and till his thumb would fill it; and he bade her to give it to him then, and to send him to Ireland, and he would know he was his son by that token. She promised to do so, and with that Cuchulain went back to Ireland.

It was not long after the child was born, word came to Aoife that Cuchulain had taken Emer to be his wife in Ireland. When she heard that, great jealousy came on her, and great anger, and her love for Cuchulain was turned to hatred; and she remembered her three champions that he had killed, and how he had overcome herself, and she determined in her mind that when her son would come to have the strength of a man, she would get her revenge through him. She told Conlaoch her son nothing of this, but brought him up like any king's son; and when he was come to sensible years, she put him under the teaching of Scathach, to be taught the use of arms and the art of war. He turned out as apt a scholar as his father, and it was not long before he had learnt all Scathach had to teach.

Then Aoife gave him the arms of a champion, and bade him go to Ireland, but first she laid three commands on him: the first never to give way to any living person, but to die sooner than be made turn back; the second, not to refuse a challenge from the greatest champion alive, but to fight him at all risks, even if he was sure to lose his life; the third, not to tell his name on any account, though he might be threatened with death for hiding it. She put him under *geasa*, that is, under bonds, not to do these things.

Then the young man, Conlaoch, set out, and it was not long before his ship brought him to Ireland, and the place he landed at was Baile's Strand, near Dundealgan.

It chanced that at that time Conchubar, the High King, was holding his court there, for it was a convenient gathering-place for his chief men, and they were settling some business that belonged to the government of that district.

When word was brought to Conchubar that there was a ship come to the strand, and a young lad in it armed as if for fighting, and armed men with him, he sent one of the chief men of his household to ask his name, and on what business he was come.

The messenger's name was Cuinaire, and he went down to the strand, and when he saw the young man he said: "A welcome to you, young hero from the east, with the merry face. It is likely, seeing you come armed as if for fighting, you are gone astray on your journey; but as you are come to Ireland, tell me your name and what your deeds have been, and your victories in the eastern bounds of the world."

"As to my name," said Conlaoch, "it is of no great account; but whatever it is, I am under bonds not to tell it to the stoutest man living."

"It is best for you to tell it at the king's desire," said Cuinaire, "before you get your death through refusing it, as many a champion from Alban and from Britain has done before now." "If that is the order you put on us when we land here, it is I will break it," said Conlaoch, "and no one will obey it any longer from this out."

So Cuinaire went back and told the king what the young lad had said. Then Conchubar said to his people: "Who will go out into the field, and drag the name and the story out of this young man?" "I will go," said Conall, for his hand was never slow in fighting. And he went out, and found the lad angry and destroying, handling his arms, and they attacked one another with a great noise of swords and shouts, and they were gripped together, and fought for a while, and then Conall was overcome, and the great name and the praise that was on Conall, it was on the head of Conlaoch it was now.

Word was sent then to where Cuchulain was, in pleasant, bright-faced Dundealgan. And the messenger told him the whole story, and he said: "Conall is lying humbled, and it is slow the help is in coming; it is a welcome there would be before the Hound."

Cuchulain rose up then and went to where Conlaoch was, and he still handling his arms. And Cuchulain asked him his name and said: "It would be well for you, young hero of unknown name, to loosen yourself from this knot, and not to bring down my hand upon you, for it will be hard for you to escape death." But Conlaoch said: "If I put you down in this fight, the way I put down your comrade, there will be a great name on me; but if I draw back now, there will be mockery on me, and it will be said I was afraid of the fight. I will never give in to any man to tell my name, or to give an account of myself. But if I was not held with a command," he said, "there is no man in the world I would sooner give it to than to yourself, since I saw your face. But do not think, brave champion of Ireland, that I will let you take away the fame I have won, for nothing."

With that they fought together, and it is seldom such a battle was seen, and all wondered that the young lad could stand so well against Cuchulain.

So they fought a long while, neither getting the better of the other, but at last Cuchulain was charged so hotly by the lad that he was forced to give way, and although he had fought so many good fights, and killed so many great champions, and understood the use of arms better than any man living, he was pressed very hard.

And he called for the Gae Bulg, and his anger came on him, and the flames of the hero-light began to shine about his head, and by that sign Conlaoch knew him to be Cuchulain, his father. And just at that time he was aiming his spear at him, and when he knew it was Cuchulain, he threw his spear crooked that it might pass beside him. But Cuchulain threw his spear, the Gae Bulg, at him with all his might, and it struck the lad in the side and went into his body, so that he fell to the ground.

And Cuchulain said: "Now, boy, tell your name and what you are, for it is short your life will be, for you will not live from that wound."

And Conlaoch showed the ring that was on his hand, and he said, "Come here where I am lying on the field, let my men from the east come round me. I am suffering for revenge. I am Conlaoch, son of the Hound, heir of dear Dundealgan; I was bound to this secret in Dun Scathach, the secret in which I have found my grief."

And Cuchulain said: "It is a pity your mother not to be here to see you brought down. She might have stretched out her hand to stop the spear that wounded you." And Conlaoch said: "My curse be on my mother, for it was she put me under bonds; it was she sent me here to try my strength against yours." And Cuchulain said: "My curse be on your mother, the woman that is full of treachery; it is through her harmful thoughts these tears have been brought on us." And Conlaoch said: "My name was never forced from my mouth till now; I never gave an account of myself to any man under the sun. But, O Cuchulain of the sharp sword, it was a pity you not to know me the time I threw the slanting spear behind you in the fight."

And then the sorrow of death came upon Conlaoch, and Cuchulain took his sword and put it through him, sooner than leave him in the pain and the punishment he was in.

And then great trouble and anguish came on Cuchulain, and he made this complaint:

"It is a pity it is, O son of Aoife, that ever you came into the province of Ulster, that you ever met with the Hound of Cuailgne.

"If I and my fair Conlaoch were doing feats of war on the one side, the men of Ireland from sea to sea would not be equal to us together. It is no wonder I to be under grief when I see the shield and the arms of Conlaoch. A pity it is there is no one at all, a pity there are not hundreds of men on whom I could get satisfaction for his death.

"If it was the king himself had hurt your fair body, it is I would have shortened his days.

"It is well for the House of the Red Branch, and for the heads of its fair army of heroes, it was not they that killed my only son.

"It is well for Laegaire of Victories it is not from him you got your heavy pain.

"It is well for the heroes of Conall they did not join in the killing of you; it is well that travelling across the plain of Macha they did not fall in with me after such a fight.

"It is well for the tall, well-shaped Forbuide; well for Dubthach, your Black Beetle of Ulster.

"It is well for you, Cormac Conloingeas, your share of arms gave no help, that it is not from your weapons he got his wound, the hard-skinned shield or the blade.

"It is a pity it was not on the plains of Munster, or in Leinster of the sharp blade, or at Cruachan of the rough fighters, that struck down my comely Conlaoch.

"It is a pity it was not in the country of the Cruithne, of the fierce Fians, you fell in a heavy quarrel, or in the country of the Greeks, or in some other place of the world, you died, and I could avenge you.

"Or in Spain, or in Sorcha, or in the country of the Saxons of the free armies; there would not then be this death in my heart.

"It is very well for the men of Alban it was not they that destroyed your fame; and it well for the men of the Gall.

"Och! It is bad that it happened; my grief it is on me is the misfortune, O Conlaoch of the Red Spear, I myself to have spilled your blood.

"I to be under defeat, without strength. It is a pity Aoife never taught you to know the power of my strength in the fight.

"It is no wonder I to be blinded after such a fight and such a defeat.

"It is no wonder I to be tired out, and without the sons of Usnach beside me.

"Without a son, without a brother, with none to come after me; without Conlaoch, without a name to keep my strength.

"To be without Naoise, without Ainnle, without Ardan; is it not with me is my fill of trouble?

"I am the father that killed his son, the fine green branch; there is no hand or shelter to help me.

"I am a raven that has no home; I am a boat going from wave to wave; I am a ship that has lost its rudder; I am the apple left on the tree; grief and sorrow will be with me from this time."

Then Cuchulain stood up and faced all the men of Ulster. "There is trouble on Cuchulain," said Conchubar; "he is after killing his own son, and if I and all my men were to go against him, by the end of the day he would destroy every man of us. Go now," he said to Cathbad, the Druid, "and bind him to go down to Baile's Strand, and to give three days fighting against the waves of the sea, rather than to kill us all."

So Cathbad put an enchantment on him, and bound him to go down. And when he came to the strand, there was a great white stone before him, and he took his sword in his right hand, and he said: "If I had the head of the woman that sent her son to his death, I would split it as I split this stone." And he made four quarters of the stone.

Then he fought with the waves three days and three nights, till he fell from hunger and weakness, so that some men said he got his death there. But it was not there he got his death, but on the plain of Muirthemne.

CHAPTER XIX

The Great Gathering at Muirthemne

Now after all the battles Cuchulain had fought, and all the men he had killed, it is no wonder he had a good share of enemies watching to get the upper hand of him. And, besides Maeve, those that had their minds most set against him were Erc, son of Cairbre Naifer, that he had killed at Rosnaree, and Lugaid, son of Curoi, that he had killed at his own house in Munster, and the three daughters of Calatin.

This, now, was the way it happened that Curoi got his death by him. He met with Blanad one time, a good while after Curoi had given him the championship of Ulster, and it is what she told him that there was not a man on the face of the earth she loved more than himself. And she bade him come, near the time of Samhain, to Curoi's dun at Finglas, and his men with him, and to bring her away by force.

So when the time came, Cuchulain set out, and his men with him, and they came to a wood near the dun, that had a stream running through it, and he sent word to Blanad he was waiting there. And Blanad sent him back word to come and bring her away at whatever time he would see the stream in the wood turning white. And when what she thought to be a good time came, when all the men of the place were sent out looking for stones to build a great new dun, she milked the three white cows with red ears Curoi had brought away by force from her father, Midhir, into the cauldron he had brought away with them, and she poured a great vessel of new milk into the stream, where it ran by the dun. And when Cuchulain saw the stream turning white, he went up to the dun. But he found Curoi there before him, and they fought, and Curoi was killed, the son of Daire, lord of the southern sea, that had a great name and great praise on him before Blanad was his wife.

Then Cuchulain brought Blanad away with him to Ulster. But Curoi's poet, Feirceirtne, followed after them to avenge his master's death. And when they were come as far as the headland of Cian Beara, he saw Blanad standing on the edge of a high rock, and she alone. And he went up to her, and took her in his arms, and threw her, and himself along with her, over the rock, and they both got their death by the fall on the moment.

And as to the children of Calatin, this is the way it was with them. At the time Cuchulain made an end of Calatin at the ford, and of all his sons with him, Calatin's wife was with child. And when her time came, there were three daughters born at the one birth, and they deformed, and each of them having but one eye.

Then Maeve came from Cruachan to visit them, and she brought away the children with her, and took the charge of them. And when they were come to sensible years, she came to see them, and she said: "Do you know who it was killed your father?" "We know well," they said, "it was Cuchulain, son of Sualtim, killed him." "That is so," said Maeve, "and let you make a journey now," she said, "through the whole world, to get knowledge of spells and enchantments from them that have it, the way you will be able to avenge your father when the time comes."

When the three one-eyed daughters of Calatin heard that, they went out into Alban, and to every other country, from the rising to the setting of the sun, and they were learning every sort of enchantment and of witchcraft. And at the end they came back to Cruachan.

And as to Maeve, she went up one morning to her sunny parlour, and from there she saw the three daughters of Calatin sitting outside on the lawn. So she took her cloak, that had beautiful embroidery on it, and put it about her, and she went out on the lawn and bade them welcome, and she sat down before them, and asked news of all they had done since they left Ireland. And they told her all they had learned. "Do you remember it all?" said Maeve. "We remember it well," they said, "and we can do many things, and we can make the appearance of terrible battles by secret words."

Maeve brought them then into the royal house, and they were attended on, and they were given every sort of food and of drink, and of good treatment.

And then Maeve sent word to Lugaid, and he came to Cruachan, and himself and Maeve began to talk together. "Do you remember," she said, "who it was killed Curoi your father?" "I remember it well," he said; "it was Cuchulain killed him." Then Erc came to her, and she asked him the same question about his father Cairbre Niafer, and he made the same answer. "What you say is true," Maeve said then, "and the children of Calatin are come back to me now, after going through the whole world, to fight against Cuchulain with their enchantments. And there is no king or chief man, or fighting man in the four provinces of Ireland, but lost his friend or his comrade, his father or his brother, by him in the war for the Bull of Cuailgne, or at some other time. And now," she said, "it is best for us to get together a great army of the men of Ireland to make an attack on him, for the men of Ulster have their weakness coming on them, and it is likely they will not be able to help him."

With that, Lugaid went away southward to the king of Munster, to bid him come, and bring his men with him; and Erc went and called to the chief men of Leinster in the same way.

Then all the provinces gathered together to Cruachan, and they stopped there with feasting and merriment for three days and three nights. And at the end of that time they went out of Cruachan. But Maeve did not bring Fergus with them this time, for she was sure the men of Ireland would never be able to make an end of Cuchulain if Fergus was along with them.

And this is the way they went, beyond Magh Finn to Athluain, and they rested there that night.

And the next day they went on their road till they came to Glean-na-loin, and from that to Glean-mor, and from that to Tailtin, and they stopped the night there; and then they went on by the borders of Magh Breagh, and Midhe, and Teathfa, and Cuailgne.

It is then Conchubar, King of Ulster, got word that the borders of his province were being robbed and destroyed by the men of Munster and Leinster, and of Connaught.

"Where is Levarcham?" said Conchubar. "I am here," she said. "Go out for me now," said Conchubar, "and bring Cuchulain here to Emain; for it is against him this army we have news of is gathered. Bid him to make no delay, but to leave Dundealgan and Muirthemne, and to come here to advise with myself, and with Cathbad and Amergin, and all the knowledgeable men. For if he can put off this battle till I myself, and Conall, and all the men of Ulster, will be ready to go out with him, we will give them a great defeat, the way they will not come into my province again. For there are many bear him ill-will," he said, "on account of all he killed. Finn, son of Ross, Fraoch, son of Idath, and Dearg, son of Conroi, and many of the best men of Ulster; and Cairbre Niafer at the battle of Rosnaree; and Curoi, son of Daire, High King of Munster, and many of the men of Munster beside him; Fircearna, and Fiamain, and Niall, and Laoc Leathbuine, and many more along with them."

Levarcham went quickly then with that message, and it is where she found Cuchulain, between sea and land, on Baile's Strand, and he trying to bring down sea-birds with his sling; but with all the birds that were flying over him and past him, he could not bring one down, but they all escaped him.

And there was heaviness on him, not to be able to hit them, for he knew it had some bad meaning. And, he had never been very happy in his mind since the death of the blossomed branch, Aoife's son, there on that strand. Then he saw Levarcham coming, and he bade her welcome. "I am glad of that welcome," said Levarcham, "and it with news from Conchubar I am come to you." "What is your news?" said Cuchulain, "I have news indeed," she said. And then she told him all that Conchubar had said, from beginning to end. "And it is what all are asking of you," she said: "chief men and fighting men, poets and learned men, women, and young girls, to keep aside from the men of Ireland that are coming here to Muirthemne, and not to go out alone against that great army." "I would sooner stop here and defend my own place," said Cuchulain. "It is best for you to go to Emain," said Laeg. So after a while he gave in to them, and they went back to Dundealgan, and Emer came out on the lawn to meet them, and they gave her the same advice, to go to Emain Macha where Conchubar and his chief men were gathered together. Then Emer got her chariot, and she sent her servants and the herds, and the cattle to Slieve Cuilenn in the North, and herself and Cuchulain set out for Emain. And that was the first time Dundealgan was emptied since Cuchulain had the sway over it.

And when Cuchulain came to Emain Macha, they brought him to the bright, sunny house. And when the women of the place heard he was there, they came and spoke sweet words, and the poets and the harpers came, and the skilled men, and they all made music, and feasting, and pleasant talk round about Cuchulain, in the wide, white, sunny house of the Red Branch; for what always quieted Cuchulain best was the singing of songs and rhymes before him. It is that way Scumac, the story-teller, quieted him one time he was vexed, and had a mind to set fire to Emain, because Conchubar had gone to a feast given by Conall, son of Gleo Glas, in Cuailgne, and had left no word for him to follow.

And Conchubar bade Cathbad, and the learned men, and the women, to keep a good watch on Cuchulain, and to mind him well. "For I leave the charge of him on you," he said, "to save him from the plans Maeve has made against him, and from the power of the children of Calatin. For if he should fall," he said, "it is certain the safety and the prosperity of Ulster will fall with him for ever." "That is true," said Cathbad, and all the others said the same.

"Well," said Geanann, Cathbad's son, "I will go now and see him." He went then to the place Cuchulain and Emer were, and the poets, and the women, and the learned men with them, and a feast laid out on the table, and all of them at drinking and pleasantness and games.

Now as to the men of Ireland, they came to the plain of Muirthemne, and they made their camp there, and they began to destroy and to take all they could find there, and in Macaire Conall; and when they knew Cuchulain had left Dundealgan, it is then the three daughters of Calatin went with the lightness and the quickness of the wind to Emain Macha. And they sat down on the lawn outside the house where Cuchulain was, and they began to tear up the earth and the grass, and by means of their witchcraft they put the appearance of troops of men and of armies, on stalks and coloured oak-leaves, and little fuzz-balls; and the sounds of fighting and striking, and the shouting of a great army were heard on every side, as if there was an attack being made on the dun.

It was bright-faced Geanann, son of Cathbad, was keeping a watch on Cuchulain that day, and he saw him sit up and look out on the lawn, and redness and shame came on his face, when he saw, as he thought, two armies fighting one another, and he put out his hand as if to take his sword, but Geanann threw his two arms about him and hindered him, and told him there was nothing before him but witchcraft and enchantment, and the appearance of fighting made up by the children of Calatin to bring him out to his death. And Cathbad and all the learned men came then and told him the same thing. But after all that, it was hardly they were able to hold him back and to persuade him.

The next day Cathbad himself came to keep a watch on him with the rest, and after a while the noise of shouting began again, and for all they could do, Cuchulain went and looked out of the window. And the first thing he thought he saw was the army of Ireland standing there upon the plain. And then he thought he saw Gradh, son of Lir, standing there; and after that he thought he heard the harp of the son of Mangur playing the sweet music of the Sidhe, and he knew when he heard those sounds that his time was come, and that his courage and his strength would soon be made an end of. And then one of the daughters of Calatin took the appearance of a crow, and came flying over him and saying mocking words, and she bade him go out and save his own house and his lands from the enemies that were destroying them. And though Cuchulain knew well by this time it was witchcraft was being worked against him, he was as ready as before to rush out when he heard the sounds and the shouting of battle; and there came trouble and confusion on his mind with the noise of striking and of fighting, and with the sweet sounds of the harp of the Sidhe. But Cathbad did his best with him, and it is what he told him, that if he would but stop quiet for another three days in Emain, the power of the enchantments would be broken, and Conall Cearnach would have come to his help, and he could go out again, and the whole world would be full of his name and of his lasting victories.

And the women of Emain and the musicians closed round him, and they sang sweet songs, and led away his mind from what he had heard, until the day drew to a close.

And on the morning of the morrow, Conchubar called for Cathbad and Bright-Faced Geanann, and the rest of the Druids. And Emer came along with them, and Celthair's daughter, Niamh, that Cuchulain loved, and the rest of the women of the House of the Red Branch. And Conchubar asked them in what way they could best keep a watch on Cuchulain through the day. "We do not know that," they said. "I will tell you what is best to do," said Conchubar then. "Bring him away with you to Glean-na-Bodhar, the Deaf Valley. For if all the men of Ireland were letting out shouts and cries of war around it, no one that would be in that valley would hear any sound at all. Bring Cuchulain there, then," he said, "and keep him there with you till their enchantments will be spent, and till Conall Cearnach will come to his help out of the island of Leodus." "King," said Niamh, "we were asking him and persuading him all through yesterday to go to that valley, but he would not go there, for all I myself or the rest of the women of Ireland could say. And let you yourself go to him now," she said, "with Cathbad, and Geanann, and the poets, and with Emer, and let you bring him into that valley, and let there be music and pleasantness made about him there, the way he will not hear the shouts and the mocking words of the children of Calatin." "It is not I will go with him," said Emer, "but let Niamh go, and my blessing with her, for it will be hard for him to refuse her." So they agreed to that, and they went to where Cuchulain was, and Conchubar's harper, Cobhtach, went along with them, making sweet music. Then Cathbad went out to Cuchulain where he was lying on the bed, and he began to ask him and to persuade him. "Dear son," he said, "come with me to-day to use the feast I am making, and all the women and the poets will come with us. And there are bonds on you not to refuse my feast." "My grief for that," said Cuchulain. "This is no fit time for me to be feasting and making merry, and the four provinces of Ireland burning and destroying Ulster, and the men of Ulster in their weakness, and Conall away, and the men of Ireland putting insults on me and reproaches, and saying I have run away before them. And but for yourself and Conchubar," he said, "and for Geanann and Amergin, I would fall on them and scatter them, that their dead would be more than their living." Then all the women persuaded him, and Emer spoke to him, and it is what she said: "Little Hound, I never hindered you until this hour from any deed or any adventure you had a mind for. So now, for my sake, my choice sweetheart, my first love and first darling of the men of the world, go with Cathbad and with Geanann, with Niamh and with the poets, to share Cathbad's feast."

Then Niamh went over to him and gave him three, fond, loving kisses; and then they all rose up, and he rose along with them, heavy and sorrowful, and in that way he went in their company into Glean-na-Bodhar. And when they came into it, he said: "My grief I ever to have come here, and I never came to any place I liked less then this; for now the men of Ireland will be saying it was to escape them I came here." "You gave me your word," said Niamh, "you would not go out to meet the men of Ireland without leave from me." "If I gave it," said Cuchulain, "it is right for me to hold to it."

Their chariots were unyoked then, and the Grey of Macha and the Black Sanglain were let loose to graze in the valley, and they all went to the house Cathbad had made ready. And there was a great feast laid out, and Cuchulain was put in the chief place, and to his right hand were Cathbad and Geanann and the poets, and on the left was Niamh, daughter of Celthair, with the women. And opposite them were the musicians and the reciters. And then they all took to feasting and drinking and to games, and they made a great show of mirth and pleasantness before Cuchulain.

But as to the three deformed, one-eyed children of Calatin, they came quickly and lightly, the way they had come on the other days, to the lawn at Emain, to the place where they had got sight of Cuchulain in the house. And when they did not see him there, they searched through the whole of Emain, but when they did not find him with Conchubar, or with the men of the Red Branch, there was great wonder on them. And then they began to think it was Cathbad was hiding him from them, and they rose up high in the air, on a blast of moaning wind they made by their enchantments, and on it they went over the whole province, searching out every wood and valley, every cave and secret path. But they found nothing, till at last they came over Glean-na-Bodhar, and there in the middle of the valley they saw the Grey of Macha and the Black Sainglain and Laeg, son of Riangabra beside them.

They knew then that Cuchulain must be in the valley, and presently they heard the sounds of music and of laughter and of women's voices, where all the people in the feasting-house were trying their best to raise the cloud and the heaviness off Cuchulain's mind.

Then the children of Calatin came down into the valley, and the same way as before they took thistle-stalks and little fuzz-balls and withered leaves, and put on them the appearance of troops of armed men, so that there seemed to be no hill or no place outside the whole valley but was filled with battalions, coming hundred by hundred. And the air was all filled with sounds of battle and shouts, and of trumpets and dreadful laughter, and the cries of wounded men. And there seemed to be fires in the country about, and a noise of the crying of women. And great dread came on all that heard that outcry, both men and women, and dogs of every kind.

But when the women that were with Cuchulain heard those shouts, they shouted back again and raised their voices, but with all they could do, they did not keep the outcry from reaching to Cuchulain. "My grief" he said, "I hear the shouts of the men of Ireland that are spoiling the whole of the province; my fame is at an end, my great name is gone from me, Ulster is put down for ever." "Let the noises pass by," said Cathbad; "it is only the noise made by the children of Calatin, that want to draw you out from where you are, to make an end of you. Stop here with us now, and put the trouble off your mind."

Cuchulain stayed quiet then, but the children of Calatin went on a long time filling the air with battle noises. But they tired of it at last, for they saw that Cathbad and the women were too much for them.

Then anger came on Badb, one of Calatin's daughters, and she said: "Go on now, making sounds of fighting in the air, and I myself will go into the valley; for even if I get my death by it, I will speak with Cuchulain."

With that, she went on in the madness of her anger to the very house where the feast was going on, and there she took the appearance of a woman of Niamh's women, and she beckoned Niamh out to speak with her.

So Niamh came out, thinking she had news to give her, and a good many of the other women of Emain with her, and Badb bade them follow her. And she led them a long way down the valley, and then by her enchantments she raised a thick mist between them and the house, so that they could not find their way, but were astray in the valley, not knowing where they were.

Then she went back to the feasting-house, and she put on herself the appearance of Niamh, and she came in to where Cuchulain was, and called out: "Rise up, Cuchulain; Dundealgan is burned, Muirthemne is destroyed, and Conaille Muirthemne. The whole province is trampled down by the men of Ireland. And it is on myself the blame will be laid," she said, "and all Ulster will say that I hindered you, and kept you back from going out to check the army, and to get satisfaction from the men of Ireland. And it is from Conchubar himself I will get my death on account of that," she said. For she knew Cuchulain had given Niamh his promise, that without leave from her, he would not go out to face the men of Ireland.

"My grief!" said Cuchulain then, "it is hard to trust in women. For I thought," he said, "that you would not have given me that leave for the whole riches of the world. But since you yourself give me leave to go out and face the men of Ireland, I will do it.' And with that he rose up to go out. And as he rose up, he threw his cloak about him, and his foot caught in the cloak, and the gold brooch that was in the cloak fell on his foot and pierced it. "Truly the brooch is a friend that gives me a warning," said Cuchulain.

He went out then, and he bade Laeg to yoke the horses and to make ready the chariot. And Cathbad, and Geanann, and the women followed him out, and took hold of him, but they were not able to stop him. For the cries of battle were still in the air, and he thought he saw a great army standing on the lawn at Emain, and the whole plain filled up and crowded with troops and bands of men, with horses and arms and armour, and he thought he heard great shouts, and that he saw all Conchubar's city burning, and all the hill ground about Emain full of things brought away, and he thought he saw Emer's sunny house thrown down, and the House of the Red Branch in one blaze, and all Emain under fire and smoke. And Cathbad tried to quiet him. "Dear son," he said, "for this day only, follow my advice, and do not go out against the men of Ireland, and I will be able to save you from all the enchantments of the children of Calatin." But Cuchulain said: "Dear master, there is no reason for me to care for my life from this out, for my time is at an end, and Niamh has given me leave to go and face the men of Ireland." And then Niamh herself came up to him and said: "My grief! my little Hound, I would never have given you that leave for all the riches of the world; and it was not I that gave you leave, but Badb, the daughter of Calatin, that took my shape on her. And stay with me now," she said, "my friend, my darling." But Cuchulain would not believe her, and he bade Laeg yoke the chariot, and put his arms in order. Laeg went to do that, but indeed that time above all others he had no mind for the work. And when he shook the bridles towards the horses as he was used to do, they went away from him; and the Grey of Macha would not let him come near him at all. "Truly," said Laeg, "this is a warning of some bad thing. And indeed, my life," he said to the Grey, "it is seldom you would not come to meet the bridle and to meet myself, up to this day." Then he went to Cuchulain and said: "I swear by the gods my people swear by, that if all the men in the province of Ulster were round about the Grey of Macha, they would not be able to bring him as far as the chariot, and I never refused you up to this," he said, "and come out now and speak to the Grey yourself."

So Cuchulain went out, and the horse turned his left side three times to his master. Then he reproached the horse. "You were not used," he said, "to behave like that to me." Then the Grey of Macha came up to him, and he let big, round tears of blood fall on Cuchulain's feet.

Then the chariot was yoked, and it was the Morrigu had unyoked it and had broken it the night before, for she did not like Cuchulain to go out and to get his death in the battle. And Cuchulain set out and came to Emain, and to the house where Emer was, and she came out and bade him come down from his chariot. "I will not," he said, "until I go first to Muirthemne, to attack the four great provinces of Ireland, and to avenge all the hurts and the insults they have put on me, and on Ulster, for I have seen their gatherings and their armies." "Those were made up by enchantments," said Emer. "I tell you, woman," he said, "and I swear by my word, I will never come back here until I have made an attack upon them in their camp."

Then he turned his chariot towards the south, by the road of Meadhon Luachair, and Levarcham cried out after him, and the hundred and fifty queens that were in Emain Macha, and that loved him, cried out upon him miserably, and struck their hands together, for they knew he would not come back to them again.

CHAPTER XX

Death of Cuchulain

Cuchulain went on then to the house of his mother, Dechtire, to bid her farewell. And she came out on the lawn to meet him, for she knew well he was going out to face the men of Ireland, and she brought out wine in a vessel to him, as her custom was when he passed that way. But when he took the vessel in his hand, it was red blood that was in it. "My grief!" he said, "my mother Dechtire, it is no wonder others to forsake me, when you yourself offer me a drink of blood." Then she filled the vessel a second, and a third time, and each time when she gave it to him, there was nothing in it but blood.

Then anger came on Cuchulain, and he dashed the vessel against a rock, and broke it, and he said: "The fault is not in yourself, my mother Dechtire, but my luck is turned against me, and my life is near its end, and I will not come back alive this time from facing the men of Ireland." Then Dechtire tried hard to persuade him to go back and to wait till he would have the help of Conall. "I will not wait," he said, "for anything you can say; for I would not give up my great name and my courage for all the riches of the world. And from the day I first took arms till this day, I have never drawn back from a fight or a battle. And it is not now I will begin to draw back," he said, "for a great name outlasts life."

Then he went on his way, and Cathbad, that had followed him, went with him. And presently they came to a ford, and there they saw a young girl, thin and white-skinned, and having yellow hair, washing and ever washing, and wringing out clothing that was stained crimson red, and she crying and keening all the time. "Little Hound," said Cathbad, "do you see what it is that young girl is doing? It is your red clothes she is washing, and crying as she washes, because she knows you are going to your death against Maeve's great army. And take the warning now and turn back again." "Dear master," said Cuchulain, "you have followed me far enough; for I will not turn back from my vengeance on the men of Ireland that are come to burn and to destroy my house and my country. And what is it to me, the woman of the Sidhe to be washing red clothing for me? It is not long till there will be clothing enough, and armour and arms, lying soaked in pools of blood, by my own sword and my spear. And if you are sorry and loth to let me go into the fight, I am glad and ready enough myself to go into it, though I know as well as you yourself I must fall in it. Do not be hindering me any more, then," he said, "for, if I stay or if I go, death will meet me all the same. But go now to Emain, to Conchubar and to Emer, and bring them life and health from me, for I will never go back to meet them again. It is my grief and my wound, I to part with them! And O Laeg!" he said, "we are going away under trouble and under darkness from Emer now, as it is often we came back to her with gladness out of strange places and far countries."

Then Cathbad left him, and he went on his way. And after a while he saw three hags, and they blind of the left eye, before him in the road, and they having a venomous hound they were cooking with charms on rods of the rowan tree. And he was going by them, for he knew it was not for his good they were there.

But one of the hags called to him: "Stop a while with us, Cuchulain." "I will not stop with you," said Cuchulain. "That is because we have nothing better than a dog to give you," said the hag. "If we had a grand, big cooking-hearth, you would stop and visit us; but because it is only a little we have to offer you, you will not stop. But he that will not show respect for the small, though he is great, he will get no respect himself."

Then he went over to her, and she gave him the shoulder-blade of the hound out of her left hand, and he ate it out of his left hand. And he put it down on his left thigh, and the hand that took it was struck down, and the thigh he put it on was struck through and through, so that the strength that was in them before left them.

Then he went down the road of Meadhon-Luachair, by Slieve Fuad, and his enemy, Erc, son of Cairbre, saw him in the chariot, and his sword shining red in his hand, and the light of his courage plain upon him, and his hair spread out like threads of gold that change their colour on the edge of the anvil, under the smith's hand, and the Crow of Battle in the air over his head.

"Cuchulain is coming at us," said Erc to the men of Ireland, "and let us be ready for him." So they made a fence of shields linked together, and Erc put a couple of the men that were strongest here and there, to let on to be fighting one another, that they might call Cuchulain to them; and he put a Druid with every couple of them, and he bid the Druid to ask Cuchulain's spears of him, for it would be hard for him to refuse a Druid. For it was in the prophecy of the children of Calatin that a king would be killed by each one of those spears in that battle.

And he bid the men of Ireland to give out shouts, and Cuchulain came against them in his chariot, doing his three thunder feats, and he used his spear and his sword in such a way, that their heads, and their hands, and their feet, and their bones, were scattered through the plain of Muirthemne, like the sands on the shore, like the stars in the sky, like the dew in May, like snow-flakes and hail-stones, like leaves of the trees, like buttercups in a meadow, like grass under the feet of cattle on a fine summer day. It is red that plain was with the slaughter Cuchulain made when he came crashing over it.

Then he saw one of the men that was put to quarrel with the other, and the Druid called to him to come and hinder them, and Cuchulain leaped towards them. "Your spear to me," cried the Druid. "I swear by the oath of my people," said Cuchulain, "you are not so much in want of it as I am in want of it myself. The men of Ireland are upon me," he said, "and I am upon them." "I will put a bad name on you if you refuse it to me," said the Druid. "There was never a bad name put on me yet, on account of any refusal of mine," said Cuchulain, and with that he threw the spear at him, and it went through his head, and it killed the men that were on the other side of him.

Then Cuchulain drove through the host, and Lugaid, son of Curoi, got the spear. "Who is it will fall by this spear, children of Calatin?" said Lugaid. "A king will fall by it," said they. Then Lugaid threw the spear at Cuchulain's chariot, and it went through and hit the driver, Laeg, son of Riangabra, and he fell back, and his bowels came out on the cushions of the chariot. "My grief!" said Laeg, "it is hard I am wounded." Then Cuchulain drew the spear out, and Laeg said his farewell to him, and Cuchulain said: "To-day I will be a fighter and a chariot-driver as well."

Then he saw the other two men that were put to quarrel with one another, and one of them called out it would be a great shame for him not to give him his help. Then Cuchulain leaped towards them. "Your spear to me, Cuchulain," said the Druid. "I swear by the oath my people swear by," said he, "you are not in such want of the spear as I am myself, for it is by my courage, and by my arms, that I have to drive out the four provinces of Ireland that are sweeping over Muir-themne to-day." "I will put a bad name upon you," said the Druid. "I am not bound to give more than one gift in the day, and I have paid what is due to my name already," said Cuchulain. Then the Druid said: "I will put a bad name on the province of Ulster, because of your refusal."

"Ulster was never dispraised yet for any refusal of mine," said Cuchulain, "or for anything I did unworthily. Though little of my life should be left to me, Ulster will not be reproached for me to-day." With that he threw his spear at him, and it went through his head, and through the heads of the nine men that were behind him, and Cuchulain went through the host as he did before.

Then Erc, son of Cairbre Niafer, took up his spear. "Who will fall by this?" he asked the children of Calatin. "A king will fall by it," they said. "I heard you say the same thing of the spear that Lugaid threw a while ago," said Erc. "That is true," said they, "and the king of the chariot-drivers of Ireland fell by it, Cuchulain's driver Laeg, son of Riangabra."

With that, Erc threw the spear, and it went through the Grey of Macha. Cuchulain drew the spear out, and they said farewell to one another. And then the Grey went away from him, with half his harness hanging from his neck, and he went into Glas-linn, the grey pool in Slieve Fuad.

Then Cuchulain drove through the host, and he saw the third couple disputing together, and he went between them as he did before. And the Druid asked his spear of him, but he refused him. "I will put a bad name on you," said the Druid. "I have paid what is due to my name to-day," said he; "my honour does not bind me to give more than one request in a day." "I will put a bad name upon Ulster because of your refusal." "I have paid what is due for the honour of Ulster," said Cuchulain. "Then I will put a bad name on your kindred," said the Druid. "The news that I have been given a bad name shall never go back to that place I am never to go back to myself; for it is little of my life that is left to me," said Cuchulain. With that he threw the spear at him, and it went through him, and through the heads of the men that were along with him.

"You do your kindness unkindly, Cuchulain," said the Druid, as he fell. Then Cuchulain drove for the last time through the host, and Lugaid took the spear, and he said: "Who will fall by this spear, children of Calatin?" "A king will fall by it," said they. "I heard you saying that a king would fall by the spear Erc threw a while ago." "That is true," they said, "and the Grey of Macha fell by it, that was the king of the horses of Ireland."

Then Lugaid threw the spear, and it went through and through Cuchulain's body, and he knew he had got his deadly wound; and his bowels came out on the cushions of the chariot, and his only horse went away from him, the Black Sainglain, with half the harness hanging from his neck, and left his master, the king of the heroes of Ireland, to die upon the plain of Muirthemne.

Then Cuchulain said: "There is great desire on me to go to that lake beyond, and to get a drink from it."

"We will give you leave to do that," they said, "if you will come back to us after."

"I will bid you come for me if I am not able to come back myself," said Cuchulain.

Then he gathered up his bowels into his body, and he went down to the lake. He drank a drink, and he washed himself, and he turned back again to his death, and he called to his enemies to come and meet him.

There was a pillar-stone west of the lake, and his eye lit on it, and he went to the pillar-stone, and he tied himself to it with his breast-belt, the way he would not meet his death lying down, but would meet it standing up. Then his enemies came round about him, but they were in dread of going close to him, for they were not sure but he might be still alive.

"It is a great shame for you," said Erc, son of Cairbre, "not to strike the head off that man, in revenge for his striking the head off my father."

Then the Grey of Macha came back to defend Cuchulain as long as there was life in him, and the hero-light was shining above him. And the Grey of Macha made three attacks against them, and he killed fifty men with his teeth, and thirty with each of his hoofs. So there is a saying: "It is not sharper work than this was done by the Grey of Macha, the time of Cuchulain's death."

Then a bird came and settled on his shoulder. "It is not on that pillar birds were used to settle," said Erc.

Then Lugaid came and lifted up Cuchulain's hair from his shoulders, and struck his head off, and the men of Ireland gave three great heavy shouts, and the sword fell from Cuchulain's hand, and as it fell, it struck off Lugaid's right hand, so that it fell to the ground. Then he cut off Cuchulain's hand, in satisfaction for it, and then the light faded away from about Cuchulain's head, and left it as pale as the snow of a single night. Then all the men of Ireland said that as it was Maeve had gathered the army, it would be right for her to bring away the head to Cruachan. "I will not bring it with me; it is for Lugaid that struck it off to bring it with him," said Maeve. And then Lugaid and his men went away, and they brought away Cuchulain's head and his right hand with them, and they went south, towards the Lífe river.

At that time the army of Ulster was gathering to attack its enemies, and Conall was out before them, and he met the Grey of Macha, and his share of blood dripping from him. And then he knew that Cuchulain was dead, and himself and the Grey of Macha went looking for Cuchulain's body. And when they saw his body at the pillar-stone, the Grey of Macha went and laid his head in Cuchulain's breast: "That body is a heavy care to the Grey of Macha," said Conall.

Then Conall went after the army, thinking in his own mind what way he could get satisfaction for Cuchulain's death. For it was a promise between himself and Cuchulain that whichever of them would be killed the first, the other would get satisfaction for his death.

"And if I am the first that is killed," said Cuchulain at that time, "how long will it be before you get satisfaction for me?"

"Before the evening of the same day," said Conall, "I will have got satisfaction for you. And if it is I that will die before you," he said, "how long will it be before you get satisfaction for me?"

"Your share of blood will not be cold on the ground," said Cuchulain, "when I will have got satisfaction for you."

So Conall followed after Lugaid to the river Life.

Lugaid was going down to bathe in the water, but he said to his chariot-driver: "Look out there over the plain, for fear would any one come to us unknown."

The chariot-driver looked around him. "There is a man coming on us," he said, "and it is in a great hurry he is coming; and you would think he has all the ravens in Ireland flying over his head, and there are flakes of snow speckling the ground before him."

"It is not in friendship the man comes that is coming like that," said Lugaid. "It is Conall Cearnach it is, with Dub-dearg, and the birds that you see after him, they are the sods the horse has scattered in the air from his hoofs, and the flakes of snow that are speckling the ground before him, they are the froth that he scatters from his mouth and from the bit of his bridle. Look again," said Lugaid, "and see what way is he coming." "It is to the ford he is coming, the same way the army passed over," said the chariot-driver. "Let him pass by us," said Lugaid, "for I have no mind to fight with him."

But when Conall came to the middle of the ford, he saw Lugaid and his chariot-driver, and he went over to them. "Welcome is the sight of a debtor's face," said Conall. "The man you owe a debt to is asking payment of you now, and I myself am that man," he said, "for the sake of my comrade, Cuchulain, that you killed. And I am standing here now, to get that debt paid."

They agreed then to fight it out on the plain of Magh Argetnas, and in the fight Conall wounded Lugaid with his spear. From that they went to a place called Ferta Lugdac. "I would like that you would give me fair play," said Lugaid. "What fair play?" said Conall Cearnach.

"That you and I should fight with one hand," said he, "for I have the use of but one hand."

"I will do that," said Conall. Then Conall's hand was bound to his side with a cord, and then they fought for a long time, and one did not get the better of the other. And when Conall was not gaining on him, his horse, Dub-dearg, that was near by, came up to Lugaid, and took a bite out of his side.

"Misfortune on me," said Lugaid, "it is not right or fair that is of you, Conall."

"It was for myself I promised to do what is right and fair," said Conall. "I made no promise for a beast, that is without training and without sense."

"It is well I know you will not leave me till you take my head, as I took Cuchulain's head from him," said Lugaid. "Take it, then, along with your own head. Put my kingdom with your kingdom, and my courage with your courage; for I would like that you would be the best champion in Ireland."

Then Conall made an end of him, and he went back, bringing Cuchulain's head along with him to the pillar-stone where his body was.

And by that time Emer had got word of all that had happened, and that her husband had got his death by the men of Ireland, and by the powers of the children of Calatin. And it was Levarcham brought her the story, for Conall Cearnach had met her on his way, and had bade her go and bring the news to Emain Macha; and there she found Emer, and she sitting in her upper room, looking over the plain for some word from the battle.

And all the women came out to meet Levarcham, and when they heard her story, they made an outcry of grief and sharp cries, with loud weeping and burning tears; and there were long dismal sounds going through Emain, and the whole country round was filled with crying. And Emer and her women went to the place where Cuchulain's body was, and they gathered round it there, and gave themselves to crying and keening.

And when Conall came back to the place, he laid the head with the body of Cuchulain, and he began to lament along with them, and it is what he said: "It is Cuchulain had prosperity on him, a root of valour from the time he was but a soft child; there never fell a better hero than the hero that fell by Lugaid of the Lands. And there are many are in want of you," he said, "and until all the chief men of Ireland have fallen by me, it is not fitting there should ever be peace.

"It is grief to me, he to have gone into the battle without Conall being at his side; it was a pity for him to go there without my body beside his body. Och! it is he was my foster-son, and now the ravens are drinking his blood; there will not be either laughter or mirth, since the Hound has gone astray from us."

"Let us bury Cuchulain now," said Emer. "It is not right to do that," said Conall, "until I have avenged him on the men of Ireland. And it is a great shouting I hear about the plain of Muirthemne, and it is full the country is of crying after Cuchulain; and it is good at keeping the country and watching the boundaries the man was that is here before me, a cross-hacked body in a pool of blood. And it is well it pleased Lugaid, son of Curoi, to be at the killing of Cuchulain, for it was Cuchulain killed the chiefs and the children of Deaguid round Famain, son of Foraoi, and round Curoi, son of Daire himself. And this shouting has taken away my wits and my memory from me," he said, "and it is hard for me, Cuchulain not to answer these cries, and I to be without him now; for there is not a champion in Ireland that was not in dread of the sword in his hand. And it is broken in halves my heart is for my brother, and I will bring my revenge through Ireland now, and I will not leave a tribe without wounding, or true blood without spilling, and the whole world will be told of my rout to the end of life and time, until the men of Munster and Connaught and Leinster will be crying for the rising they made against him. And without the spells of the children of Calatin, the whole of them would not have been able to do him to death."

After that complaint, rage and madness came on Conall, and he went forward in his chariot to follow after the rest of the men of Ireland, the same way as he had followed after Lugaid.

And Emer took the head of Cuchulain in her hands, and she washed it clean, and put a silk cloth about it, and she held it to her breast; and she began to cry heavily over it, and it is what she said:

"Ochone!" said she, "it is good the beauty of this head was, though it is low this day, and it is many of the kings and princes of the world would be keening it if they knew the way it is now, and the poets and the Druids of Ireland and of Alban; and many were the goods and the jewels and the rents and the tributes that you brought home to me from the countries of the world, with the courage and the strength of your hands!"

And she made this complaint:

"Och, head! Ochone, O head! you gave death to great heroes, to many hundreds; my head will lie in the same grave, the one stone will be made for both of us.

"Och, hand! Ochone, hand, that was once gentle. It is often it was put under my head; it is dear that hand was to me!

"Dear mouth! Ochone, kind mouth that was sweet-voiced telling stories; since the time love first came on your face, you never refused either weak or strong!

"Dear the man, dear the man, that would kill the whole of a great host; dear his cold bright hair, and dear his bright cheeks!

"Dear the king, dear the king, that never gave a refusal to any; thirty days it is to-night since my body lay beside your body.

"Och, two spears! Ochone, two spears! Och, shield! Och, deadly sword! Let them be given to Conall of the battles; there was never any wage given like that.

"I am glad, I am glad, Cuchulain of Muirthemne, I never brought red shame on your face, for any unfaithfulness against you.

"Happy are they, happy are they, who will never hear the cuckoo again for ever, now that the Hound has died from us.

"I am carried away like a branch on the stream; I will not bind up my hair to-day. From this day I have nothing to say that is better than Ochone!"

And then she said: "It is long that it was showed to me in a vision of the night, that Cuchulain would fall by the men of Ireland, and it appeared to me Dundealgan to be falling to the ground, and his shield to be split from lip to border, and his sword and his spears broken in the middle, and I saw Conall doing deeds of death before me, and myself and yourself in the one death. And oh! my love," she said, "we were often in one another's company, and it was happy for us; for if the world had been searched from the rising of the sun to sunset, the like would never have been found in one place, of the Black Sainglain and the Grey of Macha, and Laeg the chariot-driver, and myself and Cuchulain. And it is breaking my heart is in my body, to be listening to the pity and the sorrowing of women and men, and the harsh crying of the young men of Ulster keening Cuchulain, and

Ulster to be in its weakness, and without strength to revenge itself upon the men of Ireland."

And after she had made that complaint, she brought Cuchulain's body to Dundealgan; and they all cried and keened about him until such time as Conall Cearnach came back from making his red rout through the army of the men of Ireland.

For he was not satisfied to make a slaughter of the men of Munster and Connaught, without reddening his hand in the blood of the men of Leinster as well.

And when he had done that, he came to Dundealgan, and his men along with him, but they made no rejoicing when they went back that time. And he brought the heads of the men of Ireland along with him in a gad, and he laid them out on the green lawn, and the people of the house gave three great shouts when they saw the heads.

And Emer came out, and when she saw Conall Cearnach, she said: "My great esteem and my welcome before you, king of heroes, and may your many wounds not be your death; for you have avenged the treachery done on Ulster, and now what you have to do is to make our grave, and to lay us together in the grave, for I will not live after Cuchulain.

"And tell me, Conall," she said, "whose are those heads all around on the lawn, and which of the great men of Ireland did they belong to?"

And she was asking, and Conall was answering, and it is what she said:

"Tell me, Conall, whose are those heads, for surely you have reddened your arms with them. Tell me the names of the men whose heads are there upon the ground."

And Conall said: "Daughter of Forgall of the Horses, young Emer of the sweet words, it is in revenge for the Hound of Feats I brought these heads here from the south."

"Whose is the great black head, with the smooth cheek redder than a rose; it is at the far end, on the left side, the head that has not changed its colour?"

"It is the head of the king of Meath, Erc, son of Cairbre of Swift Horses; I brought his head with me from far off, in revenge for my own foster-son."

"Whose is that head there before me, with soft hair, with smooth eyebrows, its eyes like ice, its teeth like blossoms; that head is more beautiful in shape than the others?"

"A son of Maeve; a destroyer of harbours, yellow-haired Maine, man of horses; I left his body without a head; all his people fell by my hand."

"O great Conall, who did not fail us, whose head is this you hold in your hand? Since the Hound of Feats is not living, what do you bring in satisfaction for his head?"

"The head of the son of Fergus of the Horses, a destroyer in every battle-field, my sister's son of the narrow tower; I have struck his head from his body."

"Whose is that head to the west, with fair hair, the head that is spoiled with grief? I used to know his voice; I was for a while his friend."

"That is he that struck down the Hound, Lugaid, son of Curoi of the Rhymes. His body was laid out straight and fair, I struck his head off afterwards."

"Whose are those two heads farther out, great Conall of good judgment? For the sake of your friendship, do not hide the names of the men put down by your arms."

"The heads of Laigaire and Clar Cuilt, two men that fell by my wounds. It was they wounded faithful Cuchulain; I made my weapons red in their blood."

"Whose are those heads farther to the east, great Conall of bright deeds? The hair of the two is of the one colour; their cheeks are redder than a calf's blood."

"Brave Cullain and hardy Cunlaid, two that were used to overcome in their anger. There to the east, Emer, are their heads; I left their bodies in a red pool."

"Whose are those three heads with evil looks I see before me to the north? Their faces blue, their hair black; even hard Conall's eye turns from them."

"Three of the enemies of the Hound, daughters of Calatin, wise in enchantments; they are the three witches killed by me, their weapons in their hands."

"O great Conall, father of kings, whose is that head that would overcome in the battle? His bushy hair is gold-yellow; his head-dress is smooth and white like silver."

"It is the head of the son of Red-Haired Ross, son of Necht Min, that died by my strength. This, Emer, is his head; the high king of Leinster of Speckled Swords."

"O great Conall, change the story. How many of the men that harmed him fell by your hand that does not fail in satisfaction for the head of Cuchulain?"

"It is what I say, ten and seven scores of hundreds is the number that fell, back to back, by the anger of my hard sword and of my people."

"O Conall, what way are they, the women of Ireland, after the Hound? Are they mourning the son of Sualtim? are they showing respect through their grief?"

"O Emer, what shall I do without my Cuchulain, my fine nurseling, going in and out from me, tonight?"

"O Conall, lift me to the grave. Raise my stone over the grave of the Hound; since it is through grief for him I go to death, lay my mouth to the mouth of Cuchulain.

"I am Emer of the Fair Form; there is no more vengeance for me to find; I have no love for any man. It is sorrowful my stay is after the Hound."

And after that Emer bade Conall to make a wide, very deep grave for Cuchulain; and she laid herself down beside her gentle comrade, and she put her mouth to his mouth, and she said: "Love of my life, my friend, my sweetheart, my one choice of the men of the earth, many is the woman, wed or unwed, envied me till to-day: and now I will not stay living after you."

And her life went out from her, and she herself and Cuchulain were laid in the one grave by Conall. And he raised the one stone over them, and he wrote their names in Ogham, and he himself and all the men of Ulster keened them.

But the three times fifty queens that loved Cuchulain saw him appear in his Druid chariot, going through Emain Macha; and they could hear him singing the music of the Sidhe.

NOTE BY W. B. YEATS ON THE CONVERSATION OF CUCHULAIN AND EMER. (Page 351.)

This conversation, so full of strange mythological information, is an example of the poet speech of ancient Ireland. One comes upon this speech here and there in other stories and poems. One finds it in the poem attributed to Ailbhe, daughter of Cormac Mac Art, and quoted by O'Curry in "M.S. Materials," of which one verse is an allusion to a story given in Lady Gregory's book:

> "The apple tree of high Alanine,
> The yew of Baile of little land,
> Though they are put into lays,
> Rough people do not understand them."

One finds it too in the poems which Brian, Son of Tuïreann, chanted when he did not wish to be wholly understood. "That is a good poem, but I do not understand a word of its meaning," said the kings before whom he chanted; but his obscurity was more in a roundabout way of speaking than in mythological allusions. There is a description of a banquet, quoted by Professor Kuno Meyer, where hens' eggs are spoken of as "gravel of Glenn Ai," and leek, as "a tear of a fair woman," and some eatable seaweed, dulse, perhaps, as a "net of the plains of Rein"—that is to say, of the sea—and so on. He quotes also a poem that calls the sallow, "the strength of bees," and the hawthorn "the barking of hounds," and the gooseberry bush "the sweetest of trees," and the yew "the oldest of trees."

This poet speech somewhat resembles the Icelandic court poetry, as it is called, which certainly required alike for the writing and understanding of it a great traditional culture. Its descriptions of shields and tapestry, and its praises of Kings, that were first written, it seems, about the tenth century, depended for their effects on just this heaping up of mythological allusions, and the "Eddas" were written to be a granary for the makers of such poems. But by the fourteenth and fifteenth centuries they had come to be as irritating to the new Christian poets and writers who stood outside their tradition, as are the more esoteric kinds of modern verse to unlettered readers. They were called "obscure" and "speaking in riddle" and the like.

It has sometimes been thought that the Irish poet speech was indeed but a copy of this court poetry, but Professor York Powell contradicts this, and thinks it is not unlikely that the Irish poems influenced the Icelandic, and made them more mythological and obscure.

I am not scholar enough to judge the Scandinavian verse, but the Irish poet speech seems to me at worst an over-abundance of the esoterism which is an essential element in all admirable literature, and I think it a folly to make light of it, as a recent writer has done. Even now, verse no less full of symbol and myth seems to me as legitimate as, let us say, a religious picture full of symbolic detail, or the symbolic ornament of a Cathedral. Nash's—

> "Brightness falls from the air,
>   Queens have died young and fair,
>   Dust hath closed Helen's eyes"—

must seem as empty as a Scald's song, or the talk of Cuchulain and Emer, to one who has never heard of Helen, or even to one who did not fall in love with her when he was a young man. And if we were not accustomed to be stirred by Greek myth, even without remembering it very fully, "Berenice's ever burning hair" would not stir the blood, and especially if it were put into some foreign tongue, losing those resounding "b's" on the way.

The mythological events Cuchulain speaks of give mystery to the scenery of the tales, and when they are connected with the battle of Magh Tuireadh, the most tremendous of mythological battles, or anything else we know much about, they are full of poetic meaning or historical interest. The hills that had the shape of a sow's back at the coming of the Children of Miled, remind one of Borlase's conviction that the pig was the symbol of the mythological ancestry of the Firbolg, which the Children of Miled were to bring into subjection, and of his suggestion that the magical pigs that Maeve numbered were some Firbolg tribe that Maeve put down in war. And everywhere that esoteric speech brings the odour of the wild woods into our nostrils.

The earlier we get, the more copious does this traditional and symbolical element in literature become. Till Greece and Rome created a new culture, a sense of the importance of man, all that we understand by humanism, nobody wrote history, nobody described anything as we understand description. One called up the image of a thing by comparing it with something else, and partly because one was less interested in man, who did not seem to be important, than in divine revelations, in changes among the heavens and the gods, which can hardly be expressed at all, and only by myth, by symbol, by enigma. One was always losing oneself in the unknown, and rushing to the limits of the world. Imagination was all in all. Is not poetry, when all is said, but a little of this habit of mind caught as in the beryl stone of a Wizard?

NOTES

I am not enough of a scholar to read the old manuscripts from which these stories are taken, but the Irish text of the greater number has been printed either in *Irische Texte*, or the *Revue Celtique*, or by O'Curry, in *Atlantis* and elsewhere, and I have worked from this text, with the help of the translations given. In some cases, as in the greater part of "The War for the Bull of Cuailgne," the Irish text has not yet been printed, and I have had to work by comparing and piecing together various translations.

I have had to put a connecting sentence of my own here and there, and I have condensed many passages, and I have sometimes tried to give the meaning of a formula that has lost its old meaning. Thus I have exchanged for the grotesque accounts of Cuchulain's distortion—which no doubt merely meant that in time of great strain or danger he had more than human strength—the more simple formula that his appearance changed to the appearance of a god. In the same way, I have left out Levarcham's distortion, which was the recognized way of saying she was a swift messenger.

As to the date of the stories, I cannot do better than quote from Mr Alfred Nutt's "Cuchulain, the Irish Achilles":-

"It suffices to say that we possess a MS. literature of which Cuchulain and his contemporaries are the subject, the extent of which may be roughly reckoned at 2000 8vo. pages. The great bulk of this is contained in MSS. which are older than the twelfth century, or which demonstrably are copied from pre-twelfth-century MSS.; where post-twelfth-century versions alone remain, the story itself is nearly always known from earlier sources; in fact, there is hardly a single scene or incident in the whole cycle which has reached us only in MSS. of the thirteenth and following centuries. At the same time a not inconsiderable portion of the cycle comes before us altered in language, and to some extent in content, style of narrative, and characterisation, showing that the saga as a whole remained a living element of Irish culture and participated in the accidents of its evolution.

"The great bulk of this literature is, as I have said, certainly older than the twelfth century; but we can carry it back much farther, apart from any consideration based upon the subject-matter. Arguments of a nature purely philological, based upon the language of the texts, or critical, based upon the relations of the various MSS. to each other, not only allow, but compel us to date the *redaction* of the principal Cuchulain stories, substantially in the form under which they have survived, back to the seventh to ninth centuries. Whether or no they are older yet, is a question that cannot be answered without preliminary examination of the subject-matter. In the meantime it is something to know that the Cuchulain stories were put into permanent literature form at about the same date as Beowulf, some 100 to 250 years before the Scandinavian mythology crystallised into its present form, at least 200 years before the oldest Charlemagne romances, and probably 300 years before the earliest draft of the Nibelungenlied. Irish is the most ancient *vernacular* literature of modern Europe, a fact which of itself commends it to the attention of the student."

A critical account of this and the other Irish cycles is also given in Dr Douglas Hyde's "Literary History of Ireland."

The Tuatha of Danaan, or the Sidhe, so often mentioned, were the divine race, the people of the Gods of Dana, who conquered the Fomor, the powers of darkness and their helpers the Firbolgs, in the Battle of Magh Tuireadh, and possessed Ireland until they were in their turn conquered by the children of the Gael, under the leadership of the Sons of Miled. Then they became invisible, and made their home in hills and raths.

The Morrigu was their goddess of battle, and Angus Og, Son of the Dagda, their god of youth and love, and Lugh, the Master of many arts, their Hermes, their Apollo, and Manannan, Son of Lir, their Sea-god, or, as some say, the sea itself.

The spelling of Irish names for English readers is always a difficulty. I have not gone by any fixed rule, but have taken the spelling of names from various good authorities. As to pronunciation, the modern is generally used, but we know so little what the ancient pronunciation was, that we are left some freedom, and some words have taken a shape from English-speaking generations, that it is hard to change. Teamhair, for instance, has become Tara through a mistaken use of the genetive; Muirthemne is called by Irish speakers "Mur-hev-na," but others call it Muir'them-mé, and I am inclined to prefer this for the charm of the sound, and I do not see any stronger reason against using it than against sounding as we do the 's' in Paris. After all, it has not yet been definitely settled whether Trafalgar is to be spoken in the Spanish or the English way; English poets have given it one or the other emphasis. This is the approximate pronunciation of the more difficult names:-

Aedh	Ae (rhyming to "day").
Aoife	Eefa.
Badb	Bibe (as "jibe").
Cliodna	Cleevna.

Conchubar	. . . . . .	Conachoor.
Cuailgne	. . . . . .	Cooley.
Cuchulain	. . . . . .	Cuhoolin, or Cu-hullin.
Cobhthach	. . . . . .	Cowhach.
Dun Sobairce	. . . . . .	Dom Sĕvĕrka.
Emain	. . . . . .	Avvin.
Eochaid	. . . . . .	Yohee.
Eoghan	. . . . . .	Owen.
Eocho	. . . . . .	Yūchŏ.
Fernmaighe	. . . . . .	Farney.
Glen na (m) Bodhar	. . . .	Glen na Mower (as "bower").
Inbhir	. . . . . .	Inver.
Lugh	. . . . . .	Loo.
Magh Tuireadh	. . . . .	Moytirra.
Muirthemne	. . . . .	Mŭr-hĕv-na.
Niamh	. . . . . .	Nee-av.
Rudraige	. . . . . .	Rury.
Sidhe	. . . . . .	Shee.
Slieve Suidhe Laighen	. . .	Slieve see lihon.
Suibnes	. . . . . .	Sivness.
Teamhair	. . . . .	T'yower.
Tuathmumain	. . . . .	Too-moon.

I gave below some names of places that can still be identified—

Ath Firdiadh	. . . . . .	(Ferdiad's Ford). Ardee.
Ath Truim	. . . . . .	Trim.
Ath Cliath	. . . . . .	Dublin.
Beinn Edair	. . . . .	Howth.
Boinne River	. . . . .	The Boyne.
Brug Na Boinne	. . . . .	On the Boyne.
Bri Leith	. . . . . .	In Co. Longford.
Bregia	. . . . . .	Bray.
Carraige	. . . . . .	Kerry.
Cerna	. . . . . .	Probably River Muilchean, Co. Limerick.
Clartha	. . . . . .	Clara, near Mullingar.

Cleitech	On the Boyne.
Conaille—Muirthemne	Between the Cooley Mountains and the Boyne.
Cuilsilinne	South-west of Kells.
Cuailgne	Cooley, Co. Louth.
Cruachan	In Co. Roscommon.
Dun Scathach	Isle of Skye.
Dundealgan	Dundalk.
Dun Rudraige	Dundrum, Co. Down.
Dun Sobairce	Dunseverick, Co. Antrim.
Druim Criadh	Drumcree, Co. Westmeath.
Emain Macha	Navan fort, near Armagh. A description and plan of Emain Macha are given by D'Arbois de Jubainville in *Revue Celtique*, vol. xvi.
Esro	Ballyshannon.
Fearbile	In Co. Westmeath.
Femen	At Slieve na Man, Co. Tipperary.
Gairech and Ilgairech	Two hills near Mullingar.
Hill of Brughean Mor	In Parish of Drumany, Co. Westmeath.
Hy Maine	A part of Roscommon, bordering Sligo and Mayo.
Inver Colptha	Estuary of the Boyne
Loch Cuan	Strangford Loch.
Loch Riach	In Co. Galway.
Leodus, Cadd, and Ork	Lewish, Shetland, and Orkney.
Magh Ai	In Co. Roscommon.
Magh Breagh	In East Meath.
Magh Mucrime	Near Athenry, Co. Galway.

Magh Slecht	Near Ballymagauran, Co. Cavan.
Muirthemne	The part of Co. Louth bordering the sea, between the Boyne and Dundalk.
Road of Midluachair	The north-eastern road from Teamhair.
Slieve Breagh	Co. Louth.
Slieve Cuilinn	Co. Londonderry.
Slieve Fuad	Co. Armagh.
Slieve Mis	Co. Kerry.
Slieve Suidhe Laighen . . .	Mount Leinster.
Sleamhain of Meath	Near Mullingar.
Sligger Isles	Faröe Isles.
Sionnan	The Shannon.
Sudiam	Sweden.
Tailltin	Telltown.
Teamhair	Tara, Co. Meath.
Tuathmumain	Thomond.
Uaran Garad	River Cruind.
Usnech	The Hill of Usnogh in West Meath.
Wave of Cliodna	At Glandore, Co. Cork.
Wave of Assaroe	At Ballyshannon.

The following is a list of the authorities I have been chiefly helped by in putting these stories together. But I cannot make it quite accurate, for I have sometimes transferred a mere phrase, sometimes a whole passage from one story to another, where it seemed to fit better. I have occasionally used Scottish Gaelic versions, as in the account of Deirdre's birth, and the manner of her death, and in a part of "The Only Son of Aoife." "O'Curry" stands for his two books, "The Manners and Customs of Ancient Ireland," and "MS. Materials for Ancient Irish History," and his contributions to *Atlantis*.

BIRTH OF CUCHULAIN.—O'Curry; De Jubainville, "Epopée Celtique"; Nutt, "Voyage of Bran"; Kuno Meyer, *Revue Celtique*; Duvau, *Revue Celtique*, Windisch, *Irische Texte*; Stokes, *Irische Texte*.

BOY DEEDS OF CUCHULAIN.—Same as "War for the Bull of Cuailgne."

COURTING OF EMER.—Kuno Meyer, *Revue Celtique*; Kuno Meyer, *Archæological*

Review; Dr Douglas Hyde, *Literary History of Ireland*; De Jubainville, *Epopée Celtique*; O'Curry.

BRICRIU'S FEAST, AND THE CHAMPIONSHIP OF ULSTER.—Text, with Henderson's translation, published by Irish Texts Society; De Jubainville, *Epopée Celtique*; O'Curry, Windisch, *Irische Texte*.

THE HIGH KING OF IRELAND.—Whitley Stokes, *Revue Celtique*; O'Curry; Zimmer, *Keltische Studien*.

FATE OF THE CHILDREN OF USNECH.—Text and translations published by the Society for the Preservation of the Irish Language; Hyde, *Literary History of Ireland*; Hyde, *Zeitschrift Celt. Philologie*; O'Curry; Whitley Stokes, *Irische Texte*; Windisch, *Irische Texte*; Cameron, *Reliquae Celticae*; O'Flanagan, *Transactions of Gaelic Society*; O'Flanagan, *Reliquae Celticae*; Carmichael, *Transactions of Gaelic Society*; *Ultonian Ballads*; De Jubainville, *Epopée Celtique*; Dottin, *Revue Celtique*.

THE DREAM OF ANGUS.—Müller, *Revue Celtique*.

CRUACHAN.—Kuno Meyer, *Revue Celtique*; O'Beirne Crowe, *Proceedings of Royal Irish Academy*; O'Curry; Rhys, *Celtic Heathendom*.

WEDDING OF MAINE MORGOR.—Windisch, *Irische Texte*.

WAR FOR THE BULL OF CUAILGNE, and AWAKENING OF ULSTER.—MS. translations by O'Daly in Royal Irish Academy; MS. translation by O'Looney in Royal Irish Academy; O'Curry; Standish Hayes O'Grady's Synopsis in Miss Hull's *Cuchulain Saga*; Zimmer, Synopsis in *Zeitschrift für Vergleichende Sprachforschung*.

THE TWO BULLS.—Windisch, *Irische Texte*; Nutt, *Voyage of Bran*; O'Curry.

THE ONLY JEALOUSY OF EMER, and INSTRUCTION TO A PRINCE.—O'Curry, *Atlantis*; De Jubainville, *Epopée Celtique*.

THE SONS OF DOEL DERMAIT.—Windisch, *Irische Texte*; Rhys, *Hibbert Lectures*.

BATTLE OF ROSNAREE.—Text with Father Hogan's translation; Todd Lecture Series; O'Curry; Kuno Meyer, *Revue Celtique*.

ONLY SON OF AOIFE.—Keating's *History of Ireland*, Miss Brooke's *Reliques*; Curtain's *Folk Tales*; Some Gaelic Ballads.

GATHERING AT MUIRTHEMNE and DEATH OF CUCHULAIN.—"Brislech Mor Magh Muirthemne," and "Deargruatar Conaill Caernaig"—published in *Gaelic Journal*, 1901; S. Hayes O'Grady in Miss Hull's *Cuchulain Saga*; Whitley Stokes, *Revue Celtique*; an unpublished MS. in Dr. Hyde's possession.

We must be grateful to all these scholars, workers, or compilers, those who have passed away, and those who are living. And I am personally grateful to my friend Douglas Hyde for patient answering of many questions; and to my friend and critic, W. B. Yeats, for his kindness and for his severity.

A.G.